INTRODUCTION TO
CITIES

About the website

The *Introduction to Cities: How Place and Space Shape Human Experience* companion website contains a number of resources created by the authors that you will find helpful in using this book for university courses or for your own intellectual growth.

Students

List of urban studies journals presents a large number of scholarly journals that publish urban research from around the globe.

Annotated list of urban studies web resources directs you to the websites of research centers, data compilers, and nonprofit organizations working on urban questions.

Annotated documentary guide provides information about a number of films that help to illustrate many of the key themes in the book.

Instructors

Essay and discussion questions supplement the critical thinking questions included in the book.

Additional cases and examples are provided for use in the classroom, including a guide to how to pair them with the relevant chapters of the book.

INTRODUCTION TO
CITIES

HOW PLACE AND SPACE
SHAPE HUMAN EXPERIENCE

Xiangming Chen, Anthony M. Orum,
and Krista E. Paulsen

WILEY-BLACKWELL

A John Wiley & Sons, Ltd., Publication

Blackwell Publishing was acquired by John Wiley & Sons in February 2007.
Blackwell's publishing program has been merged with Wiley's global Scientific,
Technical, and Medical business to form Wiley-Blackwell.

Registered Office
John Wiley & Sons Ltd, The Atrium, Southern Gate, Chichester, West Sussex, PO19
8SQ, UK

Editorial Offices
350 Main Street, Malden, MA 02148-5020, USA
9600 Garsington Road, Oxford, OX4 2DQ, UK
The Atrium, Southern Gate, Chichester, West Sussex, PO19 8SQ, UK

For details of our global editorial offices, for customer services, and for information
about how to apply for permission to reuse the copyright material in this book please
see our website at www.wiley.com/wiley-blackwell.

Image of Anthony Orum courtesy of William Bridges. Image of Krista Paulsen
courtsey of David Wilson, UNF Center for Instructional and Research Technology.

Library of Congress Cataloging-in-Publication Data

Chen, Xiangming, 1955–
   Introduction to cities : how place and space shape human experience / Xiangming
Chen, Anthony M. Orum, and Krista E. Paulsen.
     pages cm
   Includes bibliographical references and index.
   ISBN 978-1-4051-5554-0 (pbk.)
1. Cities and towns–Social aspects.   2. Urban sociology.   3. Urbanization–Social
aspects.   I. Orum, Anthony M.   II. Paulsen, Krista E.   III. Title.
   HT119.C485 2013
   307.76–dc23

                                       2012009764

A catalogue record for this book is available from the British Library.

Set in 10/12pt Minion by SPi Publisher Services, Pondicherry, India
Printed and bound in Singapore by Markono Print Media Pte Ltd

1   2013

BRIEF CONTENTS

CONTENTS

Part I

Part II

THE CHANGING METROPOLIS 99

Part III

THE METROPOLIS
AND SOCIAL INEQUALITIES 177

8 The early metropolis as a place of inequality 178

9 Inequality and diversity in the post-World War II metropolis 204

Part IV

THE METROPOLIS IN THE
DEVELOPING WORLD 231

10 Urbanization and urban places in developing-country cities 232

Part V

CHALLENGES OF TODAY AND THE METROPOLIS OF THE FUTURE 295

List of illustrations

became a center of manufacturing and processing as well, leading to the city's unprecedented growth rate in the nineteenth and early twentieth centuries.

List of tables

List of boxes

About the authors

Xiangming Chen

Is the founding Dean and Director of the Center for Urban and Global Studies and Paul Raether Distinguished Professor of Global Urban Studies and Sociology at Trinity College, Hartford, and Distinguished Guest Professor in the School of Social Development and Public Policy at Fudan University, Shanghai. His books include *The World of Cities: Places in Comparative and Historical Perspective* (with Anthony M. Orum, Blackwell, 2003), *As Borders Bend: Transnational Spaces on the Pacific Rim* (2005), and *Shanghai Rising: State Power and Local Transformations in a Global Megacity* (ed., 2009), and *Rethinking Global Urbanism: Comparative Insights from Secondary Cities* (coed., 2012). Several of his books have been translated into Chinese.

Anthony M. Orum

Is Professor Emeritus of Sociology at the University of Illinois at Chicago. He was the founding editor of the journal *City & Community*, and has received several awards, including the 2009 Robert and Helen Lynd Award for Lifetime Achievement and Service given by the Community and Urban Sociology Section of the American Sociological Association. His publications include *City-Building in America* (1995), *The World of Cities: Places in Comparative and Historical Perspective* (with Xiangming Chen, Blackwell, 2003), and *Common Ground? Readings and Reflections on Public Space* (ed. with Zachary Neal, 2010). Several of his books have been translated into Chinese.

Krista E. Paulsen

Is Associate Professor of Sociology at the University of North Florida. She has published widely on the city, urban tradition, and the ways that places develop and maintain distinctive cultures. Her research examines the ways that homes and neighborhoods reflect and reproduce cultural ideals associated with family and community, and her teaching takes in urban sociology and urban studies, environmental sociology, community, and qualitative research methods. She is currently at work on the edited volume *Home – Place – Community: International Sociological Perspectives* (ed. with Margarethe Kusenbach and Melinda Milligan).

Acknowledgments

The authors would like to thank a number of people whose contributions and assistance made this book possible. It is no exaggeration to say that this work would not exist without the patience and enthusiasm of Justin Vaughn, our acquisitions editor at Wiley-Blackwell. The editors and production staff with Wiley-Blackwell – Louise Butler, Hazel Harris, Dave Nash, Annie Rose, and Ben Thatcher, as well as a number of others – shepherded us through this process and made innumerable contributions to the quality of this book. We are also grateful to the various anonymous scholars who reviewed this book. Their feedback was vital. In particular, we wish to acknowledge the comments of Jan Lin, Robert Kleidman, Tai-lok Lui, and Charles Jaret. Their criticisms and suggestions, which we received toward the completion of our first draft, helped us to organize the book more effectively as well as to more clearly and forcefully articulate the book's major themes of place and space. We also thank Dale Morgan at Wiley-Blackwell and Katie Song of John Wiley & Sons (Asia) in Beijing for facilitating the translation of this book into Chinese for publication by Fudan University Press toward the end of 2012. Mr. Hui Zhu in Shanghai has done a tremendous job in finishing the translation of the manuscript early enough so that the Chinese edition could and would appear soon in China after this book is officially published in the United Kingdom.

We also wish to thank a number of research assistants and other colleagues. David Boston researched and wrote a number of the boxes. Their quality reflects his broad curiosity and passion for the study of cities. Annika Hinze allowed us to use some of her observations and acute insights into the experiences of Turkish immigrant women in Germany; she prepared the box on this material that appears in Chapter 9. We urge readers to look for her new book that examines these matters in greater detail and is forthcoming in 2013 from the University of Minnesota Press. We thank several undergraduate research assistants at the Center for Urban and Global Studies of Trinity College for their contributions to this book. Curtis Stone (class of 2010) produced three beautiful charts for Chapter 11. Yuwei Xie (class of 2011) located some material for several boxes in Chapter 11 and Chapter 12. Henry Fitts (class of 2012) searched for and compiled the online urban resources for the book's website (www.wiley.com/go/cities). We also are grateful to Terry Romero, administrative assistant at the Center for Urban and Global Studies at Trinity, for indexing the book.

Individually, we wish to thank the following:

I owe another long-overdue thanks to Joel Smith for turning on my interest in studying cities in the 1980s when I was a graduate student at Duke University. My friend and former colleague Tony Orum helped to push my interest further through our joint publication of *The World of Cities* (Blackwell, 2003). That book created a wonderful opportunity for my own scholarship on Chinese and Asian cities to blend with and complement Tony's work, and that partnership is now joined with Krista's expertise in this broader collaboration. My work on this book has been enriched by conversations and collaboration with many colleagues at and through the Center for Urban and Global Studies at Trinity College over the past five years. Laura X. Hua helped to edit a few chapters and was a loving source of support. Finally, I thank the 30 students in my "From Hartford to World Cities" class in fall 2011 for reading the almost finalized chapters and collectively endorsing our shared goal to write a book that will really help students like them to understand cities.

Xiangming Chen

I embarked on the study of cities almost 30 years ago, prompted by my curiosity about the many changes I was witnessing in Austin, Texas. For me this book represents the culmination of my years of observations and reflections. I thank Xiangming and Krista for their supportive collaboration on this work, and I thank my many friends and students who across the years have helped me to better appreciate why and how *place* plays such an important role in the lives of human beings.

Anthony M. Orum

A research sabbatical granted by the University of North Florida allowed me substantial time to work on this book. My colleagues in the UNF Department of Sociology and Anthropology were a constant source of information, inspiration, and support through this process, as were the students in my courses on Urban Sociology; Race, Place and Inequality; and Community Organization, Change and Development. I also wish to thank Harvey Molotch for introducing me to urban sociology, Sharon Dunn for sparking my interest in old buildings and neighborhoods, and Nick Hudyma for his patience and support while I worked on this project. Finally, thanks to my coauthors Tony Orum and Xiangming Chen for making this collaboration so productive and enjoyable.

Krista E. Paulsen

Walk-through tour

As you read through the individual chapters in this book you'll find the following features, designed to help you develop a clear understanding of cities and their role in the human experience.

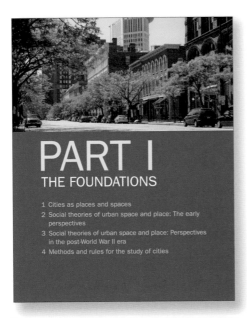

Part openers   The book is organized into five parts, and each part opens with a page listing the chapters it contains. The parts are color-coded, making them easy to identify.

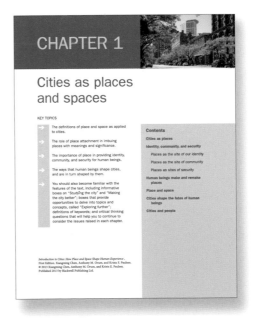

Key topics   Each chapter opens with a list of the key elements and concepts of the chapter, which will help to guide your reading.

CHAPTER 5

The metropolis and its expansion
Early insights and basic principles

Chapter table of contents   Each chapter also begins with a list of its main headings and sub-headings.

Keywords   Throughout the text, keywords are highlighted in **bold**, and you will find the definition nearby in the margin. The chapter keywords and their definitions are also collated in a glossary at the end of the book.

Exploring further   One of three types of textbox designed to enhance your reading of the book, Exploring further explains concepts or phenomena in greater depth.

Studying the city   Studying the city textboxes present distinct research techniques or findings.

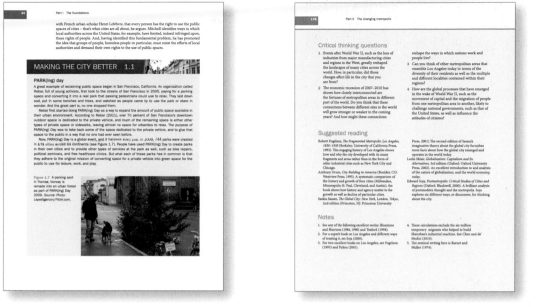

Making the city better   Making the city better textboxes focus on the efforts made throughout history to improve cities' inhabitability.

Critical thinking questions   These questions are found at the end of each chapter and help you to revisit and consider the chapter's main points.

Suggested reading   Each chapter ends with a list of suggested reading, giving you the opportunity to take your knowledge and understanding of the subject further.

Introduction

You are about to read a book about cities. We cover a number of different cities, ranging from those in the West, such as Berlin and Chicago, to those in Asia, such as Shanghai and Mumbai. We want to furnish you with as complete and as rich an introduction to the nature of cities as we can. We have written this book in a particular style – what one reviewer has said is "almost conversational." Cities are hard enough to understand without wading through a lot of difficult concepts and what critics of the social sciences often call jargon. We have tried in all instances to avoid jargon, and to make cities come alive in our prose.

Every author faces choices when writing a book, especially one like this that aims to be comprehensive. What ideas shall guide us on our journey? What ideas are important enough to make them key themes for an exposition about difficult material? We have faced those decisions and made certain choices in the narrative materials you are about to read. As you get further into this book, you will begin to learn more about our choices and why we made them. But here, at the outset, we want to share with you some of our thinking and reflections about the choices we have made.

The first choice we have made is to introduce a few basic concepts to guide us along our journey. Two concepts are essential to the way we think about cities: they are both *places* and *spaces*. Cities are places in the sense that people become connected and attached to them. The lives of people today typically occur in an urban environment, and so it is important for us to flesh out the nature and character of that environment. How do people make cities as places, whether through deliberate action or through the routines of their daily lives? And how do urban places act upon people?

We argue that cities as *places* provide three fundamental things that are important to human life and experience. They furnish a *sense of community*; they provide residents with a *sense of identity*; and they also help to establish a *sense of security* for people, a feeling that one can live in a particular neighborhood or street and be safe. As we introduce you to the specifics of cities throughout this book, we will come back again and again to emphasizing and illustrating the importance of cities as places, and of these three dimensions in particular.

In addition, we argue that cities are *spaces*. They offer a way to configure and to shape the material and natural environment of which they are composed. They have streets, houses, commercial buildings, and so on within, and their expressways and other transportation lines are configured in ways to help people move in and out of cities. Cities also provide

Introduction to Cities: How Place and Space Shape Human Experience,
First Edition. Xiangming Chen, Anthony M. Orum, and Krista E. Paulsen.
© 2013 Xiangming Chen, Anthony M. Orum, and Krista E. Paulsen.
Published 2013 by Blackwell Publishing Ltd.

public spaces – areas where their residents can come together and help to build a sense of community that is vital to the city as a place. Parks, sidewalks, and public squares are essential forms of public spaces, and they are crucial to the daily living that occurs in cities.

As you read through this book, these ideas, which at this moment are bare and abstract, will become more concrete. Indeed, the first chapter of this book is all about cities as places and spaces, and will furnish you with a number of specific examples and illustrations to make all of this clear.

There is a second critical choice we have made, and it is equally as important as the guiding concepts we have used here. This is the choice to emphasize the changing currents and elements of history as a way of showing how the theories about cities change as well as how cities themselves have become transformed, particularly over the course of the twentieth and early twenty-first centuries. One thing is certain: cities do not remain the same. They change from one time to another. Early on in the United States, for example, cities were, as some observers have said, "walking cities." They were small and people could get the things of daily life done by simply walking from one site to another. Parents could walk with their children to parks and schools; men and women could head off to work only minutes from where they lived.

In the latter part of the nineteenth century in the United States, and somewhat earlier in the United Kingdom, the world became transformed. The Industrial Revolution introduced a wide variety of changes that would affect the lives of people and also the shape of the cities and their surrounding rural environment. The space of the emerging industrial city began to expand. New industries opened, providing an opportunity for many people to migrate to the city and to find jobs. With all this expansion, and more, the character of the city began to change. One could no longer walk easily from one end to another. Eventually new forms of transportation, including buggies led by horses and later streetcars, emerged that would change the very character of a city's streets and sidewalks as well as the social and business rhythms of everyday life. The composition of cities would change too, as populations became larger and more diverse.

This change from the walking to the industrial city was momentous. Equally momentous have been the transformations of cities over the course of recent decades. Some industrial cities have lost industries that had been their foundations: cities such as Manchester or Barcelona or Detroit have seen their factories and manufacturing firms move elsewhere, often to places in Asia. On the one hand, this sort of change has emptied and altered the character of a place like Detroit, leading to the loss of people as well as industries. Those left behind have been the poor, often the black poor, and their lives have been devastated by the loss of jobs. On the other hand, Detroit's economic and manufacturing losses have turned out to be the gain of places elsewhere in the world, in China and India, for example. Over the course of the past 20 years alone, a number of new megacities have grown up in Asia. With new industries and plentiful jobs, these cities now have become the booming metropolitan areas of the early twenty-first century, just as Chicago and New York were at the beginning of the twentieth century.

Because cities have become so transformed across the globe over the course of the past century or so, we believe it important to take account of these changes in our narrative about cities and how they develop. We have done so by attending to historical forces and, where appropriate, dividing our story about cities into two historical periods: roughly before and after World War II. This is a convenient line of demarcation as many things happened after the war – economic changes as well as political changes – that would shift the patterns of urban growth across the world as well as lead to the sorts of transformations we point to above.

The other important point here to realize is that not only have cities changed over this period of time, but so, too, have theories about cities and their development. Theories of urban growth that might have made sense early in the twentieth century have been overshadowed by newer ideas that take account of the some key historical shifts of recent years. We devote two entire chapters in this book (Chapter 2 and Chapter 3) to many of the key urban theories, and how and why new ones have supplanted older ones.

We want to conclude this brief road map to our book by emphasizing the kind of sociological vision at work here. Cities are composed of structures, such as businesses and government, but, in the end, they happen because of the men and women and adults and children who live in them and breathe life into their daily activities. Some writers about cities, in our view, tend to overemphasize the structural and institutional features of cities, and to neglect the lives of the ordinary citizens who live in them. Our view of cities, as places and spaces, is intended to see the city from the bottom up – in the experiences of people making do and building communities and supporting families. We will talk a lot about structures later in this book, but ultimately we want to remind you that we view cities as rooted in the lives of human beings. It is human beings who make the city an important place in which to live and to work, and it is these same human beings who, we believe, possess the ability to change the cities in which they live, if they so wish.

Using this book

In the following chapters we provide insights into how and why cities across the globe have come to be as they are, and just how the places and spaces therein affect the lives of residents. There are five parts to the book, each of which lays out a coherent story about cities.

Part I develops the intellectual groundwork, starting with a full examination of the key concepts of space and place (Chapter 1). In Chapter 2 and Chapter 3, we introduce the ways that early and contemporary social theorists have explained problems such as why cities take the forms that they do, how the transition to an urban world affects social life, and how cities reflect and even amplify the inequalities that exist between groups. We then turn in Chapter 4 to the methods that have been used to study cities. This chapter will, we hope, provide you with the insights necessary to evaluate urban scholarship as well as some thoughts on how *you* might investigate the kinds of questions that this book will raise.

In Part II we turn, in considerable detail, to a discussion of the nature of cities and their development. In Chapter 5 we describe the development of the metropolis and its expansion. We invoke the idea of the metropolis as a way of emphasizing the size and scope of cities as they have grown over time. Chapter 6 then turns to a consideration of the nature of suburbs – when they began and how they have changed over the course of the twentieth century, in particular. Chapter 7 concludes this part by examining the broad historical changes that changed the character of the metropolis, focusing especially on the period after World War II. Here we consider such important historical events as the decline of industrial manufacturing in the United States. This decline presented major challenges to such older industrial cities as Chicago and Detroit, but it also provided great opportunities for new cities to develop in other parts of the world.

Part III turns to consider the nature of the metropolis and the social inequalities and differences that developed within it over the course of the twentieth and early twenty-first centuries. In Chapter 8, we explore how different racial and ethnic groups began to populate cities, the patterns of racial segregation that followed, and how social class intertwines with race and ethnicity in urban places. Chapter 9 pursues these matters further, tracing how social inequalities and differences changed in the period after World War II. Here we explore such important events as the movement of a wealthy middle class into the central areas of cities. The positive and negative dimensions of this process of gentrification have stirred up many political and social concerns about life in the metropolis in recent years. We also attend to the ways in which new patterns of immigration have transformed US and European cities, creating a new generation of ethnic enclaves, and consider the increase in gay and lesbian places within cities.

In Part IV, we shift our attention to the developing nations of the world and to the issues of urban development and metropolitan expansion within them. Much of the energy and dynamism in metropolitan expansion has taken place in these areas over the course of the past several decades. We present these developments with an eye to both the global forces behind them and the human impacts of this rapid urbanization. Chapter 10 and Chapter 11 go into more detail on the nature of urban development and they also consider the vital roles of the economy and the state.

Finally, in Part V, we conclude the book by considering the changes and challenges facing cities today. In Chapter 12 we consider the important issues of the broader natural environment and urban sustainability. Chapter 13 then draws the book, and our argument, to a close by re-examining and re-emphasizing the issues of place and space.

In addition to the materials in the book itself, you have access to the companion website: www.wiley.com/go/cities. This website is a way for us as authors to connect current events and other important examples and case studies to the broader concepts put forth in the text. Students will find lists of journals and web resources for Urban Studies, as well as an annotated documentary guide that details films relevant to the main themes of the book. There are also further essay and discussion questions for instructors to use, as well as additional cases and examples accompanied by a guide that shows you how to use them in conjunction with the book.

We know that this book will be used in different ways by different readers. It provides an introduction to urban studies in general and urban sociology more particularly. We hope that it provides a solid foundation to those of you who will go on to further studies in urban policy and governance, planning, social welfare, or urban sociology. For those of you for whom this book represents a first and last inquiry into urban issues, we aim to help you see places – and particularly cities – in new and more complex ways. Though few of us will make our living studying cities, most of us will make our lives in cities. It benefits us all to understand how these places came to be what they are, and to have insight into the ways that cities as places affect our own lives and those of our neighbors. We hope that this book provides resources with which you might develop such insight, and the motivation to use this knowledge in your everyday lives.

PART I
THE FOUNDATIONS

CHAPTER 1

Cities as places and spaces

KEY TOPICS

→ The definitions of place and space as applied to cities.

→ The role of place attachment in imbuing places with meanings and significance.

→ The importance of place in providing identity, community, and security for human beings.

→ The ways that human beings shape cities, and are in turn shaped by them.

→ You should also become familiar with the features of the text, including informative boxes on "Studying the city" and "Making the city better"; boxes that provide opportunities to delve into topics and concepts, called "Exploring further"; definitions of keywords; and critical thinking questions that will help you to continue to consider the issues raised in each chapter.

Contents

Introduction to Cities: How Place and Space Shape Human Experience, First Edition. Xiangming Chen, Anthony M. Orum, and Krista E. Paulsen.
© 2013 Xiangming Chen, Anthony M. Orum, and Krista E. Paulsen.
Published 2013 by Blackwell Publishing Ltd.

This is a book about cities, a topic that seems familiar enough but that most of us have not considered in any great depth. There are plenty of reasons why we should. We can estimate statistically that most of you live or have lived in a city or metropolitan area; more than half of the world's population now lives in cities (see Figure 1.1). Cities are also the centers of the world's economy. They are not only sites of production, where industries cluster, but also the central nodes in service and distribution networks and the command points from which economic decisions are made. Across the globe, wealth is increasingly generated, and spent, in cities (see Table 1.1). But cities are also the locus of profound environmental challenges (they consume two-thirds of the world's energy, and are home to many toxic industries and waste sites) and social problems ranging from pronounced poverty and uneven access to the most basic of human necessities, to crime, violence, and even warfare. Without a doubt, cities deserve our attention now more than ever.

While cities are important for all of these reasons, we argue that cities are also particularly important kinds of **places**. So what do we mean by places? Places are specific sites, whether entire cities or smaller locations within cities, that are shaped by human beings and shape the lives of human beings. Places include large metropolitan areas as well as individual homes, workplaces, playgrounds, schools, and street corners. They are all those specific and rich sites to which we feel attached, that become a part of us. As places, cities are distinct and meaningful

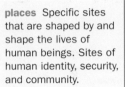

places Specific sites that are shaped by and shape the lives of human beings. Sites of human identity, security, and community.

sites in which people live out their lives. These meanings derive from the histories of places, whether the formal history found in books or the informal history that is created by individuals as they go about their daily routines. In turn, these histories reflect the uses to which places are put: who has lived in a place and how, the businesses and industries that thrived or failed there, and conflicts over just what should occur where. Histories, uses, and experiences imbue places with memories and meanings that distinguish one place from another. Places are thus inherently social creations.

Attending to the histories of places draws our eyes to the important work that individuals and groups do to make and remake places. That places are the result of human efforts may seem obvious enough, but all too often we take places as givens, assuming that they just are the way they are; that they are somehow immutable and unchanging. This is particularly common when we compare two places – two very different cities or neighborhoods, for example. An impoverished ghetto area is drastically different from a wealthy gated suburb, and these differences may appear almost natural. But, as we will explain in this book, places

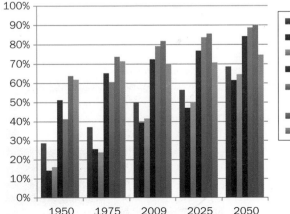

Figure 1.1 Percentage of population in urban areas by world and region, 1950–2050. *Source: Developed by David Boston from data from the UN Department of Economic and Social Affairs, Population Division, World Urbanization Prospects 2009.*

Table 1.1 Percentage of GDP generated in urban versus rural areas, 2009. *Source: Based on data from* CIA World Factbook, Field Listing: GDP – Composition by Sector.

	Urban	Rural
World	94.0	6.0
United States	98.8	1.2
United Kingdom	98.8	1.2
Japan	98.4	1.6
European Union	98.1	1.9
Canada	97.7	2.3
South Korea	97.0	3.0
Australia	95.9	4.1
Mexico	95.7	4.3
Russia	95.3	4.7
Ireland	95.0	5.0
Brazil	93.9	6.1
Turkey	90.7	9.3
Colombia	90.3	9.7
China	89.4	10.6
Iran	89.1	10.9
Egypt	86.3	13.7
Indonesia	84.7	15.3
India	83.0	17.0
Nigeria	66.9	33.1

come to be different from one another through human efforts, whether the work of individuals building their own homes on the outskirts of growing cities or the policies of nations that seek to industrialize their lagging regional economies. Culture, power, nature, resources – these and other factors affect the ways that places become what they are, and human beings are always at the helm.

Places are not only created through social processes but also fulfill an important array of social needs. Among these needs we single out three for special attention: *identity*, *community*, and *security*. As we explain in this chapter, places provide us with a sense of who we are, and we may attach the meanings associated with a place to ourselves. Telling someone where we are from becomes an important way of announcing who we are – our identity. Places are also the cradles of community. Though some communities exist and even thrive in virtual spaces (groups on Facebook and other internet networks are prime examples), the places where we live, work, and play often link us to groups that care about and share our fates. Significantly, these groups may exclude as well as include individuals, and constrain as well as support them. Identity and community are actually key constitutive elements of our third dimension of place – security. When we identify with a place and feel connected to groups there, we often feel the most secure. But security extends beyond the psychological and emotional to the material. Some places provide the kinds of environments in which humans thrive – clean air and water, shelter, and freedom from violence, as a minimum – while others deprive residents of these basic elements of a safe and decent life. Moreover, some places are vulnerable to political upheavals and environmental catastrophes that undermine the security of large populations.

spaces Geographic entities with distinct shapes, scales, and other properties that set the stage for certain kinds of human activities.

Cities are also important **spaces**. In distinguishing the ideas of place and space, we separate the particular from the general. Places are specific sites, whether structures or neighborhoods or entire metropolitan areas, to which people have attached meaning. As such, São Paulo is a place, as is Heliopolis (a slum area in São Paulo), or the block on which you grew up. But these particular places are also different kinds of spaces – geographic entities with distinct shapes, scales, and other properties that set the stage for certain kinds of human activities.

Consider, for instance, a city block. As a space it may be dense or sprawling, accessible or remote, pedestrian-friendly or designed to accommodate automobiles. These qualities of space and others may then predispose the block to becoming a certain kind of place, as human beings live out their lives and write its informal history. As you will learn in this book, the spatial forms of cities have changed dramatically in the past 50 years or so (indeed, some would argue that the word "city" is no longer appropriate for describing the sprawling urban regions that now house many millions of persons), and this has in turn affected them as places. While you will have a chance to fathom the gigantic scale of megacities later in the book, you will be guided to appreciate the microscopic meanings they also possess as places.

Finally, and perhaps most importantly, places shape our destinies. They are contexts in which lives are created, and as such they furnish many of the resources that we need to develop as human beings and to reach the opportunities to which we aspire. And, while all cities play this role as places, different cities and the neighborhoods within them do so unequally. Places are thus an important element of inequality both globally and locally. As you read this book, we ask that you keep in mind the very different and unequal types of identity, community, and security provided by urban places, and how these in turn shape the fates of individuals and groups.

In this chapter we develop these central elements of cities as places and spaces. We expand on what it means to understand cities as places, and how this will inform the material covered in the book. We then take up the points raised here in greater detail, elaborating on what it means for places to provide identity, community, and security, and the processes by which places are made and remade. We then turn to the distinction between space and place, and to some central concepts in the scholarship on urban spaces. Finally we take up the notion of how places shape our fates, previewing the great diversity of urban places that you will come to know through this book.

Cities as places

At first glance, cities seem to be an odd jumble and mixture of things. There are streets and sidewalks, possibly parks, an abundance of housing, factories, offices and government institutions, and perhaps some empty lots and vacant buildings. All kinds of vehicles fill cities – bicycles and buses, trucks and taxis, and more and more private automobiles. The landscape is largely paved, and what little bits of nature remain are probably heavily manicured or just struggling to survive. These physical features may distinguish cities from rural lands, and they certainly predispose residents to certain kinds of activities and experiences. But what makes cities places is more than the presence of these kinds of surroundings – it is the way that these surroundings become useful and meaningful over time. It is these uses and meanings that connect human beings to cities and that make cities distinct from one another. Strip away the specific everyday uses and meanings, and one city comes to look much like another.

In this book we focus on cities as places, so their uses and meanings are central. But just what do we mean by these terms? Let's first take up *uses*. Cities often develop around very different purposes. Some, like Washington, DC, or Beijing or The Hague are national and even international political capitals, and because of this they contain institutions of government and become magnets for a great deal of traffic in politics, and sometimes traffic in money and finance as well. Beijing also aspires to become an international financial center, for example. Other cities are like Miami Beach or Barcelona, sites where people often go as tourists and embrace the warmth and good life they find there. As these cities come to be known as particular kinds of places (tourist destinations or seats of power, in our examples), businesses that will flourish in these places will seek to locate there (a human rights law firm in The Hague, for instance, or a chain restaurant in Miami Beach). Migration, too, perpetuates distinctions between different kinds of cities. Cities might attract migrants with distinct kinds of knowledge and skills, and residents seeking different kinds of pleasures and opportunities. These migrants in turn may work to preserve those aspects of the city that attracted them in the first place, thus ensuring that the distinctive qualities of a place are maintained. Though not all cities are dominated in this way by a particular type of political or economic use, all have distinct mixes of uses that differentiate them from other places and can set similar chains of events in motion.

While entire cities may have different kinds of uses when examined in broad strokes, the uses of different parts of the city matter more for its residents. Over time, cities develop districts that are known for this or that – as industrial or residential or commercial, for instance. They also take on certain qualities within these kinds of distinctions. So, a residential area may be desolate and depressing, hip and fashionable, or quiet and insular. And the neighborhood that is desolate one day may be hip the next. All of this goes to show that the nature of an area reflects how it is used, and that those uses are subject to change. So, if a residential area is, for instance, a disused site of vacant lots and abandoned buildings, young house hunters seeking a bargain may buy, build, and improve properties there. Their labors, as well as their everyday comings and goings, transform the neighborhood through what is known as gentrification, as you will learn later in the book.

The uses of places furnish the primary way in which human beings come to imbue places with *meanings*. These meanings include the memories associated with places, whether first-hand experiences and stories such as those told by a long-time resident or the kinds of public memories derived from books or monuments. Meanings also include associations between a place and certain kinds of social attributes – good or bad – and the senses of what a place should be. These meanings may be quite personal, as in the case of an elderly woman who could no longer afford the property taxes on her home in a small town in upstate New York. She was one of a growing number of people who found her income in her old age did not quite match her needs. At the same time, the community in which she lived needed to raise taxes so it could fund some important public projects, including local schools. This poor, elderly woman told her story to a *New York Times* reporter and, as she did, she revealed the ways in which she and her husband, now deceased, had made her house into a home. He had built the cabinetry in the kitchen, for instance, and in doing so left a seemingly indelible imprint on the place. Thus, although to an outside observer the large, rambling, and older structure only seemed to be a building, to this woman it was a distinct place: she and her husband had invested their energies into it, and now the house had become a site of memories and meanings in her life. These kinds of attachments prove fateful in the lives of individuals and in the character of the places they inhabit (see Exploring further 1.1).

Though personal and sentimental meanings such as these are certainly important, individuals and groups attach meanings to places of much larger scales, and with much higher stakes. This can best be illustrated by the large-scale urban redevelopment over the last two decades in Shanghai, where people on entire blocks of old houses, primarily located in the urban core, have had to relocate due to the new construction of more lucrative commercial and residential projects (see Figure 1.2). An estimated one million households and up to three million people have lost their attachments to their old residences and neighborhoods. Without sufficient compensation from the government and developers, many of these displaced residents have experienced both the financial strain of buying the new and more expensive high-rise housing away from the city center and the difficulty of

EXPLORING FURTHER   1.1

Place attachment

One way to better understand how places provide security, community, and identity is to study what scholars refer to as **place attachment**. Although this term has a variety of meanings that are subject to intense debate, at its most basic, place attachment describes the emotional connections that people feel toward specific places such as buildings, neighborhoods, or cities. These connections are formed over time, through repeated positive interactions. As we live our lives, places are part of routines as well as special occasions: we drop in at a neighborhood coffee shop each morning, celebrate our birthday at

place attachment
The emotional connections that people feel toward specific places such as buildings, neighborhoods, or cities.

a local bar, or bring our newborn child home to a particular apartment. In doing so, those places become imbued with meaning and take on some importance in our lives. Attachments may be intensely personal or shared by larger groups, and may vary from the functional and practical to the social or sentimental. Scholars from fields as diverse as psychology, sociology, geography, and anthropology agree that these attachments are important for individuals and groups, but they often disagree on just how and why.

A useful starting point within the scholarship on place attachment is the research on places that are destroyed or threatened with destruction. Psychologist Marc Fried (2000), one of the first researchers to work on this problem, found that residents forcibly relocated from Boston's West End felt a strong attachment to their old neighborhood. Relocated residents grieved for their homes – structures reasonably characterized as blighted – as they would for lost loved ones. This finding was a surprise at the time of its publication in the early 1960s, as many assumed that housing quality might better predict residents' commitment to their neighborhood. Instead, Fried revealed (just as sociologist Herbert Gans also found in *The Urban Villagers* (1982 [1962]), his study of the same area) that the dense social networks of the West End fell apart as residents relocated, and that social dimensions of place had been central to residents' attachment to the area.

More recently, in a study of the Walker neighborhood of Newcastle-upon-Tyne, Alice Mah (2006) examined resistance to urban renewal projects designed to encourage economic development. Though their neighborhood scored worst in Newcastle on the year 2000 English Indices of Deprivation (and thirtieth worst for England out of over 8000 wards), the residents were firmly committed to staying in their homes. Here multiple generations of a family could be found on the same street, and residents were loyal to the few shops and pubs that remained as industry and population declined. Given the turbulent economic times in which these residents were living, and the changes to the urban environment around them, their attachment to place may have reflected a desire for stability and continuity. Moreover, uncertainty about the fate of their homes resulted in stress, depression, and anxiety, indicating the strong psychological importance of having a secure home place.

These studies by Fried and Mah, among others working in this tradition, invite an important question about the relationship between social class and place attachment. Are poor or working-class residents, including ethnic minorities and immigrants, more attached to places? Given that poorer residents are more likely to rely upon social networks within their communities (using a neighbor or nearby family member for childcare, or sharing food when times are tight economically) and the myriad dimensions of support that neighborhoods provide to new immigrants (see Chapter 8), this seems like a reasonable question. In an innovative study of communities in three regions of Poland, Maria Lewicka (2005) found that place attachment was no stronger among those with limited personal and economic resources.

But, while economic capital did not affect one's attachment to place, *cultural capital* did. In her study, residents with more education (and more educated parents) tended to be less attached to place.

Another important question that drives place attachment research is just what impacts attachments to place might have on the lives of individuals and groups, whether positive or negative. On the positive side, place attachment may be equivalent to what Jane Jacobs calls a sense of proprietorship in one's neighborhood. This sense empowers residents to act on behalf of the neighborhood, enforcing local behavioral norms and watching out for people and property. On the negative side, we might ask to what extent place attachment – which is often measured by the expressed desire to stay in a place, or the degree to which people say they would be sad to leave – leads residents to stay in places that are not good for them. This may include places devoid of economic opportunities, those polluted by hazardous substances, or those where residents are exposed to violence. In addition, we should remember that one group's attachment to place may motivate them to exclude a different group; consider, for example, the violence against immigrants in neighborhoods across the United States and Europe. If we extend this line of thinking to a broader geographic scale, we can see how place attachment might lead to national interethnic violence or ethnic cleansing.

We might also consider the degree to which people remain attached to place in an increasingly globalized world. As we move from place to place more quickly and know more of places that we have never visited in person, how much does our own place matter to us? The demands of the global economy arguably compel us toward a footloose life in which attachment to place is ever more difficult. In addition, some scholars have argued that the increasing standardization of products and places erodes place attachment (consider the identical architecture of chain stores across the United States, or the familiar menu and iconography found at McDonald's restaurants around the globe). We can contrast these pessimistic views with those of scholars who see a continuing relevance of place attachment as places constitute a greater share of our identity. Richard Florida, whose work we discuss in several chapters within this book, contends that, for individuals in creative fields such as entertainment or software design, where one lives is increasingly more important to identity than where one works. Florida's research suggests that the same global forces that may pry us from the places of our birth may also help us to locate meaningful places of choice.

accessing convenient shopping and services. More importantly, however, they have lost the emotional attachments to and social networks in the old neighborhoods that once were manifest in convenient daily encounters and casual chats across the alleys and on the street. This loss took a much heavier toll on older people, who were much more strongly and deeply attached to the old houses and neighborhoods as places (see Chapter 11).

Let's return for a moment to where this section began, with a rough inventory of the kinds of physical things that one finds in a city – the streets and sidewalks, parks and factories, and so on. While this physical landscape certainly has a hand in shaping the ways that human beings make their lives in cities, it becomes much more consequential once humans establish patterns dictating what the physical spaces mean and how they will be used. For example, who will dictate the uses of public parks? Will it be children? Or gangs? Or police? Or people who are homeless? Does the statue in a public square provide a rallying point for protestors or merely a roost for pigeons? Does the struggling industrial center erode, and thereby lose population, or do its leaders anticipate change and invest in new kinds of production? Actions and decisions, large and small, make cities the distinctive kinds of places that they are, and, as we will discuss below, allow them to in turn shape the fates of the individuals who live there.

In emphasizing the importance of place, we do not intend to overshadow the roles of other social forces in the lives of city dwellers, or to imply that all residents have the same experiences of places. Take, for example, the contrast drawn above between cities that serve primarily as tourist destinations and as seats of government. These central uses of any given city are not immediately relevant in the day-to-day lives of every resident. For instance, the lives of a low-wage service worker in Washington, DC, and one in Miami Beach might actually be quite similar. Each would likely struggle to find adequate housing and transportation, and would have little time or income to enjoy the museums and restaurants, or beaches and clubs, for which these places are internationally famous. This illustrates an important caveat when studying cities as places: it is important to keep in mind the differences between places, but larger social structures still shape the lives of residents. The types of racial/ethnic, gender, and income inequalities present in a society will extend to all places there, though the specifics of how inequalities operate will vary from one place to another.

Similarly, different people will come to associate different meanings with places, in part because they use them in very different ways. Tourists, for instance, have very different experiences of cities than locals, often because they are insulated from areas of danger or decline (see Studing the city 1.3). As a result, tourists may associate a given city with leisure, culture, or romance while locals have far more complex associations that are less universally positive. Race, class, and gender matter too in shaping the meanings that people make of places – as do immigrant status, religion, physical ability, age, sexuality, and any other dimension of inequality. One illustration of this is to be found in how differently the dwellers of Mumbai's slums and the foreign tourists who visit those slums view and feel about these places. While the residents see and experience the wretched living conditions as living quarters and as work environments for those with home businesses, the tourists walk

Figure 1.2 Redevelopment in the older areas of Shanghai has displaced an estimated one million households. This woman was one of the last remaining residents in her neighborhood, having refused to relocate. *Source: © LOOK Die Bildagentur der Fotografen GmbH/Alamy.*

through them and gaze at the people, thereby satisfying their own fleeting curiosity. *Slumdog Millionaire* (2008), the popular movie about India, helps to reinforce the curiosity that people possess as tourists and outsiders. Yet the slums remain fundamentally different places in the minds and lives of those who inhabit them.

Identity, community, and security

Places as the site of our identity

In recalling his childhood in Southie, a poor, predominantly Irish-American neighborhood in Boston, the author Michael Patrick MacDonald conveys the powerful and multi-layered ways in which young people constructed place-based identities. For them, being from Southie meant being Irish (or Irish-American), and even youth who were several generations removed from their Irish ancestors relished cultural displays such as caps and jackets bearing the University of Notre Dame's Fighting Irish name and logo. Symbols like these helped to connect the young people not only to their ancestors' home but also to the ethnic enclave from which they hailed. Southie youth also announced a specific neighborhood identity with a small tattoo on the wrist known as the "Southie dot." This indelible mark conveyed to all who understood it just where a young person was from – for better or worse. As MacDonald recounts, the dot could make one a target for gangs from outside neighborhoods or other ethnic groups. "But everyone went ahead and did the Southie dot anyway," he writes, "to prove their loyalty to the neighborhood, regardless of the consequences in the outside world" (MacDonald 2000: p. 63). Solidarity and toughness were central to what it meant to be a young person from Southie.

Although most of us do not announce our place-based identities with a tattoo, the places we are from still constitute an important part of who we are. This is in part because the meanings attached to places also attach to people. When a stranger asks you about yourself, one of the first things that you tell them is likely to be where you are from. We know that others are familiar with a variety of places, and we allow those familiarities to say something about us as individuals. What do we say about ourselves when we tell people where we're from? To start, our home places convey something about our cultural roots. For instance, one religion may predominate in a particular city, or the city may be known for a distinct set of values. Our hometown may have a well-known art or music scene of which we are a part, or it may be recognized as a place that is rabid for its sports teams. Places also announce social differences, whether high or low. Noting the city where we come from – and particularly the neighborhood – can thus serve as shorthand for our social class (this is particularly useful in countries like the United States, where people are uncomfortable talking about class status). It is important to keep in mind, however, that individuals do not identify wholesale with the cultures of their places, and that places and their residents can be stereotyped in just the same way that ethnic or racial groups are.

The sense of identity derived from places allows us to understand ourselves as well. We are socialized in specific places, and learn how to be of a place at the same time that we learn how to be members of society more generally. To return to the Southie example above, MacDonald and his friends learned a certain set of local traits and behaviors, from how to speak, stand, and dress to just whom one should trust. Our families and peers typically share the norms of our place, and in this way much of our culture is derived from, or mediated through, the places we inhabit.

Places as the site of community

Places furnish not only a sense of identity for us but also a strong sense of community – of our social connections to other people. Neighborhoods do this for people, and people become attached to those neighborhoods. The daily routine of our movements through the neighborhood, the people that we see, gives us a strong sense of a community that surrounds us. A famous student of cities and neighborhoods, Jane Jacobs, wrote at length about her neighborhood in the Greenwich Village area of New York City (see Figure 1.3). Jacobs pointed out that the various people who lived in the neighborhood provided the kind of community in which residents could feel a sense of belonging, and, especially, a sense of trust. People got to know one another in the neighborhood, and, if there was a problem or someone was in danger, neighborhood residents and business owners would help one another out. Jacobs wrote of the local delicatessen owner, Joe Cornacchia, for example, who served as the eyes of the neighborhood. Because his shop opened early, Joe kept a watchful eye over the street at hours when others were attending to matters inside their homes. Moreover, because everyone visited the delicatessen regularly, Joe acted as an important source of information in the community. He even held the keys to various buildings and residences in the neighborhood – a strong indication of the level of trust there.

Ideally, places furnish these kinds of communities with a high degree of social capital – and that is the second key element of place. Sometimes these places can be very small – for example, playgrounds where parents will gather with their children in the afternoon. They meet with other parents and their children play with one another, creating strong bonds of friendship for both generations. Alternatively, sometimes such places can simply be street corners or shopping malls where teenagers gather after school and on the weekends. Businesses are well aware of

Figure 1.3 Jane Jacobs at the White Horse Tavern in Greenwich Village in 1961. For Jacobs, the neighborhood tavern was an important place for locals and visitors alike to renew connections. *Source: Photo: Cervin Robinson/Courtesy of the Architects' Journal.*

these features of places. Sociologist Ray Oldenburg (1997) refers to places where people can gather and establish connections to one another as "third places," following home and work in their importance. He offers that pubs, taverns, and other sites outside people's homes where friends can gather on a regular basis help to create this strong sense of community. Indeed, Oldenburg was a consultant for the coffee company Starbucks, and he urged them to create not merely a site where people could get a good cup of coffee but one where they could sit around and chat with one another.

It is easy to idealize places as sites of strong and supportive communities. But, in many places, the trust and mutual support that communities provide is largely absent. This may be because populations are highly transient (although most of the residents in Jane Jacobs' neighborhood rented, they stayed in the area for many years) or because neighborhoods lack the kinds of spaces and institutions that would facilitate positive interaction among residents (no parks, no pubs, and so on). In other places, communities may have strong ties, but these ties may not extend to all members. Ethnic, racial, religious, and sexual minorities have often been excluded from place-based communities. In other places, any newcomer or new way of thinking is suspect, and as a result change occurs only very slowly. It is important to remember that, while places *can* facilitate community, we should not assume that they actually do, or that community is universally positive.

Places as sites of security

The last element so important to places is that they can furnish us with a sense of security. As discussed in the introduction to this chapter, security often follows from identity and community. When we feel connected to a place and the other people therein, we often feel secure. We know our figurative "place" in the world, and know that we are surrounded by individuals we can trust to support us. The positive implications of this type of security cannot be understated – it allows us to truly be ourselves.

But security has a more practical side as well. We need to feel that our person and our family, as well as our property, are safe. This too is fundamental to our wellbeing. Knowing that our home will be there as we left it when we return from work, or that we are safe walking to a friend's house, or that our children are able to play outside, allows us to then turn our minds to the myriad other interests and responsibilities that life presents.

The lack of such security is a major concern for city dwellers today – particularly for parents, who may feel this most acutely. Especially in large and dynamic cities, the safety and security of neighborhoods varies widely. When people choose to move to a particular place, they often do so because they have heard that that neighborhood is safe and secure, for them and their children. Anthropologist Setha Low has found that this desire to *feel* secure, even when real threats to that security are largely imagined, is a major factor behind the spread of **gated communities** in the United States and around the world (see Studying the city 1.1). Likewise, when people choose to leave neighborhoods, it often is for the very same reason – that those neighborhoods did not feel safe or secure to them. In poor neighborhoods, in particular, this sense of security is a major issue. In a study done of local residents in Milwaukee years ago, for example, the researchers found that the key reason people wanted to leave their neighborhood was that they did *not* feel safe and secure there.[1] They reported that they were worried, in particular, about the amount of crime and violence in their neighborhood.

Though crime is certainly an important threat to the security of places and individuals therein, other larger-scale forces also threaten places. Political conflicts have the potential to undermine the security of neighborhoods and even entire cities. As regimes change, large populations are displaced or killed – often to make places

gated community
A residential community surrounded by walls, fences, gates, water, and/or natural barriers that admits only residents and their guests.

STUDYING THE CITY   1.1

The globalization of gated communities

Why are we seeing more and more communities surround themselves with walls, gates, and guards' towers? Increasingly we see urban and suburban communities, whether groups of single-family homes or multi-story apartment complexes, fortified against would-be intruders. Anthropologist Setha Low (2005) studies gated communities in the United States, Latin America, and China to try and make sense of this global trend toward the increasing privatization of residential space.

The places that Low studies have very different cultural backgrounds as well as different social meanings attached to gated communities within them, so identifying what these places have in common and how this trend of residential privatization emerged almost simultaneously in each place is a daunting task. Two important perspectives that have tried to explain this global trend are the supply-side theory put forward by Chris Webster (2001) and the demand-side perspective advocated by Low.

According to Chris Webster, gated communities have been springing up globally because goods and services can be supplied most efficiently and effectively through smaller-scale local organizations, such as gated communities, and this leaves less for government to supply in the public realm. Conversely, Setha Low argues that globalization is leading to increasing heterogeneity and uneven development in cities, which in turn leads to increased perceptions of crime. When the perceived level of crime rises, people begin to feel more insecure, and the option to live somewhere safe and predictable, such as a gated community, becomes very appealing.

Whatever the reason, the increase in gated communities across the world means that more types of public space are being privatized every day. And, as many people begin to have all of their services and amenities provided through private gated communities, those people may be less likely to want their tax money spent on providing the same types of services and amenities publicly. What then might happen to those living outside the walls?

more homogeneous or to provide greater access to a privileged group. The so-called "ethnic cleansings" that occurred in the former Yugoslavia are a prime example, as are the sectarian struggles occurring in Iraq. In another example, as part of an effort to remake the nation of Cambodia, the Khmer Rouge regime purged about two million people out of Phnom Penh after it came into power in the 1970s. Environmental forces also threaten the security of places, whether the potential flooding of coastal areas due to climate change or more routine disasters such as earthquakes, wildfires, and seasonal flooding (see Chapter 12). Whatever the threat to security, it is important to keep in mind that, when people lose the places to which they are attached, they lose much more than their physical environment: they also lose the potential of that environment to generate a positive identity or community. For that reason, displacement is among the most disruptive events that an individual can experience.

Human beings make and remake places

Places, whether they are cities or their constitutive parts, are human creations. Though the age and scale of places such as London or New York City may obscure the efforts of the people who envisioned and built them, we must always remember that even these cities reflect the work of human hands, and that these hands are never idle. One generation designs one kind of city – for example, the generation of people who developed cities during the Industrial Revolution – and another generation then seeks to change and modify that city. Cities and other places must therefore be seen as fundamentally human and social constructions that change and evolve over time. As we will explain later in this book, industrial cities such as Detroit are increasingly finding that their infrastructure outstrips their current population and economic output, resulting in efforts to "downsize" the city and return urban landscapes to nature. Meanwhile, on the other side of the world, Chinese agricultural lands are now sprouting factories and worker housing as cities large and small grow outward and eat up farmland. It is estimated that between 1987 and 1992 China lost close to 100 million acres of farmland each year to urbanization and the expansion of roads and industries. Between 1990 and 2000, 74 percent of the new urban land use in the Beijing, Tianjin, and Hebei (Province) region was converted from arable land (Tan et al. 2005).

These kinds of urban changes mark important shifts in the world economy, but changes in social arrangements at the local and national levels are also visible in the forms that cities take. Consider, for instance, the patterns of segregation seen in US cities. For many years, black and white residents lived near one another, albeit often in unequal circumstances. Following the **Great Migration** of the early twentieth century, a period in which millions of African Americans moved from the rural south to industrial cities of the north, segregation became much more pronounced and was enforced by violent means. This coincided with an initial boom in suburban construction that facilitated the movement of affluent whites to the urban outskirts, where racial and ethnic minorities were denied residence by legally enforceable covenants (this process is detailed further in Chapter 6 and Chapter 8). As a result, US cities took on a form that George Clinton of the funk band Parliament characterized as "chocolate cities and vanilla suburbs."

Great Migration The movement of a large number of African Americans from the US South, especially during the interwar period.

Patterns of segregation by class, race, and ethnicity are common in cities across the globe as groups map their social positions onto the urban landscape. In South Africa, the patterns of segregation under the system of Apartheid essentially separated people by race so that black South Africans were compelled to live entirely in areas separated from the white population of Afrikaners and British. The Apartheid system was overturned partially because black South Africans began challenging these racial boundaries by moving into areas designated as white-only neighborhoods. With the end of Apartheid, legal racial segregation was eliminated. Yet today these formal barriers have been replaced, in part, by the emergence of new barriers of separation that are both race- and class-based. Thus, in metropolitan Johannesburg, one today finds enormous slums on the outskirts of the city populated by poor black South Africans but also by a flood of recent refugees from nearby Zimbabwe and migrants from countries such as Nigeria and Mozambique who have come in search of work. At the same time, wealthy white residents have deserted the central city and, along with the new black elite, have consolidated their financial and political power in nearby Sandton, a former all-white suburb that has become the new social and economic capital of metropolitan Johannesburg (Murray 2008).

Difference not only results in negative and exclusionary forms of place-making but can also foster positive outcomes. As immigrants flood into cities across the world, they create and recreate neighborhoods in ways that make them comfortable. They create, in effect, **urban enclaves** – social settlements that provide immigrants with a way to remain attached to others from their homelands and to mark and identify their place as a distinct ethnic space in their new country. Over the course of the past several decades in Chicago, for example,

urban enclaves Settlements and communities created by new immigrants to a country.

various enclaves have grown up in and around the city, enclaves that consist primarily of recent Mexican immigrants but also those from Korea and Ukraine. These immigrants develop special shops and restaurants, places where recent immigrants can come to buy the groceries and the clothing from their homelands. One particularly well-known Chicago neighborhood is Pilsen (see Figure 1.4), home to many thousands of recent immigrants from Mexico. Its residents have attempted to recreate elements of their homeland for themselves and marked the area with various public artworks and murals – a twentieth-century Mexican tradition they have reinvented in Chicago. Spanish is spoken as often as English, if not more often, in the enclave, and the whole range of institutions – from churches to schools – reflects the Mexican influence. As more and more Mexican immigrants have entered the city, in fact, they have settled in the outskirts of the metropolis, creating new and even more diverse enclaves for themselves. As you will see in Chapter 8, cities and their ethnic enclaves have long served as important points of transition for new immigrants, and these immigrants have in turn remade their cities in vital ways.

We should look at cities not merely as bricks and mortar, buildings and streets – as the work of architects and urban planners, engineers and laborers – but also as cultural and social creations providing insight into the ways and customs of the people who live in them. Cities reveal to us how people live, their power arrangements, their values and priorities, how they care for their children, and other important matters. A recent conflict over the construction of an Islamic center and mosque near the site of the former World Trade Center provides a useful illustration here. Had the area never been the target of terrorist attacks, the proposed mosque might have proceeded with little notice. But, because the area now possesses a near-sacred status, and because that status is bound up with the identity of the terrorists, in the minds of some New Yorkers the construction of a mosque nearby

Figure 1.4 Murals in Chicago's Pilsen neighborhood announce – and enhance – the area's Mexican heritage. *Source: Photo © Ralf-Finn Hestoft/Corbis.*

constituted another assault. Those supporting and opposing the mosque struggle to attach their preferred meaning to Lower Manhattan as a place: some supporters have argued that a mosque nearby would serve as a testament to US tolerance and diversity, while those opposing the development contend that it would mock the memories of those who perished nearby. Although this is a dramatic example, the meanings of all places are subject to change, whether by deliberate action or by accident. Changes in meaning are then literally cast in concrete when one type of structure or another is deemed appropriate and constructed.

Place and space

In revealing the ways that meanings are contested and attached to sites, the struggle over what kinds of uses should or should not occur near Ground Zero also illustrates ways in which space becomes place. The concepts of space and place are often used together, as each turns our attention toward the importance of land and structures, and people's connections with these. For many years, social and behavioral sciences – with the exception of geography – paid limited attention to the roles of place and space. In looking for the general patterns in human behavior, they often looked to variables that transcended locations. They knew that people might behave differently in one city or country than they did in another, but believed that this was only because other important variables – income, religion, level of education, and so on – differed in those locations. But in recent years social scientists have recognized that places and spaces differ in important ways – ways that are more than the sum of a handful of demographic or geographic variables – and that these differences have important consequences for people's lives. This has led to more cross-disciplinary discussions of the roles that place and space play in people's lives, conversations that will continue through this book.

We've said quite a bit about place but so far have not said much about space. Just how do they two differ, and how do they work together? The distinction is partly one of the general versus the particular: space is different from place in that *places represent specific locations in space* (see Table 1.2). As spaces are used and made meaningful by human beings, they become places. To illustrate this distinction, Studying the city 1.2 describes the spaces and places dedicated to tourism, a growing share of urban areas. The same location is therefore simultaneously a certain kind of space and a particular place. Thus, a plaza is a certain kind of *space*, and Mexico City's Plaza de la Constitución is a *place*.

Beneath the meanings and uses that distinguish spaces as places, spaces differ from one another in important ways. Some spaces are constructed for certain kinds of uses – ball fields, for instance, or streets – though this does not always mean that they are used for their intended purposes (indeed, a street may come to serve as a soccer pitch or baseball diamond when no proper field is available). Scale also matters, as small spaces suggest intimacy and

Table 1.2 Place versus space.

Place	Space
A specific site, whether an entire city or a smaller location therein, that is shaped by human beings and shapes the lives of human beings.	Geographic entities with distinct shapes, scales, and other properties that set the stage for certain kinds of human activities.

STUDYING THE CITY   1.2

Tourist spaces

As cities increasingly attempt to market themselves as tourist destinations, scholars have used the concepts of place and space to better understand this process. Tourism certainly capitalizes on cities as places: the distinct qualities of Vienna or Bangkok or Las Vegas motivate visitors to come and experience them. But space is also important in tourism, as tourist *places* also construct tourist *spaces* – areas designed for the comfort and pleasure of visitors (see Figure 1.5).

tourist spaces Highly controlled areas that cater specifically to the experiential, consumption, service, and aesthetic demands of tourists.

What is a **tourist space**? Within cities, we find highly controlled areas that cater specifically to the experiential, consumption, service, and aesthetic demands of tourists. They allow visitors to engage with a place's positive associations in a highly controlled environment. Informed by tourist literature and local iconography, tourism promoters essentially "script" the impression a tourist is to take away from a place. Thus, in Rome or Paris the tourist revels in culture and art, while in Jamaica or Cancun the script emphasizes tropical relaxation. Care is taken to ensure the harmony of the message, typically by removing any contradictory elements. Thus, a resort district may wall off views of nearby slums, and street vendors might be carefully controlled around museums and monuments. However, slum tourism in India's megacities (mentioned earlier in this chapter) appears to fit both in an ironic way.

Political scientist Dennis Judd (1999) observes the emergence of what he calls "tourist bubbles," a type of tourist space unique to decaying cities. Here the traveler "moves inside secured, protected, and normalized environments." Judd cites Baltimore's Harborplace development as a typical example. Harborplace's "festival marketplace" (a hybrid of shopping mall and performance space popularized in the 1980s) provides opportunities to shop, dine, and take in local sites of Baltimore's Inner Harbor in an atmosphere free of crime, decline, or interactions with urban "others" such as the homeless.

But, while Harborplace is a specific *place*, we can identify a category of locations like it – which are increasingly common across the globe – as tourist *spaces*. These would include entertainment districts, where one finds a high density of performance venues, restaurants, and pubs, as well as many historic districts, resorts, casinos, parks, and monuments. As you travel through or explore your own city, keep an eye out for *spaces* that cater to tourists and ask yourself how these kinds of spaces represent a particular *place*. What meanings are conveyed? Whose version of the place is presented?

Figure 1.5 A horse and buggy ride in front of Hoffburg Palace, Vienna. Tourist spaces often include elements that connect places to moments in the past. *Source: Photo: Hiroshi Higuchi/Getty Images.*

privacy while large spaces seem to foster anonymity. Many more qualities of spaces matter as well, as these allow spaces to facilitate some activities rather than others. And, as you will learn later in this book, even the same kinds of spaces can have qualities that make them inviting or repellant, well-loved or reviled. Jane Jacobs called attention to the ways that parks – an important type of urban space – differ from one another. Park spaces that offer a sense of enclosure, for instance, will actually be more inviting. Examining similar properties of urban space, William H. Whyte, whose work we discuss in Chapter 4, found that something as simple as the presence of movable seating will make one park or plaza more popular than another.

While some urban spaces are as small as plazas and parks, space can scale up to entire cities and metropolitan regions, whose spatial attributes are more complex and variegated. Think about the difficulty of orienting yourself spatially in downtown Shanghai, which has almost 20 million people, with its crowded high-rises and people, compared to in a small empty suburban park in the United States. Then imagine the likely scenario of Shanghai and a dozen other nearby million-plus cities growing into one another in the Yangtze River Delta and forming a megacity region of 80 million people. These gigantic spatial units make it difficult to visualize myriad concrete places such as streets and parks embedded within and across many scalar units and boundaries (see Chapter 11 for an extended discussion of this topic). From their scaled-up vantage point, cities and metropolitan regions amplify the more abstract quality of space relative to place.

One of the most important qualities of spaces is the degree to which they are freely accessible. Scholars are increasingly turning their attention to the distribution of **private spaces** and **public spaces** within urban areas. Cities have always contained private spaces, which provide a degree of protection from the outside world, and where the owner of the property may dictate just who is allowed to enter and what they may do on the premises. Homes are the major private spaces that we human beings occupy, as are those sites where we work, particularly private businesses and firms. Both family spaces and work spaces are protected by certain laws in democratic societies: they are private and thus cannot be subject to unlawful entry by public authorities such as the police. These laws, among other things, help to establish the boundaries and contents of security, and thus they provide an added layer of protection, above and beyond our own families and friends, to our sense of security in places.

private spaces
Spaces to which access is restricted by those who own the property.

public spaces
Spaces that are open and accessible to every person in a society, in particular its citizens.

But it is public spaces that in many ways represent the heart of societies – democratic societies in particular. Public spaces are, by definition, open and accessible to every person in a society, in particular to the inhabitants of that society. Such spaces include streets, parks, and plazas, and other areas that we regard as sites of gatherings. In democratic societies such public spaces enable people who are different from one another to gather and participate with others in activities that they enjoy. It is this gathering and the participation, in public, so the argument claims, that help to establish the character and quality of democratic societies. And, where such public spaces are not used, or in fact not available to everyone, then the very nature of democracies and the very quality of communities is substantially diminished, even threatened.

Both private and public spaces serve important purposes: free speech and assembly are cornerstones of democratic societies, but most of us would like to have some say regarding the uses of some spaces, particularly our homes. Of increasing concern to scholars is the degree to which the kinds of spaces that were once unambiguously public are increasingly becoming private. They refer to this process as the **privatization of space**: efforts to make space less

privatization (of space)
The shift in ownership of spaces from public to private, whether corporations, management companies, or home-owners' associations.

accessible and to curtail the freedoms of those who use it. Take the shopping mall, for instance. While it may appear to serve many of the same functions as a town square or an open-air market like that shown in Figure 1.6, malls are privately owned and the rights of those who use them are specified by owners and management. Neighborhoods, too, particularly gated communities and common-interest developments, are extending private control of space beyond individual residences to the formerly public areas of streets, sidewalks, and parks (recall Studying the city 1.1 on the global spread of gated communities; also see our extensive discussion of such communities in Chapter 6). Anthropologist Teresa Caldeira (2001) has chronicled the increasing use of walls, gates, and guards to seal off residential compounds in São Paulo, Brazil. There, what are called closed condominiums include not only residential spaces but also parks as well as sports and entertainment facilities. Even the utilities are provided independently of the surrounding city.

One of the major issues of the twenty-first century will be how the public spaces of cities, such as parks and plazas, even sidewalks and corners, are treated and preserved so that they can truly represent sites and sources of cultural diversity and democracy in the modern world. Those of a more cynical turn of mind believe that the privatization of public space will be one of the great tendencies of modern life, whereas those who seek to protect the democratic elements of modern societies believe that movements of resistance must be made in order to establish the rights of all citizens to be able to enjoy the public spaces of cities. Don Mitchell (2003), a geographer, has promoted the point of view, which originated

Figure 1.6 Attractions such as markets (this one is in Gualaceo, Ecuador) ensure that public spaces remain well-used, as the presence of people tends to attract even more people. *Source: Photo: Danita Delimont/Gallo/Getty Images.*

with French urban scholar Henri Lefebvre, that every person has the right to use the public spaces of cities – that's what cities are all about, he argues. Mitchell identifies ways in which local authorities across the United States, for example, have limited, indeed infringed upon, these rights of people. And, having identified this fundamental problem, he has promoted the idea that groups of people, homeless people in particular, must resist the efforts of local authorities and demand their own rights to the use of public spaces.

MAKING THE CITY BETTER   1.1

PARK(ing) day

A great example of reclaiming public space began in San Francisco, California. An organization called Rebar, full of young activists, first took to the streets of San Francisco in 2005, paying for a parking space and converting it into a real park that passing pedestrians could use to relax. They laid down sod, put in some benches and trees, and watched as people came by to use the park or stare in wonder. And the great part is, no one stopped them.

Rebar first started doing PARK(ing) Day as a way to expand the amount of public space available in their urban environment. According to Rebar (2011), over 70 percent of San Francisco's downtown outdoor space is dedicated to the private vehicle, and much of the remaining space is either other types of private space or sidewalks, leaving almost no space for urbanites to relax. The purpose of PARK(ing) Day was to take back some of the space dedicated to the private vehicle, and to give that space to the public in a way that no one had ever seen before.

Now, PARK(ing) Day is a global event, and it happens every year. In 2009, 744 parks were created in 141 cities across six continents (see Figure 1.7). People have used PARK(ing) Day to create parks in their own cities and to provide other types of services at the park as well, such as bike repairs, political seminars, and free healthcare clinics. But what each of these parks has in common is that they adhere to the original mission of converting space for a private vehicle into green space for the public to use for leisure, work, and play.

Figure 1.7 A parking spot in Tromsø, Norway is remade into an urban forest as part of PARK(ing) Day 2009. *Source: Photo: Lepetitgarcon/Flickr.com.*

Cities shape the fates of human beings

All of the issues touched upon in this chapter – whether qualities of space such as privatization, the ways that groups have been segregated throughout the city, or the impact of changes in the world economy on urban development – bring us to perhaps the most important lesson that you will take from this book, and from urban studies more generally: *places impact the fates of human beings*. The cities in which we live, as well as our neighborhoods, affect our material wellbeing and our security. In large part, places also provide – or deny – access to social, educational, and economic opportunities. While all social scientists take care to balance individual and societal factors when seeking to understand people's life chances, we can say with confidence that much of a person's success or suffering can be explained by looking at where they live.

This process begins at our beginnings. *Where* you are born determines, in large part, *how* you were born. Did your mother have access to prenatal care? Were you born in a well-equipped hospital? Did you first come home to a dwelling free of toxic hazards, violence, and other threats to your family's safety? What was the quality of the school you first attended? Was your journey to school an opportunity for friendly play or fraught with danger? Even by the age of five or six, qualities of place have left their mark on children, and understanding the complex ways in which they do requires an understanding of how cities work.

Take schools, for example. In the United States, schools are largely funded through property taxes. The budget available to a school thus depends on the value of homes and businesses in the area. These values turn on a number of factors: the strength of the local economy (which is increasingly tied to the global economy), the demographic composition of a city, the desirability of the kind of housing and lifestyle available in a community, and the attitudes of local leaders and residents toward taxation. To make things even more complex, property values can also turn on the quality of local schools, creating a vicious cycle for poor-performing school districts as families with the means to do so move to stronger districts. This drives up property values in communities known for strong schools and pulls them down in those areas that families with children leave behind. In turn, schools become more unequal, and the children in those schools have increasingly divergent chances for economic success later in life.

In many places, the ways that place affects our life chances are even more basic than access to education. For some, place generates exposure to environmental dangers that sharply limit chances for a good life. While many of China's northern cities, for example, have a severe shortage of water, a much worse situation happens in some small cities and towns, where the only accessible water is a nearby river, heavily polluted by urban industrialization, which makes the local children ill. Rising sea levels caused by global warming are threatening the basic livelihood of people living in Asia's large coastal cities such as Dhaka and Jakarta as well as smaller fishing villages. Indeed, across the world, melting glaciers and the resulting rising waters of seas and rivers are posing an ever-growing menace to those people who live alongside or nearby them. Such was the case in Pakistan during the summer of 2010.

The places in which we live not only shape our destinies but also influence the everyday texture of our lives. Consider this simple example. People travel to and from work across the highways and boulevards that are built as part of the city. The more people who live in a city and the more people who travel these roads, the more time it takes to get to work. In cities like Moscow or Los Angeles, for example, those who commute by car can spend upwards of two to three hours to go from their home to work, and then, at the end of the day, they must return again. It may seem a trivial thing at first, but the very system of transportation affects our daily lives, making them more difficult than they might be. We adapt, of course, as humans always do, and in the process we may invent new techniques of living – for instance, using cell phones to connect with friends and family while we each spend hours alone in our cars. In cities where people instead spend long hours on public transit, commuters devise still different strategies such as using headphones to exert some control over their auditory environment, or simply refusing to recognize other riders as fellow human beings (for an antidote to this, see Making the city better 2.1). Though the details vary from one place to another, place still determines, in large part, the constitutive elements of our daily routines as well as the kinds of practical and psychological coping strategies we will use to make the best of these.

Cities and people

Human beings and cities are inextricably intertwined. Human beings make cities, and they live and work in them. Although the pace at which cities grow and change may sometimes be so slow as to avoid detection, and while the scales of urban places may confound any sense of human efficacy, we must bear in mind that these are objects of our own making. Not only do human beings shape the physical structures of cities but they also decide what those structures will mean and, as a result, suggest how other human beings will use them. We offer these insights to stir your curiosities, and as a source of empowerment. Whatever is built by human hands is, by definition, within our power to change. Indeed, throughout the book we offer examples of individuals and groups who are working to change cities in ways that in turn improve the lives of residents.

This brings us to perhaps the most important point of this chapter, and of this book: *places, whether cities, neighborhoods, or even smaller units therein, have the power to shape human lives*. The structures of inequalities found within and across societies are quite literally made concrete in cities. Add to these a host of place-specific threats stemming from political and environmental instability, and we can trace many of the factors that diminish individuals' lives to the places where they live. Places are not the only culprit here – in many instances, places are the sites where problems stemming from larger structures manifest themselves – but understanding places allows us to understand the ways in which these forces intersect with specific populations and resources.

We hope that this chapter leaves you with a sense of why cities are compelling topics of study. Some of you likely needed little convincing: you may have had questions about why cities take the forms they do, how immigrants create communities in a new place, or why some neighborhoods are luxurious and opulent while others are sites of danger and despair. We encourage those of you who have come to this field accidentally or even reluctantly to consider cities as sites where you can readily see social processes at work, whether the construction of meanings and memories as they become attached to places or the unequal distribution of economic opportunities. Whatever path you have taken in becoming a student of cities, we hope that this book, and the concepts of space and place at its core, will help you to recognize and understand the ways that humans experience an urban world. Visit the book's companion website at www.wiley.com/go/cities for examples, case studies, and discussion questions, plus a list of useful films and other media, that are relevant to this chapter.

Critical thinking questions

1 Think of a place in your neighborhood that is particularly important to you. What makes this place important? Do you associate the place with certain events or memories? Is it a place you use every day?

2 What kinds of public spaces are there where you live? How do people use them? Do any of these spaces work as theories of public space argue – as democratic spaces? And just how does democracy play out in them? As a hint, think of public spaces like sidewalks and parks, but also things like public markets.

3 Do you live in a city that is experiencing a decline today in terms of its industry or population? Or do you live in a city that is experiencing boom times? How do these broader economic events affect the way people feel about the city and their attachment to it as a place?

4 In what ways has the city in which you live influenced your daily life? Would your life have been much different had you lived in a different kind of city? Did you ever think about relocating to another city and then move there?

5 The great economic crisis of recent years has had many profound effects across the world and in the cities in which we live. One of them, in the United States, in particular, concerns the rising number of home foreclosures. People are simply now unable to pay their mortgages and leaving their homes vacant. Do you think this will change the ways in which people think about homes and housing as places?

Suggested reading

Peter Dreier, John Mollenkopf, and Todd Swanstrom, *Place Matters* (Lawrence: University Press of Kansas, 2001). A major book on American cities that shows how and why cities, as places, matter in the lives of people.

Jane Jacobs, *The Death and Life of Great American Cities* (New York: Random House, 1961). One of the most influential works of the twentieth century. Jacobs argues that urban planners have failed to design cities that account for the way in which people live, work, and play in cities.

Henri Lefebvre, *The Production of Space*, trans. Donald Nicholson-Smith (Oxford: Blackwell,1991). One of the leading Marxist writers to re-examine issues of urbanization and the city, Lefebvre argued that space was actually produced by the capitalist institutions of the modern world.

Michael Patrick MacDonald, *All Souls: A Family Story from Southie* (New York: Ballantine Books, 2000). MacDonald's moving account of life in south Boston reveals the ways in which neighborhood, social class, and ethnicity contributed to residents' identities and how the neighborhood shaped their fates.

Yi-Fu Tuan, *Space and Place: The Perspective of Experience* (Minneapolis: University of Minnesota Press, 1977). The work that brought the importance of space and place to the attention not only of geographers but also to the whole range of social sciences.

Note

1. On a similar theme, see Glaser et al. (2003).

CHAPTER 2

Social theories of urban space and place
The early perspectives

KEY TOPICS

→ How the industrial roots of modern cities shaped theories of urban life.

→ Ferdinand Tönnies' concepts of *Gemeinschaft* and *Gesellschaft*, and how each one represents an idealized conception of social life.

→ Georg Simmel's characterization of the "mental life" of people who live in cities and his view of the style of urban social interaction.

→ The urban theories of the Chicago School of Sociology and how they were grounded in earlier German theories, especially regarding the ecology of populations.

→ Ernest Burgess' model of urban space as concentric zones that contain distinctive populations and social institutions.

→ The ways that, in the view of sociologists such as Robert Park and Ernest Burgess, competition and succession change cities.

→ How Louis Wirth depicted the metropolis in terms of "a way of life," including the distinctions between his view and the earlier views of Tönnies and Simmel.

→ Ways that urban planning has reflected the concerns of urban social theory.

Introduction to Cities: How Place and Space Shape Human Experience,
First Edition. Xiangming Chen, Anthony M. Orum, and Krista E. Paulsen.
© 2013 Xiangming Chen, Anthony M. Orum, and Krista E. Paulsen.
Published 2013 by Blackwell Publishing Ltd.

Cities, especially those in the modern world, seem to be constantly changing. Many grow larger in terms of the size of their populations, while others disappear. Some cities literally gobble up nearby towns and villages, and even other cities. This process of change can be found everywhere in the city – in new housing, businesses, and streets, for instance, and the demise of the old. The modern world in which we live is neither still nor silent. Economic and political forces constantly keep cities in flux, developing and reshaping them.

A glance upward reveals some of the most obvious indicators of urban growth and transformation: the skyscrapers that mark centers of urban commerce and investment. An architectural form that originated in North American cities – the term "skyscraper" appears to have first been used to describe buildings in New York City or Chicago – these dense vertical structures mark cities across the globe. Today many of the tallest skyscrapers in the world are now rising in the skylines of cities in Asia and Latin America. These are relatively new cities – as least as compared to many of those in Europe and the United States – and they are now growing almost like wild fire, inventing and reinventing the nature of the city itself. Furthermore, in these countries – China or India, for example – the change that is happening in the city itself is dramatic. Virtually overnight, cities such as Shanghai have changed from places that held buildings no taller than 22 storys high to ones that today contain dozens of skyscrapers, some of them among the tallest in the world.

When the city around us changes its form – whether dramatically, as when modern high-rises replace centuries-old homes in Chinese cities, or incrementally, as when one immigrant group leaves a neighborhood and another one moves in – people ask why. Often our explanations may draw on our own observations or news accounts, and may provide some insight into why things happened the way they did in our city. But social theorists take these matters even more deeply and seriously, looking beyond a single case to the kinds of forces and people that change all cities. Examining their explanations, as well as the distance between these theories and our own experiences of cities and urban life, we can begin to understand just what moves cities as spaces and places.

In this chapter and the next we provide you with an overview of the major explanations and ideas that have been used to talk about changes to the city, today as well as in the past. These explanations address the forces at work in transforming cities as places, as well as the ways that urban places affect residents' everyday lives and interactions. As you will soon discover in examining cities in detail, scholars have often developed very useful ways of understanding modern social life more generally.

In this chapter, we discuss early theories of cities and social change, beginning with those that arose as industrial cities multiplied in the late nineteenth century. These theories helped to lay the foundations for the later ones, ones that emerged in the latter part of the twentieth century and that we will discuss in Chapter 3. While these chapters will provide you with insights into key developments in urban social theory, our account is by no means exhaustive. As you will see, we call upon the ideas presented here later on in the book, in the service of relevant topics. We also encourage you to pursue the sources listed at the ends of these chapters.

The social and theoretical roots of modern urban theory

The effort to explain the nature of the city and, especially, the changes that occur in cities, began in the late nineteenth century. In a word, the world was becoming modern. This was a period of great upheaval in much of Europe and the United States. New technical inventions, such as the steam engine, and new forms for the production of goods, such as the factory system, transformed how and where people worked. Almost overnight, the cities and towns where people lived and worked began to change. Many people who worked on farms, toiling from the early morning hours to late at night, were drawn by new opportunities into the emerging centers of population, among them London and Manchester in the United Kingdom and New York City and Chicago in the United States (see Figure 2.1). There they joined thousands – even millions – of their fellows: individuals and families from different regions and countries who brought their own cultures and traditions to their new homes. Cities thus not only contained great concentrations of people and businesses but their populations were far more diverse than the towns and villages from which the migrants came.

All these developments, in business and in cities themselves, prompted scholars to ask why these changes were taking place, and how they were affecting the way in which people led their lives. Among the most famous of these theories were those of Karl

Figure 2.1 Manchester as it looked in the 1840 s (around the time that Engels was writing). As in other industrial cities of this era, Manchester's poor and working-class residents struggled to find decent housing and food, and lived with polluted air and water. These circumstances, as well as the unprecedented crowding found in growing cities, contributed to early theorists' generally bleak view of urban life. *Source: Victoria Bridge, Blackfriars, Manchester, 1843. Courtesy of Manchester Library & Information Service, Manchester City Council.*

Marx, a figure of enormous significance even today. Marx's interrogation of the relationship between power and capital would have great influence in the twentieth century, as a new generation of scholars turned their attention toward these issues. We take up those ideas in Chapter 3. Here we present some of the impressions of Marx's collaborator, Friedrich Engels, that shaped the pair's views of modern inequality (see Studying the city 2.1). In broadly influential works such as *The Communist Manifesto*, Marx and Engels characterized cities as sites where the concentration of laborers reflected not only deprivation but also great potential. Urban density set the stage for communication among workers: as they saw one another's struggles and shared their

STUDYING THE CITY   2.1

Friedrich Engels in Manchester

Alongside the worldwide trend of urbanization and industrialization, cities eventually came to be viewed as undesirable places to live, reinforcing earlier images of them. With good reason, scholars focused on the very worst dimensions of urban life, such as poverty, crime, and pollution. One of the earliest condemnations of these conditions is Friedrich Engels' description of Manchester. Engels was sent to the city by his father in order to work in the Manchester branch of a textile firm that his family partly owned. His father sent Engels there in an attempt to foster an appreciation of capitalism, but this ended up backfiring when Engels observed the horrors of city life in England.

In *The Condition of the Working-Class in England in 1844*, Engels described in great detail the "ruinous and miserable" living conditions of working-class city dwellers. He portrayed the towns as districts as "unplanned wildernesses of one- or two-storied terrace houses" that were "badly and irregularly built." "No human being," he claimed, "would willingly inhabit such dens." Sanitation posed a major problem, as streets were filled with human and animal wastes, the fetid odors of which contributed to those offered up by nearly inedible vegetables and meats for sale by local vendors. Crime also flourished in these areas. Engels wrote that, "here the worst-paid workers rub shoulders with thieves, rogues and prostitutes." But ironically, "in this nest of thieves doors are superfluous, because there is nothing worth stealing."

Presaging the concerns of early urban theorists, Engels observed that density within the inner cities of England hindered the ability of residents to enjoy an adequate quality of life. He suggested that, as people "are packed into a tiny space, the more repulsive and disgraceful becomes the brutal indifference with which they ignore their neighbors and selfishly concentrate upon their private affairs." He linked this to the injustice perpetuated by England's political and economic system by saying that people "here regard their fellows not as human beings, but as pawns in the struggle for existence. Everyone exploits his neighbor with the result that the stronger tramples the weaker under foot. The strongest of all, a tiny group of capitalists, monopolize everything, while the weakest, who are in the vast majority, succumb to the most abject poverty" (Engels 2010: 23–74).

After writing about his horrific observations in England, Engels met for a second time with Karl Marx in France on his way to Germany. The two hit it off quite well, and together would publish famous works such as the *Manifesto of the Communist Party* in order to try to address the atrocious living conditions of the urban poor through radical political and economic change. As we will see in Chapter 3, their attention to capital and conflict would also come inspire urban theorists of a later era.

stories, they would develop a class consciousness – a first, necessary step in asserting workers' power. Bringing workers together was thus a means by which industrial capitalism would, in Marx and Engels' terms, produce "its own grave diggers" (Marx and Engels 1998: 50).

As broad economic and technical transformations took place across Western countries, they began to loosen the attachments people had to the places where they lived as well as their connections to other people in those places: their *security, sense of community*, and *identity*. Young men and women who moved to the city from farms now found their lives transformed by the work they did as well as the new places where they and their families took up residence. While Marx focused on the implications for economic systems, other scholars, who themselves may have experienced this move from the countryside to the city, began to raise a simple but profound issue: how can we explain the differences that seem to be emerging between the nature of life in the countryside and the nature of life in the city?

Ferdinand Tönnies: Community and society

One of the first scholars to make an extended inquiry into the nature of the places in which people lived in the new and emerging worlds of the nineteenth century was the German social theorist, Ferdinand Tönnies. Tönnies was broadly concerned with how modern life was different from earlier forms of social life. He believed that the types of social organizations and relationships people had with one another in the modernizing world were vastly different from those in the premodern world, especially in the towns and rural settings that lay outside places like the modern metropolis. He offered a way to think about these differences that provided new insight into the nature of social life and social organizations among people.

All of us are aware, of course, of the ways in which towns and cities differ from each other. Cities are larger, more populated, more diverse, and louder. Especially for people who come to live in the city from the countryside and rural areas, cities just seem to be vastly different. The city – indeed, the large metropolis – looks as though it is likely to be a less intimate and congenial place than the towns and villages of the countryside, which are far smaller and seem to be less impersonal.

Tönnies focused his attention precisely on these differences of scale and of social organization. He used two German expressions to capture the difference: *Gemeinschaft*, a term that in German means community, and that Tönnies employed to identify small and intimate settings like towns and villages, and *Gesellschaft*, a term that in German refers to society, or to the larger social order, and that Tönnies used to capture the qualities of the new cities into which people now were moving. The smaller and intimate settings – those of *Gemeinschaft* – were the places of more intimate social ties among people (the bond between parent and child was, in his view, the purest form of *Gemeinschaft*). Those places also, he suggested, seemed to engage people in closer, more durable, and lasting social relationships. People in such settings knew the full details of one another's lives, in part because they, and their relatives, had lived there a long while, and so shared a deep and close personal bond to one another as well as to the land itself. Such places provided a great deal of warmth and security to people. Tönnies continued that these kinds of settings were to be found not merely in rural villages or towns, which were their prototype, but also in the neighborhoods of large cities.

Gemeinschaft (German) Ferdinand Tönnies' term for community. The close and intimate, as opposed to fleeting and impersonal, relationships between people.

Gesellschaft (German) Ferdinand Tönnies' term for society. The partial and impersonal, as opposed to close and intimate, relationships between people.

By contrast, however, the modern form of social organization that was emerging, and was found in the broader social order, the *Gesellschaft*, was based on an entirely different set of conditions. Here, in the modern form of organization, people did not know one another intimately. They only knew one another in a specific sphere, as a member of a particular organization, for example. Thus, the quality of these relationships was far different from that of those relationships in the rural villages and towns. People might have been members of the same business organization, or even of the same social club, and they might even have worked together for many of the same purposes – to make the business better, or to elect a certain person to political office. But these relationships extended only so far. One would in all likelihood never have become as involved with fellow club members as he, or she, would have been with a father, son, or even a close friend. In a phrase, *Gemeinschaft* was the site of the intimate connections, whereas *Gesellschaft* was the site of only secondary and impersonal relationships. Indeed, if the *Gemeinschaft* setting was exemplified in the small town, the home, or even the urban neighborhood (as Tönnies himself wrote), the *Gesellschaft* setting was embodied in the large metropolis, that place where all the action and development of modernity had begun to unfold.

Tönnies' ideas have become part of the working vocabulary of modern sociologists, and still are very helpful in understanding the qualitative differences between the social life in small towns, or even families, and social life in the larger, more distant social order of which we are a part. His method of using key concepts to define the types of social settings employs what sociologists call "ideal types," following the methodological strategy of Max Weber. Such concepts are abstractions from real life, and are used precisely to isolate and to contrast the distinguishing features of a social setting, even of a social organization (Weber 2011). This effort by Tönnies to grapple with modernity in terms of social organization and social relationships became a central concern of many sociologists, and the concern often took the form precisely of trying to imagine and conceive of how rural and urban life differed. While Tönnies' attention furnished a clear and concrete and transparent way especially of talking about the premodern forms of community, it was a fellow German scholar, Georg Simmel, who filled in important details about the modern form – the form that arose in the metropolis.

Georg Simmel: The metropolis and mental life

Like Ferdinand Tönnies, Georg Simmel, another German scholar, took a great interest in trying to fathom the nature of the changes in the nineteenth century, and especially in the ways in which the modern world had developed beyond the world on medieval estates and small villages. Simmel, however, thought more deeply about these matters than Tönnies. Like the French social theorist Emile Durkheim, Simmel wished to explore and highlight those elements of the world that were distinctively social, or, in other words, those elements that dealt with the connections between and among people. For example, he invented explanations and theories of social relationships, showing how the numbers of people in a relationship routinely influenced the way in which people acted and thought about one another.

When it came to providing a general picture of the emerging and special character of the modern world, Simmel (1964 [1903]) used the modern metropolis to depict that world. Unlike someone like Karl Marx, who talked about modernization and change in terms of the character of labor and work, Simmel believed that the life of people in cities provided a window into how the modern world actually worked. A resident himself of Berlin, Simmel seemed to take Berlin as the prototype of the modern city, and to rework the features of its everyday life into a picture and portrait of modern life itself.[1] By noting, for example, the impersonal ways in which people engaged with one another in doing business in the metropolis, he highlighted a more universal feature about how modernity shapes and transforms our social relationships.

Simmel, like Ferdinand Tönnies, found life in the city to be very different from life in the countryside – though he focused all his attention just on the city itself. He pictured life in the city as impersonal and anonymous. People dealt with one another, he believed, not as intimates, as friends or as family members, but rather in a categorical, almost distant manner. If the prototype of a social relationship in the countryside were the relationship between a parent and a child, the prototype of a social relationship in the city – the metropolis – was a relationship between a clerk and a client. Each approached one another not on the basis of specific personal knowledge of the other but, in effect, simply to do business. They held no affection for one another. Rather, when they met, in a small business or store, they met about a sale. It was all about work and not about pleasure.

To imagine this way of thinking about modern life, picture to yourself the way you deal with your friends or your brothers or sisters. You know one another. You have a long history together. You have feelings for one another – sometimes positive, sometimes angry, and sometimes, in the case of friends, romantic or of great affection. Your bonds are based on longstanding knowledge of each other and experience together, cemented by deep feelings. By contrast, think about the way you relate to a clerk in a large department store, or someone who sells you a lunch at McDonald's. Each of you may smile, but it is all business. You are there to make a purchase, and they are there to make a sale. Nothing more, nothing less is involved. The character of your relationship is the character of a business transaction: here is what I want; here is my cash; give me my goods; now I am done. So it was that Simmel portrayed modern life.

Using this imagery, then, Simmel elaborated and expanded on the modern world and life in the modern metropolis. He insisted that the nature of the way in which people thought here was in terms of calculation and rationality. Since we deal with one another exclusively in impersonal terms, and are doing business with one another, each of us is trying to get the most benefit out of our relationship. You, for example, may be trying to get the best goods for the smallest funds, whereas the clerk is trying to sell you something and make a good profit. It is all about making systematic and rational calculations in the transactions we carry on.

Life in the city for Simmel was, then, in a phrase, just about work. People did not have to know one another intimately in order to relate to one another. They simply had to know what they wanted in a particular transaction. Moreover, because the character of such life was based on impersonal criteria, certain types of people, or characters, came to represent the ideal forms of the city. In particular, Simmel said, city life gave birth to figures he termed "strangers": these were types of people, or social types, who were unknown to others and who possessed no particular social ties or relationships to them. As a result, the stranger was a foreign figure, someone who was mysterious but also alluring – someone who, because we did not know them, we would be willing to share the most intimate details with. The stranger, in effect, was someone we might meet on a train or a plane, share a few hours with during our passage, and to whom we might even tell a few stories, some secrets we would not normally reveal, precisely because we knew that we would never again see that figure. The stranger is, as Simmel put it, the embodiment of the modern world and, in particular, the modern metropolis.

For Simmel, the essence of modernization and the modern world is to be found in daily life among people in the emerging metropolis. His conception of modernization emphasized certain ideas, or concepts, of social life, and it left out all the details – the who, the where, the what, and the when. These particulars, he believed, were unnecessary to his portrait and project: if one wished to understand the energies and motion of the changes of the nineteenth century, all one had to do was to visit the city and picture it with a certain eye, or from a certain angle; look at how business transpires; see how people in a store deal with one another; examine what they are doing and how they are doing it.

Now, if we step back for a minute and compare our view of the city, with all its messy details, with that of Simmel, we will discover that he omitted certain elements. He did not talk about families or friends; he did not talk about life in neighborhoods; he did not talk about feelings such as affection or love; he did not talk about the rich particulars (i.e., the sights and the sounds) that we all know and recognize. Instead, he wrote about an idealized portrait of the city, as exemplified in the new world emerging before his eyes. It was, as Tönnies also recognized, vastly different from the traditional world on the farm, or in the village. It took a certain state of mind and of imagination to handle such a world, one that was content to deal with people in a neutral or rational manner rather than an emotional one. And it was this world – a creation of Simmel's theoretical imagination about the nature of places – that was left to us as a tool with which to think about and examine cities today.

Tönnies and Simmel: Further reflections

Ferdinand Tönnies and Georg Simmel represent the first of the modern theorists of the city – and, at the same time, they are among the first social theorists of modernity itself. They both furnished an idealized portrait of modernity, and they framed it in terms of the modern metropolis, of real places like London and Paris and Berlin. But the form that these places took in their imagination was not a historical one, but rather an idealized social image of the city, one that accentuated and abstracted those elements that both scholars believed represented the essence of the new modern life. Such life, to both of them, took the form of dealings and relationships that were impersonal, distant, unemotional, and subject, above all, to rational calculations and assessments. If life in the family represented the premodern form of life, then life in the economy represented the modern form. In this regard, among others, their concerns and ideas reflected those of other theorists of the modern world. But the twist they gave them, of course, was to focus and find those forms in the metropolis, or the city, itself. This was particularly true for Simmel, and suggested by the ideas of Tönnies.

Looking back at these explanations of the changing world, we find that they depicted this world as though it were totally different from forms found in earlier periods of history – the polar opposite. This was a nice theoretical technique, but it obviously distorted reality to some degree. Could it possibly be true that people possessed no emotions in the emerging metropolis of the modern world? Of course not. But this theoretical exaggeration permitted people to examine and analyze the modern city as a new and different form of social organization. Later scholars, who sought to extend and expand upon these writings, would come back to question some of the devices and choices made by Tönnies and Simmel.

EXPLORING FURTHER   2.1

Urban planning as a remedy for urban ills

The early-twentieth-century view of cities as places where relationships between individuals become strained was shared not only by social theorists but also by urban planners. Urban planning provides a practical counterpoint to urban theory. The scholars discussed in this chapter attempted to understand just what cities were and why they were that way. Planners used this knowledge, as well as more routine observations of urban life, to try to make cities more efficient and humane places. Much of professional urban planning concerns itself with relatively mundane elements of urban life, such as the optimal width of a sidewalk or the appropriate height of buildings in the urban core. But, just as the theorists you are reading about in this chapter pushed the boundaries of their fields, so too have a number of planners, architects, landscape architects, and urban designers. Early on, they (or their patrons) recognized the same challenges as these social theorists, and offered bold new solutions to be achieved by changing the physical form of spaces. As you will see, some have continued to improve urban environments, while others have since come to be viewed as detours on the path to a better urban future.

Ebenezer Howard, a British urban planner, attempted to avoid the typical disadvantages of the city by essentially merging the *Gemeinschaft* and *Gesellschaft* archetypes established by Ferdinand Tönnies in a single planning scheme called the "garden city" (see Figure 2.2). He imagined the city and country as exerting different and competing "pulls" on individuals. For instance, the city offered high wages and offered "places of amusement"; the country could provide natural beauty but little of interest socially. The ideal city would somehow draw the good from both city and country and leave behind the bad. Howard's goal was to create cities that were efficient yet allowed people to live without all of the clutter and social problems found in sprawling metropolises. He recommended limiting cities to 30 000 people who would also own the community through a type of cooperative socialist framework.

Figure 2.2 Ebenezer Howard's Garden City Plan attempts to unify the city and the natural world. Not only is the small city surrounded by natural and agricultural spaces but nature can also be found within the city as well in the form of parks and gardens. How different is this vision from contemporary small towns and suburbs that try to balance the advantages of urban and rural spaces? *Source: Ebenezer Howard's plan for the Radiant Garden City, from* Garden Cities of To-Morrow *(London: Swan Sonnenschein & Co., Ltd., 1902).*

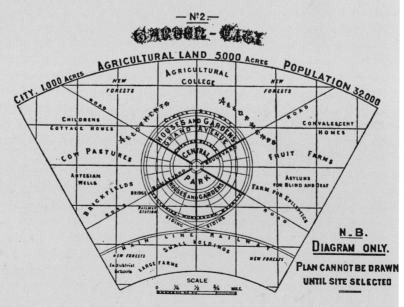

Development would be surrounded by a "greenbelt" of rural land to be used for farming purposes. These cities were to be built in the undeveloped countryside, unburdened by existing structures, high construction and renovation costs, and pollution. Howard published his ideas in 1898 in a book called *Garden Cities of To-morrow*. His ideas were very influential in Great Britain, where the first garden city, Letchworth, was built north of London. Many of Howard's ideas would also influence the plans of suburbs that sought a balance between the cultural and economic offerings of the city and the restorative and spiritual dimensions of country life.

The desire to integrate country and city can also be seen in the creation of urban parks and boulevards. Perhaps their most influential advocate was the American Frederick Law Olmsted, who, along with his collaborator Calbert Vaux (an English architect) and later through his sons John Olmsted and Frederick Jr., left his mark on countless US cities and college campuses. Olmsted's first project (begun in 1858 and completed in 1871) is still the most well known: New York City's Central Park. Here his signature naturalistic style was developed. Open meadows complemented forests and built structures to create a variety of interesting and distinct environments. The beautification of the urban environment would, in Olmsted's view, have positive effects on individuals living within the city, allowing them to unwind and enjoy the scenery. At the same time, park and boulevard systems, or any other aesthetic improvements for that matter, would increase nearby land values, stimulate private development, and bolster city budgets as property taxes increased. Despite Olmsted's good intentions, however, urban park building and the related City Beautiful movement led in part to bulldozing many "unattractive" slum neighborhoods.

While Howard and Olmsted sought a return to nature, a radically different but equally influential vision came from Le Corbusier, a French urban planner (originally from Switzerland). In the 1930s, Le Corbusier proposed the streamlined and efficient "radiant city" (see Figure 2.3). Implementation would require that entire central city districts be leveled in order to make way for huge skyscrapers, which would each be surrounded by parks and superhighways. These would allow for the swift and efficient movement of individuals and goods, a goal hampered by the narrow streets and haphazard design of older cities. To emphasize his point that much time was wasted in current urban layouts, Le Corbusier dubbed his plan for the radiant city, "a city worthy of our time." Le Corbusier's plan to improve the cities materialized in many instances of urban renewal in the mid-twentieth century,

Figure 2.3 Le Corbusier's 1925 Plan Voisin for Paris. The Isle de la Cité, at right center in this image, is one of the few recognizable features in this radical proposal. Note how the winding streets and blocks are razed and replaced with a much-larger-scale, "efficient" grid surrounding the skyscrapers. These "superblocks," combining many standard-sized city blocks, would become a hallmark of Le Corbusier-inspired planning as adopted worldwide. *Source: © FLC/ADAGP, Banque d'Images, Paris and DACS, London 2011.*

along with the construction of high-rise housing projects, many of which are now crumbling homes of last resort for the urban poor.

Urban planning continues to be a field where professionals come together to try and solve problems within the cities. And, despite the negative outcomes associated with many of these proposed solutions to urban troubles, these plans laid the foundation for addressing disadvantages associated with city life through progressive development approaches. As you will read in Chapter 13, this continues to be the goal of urban planning, although the means for doing so have dramatically changed (for instance, we invite you to contrast the goals of New Urbanism with the vision of Le Corbusier). Despite many changes in terms of what is deemed desirable in urban environments, planning continues to engage in a dialogue with urban theory.

The Chicago School of Sociology

In the late 1890s, a young journalist, Robert Park, went to study in Germany. While there he came under the influence of a number of important figures, among them Ferdinand Tönnies and, especially, Georg Simmel, both of whom were popular intellectuals at the time. Park also studied and came in contact with ideas of the new school of ecology. These represented new notions and ways for thinking about the world in terms of animal and plant life, and the manner in which new species and forms of life emerge and eventually adapt to one another. So was the stage set for yet another volley of ideas about modernization and change. But these ideas would take root and blossom in the setting of the new world – the United States – and they would eventually establish themselves as a truly original and unique way to think about social change and social life.

When Park returned from Germany, he was invited to join the relatively new Department of Sociology at the University of Chicago (Bulmer 1986). The university had been built in the late 1890s with a major gift from John Rockefeller, and it soon became known as a bastion of new and exciting ideas about the world across a range of different academic disciplines. Park was joined in the Department of Sociology by several other notable figures, men who would go on to become quite famous for their writings on the nature of social life in the modern world. They included W. I. Thomas, who gave birth to the idea of self-fulfilling prophecies and who also helped to invent new and special methods for the study of social life, including detailed examinations of the ways in which people adapt to life in the city.

Just as change had propelled the ideas of Tönnies and Simmel, it would have the same effect on the writings and ideas of Park and his colleagues. Chicago, like New York City, had begun to change dramatically at the end of the nineteenth century. New forms of business and modern capitalism began to arise in the city, and soon, because of its central location in the United States and the many railroads that entered and left Union Station in its downtown, Chicago had become one of America's most booming and dynamic metropolises. By the beginning of the twentieth century, it housed over one million people, many of them immigrants from Europe as well as from the rural farmlands of the United States.

Its new residents and diverse populations resulted in a polyglot city, a place where a variety of languages were spoken and where people of different cultures came in contact with one another on a daily basis. Like others who left Europe, those men and women (and their families) who came to Chicago came for its jobs and for new opportunities, often leaving behind their lives in small villages and towns. The relocation of these tens of thousands of people was like that in Europe, but in the United States it involved vast distances and created a much more diverse, new, and (in the words of many observers) uprooted population. These were people who had, of course, not simply left the countryside but left their homelands. And they had come to a country so different that it offered not only new opportunities but also challenges that were equally as great and often simply overwhelming.

The city as social space

In the midst of this social ferment, Robert Park and his colleagues, among them Ernest Burgess and Louis Wirth, invented a new way of thinking about the social change they saw around them every day in Chicago (Park 1936; Park et al., 1967). Chicago became for them the model, the prototype, of the modern city. By virtue of the new businesses being established there and of the booming economy, Chicago in general seemed to possess all those qualities that Park had observed in the great European cities, but with US variations: an expanding population; an ever-expanding number and array of new industries; and a flood of immigrants, both from nearby villages and from abroad. And, in this effort to invent a new way of thinking about the social world, Park drew on his education abroad, reworking what might appear to be unrelated ideas about ecology and plant life.

One of the most lasting and enduring images created by this group of creative scholars was the image of the city itself. Time and history, which were so dominant in the writings of the great European scholars, such as Karl Marx and Georg Wilhelm Friedrich Hegel, played a far less significant role in the explanations of the social theorists at the University of Chicago. Instead, space became the dominant motif – how the city itself was organized in space and the various key social groups and institutions represented therein. Burgess, who was a student at the time, left the most lasting visual impression of Chicago as a **social space**. He created a social map of the city (see Figure 2.4), showing its various regions and social groups as well as the locations of specific neighborhoods and ethnic groups (Burgess 1961 [1925]). His image of the social space took the form of a series of concentric circles, or zones, as he called them, and in each zone he identified the dominant social institutions and forces. Thus, for example, he identified the "red light" district in the city of Chicago as well as the Italian neighborhood just west of the downtown area, or the Loop, as it was commonly identified. The map provided a view of the city as it stretched from its center to those areas at the farthest remove. Thus, on the outskirts, one found the zone of commuters, for example, in those areas known as Highland Park and Wilmette (in Chapter 4 we consider this chart at greater length).

social space The ways in which the spatial patterns and areas of cities are shaped, and influenced, by their residents.

Burgess' rendering of Chicago was a map absolutely unlike any other map of the time (Figure 2.4). It did not have the spatial coordinates of geographers but located real social groups and institutions in a social space. It seemed to imply that all cities looked like the city of Chicago, having a series of **concentric zones** or rings, each containing distinctly dominant groups. The map eventually would take on a life of its own, as new scholars and researchers across the world sought to discover whether their particular location – whether Paris or Shanghai,

concentric zones theory Ernest Burgess and Robert Park's theory of metropolitan areas being in a set of circular areas radiating from the center.

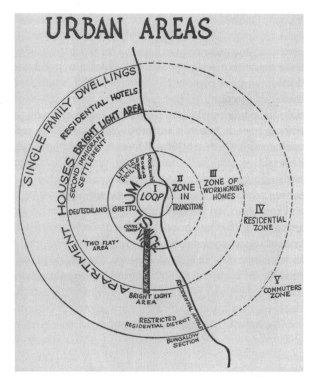

Figure 2.4 Ernest Burgess' map of Chicago's "concentric zones." The Central Business District, in Chicago known as "the Loop" after the elevated railway that circles it, is Zone 1. From this dense center we move to decreasingly dense outer areas at the city's edge. As applied to Chicago, the zones or rings are really semi-circles. The wavy line that vertically bisects this figure represents the shore of Lake Michigan. *Source: Robert Ezra Park and Ernest Watson Burgess,* Contained in the City: Suggestions for Investigation of Human Behavior in the Urban Environment *(Chicago, IL: University of Chicago Press, 1925 and 1967).*

Bombay or Mexico City – showed the same kinds of spatial characteristics and distributions of people as the city of Chicago. In the same way that Berlin had furnished the prototype of the modern city for the writings of Georg Simmel, Chicago provided the prototype model of the modern city for Park and his colleagues, plus countless other sociologists across the world.

The city, social change, and social order

The social map of the city of Chicago not only provided a sense of social space but also implied a perspective on change. One area of the city was identified as the zone of transition, suggesting that somehow a change took place between the central portions of Chicago and its external portions. In fact, Park and his colleagues moved beyond a mere spatial representation of the city to provide a broader social theory of the city and its inhabitants. For this novel work, they drew upon Park's scholarship and learning from Germany.

The writings of the plant and animal ecologists in Germany provided the main inspiration for the ideas of Park and his colleagues about social change. Such ideas focused on the plants and animals in natural habitats, and showed how these living things adapted to one another and evolved over time. The Chicago sociologists modified and reworked these ideas, adding social life and social institutions to the original focus of the ecologists. The Chicago sociologists created a picture of the social world in which social institutions were somehow built on the foundations of all life as rooted in biology. And to this they also added an economic dimension, one suggesting that, in addition to biological drives and mechanisms, social life also had an economic basis and foundation. This eventually became a very complicated picture of the social world and social change – and obviously it was a portrait far removed from the messiness and detail of the world they saw around them daily in the city of Chicago. But it had a central purpose. It represented an effort to create a new social science of the world, one that would do for sociology what the German scholarship had done for the work of the ecologists. This new science would take the name of **human ecology** (Park and Burgess 1924; Park et al. 1967).

> **human ecology**
> The view that change in cities can be construed in terms of the rivalries among different population groups.

This new portrait of the social world created and drew upon an entirely new and different set of concepts. It depicted not actual people, social actors, or human beings, but rather *populations of people*. It depicted such populations in terms of their aggregate characteristics, as though they were the real actors in history – not kings and paupers or even, as Marx had suggested, social classes. Such aggregates, this new portrait claimed, *competed* with one another to become dominant in the social spaces of the city. Just as the Italians, for instance, had come to dominate a particular neighborhood in downtown Chicago, so, too, one could think in general of Italians, or Poles, or Irish – all of them real groups that had recently arrived in Chicago – as an aggregate of people who took their place within the broader social space of the city of Chicago.

Added to this picture of the groups and institutions of the city were the dynamic mechanisms that drove the city to expand and to develop. The central mechanism for the development of the city, Park claimed, was that of *competition for social space*, a notion that he adopted from the work of the ecologists. These real groups, many of them recent immigrants, he suggested, competed with one another to gain social dominance in a particular area of the city. Once such a group took up residence in a particular space, it could become the dominant force there, establishing families, homes, new social institutions, and organizations. And, once that had happened, the area could take on a special social identity, becoming known, for example, as the Italian neighborhood of the city. However, like the forces of modernization themselves, the dominance of a particular group in a particular neighborhood was neither certain nor permanent. As the city expanded in size, groups and institutions throughout this social order constantly competed with one another to become powerful and to establish their own rules and institutions within a particular area. The language of Park and his associates imagined the world they saw in terms of constant change and movement, but change with an edge: new groups (say, for example, Italians) might challenge old groups (say, Irish) to become dominant in a particular area of the city. As the new group moved into the area, they *invaded* it. If the Italians replaced the Irish, they *succeeded* them. In these terms, change and movement in the city represented a constant dynamic motif of competition, invasion, and succession, one group by another.

Park and his colleagues used other ideas to capture the economic dynamics of the city. They argued, in particular, that the central portions of the city were the most valuable ones: these were the areas where the major financial and commercial institutions were located, and the areas, therefore, where the price of land was the highest. Employing the imagery of both the ecologists and economists such as Adam Smith, the Chicago sociologists saw in the city a natural order where the dominant institutions and groups – those most central to the workings of the modern order itself – occupied the central areas of the city; and their power was evident in the value that attached itself to the land there. It was a nice and neat portrait of the way in which the social order of the city seemed to work like the natural order of plants and animals: the institutions and groups best suited to a particular piece of land would flourish there, thus out-competing other institutions and groups who would, in turn, move elsewhere. In this way, Park and his colleagues fit social institutions into a broader pattern and meaning of life, and one could set about making new and challenging discoveries based on these simple yet elegant principles. Groups competed; over time some won, some lost; and their spatial arrangement in the city reflected their place in the broader social order.

STUDYING THE CITY   2.2

Walter Firey on sentiment and symbolism

While Park, Burgess, and others made important advances in understanding cities as social spaces, their theories have been viewed by many as devaluing the role of human action or agency in shaping the urban landscape. As we will discuss in Chapter 3, neo-Marxists made this critique quite powerfully in the 1970s. But, many years prior, a fellow urban ecologist began calling attention to how human action, motivated by culture rather than economic interests, was just as powerful a force in shaping cities.

In the 1940s, Walter Firey sought to correct what he saw as an overly economic ecological perspective as articulated by the likes of Park and Burgess. They had emphasized the capacity of people and institutions to make "efficient" use of space, but without acknowledging how a given location might come to possess the qualities that led to that efficiency. In other words, they took space as a given, when instead we should view the capacity of spaces to provide for human needs as the result of purposeful action. To Firey, a key element of that action was the tendency of humans to imbue places with meaning – in our framing, to transform spaces into places.

To make his case, Firey studied two areas in central Boston: Boston Common, an open green that originally served as a common pasture, and Beacon Hill, a historic neighborhood home to many of the city's social elite. Given the proximity of each to an expanding central business district (the first ring in Burgess' concentric zone model – see Figure 2.4), an urban ecologist might predict that commercial uses would "out-compete" and then "succeed" the open space and historic neighborhood. Indeed, a real estate developer could secure tremendous profits by replacing open spaces or row houses with office towers. That this was not these places' fate does not reflect a lack of trying; modern redevelopment plans had been proposed there, and had succeeded in nearby areas (see Studying the city 3.1). Instead, the Common and Beacon Hill remain intact due to the efforts of individuals and organizations with strong attachments to place. These constitute early examples of urban movements that are now commonplace but have not always been so.

As a pioneer in acknowledging the roles of culture and meaning in shaping cities, Firey crafted a new lexicon for speaking of cities, emphasizing what he called **sentiment** and **symbolism** (see Figure 2.5).

sentiment Walter Firey's term for a set of attachments people have to places, whether aesthetic, historical, or familial.

symbolism In Walter Firey's conception, what a place represents as compared to other places.

By sentiment he meant a set of attachments people have to places, whether aesthetic, historical, or familial. Symbolism referred to what a place represents as compared to other places. Beacon Hill addresses conveyed a high degree of social status, even when new developments attempted to promise the same thing. Firey's methods also pioneered ways of studying the meanings attached to places: for instance, he gauged the status associated with Beacon Hill by examining the addresses listed in Boston's Social Register, and considered treatments of these areas in literature and poetry as important data. Contemporary urban scholars are increasingly turning to these kinds of measures to capture otherwise elusive qualities of place.

Figure 2.5 Row houses along Acorn Street in Boston's Beacon Hill neighborhood. Although the narrow cobblestone streets confounded modern standards of efficiency, for residents and visitors they held great sentimental value. *Source: Photo © Chee-Onn Leong/Fotolia.*

Life in the city as a way of life

Robert Park had employed his knowledge of ecology, acquired during his studies in Germany, to fashion an entirely new and different way of thinking about the modern world and modernization. Groups of people became aggregates of population; life in the city became a matter of one group competing with another; the social space within the city mirrored positions within the social order. But Park's was not the only view of life in Chicago to emerge during this time of creative ferment at the University of Chicago. Louis Wirth, one of Park's colleagues, provided yet another portrait, one that echoed many of the themes and ideas found first in the writings of Georg Simmel.

Wirth was one of the many new immigrants to come to Chicago. Born in Gemünden im Hünsruck, Germany in 1897, he moved to the United States to live with his older sister at an uncle's home in Omaha in 1911. His Jewish roots were reflected, in part, in his ideas and concerns as a sociologist. Using Chicago as a prototype of the modern city, he studied the emergence and development of the Jewish community there. He took up the idea of the "ghetto" to capture the quality of life among the Jews in Chicago, and in so doing he returned to earlier periods in history to unearth, for example, the nature of other Jewish settlements in places in Europe and find a model of the Jewish community (Wirth 1928). His writing, like that of his contemporaries at the University of Chicago, helped to flesh out the inner workings of these communities among new immigrants. But Wirth's most lasting contribution to explanations of the city and the modern world took the form of an extended and widely heralded theoretical essay about life in the city, a theory he termed "**urbanism as a way of life.**"

urbanism as a way of life Louis Wirth's view of life in the city as impersonal and anonymous.

Wirth extended the idea of the city as the novel and central social form of the modern world (Wirth 1938).[2] He idealized it in the same manner as Tönnies and Simmel, but he filled in important details they had missed. The city, he argued, was a large and complex site, one of new and dynamic social institutions. It had grown and developed as the world of the nineteenth and twentieth centuries emerged. Its institutions and other social forms were entirely new, a distinct break with the past. People knew one another not in an intimate and personal fashion but rather in a secondary and impersonal one – thus echoing the claims of Simmel and Tönnies. More than that, he insisted, people, in effect, become lost in the city. Taking the idea of the stranger to an extreme, he viewed the city as a place where one did not act as a member of a community or family but rather as a lone individual. Compared to the villages and towns from which most migrants had emigrated, the city did not furnish the close ties and warm comfort so characteristic of a happy and contented social life. People simply did not know one another very well in the city. They knew one another not as full and whole people but only as partial people – someone who belonged to the same social club, or worked in the same factory. The city was not a place, in other words, where people could find *security* and *community* – as we have insisted as part of our definition of places – but, in fact, it was the very opposite.

As a result of this sense of detachment and loneliness in the city, people could come to feel distant from one another. The great paradox of urban life was that it provided close physical contact among people who at the same time knew virtually nothing about one another. It was as though the daily sidewalk traffic in Lower Manhattan became the metaphor for all life in the city (see Figure 2.6). Losing close contact with one another, then, people could come to feel disoriented and anonymous. Instead of being an exciting and challenging new place where people could pursue and enrich their lives among other newcomers, the city, in Wirth's eyes, harbored all the ills and dangers of the modern world.

The character of this way of life, as Wirth put it, could unleash the dark side of humanity, in the form of various symptoms and types of social disorder. Lacking the social ties and security of life in the rural settings, crime, divorce, and other features of life became central byproducts of modernization and, in particular, of the new, emerging metropolis. To maintain social order, in fact, formal institutions, such as the police force, arose, providing the urban equivalent of the family, small friendship groups, or even the church of rural areas. Moreover, city residents lost interest in one another. Their transitory lives discouraged neighborly bonds, and the dense, diverse environment with which they were confronted each day demanded emotional reserve.

Louis Wirth's vision of the city as the idealized form of modern life revealed modernity's dark side along with its accomplishments. Modernization was, Wirth seemed to suggest, not all it had been cracked up to be by its proponents – by the wealthy and by the champions of modern life. People were free; they had been liberated from the tedium and labor of life on the farms – but free to do what and to become what? Free to be alone and isolated, detached from the intimate and secure bonds of their rural homes and villages.

Figure 2.6 As this scene from a Manhattan sidewalk reveals, the density of urban environments brings people into close contact with one another even when they have no social or emotional connections. Wirth argued that this proximity, and the resulting overstimulation, leads city dwellers to adopt a blasé attitude as a means of defense. *Source: Photo by George Marks/ Retrofile/Getty Images.*

MAKING THE CITY BETTER   2.1

Technology and urban isolation

Early theorists such as Tönnies, Simmel, and Wirth painted a particularly bleak picture of the city, but one that nevertheless may resonate with city dwellers today. These theorists suggested that, even though urban residents live closer together in physical terms than at any point in human history, they are emotionally more distant. In addition, Wirth called attention to the ways in which technologies compound our social distance and create new sources of anxiety. Consider the following passage from "Urbanism as a Way of Life":

> Frequent close physical contact, coupled with great social distance, accentuates the reserve of unattached individuals toward one another and, unless compensated for by other opportunities for response, gives rise to loneliness. The necessary frequent movement of great numbers of individuals in a congested habitat gives occasion to friction and irritation. Nervous tensions which derive from such personal frustrations are accentuated by the rapid tempo and the complicated technology under which life in dense areas must be lived. (Wirth 1938: 16)

You can imagine that Wirth was describing the simultaneous isolation and contact that occurs in urban spaces such as subway cars, though his mention of "friction and irritation" could just as easily apply to other means of transportation as well (road rage comes to mind).

Given this pessimistic view of urban life, it's noteworthy that the very kinds of technologies that may be creating social distance between city dwellers are also fostering new ways of forging connections. For instance, flash mobs use the internet and text messages to communicate a time and place in which members of an extended social network can come together to engage in fun and creative events. International Pillow Fight Day is one variation in which people have come together in cities from Accra, Ghana to Zurich, Switzerland for a playful battle (see http://www.pillowfightday.com; Figure 2.7). Another variation is what is called "silent disco," in which individuals listen to their own choice of music (using iPods and the like) but dance together. Perhaps the best-known silent disco event took place at London's Victoria station, where some 4000 people participated.

Figure 2.7 International Pillow Fight Day 2010, as observed in Brussels.
Source: © Nathan Fougnies.

In London and New York, a group of street theater artists calling themselves the Love Police seek to spread love and good feelings in urban spaces that might otherwise be bleak and isolating. One of their most ingenious stunts – and one that turns Wirth's observations squarely on their head – designates a single subway car or carriage as the "happy carriage." Using a megaphone, the Love Police proclaim that wearing headphones and reading the newspaper are forbidden, and smiling is mandatory (if you do not wish to smile, you must move to another carriage). At each stop, riders are encouraged to applaud new passengers "just for being human," recognizing the very qualities that Wirth claimed we had forgotten.

Early social theories of urban life

Cities, by definition, are not orderly and neat places; they are in fact disorderly ones. Yet social theorists of the city typically have tried to give the city a sense of order and a sense of movement and change in their theoretical work. All of this is done to simplify and make the analysis of cities easier. If we work with imagined portraits of the modern city, we can compare our portraits with both real cities and premodern settings to gain new insights.

Robert Park, Ernest Burgess, and Louis Wirth all came up with novel ideas about modernity, social change, and the modern city, ideas that we have suggested built on the earlier insights of Georg Simmel. Park and Burgess created a model of the city in which social space was its most prominent feature. People and institutions were not randomly scattered throughout the city, but they were located within it, based on the social groups to which they belonged. The key players in the life of the modern city, Park and Burgess claimed, were mainly the new immigrant groups that entered the city. And the key social institutions were mainly the economic institutions, the ones that generated the jobs and the cash that kept the modern city going. Louis Wirth developed his own picture of the city and its way of life, or lifestyle; and it clearly owed a great debt to the inspired portrait invented years earlier by Georg Simmel. But Wirth also brought to light the darker sides of modern life – the anonymity of life in the city, the sense that people actually could become lost among the messiness and complexity of this new and vital form of social organization. Whereas Simmel had pictured the city in terms of the liveliness of thought and the overwhelming mark of business and rational calculations, Wirth invented a city in which the warm and fuzzy features of premodern life virtually disappeared – only to be replaced by various forms of crime and the like.

These portraits and ideas fashioned by the Chicago sociologists have had a lasting impact on the way that we as social scientists think even today about the city. The notion that the city is nothing but a collection of economic institutions, social groups, and areas remains a device that urban scholars routinely invoke to talk about the modern city. But this picture also omits some key features and institutions. Why, for example, did the Chicago sociologists talk only about immigrant groups and not social classes? And why did they not explore more deeply the social and economic roots of the obvious poverty and forlorn quality of life of so many immigrants – men, women, and often children – who toiled in the factories of Chicago? These were issues that came to preoccupy other residents of the city, especially the great champion of the new immigrants, Jane Addams (see Chapter 7). But they were of little concern to the original Chicago sociologists. And it required new developments, new social changes, and some strong intellectual advocacy to put these matters back on the table for students of the city. In Chapter 3 we will take up these issues at length. Visit the book's companion website at www.wiley.com/go/cities for examples, case studies, and discussion questions, plus a list of useful films and other media, that are relevant to this chapter.

Critical thinking questions

1 What is your overall image of life in cities: is life in the city cold, rational, and calculating, or is it filled with close contacts and friendships? How different is city life today from life in suburbs and small towns? What advantages do each have?

2 What evidence do you see of social change in the city today? Does social change happen so rapidly and dramatically as Simmel seemed to believe?

3 Robert Park and Ernest Burgess seemed to see the city in terms of specific residential and commercial areas. Do you think cities are organized in the same way today? How have they changed, if at all?

4 Park was very concerned about the emerging patterns of segregation between groups in the city. Is that still a concern today? Do you think the types of segregation that exist today are different from those of the past?

Suggested reading

Martin Bulmer, *The Chicago School of Sociology* (Chicago, IL: University of Chicago Press, 1986). One of the best books on the Chicago School of Sociology, it traces the development of the school, its major ideas, and its leading figures, including Robert Park.

Peter Hall, *Cities of Tomorrow: An Intellectual History of Urban Planning and Design in the Twentieth Century* (Oxford and Malden, MA: Blackwell, 2002). Hall provides a comprehensive view of the origins and variations of approaches to urban planning from the earliest efforts through the end of the twentieth century.

Amos Hawley, *Human Ecology* (New York: Ronald Press Co., 1950). The most sophisticated and imaginative exposition of human ecology ever written. Hawley examines and theorizes cities using such basic elements as population and social organization.

Robert E. Park, Ernest W. Burgess, and Roderick McKenzie, *The City* (Chicago, IL: University of Chicago Press, 1967). The basic perspective about cities in terms of the original view of human ecology. Required reading for anyone interested in the history of this field.

Louis Wirth, "Urbanism as a Way of Life" (*American Journal of Sociology* 44(1): 1–24; 1938). In this relatively brief article, Wirth created a theoretical template about cities that drew upon the writings of Georg Simmel and linked elements of population and urban life to their consequences for the lives of urban residents.

Kurt H. Wolff, *The Sociology of Georg Simmel* (New York: Free Press of Glencoe, 1964 [1903]). The major collection of the writings of Georg Simmel. It includes his brilliant essay on the modern metropolis – which is also a theory of modernization.

Notes

1. See the interesting article by Dietmar Jazbinsek (2003) on this subject.

2. For an excellent treatment of this article, see Saunders (1981: Chapter 3).

CHAPTER 3

Social theories of urban space and place
Perspectives in the post-World War II era

KEY TOPICS

→ How the writings of Karl Marx were used to promote a revolution in thinking about cities and issues such as social justice and inequality. In particular we will introduce you to the following authors and their central contributions:

- Manuel Castells' critique of the Chicago School of Sociology;
- David Harvey on justice and the uneven development of the metropolis; and
- Harvey Molotch and John Logan's model of the city as a growth machine.

→ The rediscovery (or perhaps discovery) of community in cities through the work of Jane Jacobs and Herbert Gans.

→ Sharon Zukin's contributions on the role of culture and consumption in shaping urban growth and redevelopment, as well as the experience of urban life.

→ Theories, particularly those of John Friedmann and Saskia Sassen, of globalization's impact on cities.

→ How different theories of the city compare, and some analytical tools you can use to evaluate urban theories.

Introduction to Cities: How Place and Space Shape Human Experience,
First Edition. Xiangming Chen, Anthony M. Orum, and Krista E. Paulsen.
© 2013 Xiangming Chen, Anthony M. Orum, and Krista E. Paulsen.
Published 2013 by Blackwell Publishing Ltd.

Contents

Theoretical descendents of Marx

Manuel Castells and the urban question

David Harvey: Injustice and inequality in the city

John Logan and Harvey Molotch: The city as a growth machine

Further reflections: Marx and the critique of modern cities

The return to place and the turn to culture

Jane Jacobs and the discovery of community in the modern metropolis

Sharon Zukin and the turn to culture

Going global: The 1980s and the creation of the global city

Evaluating theories of the city

The European theorists' and Chicago School sociologists' ideas about cities, described in Chapter 2, remained the leading urban theories through the 1950s. They furnished a set of concepts that could be used to explore how social order emerged and how social change took place. They also relied on some basic concepts, especially the concept of social space, which originated with and was used with great insight by sociologists such as Robert Park and Ernest Burgess. Though some scholars took issue with just what types of forces mattered in the ecology of cities (recall Walter Firey's contribution, outlined in Studying the city 2.2), the ecological model held fast for decades.

But just as the social changes in Europe and America had once fostered and promoted the new ideas of Georg Simmel and Louis Wirth, so, too, change would begin to erode the dominance of old frameworks among social scientists. The beginnings of a shift can be traced to the 1960s, a period of great intellectual and political upheaval across the world. A spirit of revolution was in the air, and it took various manifestations. The year 1968 was particularly significant; students across the world, from Chicago to Prague, from New York City to Paris, took to the streets in protest. In May of that year, millions of workers as well as students called a general wildcat strike in France, the largest such strike ever against an advanced industrial society. A new generation of young people helped to lead the assault on the ideas of the past, urging that such ideas be overthrown and, as in the case of the Students for a Democratic Society in the United States, that new forms of democracy – participatory democracy – arise. The swirl of new ideas, advanced by young college students, had roots in the resistance to the war in Vietnam, in the forms of racial and gender inequalities newly disclosed in America, and in resistance to the new consumer societies emerging across the world.

Eventually this spirit of revolution invaded the halls of academia itself. If young people could challenge the government because of wars fought abroad, they could challenge the older ideas and theories of university departments and professors as well. The university itself came under attack: campuses at the University of California at Berkeley, the University of Wisconsin in Madison, Columbia University in New York, and the Sorbonne in Paris became sites where radical students mobilized and faced off against the local – and, in Paris, national – authorities. Tear down the old, students proclaimed, and replace it with the new – new ideas, new theories, even new forms of criticism about the military–industrial complex that was called America. Ironically, this spirit of revolution reached back into the nineteenth century in order to find a voice with which to criticize current conditions. It resurrected the voice and passion of Karl Marx. Marx, the theorist of nineteenth-century political economy, became the inspiration for challenging the conventional wisdom of urban social science in the twentieth century.

Theoretical descendents of Marx

Manuel Castells and the urban question

A direct assault was launched by a young Spanish intellectual who had embraced and helped to rework the fundamental ideas of Karl Marx, and then applied them to thinking about the city. His name was Manuel Castells, and his work helped to inspire a new wave of thinking about cities and how they worked. Marx, in fact, never wrote about cities directly. Instead, he was primarily concerned with how the institutions of modern capitalism arose and how they worked. Now, if that were so, how could one actually use Marx to talk about cities? This became the intellectual project of Castells (1977).

Castells began with a critique of the older forms of urban thinking. He argued that figures such as Robert Park and Ernest Burgess had misconstrued the fundamental nature of cities and of modern urban life. Though they had written about urban institutions and the various forms of social disorganization that arose within cities, Castells insisted that they had missed the central feature of modern society and, thus, the modern city. Whereas Park and Burgess had urged scholars to examine the city through the lens of how a population of people tried to adapt to the city (see Chapter 2), Castells claimed that it was modern capitalism that dominated everything that took place within the city. The motor force for the modern metropolis everywhere had become, or was becoming, the machinery of the market – in a phrase, the single-minded pursuit of profit by people.

The daily lives of the people residing in cities, Castells insisted, could be not understood in terms of the competition between groups for dominance in social space, as Park had claimed. Nor could one simply think of urban living, as Wirth had, in terms of social relationships and the unique nature of such relationships in the modern city, even though those relationships might reflect the nature of economic exchanges, as Simmel had argued. Rather, one had to turn to the economic processes of the larger social world itself and to look therein to understand what cities and metropolitan life were all about. And Castells went further. Because modern capitalism itself clearly had changed in important ways since the days when Marx had observed and written about it, one also had to update one's understanding of the nature of such capitalism. In particular, Castells built on the work of recent neo-Marxists, such as Louis Althusser and Nicos Poulantzas, insisting on the necessity of picturing the world of the 1960s and 1970s in terms of broad social structures, not simply classes of people.[1] Such structures included, for example, the political (i.e., the state) and the ideological – those institutions that focus on basic values, such as the importance of human rights. Moreover, Castells said, one also had to fundamentally shift attention away from the ways in which things were produced – that is to say, manufacturing and production – to the ways in which those things were now consumed. He was especially intent on shifting the attention of urban study to the way in which people lived in the city, and to their patterns of housing. He argued that urban analysts should move to thinking of urban life in terms of the ways in which people consumed things rather than the ways in which they produced them. Indeed, within a matter of decades, the study of cities, especially in the West, would shift from critical analyses of factories and the exploitation of workers to critical analyses of new lifestyles and the emergence of a new, and dominant, urban middle class.

Castells' perspective quickly became widely known and highly celebrated among students of cities and metropolitan areas. But it also was put forth in very abstract and complex terms, using some of the ideas and techniques of neo-Marxists such as Althusser. Though Castells helped to initiate a new wave of neo-Marxist thinking among urbanists, it was left to other scholars to make the ideas of Marx more lucid and directly applicable to the workings of the city in contemporary times.

David Harvey: Injustice and inequality in the city

One of those scholars was a young English geographer, David Harvey. Trained in the orthodox ways of geography in the late 1960s – at the same time that others were taking more radical ideas to heart – Harvey embraced the ideas of Karl Marx. He has used them ever since in systematic and often ingenious ways to offer new ideas for thinking about cities and their residents.

Harvey's major insight was to suggest that a Marxist view helped to reveal the blind spots in the conventional ways in which sociologists and geographers talked about cities (Harvey 1973, 1989, 2008). In particular, he argues, the city in modern capitalist societies is fraught with various problems and issues, the root of which is the basic character of capitalism itself. Capitalist enterprises constantly require profit, and, in the process of securing such profits, those enterprises gain while many residents of the city lose. One can look at the spatial development of any modernizing city, for example, and notice that certain parts of the city are undergoing growth and new development, while other parts – especially the inner, or central, city – are left to decline. This is because, Harvey says, capitalism is intent on the process of gaining profit not only through manufacturing but also and equally through the process of promoting urban growth in the form of new housing and commercial properties.

All sectors of capitalism, he argues, essentially work in tandem so that, when the profit-making in one sector (e.g., manufacturing) slows down, another (e.g., real estate and property development) can take up the slack. The optimum way in which such profits can occur is for real estate developers and bankers, along with their allies, to buy new land, build new houses, and sell those properties. Capital, in effect, always looks for the best investment and the biggest dollar. And that can only happen with the purchase of new

uneven growth of the city The unequal spatial development of cities, with older portions left to decline and new growth occurs elsewhere.

land, often on the periphery of growing cities, and the creation of new residential and commercial properties. Such land is typically cheaper, of course, because it lies at the outskirts of cities – an insight offered by human ecologists as well – and its development is less costly because it does not require the replacement of older and declining properties. As a result, the space of the city, itself, Harvey argues, displays **uneven growth** and development, with a great deal of money being spent on housing and commercial properties in outlying areas and very little on developments in the older, central portions of the city (see Figure 3.1).

Figure 3.1 A child walks through the Islington area of London, 1966. At the time of Harvey's early writings, conditions for the urban poor of many developed nations were no better than those of their counterparts in the nineteenth century. *Source: Photo: Popperfoto/Getty Images.*

The beauty of Harvey's imagery is that it fits the circumstances of so many actual cities in the older, industrialized countries of the world, such as England, France, and the United States. In the late 1960s and early 1970s, many such cities – for example, London, Paris, New York City, and Philadelphia – displayed precisely this pattern of uneven development: new growth at the outskirts and material decay and decline within the central city. Harvey's argument seems to capture the very essence of modern capitalism. The institutions of capitalism always look for profit, and try to identify where the most profitable investments can be made in land and other forms of property.

Yet, unlike the conventional economists, Harvey's view also reveals the underbelly of modern capitalism. Just as Marx talked about the winners and losers in the modern world – that is, the wealthy institutions and people on the one hand and the workers and their families on the other – Harvey insists that there are winners and losers in the modern city as well. The winners are all those people and enterprises who hold capital and invest it in property (the bankers and real estate developers), whereas the losers are residents, who must pay the high prices charged by the banks and the holders of mortgages. In fact, Harvey argues – and much other evidence now shows him to be right – it is the very poorest residents of cities who are the most vulnerable and who end up being charged the highest rates for their mortgages.

The next stage of Harvey's argument was to extend Marx's ideas about private property and exploitation and use them to talk about the uneven economic growth and development in the city, as well as the forms of economic and social injustice that arose as a result. Capital stood on one side of the transactions over land and property in the form of the bankers, the real estate figures, and their allies, and the bulk of urban residents stood on the other side, in the form of homeowners and those who held commercial property, such as small businesses. And, just as Marx used the notion of exploitation to argue that workers are exploited by business owners, so Harvey insisted that homeowners and renters are exploited in the transactions they carry out with bankers, developers, and real estate companies. The worldwide sub-prime mortgage crisis of 2008, a crisis partly rooted in the shady business practices of mortgage companies and their agents, provides a telling illustration of this theoretical argument.

John Logan and Harvey Molotch: The city as a growth machine

In the United States, the ideas of Marx caught on as well. A young sociologist trained at the University of Chicago, Harvey Molotch, challenged the writings of the earlier Chicago sociologists. Like Manuel Castells, Molotch believed that Park and his colleagues did not truly grasp the way in which cities worked. In particular, he argued, the old Chicago School had spoken of social institutions and the spatial competition among varying groups of people, but their theories never talked about real people, whether average residents or those who wield sufficient power to transform urban places. Hearkening back to earlier concerns of other social scientists that lived and worked in Chicago, among them Jane Addams (see Making the city better 8.1), Molotch reasserted the need for urban scholars to pay more attention to the lives of real people who lived and worked in cities. Like David Harvey, he saw these people becoming winners and losers as cities grew and changed, but he offered a unique insight into how urban growth occurred.

Molotch claims that we should think of cities metaphorically – or, as he said, we should think of the **city as a growth machine** (1976). What he means is that

> **city as a growth machine** A concept, developed by Molotch and Logan, that interprets the city as a machine whose sole purpose is growth.

MAKING THE CITY BETTER   3.1

The Los Angeles Bus Riders Union

The Marxist perspective of urban scholars such as David Harvey has been widely adopted by social and community activists working to improve the quality of life in cities. Poor and working-class citizens play a substantial role in keeping cities running, but little of the wealth generated in cities returns to these workers. As activists have made clear, the poor often struggle for the bare necessities such as decent housing, childcare, nutritious food, and access to transportation. In some cases, the poor are even asked to subsidize urban services that will be used by more affluent citizens.

Such was the case in Los Angeles during the 1990s. Los Angeles is a notoriously large and sprawling city in which access to economic opportunities depends upon access to reliable transportation. Roads and highways are routinely clogged with private cars, while overburdened buses provide the only viable alternative for those without them. The regional transit authority sought to increase transit ridership by constructing a clean, fast subway and light rail system that might lure commuters out of their cars. While such a proposal certainly had merit, it also required significant expenditure – $300 million per mile in the case of the Los Angeles Red Line subway. Where would the money come from? In part, from a fare increase for bus riders, who were primarily racial and ethnic minorities, and included large numbers of young, elderly, and disabled passengers. Routes would also be cut, including the late night runs that janitors, hotel staff, and other night shift workers relied upon.

In 1994, the Los Angeles Bus Riders Union (a grassroots transit advocacy group), in conjunction with the Labor/Community Strategy Center, the NAACP Legal Defense and Education Fund, and other labor and immigrant rights organizations, sued the Los Angeles Metropolitan Transit Authority (MTA) for using its funds in a discriminatory manner (see Figure 3.2). Poor, minority bus riders were paying more and receiving less when compared to primarily white rail passengers. They won their suit, resulting in a court order that the MTA issue low-fare monthly passes, purchase new clean-fuel buses, and increase service. While the campaign to ensure access to affordable and reliable public transportation is ongoing, it reflects an important step in efforts to ensure equity for all citizens.

Figure 3.2 Many types of community organizing and urban protest movements build on the critiques of urban inequality put forth by David Harvey. Here protestors from Los Angeles' Bus Riders Union pressure the Metropolitan Transit Authority to end a mechanics' strike in 2003. *Source: Photo: Hector Mata/ AFP/Getty Images.*

the modern city's central purpose is growth, or expansion. Once we grasp this basic insight, many other things about urban life become clear. In particular, he notes, there is a group of diverse officials and institutions in the city. This **growth coalition** includes the mayor and local government, as well as banks, real estate developers, and even the local media, such as newspapers. Though the members of the coalition are different and have different occupational pursuits, they are all aligned in favor of the growth of the city, and each of these major officials and institutions stand to benefit from such expansion. Political officials benefit if more people move into the city because their base of political power can expand. Bankers benefit because greater numbers of people and business enterprises can increase their assets. And, of course, real estate agents and, especially, those figures that develop large residential or commercial projects also benefit through the profit they secure by the sale of property. Growth, in other words, is not merely an economic fact of life in cities but also a major political fact, something that creates alliances among the most powerful of urban institutions and groups.

> **growth coalition**
> A group of individuals and organizations who come together in support of urban growth.

After the publication of his original argument, Molotch and a colleague, John Logan, expanded this basic insight into a full-blown argument about the nature of cities in the modern United States (Logan and Molotch 1987). They argued that, while bankers, politicians, and developers all gain from the expansion of the city, there are losers as well – and they are primarily the residents of the city. Here they echoed a similar argument made by David Harvey, using a notion first developed by Marx. Let us take a moment to explain this notion.

Marx insisted that, under capitalism, commodities, or the goods and products that are created, have two values. One is the value they possess as useful items. For example, someone, let us say Peter, might decide to make a desk for himself, and so Peter takes wood, a lathe, and other tools and creates a desk. Peter does so for the utility, or **use value**, it provides him. But a desk can possess another value as well, a value characteristic of all products of modern capitalism. If Peter decides, for example, that he wants to make other desks, even though he has no use for them, he can sell them on the open market. Such desks no longer have utility for him because he already has a desk, but those that he sells now will have a second value, an **exchange value**. Exchange value, or "price," as we can think of it in simple terms, is the value of desks, and all products in general, created for sale under capitalism. The products of a capitalist economy thus have two values – a use value and an exchange value. And therein lies the secret of modern capitalism, Marx insisted. Workers and residents attach one set of values to those things we use, such as desks or housing, but capitalists, such as banks and realtors, attach another and a competing set of values – an exchange value, or price – to those very same things.

> **use value** Marx's concept valuing the use of a thing; residents' primary concern regarding their neighborhoods.
>
> **exchange value** Marx's concept of the market value of commodities; the primary interest of real estate developers.

Logan and Molotch ingeniously applied this distinction between use values and exchange values to clarify the way in which growth and expansion happen in cities, and just why growth so often seems to involve a set of conflicts between residents and local officials and developers. First, they reiterated, the very nature of the modern capitalist city is growth and expansion. This is the character of capitalism itself, and therefore it is also the character of major human enterprises under capitalism, such as the city. Second, they argued that in the course of such expansion, those aligned on the side of growth and capital – namely, the local government and banks – often come to loggerheads with local residents as well as many local small businesses. This happens because the residents have an attachment to their homes and neighborhoods in the sense that those things have a use value for them.

We can also frame this argument in terms with which we are already familiar in this book: *homes and neighborhoods take on the value of places for us*. Homes are where we live and raise families; they are places where we feel a *sense of security*. Neighborhoods are where we have social gatherings and where we spend much of our time and leisure outside work; they are places where we establish our *ties to community*. But banks, realtors, and local officials see all those things in an entirely different light – as exchange values. At those sites where we become attached to and enjoy our local parks or streets as *places*, a realtor envisions the opportunity to build another housing development or develop a large commercial property. Conflicts over the fates of places thus reflect the very different meanings they have for residents as opposed to those seeking to profit from places.

Just as David Harvey used the ideas of Marx to talk about the obvious uneven growth and development in modern cities, Logan and Molotch used Marx's ideas to pinpoint other fundamental inequities and basic conflicts in those same cities. And, just as Harvey's explanations seemed to fit so many of the real-life circumstances in the changing urban environment of the 1960s and 1970s, so, too, did the work of Logan and Molotch capture the realities of the many clashes across US cities about growth. Whether in London or Los Angeles, countless clashes occurred in this era between neighborhood associations, seeking to protect the rights of residents, and local governments, backed by developers and seeking to find and develop new pieces of property in the city. Indeed, not only did the metaphor of the city as a growth machine work as an interpretive theory but it also seemed to work even more effectively as a political theory. By the 1980s and 1990s, the political forces of resistance to urban growth had arisen across many of the newer cities in the West and Southwest, such as Phoenix, all of them loudly proclaiming their attack on the local "growth machines."

MAKING THE CITY BETTER   3.2

International sporting mega-events

The bidding for and hosting of international sporting mega-events, such as the Olympics and World Cup, is one of the many ways that urban growth coalitions attempt to gain positive national or international attention for their cities, and in turn attract growth and investment. Logan and Molotch suggest that these events, like the presence of major league sports franchises, announce to the world that a city has "arrived." Much of the media attention lavished on these mega-events showcases beautiful local scenery, sparkling new athletic venues, and interesting elements of local culture – promotions that show a place in its best light. Urban problems such as poverty and homelessness have no place in this picture.

Not only do sporting mega-events obscure urban problems but they also have a track record of leaving local low-income populations worse off while profits are funneled into growth coalitions. Often local communities will resist the changes that come with a city hosting an international sporting mega-event. For instance, protests around the 2010 Winter Olympics in Vancouver sought to call attention to local poverty and downtown gentrification, among other issues.

The Center on Housing Rights and Evictions (COHRE) is an independent, not-for-profit human rights organization based in Geneva that focuses on the human right to housing and on forced evictions at the international level. According to COHRE (2007), well over two million people have been displaced as a result of the Olympic Games since the 1980s.

For example, during the 1988 Seoul Olympic Games, about 750 000 people were displaced in order to build Olympic facilities and make the South Korean capital more presentable to the international audience. *Twice* that number were displaced as a result of preparations for the 2008 Beijing Olympics and many of these people didn't even lose their homes to make way for Olympic facilities:

large tracts of slum housing were cleared to build attractive skyscrapers filled with luxury apartments signifying China's status as a rising economic power, but the apartments were left completely vacant.

Also according to COHRE, in the United States during the 1996 Atlanta Olympic Games, low-income African American residents were hit on several fronts. Many residents were made homeless when 30000 people were displaced to make room for 9000 parking spots and other Olympic facilities. Three Atlanta homeless shelters were closed to build Centennial Olympic Park and the Olympic Village, and the use of sleep-proof benches and intermittent sprinklers and a lack of public restrooms told the homeless that they were not welcome in the area. Finally, Atlanta police issued arrest warrants for thousands of homeless individuals; they transported others to shelters outside the city and threatened them with a three-month prison sentence if they returned.

If international sports events are truly to make cities better for all, they must be conducted in equitable ways. Some attempts are being made to see that this is the case – for instance, projects that built soccer fields in poor areas of South Africa in conjunction with that country's hosting of the World Cup (see Figure 3.3). But important questions remain about how the benefits of such events will improve citizens' everyday experience of their cities.

Figure 3.3 Soccer City Stadium in Johannesburg, constructed for the 2010 World Cup. Sporting "mega-events" are one way in which cities can generate positive attention in the hopes of attracting growth and investment, but this often comes at a cost for residents. *Source: Photo © AfriPics.com/Alamy.*

Further reflections: Marx and the critique of modern cities

Although socialist systems across the world have disappeared since the fall of the Soviet Union in 1991, the ideas of Karl Marx, the icon on which such socialism was built, remain as powerful and important as ever. Marx offered major insights into the workings and inequalities of modern capitalism. The scholars discussed in this section – Manuel Castells, David Harvey, John Logan, and Harvey Molotch – all used those ideas in novel fashion to provide new ways of examining and thinking about cities in the modern world. At the same time, these thinkers collectively challenged and replaced the frameworks they inherited from the Chicago School of Sociology.

Today these new ideas remain as important as ever. They provide a platform from which people can continue to criticize the workings of the modern city, especially the ways in which both the working and the middle classes are exploited by ruthless bankers and real estate developers. The devastating global financial crises of 2008 provide further ammunition for those critics who single out bankers and their allies for the ways in which they financially exploit homeowners.

Yet, just as the ideas of Robert Park and his colleagues were limited and missed key developments in the modern world, so, too, do these ideas of the neo-Marxists. By turning our attention primarily to the economic workings of the modern city and the ways in which those principles manifest themselves in politics as well, they ignore other new developments in the modern city. For example, they neglect to spend much time on the ways in which people form their neighborhoods and develop lively communities. In this sense, they share the same flaw as the earlier work of Louis Wirth, among others. They also miss out on other important social changes that have taken place over the course of the late twentieth and early twenty-first centuries. As Castells suggested, the city is no longer a site simply of production but is above all else a site of consumption. It is such consumption, and related features of culture, that require more study and new theories.

The return to place and the turn to culture

Changing circumstances in the world and in cities promote the need to consider why they have so changed – a quest that always lies behind the work of social theory. So we have argued throughout this chapter. But sometimes change and even the passage of time can bring to light hidden features of cities, things that demand explanation. Thus it was that the idea of community, first explored in the writings of Ferdinand Tönnies, reappeared in the writings of later urban scholars. Those writings made clear that cities are not simply about a new way of life, as Louis Wirth had insisted, but are also about the ways in which people actually create and sustain human communities within the city. In other words, they are about the importance of cities as places, and places as the sites of community for human beings.

Jane Jacobs and the discovery of community in the modern metropolis

In the 1950s and 1960s, the older industrial cities across the world began to show their age. From New York City to Manchester, from Barcelona to Boston, cities began to show evidence of decline both in their economies and in their infrastructures, including the old warehouses and plants, among other things. Many of their buildings and highways had been created in the late nineteenth century and now, more than half a century later, they were showing signs of wear and tear. Old factories had become abandoned in some cities, such as Detroit, as those businesses that had once occupied them left for greener pastures in the South, the suburbs, or overseas. The housing in older neighborhoods had begun to fall apart, and the older tenement buildings no longer seemed to fit the lifestyle circumstances of families that now were moving out of the working class into the middle class. In the United States, the federal government and local officials, noting these kinds of changes, embarked on a program to undertake a massive rehabilitation of the older areas of cities. This program, which became known as **urban renewal**, took place across the older parts of America. Urban renewal areas deemed "blighted" or "slums" were razed to make way for highways, sports stadiums, and office and entertainment complexes (Studying the city 3.1 describes sociologist Herbert Gans' research on the impact of urban renewal in Boston).

urban renewal
Large-scale, government-funded efforts to remake older areas of cities.

For a period of time, urban renewal massively reshaped the older and declining areas, while, at the same time, uprooting many poorer people from places, such as neighborhoods where, despite the age of buildings, people had become firmly entrenched in the security and comfort of their own local communities.

Spearheading these changes were many of the important urban planners of the time. They wanted to remake the urban landscape, using principles they had learned in graduate school. They thought that big buildings were the solution to the overcrowding of the booming metropolis (see Exploring further 2.1, particularly the discussion of Le Corbusier). They also employed new principles of street design, ones that tried to create streets more accommodating to the increasing numbers of cars and trucks that now entered cities. Altogether, they desired to use this wave of urban change and renewal to make the city into a place they thought would be far more functional and useful for its various residents. Yet they ran into a major critic, someone who would bedevil them for many decades and who would become a voice for asserting the importance of place and neighborhood in modern urban life.

Her name was Jane Jacobs. While she never trained as a professional planner or social scientist, her work has had lasting theoretical importance for the social sciences. Jacobs lived with her husband and their children in Greenwich Village, New York City. She became a vocal critic of planning in the city, particularly the efforts of Robert Moses, who was the mastermind and "powerbroker" behind many of the city's parks and public buildings,

STUDYING THE CITY   3.1

The Urban Villagers

Jane Jacobs was not alone in her quest to reveal the pro-social dimensions of urban life. A number of scholars sought to combat the notion that cities were primarily sites of decline or hotbeds of crime (also see William H. Whyte's work on urban space, discussed in Exploring further 4.1). In Boston in the late 1950s, sociologist Herbert Gans sought to understand a neighborhood slated for destruction and redevelopment through urban renewal. The West End was home to predominantly first- and second-generation immigrants of Italian descent, but also Jews, Polish immigrants, and some of Irish descent. The housing stock was primarily old and run-down tenements, and the relatively poor condition of the housing constituted one reason that the area was to be demolished. A second motive for destroying the neighborhood was the perception of the people who lived there: they were poor and held more closely to their ethnic identities and were, in the view of social scientists of the day, socially disorganized – a term describing a lack of core values that can in turn lead to delinquency and crime.

Gans moved into an apartment in the West End to conduct his study, interviewing and observing his neighbors while engaged in other forms of research (for instance, using Census data, church records, and library memberships to track demographic changes in the area). He observed the patterns of residents' daily and weekly routines, shared meals in their homes, and attended social functions. Gans' thorough knowledge of the community established his book *The Urban Villagers* as a model of the urban ethnographic case study (see Chapter 4).

Contrary to the views of outsiders, Gans found that the West End was a tight-knit and stable community in which neighbors knew and supported one another. This was not a disorganized community – just the opposite. Gans credited the stability of the West End's population with the sharing of widely held values. As Gans said, "Everyone might not know everyone else; but, as they did know something about everyone, the net effect was the same … For most West Enders, then, life in the area resembled that found in the village or small town, or even the suburb" (1982 [1962]: p. 15). The major threat to the community came not from a lack of values within but from the lack of recognition of the neighborhood from outsiders. Despite protests from well-organized residents, the community was largely demolished by the 1960s.

bridges, and highways. Jacobs took on Moses and others, arguing that the life of cities could be found not in the design of the major highways nor in the large skyscrapers, but rather in the people and their neighborhoods across the city.

In particular, Jacobs claimed that neighborhoods like hers provided all the important elements of the everyday community life of people. As we discussed in Chapter 1, Jacobs felt that strong urban neighborhoods furnished the everyday elements of community in the form of people who one saw on a regular basis – such as the butcher down the street, the baker on the corner, even just the pedestrians who one passed by every day. People living in these neighborhoods, she claimed, could feel secure and comfortable with one another because they saw and spoke with one another on a regular basis – on the corner, at the market, or even in schools to which they took their children.

More than that, however, neighborhoods provided the kinds of urban architecture that really mattered – not big buildings but sidewalks and parks where children could play and parents could gather. Sidewalks (also known as pavements in the United Kingdom) were to Jacobs a special site of community life. Though built so that people could walk on them throughout cities, in many neighborhoods across the city such sidewalks actually provided places where children could play (see Figure 3.4). The stone steps that connected the sidewalks to houses had a particular benefit in the lives of New York City schoolchildren. Young children learned to play games such as stickball against the steps, using both the sidewalks and the streets for their games, and furnishing lively entertainment every day for themselves as well as for parents and other adults.

While Louis Wirth had argued for the importance of the police force as a means for furnishing the basis of compliance and social order in the modern city, Jacobs demurred,

Figure 3.4 Children at play on a New York City sidewalk. While playing in the street was often derided as akin to juvenile delinquency, many urban children had few other places to play. Jane Jacobs made the case that streets and sidewalks provided play spaces that adults could easily supervise from steps or windows, thus decreasing the likelihood that children would get into trouble. *Source: Photo by Walker Evans, Library of Congress, Prints and Photographs Division, LC-USF3301–006721-M5.*

claiming that social order was a regular part of neighborhood life. The grocer on the corner and the local busybody, poking about in everyone and anyone's business, were the key elements of maintaining social order and thus securing communities in the city. Indeed, Jacobs seemed to suggest that the police force was almost an unnecessary afterthought, and that cities never would work properly if the essential social and personal elements of the neighborhood were not present and did not do their job.

Jacobs' penetrating insights, published in one of the great non-fiction works of the twentieth century, *The Death and Life of Great American Cities*, provided an important corrective to the ideas of the old Chicago School theorists, and actually echoed an argument first made by Ferdinand Tönnies in his seminal work (Jacobs 1961; see also the discussion of Tönnies in Chapter 2). Tönnies insisted that community life, in the form of *Gemeinschaft*, could be discovered in the modern metropolis, and precisely at the spot where Jacobs found it – in the neighborhood. But, for over half a century, this simple claim was ignored by other writers intent on discovering something novel in the modern metropolis. Jacobs, however, found community within the city, and, lo and behold, it was there where we all knew it had been lurking – in front of our eyes. It was down the street, on the sidewalk, in the parks, among the children, shared by adults, and protected by the local busybody, Mrs. O'Reilly, who sat in her window every day, observing people (but actually protecting them).

The local community that Jacobs discovered not only served as an important critique of the work of modern urban planners but also helped to revive the work of urban sociology. It made everyday social life a vital element in the workings of the modern city – certainly as important as the way in which local economies worked. Today, in fact, the ideas of Jane Jacobs, which had disappeared from the theoretical work of urban scholars for a while, have re-emerged. They provide the foundations for some of the most interesting and exciting research and important social policy taking place in the early years of the twenty-first century.

Sharon Zukin and the turn to culture

The 1950s and 1960s were a period of great social change, as we have noted throughout this chapter. Among other things, such change involved efforts to rehabilitate the inner core of cities, as in the case of urban renewal programs; other change took the form of political resistance to the status quo, as in the various rebellions led by young people. But there was an additional form, and it involved fundamental structural changes to societies and to the city itself. This was the change Manuel Castells first identified – the transformation of modern capitalism from an economy that was based primarily on the production of goods to one that emphasized the consumption of goods as much as, if not more than, the production of them.

By the early years of the 1960s, it was clear that many manufacturing businesses in the West, in cities such as Chicago, Manchester, Barcelona, and Philadelphia, had begun to decline. They confronted dwindling profits, in part because of the effectiveness of labor unions in gaining better wages for their workers and in part because costs – particularly for energy – were rapidly increasing. As the factory system of production was becoming less and less profitable in the West, advancing communication and transportation technologies, as well as new trade agreements, made overseas manufacturing more feasible. Firms feeling the profit squeeze began to move their operations elsewhere, whether to developing nations with lower wages or to areas beyond traditional industrial cities. This transformed economy required a very different kind of labor force. Once composed primarily of blue-collar workers who toiled away on the floors of massive factories, now the labor force in the United States and in many European countries began to change into one that was composed of many white-collar workers. These were men and women who worked in office jobs, earning salaries that provided them with new and comfortable lifestyles.

When manufacturing firms left a city, whether it was Chicago or St. Louis, they left behind a major void. Many laid-off workers could not find jobs. Families were devastated. And the material environment of the city changed, too. Factories that once relentlessly turned out dresses or cars were now empty, left like the decaying carcasses of a dying civilization. Urban renewal efforts remade parts of the city, but other parts simply were abandoned. In the United Kingdom, industrial cities such as Manchester and Newcastle saw their fortunes decline. Across the United States (see Figure 3.5), there were empty buildings and vacant lots, sites protected from vandals by tall fences lined with barbed wire. In cities such as Detroit, the downtown area looked as though it had been through an aerial bombardment, a state only aggravated by the financial crisis of 2008 (see Chapter 13). City officials bemoaned this state of affairs. They were in a bind. The tax revenues that the manufacturing enterprises had provided to local government disappeared, leaving officials to wonder how they could continue to fund public services from roads to schools. But the problem of unused urban space would soon prove a benefit, as new uses emerged that would help to solve the financial crisis of the city and also to transform its character.

Change came in the form of new ways to use the old factories left behind by the departed manufacturers. Clever real estate developers along with shrewd city officials remade the old structures into new forms of residences and consumption spaces (see Exploring further 3.1).

Figure 3.5 New York's SoHo district in 1970. While this street still bustles with commercial activity, garment manufacturing was on the wane and the area was becoming home to more and more of the artists that would transform its character. Note the "Loft for Rent" sign on the pole at the right. *Source: Photo: John Dominis/Time Life Pictures/Getty Images.*

EXPLORING FURTHER 3.1

From spaces of production to spaces of consumption

As Sharon Zukin and Saskia Sassen (discussed later in this chapter) have argued, transformations in local and global economies are radically transforming urban spaces. Economies of scale have become economies of precision as technology becomes more advanced, transportation methods become cheaper, and corporations within developed countries move factories and other spaces of production to countries with lower wages. During the most intense period of this transition in the mid- to late-twentieth century, growth coalitions within cities of developed countries worked to make spaces of production into spaces of consumption and command centers for the global economy. Sharon Zukin famously called attention to this in her book *Loft Living*, which detailed the takeover of garment manufacturing spaces in New York City's SoHo by artists looking for live–work space. Galleries soon followed, and now, decades later, the area is dominated by high-end boutiques and restaurants. But examples of this kind of redevelopment can be found all over the world, from the Docklands in London to Kitakyushu, an industrial city in Japan.

The Docklands experienced their end as spaces of production with the development of containerized shipping in the 1960s. This required much larger ships to bring cargo into much deeper ports, and the Docklands didn't fit the bill. Over the next 20 years, the area fell into a slum-like state of poverty and crime as dock employment fell from 25 000 to 4100 jobs. In 1980, Britain's Chancellor of the Exchequer announced the creation of enterprise zones – development areas with special tax incentives and relaxed planning regulations – to generate employment and investment in depressed areas, including the Docklands. Since then, the five boroughs that constitute the Docklands have been broadly remade into spaces more congruent with a postindustrial economy (Church 1988).

Canary Wharf, a major shipping terminal before the container era, was redeveloped as a financial services district. Here one finds many of the tallest buildings in London, home to firms including Barclays, HSBC, and Credit Suisse (see Figure 3.6). In the Southwark Borough of London, across the Thames, are the Oxo Tower Building and the Tate Modern. Both of these buildings were originally power stations, and, while Bankside Power Station (which became the Tate Modern) remained a power station until 1981, when it closed, the Oxo Tower was converted to a warehouse for beef stock under the ownership of Liebig Extract of Meat Company, and it remained that way for most of its existence. In the 1980s and early 1990s, following the trend of spaces of production transforming into spaces of consumption, the Oxo Tower Building was refurbished to include art stores, residential apartments, and the famous Oxo Tower Restaurant, and the Tate Modern building became Britain's national museum of international modern art. Gentrifying changes such as these made the Docklands much more sought after, but did little to aid the living conditions of the pre-existing local population. For this reason, efforts like these have prompted resistance from local residents and displaced workers (Short 1989).

Across the Atlantic, many of Toronto's old warehouses and grain elevators have been demolished, but others have been adapted to new uses. One such building is the Queen's Quay Terminal warehouse, a cold storage facility that was renovated in 1983. The building is now home to condominiums, shops, galleries, restaurants, and a dance theater. The original art deco style of the space has been preserved, providing the sense of authenticity that Richard Florida argues is attractive to the creative class but that is often a casualty of larger-scale redevelopment efforts (Gordon 1996).

The city of Kitakyushu in Japan's Kyushu region provides a unique example of an industrial city transforming to create spaces for consumption. Here Nippon Steel attempted to help the city to diversify its traditionally industrial economy as steel production declined. This included converting spaces of production into spaces of consumption: the company built Space World, a theme park, on the site of one of its former blast furnaces. Although the theme park employed some 80 former Nippon Steel workers, the wages were below those paid at McDonald's restaurants in Japan. The city of Kitakyushu has aims beyond tourism, and seeks to develop high-technology research and development and manufacturing, but has struggled to overcome the "smokestack" image associated with being a major steel producer (Shapira 1990).

Regarding cities of the less developed world, Buenos Aires, the capital of Argentina, offers a delayed example of converting formerly shipping and warehousing spaces into different non-production uses. At one time an old port on the Rio de la Plata, running through the city, Puerto Madero had to wait until 1990 before the municipal and federal governments of Argentina agreed to a master plan that led to the development of millions of square meters of new office, residential, cultural, and recreational spaces. The project has largely been completed according to the plan, despite the collapse of Argentina's economy in 2001. While some Buenos Aires residents have complained about Puerto Madero as a residential and recreational enclave for the rich and tourists and not "Argentine" in an authentic local sense, Puerto Madero stands as a striking example of redeveloping industrial and shipping warehouses into new consumption spaces.

While many other cities have transformed from spaces of production to spaces of consumption in a slightly less dramatic fashion, the examples provided here are all part of a global trend that can be found in major cities of developed countries everywhere. While often the transformation is a costly process and cities may ultimately be successful by some measures, the process will usually, at least locally, create losers as well as winners. As spaces of production are lost, people with limited skills lose jobs, and, when spaces of consumption take their place, jobs pay less and housing is often unaffordable. The transition is an urban process that is still being studied so that redevelopment may happen in a way that causes as little negative social impact as possible.

Figure 3.6 Canary Wharf in London epitomizes the urban impact of global economic transformations that Sassen calls attention to. Once a working dock, the wharf's navigational use faded with the shift to container shipping that accompanied economic globalization. The area has since been redeveloped as a financial services center. *Source: http://commons.wikimedia.org/wiki/File:Canary_Wharf_Wide_View_2,_London_-_July_2009-2.jpg. Photo © David Liff. This file is licensed under the Creative Commons Attribution-Share Alike 3.0 Unported license.*

The result of these efforts was to change the character of the city itself from an old industrial form, in which factory life dominated the landscape, to a new form in which people became concerned as much about how to use their growing leisure time as about work itself. All of these changes in the city mirrored the broader change taking place in the industrial economy. The industrial United States had begun to change from a country in which much of its gross domestic product was based on production to one in which eventually two-thirds of that product would be based upon what people consumed – in cars, housing, and clothing, among other things.

Various theories and theorists tried to make sense of these changes to the city, just as earlier theorists, such as Georg Simmel and Robert Park, had sought to understand the period of the great industrial revolutions in Europe and the United States. Among the most distinguished is sociologist Sharon Zukin. Zukin helped to spearhead and develop a new line of urban scholarship devoted not so much to issues of the economy and production but rather to issues of culture and consumption. In a series of books, she explored how the new patterns of consumption and lifestyles in cities – and in New York City in particular – were reshaping the industrial city of the past (Zukin 1982, 1991, 1995). She argued, for example, that the new residential use of the old factory warehouses in New York City had important consequences for the city as a whole. It provided a new kind of energy for the growth of the city, one based on the work and vitality of young artists, many of whom had taken up residence in an area of old factories, SoHo. Here Zukin discovered a large and growing community of people who made their living off the arts, and who therefore seemed to represent an entirely novel form of neighborhood development.

Zukin also showed how the redevelopment of these older areas of factories could reshape the city in even more profound ways. As the old areas of manufacturing were changed into new areas of residence, they became increasingly desirable residences for wealthier people. The artists, who originally settled in them soon after the redevelopment, could no longer afford the higher rents and costs. Hence, such areas became the sites where the richer residents of the city could now move – people who otherwise might have moved to the suburbs. This all became a part of the process of **gentrification**, and of the fundamental transformation of the inner city of many metropolitan areas across America from one of decline to one of wealthy and lively residential developments.

> **gentrification**
> Redevelopment of older residential and/or industrial districts of the metropolis; marked by increased land values and population changes.

Zukin's thinking evolved in ways that paralleled the growth and evolution of the modern city. She turned her attention, for instance, to the ways in which people consumed in the city, identifying new markets and shopping sites. She wrote about new areas within New York City that arose: places that were no longer simple sites of security or even community but ones that, to all appearances, were sites of high fashion and lifestyle. As the wealth of urban residents grew, so too did their appetite for new and varied forms of consumption. Thus, Zukin depicted the era of the new coffee houses and the bodegas where people could spend lots of money on quaint and exotic consumer goods. She was also among the first sociologists to draw attention to the simulated urban, or tourist, environment. Disneyland became a favorite example for her of the ways in which the urban landscape had been remade from one of nature and buildings to one of sheer artifice and invention. The urban environment itself was transformed: once a place where people simply worked, ate, and slept, it had changed into a place where their fantasies could become fulfilled. Children could go to Disneyland and spend time with Cinderella, up close and personal. Their parents, meanwhile, could visit Las Vegas and gamble away their life savings at the foot of the Eiffel Tower without ever actually having to set foot in Paris! One could no longer distinguish the real from the artificial city.

The elements of culture in the hands of Zukin and many other sociologists have now become a major tool for understanding the whys and wherefores of the city in contemporary times. Art and music – whether in the form of urban graffiti or Brahms or Broadway – are, we find, as essential to the urban experience as anything else. And this new focus on culture has come along at just the right time, as cities themselves are changing in part to retain their role as vibrant enterprises in a rapidly changing world. From Prague to Los Angeles, cities have begun to rebuild themselves with great, towering edifices, one skyscraper aiming to be taller than another. They compete with one another to secure the talents of the most daring and imaginative urban architects, many of them turning to the Los Angeles architect Frank Gehry, who designed the spectacular Guggenheim Museum in Bilbao (see Figure 3.7). All such creative activities have become so central to the evolving metropolis in this new world that some urban theorists, such as Richard Florida (2005a), have even insisted on talking about a new "creative economy" and the new "creative class" of the cities.

This line of argument adds, then, to the ways in which social scientists can use the tools of their discipline to explore and further our insight into the developing metropolis. It has helped us to grapple with the issues of taste and lifestyle as they emerge in cities now that the city itself has been cut free from its old industrial anchors. Urban life has become immensely richer and more varied than a century ago – but also considerably more challenging to decipher.

Going global
The 1980s and the creation of the global city

In the early 1980s, Saskia Sassen began integrating important ideas from different theoretical traditions in order to understand how fundamental transformations of the economy were having similar effects across the world. She believed that a new kind of global system of

Figure 3.7 The Guggenheim Museum in Bilbao, designed by Frank Gehry. The museum has helped a city once known for mining and shipbuilding to redefine itself as a center of art, culture, and, of course, tourism. *Source: Photo: Dorota and Mariusz Jarymowicz/Getty Images.*

cities was emerging, one in which the city itself served as a strategic point in the economic process. She was not the only social scientist to take this point of view. Earlier, the prominent geographer and urban planner John Friedmann (1986) was actually the first to proclaim a working hypothesis about the emerging new system among cities across the world (see also Knox and Taylor 1995). But Sassen was the one scholar to take the idea seriously and to engage in an extensive and long research effort to plumb the depths of this new system, and this research resulted in her famous book, *The Global City* (2001; see also 2006).

Both Sassen and Friedmann insisted that, beginning in the 1980s, cities across the world were becoming ordered into a new hierarchy. This hypothesis had an earlier and more primitive history among urbanists, in the work of Roderick McKenzie (1968), who wrote of the relationships and hierarchy of cities within nations. But, in the new argument, such relationships and the hierarchy itself were said to be emerging on a much more expansive scale. The city, and certain cities in particular, such as New York City and London, were claimed to be sites, or places, where various key economic functions in finance and banking had become located. In particular, Sassen argued that as the multinational corporations now found themselves locating various parts of their operations in countries across the world – for instance, manufacturing finished products in China – such a dispersal of operations required some point of coordination and control. As the dispersal of activities in a firm's operations continued, in fact, the need grew simultaneously to find a point where those operations could be coordinated. And that point took place in a certain set of cities, cities that were not simply large but that would become the centers of financial and producer service operations, such as legal services, as well.

The city in the 1980s, Sassen insisted, became even more important than in the past, primarily because it now served a function that was central to the work of the interdependent global economy. Moreover, the concentration of capital and of producer service industries in such cities was not evenly distributed – only a few key cities had by the early 1980s appeared as the key nodes of this new system of global cities. Yet, by the early part of the twenty-first century, as the world's economy grew to take in more and more people (and with it more and countries), newer cities, such as São Paulo and Shanghai, were brought into this new world system. The growth of the global, or world, economy increased at such a rapid pace over the course of these 20 or so years that within a short span of time a whole range and variety of cities came to be fixed within the system. Moreover, other cities within specific countries – smaller cities or primate cities – began to change their function as well, shifting into national or regional centers – not quite on the scope or level of the global cities, but significant nonetheless for the work of cities, the economy, and citizens as well.

There were other important features of this new global economy of places. Sassen argued that financial and service functions had become concentrated in and controlled by a small number of global cities – New York City, London, and Tokyo – rather than in a small set of countries, as they had been in the past. Moreover, with the inception of new free trade zones and agreements, such as the North American Free Trade Act, which promoted free trade between Mexico, the United States, and Canada, it appeared to her that the economy itself had been liberated from its restrictions and regulations by the state – that is, by specific states such as the United States and the United Kingdom. And, as trade and financial operations flowed freely across borders, so, too, did people: immigrants from one country began to move more easily into others. The emergence of the European Union provided the best indication of the new kind of economic freedom at work across state boundaries and the likely shape of the political future as well.

One might wonder why this new global economy took off in the early 1980s – whether, for example, there was something necessarily at work in the development of the new economic forces themselves. In part, there was. With the rise of telecommunications and the spread of new computer technologies across the world, economic transactions that previously had taken days to complete now occurred in the course of hours, if not minutes. The time required for economic transactions became shortened, and the spaces across which those transactions occurred increased. But there was something else at work as well, something that was fundamentally built into the global economy. This was the new policy of deregulation of economic activity, a policy decisively shaped by the governments of Margaret Thatcher and Ronald Reagan. Both political figures insisted that the economy worked best with little, if any, government interference, a doctrine espoused with great force by the economist Milton Friedman. This policy would later become enshrined, in 1990, as the "Washington consensus," a set of directives designed to guide and shape economic activity among the states and key economic actors of the world.

Unleashed, then, the global economy grew by leaps and bounds, and with it so, too, did the economic forces and activities in global cities. Key businesses in these places included finance and real estate operations as well as other supporting services, such as legal, accounting, and related activities. As financial operations in banks grew, especially investment banks such as Lehman Brothers, so, too, did the need for services that could support this work. And, as we now all know too well, there were new financial instruments created, called derivatives, used and packaged by banks and then transformed into securities that were spread into financial institutions across the world. All of this happened, in part, because, in fact, the ability to carry out such transactions had spread and become integrated across the globe. And, at the heart of those activities were the global cities themselves: Sassen insisted that the state had naturally receded from the workings of the world, and that the new economy now was reshaping the state as well as cities.

There were a host of consequences that flowed from the construction of the new global cities and the system that arose to connect cities with each other. The nature of work and production now changed in the major cities. Financial operations were key, as were their supporting services. But, as a wealthy class of financiers arose in the city, so, too, did a need for people to provide them with services – nannies, restaurant workers, gardeners, and the like. In addition, as industrial manufacturing left cities in the West, moving abroad to Asia, new kinds of workplaces emerged to replace them. Of course there were the producer services, but there was also an informal economy, especially for those immigrants who now came into the major cities such as New York City. Unskilled, many of them found work off the books – small jobs, work in their own households, any kind of work that would keep them alive. Some came to occupy special niches in the emerging urban labor markets, such as in the garment industry or as taxi cab drivers. Ultimately, this process of reshaping production and work in global cities created a bifurcated system of social stratification – at the top a small group of very wealthy people working in the banks and related industries, and below them a larger and growing group of the working poor, many of them immigrants. And thus, Sassen shows, income inequalities grew within global cities and other major cities over the course of the 1980s and 1990s, a result that had also been projected by Friedmann.

Sassen's thesis provides a very comprehensive and timely assessment of cities today – and not merely in one country or two countries but, as her data clearly show, across the globe. It is enormously provocative and synthetic, drawing on a wide range of literatures and integrating them into a coherent whole. Moreover, it has gained great appeal across the world precisely because it seems to provide such a clear and compelling interpretation both of the new world economy and of the city.

Yet it possesses one potential flaw: it is based on the nature of the world and of its economy at that time when the policy of state leaders was to trim the regulation of industry, allowing it therefore to be free to work its magic. Many analysts point out that the financial crisis of 2008 came about precisely because of too little regulation of economic activity by the state. Governments, from the United Kingdom to Germany to the United States to the European Union, have had to step in to provide the ultimate backup to the failure of the economy, by nationalizing banks, for example.

The question, therefore, remains: will the global economy and the global cities continue to operate as Sassen, and Friedmann, discovered, or will they change as a result of the new constraints and regulations provided by governments? However powerful this view of global cities, it remains to be tested by circumstances in the coming years of the twenty-first century.

Evaluating theories of the city

In this chapter and Chapter 2 we have introduced you to the leading theories of the city. By now you may feel overwhelmed with all this theory, and wonder how you can distinguish between a good theory of the city and a bad one. We want to offer you some guidelines – principles that can be used to compare and contrast the theories we have presented here.

Some principles are matters of intellectual taste or aesthetics. A good theory, we believe, is a theory that is *simple and easy to capture in a few leading ideas.* The theory of the city as a growth machine is an illustration of such a theory. It has a few key components and ideas, such as the idea that leading figures of the city coalesce around the importance of growth and development. With this claim as well as a few others, it offers a way to understand the workings of the modern city, both in terms of the local economy and the local politics. A second principle is that of *comprehensiveness*. A good theory should capture most of the elements that are part and parcel of the modern city. Does the theory take account of the local economy, for example? Does it capture and explain the spatial nature of the city, and how some parts are left to decline while others grow at a rapid rate? David Harvey's interpretation of Marx provides an excellent illustration of how a theory can be simple but also capture many of the elements of the modern city. And so, too, does the theory of the **global city** advanced by Saskia Sassen, which has been criticized by some as not comprehensive but too economically functional.

> **global city** Saskia Sassen's term for major cities that act as control centers for the global economy.

A third principle is that the theory should be *plausible*. Does the theory offer a way of understanding the city that seems credible and consistent with our observations of reality? By this reckoning, we believe that Jane Jacobs' ideas about the importance of neighborhoods as communities is a very plausible and realistic view of the city. By the same token, we also believe that the earlier theory of Louis Wirth, which stressed the loneliness and isolation of individuals in the city, was not very plausible. Wirth frankly just looked at the city, as we suggested, as though it were a sidewalk filled with pedestrians, none of whom knew one another. That view missed a whole and real part of the actual life of people in cities.

Besides these principles, it is also important that any theory *provide a set of tools* with which to examine how cities work, and even how cities differ from one another. The theory must open our eyes to new and effective ways of thinking about cities and, at the same time, it must also provide a means for confirming, or disconfirming, itself. Does the theory direct our attention to a clear set of empirical facts about city life? Can we learn more about the workings of the city by following the leads furnished by the theory? Here, again, a theory such as that of Jane Jacobs is very useful because it directs our attention to the way in which neighborhoods develop small communities and provide those essential elements of security and safety in the city, but also tells us how streets, sidewalks, and parks can figure in the shaping of a satisfying and important life among neighbors and residents. Any good theory must provide such a set of tools.

In the end, the principles of *simplicity, comprehensiveness, plausibility,* and *scientific insight* are the means that you can use to test and compare different theories of cities. On these grounds, most of the recent theories we have discussed in this chapter measure up well. Finally, as we have tried to show throughout this chapter, it is always important to consider the social and historical contexts in which a theory is developed. Such contexts help us to reach a fuller understanding of the nature of theories of the city, and why and how specific theories are developed at a particular moment in time. Visit the book's companion website at www.wiley.com/go/cities for examples, case studies, and discussion questions, plus a list of useful films and other media, that are relevant to this chapter.

Critical thinking questions

1 Of the several theories we discussed in this chapter and Chapter 2, which theory do you find most the compelling? Why? Does this theory satisfy the criteria we suggested for evaluating the utility and effectiveness of a social theory?

2 What are the use values associated with your home and neighborhood? In what ways are those reflected or not reflected in their exchange values?

3 Consider a conversation between scholars such as Jane Jacobs and Herbert Gans, who saw cities as places with thriving communities, and Georg Simmel and Louis Wirth, who saw cities as undermining social bonds. How might each group try to convince the other that its views are correct?

4 When you look around your city, do you see development initiatives that reflect the emphasis on culture put forth by scholars such as Sharon Zukin? How do these differ from urban development strategies of years past?

5 How would you modify a theory of the city to take account of the significant changes in the global economy over the past several years?

6 Are there any social or economic developments in your city or neighborhood that are not captured by any of the main social theories of the city? What are they? Can you invent, or modify, a current theory to explain those developments?

Suggested reading

David Harvey, *Social Justice and the City* (Baltimore, MD: Johns Hopkins University Press, 1973). This book represents Harvey's break with the traditional geographical perspective on cities and his initial effort to apply Marx's theory of political economy to an understanding of cities, including issues of social justice and inequality.

John Logan and Harvey Molotch, *Urban Fortunes: The Political Economy of Place* (Berkeley: University of California Press, 1987). In this thorough exposition of the city as a growth machine, Logan and Molotch provide great insight into the economic and political dynamics of many US cities today, especially those in the Sunbelt.

Saskia Sassen, *Cities in a World Economy* (Thousand Oaks, CA: Pine Forge Press, 2006). A clear and readable introduction to Sassen's theory of globalization and of the nature of global cities today.

Sharon Zukin, *The Cultures of Cities* (Oxford: Blackwell, 1995). Zukin addresses the diverse cultures and residents of cities in this book, and introduces the notion of a symbolic economy of cities that parallels in some sense the city's political economy.

Note

1. For a discussion of the writings of Nicos Poulantzas, see Orum and Dale (2008: Chapter 2).

CHAPTER 4

Methods and rules for the study of cities

KEY TOPICS

→ The rules of validity and reliability in social science research, and how these apply to urban research in particular.

→ Strategies for approaching cities as case studies, such as using a city as a typical or prototypical case.

→ Basic concerns when using quantitative data to learn about cities, and sources of quantitative demographic data.

→ The fundamentals of ethnographic and historic approaches to studying cities.

→ How single urban case studies can be expanded to multiple cases and thus can be generalized.

→ The relationship between theory and methods in urban social science research.

→ Ways in which urban research is used to improve the condition of cities, whether in the design of public spaces or through applied research projects.

Contents

Introduction to Cities: How Place and Space Shape Human Experience, First Edition. Xiangming Chen, Anthony M. Orum, and Krista E. Paulsen. © 2013 Xiangming Chen, Anthony M. Orum, and Krista E. Paulsen. Published 2013 by Blackwell Publishing Ltd.

Suppose you sit down and read a book about cities. Let's say it's a famous book, such as Jane Jacobs' *The Death and Life of Great American Cities*. By any measure, this has been one of the most influential books ever written about cities – how they work and what keeps them ticking. As you begin to read the book, you will find that Jacobs writes a lot about her neighborhood. She mentions major concerns, such as issues of security in the neighborhood, and, more broadly, in the city. She is such a good writer that you feel at once you know her neighborhood – the local grocer, the tavern owner, the neighbor who sits and looks out at everyone on the street from her window.

Jacobs takes you deeply into the life of her neighborhood, showing you what makes that place so special and why she felt so strongly about the people who lived there. But, being a curious person, you may wonder: is her neighborhood like mine? Do I feel the same sense of trust and security that she describes in her neighborhood? Can children play and romp around the streets and sidewalks as they did in Greenwich Village? What is there about her neighborhood that might make it unique – or even very different from the neighborhood in which I live?

This is the kind of question all of us – teachers, students, and ordinary folks – must naturally ask ourselves when we read a book about cities, about the neighborhoods and people who reside in them. After all, we are not reading a novel (say a work by Charles Dickens) with the view of discovering some special elements of nineteenth-century London but are reading a work of non-fiction to discover some important and general ideas that help to make cities, and neighborhoods, what they are. Our concepts of place and space that we have used here help to guide us into the general issues, and give a sense of the theory about how cities work – why, for example, they are important to us in furnishing a sense of our own *identity*. But we need something far more than just theory to guide us. We also need some kind of methodological guidelines that permit us to make judgments about what we read and learn about cities – to know that, in fact, the materials used to describe a city or a neighborhood (e.g., Jacobs' work on her neighborhood) are good ones and, in an old-fashioned intellectual sense, somehow and somewhat true.

To move from a description of a city, or places in a city, to make general and reliable claims about a city, we require some basic rules – methodological rules, if you will forgive a rather formal expression – about what constitutes sound social scientific knowledge, and how we ourselves might actually generate such knowledge when we walk out our door and into the city, and begin to observe and to judge what we see around us. In this chapter, then, we want to discuss the kinds of general strategies and assumptions that social scientists employ to study cities as well as the various places and spaces within them.

In particular, we want to furnish you with a practical and working sense of how social scientists approach their studies of the city, the questions they address, the assumptions they make, and the way they accumulate knowledge – **valid** and **reliable** knowledge about the city. Once you get a better sense of how good research can be done, you will be more adept at making judgments about good and bad social scientific knowledge about the city – and, we hope, you will also be able to set out on your own, even in an informal way, and begin to employ those principles to create verifiable and reliable observations about such things as your own neighborhood. The methods and rules, we hope, also will lead to a broader generalization about other neighborhoods or cities as places and spaces.

validity The verifiable assumption that the measures of, or information about, a particular phenomenon actually represent that phenomenon.

reliablility Measures of, or information about, a particular phenomenon that can be replicated by observers.

First rules for doing a social science of cities

We begin, then, with two basic rules that always guide the work of social scientists. But here we shall tailor them specifically to research about cities.

The rule of validity

The first rule we follow is that we must aim to generate valid and authentic information about the city. This is a very simple principle, but it is one that we must always invoke. To be valid, the information we collect must accurately portray the particular thing we wish to say about a city, or about a particular place. Let's take an example to see how this rule works. Suppose we are studying the ways in which the older neighborhoods of a city are becoming home to more and more middle-class or upper-middle-class residents, forcing the current residents, who are less wealthy, to move out. This kind of concern is found in the work of a number of urban scholars today, and it is typically captured in the term, or concept, of gentrification (see the excellent book edited by Brown-Saracino 2010). It refers to the ways in which the older parts of a city are taken over by wealthier residents, thereby changing neighborhoods and compelling poorer residents, who may no longer be able to afford the rents or the prices of local services and goods, to leave.

If we actually want to demonstrate that such a process is happening, we must be able to assemble lots of information on older neighborhoods, especially some historical information on the pregentrification stage – for example, who occupies such neighborhoods, and how there is a displacement of the older, poorer residents by younger, wealthier ones. So, we could go out and make observations about a select group of neighborhoods – those places in the city where we believe the process is taking place. If we interview a few people, get a history of the sites through their eyes, and then begin to build a case of how a particular neighborhood (or several neighborhoods) seems to be undergoing the process of gentrification, that represents an excellent start in obtaining valid knowledge – knowledge of the process of gentrification. But we need to dig deeper. We also need to collect other, objective information – information on how the neighborhood has actually changed in terms of the incomes and wealth of families. If, for example, we interview people, especially aging, long-time residents whose memories might be faulty or biased, then we could very easily draw false conclusions about the process of gentrification.

Thus, to obtain valid knowledge of possible gentrification, we would turn to a body of information available about cities – for example, a census of the national population or, in the case of the United States, something called the American Community Survey. This information, generated on a regular basis, is designed to uncover the facts about the people who live in the urbanized areas of a country. It is based on very precise estimates, and it can help us to determine the wealth of families in a particular place at present, but also in the past. So, if we identify our neighborhoods clearly (their boundaries and where they are located), the United States Census, for instance, can give us the information about families and wealth as well as past patterns that will enable us to determine quite clearly whether or not the families who live in a specific area at the present time are generally wealthier than those who lived there in the past. And not only that: the proportions of families that are wealthy and of families that are poor can also be determined. Are they really growing in numbers and do they dominate a particular neighborhood, or are there simply small proportions of wealthy families? Of course, we need to be sensitive to how changes and shifts in neighborhood boundaries and their adjustments in Census tracts may complicate our observation and perception of the gentrification process (see Figure 4.1).

In other words, to secure accurate and valid information, we must not simply rely on what our eyes show us. Nor can we rely simply on what residents tell us. We must rely on various pieces of evidence in order to make any judgment about whether gentrification is actually taking place or not. Our own eyes and observations, of course, are extremely important, and help us as a first step to drawing conclusions. But they can mislead us, so we also turn to interviews with local residents. Yet residents, too, might have faulty memories. Thus, we turn to yet another piece of evidence (the most objective and useful for many students of cities): evidence on the numbers and types and wealth of local families, and how these may vary across time. The United States Census provides this kind of evidence. And, while it may not always get us to the exact neighborhood (or place) we are studying, it can give us very close estimates and thereby tell us whether poorer people have moved out and wealthier people have moved into a particular place in the city.

The claims we read about cities, if made carefully and systematically, are based on information that comes from a variety of sources – observations, interviews, and statistical evidence – all of which collectively allows us to assess whether the thing that a social scientist claims to be true actually is so. This also means, then, that if we are to be a tough and strong judge of the claims of the social scientists about cities, we must be able to take these standards of evidence and apply them to the arguments that the writer makes.

Jane Jacobs, for example, claimed that trust and security were important to the workings of her little neighborhood. How did she demonstrate that her claims were valid? By providing us with detailed information about the people who lived there and furnishing us with

Figure 4.1 A new Whole Foods market opened in New York City's Bowery neighborhood in 2010. While the area was once synonymous with vagrancy and crime, it is now home to upscale retailers such as Whole Foods, which specializes in organic and natural products. A systematic inventory of the retail and service offerings in a neighborhood can be one means of documenting changes associated with gentrification. *Source: Photo: Tom Starkweather/Bloomberg/Getty Images.*

specific illustrations of what had happened to her neighborhood. She showed us various examples – specific and rich instances of trust and of security – and thus led us to believe that these things really existed. Trust and security, of course, are not easily turned into statistics, so Jacobs felt compelled to demonstrate that her claims were valid by furnishing us with enough actual examples and illustrations – stories, in other words – to make us believe her. In the end, it was the richness of her illustrations that made her argument so plausible and compelling. One does not always have to use the Census or other forms of statistics to make a good strong case about something happening in a city or in your neighborhood. Those materials help, of course, but sometimes theoretical arguments can also be supported by other data, such as stories and interviews that portray the depths of life in the city.

The rule of reliability

The second important rule we must follow is that the information we gather about a particular process or a particular place must be reliable. Of course, we all want to make reliable claims – claims that people other than ourselves can believe. But what precisely does this mean? How can we possibly convince other people that we have uncovered the truth, so to speak, when we write something about a city or about a particular site within it?

The clue to the matter of reliability lies in its definition: we must be able to convince other people that what we have found – say, about gentrification in a neighborhood – is actually correct. So, while we, ourselves, might be the best observer – even perhaps the best theorist – in the world (or so we think), naturally it would be helpful if we had some other eyes and ears available to record what we are observing. This is precisely what good social scientists do, and they pursue this strategy in at least two ways.

The first is to make repeated observations and examinations of the thing they are studying. If, for example, we want to argue that the people in a particular neighborhood seem to socialize a lot with one another, especially in the open spaces, such as parks and sidewalks, then we need to make a number of observations of such spaces and how people relate to one another in them. Thus, for example, we could choose a specific park and look at the groups of people who gather there; observe what they are doing and whether they are, in fact, truly socializing. Do they sit and chat? Do they play games, such as chess, with one another? More than that, however, we would want to make our observations at different times of the day, as well as on different days of the week. We would want to make and record as many observations as possible in order to ensure that our conclusions were reliable – and to convince other people of our conclusions.

And this leads to the second strategy for gaining reliable information about the city, an obvious one: we could (and often *should*) work with other researchers – other students like ourselves – and each, independently, observe and record the activities of people in open spaces. Then we could compare our notes with those other eyes and ears and ask a simple question: did we all make the same kinds of observations? Did we all find that people seemed to socialize, as we claimed they did? If not, why not? The answers could be very helpful and lead to further insight. Perhaps those of us who made observations at noon found a great deal of socializing in the park, whereas those who observed in the early morning hours did not. So, we could draw the conclusion that, while socializing does take place in open spaces, such as parks, it can also vary according to the time of day.

To put all this another way, to gain truthful observations in the sense of reliability, we need to make repeated observations. We can do so by ourselves, if we are working alone; but, to be more efficient and practical, we can add the reports of other people. It all makes great sense. If we want to ensure that other people believe what we claim about the city,

EXPLORING FURTHER   4.1

Validity and reliability in the study of public spaces

In 1970, William H. Whyte Jr. and a group of researchers called the Street Life Project set out to understand the condition of urban spaces. To understand the aim of this work, it is important to think back to the time it was conducted. As you read in Chapter 3, the 1960s and 1970s posed new challenges to cities as expanding suburbs drew residents and businesses to the urban edge. This occurred in part because cities were presumed to be too crowded, and crowding was presumed to be a bad thing. Whyte and his team sought to ascertain whether either of these claims was correct. In doing so, it was imperative that they developed measures of the use of space that were both valid and reliable.

Much of the distress over urban density had been extrapolated from studies of animals in overcrowded environments or institutionalized populations that had been driven to anti-social behavior – not particularly valid measures of the effects crowding might have on free, human populations. But, at the same time, "common sense" and anecdotal accounts – plus the ongoing trend toward suburbanization – suggested that people seek to *escape* from crowds. The "evidence" might seem convincing, but were these claims appropriate and true?

To find valid and reliable answers regarding the degree of urban crowding and its implications, Whyte and his team set up cameras at key public spaces first in Manhattan and later in other cities, including Montreal and Tokyo (see Figure 4.2). Using stop-motion photography, they documented how people used sidewalks, parks, and plazas; how they came and went from doorways; and how and where they sat. The results proved valid in that they detailed just the behaviors the researchers sought to understand, eschewing limited recollections that might be introduced by interviewing people about their uses of space, or the biases experts might have about the ways people *should* use spaces. They were also reliable in that the research team used measures that all could agree were correct, and correct across multiple circumstances.

A small element of Whyte's study provides a useful example: the examination of just where on a busy sidewalk people engage in conversation. "Common sense" might suggest that when we bump into a friend or acquaintance we step to the side, out of the flow of traffic. Whyte's team found just the opposite. His team set up cameras outside a busy department store on Fifth Avenue and Fiftieth Street in New York. They looked for instances of conversations, defined as interactions lasting more than one minute (this allowed them to omit from their sample individuals who were simply waiting at a corner for the light to change). Rather than occurring near the curb or against the side of the building, the bulk of conversations (57 percent of the 133 that they recorded) clustered in the areas with the heaviest pedestrian traffic – at the street corner or outside the department store entrance. Scholars in Australia and Denmark have found similar patterns.

The thorough documentation of urban interaction provided by the Street Life Project provides much of the study's strength. Not only did the team use cameras in novel ways but they also recorded their observations of uses of spaces and interactions therein with great care. This required tracking the general patterns of use, such as who was there (male or female? young or old? rich or poor?), what they were doing (eating lunch? reading the paper? waiting on a friend?), and how long they stayed. These recordings, typically plotted on maps of the site under investigation, revealed how spaces were used in relatively broad strokes. But the team went further, examining the nuances of what people do and do not do. One of the team's most interesting findings concerns a group Whyte calls the "girl watchers." In parks and plazas, Whyte's team found that males often occupy the seats nearest the

Figure 4.2 The Street Life Project made innovative use of cameras to capture what really happens in public spaces such as street corners and plazas. Whyte and his team would analyze the film, frame by frame, to see how many people were present in a space, how long they stayed, and the kinds of interactions they engaged in.
Source: Courtesy of the Project for Public Spaces.

entrance, and that they take careful note of the women who walk by (Whyte found that, even when these men make a deliberate show of *not* noticing women, subtle movements and glances give them away). But watch is all they do – in all their observations, the team never saw one of these men strike up a conversation with an unknown woman.

While the details of these studies are endlessly interesting (and we highly recommend that you read Whyte's *City: Rediscovering the Center*), the core finding of the Street Life Project's work concerns the question of crowding. As the team revealed, not only is crowding a surprisingly *uncommon* urban experience (many urban spaces, even those ostensibly designed to attract people, sit empty), it is often a *positive* experience. As Whyte states, "What attracts people most, it would appear, is other people" (2000: p. 256). Plazas that for whatever reason have failed to attract a crowd will remain empty; the sidewalk that bustles with pedestrians will draw even more. Regardless of what people may say they like, people like to be around other people.

or about a place, the more numerous and varied are the people who engage in our research, the better. We can compare notes and hope to find our observations confirmed. Yet, if we differ from one another, as the illustration above shows, that difference can be used fruitfully to expand our conclusions and insights into the way the particular thing we are studying – whether it is gentrification or the socializing of people in public space – actually works.

Cities and the question of numbers

The biggest challenge that faces people who study cities concerns numbers. How many cities must one select to study in order to furnish evidence for a particular theory or argument about how a city works? Most social scientists deal directly with people – their attitudes, behavior, and predispositions – and so they can select a large sample of people to study and provide evidence for their arguments. But what can one do if one is studying cities and how they work – how many examples of a city must we choose in order to say "this is how the city and its residents work and how they operate under these conditions."

This is a constant conundrum that confronts urban scholars. Living in cities, we look around us, observe some particular fact or set of facts (say, about the growth of the city or the numbers of people moving into the downtown area from suburban areas), and then make claims about all of this as a particular feature of urban life. Some urban issues lend themselves rather easily to the assembly of facts about cities in terms of numbers. For example, if we want to talk about the relative decline of people living in suburban areas compared to the central city of a metropolis, we can define the central city and suburban areas separately, using the Census, and then compare the relative size of the populations of these two segments for a large number of cities over a specific period of time. Using such data, we can make estimates about whether or not there has been a relative decline of people who are living in the suburbs compared with the city centers.

Yet this sort of problem is a comparatively easy one to sort out. It is a problem simply of collecting the appropriate data from the Census and then comparing numbers across a wide array of different cities. But what if one wants to talk about something that does not lend itself so easily to numbers but is nevertheless a striking and important event or circumstance in the life of a city? In recent decades, for example, thousands of foreign immigrants have entered countless cities across the Western hemisphere and they have begun to change the urban culture and institutions in these cities. In cities such as Los Angeles and London, migrants have come in, settled in areas such as Brixton in London or Orange County outside Los Angeles, created new enclaves for themselves that often span traditional neighborhood boundaries, and reshaped the local areas in dramatic ways. How many examples of cities do we need to assemble if we wish to make an argument about how immigrants are reshaping the urban landscape in this manner?

It is common practice among students of cities to select one instance of a chosen issue for study, or at most two or three, to provide evidence for their claims. They do so primarily because of the sheer magnitude of data collection that is involved. Suppose that you want to argue that immigrants have changed a particular part of the city in which you live, and to do so you need to demonstrate how this change has come about. In order to make your case, you must assemble historical data on the arrival of the immigrants, where they came from,

STUDYING THE CITY   4.1

Finding demographic data

Governments collect a great deal of data about their citizens, and much of these can be of use to urban researchers. Below we provide links to national statistical databases for a number of countries; others can be located using the links at the bottom of the list.

- Australia: Australian Bureau of Statistics (http://www.abs.gov.au)
- Canada: Statistics Canada (http://www.statscan.gc.ca)
- China: National Bureau of Statistics (http://www.stats.gov.cn/english/index.htm)

- France: National Institute of Statistics and Economic Studies (http://www.insee.fr/en/insee-statistique-publique/default.asp)
- Germany: Statistisches Bundesamt Deutschland (http://www.destatis.de/jetspeed/portal/cms)
- Ireland: Central Statistics Office (http://www.cso.ie/census)
- Italy: ISTAT (http://www.istat.it)
- Japan: Statistics Bureau (http://www.stat.go.jp/english/index.htm)
- Korea: Statistics Korea (http://kostat.go.kr/portal/english/index.action)
- New Zealand: Statistics New Zealand (http://www.stats.govt.nz)
- Spain: Instituto Nacional de Estadística (http://www.ine.es)
- United Kingdom:
  - England and Wales: Office for National Statistics (http://www.statistics.gov.uk/default.asp)
  - Northern Ireland: Northern Ireland Statistics & Research Agency (http://www.nisra.gov.uk)
  - Scotland: General Register Office for Scotland (http://www.gro-scotland.gov.uk/index.html)
- United States: United States Census Bureau (http://www.census.gov)

Other useful links:

- European Union: Eurostat (http://epp.eurostat.ec.europa.eu/portal/page/portal/eurostat/home)
- United Nations: World Population and Housing Census Programme (http://unstats.un.org/unsd/demographic/sources/census/censusdates.htm) – lists the census equivalent for nearly every participating country

when they entered a particular area, how the area changed once they settled there, the new culture they adopted, the changes in the built environment that ensued, and so forth. To address this issue, in other words, you must assemble a great deal of information, and to do so will require a great deal of legwork and time. How could you possibly invest the effort required to study more than one or two instances of how immigrants have settled in and changed a particular part of the city?

In fact, in taking on a task such as this you will almost be compelled to limit yourself to only a couple of good examples to make your claims. Indeed, in general, whenever a student of cities takes on these rather complex arguments, involving time and change in the nature of places and how people have changed such places, she is compelled to reduce the number of instances studied and base her argument about the significance of the findings on the claim that her particular case – or, even, her handful of cases – is an especially timely or appropriate example of, in this instance, how new immigrants to the city are reshaping the city's landscape and changing its institutions.

The city as a case study

Much of the important research that has been done on cities has been based on the close and careful examination of a single case, or at most a handful of cases. Take the work of Jane Jacobs, for example. In some sense, her deepest insights came from the study of her own, single neighborhood in Greenwich Village. It was here that she observed how people related to one another on the streets, how neighbors protected one another, how the corner grocer kept his "eyes on the street," and how trust developed among people who were neighbors. Even when she moved beyond her neighborhood, she did not go far – she only moved her imagination elsewhere in New York City to talk about the nature of everyday life on the streets and how the work of the urban planners actually infringed and impeded the natural flow of such social life. To take another, contemporary, example, consider the work of Saskia Sassen and the growth of the global city (Sassen 2001). Though her latest work includes a range of cities across the world, her first and major observations about the growing importance of financial centers were based on her detailed and careful studies of only three cities – New York, London, and Tokyo. It was these cities, she insisted, that provided significant insights into the workings of global capitalism, and how the centers of such capitalism came to be rooted in just this small group of cities.

Individual cases, or, in other words, single instances of cities constitute the basic methodological tools that urban scholars use to generate their most important and significant ideas. How shall we define a case? A case is a clear and well-defined example that provides evidence for the particular phenomenon the researcher of cities is studying and the analysis of which can be generalized to other similar cases (see Feagin et al. 1991; Yin 2008). It can be defined not only theoretically but also, more importantly, empirically, so that one can go out and identify it – touch it, see it, smell it, feel it, hear it, and know, in other words, that it exists. Cities, like people, seem to be perfectly clear examples of cases. But are they? Are we talking about the central city or the broad metropolitan area? Are we using definitions provided by the Census or definitions imposed by our particular question or problem? In other words, we must *always define the boundaries and substance* of the thing we are calling a city, or metropolis, clearly.

Though we lose a certain breadth to our claims when we study a single case, or even a handful of cases, as the seminal significance of work like Jacobs' shows, if we study the case carefully, assemble our observations systematically, and pose our questions properly, a single case can provide great insight into the workings of cities. The study of a neighborhood, as with Jacobs, or a clearly defined suburb, as in the work of the sociologist M. P. Baumgartner, can help to offset the absence of breadth with the presence of depth (Baumgartner 1988). It permits the researcher to examine a particular question in great depth, to do so often over a period of time, and to assemble a wide variety of evidence that in all likelihood would be impossible to assemble over a large number of cases. It is never a complete substitute, for one will always wonder whether the claims, or arguments, of the scholar would hold up in some other city, in another case.

The choice we make of a particular case always involves certain assumptions about what the case represents. Jacobs believed that her neighborhood was like all neighborhoods, or at least successful ones; Baumgartner believed that her suburb illustrated certain basic tendencies characteristic of all suburbs; and Sassen believed that New York City, London, and Tokyo showed how global capitalism developed in the contemporary world, taking root primarily in these three cities. The city, as a case, in other words, is claimed to represent a particular type of case. As we discuss further below, it may be the first of its kind, or **prototypical**, or it may be a deliberately unremarkable example of an important type – what we refer to as typical but that sociologist Neil

prototypical case
A case study of the first city of a given type that is soon to become more common.

Table 4.1 Approaches to urban case studies. This table, adapted from work by sociologist Neil Brenner, presents different ways in which the study of a single city might be approached. As a case, a city may draw interest as the first of a kind (prototypical) or as an extreme or common expression of a trend (archetypical and stereotypical, respectively). *Source: Adapted from Neil Brenner, "Stereotypes, Archetypes, and Prototypes: Three Uses of Superlatives in Contemporary Urban Studies" (City & Community 2(3): 205–216; 2003; Wiley-Blackwell).*

	Prototypical	**Archetypical**	**Stereotypical**
Definition	The first case of a given development that is soon to become more generalized.	A unique or exceptional case; or, an extreme case of a more general development.	A typical case of a more general development.
Example	Los Angeles: "A polyglot, polycentric, polycultural pastiche that is somehow engaged in the rewriting of the American social contract."	Miami: "No other city has an absolute majority of recent immigrants."	Johannesburg: "A litmus test for urban reconstruction in divided cities everywhere."

Brenner calls stereotypical (see Table 4.1). Bridging the exceptional and the mundane are cases we might call archetypical.

The city as the typical case

Assuming that one wants to study a particular city, and chooses to do so out of convenience – it may the place where one lives, for example – one must still offer a strong and convincing argument to demonstrate why that city is in some way representative of other cities. Why choose this particular city rather than another particular example? You could always simply be honest and say, well, it's a matter of convenience. But social science requires that we make strong and foolproof arguments – arguments that can provide the foundations for the work of other researchers and that permit them to draw either empirical or theoretical conclusions based on the work we have done, and to compare them with their own.

Many social scientists advance the claim, then, that the city they are studying is an example of other cities, a **typical case** that shows the tendencies or forces at work in other cities. Suppose we want to talk about class and power in a modern US city, and decide to study a particular city, one in which we live. How can we actually claim that the results we find will be similar to those in other cities? If one chooses a large number of cases, this is much less of a problem: one draws out the empirical evidence and then argues that the cities provide a representative sample of all cities, and therefore any conclusions to be drawn will pertain systematically to all such cities.

typical case A case that represents the typical, or common, features of all cities, or communities, at that time and/or in that country.

But this does not work if one is examining a single case, and so one must advance the argument about typicality on other grounds. Perhaps one of the earliest of these arguments comes from the seminal work done by Robert and Helen Lynd in the 1930s (Lynd and Lynd 1959, 1965).[1] The Lynds wanted to examine how class and power operated in the United States, and they chose to do so by studying the lives of people and groups in a specific city. But which city should they choose? And on what grounds should they choose it? They chose to study Muncie, Indiana because, they claimed, it represented the typical American city at the time – being a relatively small town located virtually in the geographic center of the United States – and would therefore provide insights into how class and power worked in the typical American city. Note: they did not choose New York City, Boston, or even Chicago because, while large and complex, such cities did not represent, in the eyes of the Lynds, the typical American city. They called their books *Middletown*, precisely to emphasize that this city was meant to represent average America, the general tendencies at work in most other cities (see Figure 4.3).

The Lynds wrote two books about the people and their lives in Muncie, beginning with a description simply of the nature and recent history of the inhabitants, and then going back several years later to study how the town had changed over roughly a decade. Many years later, other researchers, under the leadership of Theodore Caplow and Howard Bahr,

Figure 4.3 School children in Muncie, Indiana around the time of the Middletown study. The Lynds and their assistants focused on ordinary facets of town life, including who went to school and what the school day was like. In doing so, they emphasized the typicality of Muncie, stating in their introduction that "a typical city, strictly speaking, does not exist, but the city studied was selected as having many features common to a wide group of communities" (Lynd and Lynd 1959: p. 3). *Source: W. A. Swift Collection, Ball State University Libraries.*

returned to Muncie and did follow-up work on change. Much of social science hopes to systematically observe and record change, but most of it is unable to do so owing to the limitations of data and time; yet here was a case where data had been assembled in the 1930s, looked at a few years later to discover changes, and then examined again decades later to probe even more deeply into substantial historical changes. The facts of life in Muncie are not so important as to warrant coverage here, though it is notable that the Lynds uncovered one family of considerable power and influence in the town, and made other important discoveries about work life, family life, and social class.

The Lynds had yet another special trick up their sleeves. It was one that would give the appearance that their discoveries really were about the lives of people in a typical American city. They actually disguised the name of the town, as we have indicated, and treated those who held power and the nature of the specific social classes in very general terms. They named the leading family "the X family," when, in reality, it was the Ball family. They did this so that readers would not confuse the particular social and historical details of those involved with the more general lessons the Lynds wished to convey. In other words, the Lynds wanted to speak about people living in the typical city of America – typical and average Americans, in other words – and so they eliminated all possible specific historical and particular references to the city and to the people involved. By doing so, of course, they also made the city appear as though it was typical so that readers would not confuse specific details, such as its location, with the more general social and economic lessons they sought to convey.

This method, of taking one city or town and using it to illustrate more general tendencies, characteristic of all cities and towns, is one that has been used time and again by social scientists. Let's consider another supremely good example. This one is found in the work of the sociologist M. P. Baumgartner, who wrote a wonderful book on the social and moral lives of people living in a suburb. She investigated how people lived and related to one another in a very small US suburb, of about 17 000 people (Baumgartner 1988). She removed all the concrete details of her case, and in so doing offered an argument not just about the particular place she studied but also more generally about life in the suburbs. Her research became an excellent and compelling example of how one case can be used to explore and to derive imaginative interpretations of life in a place, regarded by the social scientist as a typical place.

Yet one more illustration of this same method is to be found in the equally illustrative and compelling work of the sociologist Elijah Anderson (1990). Anderson lived in an area of Philadelphia for many years. During that time he studied the personal and public lives of both blacks and whites in the area. Eventually he put all of his years of observation and interviews into some pioneering books – altogether he spent almost two decades doing this on-site fieldwork. He was especially interested in the social dynamics that evolved out in two adjoining areas where he lived: one an upper-class primarily white area and the other an area consisting both of blacks and whites. He drew special attention to the everyday interactions of people of different races on the street, but also to how special figures in the black community treated other blacks, sometimes serving as role models.

Just as the Lynds and Baumgartner hoped to achieve broad and general insights, Anderson wanted his sociology to transcend the particular sites he studied. He regarded the sites as typical examples of other such similar cases – areas of a large city in which blacks and whites lived – so, like his fellow social scientists, he disguised their identity by calling them different names: specifically, Northton and the Village. He also never referred to specific people by name, but rather spoke of elements such as their gender, their age, and, naturally, the types of social interactions they had in public areas such as streets and sidewalks. All of this was done so that he could speak about how people of different races related to one another in the public areas of a neighborhood. But it was also done in order that his readers and fellow social scientists could draw out the more general lessons of what he observed, not mistaking the particulars of the people or sites with his general sociological insights.

All three of the above urban studies thus represent examples of how a student of the city, and of its people, uses a particular case to gather evidence and make claims about how life in the city or the neighborhood or the suburb works. And the authors all chose the same technique to get across their more general insights – that power and class in Middletown reflected more general tendencies in the United States in the 1930s; that the moral and social life of people in a suburb in the 1980s was like life in all suburbs; and that the public and personal lives of blacks and whites living near to one another in a major city were like the lives of such people in all such areas.

There was one more thing, apart from the choice of cases, that made all three works seminal pieces of research. Each piece of work was done by a meticulous and careful researcher who, relying on the first principles of validity and reliability, collected and assembled massive amounts of materials over a period of at least two years. The work was directed and based on important sociological problems/questions – for example, how people of different races relate to one another in public, or the public life of people living in suburbs – and it produced manuscripts of great and compelling insights. The cases were carefully selected and the claims made with care, but also with considerable attention to the theory at work.

Yet, for all the wonder and power of these kinds of works, we must also weigh their advantages against an obvious drawback. By disguising the urban sites, by eliminating the names and identities, by removing all the particular details at work, one also loses some of the richness of historical and cultural context – of why, possibly, Muncie is not Milwaukee, or, more obviously, why Muncie is not Mannheim, Germany. Social scientists are divided over, and often contest, these matters: some like their history rich, some like their sociological insights broad and general, and it is simply difficult to combine the two into one masterwork, though some people, such as Jane Jacobs, have done it. There are choices to be made here, and one must always be acutely aware that taking one methodological path – for example, the typical case – may preclude taking another path – the historical and cultural context. Sometimes, though not often, they can be combined into one case, through sheer energy and brilliance, as we suggest next.

The city as a prototypical case[2]

One of the most famous and influential pieces of social science research – actually social science history – was the study of democracy in the United States during the nineteenth century by the French aristocrat Comte Alexis de Tocqueville (1945). Tocqueville spent about a year in the United States in the 1830s. He then returned home to write what would become a masterpiece about American society and American democracy. He wrote about the special "habits of the heart" of Americans – the cultural norms and practices that guided people living there. He also wrote about the institutions of the society, in general, such as the government. And he provided some penetrating insights into the workings of capitalism and slavery in the United States, noting that if "ever America undergoes great revolutions, they will be brought about by the presence of the black race on the soil of the United States; that is to say, they will owe their origin, not to the equality, but to the inequality of condition" (de Tocqueville 1945: vol. II, p. 210).

But here in our discussion it is not his lessons of substance about democracy and capitalism that count for us but rather how he construed the United States as, in our terms, a particular case of study. He did not see the society as average or typical but rather, in his own words, as the prototype of the coming age of democracy in the world. He believed that if he could understand how American society and democracy worked, and how it compared to the workings of European societies, then everyone, but especially those in positions of authority, would better understand – and be able to promote – the specific sets of conditions that could lead to more democratic governments. The circumstances and conditions of democracy in the United States, Tocqueville maintained, represented the conditions that eventually would be found across the world – he believed that other countries would come to replicate the American experience or, at the very least, that the sorts of things that worked in the United States might be manipulated so as to promote democratic institutions in other countries.

This same sort of argument, we know, was made as the United States entered Iraq in 2003. The Bush Administration hoped to create democratic institutions there. But, unlike the ideological presuppositions that underlay the Bush policies, the argument of Tocqueville was that the United States in the nineteenth century served as the prototype of what a democratic society – a real democracy – would look like. Despite the conditions of wealth, for example, and despite the heavy toll of slavery, he believed that a strong involvement of citizens in associations and a strong connection of people with their government were two key conditions that promoted a democratic society in the real world. And the United States was the first of all the world's nations to show the way that this could be done.

This notion that a case can be a prototype for the way the world is likely to develop – a model that other societies can follow – has been employed as a method by students of cities as well. Take the work of the Chicago School of Sociology, for example. Robert Park and Ernest Burgess, among others, believed that the city of Chicago in the early twentieth century was the prototype of the industrial city of that age (see Chapter 2). The economy was booming, jobs were being created in abundance, and the composition of the population was being changed incessantly as more and different groups of immigrants from Europe entered the city. Chicago, at least to scholars such as Park and Burgess, epitomized the industrial city of the age; thus, they reasoned, sociological studies of the growth and development of the city – resulting, for example, in the famous concentric circle social map of the city – provided a portrait *not simply* of Chicago but of all major industrial US cities at the time. It represented a prototype of the industrial city and, therefore, any studies of it, but especially of how it grew and expanded, could be viewed as forecasts of how the same things would take place in other industrializing cities, such as New York or Philadelphia.

The assumption, then, of *prototypicality* – not just typicality – was fundamental to these scholars' work, and it furnished the methodological grounds for the claims they made about the specific social and demographic facts they uncovered. It also came to be the method that other students of cities at the time employed. And, as we have indicated in Chapter 2, the detailed findings uncovered in Chicago eventually provided other urban scholars with material they could actually use to test and discover whether Chicago was, or was not, the prototypical American industrial city.

globalization
The growing integration of countries, firms, individuals, goods, and information across the world.

Today, a similar analytical strategy is used by contemporary urban and social science scholars who, acknowledging the problem of numbers, choose to study one particular case as a prototype of specific trends and tendencies in the world. Saskia Sassen, one of the foremost students of **globalization** today in the world, argued that three cities in particular represented "the global city" in the contemporary world (see our discussion of Sassen's work in Chapter 3). New York, London, and Tokyo, specifically, she claimed in *The Global*

City (2001), were the centers of modern capitalism. In particular, in each city, major financial institutions, with global reach and influence, were concentrated. They included banks and an array of other financial firms, all of which exercised great influence not simply within the city, nor even the specific country, but across the globe. She also claimed that these global cities tended to divide themselves into two different social classes – at the top the very wealthy people whose careers were based on banking and finance and at the bottom those people who held jobs in the service industries – and that over time the people in the middle classes would tend to diminish in numbers. In other words, a sharp economic inequality was developing in these global cities. Besides all this, too, the service jobs were attracting more and more people from abroad, adding to an increasingly diverse immigrant population.

Sassen's main methodological assumption and argument was very simple. Since these three cities represented the sites where modern capitalism had become concentrated, and where the consequences of such developments unfolded, they thus provided prototypes of what was likely to take place in other cities as they, themselves, moved closer to the global city model. Her argument has become so popular and famous that she has been hosted by municipal governments across the world, all of whom wish to emulate the conditions and circumstances that promoted global capitalism in her three major prototypes. Yet it is her simple methodological assumption that has led other scholars to examine the more complex variations of the global city model, especially in the local contexts of the global South.

Other contemporary scholars also work from the same basic assumption of prototypicality as Sassen has done. A number of them, particularly urban geographers, have come to believe that Los Angeles may be the prototype of the great metropolis today. Scholars such as Edward Soja and Michael Dear, among others, write about the postmodern city and how it has become fragmented into many different parts. This condition of fragmentation has been labeled by Dear as "heterotopia," a metropolitan condition in which the central urban area, so characteristic of the earlier industrial city, disappears and is replaced by a dizzying array of different business and social districts. Los Angeles appears to be the perfect prototype of the postmodern city, not only because of the fragmentation of its spaces but also because it possesses some of the most dramatic and alluring examples of postmodern architecture, evident in the dazzling work of the architect Frank Gehry.[3]

Cities as prototypes, thus, come to serve as very important methodological devices for urban scholars. Naturally there always will be some question as to whether and how a city, such as New York or London or Los Angeles, actually provides a prototype of developing trends or tendencies in the world. But, given the challenge of numbers, the assumption can be a productive one; and, as the work done following the research by the Chicago School clearly demonstrates, the assumption of prototypicality can always be put to the test.

Ethnographic and historical case studies

Ethnographic case studies

case study A clear and well-defined example that furnishes evidence of the particular phenomenon that a researcher is studying.

Just as there are different types of case studies that one may pursue, so, too, there are different ways of actually executing a **case study** of cities. One common way to study the city, or metropolis, today is to examine some contemporary pattern that is taking place; for example, the various ways that people act toward one another in the city – much as Jacobs, Baumgartner, and Anderson did. This sort of work seeks to provide rich and vivid details about the operations of people – how they act toward and with one another, how trust develops among them – and the investigator assembles extensive material on the relationships of people in public. It is commonly called the **ethnographic case study**. Both Anderson and Baumgartner, for example, spent considerable time studying their respective cases and collecting data on the way in which people treated one another – for instance, on sidewalks and in other public spaces. They were eventually able to develop high-level generalizations about the important elements of such relationships, or what some sociologists call "grounded social theory" because it is based on close and careful observations of how people actually behave. It is built, in other words, literally from the ground up.

ethnographic case study A case study using field methods to investigate a particular social phenomenon that reflects the circumstances of a group.

To do such work, sociologists carry out their research in the field, in the sites where they are studying the behavior of people in specific places or spaces (see Figure 4.4). This kind of work also goes by the name of "ethnographic research," which is the effort to understand the actions and behavior of specific groups of people living in specific sites. It is most commonly used by social and cultural anthropologists, but today is also frequently employed by sociologists who study cities and metropolitan life. The purpose of such work is to produce rich, qualitative data and to use those data to generate insights in the form of grounded social theory. The work of Jacobs is a perfect example of such research, but, so, too,

Figure 4.4 Many urban scholars and practitioners make use of photography to reveal aspects of life in cities that are otherwise hard to capture. Joan Kadri Zald, a social worker and photographer, documented homeless individuals in Tucson and Ann Arbor, calling attention to complex dimensions of their lives and backgrounds. This married couple was among the large number of homeless families that Zald encountered in her work. *Source: Photo © Joan Kadri Zald.*

are the writings of many other important students of cities, today including figures such as Mitchell Duneier (Duneier et al. 2000) and Sharon Zukin (1995).

One of the most vivid of the current examples of such research can be found in the writings of the sociologist Mary Pattillo. Pattillo wanted to examine the social dynamics involved in an area of Chicago as it underwent change, primarily from a poor black neighborhood to one that gradually incorporated more and more black middle-class residents. The area she studied, known as the North Kenwood-Oakland section of Chicago, had once been home to some of the most important and influential figures and institutions of African Americans in the city, its strengths highlighted in the famous book by St. Clair Drake and Horace Cayton, *Black Metropolis* (1945). Over the years it began to decline and, by the 1970s, it was not only poor but overrun by gangs, drugs, and violence – the sort of toxic urban mixture found in many urban neighborhoods across the country. By the 1980s, an effort had begun to restore and to improve the neighborhood by creating new public housing as well as new and attractive single homes for residences. With these improvements, more middle-class black residents started to move into the area, and a social experiment began in the restoration of a formerly urban slum.

STUDYING THE CITY   4.2

The go-along

In order for urban researchers to truly understand cities as human environments, we must possess a detailed understanding of how people live in them. Ethnographic methods, including in-depth interviews and participant observation (spending time in a setting in order to get to know its members) are conventional – and very useful – strategies for gaining this type of knowledge. A promising new twist on these methods is proposed by Margarethe Kusenbach in her article "Street Phenomenology: The Go-Along as Ethnographic Research Tool." She describes a method in which "fieldworkers accompany individual informants on their 'natural' outings, and – through asking questions, listening and observing – actively explore their subjects' stream of experiences and practices as they move through, and interact with, their physical and social environment" (Kusenbach 2003: p. 463). This might include accompanying subjects as they walk their dog, pick up children from school, or commute to work – typical ways that individuals experience places that are nevertheless rich with memory, history, and meaning (see Figure 4.5).

The go-along method has certain benefits when compared to other ethnographic research methods. While participant observation, or "hanging out" with members of the population, can produce a very detailed and rich understanding of what life is like for a few informants, the informants that the researcher has contact with, and the surroundings that are observed, are relatively limited. The go-along, as Kusenbach explains, is a "more systematic and outcome-oriented version of 'hanging out' with key informants" (2003: p. 463). With the go-along, instead of being around a few informants for very extended periods, you can meet and walk with them for very specific periods of time with the aim of understanding a particular aspect of their life. This method can then be repeated with other community members.

Kusenbach suggests that the go-along is also more useful than a standard interview. During an interview, informants may refuse to talk about, or may not think to mention, many aspects of their daily lives that can actually be very important to the interviewer. Another shortcoming of interviews is that they are unnatural by nature, and many elements of subjects' daily lives will be pushed to the background by the interviewee in order to focus on talking to the researcher. As Kusenbach puts it, "in short, the particular interactional dynamics and the physical constraints of most ethnographic interview encounters separate informants from their routine experiences and practices in 'natural' environments" (2003: p. 462). The go-along seeks to correct this.

Through use of the go-along, researchers are able to interact with informants during their natural daily rounds throughout the city in a way that balances the strengths of observational and interview techniques. You might try a go-along interview with a friend, neighbor, or family member.

Figure 4.5 Walking the dog is a routine activity that brings individuals into contact with places and one another. Sociologist Margarethe Kusenbach suggests that accompanying people on these outings can be a productive research strategy. *Source: Photo © Gabor Izso/istockphoto.*

Pattillo is a gifted observer. She produces many rich insights by focusing her work on the ethnographic details of the changes, among them that, despite being of a common racial background, tensions broke out between the older, poorer residents and the newer, middle-class residents – tensions that no one could have easily foretold. She does a wonderful job of using her research locale as a way of revealing many of the unintended consequences of neighborhood improvement – efforts that were designed to lift up the lives of poorer residents but created some unexpected tensions instead.

Historical case studies

There is a second form of case study as well, one that we can call the **historical case study**. Instead of focusing on the rich detail of contemporary circumstances – how, for instance, people behave toward one another in a specific space or place – researchers will examine specific cases in great historical depth, seeking to uncover and reveal the workings of a place by virtue of its special historical circumstances. The purpose of the historical case study is to investigate a specific question whose answer rests on the broad circumstances and conditions that have made a particular city the way it is. It parallels the research of Alexis de Tocqueville into the origins of democracy in the United States. Tocqueville believed that the democratic government in the United States, based on the commitment of people to equality and freedom, could only be explained by the specific and unique conditions of the people themselves – and thus he sought to trace them both historically and to compare them with those conditions in European countries where democracy was

historical case study
A study of a particular area or city that focuses on how historical circumstances have shaped life there.

not yet found. He famously claimed, for instance, that the absence of a feudal past in the United States as compared to European countries helped to promote a sense of freedom and equality in the former.

The work of Robert and Helen Lynd represents one of the earliest forms of a historical case study, designed, as it was, to probe the historical conditions leading to the emergence and development of Middletown. However, perhaps the single best recent such study is to be found in the pioneering research of the environmental historian William Cronon (1991). Cronon produced a masterpiece in his study of Chicago, and he did so by examining how Chicago, as home to major financial and transportation institutions, developed over the course of the nineteenth century (see Figure 4.6). His work revealed how the emergence of this great metropolis depended on its intimate ties with and exploitation of the hinterlands that surrounded it. In particular, it demonstrated the ability of the city to draw on the forests of Wisconsin and the grains of Iowa, and to turn these natural elements not only into the building blocks for its residents but also into commodities that became the basis for an energetic and far-reaching capitalist economy centered in the Midwestern United States. The work is rich both in its detail regarding the nature of the hinterlands that surrounded it (see Chapter 5 for a discussion of hinterlands and the metropolis) and also in its close attention to theoretical details – specifically, how nature became transformed into commodities, or things that, in Karl Marx's terms, became the foundation for the modern capitalist economy.

hinterland A generally rural or agricultural area or region that surrounds a highly urbanized city.

Cronon's work illustrates the second kind of case, a historical prototype of a city whose unparalleled growth in the industrial age illuminates the ways in which nature and man are connected, one to another. And, again, as in all instances, the specific attention to Chicago provides a magnificent study not simply into the way that history has shaped the emergence of this particular place but also of other historical cases in which industrialization grew over the course of the nineteenth century.

From one to multiple cases

Sometimes social scientists are fortunate and are able to use multiple cases as a way to gather evidence and gain insight into a particular question or idea. One of the best illustrations recently of the productive use of multiple cases can be found in research by Richard Florida, a student of urban economics and metropolitan growth. Florida (2005a) was interested in why some places are more productive and dynamic than others – why they grow and flourish today rather than simply decline. This is a question that has come to interest many students of cities, especially in the latter part of the twentieth and early part of the twenty-first centuries, when so many cities in the United States and other Western nations have suffered the ravages of industrial decline and a growth in poverty.

Many answers have been proposed to the problem, among them that cities must develop a stronger sense of community and a more vital civic life in order to create the necessary dynamic for growth and development. But Florida had a different idea. He insisted that the driving force behind metropolitan growth is a particular kind of social class, or what he called "the creative class." This, he insisted, is a class of highly creative people – men and women who are engaged in a variety of professional and technical pursuits in education, engineering, and business – who represent the leaders of the new economy in the world. These are people such as Bill Gates, Michael Dell, or the late Steve Jobs – leading figures in the world of high technology especially. And successful cities are those that are able either to grow such a class on their own – for example, Seattle – or to be effective in attracting such a class through their industries and economies. Cities that succeed today, Florida insisted, are cities with a strong and vibrant creative class, whereas those that fail do not possess such a class.

Figure 4.6 Railroads play a central role in Cronon's analysis of Chicago. In this 1870 map you can see that by the time of the Great Chicago Fire the city had established itself as a central transportation node connecting the productive lands of the American West to the markets of the eastern seaboard and Europe. It then became a center of manufacturing and processing as well, leading to the city's unprecedented growth rate in the nineteenth and early twentieth centuries. *Source: Library of Congress, Geography and Map Division, Digital ID g3701p rr000500.*

But it is not only the talents of this class of people that are important in creating vibrant places, such as Seattle and Austin; it is also a kind of intellectual synergy that the class itself promotes. Where there is such a creative class, the community itself tends to be a more tolerant and diverse place to live, Florida and other researchers found. The creative class, in other words, not only promotes growth in the local economy but also generates a kind of local civic and social order that is attractive and sustains the interests and activity of people who live there – or who want to live there.

Now, if Florida only had a single case, let us say, only Seattle or San Francisco, then he might have examined it deeply and come up with some general explanation about why this particular place promoted growth and how unique its local culture and creative class were. But this would have been a hard sell, and a very difficult argument to make. He would have needed at least two cases – one a flourishing city, the other a dying city – to furnish the necessary comparative data to discover whether growth, or decline, was actually caused by a flourishing and vital creative class. But Florida was able to do a lot better than that. He managed to develop quantitative measures (see Table 4.2) of each of his key variables – the creative class, the tolerance of the city, and the city's diversity – and to demonstrate that, the more sizeable the creative class in a city, the more tolerant it was and the greater was its actual social and ethnic diversity. But, more than that, he was also able to highlight specific cases of cities that illustrated his general argument. Thus, Seattle, San Francisco, and Austin each served as prototypes of places where a creative class developed, the city grew, and the conditions of a lively and vibrant civic life also developed.

Although Florida has many detractors (many of whom seem envious of his fame and worldwide influence), the simplicity and elegance of his arguments, along with his many cases, have proven overwhelmingly attractive to municipal officials across the globe, all of whom, of course, want to build the next creative class and the next creative city – ones that would emulate, if not rival, places like Seattle and Austin. Florida's theories, moreover, have caught on across the world, in cities in Japan as well as in city-states such as Singapore. His work illustrates how one can employ multiple cases of cities and use them to provide evidence for a good idea and a good theory. And the reason Florida was able to do so is that he could use statistical measures of the various elements of his theory – for example, the size of the creative class, the tolerance for diversity – and deploy them systematically to compare cities across the United States, ultimately showing a clear link between the number of talented people in the local population and the growth of the local economy, among other things.

Table 4.2 Rankings for tolerance and creativity; US urban regions. Richard Florida's investigation of the cities in which creative professionals cluster led him to a variety of novel measures. The Gay Index, developed by Florida's collaborator Gary Gates, ranks cities in terms of their concentration of gay and lesbian adults based on 2000 US Census data. This closely corresponds to the Creativity Index, which combines multiple indicators of creative and high-tech productivity in an urban area. *Source: Richard Florida,* Cities and the Creative Class *(New York: Routledge, 2004).*

Tolerance (Gay Index)	Rank	Creativity Index
San Francisco	1	San Francisco
San Diego	2	Austin
Los Angeles	3	Boston
Austin	4	San Diego
Seattle	5	Seattle
Sacramento	6	Raleigh-Durham
Madison, WI	7	Houston
Washington, DC	8	Albuquerque
Atlanta	9	Washington, DC
Minneapolis	10	New York

STUDYING THE CITY   4.3

Applied sociology and action research

Many of the research strategies addressed in this chapter presume a desire to gain knowledge for knowledge's sake. Yet this is certainly not the only reason that we study cities. Much of the research conducted in and on cities and urban communities is intended to help urban populations or solve urban problems – for instance, Richard Florida's work stemmed in part from his curiosities about Pittsburgh (then his home) and its inability to retain high-tech companies, and his findings have since influenced many urban economic development agencies. Scholars and professionals from a range of different disciplinary and organizational backgrounds engage in these studies, including planners and urban administrators, political scientists, community organizers, sociologists, and social workers.

While some questions or problems may be endlessly interesting to scholars in universities, people living in communities have questions of their own that need answering – and those questions often stem from serious situations in which community members find themselves. Applied sociology and action research seek to bridge the gaps that often develop between the interests of academia and the interests of communities. Applied sociology is a subfield within the discipline that seeks to use sociological research techniques and theories to gain insight into problems faced by individuals, communities, and organizations. Action research also responds to community problems, with an explicit emphasis on social change. Both are used extensively in urban communities.

The Annual Homeless Census and Survey conducted in Jacksonville, Florida provides a great example of an applied sociology project linking academia and the community. For several years, sociology faculty and students and community volunteers, together with homeless shelters and other support agencies, have attempted to count and survey individuals whose voices are otherwise not heard. The data gathered help local agencies know how many homeless individuals are in need of services, and just what kinds of services, and provide necessary documentation for obtaining federal aid monies. The survey also provides information on why individuals are homeless: for instance, a recent survey revealed an increase in homelessness in Jacksonville of almost 20 percent during the 2009 recession, and more than 55 percent of respondents to the survey indicated that the economic crisis was the primary reason for their plight.

In Omaha, a class-based action research project paired university students with members of a community-based organization seeking to decrease childhood lead exposure in the city's poor urban neighborhoods (Rajaram 2007). The community organization knew that several neighborhoods had high lead exposure due to lead paint in aging dwellings and nearby industrial pollution, but they did not know whether residents understood these hazards or how best to reach residents who might need more information. Working with faculty and students, the researchers were able to answer these questions and to tailor their future education efforts in ways that would reach key populations.

A last but very important rule on doing a good social science of cities
Fitting good theory to good methods

In Chapter 3, we spoke at length about the varieties of sociological theories about cities, ranging from those produced in the nineteenth century to those of the most recent decades. The trick for a good social science of cities is to be able to weave together good theory and good methods, to put together the best of the theories available about cities with the best of the methods.

One's theory is always necessarily connected to one's method in the study of cities. Take our most recent example here – Richard Florida's theory of the creative class. Florida's work *could not have been done* with only one city, nor could it have been accomplished with even a handful of cities. His argument was that urban growth and development in contemporary times are driven by a creative class, a class that not only brings economic energy to the city but also helps in the creation of a set of other attractive conditions: amenities such as good music, as in Austin or Seattle, and a high degree of diversity and tolerance for other people. One could only make this argument by showing an array of cities, ones that possessed a large creative class (and hence the other conditions) compared to ones that did not (typically those older industrial cities that declined in the latter part of the twentieth century). His theory became compelling, not simply based on a plausible argument but chiefly based on the wide array of cities he included. His methods were appropriate to his theory; or, equally, his theory dictated the kind of methods he needed to have.

But multiple cases, as we have shown, are not always required, even in our times, when it is easier to accumulate data than in earlier ages. Elijah Anderson's interpretations of life on the streets and sidewalks of the Village and Northton used only two cases – those two parts of Philadelphia – and yet his theory carried a great deal of weight and plausibility: it seemed correct and real. Why? Sometimes it only takes a few cases to demonstrate the wisdom of a particular sociological theory about cities. And, in Anderson's case, his work was devoted to exploring social relationships, between and among blacks and whites, in his two neighborhoods. So, in fact, although he was dealing with only two areas, he really was examining multiple instances and examples of social relationships on the streets and sidewalks, collecting a wide array of observations and doing so over time. Place and space were very important to him – they provided the setting and the stage on which such relationships occurred – and hence made the urban setting key to his work. But it was the nature of the social relationships themselves that it was important for him to uncover.

In other words, then, his theory, about the relations in public of people, required that he should look at people who lived and interacted in urban neighborhoods, but his focus was on the relationships, and so he looked at countless such relationships. His work became compelling because of the evidence he assembled on such relationships, and because his specific cases were not cities per se but the social happenings that took place in them. The lesson of Anderson's work, then, is that *one must always specify the theoretical object of focus in doing work on cities*. Is it the city itself, as in the case of Florida's research, or is it things that take place on the sidewalks and streets of the city, as in Anderson's work as well as in the seminal research of Jane Jacobs? In the end, this theoretical focus must work hand in hand with the choice of methods, dictating not only what to look at but also how many cities one necessarily has to choose for one's work.

And what about insight?

In this chapter we have shown you the ways in which students of cities go about their work, and the principles that help to guide this research. The best research on cities studies cases, or examples, of cities and seeks to generalize from those cases to some larger population of cities. Cities are chosen either because they are typical, or an average, of all cities (like Middletown) or because they represent the prototype of the age, as Chicago represented at one time all industrial cities, or as London is claimed by Sassen to represent the features of the global city today. The prototype is indeed a very important strategy to use, in part because it enables other scholars to determine whether the features of the prototype are to be found in other cities as well.

One thing we cannot easily account for is why some good ideas become more compelling than other good ideas, even when scholars use all the good methodological advice we have offered here in this chapter. It turns out that, while we all can use the same methods, some of us have more insight than others. Many writers have tried to duplicate the work of Alexis de Tocqueville, for example, but no one has succeeded as well as he did in depicting both the nature and the preconditions of democracy in the United States. So, too, the writings of figures such as Elijah Anderson and Mary Pattillo stand as exemplars of newer work on cities – illustrations of how sensitive and insightful social observers can make sense of cities in terms of their residents, neighborhoods, and interior social and political life. What we can try to do ourselves is to pick the right methods, choose the research of exemplars and study them carefully, and ultimately hope through our own experience and insight to penetrate deeply into the core of urban issues and problems today. Visit the book's companion website at www.wiley.com/go/cities for examples, case studies, and discussion questions, plus a list of useful films and other media, that are relevant to methods of studying cities.

Critical thinking questions

1 What is a case study? Does it only refer to cities or does it refer to other things as well? How so?

2 How do you decide the number of cities to study if you are trying to answer a specific question about cities?

3 Suppose you are living in Paris and you want to study how people of different ethnic and racial backgrounds relate to one another there. If you wish to generalize to other cities, what kinds of assumptions must you make in your research?

4 Can you think of one city – any city – that is a prototype of certain important social and economic processes today? Why is it so?

5 Suppose you want to compare the experiences of immigrants living in an Asian city and those living in a European city? How many cases would you choose, and why?

Suggested reading

Neil Brenner, "Stereotypes, Archetypes and Prototypes: The Uses of Superlatives in Contemporary Urban Studies" (*City & Community* 2(3): 205–216; 2003). A brilliant article that explores the different ways in which urban scholars employ case studies.

William Cronon, *Nature's Metropolis: Chicago and the Great West* (New York: W. W. Norton & Company, 1991). Perhaps one of the best books ever written about a single city, *Nature's Metropolis* provides a rich and deep exploration of the origins and character of Chicago up to the end of the nineteenth century.

Mitchell Duneier, Hakin Hassan, and Ovie Carter, *Sidewalk* (New York: Farrar, Straus and Giroux, 2000). One of the most important recent ethnographies (by one of its best practitioners), this book shows how people come to populate sidewalks and to create a habitat there for themselves.

Joe R. Feagin, Anthony M. Orum and Gideon Sjoberg, editors, *A Case for the Case Study* (Chapel Hill: University of North Carolina Press, 1991). This book helped to reinvigorate and restore interest in case studies today, and provides a variety of ways in which

case studies are useful and important to the work of social scientists.

Richard Florida, *Cities and the Creative Class* (New York: Routledge, 2005). Florida's exposition of his theory about the creative class. It shows how and why some cities, such as Austin, Texas, are able to develop such a class while others cannot.

Robert S. Lynd and Helen Merrell Lynd, *Middletown: A Study in American Culture* (New York: Harcourt, Brace & Company, 1959). A classic study done in the 1930s of Muncie, Indiana, *Middletown* represents an effort to understand American society and culture by focusing on a city claimed to be typical of the United States at the time.

William H. Whyte, *City: Rediscovering the Center* (New York: Doubleday, 1988). This creative and careful study examines just how people use urban spaces, revealing sometimes surprising patterns.

Robert K. Yin, *Case Study Research: Design and Methods*, 4th edition (Thousand Oaks, CA: Sage Publishers, 2008). The best book available on the nature of case studies in general, including their strengths and weaknesses.

Notes

1. For important follow-up research on the same place, see Caplow et al. (1982).

2. See the illuminating discussion of the various forms of cities as cases, and types, in Beauregard (2003) and Brenner (2003).

3. See the various articles by Dear and others in *City & Community* 1(1); 2002. See also Dear (2002).

PART II
THE CHANGING METROPOLIS

CHAPTER 5

The metropolis and its expansion
Early insights and basic principles

KEY TOPICS

→ The distinction between a city and a metropolis.

→ Basic patterns in the growth of the metropolis.

→ A deeper understanding of how Burgess' concentric zone map of Chicago describes and analyzes urban growth.

→ Alternatives to the concentric zone model and the reasons why these have been pursued.

→ The concept of the natural area and its manifestations, as well as how natural areas come to be and how they have been studied.

→ How and why people have migrated to the metropolis.

→ How the metropolis is linked to surrounding areas.

→ The role of human agency in creating and reshaping the metropolis through both physical and political processes.

Introduction to Cities: How Place and Space Shape Human Experience,
First Edition. Xiangming Chen, Anthony M. Orum, and Krista E. Paulsen.
© 2013 Xiangming Chen, Anthony M. Orum, and Krista E. Paulsen.
Published 2013 by Blackwell Publishing Ltd.

Contents

So far in this book we have written about urban areas as cities. We have depicted them as both places and spaces. Now we want to broaden our discussion a bit more, to consider urban issues in a more complex way. One way for you to think about this greater complexity is to imagine the settlements of people as they expand from very small towns and villages to very large areas across a wide geographic space. Until now we have assumed that all such places are pretty much the same – as though the size of their populations and complexity of their social institutions made no difference. But of course that is not true. Or rather, to put it more precisely, students of urban settlements have not found that to be true. There is a great deal more complexity – richness, variety, diversity, inequality, and political struggle – to those very large urban settlements, such as Tokyo or Mexico City, than there is to the ones of a much smaller scale, such as St. Ives in Cornwall or Peoria, Illinois.

Students of cities have invented a particular term to capture this difference of scale and complexity in human settlements. This is **metropolis**, a term used, for instance, by Georg Simmel to characterize how the forces of modernization changed the social forms and everyday tempo of urban settlements. The idea of the metropolis is intended to capture its scale, as well as the range in the concentrations of people and the variety and history of their social institutions. The metropolis also can be thought of as having a center – the downtown or the central city – as well as having a range of communities and neighborhoods that expand outward from the central city and into the fringe areas or outskirts, such as suburbs. Moreover, the metropolis – or "metropolitan area," as some prefer – may also include smaller settlements of people living in towns and villages far from the central city. Urban sociologists as well as geographers have shown that, even though particular places may lie on the fringe of the metropolitan area – indeed, even in rural settings – a strong interdependence eventually develops between the core and the periphery: there are links of trade, communication, and even transportation that tie people in the central parts to those in the fringe areas.

> **metropolis** A vast settlement of people and various organizations that can consist of countless cities and towns.

Thus, if we wished to capture the complexity of the range of places and spaces that coexist in the metropolitan area of Los Angeles, California, for instance, we would include the core area of downtown Los Angeles but also the range and variety of smaller cities that exist within this area. Altogether, in fact, there are almost 180 cities within this metropolitan area; it includes 16 million people and covers 14 000 square miles. Metropolitan Los Angeles includes cities such as Irvine, California in Orange County but also cities such as Long Beach and Santa Monica. Or, to take the case of the Chicago metropolitan area, one would include the downtown area of Chicago but also areas that lie many miles away, such as Naperville, Illinois to the west or, for some purposes, even Gary, Indiana, which lies to the southeast of downtown Chicago. The metropolis, in other words, can encompass a wide range of many places, cities, and towns (see Figure 5.1). And it makes good sense to talk of the social and economic processes across these wider areas, especially when one is interested in the workings of the economy or even the processes of politics.

Here, in this first chapter on the metropolis, we want to share with you some of first principles and early insights into the basic workings of the metropolis, insights that come mainly from the ideas and research of human ecologists. We also want to re-emphasize to you that the basic elements of place and space continue to lie at the root of life and work in such sites. People still seek to find their own sense of security and identity in the metropolis, but in the smaller spaces therein – the neighborhoods, the villages, and even the local bars.

Figure 5.1 Sprawling Mexico City is among the many cities that are now most appropriately understood as a metropolis. *Source:* © *Hector Fernandez/Fotolia.*

Likewise, the metropolis remains a key and vital social space, where various groups and institutions act and compete with one another, thereby promoting the vitality of the metropolis in its rich and varied landscape, from its movies to its arts to its many thriving economic enterprises.

We begin by talking about the growth of people – the population – and thus the growth and expansion of the metropolis itself. Then we will move on to details, and some of the elementary principles and processes that help to guide expansion.

Metropolitan growth
Basic features

Across the broad swath of human history, the tendency of human beings to live and work in specific villages, towns, and cities has grown. This tendency has become particularly prominent in just the last two centuries, but has accelerated over the course of the past several decades. Since 1950, the number of people living in urban areas, or dense populations of people, has grown worldwide from 736 million to almost 3.5 billion.[1] The percentage of people living in urban centers has grown over this time from about 29 percent in 1950 to slightly above 50 percent in 2010 (the last a projected estimate from 2009). In the United States, the respective proportions in 1950 and 2010 were 64 percent and 82 percent. And this is by no means simply a Western phenomenon. In the less developed regions of the world, such as Asia and Africa, 18 percent of people lived in urban centers in 1950 compared to an estimate of 40 percent in 2010 (see Table 5.1).

In the mid-twentieth century, there were a wide range of metropolitan areas across the globe. For example, in 1950, Tokyo had a population estimated to be 11.2 million; by 2010 it is estimated to have been three times as great, or 36 million. In 1950 Mexico City had a population of 2.8 million, and 60 years later it had grown nearly sevenfold to almost 20 million people. And Moscow, the major metropolis of Soviet Russia, held about 5.5 million people in 1950 but double that number by 2010. The other major Russian city, St. Petersburg, had a population of 4.5 million people by 2010.

Table 5.1 Projected populations of the world's largest urban agglomerations in 2025. Where the rounding of populations led to equal figures, the ranks are based on the unrounded data. *Source: Based on data from United Nations Population Division Department of Economic and Social Affairs. "Urban Agglomerations 2007." http://www.un.org/esa/population/publications/wup2007/2007urban_agglo.htm.*

Urban Agglomeration	Country	Population in Millions			Rank		
		1975	2007	2025	1975	2007	2025
Tokyo	Japan	26.6	35.7	36.4	1	1	1
Mumbai (Bombay)	India	7.1	19.0	26.4	15	4	2
Delhi	India	4.4	15.9	22.5	23	6	3
Dhaka	Bangladesh	2.2	13.5	22.0	65	9	4
São Paulo	Brazil	9.6	18.8	21.4	5	5	5
Ciudad de México (Mexico City)	Mexico	10.7	19.0	21.0	3	3	6
New York–Newark	United States	15.9	19.0	20.6	2	2	7
Kolkata (Calcutta)	India	7.9	14.8	20.6	9	8	8
Shanghai	China	7.3	15.0	19.4	13	7	9
Karachi	Pakistan	4.0	12.1	19.1	26	12	10
Kinshasa	Democratic Republic of the Congo	1.5	7.8	16.8	116	29	11
Lagos	Nigeria	1.9	9.5	15.8	81	22	12
Al-Qahirah (Cairo)	Egypt	6.4	11.9	15.6	17	13	13
Manila	Philippines	5.0	11.1	14.8	19	17	14
Beijing	China	6.0	11.1	14.5	18	16	15
Buenos Aires	Argentina	8.7	12.8	13.8	7	10	16
Los Angeles–Long Beach–Santa Ana	United States	8.9	12.5	13.7	6	11	17
Rio de Janeiro	Brazil	7.6	11.7	13.4	11	14	18
Jakarta	Indonesia	4.8	9.1	12.4	21	23	19
Istanbul	Turkey	3.6	10.1	12.1	35	19	20

Now, you might ask yourself why it is that people tend to move into these very large metropolitan areas, and what it is that makes this movement so universal, across time as well as nations and cultures. These clearly are among the most important questions facing those men and women who study the growth of population and the concentration of people into dense settlements. Some of the material we cover in this chapter will address precisely these questions, and we will address them with a more explicit focus on developing-country cities in Chapter 10, but here at the start we can offer you a few important hints.

In the modern world, which many historians date from around the end of the eighteenth century or the beginning of the nineteenth in the West, the city became the center for the production of goods and knowledge and the creation of capital (see e.g., Tilly 1990). Cities held most of the major institutions of civilization at the time – the factories, the banks, the small shops, even many colleges or universities. And, as cities grew into metropolitan areas, they provided the livelihood for tens of thousands of people through the growth of new industries and the creation of new jobs. It became socially easier and economically more efficient for people to live in close physical proximity to one another than to live apart at great distances. In the absence of modern telecommunications, it was necessary for people to deal with one another face to face – to buy, to sell, and to develop the social relationships so necessary to the common human experience.

In countries such as the United States, one might think that people could live anywhere, given the great expanse of land and territory. But a great deal of this territory is inhospitable to human beings; for example, the vast stretches of mountains and deserts in the west of the country. Moreover, there are certain topographical features of an area that make some physical places more likely to provide the seeds for the growth of settlements. For example, sites along rivers typically lend themselves to the emergence of towns and villages because rivers furnish the means for transporting goods that can be bought and sold, thus sustaining the livelihoods of people. And, as industry grows and develops, the ease of transportation becomes very important. Again, to take another illustration, the city of Chicago in the United States expanded largely because it became a center where various branches of rail transportation merged.

These various factors – the growth of industry, the development of jobs, the concentration of capital, and the emergence of key transportation routes – all contribute in major fashion to the creation of settlement in urban areas, across the globe. And thus, as they develop, as the forces of capitalism unfold, they bring more and more people together into the same central locations. Thus, one way to tell the story of the modern world, or of modernization, is to say it is all about the growth and concentration of people into central locations (or the metropolis) and the development of this metropolis into a rich and varied site where millions of people can live, work, and raise families.

The metropolis and its expansion

At first glance, the topic of the metropolis and its expansion would seem to be fairly straightforward: simply portray the growth of the population and then depict how people move across the wide swath of a metropolitan area. Moreover, there is a very simple general rule that captures the distribution of people in the area: the density of the population across the metropolis varies from high at the center to smaller concentrations on the outskirts, or the periphery (Frisbie and Kasarda 1988). Density, in other words, diminishes with distance from the center of the metropolis – which is something you have probably noticed.

But those social scientists interested in how the metropolis, like any social space, is constructed by people wish to develop a kind of map of its social and economic tendencies. So, what kind of map should they choose? Should it just be any kind of map? Will each place in the world have a different kind of map? In fact, the first answer proposed to these questions came from the hands of a sociologist connected with the Chicago School of Sociology, Ernest Burgess. In Chapter 2 we briefly discussed Burgess and his map of Chicago's concentric zones, but in this chapter we want to spend more time on it, in part because it has exercised a great deal of influence over the thinking of social scientists about how the metropolis expands and becomes more diverse.

The center of the city

Let's begin by taking one more look at Burgess' portrait of Chicago (see Figure 2.4). And let's start from the center – the area known famously in Chicago as the Loop – and move outward. At the center are the major institutions of the city, the financial enterprises and the major retail stores. These are the institutions that form the core of the city, the ones that are the most central to its workings as both an economic and a political enterprise. Here, too, one discovers an important fact about all major metropolitan areas, one that you probably already know. The price of land takes on different values in a metropolitan area: in some places the cost of land is very high, whereas in others it tends to be low.

The early human ecologists argued that the cost of land, otherwise known as the land value, was the highest at the center of the city but lower at the fringes. And then they asked why. They concluded that it had come about because, they claimed, land acquires its value from the *competition* for it. Banks and major business enterprises wish to be in the center of the city for it is there that the daily life of the metropolis is the most active: large numbers of people work in the central locations and the political offices of the metropolis are there to concentrate and use their power. Moreover, in the days of industrial growth, railroads entered the city at the center, thereby providing easy access for the purchase and sale of goods. Hence, the early human ecologists concluded that, where competition for land is high, the value of that land also will be high. And only those businesses and commercial enterprises that can pay those costs will be able to locate there and gain easy access to goods and to people. Thus it came to be that banks and other major economic enterprises will locate in the central portions of the metropolis.

This notion of an underlying and enduring competition among people and institutions for land, and for space in the city, became a key scientific principle of the Chicago School of Sociology (Park 1936). The movement of people and organizations across space grew out of the competition among them for land: those that won out in the competition generally were the most powerful and the most able to pay a pretty penny for the land. Yet, as the history of the metropolis unfolded in the twentieth century, social scientists amended and elaborated on this theory of competition. They observed that the whole process was not simply the workings of the invisible hand of competitive capitalism, as the great economist Adam Smith had once argued. Rather, it owed a great deal to the machinations of, among others, real estate developers who could help to set the price, or value, of land, and thus exercise a great deal of control over who settled where in the city (see e.g., Harvey 1973; Logan and Molotch 1987; Gottdiener 1994). We shall say more about this later in the chapter.

The zone of transition

Beyond the center of the city came the zone of transition. Being the social area of the city, where residential settlements began to appear among the commercial ones, it became known as the zone of transition. There may have been warehouses here as well as commercial enterprises that were wholesale rather than retail firms; in other words, ones that sold large quantities of goods to retail stores such as Macy's or Woolworth's. It was also the area where the red light district of the city existed, and where men and women would gather for their nightly or weekend dalliances. The other key feature of the zone of transition is that it is where the immigrant settlements arose – the neighborhoods created by the immigrants who arrived in Chicago at the end of the nineteenth and beginning of the twentieth centuries (the Irish, Italians, and the Polish).

Of course, you will wonder why settlements grew there rather than in some other place. There was one very simple reason. This was the area where the railroad stations of the metropolis lay, and hence the site where, during the era of the railroads, newcomers to the city disembarked for the first time. And, lacking both funds and knowledge of the city, it became almost inevitable that small numbers of immigrants would settle close to the stations and eventually that the institutions of the immigrant community would arise. The proximity of these neighborhoods to commercial and industrial uses also attracted new immigrants as housing prices tended to be low and nearby work opportunities numerous. This happened across many US metropolitan areas, in fact, ranging from Philadelphia to New York to Chicago.

The zone of commuters

Further from the center, the nature of the area began to change even more. There were the homes of the working-class members of the labor force, many of them immigrants. Most, if not all, of this housing consisted of tenements: two- or three-story buildings where people could live together, often with many of them in cramped quarters. Rooms were comparatively cheap, but, more than that, these buildings were close to the factories and retail shops, and hence people could travel back and forth from home to work cheaply and easily. Finally, at the outer fringes of the city lay some of the more expensive housing: this was the zone of the commuters, the inhabitants who took the train into the city in the morning and returned at night. The outer zones would become the site of the suburban residents who, when the automobile replaced the train as the chief form of transportation, would commute to and from the city by car.

Assessing the concentric zone theory

This map of the expansion of the metropolis is exquisite for its clarity and simplicity. Burgess created it not so much to show a hard-and-fast view of the city but rather to provide a means for promoting further inquiry into it. Moreover, this map was intended to show how the metropolis expanded not in terms of the raw numbers of people and institutions but rather in terms of the way they were distributed across specific spaces within the city. And Burgess did claim that, as the map seemed to show, "the resulting differentiation of the cosmopolitan American city into areas is typically all from one pattern, with only minor modifications" (Burgess 1961 [1925]: p. 41).

This portrait eventually became very famous. Social scientists interpreted it to mean that all cities consisted of a series of social and economic zones that were concentric circles, or semicircles (like Chicago) organized around the center of the city. The map showed that the key political and economic activities were located at the center, while many of the residential areas lay at the fringes. It also suggested seeming principles underlying the historic development of the expansion of the metropolis, among them the existence of the various ethnic and immigrant neighborhoods. Finally, this picture identified key elements to the economy of the city, showing where the major financial institutions of the city were located as well as those of various forms of commercial enterprise. The map became so popular in the early days of urban social science that it provided the basis for countless efforts by other researchers to see whether other metropolitan areas actually expanded as Chicago had. And, in fact, in many cases they did: Chicago had become, in effect, the prototype for the emerging industrial city, not only in the Unites States but in Western Europe as well. This map portrayed not only how the expansion of the metropolis had taken place but also how it would continue to take place in many cities other than Chicago.

The natural areas of the city

There was yet one other important feature of this portrait of the city. It suggested that people and institutions did not distribute themselves randomly across the city. Rather, certain kinds of people were distributed in one place – for example, the immigrants – and certain kinds of institutions in others, such as the wholesale district. These became known as the **natural areas** of the city. Hence, it was concluded that people and institutions that shared the same traits, though in competition with one another, would tend to concentrate in roughly the same geographical areas of the city, thus also making these areas into important and distinctive social and economic places of the city. If one then looked at the city through the lens of the map, the best areas to live were on the fringes, if one could afford the cost. But the worst areas were those in the center of the city, near the major business district. These were the areas of high poverty and many tenements, the areas of "social disorganization" (so called by Burgess and his colleagues), and University of Chicago sociologists would continue over the course of many decades to try to unravel how and why both crime and poverty coexisted in these particular social areas of the metropolis. Was all of this some kind of ineluctable social – indeed social scientific – fact? Or was it a mere artifact of the way in which events unfolded historically in the growth of the metropolis?

> **natural areas of the metropolis** Those specific spaces in the metropolis where distinctive groups of people and/or organizations congregate.

   Ultimately Burgess and Park proposed that the different social areas of the city were natural areas, not created by a series of historical events but rather by the positioning of people, groups, and functions in certain areas of the city that were natural places for them to be located. This view of the city as a space in which natural areas formed was entirely consistent with the larger purposes of the human ecology paradigm: the city was a natural setting and environment – as natural, say, as the human organism is for biologists. Indeed, the city, in the eyes of the Chicago School, was roughly the equivalent of the human organism – but this was a social and ecological fact, not a biological one.

Alternative views of the city

A key question raised by urban scholars who examined the map was whether all emerging metropolitan areas actually developed in the form of concentric zones or whether there were other patterns of expansion and development that took place. In fact, other research showed that there could be alternative patterns in the expansion of the city and the metropolis (see Figure 5.2). The expansion of some metropolitan areas took place in terms of multiple centers and areas of development, a pattern that did not at all follow Burgess' map of Chicago (Harris and Ullman 2005 [1945]: p. 52). Thus, there were metropolitan areas, such as Seattle, Washington, that displayed a different pattern regarding the shape and location of their social areas and social institutions. These had specific areas where retail shops were concentrated as well as upper-income residential areas, but not in the form of concentric zones. And sometimes they did not even include any specific immigrant settlements.

STUDYING THE CITY   5.1

The Chicago School's natural area studies

Viewing the city as comprised of natural areas led scholars of the Chicago School to study those areas in detail, examining human behavior as it occurred in natural settings. This included studies of the neighborhoods that comprised these natural areas, as well as the distinct institutions and behaviors found therein.

Harvey Zorbaugh, who elaborated on the concept of the natural area, is one of the best-known scholars working in this tradition. He defined a natural area as a geographical area characterized both by a physical individuality and the cultural characteristics of the people who live in it (Zorbaugh 2005 [1926]). Zorbaugh proposed that a city develops as a result of the free market naturally sorting residents into enclaves, and therefore that racial segregation is a natural result of the market moving people to the areas in which they are predestined to live. Though some of Zorbaugh's views were misguided, he did point out that overly mobile populations in disadvantaged communities were hurting chances of upward mobility. He also suggested that city planners and politicians were not meeting the needs of many city residents because they did not recognize the differences between natural areas of the city. His study of Chicago's adjacent poor and wealthy areas, *The Gold Coast and the Slum* (1983 [1929]), is still widely read.

Zorbaugh's colleagues at the University of Chicago turned the same attention to detail and interest in the everyday lives of urban dwellers to other areas of the city – particularly those that differed from white middle-class experiences. Nels Anderson's *The Hobo* (1923), for instance, chronicled the lives of homeless men in Chicago, from the "jungles" or camps on the shore of Lake Michigan where they passed the summers to the roach-infested flophouses where they spent winter nights (a dedicated urban ethnographer, Anderson spent the night in one of these flophouses and presents all the harrowing details). Clifford Shaw's *The Jack Roller* (1966) presents the case study of a "delinquent" who made his living by robbing drunks; it was revolutionary at the time for its use of the young man's own perspective.

St. Clair Drake and Horace Cayton's *Black Metropolis* (1945) is certainly among the most ambitious and important studies to come out of this tradition. Through their study of African American life in Chicago, Drake and Cayton were some of the first researchers to reveal the relationships between African Americans and white residents in urban areas, and to point out how these relationships affected the personalities and institutions that African Americans were able to cultivate under their separate and subordinate status within the city. Drake and Cayton scientifically exposed problems related to religion, crime, low literacy rates, unemployment, and a variety of other factors to paint a picture of African American urban life richer than any previously known, and to influence and stimulate activism and further research on the problem of racial inequality for generations to come.

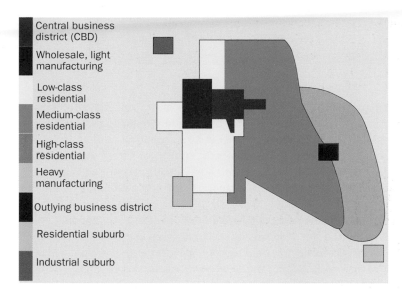

Central business district (CBD)

Wholesale, light manufacturing

Low-class residential

Medium-class residential

High-class residential

Heavy manufacturing

Outlying business district

Residential suburb

Industrial suburb

Figure 5.2 Harris and Ullman's multiple nuclei model. *Source: From Chauncy D. Harris and Edward L. Ullman, "The Nature of Cities." In Nicholas R. Fyfe and Judith T. Kenny, eds.* The Urban Geography Reader *(London and New York: Routledge, 2005 [1945], pp. 46–55, at p. 52).*

The mobility of people and groups in the metropolis

Cities and metropolitan areas, we have insisted, are all about change and movement. People like yourself grow up in one area of the city, and you and your family may during your lifetime move to another area (the typical American moves about six times during his or her lifetime). What is true about your own experiences turns out also to be true of the experiences of other people like you and your family. One of the important implications of the concentric zone portrait of the metropolis produced by Ernest Burgess is that different parts of the metropolis take on different social and economic characters. For example, as we have said, wealthy residents tend to live in the outer rings of the metropolis while poorer residents live in the inner portions. This pattern of the location of people seems to imply something more – that, as families who live in the city become wealthier, they will tend to move out to and congregate with others like themselves in the wealthier districts. It seemed to be an obvious deduction from the social map. But was it true or not?

Social differences and migration in the metropolis

In fact, a range of studies, especially of the early immigrant groups, showed that the wealth of families was strongly correlated with their movement to the outer fringes of the city (see e.g., Massey 1985; Massey and Denton 1985; Fong and Wilkes 1999). Thus, if an Irish or Italian family came to the United States and settled near the center of a city at the turn of the century, as many did, it was entirely possible that the next generation of that same family, having gained a certain amount of wealth and facility with American customs, would move to the outlying areas of the metropolis – the fringe or suburban areas. This was a pattern that seemed to be repeated over and over for different ethnic and immigrant groups. It was an avenue of geographic mobility as well as social integration that moved the second and third generations of families who had originally disembarked at the center of the city outward to the wealthier suburban areas. Indeed, it suggested a critical and vital social connection between geographic and social mobility in the metropolis: the longer your

EXPLORING FURTHER   5.1

Beyond concentric zones

The concentric zone model developed by Ernest Burgess outlined the layers of Chicago quite effectively, showing how land uses changed as they moved from one ring to the next outward from the Loop, Chicago's central business district. But, when this model was applied to other cities, it was less effective. This was especially true when the model was applied to cities within the United States that developed postindustrially, or to many major cities outside the United States, where the most affluent residents tend to prefer to live in the inner city instead of suburbs on the outskirts.

In response, several urban scholars attempted to fix this problem by developing new models of their own. The first of these alternative models was proposed by Homer Hoyt, an economist, who put forward his sector model in 1939. While the concentric zone model separated areas of the city as rings surrounding the central business district, Hoyt's sector model also separated areas of the city, but as wedges, like slices of a pie, extending from the central business district all the way to the periphery. Hoyt created his sector model as a result of a study involving 142 US cities that looked at the location of rent areas within the cities. In this context, "rent" refers to any money paid toward a home, so mortgage payments are considered rent.

Though Hoyt did not discredit the concentric zones model, he claimed that some cities may have an urban structure closer to the wedge-shaped rent separations proposed in his model. He believed that each type of rent area could be found all the way from the central business district to the periphery. Many industrial land uses, Hoyt claimed, could be found extending from the central business district along transportation routes that would bring raw materials and manufactured goods in and out of the city, such as railroad tracks.

Residential land uses would then extend from both sides of the industrial wedge from low-rent sectors to high-rent sectors. Low-rent sectors could be found closest to the industrial areas, because poor residents would not be able to travel great distances to and from work and would therefore live close to where they work. Hoyt also pointed out that residential areas closest to the industrial sector were in the lowest demand due to problems such as noise and pollution.

Intermediate-rent sectors would then extend from the central business district all the way to the periphery, adjacent to low-rent sectors from the side farthest from the industrial sector. These residential areas would be able to avoid the problems associated with land next to industry, but their residents would miss out on attractions enjoyed by the affluent living in high-rent sectors.

High-rent sectors, Hoyt explains, would extend from the central business district along very particular routes. They would almost always be on the opposite side of the circle, and farthest away from the industrial and low-rent sectors. High-rent sectors would also frequently develop on non-industrial waterfronts, toward or along high ground, or along a path radiating outward toward a side of the city containing open countryside. Though Hoyt claimed that these high-rent sectors remained relatively stable in their location within the city, he stated that their position could be altered by the activities of private developers. Here we see some early attention to the kinds of urban manipulations that Logan and Molotch would later put at the center of their analysis of cities (see Chapter 3).

Though Hoyt's model made logical sense, and there were several cities found to have urban structures similar to the sector model, they were still mainly old industrial US cities of the northeast and Midwest, and many cities didn't fit the bill. In an attempt to address this problem, urban geographers Chauncy Harris and Edward Ullman developed the **multiple nuclei** model in 1945 (see Harris and Ullman 2005 [1945]).

> **multiple nuclei** The claim that metropolitan areas consist of different centers that can compete with one another in development.

In the multiple nuclei model, a city may have had a central business district at one point, or may not have, but there are now numerous centers within cities for different specialized land uses. As an example, the London metropolitan area developed with two distinct nuclei from the beginning. The city of London and the city of Westminster started out as separate urban developments, each surrounded by countryside, one being the center of regional commerce and the other the center of political activity. Today the two are joined and the London metropolitan area essentially has two very major nuclei.

Harris and Ullman explain that in other cases cities may develop multiple nuclei over time as a result of four different causal factors. First, certain activities require specialized facilities (for instance, law offices cluster near courthouses); second, certain similar activities group together because they profit from cohesion; third, certain unlike activities are detrimental to each other; and fourth, many activities are unable to afford the high rents of the most desirable areas. These factors may work in conjunction with one another. For example, retail districts will be located in the most easily accessible areas of the city, and will often cluster together to form a district or nucleus where rents are relatively high; at the same time, other nuclei will form in areas they can afford and that are suitable to their needs while attracting and opposing other land uses.

Neither of these alternative models can be applied accurately to portray the urban structure of most cities, but they are not meant to. The purpose of such models is to encourage thought and discourse over the development of major urban areas, and to find valuable similarities where possible without claiming that one model will fit all. After all, the development and structure of urban areas is a very complex topic, and can never easily be reconstructed in the form of a model.

family was in the metropolis, the wealthier it was likely to become and the more likely it was that future generations would move to the better districts – those possessing big yards and open green spaces, and houses with white picket fences.

Thus, the expansion of the metropolis also implied the social and geographic mobility of families; the two processes seemed to be intimately connected with one another. And they were processes that happened not just in the metropolitan area of Chicago – though this proved to be one of the most studied of the United States' metropolises – but also in the New York metropolitan area as well as places such as Philadelphia. And stories grew up among the immigrant families and within the emerging ethnic communities of how Uncle Abe and his wife, or Peter and his family, or the third generation of the Connors moved out to the suburbs, seeking to capture their part of the American Dream. But, in doing so, they became a part of the growth and history of the metropolis, revealing that individual stories, even of distinct ethnic groups, seemed to repeat themselves again and again. As these individual mobilities multiplied and aggregated, they translated into a constantly shifting mosaic of the metropolitan residential landscape.

However, this pattern of mobility did not reflect the lives and experiences of all new immigrants to the city in the United States, especially not those of African Americans (see e.g., Massey and Mullan 1984; Massey and Denton 1993). Their journey had been centuries in the making, but from the 1920s African Americans started to move to the major US cities in the north (Lemann 1992). They left the plantations and small farms in the South and began to move northward to cities such as St. Louis or Detroit or Cleveland in search of new job opportunities. It was a pattern of movement into the metropolis that replicated the pattern of the European immigrants. Yet, once they reached the metropolis, they found barriers that blocked their way, across generations and across the space of the city, into the outer regions, the suburbs, the sites of white picket fences. While their coinhabitants of the central city could ship their children and grandchildren to the better areas, African Americans simply were unable to do so.

Thus, just as insights into the geographic mobility of various European immigrants would come to be established as fact by the earliest urban social science, so the immobility of and impediments to the movement of African Americans would become another fact – and one that preoccupied the work and thought of many social scientists. The United States, from its origins, was a land of immigrants, and so the patterns of mobility were first to be observed there. But what about in other countries, particularly Western nations? Did the same patterns hold up there? To some extent they did, but, at least prior to World War II (the era with which we are concerned in this chapter), the numbers were far fewer than in the United States because such countries would only become home to massive numbers of immigrants after World War II.

Take the case of the East End of London, which for decades was where immigrants first entered England. It was here that Russian Jews, escaping the terrors that targeted them during the reign of Tsar Nicholas (1894–1917), first set foot on British soil. And, later, other immigrants would disembark in the same quarters. As in Chicago, New York, or even Philadelphia, many people remained at the first place where they set foot – and in London it was in the area of the East End along Petticoat Lane. In the mid-1990s, Anthony Orum had the opportunity to spend a great deal of time in this area. He found remarkable traces of the history of waves of immigrants and settlement in this particular site. They are etched into the history of one building in particular. This building was constructed in the nineteenth century and was at first home to new Jewish settlers. It became their first synagogue in London. Later, as the Jews moved to outer regions of the London metropolis, they were replaced by yet another immigrant group, Catholic refugees from Ireland. The synagogue, a substantial and proud building, was transformed into an Irish Catholic church. The Catholics, continuing the pattern of mobility, eventually moved out, and today that church is now a mosque, home to the latest generation of immigrants to England, including many Muslims from Bangladesh.

There is yet another important twist, and hence insight, concerning the ways in which the origins of people and their place in the city carve themselves into the metropolis. While second- and third-generation immigrants often took every opportunity to escape the central areas of the metropolis for the fresh air and verdant landscape, many of the sites they left behind remained vibrant and booming ethnic neighborhoods. Here is an instance where the attachments of people to place really make a difference, and not just in a temporary fashion but in a permanent one. The neighborhoods that had been created in the central areas of places such as Chicago, Milwaukee, or Pittsburgh often retained, for lack of a better word, their ethnic and immigrant flavor. Look back, for example, at the location of Chinatown on Ernest Burgess' map of Chicago. This area first took root in the earliest years of the twentieth century, when a small number of immigrants from China settled there. Over time, it became known across the city and among immigrants from China as Chinatown. Thus, it became the site where new Chinese immigrants would first take up residence in the city.

Eventually, of course, a whole range of institutions – small shops that sold Chinese food, bakeries catering to Chinese tastes, and places of worship – grew up in the area. It became home in a new country to people from abroad; and they remade it in a site that furnished them, as all places do, with a sense of security, community, and identity. Once the younger generation had grown up, many moved out; but some did not, and they remained with their grandparents and parents within the older area of Chinatown. This was because many of them came from a particular part of Guangdong province in China and spoke only a local dialect. In Chicago, that area today remains a site where many immigrants from the People's Republic of China, Taiwan, and Hong Kong settle, set up shops, and engage in other activities. This entry of more recent Chinese immigrants has contributed to some housing expansion around the edges of Chinatown. The old Chinatown in New York, which has been there for nearly a century, has undergone a similar expansion in recent years. Likewise, in Chicago, the original Italian area (settled about the same time) retains some of its original ethnic flavor, with various restaurants and even some of the relatives of the earliest Italian settlers in the city.

Thus, as Burgess and his fellow human ecologists at Chicago first argued, mobility was, and remains to this day, a very important part of the expansion of the metropolis. People move in and they move out. It is a bit like the Grand Hotel in the famous movie of the same name: there is constant movement through the doors of the city, people coming in and others moving out, new areas created, and second and third generations of immigrants taking a well-worn path to the outer fringes of the metropolis. In the process, the pattern would in the period prior to World War II be repeated again and again for different immigrants to the city. But, even as they left the central portions, there were, as we suggested, important traces of those areas left behind, in the form of shops and religious institutions. Many, though not all, stood the test of time, remaining there not simply as part of the constructed, or built, environment but as living social institutions, ready to welcome yet another generation of immigrants. It was mainly, if not exclusively, against the African American immigrants to the city that the avenues to the suburbs would be barricaded. And they were barricades that provided both the intellectual and the policy fodder for the work of urban social scientists.

Migration and the expansion of the metropolis

There are two ways in which a metropolis, or any specific human settlement, can grow. One is by what demographers call **natural increase** or expansion, and it is determined in a very simple fashion. The formula for it is very simple: the size of the current population, plus the number of births minus the number of deaths in the population. Hence, if there are more births than deaths the size of the population will expand, whereas if deaths outnumber births the size will diminish. Very simple, very elegant, and it has proved central to the work of demographers, or students of population, for years.

natural increase
The crude birth rate minus the death rate of a population. Usually positive, but may be negative.

But a more interesting and productive line of intellectual reasoning sees the matter of growth, or decline, from a different angle. Here the increase, or decrease, of the population is determined by the number of immigrants, or people who enter the metropolis, minus the number of emigrants, or people who leave the metropolis. Metropolitan areas that are booming with job opportunities tend to attract more of the immigrants and lose fewer people to migration elsewhere, whereas areas that are losing jobs will tend to lose more people than they gain. The story of how and why this process of migration unfolds in this manner has proven of great interest to students of the metropolis because it provides insight into the history as well as the internal social and economic dynamics of the metropolis itself.

In the latter part of the nineteenth century and early part of the twentieth century, millions and millions of people entered various US metropolitan areas just at the moment that new industries were developing and taking root in the cities. They came from nations as far away as Russia and Greece and Ireland. But why did they actually come? How can we explain why thousands of people would leave one country and come to another, and thereby contribute to the actual growth of the US metropolis? One line of explanation is very straightforward: people leave their homelands because they face difficult circumstances – they cannot find a job or they and their families are confronted by a devastating famine – and they flee to where such opportunities exist, to other European countries such as England or abroad to the United States or Canada. Here, as history shows, the new immigrants are able to enter the labor market easily and to find jobs, and eventually housing, for themselves and their families. Some social scientists have interpreted this sequence of events as a "push-pull" process: people are pushed from where they live because of the absence of opportunities, and they are pulled to other sites where such opportunities exist. This is a fairly simple and straightforward way of explaining why people move or are mobile across great distances, and why some places gain population and other places lose population. It is an elegant and, for ecologists and economists, a simple and powerful way to explain migration and the growth and expansion of the metropolis.

But the story proves to be somewhat more complex than that, and it serves to illustrate the critical role of sociological factors in the stories of migration. Although migrants contribute to the growth and expansion of the metropolis, net of other factors, it is not simply jobs or economic opportunities that prove to be the central and motivating feature behind their movement. As sociologists and historians have shown, it is also the links of people to one another – their social networks – that help to furnish the stream of migrants and create ever-expanding metropolitan growth of the kind that occurred in the United States at the turn of the twentieth century. These networks help to explain, for example, why Germans would leave Germany and settle in Milwaukee, Wisconsin, or Cincinnati, Ohio, or St. Louis, Missouri, rather than other places. Migration, in other words, is not random at all, and it goes well beyond job opportunities themselves. People leave one country and go to another where there are other people like themselves – other people who are German, or, in the case of Chicago, other people who are Irish or Polish. In other words, the flow of migrants follows a path of social connections – sometimes family, sometimes friends – that link people with one another.

The notion of job opportunities within the metropolis was thus essential to the early industrial growth of areas of the United States, or Canada, in the twentieth century, but, more than that, it was also the social networks – the ties among friends and relatives – that contributed to this growth, that made people from one country, even one village, settle among others like themselves in a particular metropolitan area in the United States. Moreover, in the process of migration and settlement in the new metropolis, many of the customs and ideas of the new settlers would become reproduced in the new US, or Canadian, or English metropolis. The church, or temple, often was the first major immigrant institution established in the center of the metropolis. And, later, it created its own social and political offspring, including various kinds of voluntary and economic groups. Indeed, across the various immigrant groups that entered the metropolis in the early part of the twentieth century, religion was almost always the central institutional vehicle and home created by the newcomers, whether they were Italian, Irish, or Polish. In Chapter 8 and Chapter 9 of this book, we discuss these matters about immigration, immigrants, and social inequalities in much greater detail.

metropolitan expansion (or contraction) The growth (or decline) of a city-region, which depends on births versus deaths and the rate of immigration/ emigration.

The process of migration, which as we have seen here in this chapter can be such an important part of **metropolitan expansion**, helps to explain the rapid and substantial growth of many American and Canadian cities and surrounding areas during the first part of the twentieth century. Industrial expansion was substantial, and brought people in; but the actual people, the specific new immigrants, came to specific sites because they possessed social connections to other people there. In effect, to use concepts we have employed before in this book, a community and a sense of security had already been established for them, and they transplanted themselves from one site to another, retaining their ethnic identity as they did so.

Economic underpinnings and social connections, thus, are important principles for you to understand in order to appreciate the population dynamics of metropolitan growth. But there are other principles as well. And we turn now to examine some of these, in the process adding to our insight and knowledge of the expansion of the metropolis.

The metropolitan center and its links to the hinterlands

As the metropolis expands, as new people arrive and new institutions are built, it becomes a more varied social and geographic site: it comes to display different kinds of spaces and places, different neighborhoods, and different economic districts (of arts and culture, but also of warehouses and banks). Now, while these different social and economic activities lie in different spaces of the metropolis, they are not entirely disconnected from one another. Indeed, certain patterns of interdependence grow up and develop, connecting the sites to one another. To take a very simple example, the earliest immigrants to metropolitan areas in the United States settled in the inner areas of the city partly because that is where the trains left them but partly also because those sites were close to factories and stores, offering easy access to the places they found work. The location of the residential area, in other words, was dependent on the location of the places of work. One part of the city, the site of residences, was dependent on another part of the city, the site of work.

This notion of the interdependence of the parts of the metropolis with one another is absolutely fundamental to understanding the workings of the metropolis itself. And it happens in many and varied ways, as the research and writings of students of cities show. One of the most important ways is through the connection between activities that occur in the outlying sections of the metropolis and those that take place at its center. Let's consider a fairly simple example, from the twentieth century. Major newspapers, such as the *Cleveland Plain Dealer*, the *St. Louis Post-Dispatch*, or the *Minneapolis Star Tribune*, were printed in the downtown areas of these larger metropolises. Though there were various local and neighborhood newspapers, these larger ones dominated the news across the metropolitan area. They furnished the information about who was selling what and where, as well as the local weather, the workings of the financial district, and the like. The newspapers thus furnished the news of the metropolis, keeping everyone, including those people at the outskirts, informed about everyday happenings and events.

But, in turn, the newspapers were dependent on the lumber that came from outside the central city, sometimes at a far remove from the metropolitan area. The trees and forests, as well as the ink supplies, all had to be furnished from the fringe or rural areas, or what are sometimes called the hinterlands of the metropolitan area. A type of interdependence thus emerged: people in the hinterlands relied on the metropolis for the news, while the papers relied on the hinterlands for the raw materials that went into their production. This kind of connection was reproduced over and over again, between the workings at the center of the metropolis and those in the hinterlands: the livelihood and energies of people and institutions in the two areas thus were intimately connected to one another – and not just in good times but especially in bad times. If there was a major strike or shutdown of the major newspapers, people in the hinterlands would not learn news critical to their daily lives; and, by the same token, the newspapers could not be produced if the forests and trees disappeared or if it proved impossible to import lumber.

Across the metropolis, then, various kinds of interdependencies grew up, ones that shaped the early twentieth-century metropolis in various ways. For a long while, the downtown area was the major location of big department stores, and thus people had to travel downtown to purchase their clothing and their major appliances. Likewise, if a small shop owner needed funds to continue the operations of his business, he would have to travel downtown, to a major bank, in order to open a bank account for such funds. A constant movement of people and goods thus emerged across the metropolis, linking the parts and making them interdependent. Ultimately, human ecologists as well as geographers would begin to invent new and more complex models to depict the complexity of the metropolis itself – ones that invoked notions of trade routes between the factories in the center and the producers of raw materials in the hinterlands. The metropolis thus became in the minds of these urban scholars a sort of working organism that could only be understood by appreciating the fuller and complete interdependence of its various neighborhoods, businesses, and producers of its raw materials.

None of this is to suggest that notions of place and space would lose their hold and force over the lives of human beings in the metropolis. Rather, it is to suggest that the idea of place remained vital to the inhabitants of the city, for reasons we have suggested, and also that any effort to understand – or, especially, to modify or alter – such things as where new factories or new shops were located had to take into account both the attachments of people to their work and home sites and the complex processes of moving people and goods back and forth across the large expanse of the metropolis.

Human agents and social institutions in the expansion of the metropolis

In the early days of the Chicago School, the sociologists there plus many other social scientists came to believe that the operations of the metropolis depended almost exclusively on certain fundamental ecological principles that worked to distribute people, organizations, and places across the metropolis. Competition and density were thought to be fundamental and unalterable features of the development and growth of the metropolis, elements subject to certain scientific rhythms and principles. Yet, as time has gone by, and as we have learned more and more about the actual workings of the metropolis, we find that key individuals and various groups of people frequently shape what happens in the metropolis and how it actually expands. Human agency and human agents play a big part not merely in the life of the metropolis but also, if not primarily, in its expansion. And they play a much larger role than the early human ecologists admitted.

Let's consider one classic illustration of how people can shape the expansion of the metropolis. It concerns the efforts of one man, Robert Moses (see Figure 5.3), who played an absolutely essential role in shaping the way that the New York metropolitan area looks today.[2] Moses became active in New York politics in the early part of the twentieth century, and from about the 1930s to the 1960s he had a hand in every major project in the metropolitan area, from the creation of new bridges that linked one part to another, to the creation of major new expressways. He controlled huge sums of money, employed tens of thousands of people to work on his projects, and was responsible for the selection of New York City as the headquarters for the United Nations. He was, in effect, the tsar of New York City, making decisions daily that affected the lives of millions of people. Many of his decisions proved vital to the expansion of the metropolis after the Great Depression, yet many revealed the hand of a man who catered to the whims of the wealthy and neglected the fates of poor people. Some highways were designed to avoid the estates of rich magnates like J. Pierpont Morgan, but they displaced tens of thousands of poorer residents, sending them across the city and of course destroying both the sense of community and the places they had built.

STUDYING THE CITY   5.2

Hinterlands as empire

Throughout history, major cities have depended upon their hinterlands for resources such as food, building supplies, and water, and for new land to facilitate their growth and outward expansion. People living in the hinterlands benefit in turn from the manufactured goods, financial institutions, and sources of information that cities provide. Neither the central cities nor the hinterlands could function effectively without the other; the two areas are truly interdependent.

Historical geographer Gray Brechin (2006) contends that the great fortunes made in San Francisco – and much of the development of the city itself – depended on the exploitation of the surrounding hinterland. Those who visit the city today can be excused for forgetting its past as a mining center, but this was the industry that propelled the city's early growth. As Brechin argues, the wealthiest families in the city depended on mining and associated services (for instance, selling supplies to miners or investing the wealth that they brought back to San Francisco's banks). Mining stoked the city's growth in other ways as well – for instance, the iconic cable cars used technologies adapted from mining to make the city's hills more accessible and thus increase land values. The hinterland – which in the case of mining included the Sierra Nevada mountain range to the east of the city – suffered environmental damage that still scars the land today.

In studying the growth of cities and their relationships with the hinterlands that surround them, Brechin continuously poses the question, "was it worth it?" He argues that central cities will often damage or disrupt the surrounding ecosystem in their quest for growth. They will extract food, water, minerals, and timber from the hinterlands until there is nothing left, and then move on to seek out new sources to fuel their outward expansion. In the case of San Francisco, this meant looking across the Pacific to Asia. San Francisco's wealthy industrialists, with the aid of newspaper publisher William Randolph Hearst, advocated imperial domination of the Philippines. Not only would this provide new agricultural territory for the city's sugar barons but conquest of Asian lands would also benefit those families who made their fortunes in munitions.

A growing central city does offer many benefits to residents living within the city's hinterlands, but at a price. And, in some cases, residents within the hinterlands decide that the price is too high. For example, residents of Owens Valley, California attempted to protest against and sabotage an aqueduct sapping their home dry to satisfy water needs in the growing city of Los Angeles (Reisner 1986; see Chapter 12). But, to some extent, the relationships between central cities and their hinterlands are mutually beneficial as people, goods, and services pass from one to the other on a regular basis to create the life that most people in the Global North are used to.

But Robert Moses was only one example of an urban booster, albeit a figure of historic proportions. Many other such figures proved to be important to the early growth and expansion of metropolitan areas in the United States as well as in Europe. Daniel Burnham, for example, was a major figure in the development of many of the buildings as well as the lakefront area in Chicago. He played an important part in securing and developing the buildings for the Columbia Exposition in Chicago in 1893, an event that helped Chicago to escape the tragedy of its great fire in 1871 and eventually become a major American metropolis. Like Moses, Burnham did everything on a big scale, and today he is remembered for his famous claim, still echoing across the many years of Chicago's history, "Make no little plans" – a claim that seemed to animate the efforts of the recently retired and longest-serving mayor of Chicago, Richard M. Daley, including his effort to secure the 2016 Olympics for his city.

Across the Atlantic in the nineteenth century, Georges-Eugène Haussmann would help to shape the great boulevards and green areas of central Paris, effectively replacing the older medieval city with the elements of a new modern metropolis and paving the way for twentieth-century Paris (see Figure 5.4). Haussmann designed, among other things, the great avenues of Paris, the 12 of which radiate today from the center of the city. And, just as Moses' plans had reshaped parts of metropolitan New York, displacing thousands of poorer residents, so, too, Haussmann's designs fundamentally remade Paris. They seemed to serve the interests of the wealthy and to particularly neglect the poor and those who were attached to the older historic institutions of medieval Paris. They also gave a glimpse into the many and diverse efforts in the twentieth and twenty-first centuries both to destroy and to remake metropolitan areas. Thus, for example, the massive changes in Paris under the direction of Haussmann have their parallels today in many metropolitan areas, among them Berlin and Shanghai.

Figure 5.3 New York City's Director of Public Works Robert Moses tours a new housing project being built in the city (Moses is on the right). While some of Moses' works were praised – particularly recreational amenities such as Jones Beach – others, such as the Cross Bronx Expressway, were broadly criticized for the number of homes destroyed and communities disrupted. *Source: Library of Congress, Prints and Photographs Division, LC-USZ62–1337834. Photograph by Walter Albertin*.

Nevertheless, it is not only single men and women, however heroic they might seem, who prove central to the growth of metropolitan areas. History, unlike the workings of the theories of the human ecologists, shows that it is also various groups and organizations that play a key role in shaping the metropolitan area – in helping to define the nature of the businesses that take root in a city, or the location of the highways and expressways, or the construction of new residential developments that take place at the outskirts. Consider one illustration. A history of the emergence of the greater Austin metropolitan area in central Texas, for example, reveals that the pivotal decision in its expansion and growth was the construction of dams on the Colorado River, begun in the late 1930s and completed more than a decade later. But actually the effort to build dams had begun years earlier, at the turn of the twentieth century, prompted by a number of local residents who were beleaguered by the constant floods that ravaged homes and businesses. Over the course of almost half a century, various groups and agencies became involved in this affair, among them the Austin Chamber of Commerce, which lobbied for dams both in Texas and in Washington, DC. When the dams were finally built and the city began an unprecedented era of expansion and growth, it was thanks to all those who had had a hand in their construction: a collection of groups and organizations that ranged from the local municipal government to the US Congress. Human agents and agencies, in other words, were responsible for the expansion of this particular place in ways that the theories of the human ecologists tended to mask.

The work of Moses, Haussmann, and countless others illustrates how powerful and dominant the active hand of human agents can be in the development of the metropolis. Highways do not just occur anywhere but take root in very specific places as a result of

Figure 5.4 Paris, as remade by Haussmann, seen here from a balloon in 1889. The familiar radial form of the city, with its wide boulevards and monuments, is actually one of the first examples of a broad-scale urban renewal project. *Source: Library of Congress, Prints and Photographs Division, LC-USZ62–94572.*

political calculations – and often at sites in which live the most vulnerable and powerless people, who are thus unable by themselves to oppose or resist such construction. People and groups contest the location of those highways. And often, as the history of urban renewal has vividly shown in the United States, unfortunately, those people who have tended to lose out in the planning process tend to be those who are poorer and stand to lose the most from the process itself.

We shall learn even more about the details of this story in the following two chapters, which discuss the origins of suburbs as well as the great changes that took place across the globe and to the metropolis after World War II.

MAKING THE CITY BETTER   5.1

Zoning

While the market plays a considerable role in determining land use arrangements within urban areas, local governments have regulated land use within their jurisdictions for a long time. Most of the earlier cases of land use regulation involved municipal governments passing ordinances in order to criminalize land uses that the government, and usually the majority of local property owners, found undesirable. In the United Kingdom, for instance, many such regulations originated from the common law concept of nuisance, which prevented property owners from using their land in a way that injured other property owners.

However, in the early twentieth century a new concept arose called "zoning." Unlike previous land use regulation, in which local governments would exercise police power to outlaw pre-existing threats to public health and safety, zoning ordinances are preventative in nature because they designate land for particular purposes without outlawing land uses that already exist. In other words, zoning establishes and preserves the status quo for each particular area of the city.

In 1916, New York City passed what is generally considered to be the first modern zoning ordinance. The ordinance came about as a result of complaints from wealthy residents over Jewish garment makers and their employees moving into neighborhoods, and high buildings blocking out sunshine and air, both of which lowered residential property values. The ordinance effectively separated areas of New York City into districts and mandated that new development of certain types only take place in certain districts. So, while garment makers did not have to leave areas of the city that were zoned for residential, single-family, or two-family dwellings only, no more garment makers could move in. This distinction was mainly included as a way for zoning to achieve one of its primary objectives – keeping out unwanted neighbors – while still maintaining a defendable level of constitutionality.

One strong criticism of zoning is that it began as, and remains today, a tool frequently used to protect affluent property owners from anything, or anyone, who may lower property values. When the concept of zoning first arose, many planners and landowners in favor of zoning saw it as tool capable of protecting the suburban home against the encroachment of urban blight and danger. By separating land uses deemed "incompatible," single-family homes were essentially severed from everything except for other single-family homes, including high-rise apartment buildings and other cramped living environments that minorities could afford to call home. As a result, large-scale suburban developments for white, single-family households flourished, while poor and minority residents were left with fewer areas zoned for their existence – all in the name of protecting property values. See Cullingworth and Caves (2009) for further discussion of the themes presented in this box.

Urban growth, institutions, and human agents

Cities can become very large and complex places, sites that turn into vast and extensive numbers of businesses, people, and the various communities they create. When this happens, it is useful to change our orientation from thinking simply about cities as places that range between small (e.g., the town or village down the road from where you live) and large settlements (or what we have come to call the metropolis). In this chapter we have looked at the metropolis in greater detail, covering the social and spatial map created decades ago by Ernest Burgess through to the ideas and concepts that we use to talk about the expansion of the metropolis. Like all cities, metropolitan areas constantly change, and today they often grow and expand enormously. Some of this expansion is caused by the dynamics of the social and economic institutions of the city, particularly the growth of businesses and economic enterprises. But some is very much due to the work of particular individuals, such as Robert Moses, or groups – small clusters of people who become the entrepreneurs and driving forces of the city. Other metropolitan areas, however, are stretched and expanded primarily by powerful local governments, as in China (see Chapter 11). These and other principles we have discussed in this chapter provide the basic concepts with which you can begin to think about metropolitan growth in general. Visit the book's companion website at www.wiley.com/go/cities for examples, case studies, and discussion questions, plus a list of useful films and other media, that are relevant to this chapter.

Critical thinking questions

1 Does the metropolis where you live look anything like the concentric zone map that Ernest Burgess used to describe industrial Chicago?

2 Are there distinctive "natural areas" in the place where you live? How would you describe them? What makes them "natural"?

3 In some metropolitan areas, such as Paris, the wealthier districts tend to be located toward the center whereas the poorer areas tend to be located on the periphery? Why do you think there is a difference between this pattern and that found in many US metropolitan areas?

4 Finally, can the principles invoked by the human ecologists, such as competition for space and density, still be used to depict the expansion of metropolitan areas, especially in non-Western settings?

Suggested reading

Nels Anderson, *The Hobo: The Sociology of the Homeless Man* (Chicago, IL: University of Chicago Press, 1923). An engaging and path-breaking account of the places where Chicago's homeless men made their lives in the 1920s.

Robert Caro, *Power Broker: Robert Moses and the Fall of New York* (New York: Vintage, 1975). Considered one of the most influential works written during the twentieth century, this book shows the many ways in which one figure, Robert Moses, helped to shape the development of New York City and its nearby regions.

David Harvey, *The Urban Experience* (Baltimore, MD: Johns Hopkins University Press, 1989). Provides an excellent review of Harvey's neo-Marxist interpretations of the contemporary metropolis.

Amos Hawley, *Human Ecology* (New York: Ronald Press Co., 1950). The most sophisticated and imaginative exposition of human ecology ever written. Hawley examines and theorizes cities using such basic elements as population and social organization.

Notes

1. These and the following numbers on population can be found online, identified as "World Urbanization Prospects: The 2007 Revision/ Population Database" on the United Nations website. The data can be easily accessed and manipulated to obtain a range of information on the world population today.

2. For a fascinating view of the work of Robert Moses and his great influence in shaping metropolitan New York City, see Caro (1975).

CHAPTER 6

The origins and development of suburbs

KEY TOPICS

→ The definition of the suburb, and the various forms that suburban development has taken across time and from one society to another.

→ The ways that suburbs conform to, and deviate from, conventional assumptions regarding social homogeneity.

→ The role of culture in creating demand for suburban housing.

→ The roles of technology, policy, and new construction techniques in generating the supply of suburban housing.

→ How suburbanization and increased homeownership affected families' social and economic wellbeing.

→ Changes in contemporary suburbs, such as the increase in gated and privatized communities.

→ Ways that suburbs as places provide security, community, and identity.

Contents

Introduction to Cities: How Place and Space Shape Human Experience,
First Edition. Xiangming Chen, Anthony M. Orum, and Krista E. Paulsen.
© 2013 Xiangming Chen, Anthony M. Orum, and Krista E. Paulsen.
Published 2013 by Blackwell Publishing Ltd.

The word "suburb" often conjures up visions of identical houses with expansive lawns, occupied by white, middle- and upper-middle-class families with 2.5 children. In both popular culture and academic literature, we can find suburbs portrayed as homogeneous places devoid of the character and texture typical of cities (see Figure 6.1). While this stereotype denies the diversity found both within and among suburbs, it is rooted in real distinctions that exist between suburbs – at least in their ideal form – and cities. As this chapter will discuss, suburbs have long promised an antidote to the least desirable qualities of urban living, including crowding, substandard housing, and unwelcome forms of social diversity. This promise is one that resonates with many families (a majority in some societies), but its fulfillment has brought with it a fair share of unintended consequences. The extension of urban boundaries into the surrounding countryside transformed both the physical and social landscape of metropolitan areas.

This chapter first takes up the difficult work of defining the term suburb, a task complicated by the variety of communities understood as suburban and the dynamic nature of suburbs. In doing so, we contrast the low-density, primarily residential communities central to this chapter with other kinds of development found on the urban periphery in some societies. We then move on to a history of the suburb, from the eighteenth-century retreat of wealthy industrialists to the expansion of suburban living to the middle classes in the nineteenth century, through the booms in suburban housing construction occurring in 1930s Britain and the postwar United States to the current challenges facing suburbs old

Figure 6.1 The mass-produced tract homes that constitute the stereotypical image of the suburb. In reality, suburbs and their residents have always been more diverse than images like this suggest. *Source: Photo by IDuke, November 2005. http://commons.wikimedia.org/wiki/ File:Markham-suburbs.id.jpg.jpg. Licensed under the Creative Commons Attribution-Share Alike 2.5 Generic license.*

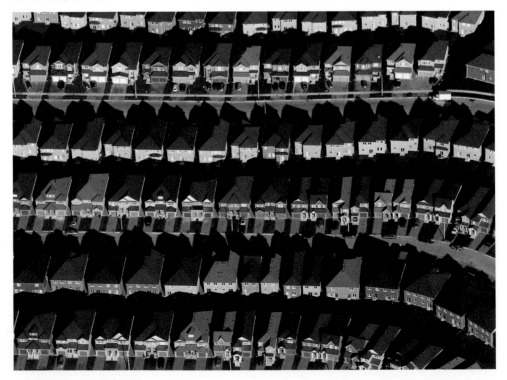

and new. We pay particular attention to the role of culture and urban living conditions in generating demand for suburban housing, and of transportation technologies and governmental policies in helping to produce the supply. We close with a discussion of suburbs as distinct kinds of places, examining how they provide identity, security, and community.

What is a suburb?
Definitions and variations

The Latin roots of the term "suburb" refer to a place under the city. This meaning likely reflected the original form of suburbs – places where marginal populations lived outside the protection and economic opportunity afforded by early walled cities. But contemporary definitions of the term are varied and often conflicting, due in part to the increasing diversity of suburban forms and functions.

The archetypical **suburb** is primarily a residential district located adjacent to, and existing in a dependent relationship with, a large city. These areas provide little in the way of employment outside the retail and service establishments that cater to residents. For most working residents, then, a substantial daily commute to the city is part of the suburban experience. The colloquial term "bedroom community" is sometimes used to characterize this type of suburb – a residential area where people sleep but don't typically work. Of course, this term neglects the fact that many suburban residents, particularly children and homemakers, spend almost of all their waking hours in suburbs, and makes invisible the service employees who live and work there. This archetypical suburb corresponds to the definition offered by historian Kenneth T. Jackson, who is among the leading experts on US suburbs. His work *Crabgrass Frontier* characterizes suburbs as having a primarily residential function and being a substantial distance from workplaces; housing residents of middle- to upper-class status; and exhibiting low density in their spatial form (Jackson 1985: p. 11). In making this characterization, Jackson calls attention to many of the qualities of suburbs that have most concerned urban scholars, including their tendency toward social homogeneity, economic dependence on cities, and sprawling geographic form.

> **suburbs** Areas on the periphery of cities, traditionally considered to contain primarily low-density residential development.

It is important to examine each of these dimensions of suburbs with a critical eye, and to measure each against what we know of suburbs both historically and today. In examining social homogeneity, the early railroad suburbs surrounding Chicago, New York City, Boston, and Philadelphia illustrate the utility and the shortcomings of such a definition. Founded as residential retreats for affluent businessmen and their families, communities such as Scarsdale, outside New York City, and Brookline, near Boston, were home to the very wealthy as well as the domestics, gardeners, and laborers who served their homes and families. Thus, while the landholding class was relatively affluent and racially homogeneous, their suburban lifestyle necessitated the presence of a substantial working class too. As smaller bungalow-style homes designed to be cared for without the help of servants came to predominate in the 1920s and 1930s, suburbs became more homogeneous in terms of social class. The continuing expansion of suburban homeownership to middle- and working-class families after World War II further deepened this pattern, and today it is common to see suburban neighborhoods where houses are within only a very narrow price range.

How do suburbs look when we examine other dimensions of social diversity, such as religion or race and ethnicity? For reasons detailed below (see "The role of policy in suburban expansion"), many suburbs were, by design, off limits to racial, ethnic, and religious minorities. Again, the early US railroad suburbs complicate this model, as the servant class did not necessarily share the white Anglo-Saxon Protestant background of their employers. Servants were more likely to be recent immigrants and Catholics. In his extensive research on African American suburbanization, historian Andrew Wiese finds that affluent suburbs were home to significant numbers of black domestics; elsewhere, African Americans built or bought suburban homes in subdivisions that ranged from unplanned communities with minimal municipal services to elite (though still segregated) areas with all the amenities of similar white suburbs (Wiese 2004). Today we see that racial and ethic minorities, including a large number of immigrants, make their homes in suburban communities, particularly "first ring" or near-in suburbs.

In emphasizing suburbs' economic dependence on cities, we risk losing sight of other dimensions of suburban diversity. Early suburbs that provided bedroom communities for affluent whites *incidentally* provided workplaces for many others, but a number of suburbs were created *expressly* as workplaces. **Industrial suburbs**, communities anchored by large factories, were actually among the earliest forms of suburban expansion, dating from the nineteenth century. Here the intent was not to create distance between home and work but quite the opposite: Factories and housing could be built near each another on previously undeveloped land, providing potential benefits to employers and workers alike.

industrial suburbs Developments on the metropolitan periphery anchored by manufacturing or other industrial facilities, typically including worker housing as well.

edge city Joel Garreau's term for clusters of dense commercial and residential land use located at the urban periphery.

technoburb Robert Fishman's term for areas on the urban periphery that have developed their own socioeconomic viability.

A contemporary manifestation of the economically self-sufficient suburb is the **edge city**, a concept offered by journalist Joel Garreau to describe large, multi-faceted developments on the outskirts of cities such as Boston, Washington, DC, and Atlanta. Responding to the same phenomenon, historian Robert Fishman applies the term **technoburb** to socioeconomically viable areas that are peripheral to central cities (Fishman 1987b; Garreau 1992). These concepts describe an important shift in the suburban form toward increased autonomy: edge cities and technoburbs provide substantial commercial, office, and retail space in addition to residences. Typically built along interstates or other substantial transportation corridors, these new quasi-urban spaces often take shape on land that was forest or farm just a few decades ago. Tyson's Corner, located outside Washington, DC, is often mentioned as an early and archetypical model of the edge city; Fishman offers California's Silicon Valley or Massachusetts' Route 128 corridor as archetypical technoburbs. In such places, the shopping mall takes the place of the main street, providing the retail, service, and entertainment options found in other types of towns but enclosing them all within private spaces. Surrounding these malls are sparkling office towers or sprawling corporate campuses, with plenty of parking and, in some cases, a mass transit hub. This development pattern has become common across the United States, and can also describe far-flung districts such as La Defense outside Paris (see Figure 6.2), Sandton outside Johannesburg, Santa Fe in suburban Mexico City, and Anting outside Shanghai (see Chapter 11).

Autonomous peripheral developments such as these call attention not only to the increasing economic self-sufficiency of suburbs but also to the third element of Jackson's definition: their sprawling geographic form. **Sprawl**, or suburban sprawl, refers to often minimally planned, low-density urban development, typically expanding beyond recognizable boundaries (Bruegmann 2005). As suburbs grow, they continually extend the boundary between developed and undeveloped land. Older suburbs that were once at the periphery may age in undesirable ways, often due to disinvestment, and newer developments on the outskirts may attract investment. As geographer David Harvey has pointed out, greater profits can typically be made by building on new land than by maintaining or restoring older properties,

sprawl The extensive growth and spread of people and institutions across metropolitan areas.

motivating the continual encroachment into what was once countryside. A similar pattern can be seen with the spread of residential areas, as new developments offering the latest amenities are built on increasingly distant undeveloped parcels. New communities are often assumed to be free from the kinds of problems found in older and urban neighborhoods, and demand for them depresses the prices of older housing. Responding to recent dramatic increases in fuel prices, some urban scholars have suggested that the pattern of suburban sprawl may radically change as higher commute costs make central-city residences more attractive. Such a turn might be mediated, however, by the benefits associated with newer dwellings and suburban school districts (Leinberger 2008).

Alternative suburban forms

So far we have described the type of suburban development most common in Canada, the United Kingdom, and the United States. This is in part an artifact of the concept of the suburb, which in its common usage describes the kind of development typically found there. Moreover, the suburban form is so common in these countries that sustained scholarly attention has been focused there on the development of suburbs and their impact on cities and societies. But it is worth taking a moment here to contrast the familiar suburban form at the core of this chapter with the types of development seen elsewhere.

The forms that development takes on the edges of African, Asian, European, and Latin American cities further complicate conventional definitions of the suburb. For instance,

Figure 6.2 The edge city mode of development is not limited to the United States. In Paris, La Defense conforms to Garreau's definition of an edge city, as do areas in other major European and Asian cities. *Source: http://commons.wikimedia.org/wiki/File:Esplanade-de-la-defense.jpg. Wikimedia Commons.*

suburbs in these regions are more likely to have multi-family structures, including high-rise developments. In some cases these are part of relatively dense suburban communities, and in others a small number of towers are surrounded by green spaces in plans reminiscent of Le Corbusier's radiant city (see Exploring further 2.1). The relative lack of multi-family and attached dwellings in US suburbs illustrates the exceptional importance that Americans place on the freestanding single-family home and the private yard or garden.

In many European cities, suburbs are home to the poor and working class. During the late 1960s and early 1970s, Sweden's Million Programme provided over one million government-funded homes and apartments, often at the edge of cites (see Figure 6.3). While the architecture of what came to be called the "concrete suburbs" was criticized, the project provided homes for families of a variety of means during a time when private units were scarce. As private housing units became more available, those with the means to choose their housing left, and many immigrants moved into vacant Programme units. Programme housing was subsequently associated with crime, unemployment, and social isolation, but has since become the site of increased investment in both social programs and the physical plant (Hall and Vidén 2005; Demsteader 2007). Similarly, French *banlieues* are suburban areas crowded with public or council housing. Like the Swedish suburbs, the *banlieues* are home to significant immigrant populations and sites of economic disadvantage. In 2005 they were sites of uprisings in which local youths, whose unemployment rate was some *four times* the French average, set nearly 9000 cars ablaze during three weeks of violence (BBC News 2005). These events called

Figure 6.3 Swedish Programme housing in Malmö. High-rise apartments are common in European suburbs and elsewhere, but epitomize the density that Americans were seeking to avoid in moving to the city's edge. *Source: Photo by Fred J. http://commons.wikimedia.org/wiki/ User:Fred_J. This image is licensed under the Creative Commons Attribution 1.0 Generic license.*

attention to the very different life chances of *banlieue* residents, where limited educational and employment opportunities and police practices perceived as heavy-handed find their US parallel in inner-city ghettos rather than suburbs.

The same pattern of suburban poverty can be found in a number of other cities, including many in developing nations (see Chapter 10). Populations with limited resources have often made their own housing and communities on pockets of otherwise unoccupied land, and this is most likely found on the urban fringe. Although these residents may not hold title to their homes, and are in some instances considered squatters, some of their communities have endured for many years – for instance, Morro de Providencia, a *favela* in Rio de Janeiro, dates from the 1880s. In other cases, poor or powerless populations have been forced to live outside more economically and politically powerful cities. The South African Apartheid regime forced black Africans out of cities and into townships on the urban periphery (Davis 2006). These townships were often located near mines and other industries that relied upon a largely black labor force. As is the case with the French *banlieues*, *favelas* and townships occupy the same geographic proximity to major cities as conventional suburbs, and, while their residents often depend on these cities for employment, they differ vastly in the quality of life enjoyed by residents and the political power wielded by these communities.

Suburban development of a different kind in rapidly urbanizing countries such as China and India is associated with both the high and lower ends of the class spectrum (see Chapter 10). In recent years, globalization has led to the export of American-style suburbs across the globe. For instance, about an hour outside Beijing one can find the *other* Orange County – a community of American-style stucco townhouses and single-family homes designed by a Southern California architect. This transplanted suburban landscape symbolizes a double transfer of influence from the core to the periphery: America to China and central city to suburb.

The diversity of forms that development on the urban edge can take complicates any definition of suburbs. Although all of the variations examined here share some of the conventional dimensions of a suburb – social homogeneity, economic dependence upon cities, and sprawling geographic forms – they do not necessarily reflect all of those dimensions at once, nor do they reflect them in conventional ways. For instance, edge cities or technoburbs undermine the assumption that suburbs depend economically upon older central cities, but they adopt the sprawling form indicative of suburban development. Furthermore, these types of places might rely upon older central cities for something other than employment – for instance, those who live and work in the edge city may adopt the identity associated with the central city (i.e., cheering for the city's sports teams, or saying they hail from Atlanta or Milan or Johannesburg). An important question is how we might adapt a definition of the term suburb to acknowledge suburbs' diverse economies, geographies, and populations while still keeping it focused enough to be useful. We invite you to take up that question as we detail the origin and proliferation of suburban development.

A brief history of suburban development

The original suburbs

In the **walking cities** of the early United States and Europe, economic and social opportunities depended upon proximity to the urban center. Thus, wealthy residents both lived and worked in the city proper, where the most fashionable addresses could be found. For most merchants and entrepreneurs, home and work

walking city The dense, compact forms that cities took before the wide adoption of powered transportation technologies.

combined in one building, and access to markets required working and living in the central city. In a time when transportation depended on muscle power (horses for the affluent; walking for everyone else), these urban centers were quite compact – far smaller than contemporary central business districts. For instance, the mercantile district known as the "City of London" was about one mile square, and understandably quite dense. Like other walking cities, including early New York City, London's outskirts were left to those who could not afford to live in town, and to enterprises that required extensive land holdings. These included diverse and often noxious land uses such as slaughterhouses, tanneries, and other industry, as well as agriculture and shantytowns – certainly not the setting one associates with the contemporary suburban ideal.

It may come as a surprise, then, that the first emergence of what we would recognize as a residential suburb can be traced to eighteenth-century London. While urban locations were economically beneficial to the growing merchant class, the radical diversity of the central city proved challenging socially. Here the affluent mingled with laborers and beggars, and the most respectable families lived in proximity to dubious urban entertainments. Historian Robert Fishman cites cultural change within the upper classes – specifically, an increased desire for privacy, and a belief that women and children should be sheltered from the public realm, both related to teachings of Evangelical Christianity at that time – with the move to more rural parcels outside the city limits.

Weekend country homes or villas provided affluent families with a means of escaping the city's less desirable qualities, and flourished during the early 1700s. These were essentially second homes, used as a retreat from the primary residence in town. Drawing inspiration from villas outside Rome and Florence, as well as from the estates of the English aristocracy, these large homes with expansive grounds bolstered the class status of their owners by providing physical distance from the poor. Furthermore, families whose fortunes came from shipping, banking, or manufacturing could live a life that looked very much like that of the landed nobility. Around 1790, men began commuting by carriage to work in the city, returning home to their families in the evening (Fishman 1987b). Still, a full-time suburban lifestyle was not immediately adopted by everyone who could afford to do so. For instance, in Manchester, industrialists continued to build townhouses near their urban warehouses until the 1820s. But, by the time Engels wrote his famous work in the 1840s (see Studying the city 2.1), they too had decamped to the countryside, turning a tidy profit as they converted their former townhouses into office and industrial space (Fishman 1987a).

In the United States, too, development of commuter suburbs was preceded by the construction of opulent country homes a relatively short distance from major cities. As in Britain, these ostentatious estates allowed their owners to solidify their class status by emulating the European aristocracy, often through the use of architectural styles that mimicked the homes of the nobility. The mansions of the Gold Coast section of New York's Long Island are indicative of this model (see Figure 6.4). Here F. W. Woolworth, Marshall Field, Otto Kahn, William K. Vanderbilt, and Payne Whitney, among other wealthy retailers, investors, and industrialists, spent their fortunes on lavish homes with pools, tennis courts, formal gardens, and game preserves. Both the mansions and the elaborate parties hosted there were pinnacles of ostentation and consumption (Baxandall and Ewen 2001).

The first gated communities in the United States arose around this time. Older gated communities can be argued to have existed in Europe and other places, when cities relied on walls, moats, and gates to protect their populations from potential invasions, but, if we understand a gated community as an exclusive residential enclave surrounded by walls or natural barriers, the first cases are typically attributed to the late-nineteenth-century United

States. These included Tuxedo Park, New York, which resembled contemporary elite gated communities not only in its use of gates and fences but also in its simultaneous development of a country club that all residents were expected to join. In St. Louis, private streets insulated the homes of the wealthy, as did gates in the residential enclaves favored by Hollywood's elite in Los Angeles (Jackson 1985; Blakely and Snyder 1998). Although gated communities were not typical during this early era, their exclusivity helped to associate gates with social status and encouraged the proliferation of gated communities in the late twentieth century.

Culture and the demand for suburban living

Although early elite suburbs housed relatively few residents, and many provided only part-time residences, their existence and association with the good life helped to elevate suburban living as a cultural ideal. This was supported by nineteenth-century popular literature and advice books emphasizing the benefits of suburban living for families. Fresh air, the argument went, would benefit children's health and development, and husbands and wives would become happy helpmates as they worked together in home and garden. These works emphasized the pleasures of homeownership, glorifying simple tasks such as yard work and home repair (Nicolaides and Wiese 2006). The values of self-sufficiency and entrepreneurialism, and the benefits of a quasi-rural environment, were also reflected in urban planning theory of the time. As discussed in Exploring further 2.1, Ebenezer Howard's Garden City plan promised a delicate balance of the finest qualities of the city – culture, science, and social support – and of the country, which he saw as the source of both industry and inspiration. Residents of this utopia, a diverse mix of professionals and tradespersons, would construct their own homes with financing from

Figure 6.4 The former Phipps home on Long Island (now Old Westbury Gardens) is typical of the mansions built by US industrialists to mimic the estates of the English nobility. This model of the suburban "good life" is reproduced through the current era in the United States and globally. Source: Photo © Jim Lopes/istockphoto.

small mutual aid societies (Howard 1902; Hall 2002). This ideal still shapes what many homeseekers hope to find in suburban communities.

The plans of Ebenezer Howard and his peers, and the literature and advice books of their era, suggested that nature was benevolent and restorative. In early US and Canadian history, nature had provided a source of livelihood to rural residents and a source of anxiety to pioneers. The closing of the frontier and increasing shift to an industrialized economy meant that for many people – particularly city residents – the natural world became something of a novelty. Romanticized images of the home surrounded by a domesticated natural landscape suggested to city dwellers that suburbs were indeed the antidote to city life. Although the spatial forms of suburbs vary, green spaces in the form of lawns and gardens, landscaped boulevards, or wooded perimeters continue to provide residents with a connection with some form of nature (see Making the city better 6.1). Importantly, this was not the nature of the wild frontier but a carefully manicured version of nature, tamed and benign. The suburbs promised a house in a park, where nature would give her gifts but withhold her threats. Snakes and rodents could hardly hide in carefully mowed lawns, and wild beasts would find no place to lurk in meticulous flowerbeds. Even the architecture of the suburbs contributed to the prominence of nature. The bungalow, the most popular home style during the suburban expansion of the interwar years, combined a low, earthbound exterior with an interior that showcased the beauty of natural materials. Homes derived from this style populated many of the first mass-produced suburbs throughout the 1920s and 1930s.

The ideal of benevolent nature contrasted with definitions of cities as unsafe or undesirable. Crowding presented one problem, as it deprived families of privacy and thus compromised ideals of morality. Traces of this ideology can be seen in the work of social activists who railed against tenement conditions in the cities (see Chapter 8). In urban apartments, many family members, often representing multiple generations, would crowd into just a few rooms; bathroom facilities were often shared with another family; and access to fresh air and natural light was limited (Wright 1983). These conditions facilitated the spread of disease, as did the poor quality of sanitation and water supplies.

Crowding was not the only problem associated with cities. Popular-culture representations of cities portrayed them as moral wastelands where the otherwise upright citizens would be tempted by gambling, drugs, and illicit sex. Hustlers and pickpockets were presumed to lurk around every corner, waiting for their next mark (Cronon 1991). While crime is certainly a rational fear, urban crime was often blamed on the immigrants and racial/ethnic or religious minorities who populated cities. Urban diversity increased the likelihood that residents would not share common values, or even a common language. This diversity caused tensions among neighbors living in very close quarters, and became the basis for stereotyping and scapegoating. It also motivated the racial and ethnic exclusion that, as we discuss below, ensured a high degree of homogeneity in suburbs.

Developers also cultivated demand for suburban homes by playing upon ideals of self-sufficiency and thrift. Advertisements for tract homes asked "Why pay rent?" and emphasized low monthly payments while neglecting high interest rates and other difficult financing conditions. As a result of deceptive advertisements and exploitative lending practices, many households found themselves overextended and lost their homes to foreclosure – a tragic outcome repeated in the early twenty-first century (Hayden 2003). But, at the same time, the availability of homes on credit and the comparison to renting made the acquisition of a home a symbol of having arrived financially. Some scholars have argued that the expansion of suburban homeownership also served efforts to curb the spread of socialist and communist movements in the United States. Homeownership would, the argument goes, provide citizens

MAKING THE CITY BETTER   6.1

The lawn

The notion of having a lawn surrounding every house is one so taken for granted that many believe this has always been the suburban way. But this is not the case. While English landowners were the first to regularly tend plots of land resembling the modern-day lawn, maintaining such property was an expensive process, and lawns were typically only utilized as venues for large social events. Early lawns were cut with a scythe or grazed down by sheep or goats, and most early suburbanites did not possess the time, money, or skills required to maintain a lawn through such methods (Jenkins 1994).

During the late nineteenth century, new inventions such as the inexpensively manufactured lawnmower and the garden hose, as well as the proliferation of cheap meadow-like grass seeds from Europe, caused lawns to explode in popularity, particularly in the United States (Jenkins 1994). As suburban development spread across North America and more people fled the cities every year in favor of their own suburban plot, it became highly desirable to own, maintain, and show off lawns – so desirable, in fact, that the American Frank J. Scott had the following to say about lawns in 1870:

> Whoever spends the early hours of one summer, while the dew spangles the grass, in pushing these grass-cutters over a velvety lawn, breathing the fresh sweetness of the morning air and the perfume of new mown hay, will never rest contented again in the city. (Quoted in Teyssot 1991: p. 1)

In the United States today, the zoning of residential land so as to ensure very large lawns and gardens is a way of keeping neighborhoods economically segregated. And, to ensure aesthetic harmony among homes in a development, many homeowners' associations also specify the type and even the shade of grass that residents must maintain in their lawns. Failure to maintain grass of the proper length, hue, and species can result in stiff fines. In the United States alone, about $6 billion a year is spent maintaining lawns, the majority of metropolitan water is used watering lawns, and massive amounts of pesticides and fertilizers drain into local waterways, threatening natural habitats and drinking water supplies (*E Magazine* 2001). In attempting to make the city better, advocates of the carefully manicured lawn have created a host of unintended consequences.

In response to this problem, many neighborhood activists have started movements to replace lawns with more productive and environmentally friendly alternatives. Author and designer Fritz Haeg encourages people to "eat their lawns," replacing typical grass with vegetable gardens to improve health, help the environment, and counter the boring homogeneity of suburban landscapes (GlimmerGuy 2010). Other alternatives include eliminating the needs for watering and fertilizer by encouraging natural plant life to grow, or developing neighborhoods with far less lawn space to begin with. While each of these options promises to make suburban neighborhoods more environmentally sustainable, they struggle against over a century of cultural preferences. It remains to be seen whether the bulk of American homeseekers in particular will accept a suburban home without the requisite lawn.

with a stake in the capitalist economy. A 20- to 30-year mortgage meant that any interruption in salary – such as that potentially created by a strike – would jeopardize one's home as well as the investment therein. Suburban developer William Levitt had a slightly different take on the issue. He is reported to have said, "No man who owns a house and lot can be a communist. He has too much to do" (Hayden 2006: p. 276).

EXPLORING FURTHER   6.1

Gender and suburban life

As we learn about cities and suburbs, it is important to keep in mind that these places were and are experienced differently by men and women, adults and children. This was certainly the case for the houses, business, and streets of the walking city, but it was suburban expansion that began drawing new attention to the ways in which gender would be mapped onto the metropolitan form. With the transition from cities to suburbs, the cramped dwellings that had ensured men and women would share the same spaces within the home gave way to spacious houses where the genders might live nearly separate lives. Furthermore, the conventional bedroom-community type of suburb became relatively sex-segregated as husbands and fathers went to work in the morning leaving women and children on their own for the day.

Scholars Daphne Spain (1992) and Gwendolyn Wright (1983) have explored the ways in which suburban house styles of different eras reflect changing assumptions about gender and family. For instance, the Victorian home was designed to emphasize privacy, in keeping with the kinds of moral concerns discussed in this chapter. Design features such as large entry halls prevented solicitors and casual callers from seeing the family in their private realm. The genders were also kept apart through the use of separate leisure spaces: after dinner, women would "withdraw" to the drawing room, while men kept company with one another in the library. In the early twentieth century, when suburbs expanded to include less affluent families and privacy concerns relaxed, the popular bungalow style would allow visitors to enter directly into the familial space of the "living room."

In the 1950s, the ranch-style home presented another turn. The Victorians and the bungalow had walled off the kitchen from the home's other living spaces, but the ranch introduced an open floor plan that allowed the homemaker to interact with her family while she cooked meals or cleaned up afterward. While the assumption that the woman of the house *would* be the one to perform these roles remained steadfast, the open floor plan placed her on a slightly more equal footing by allowing her to interact with others as she did so. Contemporary suburban homebuilders now recognize that women are responsible for the great majority of home-buying decisions. Builders and marketers both cater to and flatter women's roles in the home with features such as "command centers" (small desks in the kitchen) and spaces and features that allow for presumably feminine indulgences (such as wine coolers and jetted tubs) (Paulsen 2008).

Suburbs changed not only women's place within the home but also their place within the community. Cities had allowed extended families to live in close proximity (often in the same unit) but the suburban single-family home was designed to shelter a smaller nuclear family of parents and their minor children. As such, women – who were at home with the children for much of the day – were isolated from their own mothers and sisters and the assistance and knowledge that they might provide.

Isolation figures prominently in accounts of women's lives in the suburbs, whether fact or fiction. In some cases the isolation caused practical frustrations, as shopping and other errands almost always required a car and many households' cars were used by men to commute to work. The consequences of this could be nothing short of tragic. D. J. Waldie writes in *Holy Land: A Suburban Memoir* (1996) of the neighbor and friend of his mother who came to the door one day in a panic after her baby had stopped breathing. Without cars or phones, the women could do nothing to save the infant.

Isolation took a psychological toll, too, as women were largely disconnected from the public realm and thus from the majority of pursuits recognized as important or consequential. Author Betty Friedan spoke of a "problem that has no name," or women's (particularly white, middle-class women's) dissatisfaction with a life that would seem gratifying in material terms but provided little spiritual or intellectual sustenance. Despite an abundance of new consumer goods designed to improve their lives – color-coordinated kitchen appliances and the like – women felt increasingly frustrated. As Friedan wrote:

> The problem lay buried, unspoken for many years in the minds of American women. It was a strange stirring, a sense of dissatisfaction, a yearning that women suffered in the middle of the twentieth century in the United States. Each suburban housewife struggled with it alone. As she made the beds, shopped for groceries, matched slipcover material, ate peanut butter sandwiches with her children, chauffeured Cub Scouts and Brownies, lay beside her husband at night, she was afraid to ask even of herself the silent question: "Is this all?" (Friedan 2001 [1963]: p. 1)

The second wave of the feminist movement in the United States was in part an effort to name, and correct, this problem. One strategy was consciousness-raising, wherein women would meet in their homes, often over coffee, to discuss problems that might seem explicitly private – such as domestic abuse – but that would, through the efforts of feminist activists, come to be seen as public issues.

In calling attention to the problems that suburban expansion posed to gender equality and gender relations, it is easy to lose sight of the ways in which suburbs improved the lives of those who lived there – including women. Single-family suburban homes certainly provided many more material comforts than urban tenement apartments. And, while new appliances and the like may not provide much spiritual sustenance, they did free women from certain types of domestic drudgery. Many women also found pleasure in the creative expressions that homeownership afforded, whether decorating, gardening, or cooking. It is also important to keep in mind that the kinds of troubles experienced by suburban women are rooted in race and class privilege. The isolated, overly sheltered life of the white middle-class suburban housewife often looked quite appealing to women who lacked decent housing or who had no choice *but* to work outside the home.

Early suburban diversity

The grand estates of the wealthy and early planned communities such as Tuxedo Park were certainly not the only types of communities to be found on the urban periphery. The late nineteenth and early twentieth centuries also saw the proliferation of industrial suburbs. Industrial development extended to the peripheries of cities such as Chicago, Detroit, and Montreal, and workers followed. The accompanying suburban developments took a number of forms. In some cases, workers continued to live in cities and made use of the same transit lines that moved white-collar suburbanites to their urban jobs. At the beginning and end of the workday, professionals living in the suburbs and working in the city rode the trains one way, and city-dwelling factory workers rode the same lines in the opposite direction. In Flint, near Detroit, workers inhabited a "tent city" outside the General Motors plants until residential construction caught up with demand. Pullman, south of Chicago, served as something of a model town until the 1880s. The Pullman Palace Car Company, a manufacturer of luxury railroad cars, provided factory workers with carefully planned housing and municipal services in the vain hope that this might forestall labor unrest. In Montreal, working-class suburbs provided the labor necessary to expand industry outside

owner-built suburb
Areas outside cities
where property owners
have constructed their
own dwellings.

the urban center. Although Montreal's suburbs were far different than the uniformly wealthy suburbs simultaneously appearing throughout North America, they developed their own form of homogeneity as ethnic segregation within industries led to segregation within nearby neighborhoods (Lewis 2001; Nicolaides and Wiese 2006: pp. 147–150).

Throughout the twentieth century, **owner-built suburbs** provided another alternative to the thoughtfully planned and relatively affluent communities associated with idealized suburbs. As they had in the days of walking cities, poor and working-class people, hopeful of finding a home of their own, continued to make their way to the urban edge. The places they found often lacked infrastructure such as water, gas, and paved roads but could offer inexpensive land and freedom from the building and ownership restrictions then typical of planned suburban communities. During the Great Migration, owner-built African American suburbs could be found adjacent to most northern US cities; in the southwest, owner-built suburbs also provided housing for Latinos. In Toronto, the abundance of owner-built dwellings in the early twentieth century has been credited with giving a distinctly working-class cast to suburbs (Harris 1996).

Construction typically proceeded slowly, for property owners would build only as time and finances allowed. Homes might be built one room at a time or the garage might be built first, providing the family with shelter during construction of the main dwelling. The lack of coordination, planning, and infrastructure showed in these communities' appearances, and the uses put to yards there created a distinctive landscape. Whereas more affluent planned suburbs used land and nature primarily as a restorative, aesthetic resource, working-class suburbanites often filled their yards with vegetable gardens and small livestock, as well as cast-off goods that might someday find another use (Wiese 2004; Nicolaides and Wiese 2006). Perhaps it is because of this more disorganized appearance that owner-built suburbs are often overlooked in considering the suburban experience. Still, they provided an important dimension of suburban expansion, and for the families who built them an important source of financial security.

Transportation technologies and suburban expansion

Realization of the suburban dream was only practical to the extent that transportation technologies could efficiently bridge the distance between homes on the leafy outskirts of town and workplaces in the city. The earliest suburbs relied upon existing transportation technologies: ferries, for instance, allowed Manhattan workers to live in Brooklyn suburbs from the 1810s onwards (Jackson 1985). But, as the boundaries of suburbs continued to be pushed outward, new technologies were developed to make homes on the city's edge viable alternatives for urban workers. The omnibus, a horse-drawn carriage that could transport multiple passengers along a predictable route, aided in the expansion of suburbs in Boston and elsewhere. It became a familiar site in nineteenth-century cities despite its notoriously bumpy and uncomfortable ride. Railroads, too, found new markets as early suburbs developed (recall the discussion of industrial suburbs, above). Although railroads were constructed for long-distance travel and transport, their operators found that the demand for suburban passenger service coincided with a need for increased revenues. Railroads then began constructing suburban stations and scheduling regular service aimed at those who worked in the city. All of these transportation developments went hand-in-hand with the subdivision of once-remote parcels into house lots, and the promotion of these new suburbs based on their access to reliable transportation (Binford 1985).

As suburbs become an increasingly popular residential option, transportation technologies adapted to serve this growing market. Horse-drawn streetcars that pulled passenger cars along metal rails came to replace the rough ride of the omnibus. With the expansion of commercial power lines, electric streetcars (also called trams or trolleys, or light rail in contemporary parlance) became a familiar site in cities throughout the United States and the United Kingdom. Over 2000 miles of tram lines were built in England and Wales in the first years of the twentieth century (Nagle 1998). Not only did the streetcars serve commuters but the streetcar companies became important forces in suburban development. Perhaps the most prominent among the owners of these companies was Henry Huntington, owner of Los Angeles' Pacific Electric Railway (see Figure 6.5). Beginning in the late nineteenth century, Huntington's "red cars" connected points as far distant as Santa Monica and San Bernardino (nearly 80 miles or 128 kilometers). But the streetcar fares were not what made Huntington's vast fortune. Instead, he used the streetcar lines to increase the value of his vast property holdings. After studying where riders took the red cars for weekend pleasure trips, Huntington determined the most attractive sites for residential developments and subdivided those parcels into house lots (Jackson 1985: p. 122). He soon became one of the wealthiest real estate developers in Los Angeles, and shaped the pattern of far-flung suburban

Figure 6.5 A streetcar in suburban Los Angeles. Electric and horse-drawn streetcar lines gave form to early suburban expansion. Streetcar lines were usually privately owned, and many owners (such as Henry Huntington, who owned the Pacific Electric Railway line seen here) made the bulk of their fortunes as real estate developers. *Source: Courtesy of The Pacific Electric Railway Historical Society/Donald Duke/Jack Finn Collection/www.peryhs.org.*

development that persists today. The active role that streetcar operators such as Huntington and his counterparts across North America took in developing the suburbs suggests that the interests of developers, not simply the availability of transportation technology, advanced the explosive growth of suburbs.

Mass transit was particularly important in the development of English suburbs. There, the greatest suburban expansion occurred during the 1930s, when private automobile ownership was still outside the reach of all but the most affluent English households. Access to public transportation, whether tram line, rail, bus, or underground subway, was key to making residential parcels on the outskirts appealing to those who worked in the city. Historian Robert Fishman has argued that, because mass transit coverage in the London suburbs was so thorough, it facilitated suburban development at the low densities (eight to ten homes per acre) typically associated with US automobile suburbs (Fishman 1987a).

In the United States, the automobile was arguably the most important technology in facilitating suburban expansion. Once a novelty, automobiles became a fixture of American households by the 1930s (nationwide, 8000 automobiles were registered in 1905, or one for every 1000 or so residents; in 1935, over 22 million were registered – one for every five residents). This coincided with both a decline in public transportation and significant suburban expansion: between 1920 and 1930, suburbs of the largest US cities were growing twice as fast as their urban cores. The automobile facilitated this growth, as it opened up the possibility of developing land further from public transportation. Highways and freeways pushed the limits of suburban development even further, as the distance one could cover in a commute of reasonable time increased. In 1956, the US Interstate Highway Act provided a $26 billion federal investment in freeway construction that further subsidized suburban expansion (Jackson 1985).

Technological changes in transportation are not solely responsible for the growth of suburban communities. Such a technologically determinist view would neglect the important role of demand for this type of living arrangement. But the *kinds* of transportation upon which individual suburbs initially depended certainly played a large role in the spatial forms they took, and, in many instances, the forms they retain. The early railroad suburbs were initially isolated from one another because the stopping distance of trains required that stations be some distance apart. As a result, suburban communities looked like small towns strung out along the rail line.

streetcar suburbs
Samuel Bass Warner, Jr.'s term for communities developed as a result of streetcar, tram, or light rail lines.

Streetcar suburbs – suburban developments of the 1920s and 1930s that followed streetcar and electric railway lines – were designed to rely upon a combination of public transportation and walking. Commuters walked from home to a station or stop, and these stations in turn anchored small retail and service districts with restaurants, laundries, hair salons, drug stores, and other retailers and services one might use on the way to or from work. In many communities, these commercial districts have outlasted the presence of the streetcar stations. A similar pattern can be seen in urban areas where subways, or a mix of under- and above-ground trains, service outlying residential areas. In New York City, London, and other major metropolitan areas, subway and train stations mark the center of suburban (or formerly suburban) commercial districts, and may provide a name and identity to the neighborhoods they serve.

Suburbs designed around automobiles, particularly those built adjacent to major expressways, take a very different form. These developments have lower densities and larger lot sizes than the streetcar suburbs, and the garage or carport becomes a dominant architectural feature. Often marked by gates or entry monuments (low walls or pillars that proclaim the

MAKING THE CITY BETTER 6.2

Accommodating automobiles

The familiar suburban form of cul-de-sacs and curvilinear boulevards is certainly not the only way to accommodate the automobile. Designed in the 1920s, Radburn, New Jersey proposed a novel way in which homes, families, and automobiles might coexist. In essence, Radburn turned the conventional auto-centered design of suburbs inside out. Rather than placing streets at the center, Radburn's core was a broad green space lined with paths for bicycles and pedestrians. And, whereas many suburban plans place the garage at the front of the home, Radburn's houses faced auto-free gardens and parks, while small service alleys provided the only automotive access. Although the Depression stalled construction before Radburn was fully completed, it nevertheless models one way in which cars might be accommodated and de-emphasized.

Another model comes to us from New Urbanism, a movement of architects and scholars who promote urban design on a human scale, and, drawing upon the work of Jane Jacobs, seek to encourage both diversity and density in urban settings. They advocate a return to the gridiron plan, or at least a version of it, and suggest that design features such as narrower streets and visual interest may help to slow down traffic. And, as in the Radburn plan, New Urbanists typically send cars to the rear of homes and businesses (see Figure 6.6). This leaves the front of homes open to porches that might invite social interaction, and ensures that businesses are pedestrian-friendly rather than hiding behind a sea of parking.

Figure 6.6 Houses in suburban Kentlands, Maryland face a common green space; cars are relegated to the rear. Designed by New Urbanist firm Duany Plater-Zyberk, Kentlands demonstrates how contemporary suburban communities can encourage density and walkability. *Source: Courtesy of Duany Plater-Zyberk & Company.*

name of the development), auto-dependent suburbs have prominent borders but lack centers. Clubhouses, parks, and pools may provide gathering places for some neighborhoods, but commercial districts are generally located outside neighborhood boundaries and out of walking distance. While early suburbs generally relied on the urban "gridiron" plan, or used a modified grid in which streets curved to accentuate natural features, contemporary suburban developers (and homeseekers) tend to view the grid as inviting outsiders and permitting drivers to race through at dangerous speeds. To manage traffic and control vehicle speeds, developers rely on limited access points, cul-de-sacs, dead-end streets, and roundabouts. While these design features successfully slow traffic – a real concern for families who hope suburbs will provide safe spaces for children to play – they limit the routes one might take from one point to another, and may increase driving distances between places that are quite close when measured "as the crow flies." They may also pose a danger when emergencies such as fires and storms demand quick evacuation.

The role of policy in suburban expansion

In many places, the transportation infrastructure that facilitated suburban expansion in the United States is still in place – and may still be used on a daily basis. This makes it easy to see how roads, railways, and subways helped to create the patterns of suburban development found in metropolitan areas. Just as important was a second, invisible type of infrastructure – the policies that encouraged suburban development to take distinctive forms. These included housing subsidies to buyers, renters, or builders; support for exclusionary measures; or land use regulations. In short, the legal landscape facilitated a certain kind of metropolitan landscape.

The United Kingdom undertook a major effort to improve its housing stock in the wake of World War I. Government subsidies facilitated construction by both local housing authorities and private builders; subsidized construction accounted for about 40 percent of new homes built in the interwar period (Nagle 1998). Despite these public efforts, the United Kingdom's largest suburban expansion, during the 1930s, was largely a product of private builders working without subsidies. And build they did – some 2.7 million homes were built during the decade in England and Wales. A variety of factors propelled this expansion: pent-up demand for housing, an agricultural depression that reduced prices for rural land, and a surfeit of private savings with few investment options. These savings accounts were loaned out as 20-some-year mortgages that would make homeownership affordable to a new class of English suburbanite (Fishman 1987a). So what of policy? By the late 1930s, what had largely been countryside surrounding England's major cities – especially London – was transformed into a sprawling metropolitan fringe. Without some sort of regulatory intervention, private development could, it was feared, extend this sprawl indefinitely.

The Town and Country Planning Act of 1947 radically curtailed suburban development, as well as private land development more generally. The aim was to prevent the continual expansion of metropolitan areas, and to channel new growth into smaller cities scattered around the nation. The Act drew boundaries at the outer edge of existing suburban development, declaring the surrounding rural parcels to be protected greenbelt. This early version of what is currently referred to as an **urban limit line** curtailed further sprawl and instead channeled development back into the metropolis. The density of English suburbs thus increased at the same time that US suburbs were becoming far less dense. The Act presaged a growth control strategy that would become popular late in the twentieth century, but it also had unintended consequences. Many of those who now work in London cannot find affordable housing in the city or its near suburbs, and so must spend long hours commuting from homes outside the greenbelt to jobs in the city. Thus, while sprawl has been curtailed, many of its social costs have remained (Fishman 1987a).

urban limit line
A planning device that aims to curtail sprawl by designating boundaries between developed and undeveloped, or rural, areas.

Unlike most other developed nations, the United States lacks any substantial centralized control over land uses. What type of land use will go where is generally decided by local officials or left to the market. But this does not mean that decisions at the federal level leave no mark on locales. Most scholars of US cities and suburbs agree that federal subsidies for home mortgages were among the most important factors leading to suburban expansion, and that these are also responsible for exacerbating racial and ethnic inequalities.

Anyone who has even considered buying a home knows that financing this purchase is no easy task. But the terms of a contemporary mortgage are much easier than they once were. The familiar 20 percent (or less) down payment followed by 30 years of monthly installments reflects a restructuring of the home loan dating from the 1930s. Before that time, borrowers were accustomed to 40 percent down payments and loan terms of 2 to 11 years. At the end of that term, borrowers paid the balance as a "balloon" payment or refinanced, if possible (Jackson 1985; Schwartz 2006). During the Great Depression, when homeowners could not easily refinance, these terms led to skyrocketing foreclosures (a trend repeated in the financial crisis of 2008–2010). To minimize foreclosures and stimulate construction, President Roosevelt's "New Deal" policies included new means of borrowing for a home. The first initiative was the Home Owners' Loan Corporation (HOLC), begun in 1933, which essentially acted as a federally subsidized bank. The HOLC made loans with terms very similar to those seen for contemporary mortgages: the buyer would provide 20 percent of the home price as a down payment and make equal monthly payments for the duration of the loan (usually 15 years). Within a year, the HOLC was replaced by the Federal Housing Administration (FHA). Unlike the HOLC, the FHA did not directly loan money to homebuyers; instead, it guaranteed loans made by private banks. Should a homebuyer default on his or her mortgage, the FHA would protect the bank against losses. This allowed banks to issue more loans, expanding the pool of would-be homebuyers. The terms of the FHA also permitted a larger portion of the home's value to be financed, and extended the length of the loan to the now familiar 30 years.

You might reasonably wonder why these changes in mortgage policies and practices led to the growth of suburbs; they might just as easily have led to increased investment in urban housing. The answer lies in the *types of dwellings* that the FHA preferred for its secured mortgages. Like any party with a stake in a loan, the FHA (and HOLC before it) needed to have confidence in the value of the property it was standing behind. If a homeowner defaulted 10 or 12 years into a mortgage, would the property's value still outweigh the balance of the loan? To make sure this was the case, the FHA used a rigorous set of assessment criteria. It enforced minimum construction standards on dwellings, and evaluated neighborhoods for desirability and stability. While the first measure is regarded quite positively (although it created a bias against older properties in central cities), the second takes a great deal of the blame for increasing residential segregation in the United States. When evaluating neighborhoods, FHA assessors took into account not only physical aspects of the area – such as the age and quality of housing stock, the likelihood of flooding, the number of occupied versus vacant properties, and the like – but also social dimensions including the race, immigrant status, social class, and occupation of residents. Each neighborhood was then ranked from A down through D, corresponding to color ratings of green for the highest quality to red for the lowest. Many of these evaluations were blatantly racist – for instance, remarking on the "infiltration of goats, rabbits, and dark skinned babies" in one San Gabriel, California neighborhood (Nicolaides and Wiese 2006: p. 243) – while others simply used the presence of minorities and immigrants to justify low ratings. Homes in neighborhoods coded D, or "red," were routinely denied

redlining The
systematic denial of
mortgages and other
forms of lending in
minority communities.

restrictive covenants
Agreements prohibiting
the sale of property to
members of racial,
ethnic, or religious
minorities.

mortgages, and the term **redlining** is thus used to describe the systematic denial of mortgages and other forms of credit in minority neighborhoods.

The biases inherent in the FHA lending standards worked in tandem with a second set of exclusionary practices. **Restrictive covenants** (also called deed restrictions) prohibited the sale of a given property to specified ethnic, racial, and religious minorities. These regulations could be drawn up at the time a parcel was subdivided and developed, or instituted later by homeowners' associations that feared changes in the area's racial makeup. Penalties were stiff, as this example from a San Diego subdivision attests:

> This property shall not be sold, leased or rented to or occupied by any person other than one of the Caucasian Race … [or] the title to the premises herein conveyed shall revert to the grantor, and the said grantor, its legal representatives, successors, or assigns, shall have the right to reenter upon and possess said premises with their privileges and appurtenances and hold the same forever. (Deed to lots 12 and 13, Fairmont Addition to City Heights, East San Diego, California; Office of the County Recorder, 1911. Reprinted in Nicolaides and Wiese 2006: p. 235)

In other words, selling to a racial minority would lead one to forfeit one's property. Until 1948, these covenants were enforceable using US federal courts, and the FHA continued to insure properties subject to restrictive covenants through 1950. Restrictive covenants actually preceded the FHA by a number of years: the above example was drafted in 1911. Indeed, FHA appraisers positively noted the presence of restrictions in their assessments of neighborhoods, and developers boasted about restrictions on billboards and other promotional materials. And these restrictions were not unusual, particularly in suburbs. By one estimate, some 95 percent of housing in 1920s Los Angeles was off limits to African Americans and Asians as a result of restrictive covenants (Davis 1990).

To understand just how lending practices and restrictive covenants contributed to racial and ethnic exclusion, consider the barriers faced by a hypothetical African American family seeking a home in the 1940s (see also the case of Ossian Sweet in Chapter 8). This family might aim to buy a house or apartment in a racially mixed urban neighborhood, but lending restrictions biased against mixed neighborhoods and older dwellings would make securing a mortgage difficult. If they could get a loan – certainly not an easy task – they might find themselves paying a higher interest rate. The homes with easier lending terms were in new suburbs, but these communities were covered by restrictive covenants; African Americans simply could not buy there. This effectively barred the path to homeownership for African Americans, as well as other racial and ethnic minorities, at a time when unprecedented numbers of white families were purchasing suburban homes.

The mass production of US suburbs

Restrictive covenants and the FHA appraisal system were thoroughly entrenched by the time that soldiers returned from World War II. Residential construction had largely stalled during the war, and, although GIs hoped to rejoin or begin families upon returning, they often had no place to do so. Demand for new homes and the availability of financing – including a veterans' package that mimicked the FHA process with even lower down payments (Schwartz 2006) – encouraged construction of small, single-family homes in racially restricted communities. These new homes would meet the construction codes and provide the neighborhood homogeneity deemed desirable by mortgage underwriters. With special veterans' financing, white GI families could purchase homes in new communities for less than they would pay to rent in central cities.

Builders and developers seized upon this opportunity, dramatically expanding the suburban landscape. Prototypical developments included those built by Levitt and Sons in New York, New Jersey, and Pennsylvania. "Levittowns" consisted of small (less than 1000 square feet) Cape Cod-style single-family homes surrounded by lawns. The architectural design was relatively repetitive, with minor variations in the placement of windows and doors or in paint colors. Using building methods adapted from assembly lines, and buying fixtures and materials in bulk, the Levitts could keep prices to a minimum (see Figure 6.7). With FHA financing, mortgage payments were about $60 per month. Buyers lined up to purchase the homes, which undersold the competition by $15 000 but still netted a $1000 profit (Jackson 1985). On the West Coast, Lakewood (a Los Angeles suburb near Long Beach) mimicked the mass production of Levittown, creating a city of nearly 80 000 residents within just a few years. Like Levittown, Lakewood provided small (1100-square-foot) homes on small lots, incorporating modern appliances and fixtures into the home. But, unlike the Levitts, Lakewood's developers included a major mall within their plan, as well as a number of smaller shopping centers with grocery stores (Hayden 2003). As a result, Lakewood was more walkable, but still highly dependent on automobiles.

Figure 6.7 The components of a house to be built in Levittown on New York's Long Island in 1948. Builder Levitt and Sons popularized a type of assembly line construction that, together with federally subsidized mortgages, made owning a suburban home far less expensive than renting in the city – at least for those who were not excluded by racially restrictive covenants. *Source: Photo: Tony Linck/Time Life Pictures/Getty Images.*

Although most suburban developments were smaller in scale than Lakewood or the Levittowns, these mass-produced developments made an important impact on the form and architecture of suburbs. Bulk developers revealed means through which design and construction practices could minimize costs, and exerted downward pressure on the price of homes in competing developments. For example, urban historian Dolores Hayden notes that in Park Forest, outside Chicago, houses were moved closer to the street and sidewalks were combined with curbs to minimize the costs of piping and concrete, respectively. As a result, the community has a very different look from that of more expensive developments where substantial setbacks from the street created a leafy, verdant appearance. Mass production also eliminated the diversity of design seen in both streetcar and owner-built suburbs. This uniformity of design and upkeep is a hotly debated dimension of suburban living – critics claim it undermines diversity but many homeowners feel it safeguards property values. Regardless of one's position on architectural homogeneity, most urban scholars agree that the social homogeneity encouraged by Levittowns and similar developments has been of much greater concern.

By building homes nearly identical in price and size, developers catered to a relatively narrow segment of the homeseeking population. In the case of the postwar boom, this primarily meant young couples and families with small children attracted by features such as modern kitchens and private yards, as well as the low prices. Although the families who moved to these new towns had similar incomes, their class backgrounds varied – blue-collar workers in skilled trades lived alongside young professionals and managerial types. Households also differed in their religious traditions and ethnic backgrounds. Levittowns were considered relatively open because they did not bar Jews or Catholics, but this openness did not extend to African Americans. Some scholars have argued that the ability of whites to live together and share the common experiences of suburbia contributed to the creation of "white" as a racial category, replacing the ethnic and religious distinctions that had been as important as racial distinctions throughout much of US history (see *Race: The Power of an Illusion* 2003).

Changes and challenges in contemporary suburbs

As the suburban boom of the 1950s and 1960s gave way to the urban challenges of the 1970s and 1980s (see Chapter 7), suburbs became both more like and more unlike the typical suburbs we have described here. Some new suburban developments took the ideals of aesthetic control and narrow market segmentation to unprecedented levels, and the increasing number of gated communities extended suburban exclusivity beyond that seen in the early years or postwar boom. At the same time, more suburban communities became home to minority and immigrant groups – some almost exclusively. Indeed, in the 1990 US census, Monterrey Park, a suburban city near Los Angeles, was found to be the first majority Asian city in the United States. In Southern California and other parts of the United States, older suburbs started to become more diverse as they aged, but many newer suburbs remained destinations for "white flight" (Frey 2002).

Privatization and gated communities

Perhaps the most pressing concern in contemporary suburban areas (and many *urban* areas, for that matter) is that of the increase in gated communities. These are typically subdivisions surrounded by walls, fences, or other barriers or by somewhat impenetrable natural features such as woodlands or water. Automobile access is limited by the use of gates that range from those primarily standing open (particularly during the day) to those that are staffed by security guards 24 hours a day. Although the archetypal gated community consists of detached single-family homes built for affluent residents, increasingly we see that apartment complexes, condominiums, retirement communities, and working-class areas also use gates. Gates and barriers not only limit access to the homes inside but also restrict access to the parks, swimming pools, community clubhouses, and other amenities found there. Gating thus prevents residents of nearby communities from using what may be the closest recreational facilities, and, if gates bar access to streets within these communities, prevents potentially pro-democratic activities such as door-to-door canvassing. The term "gated community" is thus a controversial one, as critics doubt whether these residential developments facilitate the interactions indicative of strong communities (Low 2003).

Blakeley and Snyder, planners who were among the first to turn sustained attention to the growing phenomenon of gating, observed three forms of gated communities (see Figure 6.8). *Lifestyle communities* offer a number of amenities, such as pools and golf courses, and these include a number of retirement communities. In *prestige communities*, the gate is the primary common amenity, and its presence lends a degree of status to the development and its residents. Blakely and Snyder also note that some older communities erect gates and barriers in response to concerns about crime or traffic. *Security zones*, as they call these, may be conventional suburban subdivisions or older urban neighborhoods (Blakely and Snyder 1997). Gated communities have also spread far beyond the US suburbs to take root in places as far away as Ghana's capital city, Accra. There they have taken on

Figure 6.8 While some gated communities contain modest single-family homes or apartments, others are among the most opulent of suburban developments. Amenities including pools and golf courses abound, and the increased security, or at least the impression of security, is also sold as an amenity. Here a security guard checks a car at a gated subdivision outside Seattle. *Source: Photo © Dan Lamont/CORBIS.*

names such as The King, The Emperor, and The President, a bizarre mix of historical and political references with high economic status (Grant 2005).

The increasing popularity of gated communities is often associated with residents' fears – of decreasing property values, of crime, or of diminishing status. These fears are interrelated, as status derives in part from the value attached to one's home and property values reflect neighborhood quality-of-life issues, including crime. Anthropologist Setha Low has studied these fears in her ethnography of gated communities and their residents. Even though the residents she spoke with lived in gated communities located within low crime areas, she found that many residents feared crime, including statistically rare crimes such as kidnapping. She found that children may become especially fearful. These fears extended to the kinds of people they associated with crime – particularly racial and ethnic minorities. Because gated communities are often segregated communities, outsiders, or those whose appearances mark them as would-be outsiders, are closely monitored. Moreover, moving to a gated community is, for some residents, a way of moving away from the diversity associated with urban crime (Low 2003).

common-interest development (CID)
A residential community that uses fees levied on homeowners to fund privately held infrastructure and amenities.

Gated communities provide the most extreme illustration of a shift toward privatization in suburban development. In gated and non-gated developments, a legal device called the **common-interest development (CID)** creates what are, for many purposes, miniature cities. Such CIDs possess the authority to collect revenues (dues or fees) from homeowners – akin to a tax – and to channel these funds toward projects that benefit the community. In suburban communities with amenities such as pools, tennis courts, and golf courses, the developer recoups the initial cost of those common goods though CID payments collected over a number of years. Services such as security officers (including gate attendants), street and landscape maintenance, and trash collection may also be funded through CID payments. An important question concerns the degree to which paying CID fees influences homeowners' willingness to support property tax increases. Residents of CIDs may feel that they are paying twice for similar services – once for the parks and security within their development and again for parks and security (among other things) outside. For these reasons, CID communities may be built in unincorporated areas where property taxes are lower, luring affluent residents and their tax contributions out of central cities. Economist Robert Reich called this pattern, wherein the affluent move to places where they will pay for private amenities but not public goods, such as parks, the "secession of the successful" (Reich 1991).

Homeowners' associations are the governing bodies guiding CIDs. Although these groups have always had an important role in suburban communities – for instance, in drafting and enforcing restrictive covenants – in CIDs the power of the homeowners' association multiplies. Critics argue that, through the use of CIDs, developers enjoy a double advantage. First, by creating what is considered a "private" development they are able to skirt some local regulations regarding infrastructure and planning (for instance, increased densities or narrower streets). This keeps costs down for the developer. Second, when the community is completely built and the developer has moved on to other projects, the developer leaves the homeowners' association responsible for the upkeep of open spaces, pools, and parks – the "common" properties of the CID. Any difficulties associated with these properties, such as a leaky pool or roads full of potholes, become the responsibility of the homeowners' association and, financially, the homeowners themselves. Homeowners' association fees that start out low to entice buyers may therefore quickly inflate.

In most new communities, the developer initially drafts the basic regulations, otherwise known as covenants, codes, and restrictions. The responsibility for enforcing the rules then turns to the homeowners' association. The regulations often specify the aesthetic and behavioral norms of a community. They may govern relatively trivial things like the color you can paint your house or how long you or your guests may park on the street. But they also govern the modes of political expression (the use of yard signs or flag poles); the composition of the household (retirement communities use their covenants to restrict permanent populations to those aged 55 and above, the last legal type of residential discrimination in the United States); how you can improve your property (building additions, changing windows); and even whether or not you may have firearms in the house. While many residents like the idea that regulations will protect them from the potentially offensive tastes and behaviors of their neighbors, these same individuals may resent that they, too, must comply with the rules. The structure of the homeowners' associations and CIDs can also lead to a type of community that sociologist M. P. Baumgartner has called "moral minimalism." She argues that relationships among residents of affluent suburbs are limited, which minimizes conflict along with intimacy. The formal rules, such as those contained in the covenants and codes, further reduce the need for residents to share common ideals (Baumgartner 1988).

The varied fates of older suburbs

While the urban edge of the metropolis continues to expand, older suburbs (generally those built before or during the 1950s), variously called "**first-ring**" or "inner" suburbs, have taken a variety of paths. It is no easier to characterize older suburbs than it is to characterize suburbs as a whole. Some older suburbs contain thriving and desirable neighborhoods; others face problems such as poverty, crime, homelessness, and population aging at levels similar to those found in central cities. Escalating property values in some first-ring suburbs, such as those in Los Angeles and Vancouver, have motivated residents and speculators to tear down existing structures, typically small bungalow-style homes, and replace them with much larger dwellings that fill their lots. Condominium developments provide a second means of maximizing profits from development in desirable first-ring suburbs, particularly those near transit routes (see Figure 6.9). But a number of first-ring suburbs have seen their populations decline – particularly those near cities with stagnant declining populations. Thus, in cities such as Cleveland and Pittsburgh, where deindustrialization has eroded the economic base, both urban and suburban populations are in decline (see Figure 6.10); indeed, many suburbs have rates of decline that outpace those of the cities. Another concern is declining infrastructure. As roads, sewers, and electrical systems age, the cost of their upkeep escalates, often beyond the reach of municipal or county budgets.

> **first-ring suburbs**
> The older suburbs of metropolitan areas. Such suburbs in recent years have shown some evidence of decline in population and housing stock – the same kind of decline that has taken place in the central areas of the metropolis.

Changes in the populations of suburbs present another series of challenges. A major concern is that the population of first-ring suburbs is increasingly composed of elderly residents, particularly in those suburbs that have stagnant or declining populations. In communities dominated by single-family housing, elderly residents may find they face a difficult choice between remaining in a home that is too large and, potentially, too expensive or relocating to a smaller home or apartment in an unfamiliar neighborhood. In first-ring suburbs where populations are expanding, primarily those in the US South and southwest, growth is occurring in large part as a result of increases in minority and immigrant populations. In fact, about as many immigrants live in first-ring suburbs as in central cities – a real change from what we saw in the late-nineteenth and early-twentieth centuries. These new populations bring vitality to areas that would otherwise decline, but may bring with them needs that communities are ill equipped to meet (Puentes and Warren 2006). For example, schools, hospitals, and other community institutions must serve those with limited English-language skills.

Figure 6.9 Transit-oriented development in the Seattle suburb of Redmond (note the "Park & Ride" sign, indicating that cars can be left here for the day while commuters take the bus into the city). Like many first-ring suburbs in growing metropolitan areas, Redmond's density is increasing. *Source: Photo Ned Ahrens, King County Department of Transportation.*

Figure 6.10 Demolition of a home in Cuyahoga County, outside Cleveland. A number of suburban communities here took advantage of federal funds to eliminate vacant, abandoned, and blighted homes in once thriving suburbs. *Source: Photo © Chuck Crow/Plain Dealer.*

An advantage that first-ring suburbs have over new developments, and one that keeps housing prices relatively high, is their proximity to central cities. In most metropolitan areas, new development occurs on the urban periphery, extending the suburbs ever further into environmentally sensitive areas. Infill projects, such as Baldwin Park in Orlando, a community built on a decommissioned Air Force base, provide some exceptions, but parcels large enough for major developments are rare within major cities. Some residents of the far-reaching suburbs may work in the suburbs, too – recall that edge cities contain substantial commercial space – but many suburban residents face very long commutes and limited access to public transportation. For these reasons, as well as financial concerns (the price of new homes, plus the added expenses associated with living in CIDs), homebuyers may return to older suburbs. To the extent that this pattern continues, older suburbs may find that they have the financial means to address their increasingly "urban" problems.

Suburbs as places

To understand suburbs as distinctive kinds of places, we should establish just which qualities differentiate them from other urban forms. While some of these qualities are revealed in the various definitions of suburbs – locations on the periphery of major urban centers, the predominance of single-family detached homes, a primarily residential function, and so on – most definitions stop short of revealing the character of suburban areas. We close this chapter by revisiting the three qualities of place that guide this book: identity, security, and community. Suburbs, we contend, are places where the illusion of a homogenous identity masks deeper diversity, where the desire for security continually motivates new forms of exclusion, and where distinct spatial, political, and demographic features can challenge the sense of community.

We opened this chapter with a stereotypical image: the suburban home surrounded by an expansive lawn and inhabited by an affluent white family with 2.5 children. This is certainly an exaggeration of the suburban norm, but it reflects some truth about who lives in suburbs and why. In North America and the United Kingdom, in particular, suburbs are seen as ideal places to raise children. This derives in part from the presumption that suburbs are safe (a point elaborated below) but also from the fact that suburbs in these countries are dominated by detached or semi-detached single-family homes with private yards. Here children can play in a quasi-natural environment while under the close supervision of a parent. From the nineteenth century onward, popular culture has affirmed this ideal for child rearing, and the presumed appropriateness of suburban single-family homes for young families is so entrenched that you will always see rooms decorated for children in the model homes that builders use to sell new suburban houses. Although one could just as easily make the case that children benefit from the diversity and cultural opportunities found in cities, this argument has not gained much traction. Commitment to family, particularly children, remains an important dimension of the suburban identity, and political movements associated with "family values" often look to the suburbs to find their constituents.

A second dimension of suburban identity, the association of suburbs with whiteness, also has its roots in reality. Suburbs were created, in part, as places to escape from diversity. And, as we have seen, many suburbs explicitly excluded racial and ethnic minorities by using restrictive covenants. Although this became illegal in the United States in 1948, and the Fair Housing Act of 1968 outlawed all forms of residential discrimination, subtle forms of discrimination persist, as do individual preferences to live among one's own racial group.

Importantly, this so-called in-group preference is much more pronounced among whites than among people of color (Charles 2003). But the assumption that suburbs are uniformly white is complicated by the pronounced diversity of older suburbs – indeed, these communities are becoming some of the most diverse places in the metropolis. We also see the development of predominantly minority suburbs, whether the Asian communities of Monterrey Park and Arcadia, near Los Angeles, or the majority African American suburbs of Atlanta or Prince George's County (outside Washington, DC). Despite increasing diversity, culture plays a part in perpetuating the myth that suburbs are white. As "urban" increasingly becomes a shorthand for African American culture, particularly that associated with hip-hop, suburbs are becoming associated with whiteness by default. An important question is to what degree this association, and the accompanying assumption that suburbs are uniformly affluent, will persist as suburban demographics change.

The desire for security has long motivated the move to the suburbs. Definitions of the city as unsavory and unsafe drew residents to early suburbs, and the presentation of suburbs as idyllic retreats continues today. Advertisements for new suburban developments promise a different quality of life, one that harks back to idealized small towns in which, the reader might infer, no one ever need lock their doors. Suburbs have typically promised residents a second form of security, too: financial security. Home equity is many families' greatest financial asset. Physical and financial security are tightly intertwined, as it was the fear not only of a racialized other but also of the effect this other might have on property values that led to the use of exclusionary devices such as restrictive covenants and to residential appraisal standards that rewarded racial homogeneity. These devices helped to ensure that white families could realize financial security through investments in their homes but blocked this avenue to wealth creation for families of color (Oliver and Shapiro 1997). In the early twenty-first century, the expansion of homeownership facilitated by new types of mortgages – including those requiring no or low down payments, variable rate mortgages, and interest-only loans – promised to extend homeownership to more and more households and to close the homeownership gap. But again, minority communities were often deliberately targeted for deceptive or predatory loans, and they now suffer from some of the highest foreclosure rates.

Finally, what can we make of the type of community provided by suburbs? Almost from their inception, suburbs have been the object of scorn for their perceived *lack* of community. Popular-culture representations often characterize suburbs as places where competitive consumption and hyper-conformity conceal deeper isolation (see Studying the city 6.1). Scholars have been more mixed in their evaluations. In the 1950s and 1960s, sociologists found that residents of new suburbs belonged to a number of social and voluntary organizations, and that residents shared intimate friendships in their neighborhood. All was not ideal, however; women often felt isolated and disconnected, children – particularly adolescents – were often bored or overlooked, and those who did not fit in found themselves especially lonely (Whyte 1956; Gans 1967).

An important question concerns the extent to which the presence or absence of a sense of community is the product of the suburban form. The sprawling design and auto-dependency of suburbs has taken its share of blame for the erosion of community. The suburban ranch house with attached garage common throughout North America allows one to drive directly into the home, thus minimizing chance interactions with neighbors. A larger issue is the commute often associated with suburban living. Not only do long commutes separate work and home lives, placing people in different communities during the day and the evening, but they also take up time that might be spent in other social activities. In his account of declining social capital, political

STUDYING THE CITY   6.1

City and suburb in popular culture

As we have explained in this chapter, understanding why people seek to live where they do requires an understanding of cultural messages about home and the good life. At different times, city and suburb have been cast as idyllic or terrifying – and, in some cases, both.

In explaining how Los Angeles transformed from a diverse and integrated city into a highly segregated and suburban metropolis, historian Eric Avila (2004) points to the ways in which city and suburb were represented in film. Many of the films produced in Los Angeles just before the area's postwar suburban boom – particularly the *film noir* genre at its zenith in the late 1930s and 1940s – cast the city as home to criminals and degenerates eager to prey on the innocent. Through the use of location filming (popular due to wartime shortages of energy and materials), real urban places, particularly poor mixed neighborhoods and downtown streets, became home to cinema villains. Many films used Los Angeles' diverse Bunker Hill neighborhood as a backdrop (the area was later razed in a major urban renewal scheme), and in a remake of Fritz Lang's *M* a mob chases a child killer past a number of downtown landmarks. Avila argues that these negative associations not only alienated affluent white residents from Los Angeles' urban areas but also carried negative messages about cities throughout the United States and the world. These messages then echoed earlier assumptions that cities were dangerous and undesirable places, particularly for families.

Suburbs take their fair share of on-screen abuse as well, though the message hasn't always been read as intended. Urban historian Dolores Hayden (2003) chronicles the unintended consequences of the 1948 Cary Grant film *Mr. Blandings Builds his Dream House*, which presents the endless stream of misfortunes befalling a family as they attempt to rehabilitate a farmhouse in the New York City suburbs. Rather than putting off would-be suburbanites, the film spawned some 70 Blandings-replica homes in suburbs around the United States that builders successfully used as promotional devices.

By the 1970s, films came to present suburbs as places where surface perfection masked deeply disturbing truths. The 1975 film *The Stepford Wives*, based on an Ira Levin novel, presented a community in which housewives were *literally* turned into man-pleasing automatons (a 2004 remake plays this to humorous ends, but the original fits more neatly in the horror genre). *Over The Edge*, released in 1979, was inspired by true events in a seemingly perfect suburb where no provision was made for the interests of adolescents. Without any formal outlets, they turn to drugs, alcohol, sex, and violence. By the 1980s, the suburbs were routine settings for horror, whether the after-effects of unscrupulous developers portrayed in *Poltergeist* or fears of murderous neighbors in *The 'Burbs*. An entire subgenre of highly acclaimed contemporary films takes on the subject of suburban angst and ennui – *American Beauty*, *The Ice Storm*, and *Revolutionary Road* all fit this mold. As film historian Davis DeWilt (2006) observes, films such as these center on the empty lives of individuals who seem, at least by material standards, to have achieved the American Dream.

scientist Robert Putnam places some of the blame for declining voluntary participation on these dimensions of suburban sprawl. He also points to the lack of community boundaries that is a byproduct of sprawl (Putnam 2000). If we do not have a clear sense of where our community begins and ends, how can we develop connections to that place or recognize our fellow community members? This may change as suburban planners increasingly turn to design features that encourage walking and facilitate a distinct sense of place. Early studies of Celebration, a New Urbanist development near

Orlando, suggest that a combination of conscientious design and residents' self-selecting for community-mindedness can produce a strong sense of solidarity (Ross 2000).

As you continue to make your way through this book, it is important to keep in mind the ways in which suburbs changed cities. They radically changed the way that people live within cities by increasing privacy and facilitating homeownership. The household – as opposed to the community – became an increasingly important unit within urban areas. Suburbanization also played a role in increasing inequalities. Existing social inequalities, particularly those related to race and ethnicity in the United States, were exacerbated by different levels of access to homeownership. Moreover, suburban expansion brought tremendous investment in suburban infrastructure, as well as private homes. This resulted in inequalities between suburbs and inner cities that had damning effects on many inner-city communities. Finally, the expansion of suburbs changed what a city *is*. No longer compact and tightly bounded places, cities spilled out into the countryside, often bumping up against one another as they did. Suburbanization thus helped to transform the city into the metropolis, an urban form that reached unprecedented size in the second half of the twentieth century. We shall describe that process next, in Chapter 7. Visit the book's companion website at www.wiley.com/go/cities for examples, case studies, and discussion questions, plus a list of useful films and other media, that are relevant to this chapter.

Critical thinking questions

1 Consider what you have learned about nineteenth-century cities in this book. With that in mind, to what degree do you feel that early suburbanites' anxieties about urban living were based on real conditions? What role might racism or xenophobia have played?

2 What kinds of cultural messages do you see or hear now that make urban or suburban living seem particularly desirable? Is one made to seem undesirable and, if so, why?

3 Looking around the cities and suburbs in your area, can you see the ways in which transportation infrastructure has shaped development? In what ways does it continue to do so?

4 Do you believe that suburban living leads to social isolation? How might this vary among people of different social classes, racial/ethnic groups, genders, or ages?

5 What kinds of advantages does suburban homeownership provide to families? What kinds of costs? How does homeownership or the lack thereof perpetuate social inequality?

Suggested reading

Dolores Hayden. *Building Suburbia: Green Fields and Urban Growth, 1820–2000* (New York: Vintage Books, 2003). Hayden's thorough account of suburban growth pays particular attention to gender and culture, and to urban and house design.

Alan A. Jackson, *Semi-Detached London: Suburban Development, Life and Transport, 1930–39* (London: Allen & Unwin, 1973). Jackson details the roots and results of England's largest suburban expansion with a focus on Greater London.

Kenneth T. Jackson, *Crabgrass Frontier: The Suburbanization of the United States* (New York and Oxford: Oxford University Press, 1985). A detailed history of suburbanization in the United States from the country's founding through the 1970s, with particular attention to the roles of policy and transportation.

Andrew Wiese, *Places of their Own: African American Suburbanization in the Twentieth Century* (Chicago, IL: University of Chicago Press, 2004). By examining the history of African Americans in US suburbs, Wiese challenges the definition of "suburb" and assumptions about suburbs' role in racial inequality.

CHAPTER 7

Changing metropolitan landscapes after World War II

KEY TOPICS

→ The emergence of a global economy after World War II and how it has altered the metropolitan landscapes of cities.

→ The simultaneous rise and decline of cities across the United States and the globe, and the impact on the people and industries of those cities.

→ The emergence of a new postindustrial and postmodern city – a city of social fragments, of great ethnic diversity, and of a growing gap between the rich and poor – and how the city of Los Angeles today exemplifies these trends.

→ The importance of considering how broad global changes, especially to the world economy, impact the lives and times of real people existing in the spaces and places of cities today.

Introduction to Cities: How Place and Space Shape Human Experience, First Edition. Xiangming Chen, Anthony M. Orum, and Krista E. Paulsen.
© 2013 Xiangming Chen, Anthony M. Orum, and Krista E. Paulsen.
Published 2013 by Blackwell Publishing Ltd.

Cities and the larger metropolises within which they lie are constantly being transformed. This is especially so today. Many such changes are the result of the workings of broad forces over which cities and their institutions exercise little control. Only a few years after the end of World War II, many cities in the United States and in other Western nations began to suffer the loss and decline of their home-grown manufacturing enterprises. This had an effect that cascaded across the metropolis and dramatically altered the lives of its residents: beginning in the late 1960s and early 1970s, many workers – men and women who had labored for major manufacturing firms for decades – were fired and would never again find employment. The change would eventually transform the economic base of the United States and its cities so that by the turn of the century a far smaller percentage of the American workforce was engaged in high-paying industrial jobs.[1] The net result was to deplete the resources of local governments, which rely on the taxes paid both by firms and by individuals, and eventually to diminish the resources such governments could use to furnish their residents with important public services such as schools and parks.

In this chapter we consider the changes that took place in the period from the late 1940s through the present time. We describe many of the changes themselves and show how they came to alter the metropolitan environment within which local governments work and the local residents live. To do so we shall draw on the experiences of people and institutions in a number of different cities, many in the United States, such as Chicago and Detroit, among others. While cities such as these and many others would suffer a major decline and transformation, they only represented one wing and type of metropolis, the older, declining industrial metropolis. There were many other cities in the United States that would in fact boom and flourish in the postwar period, the large majority of which were located in the South, the west, and the southwest – cities such as Dallas and San Antonio, Texas, for example, but also Phoenix and Santa Fe as well as a host of cities on the West Coast, especially in California (Bernard and Rice 1984).

Yet our story in this chapter would be incomplete if we only focused our attention on cities and metropolitan regions in the United States. Changes to the economic foundations of the metropolis happened in Western Europe as well, and here we shall give examples, many of which parallel those of the story in the United States. But another portion of our story here has to do with the way in which the world and its metropolitan regions have developed in recent years. Cities have sprung up and mushroomed across the globe, making the world a much smaller site, a place where people can easily connect with one another in space of a few seconds, via phone or computer. Transactions take place routinely across many thousands of miles of space, linking businesses that produce to businesses that buy and creating links not only between people but also between commodities that are produced in various parts of the world. A global economy has emerged, one that may not be entirely new but whose links vitally connect people in Mumbai with those in Chicago and people in Toronto with those in Hong Kong. The growth of this newly energized global economy has influenced us all, and it makes its presence felt strongly, though not exclusively, in the way in which metropolitan regions work today. Thus, a part of our story in this chapter will be about the emergence of this global economy. Subsequent chapters will consider many different cities across the globe and furnish you with additional insights into how cities today work within the emerging global economy.

We begin our story, then, with one metropolis in particular: Los Angeles, California. Though Los Angeles has a history that dates to the nineteenth century, its development after World War II made it into the prototype of the major metropolitan area today. Other cities, such as Mumbai or Shanghai, could vie for that title, but Los Angeles furnishes a rich mixture of many of the major tendencies and trends and can be treated, in effect, as the

postmodernism The movement in contemporary scholarship that emphasizes fragmentation and de-centering both in intellectual thought and material projects.

great postindustrial, even **postmodern**, metropolis of the contemporary era – a prototype of this era just as Chicago was for most of the twentieth century (see Chapter 5).[2] We then situate Los Angeles in a context of changes across the urban landscape of the United States, particularly the emergence of the Sunbelt as a site of urban growth and expansion. Finally, we broaden our perspective to examine how global economic forces reconfigured the ranking of cities and reshaped the lives of their residents.

Los Angeles
The prototype of the postwar metropolis

Los Angeles (see Figure 7.1), the City of Angels, has a long and richly storied history.[3] Some of this history is easily available through movies, one of the most popular of which is *Chinatown* (1974), starring Jack Nicholson and Faye Dunaway. The movie tells the story of how water shaped the creation of Los Angeles and of the entire region in which it lies. Those who controlled and manipulated the water, including key officials in the city, exercised great power over the residents, and in order to do so they often had to resort to rather shady and illegal practices to sustain this power. Even today, the availability of water continues to

Figure 7.1 Los Angeles, as seen from a satellite. Nearly every developable parcel within this 100 mile stretch is covered by houses, businesses, and roads. *Source: Earth Satellite Corporation/MDA Information Services/Science Photo Library.*

be a problem that plagues the region; Los Angeles, though bordering the Pacific Ocean, has the difficult and challenging task of obtaining enough water for its residents, and when such water is lacking the city can become prey to major outbreaks of fires, the most recent of which took place during August of 2009.

One of the more striking features of modern Los Angeles is that it lacks a vibrant and thriving downtown, one filled with a host of stores and businesses and one to which people – local residents and visitors – travel to shop and where foreign tourists regularly come (Fogelson 1993). Unlike the older industrial cities such as Chicago, or even major metropolitan areas such as New York City, there is no major center to Los Angeles. Instead, the city limits of Los Angeles encompass nearly 500 square miles (the metropolitan area is ten times that size), and the city includes a number of substantial business districts. Views of the city from the sky reveal just far it stretches, how densely populated it has become, and how many different seemingly small urban centers exist. Indeed, as we noted in Chapter 5, the Los Angeles region stretches across several counties, the most famous of which are Los Angeles and Orange Counties, and it contains a host of small metropolitan areas, such as Irvine, California.

The Los Angeles region, in fact, does not look anything like the concentric zone picture that the original Chicago School of Sociology drew up of the typical metropolis. Rather, it looks much more like the portrait of the multiple nuclei that was first developed by the urban geographers Chauncy Harris and Edward Ullman. But, more than that, today Los Angeles does not contain obvious demarcations in its social spaces: there are no clear boundaries between urban center, suburban fringe areas, and hinterlands of the sort we portrayed in Chapter 5 (on the metropolis and its basic principles). Rather, it consists of a wide array of small urban centers and tens of thousands of people and enterprises that stretch across a seemingly endless landscape. And, unlike the older industrial cities of Pittsburgh or Detroit, the rivalries that dot its political landscape are not so much between the urban authorities and suburban governments as between the rival urban centers and contending political authorities across the region (Fulton 2001).

How did Los Angeles come to look so different from the older industrial US cities such as Chicago? And how did the absence of a center and the many seemingly disparate fragments of which Los Angeles consists – both qualities that make it in the eyes of many the prototypical **postmodern metropolis** – come to compose the region? An important part of the story of its growth and expansion lies in the peculiar history of the way the region began. Some of the current small urban centers simply began as villages independent of one another. Others originated as homes of different groups of immigrants, each of which settled and made their own new homes in the United States. Moreover, since Los Angeles lacked the kind of major industrial forces and developments that came to characterize the cities of the northeast, such as Philadelphia, or the Midwest, such as Detroit, there was no dominant kind of industry that could draw people into the center and, in the absence of easy transportation, lead workers to live in close proximity to the factories where they worked.

> **postmodern metropolis**
> A postindustrial city characterized by social fragmentation.

Above and beyond that, however, there are two forces that are more important than all others: the nature of the light rail system and the highway system (see especially Fishman 1987b: Chapter 6; Fogelson 1993). Transportation, in other words, as it always has, played a major role in the expansion and development of the region. As we discussed in Chapter 6, those figures that controlled the building of the light rail system (also called "streetcars") within the city came to exercise great control over how it would expand. Though they would be challenged by other authorities, eventually their work to develop a public transit system that took people across the region helped to make the metropolis far larger and more

Table 7.1 Racial/ethnic composition of places in the Los Angeles metropolitan area, 1960–2000. The Los Angeles area, including suburban Orange County, became much more diverse over this 40-year period. Although we have collapsed a number of minority categories here due to limitations in the data reporting (particularly in the early years), the pattern reflects a pronounced increase in immigrants from Latin America and Asia. *Source: Based on US Census data.*

Place	Race/Ethnicity	1960		1980		2000	
City of Los Angeles	White	2 061 808	83.2%	1 816 761	61.2%	1 734 036	46.9%
	Non-white	417 207	16.8%	1 151 818	38.8%	1 960 784	53.1%
	Hispanics of any race	Not available		816 076	27.5%	1 719 073	46.5%
Los Angeles County	White	5 453 866	90.3%	5 135 540	68.7%	4 637 062	48.7%
	Non-white	584 905	9.7%	2 341 963	31.3%	4 882 276	51.3%
	Hispanics of any race	Not available		4 046 973	54.1%	4 242 213	44.6%
Orange County	White	694 354	98.6%	1 684 906	87.2%	1 844 652	64.8%
	Non-white	9 571	1.4%	247 803	12.8%	1 001 637	35.2%
	Hispanics of any race	Not available		562 984	29.1%	875 579	30.8%

dispersed than many others. The vast system of highways that connected one part of the region to another also led to a rapid and easy dispersal of people across the area. It meant that people could travel easily across long distances but it also meant that there would be no single and dominant urban center that would act as a magnet for people and businesses, unlike the typical industrial cities where people came into the downtown for work and traveled home to the residential suburbs at the end of the day.

Los Angeles also became a magnet for people who wanted to travel and to relocate themselves and their families, especially in the years after the end of World War II. Over the several decades after the end of the war in 1945, the metropolitan region doubled its numbers. Many were attracted by new jobs in defense and aerospace, in plants located far from the urban core. By 1975, it had become one of the leading metropolitan centers in the United States, overtaking older areas such as Philadelphia and Boston. It had come to symbolize the shift of the American population in general from the East Coast to the West Coast. Like Hollywood itself, Los Angeles became the magical site where people wanted to move to make new fortunes and where young people hoped to exercise their entrepreneurial skills. Over the course of the next several decades, millions of immigrants would enter the region (see Table 7.1). Initially, most these migrants came from within the United States itself. But eventually the Los Angeles region became one of the most polyglot metropolitan empires in the United States. Its residents came from Mexico but also from China, Korea, and other places abroad (see Waldinger and Bozorgmehr 1996). Today, in fact, the city consists of people from multiple national origins, many of whom have remade parts of the Los Angeles metropolitan area into sites that resemble their hometowns abroad. The Vietnamese, for example, have settled into Los Angeles and created an area within which they have developed their own stores and their own ethnic economy. The same is true for those immigrants who have come to the region from China as well as Hong Kong and Taiwan (see e.g., Light and Bonacich 1991).

Just as Los Angeles, with its lack of a distinctive and thriving center, its collection of social fragments, and its vast stretches of a very dense population over many hundreds of square miles, is the prototype of today's metropolis, it also represents some of the major challenges that grow out of this dense and highly diverse population. One of the single most devastating race riots in the postwar period happened in 1965 in the area of Watts, a site in East Los Angeles that is home to thousands of people of color. The experience was wrenching for the region and its residents: it came to symbolize the sharp differences and inequalities that existed, and it cast shadows over the celluloid quality to the city that Hollywood had manufactured. Decades later, the city again came to symbolize some of the sharp differences that have grown up in postwar America when Rodney King, an African American, was shown being mercilessly beaten by Los Angeles police officers (Soja 2000).

King soon became a symbol of the other side of Los Angeles, the dark and cruel side, an example of what critics of the modern metropolis such as Mike Davis have come to call the "carceral city" (Davis 1990). This is the Los Angeles of police and squad cars, of an effort to control local residents by the use of force, not a city in which democratic and civil politics reigns. It is the Los Angeles of police chasing O. J. Simpson across endless stretches of highways and of police helicopters shining their lights from above on people running across lawns. In this respect, as in so many others, Los Angeles has become the prototype of the thickly settled metropolitan contemporary region, one where something like a police state exists and where poor people of color seemingly are constantly harassed. That force and poverty exist alongside the wealth of places such as Laguna Beach and the images of a perfect world churned out by the Hollywood movie machine only adds to the disparate and disjunctive character of this postmodern metropolitan region.

Immense numbers of people; a population of various and countless fragments; diversity in terms of the origins and homelands of people; sharp economic and social inequalities; a region without an obvious center: these are the qualities that make Los Angeles feel like a prototype of the metropolitan region in the post-World War II period. Moreover, the factors and forces that gave rise to this region, especially the highway system and the use of cars in the absence of a comprehensive and efficient system of public transportation, also make the city a touchstone of how to decipher and understand life in our age. The car and the highway are the symbols of this time, and they are its menace as well. Urban planners today seek to alter the nature of the built and created landscape, especially by trying to determine how to establish viable and effective communities of people – and they do so by castigating the system of highways and the relentless use of cars. Beyond this, the sheer growth of the population, all of whom live across miles and miles of a region, is particularly symptomatic of the new metropolitan regions that are now arising across the world (see, for example, the distinctive case of Shanghai that we discuss in Chapter 11).

EXPLORING FURTHER   7.1

The unwieldy metropolis

In many countries around the world, urban populations are beginning to reach levels that have never been witnessed before, and the metropolis is beginning to grow to unprecedented sizes. This rapid growth and expansion of urban populations is bringing about several developments concerning the metropolis as we know it. In a few cases, huge regions consisting of many cities are beginning to be justifiably recognized as single economic and cultural entities with personalities of their own. On the flip side, some metropolises are becoming so large that they are beginning to break apart through a process known as urban fragmentation. And all of this growth, either way, is likely to contribute to an urban process known as sprawl.

Geographer Jean Gottmann (1957, 1961) first brought to public attention the development of regions and the relatively dense concentration of people across many miles of space. He noted, in a book published in 1961, the growth of something he called the **megalopolis**, an area that he defined as a highly dense site, stretching across thousands of acres of land, that connected people and enterprises in different cities and towns. The first of these, he insisted, occurred in the northeastern United States, in a corridor that housed millions of people and stretched from Boston all the way to Washington, DC. The unique and special quality of such sites, Gottmann argued, was that the sheer growth and density of people forced governments – municipal, state, and federal – to take such populations into account and to create a variety of cooperative enterprises among themselves.

megalopolis A very large and highly dense population site connecting people and enterprises in different cities and towns.

The reasons that such a rapidly expanding megalopolis came to be in the first place are, as Gottmann explains, tripartite: first, that the megalopolis relies on multiple nuclei; second, that these major cities all competed with one another until their growth joined them together; and third, that each of these nuclei had access to a unique hinge of the US economy – for example, easy access to the Atlantic Ocean. Other soon-to-be megalopolises that Gottmann identified in the 1950s included the metropolitan area stretching across Ohio from Cleveland to Pittsburgh and the region surrounding Chicago to the shores of Lake Michigan.

urban fragmentation The proliferation of municipalities and other governmental units within a metropolitan area.

That same kind of growth and density exists today in the Los Angeles region. At times it works to the benefit of local residents and their needs, in the form of various sorts of cooperation, yet at other times it seems to divide the region into endless municipalities and local turf wars. When this happens, it can be referred to as **urban fragmentation**, the process of a metropolitan area being split up into many separate competing governmental entities. Often, this problem arises because suburban areas recognize incentives to incorporate as separate cities. Motives include defending property values, capturing property taxes so that tax revenue can be spent on local-only projects, and locally controlling land use decisions to effectively zone out any developments that might hurt property values and tax revenues – such as low-income housing units (Miller 2002).

One major problem is that, once the process of urban fragmentation becomes too widespread, many regional planning efforts are confounded. Plans for transportation, infrastructure, and the provision of public services are best handled at the metropolitan level to make sure that cities aren't duplicating the services, utilities, or infrastructure provided by the municipality next door. But, in metropolitan areas that include large numbers of cities in a relatively small geographic space, this planning process becomes extremely complicated.

In an effort to combat the negative effects of urban fragmentation in the Los Angeles metropolitan area, the Southern California Association of Governments (SCAG) was created. SCAG currently has well over 150 member cities, one of which is Los Angeles, and six member counties. To make the regional planning process simpler and to avoid wasting significant amounts of tax money, SCAG set up committees to address metropolitan issues such as community development, energy, and transportation.

Whether this rapid urbanization and expansion of metropolitan areas happens in a way that develops a single megalopolis-like entity joined by the suburbs of multiple nuclei or in a way that develops many separate and fragmented suburban governments, sprawl is likely to occur. Sprawl refers to the process of suburban neighborhoods developing in lower-density areas and expanding outward from a central city.

According to Robert Bruegmann (2005), sprawl is described by critics as an urban problem that must be stopped for economic and environmental reasons. Indeed, if sprawl is viewed as the unplanned expansion of central cities fueled by developers seeking to build on the cheapest land possible and advertise their development as an attractive escape from the city without being too long a drive away, then it comes with many problems. Economically, this is a problem because often cities will prefer to invest infrastructure money into its suburban and property-tax-rich sectors while ignoring central city transportation, housing, and infrastructure needs. And, in line with urban fragmentation, these suburban developments may even try to incorporate themselves separately to avoid contributing any tax money at all to the central city. Environmentally, this is also a problem because sprawl takes the place of agricultural parcels and undeveloped natural spaces. The real kicker, however, is that people living in these outer suburban neighborhoods have to rely on automobiles every day to move relatively long distances from their homes to the city, contributing massive amounts of air pollution and fuel consumption (see Exploring further 12.1).

However, Bruegmann argues that this isn't the whole picture. In many cases, critics of sprawl neglect that many historic inner-city neighborhoods of today could have once been considered sprawl, and this notion implies that sprawl is more of a transitional phase associated with a high rate of urbanization than a permanent planning error. Bruegmann also points to evidence that suburban neighborhoods are actually becoming denser, as opposed to the assumption that wealthier residents are constantly moving outward to lower-density areas.

Whatever the case may be, sprawl, along with the concepts of the megalopolis and urban fragmentation, are important pieces in a larger puzzle. These issues are of paramount concern not only to urban scholars but also to planners and government officials, as well as those who make their home in metropolitan regions.

The changing metropolitan order

The decline of older industrial cities

A major feature of the post-World War II period has been the decline of the industrial city and of the region that surrounds it. Symbols of this industrial city – for example, Chicago, Detroit, and St. Louis in the United States, Manchester in England, Barcelona in Spain, and countless other sites – are no longer centers of flourishing factories where thousands of people labor. Detroit has come to represent much of this loss and decline (Sugrue 2005). By the early part of the twentieth century, thanks to the inventions and imagination of figures such as Henry Ford, the factories of Detroit employed many thousands of people, their machines humming with energy and their products selling across the world. Men and women could move to Detroit, find a job, make a great living, and raise a family. Especially for many black Americans, who would see their jobs and livelihoods disappear early in the twentieth century with the decline of the plantation economy, the factories of Detroit furnished a countless wealth of opportunities.

Many of these changes took place almost incrementally in the years just after the war, a time when the landscape of the metropolis itself was changing as well. Men came home to take on jobs in the factories, and for a time those factories continued to boom and to employ countless numbers of people. But, by the early 1960s, the industries themselves began to suffer. The stories of places such as Milwaukee are illustrative of many of these changes (see Orum 1995; see also Teaford 1994). Milwaukee had become home to several key industries, among them brewing, the manufacture of equipment and electrical devices, and the production of fine leather goods. Milwaukee was known across the United States as the city that beer made famous, and its brands, such as Schlitz, Pabst, or Miller High Life, were sold worldwide. The various factories furnished employment for many thousands of workers over a period of close to a century. Yet, by mid-twentieth century, the profits of the companies had begun to dry up, partly as a result of the challenges from firms outside Milwaukee in other parts of the United States.

This story of loss and decline happened to countless industries, countless industrial cities, and, in the end, hundreds of thousands of workers and their families across the United States. The city of Pittsburgh, once home to some of the leading steel manufacturers in the United States, such as Bethlehem Steel, would see its industries disappear over the course of several decades, leaving tens of thousands of people unemployed (see Figure 7.2). Chicago's steel manufacturing firms suffered a similar fate; US Steelworks, which was located at the southern tip of the city, eventually left, and in its wake many of thousands of people were left unemployed. St. Louis, once one of the liveliest and most flourishing of American cities, lost a number of its industries during the 1960s and 1970s, and soon, like the others, it housed countless numbers of people, many of them in their forties and fifties, who could no longer find a job simply because there were no longer any industries to employ them.

deindustrialization The movement of industrial enterprises out of older metropolitan areas during the period after World War II.

The story of **deindustrialization** was repeated not only in the United States but also across Europe. Firms and factories in various cities were no longer able to sustain their profits from local labor and thus were compelled to move their plants and production sites abroad. As they moved out, they left behind a city and

Figure 7.2 Demolition proceeds on a Pittsburgh steel mill in the early 1980s. Like many cities in the Midwest and northeast, Pittsburgh's economy was radically transformed by the closure of mills and related industrial plants. *Source: Photo: Lynn Johnson/National Geographic/Getty Images.*

many thousands of residents who would eventually become destitute and impoverished. Manufacturing had provided the economic foundation of many of these sites, cities that grew up during the industrial age; and, as industry disappeared, so the city itself became diminished. But, for every city that suffered a decline and for every industry that left, there were new ones that would arise – and often in other parts of the world.

The rise of the postindustrial/postmodern metropolitan regions

Just as Los Angeles had become a magnet for considerable population growth after World War II, there were countless other cities, many of them in the so-called **Sunbelt** of the United States, that would also grow and expand (Bernard and Rice 1984; see also Orum 2002). The center of the American population slowly began to move from the northeast and the Midwest to the southern rim of the country. Florida became a state where many people began to move, some of them those older men and women who had lost their jobs in cities such as Milwaukee and St. Louis, and who decided to retire to a warmer climate. But many other cities arose as a result of the emergence of new industries and the active role of the federal government. The latter had, for example, established naval bases and facilities in areas of California, and it was in these areas that cities such as San Diego began to grow and flourish (Markusen et al. 1991). The same thing happened in Texas, where the federal government had established army sites during the war in places near Austin and San Antonio. Moreover, in Texas, the federal government had also provided funds for the development of important infrastructure facilities, especially the construction of dams along the Colorado River, a move that made possible the migration of tens of thousands of people into areas that previously

Sunbelt The southern and western portions of the United States where many people and firms relocated after World War II.

had been virtually uninhabitable. Similar developments, also initiated by the federal government, led thousands of other families to move to states such as Arizona and New Mexico, sites previously inhospitable to all but the most determined of Americans.

Yet it was not merely a shift of people that occurred but also a shift in the energies of the US population. Many of the people who moved from the older industrial cities were young men and women who, sensing that their futures could not be fulfilled by the industries disappearing before their eyes, decided to do as their ancestors had done – move west in search of their own fortunes. Relatively small cities such as Austin, Texas, which had been known primarily for its university and also as the site of state government, seemed to explode almost overnight. In 1960 the population of Austin totaled about a quarter of a million people. Only decades later, the Austin metropolitan region held more than one million people (Orum 2002). Similar stories happened across both the southern and western United States. In California, for example, in the Bay area, cities such as San Jose mushroomed rapidly. The same thing happened to Seattle, beginning in the early 1980s, driven primarily by the development and growth of the Microsoft Corporation. Indeed, there were two signal features about the growth of many of these new exploding metropolitan regions in the United States. First, often they were located in the vicinity of good universities – as in the case of Hewlett-Packard: the firm was a spinoff of the work begun by two professors at Stanford. Second, the driving economic force behind the urban growth lay in the energy and vitality of the new high-tech industry. Though much of this new urban growth and energy was found in the southwest and the west, there were places located elsewhere – such as Columbus, Ohio and Madison, Wisconsin in the Midwest – that became home to the new industries and lured many young men and women hoping to make their own private fortunes (see e.g., Florida 2005a).

The importance of transportation, again

Why did such changes take place? Why was there such a massive shift in the population of the United States, one that would begin to move the population center of the country to the west and to the south? The obvious answer is an economic one: some industries began to decline, in part owing to the competition they faced in other parts of the country as well as the rest of the world, whereas other industries began to grow, in part aided by the actions of the federal government. If we wish to take a thin economic determinist view of history, then this is the story – finished, final, the end. But, we believe, the story is far more complicated than one simply of economic determinism. A very important factor is transportation – always a critical feature in where cities and metropolitan areas will locate.

After World War II, the federal government established a vast and important system of highways that stretched across the country, from New York to California. The highways were designed to allow firms and corporations to transport their goods more efficiently and rapidly than the rail system would allow. Moreover, within specific urban centers, the plans for new highways, it was hoped, would accelerate the growth and development of the older downtown areas, sites that had lost not only their manufacturing industries but also much of their charm and glamour during the war years. Once in place, those new expressways enabled masses of people to move easily across the United States, to take up residence and jobs outside the older population centers such as Philadelphia, and to move to sites such as Dallas or Phoenix. They also proved to have an unintended consequence within metropolitan regions: rather than simply bringing shoppers and consumers into the downtowns, they helped to facilitate the growth of the new suburbs and the fringe areas, allowing people not only to move there but also to commute back and forth regularly between their place of work and their residence in the suburbs. And as we saw in Chapter 6, these new transportation routes would allow residents and business to bypass central cities entirely through the construction of new edge cities.

The remaking of places and spaces: The profound human and political consequences

These various events had a profound impact on the lives of residents and on the metropolitan region itself. In the declining areas, the consequences were immediate and far-reaching. The loss of major industries that had provided employment and jobs for so many thousands of people over many decades left many residents unemployed, the older of whom would never be able to regain a new job – just as in the case of the recent global recession. At the same time, there were other people, many of them recent migrants of color, who had entered a metropolis such as Milwaukee or Chicago hoping to find employment but discovered that there was little to be found. Moreover, many of the jobs that now were available in the late 1960s and early 1970s were no longer the high-paying industrial jobs, jobs whose wages might have been protected by unions – which not so coincidentally had also begun to disappear. Instead, the jobs were in the service industry, in places such as McDonald's or local coffee shops; and they were jobs that typically paid far less than the jobs at plants such as Ford or Schlitz.

The growth of the unemployed workforce, especially among racial and ethnic minorities, revealed how closely the fortunes of cities were tied to the broader economic developments in the world. Local governments rely on tax revenues both from firms and from families in order to operate, especially in a country like the United States, where local governments typically have had greater autonomy and authority than in European countries, where the state exercises more local control over both resources and people. As the funds for local governments dried up, so, too, did the local services. Garbage services were temporarily suspended in various cities across the United States during the late 1970s. The city of Cleveland actually had to declare bankruptcy and suffered the loss of important services for a period of time. New York City had to be bailed out with funds from the federal government, a fact that led many to believe that this great city would never again be the same (Peterson 1981: Chapter 10; Swanstrom 1985).

These broad economic developments ultimately began to shape the places where people lived as well as the broader social spaces within which they lived. The places themselves – the neighborhoods, the homes, the stores, and the residents – all began to change as the fortunes of the older industrial cities declined. People who had grown accustomed to working at the same plant and for the same firm now saw not only their own jobs disappear but also the plants close down. The departure of the company meant not merely the loss of a job but also the loss of a whole way of life. Younger people might be able to move, but the older residents, those who had worked on the assembly line manufacturing cars or leather purses, could not leave, and it was many of them who suffered the most from these declines. Capital can move easily, we learned, but people who hold jobs cannot. Place is important, we have said throughout this book, because it enables us to build a sense of community and to develop a sense of identity for ourselves – and, as places changed, as jobs were lost and companies left, many people were set adrift, losing both a chunk of their own communities and a strong sense of their own identities as workers and human beings.

In response to the growing crisis during the 1960s and 1970s, a number of political activities arose across the United States. Knowing the importance that the idea of place has to people, many local political organizers used the idea of place to help organize resistance to the economic downturn and the effect it was having on the lives of local residents. Some of them targeted their efforts at protesting the cost of housing in cities. In New York City, for example, rent strikes were organized during the 1970s to protest the continuing high cost of housing. Other organizers targeted their efforts at helping the growing number of newly impoverished people and those who had recently been displaced from work. Some were intended to help people who not only were poor but also who had been left homeless in this period. Homelessness itself became a major issue, not only in US cities but also in major metropolitan areas such as London, where the Prime Minister, John Major, once attacked the homeless population as somehow being the cause of their own lack of employment and absence of shelter. Moreover, a new organization arose during this period of time in the United States, the Association of Community Organizations for Reform Now, or ACORN, and it targeted its efforts at organizing people in local communities to protest the effects that the new downturn was having on individual workers as well as families.

At the other end of the spectrum of growth and expansion, among the newly emerging cities in the Sunbelt, there were other sorts of political issues and problems, and a different set of political movements and organizations was arising. Here the problems faced by urban residents were not ones of the loss of employment and industry but rather the challenges posed by unfettered growth of the population itself. Local residents became concerned

MAKING THE CITY BETTER   7.1

Community organizing

Urban unrest became prevalent throughout the 1960s in almost every major city as people took to the streets and demanded their rights after years of unfair stratification and oppression. In recognition, the US federal government began supporting community-based efforts to organize residents, services, and programs at the local level within impoverished neighborhoods. The profession of community organizing emerged as a result of this synergy between local efforts and federal funding, and many neighborhood activists worked to improve their communities and empower local citizens.

The goals that professional community organizers strove for included increasing educational and occupational mobility, obtaining necessary local services, fighting the negative effects of poverty, and increasing the influence of the poor and oppressed though voter education, outreach programs, and pressure on city officials. And, since these neighborhood efforts were supported financially by the federal government, thousands of community organizations began springing up all across the country. In fact, by 1978 the National Commission on Neighborhoods had compiled a list of 8000 neighborhood-based organizations.

In most community-organizing models, success depends on community empowerment and structural transformation. The community should not come to depend upon the organizer but should instead develop social and organizational structures that allow it to meet its own needs. Generally, after a community organizer finished equipping neighborhoods with the ability to fight for their own rights, the organizer would move on, or, if he or she was a local resident, step back and work with the group in a normal membership role.

Throughout mostly Western countries, community organizers took the urban unrest of the 1960s and turned it into productive energy that could be harnessed to create real and lasting local change. Probably the most well-known community organizer in the world today is Barack Obama, the current

President of the United States, who helped to improve neighborhoods in the South Side of Chicago (see Figure 7.3). Others who worked as community organizers before becoming well known for their national political activism include César Chávez, Martin Luther King Jr., and Ralph Nader.

Community organization continues to be an important source of positive change in urban neighborhoods. Contemporary community organizers often act as mediators between philanthropic and government agencies on one side and community members on the other. Common types of projects include the construction of affordable housing and neighborhood economic development (particularly that aimed at attracting necessary services and retail, such as banks, grocery stores, and childcare facilities). They may also face new kinds of challenges – for instance, ensuring that housing remains affordable in gentrifying neighborhoods or cleaning up after decades of environmental racism (see Chapter 12). The goals remain the same, however – to improve the qualities of neighborhoods as places and to prepare community members to lead themselves.

Figure 7.3 President Barack Obama's biography has brought new attention to community organizing, a strategy for improving urban neighborhoods that became widespread in the 1960s. Obama worked in neighborhoods on the South Side of Chicago, an area devastated by deindustrialization. *Source: Photo: AP Photo/Obama Presidential Campaign/PA Photos.*

about the ways in which real estate developers moved into local neighborhoods and sought to change zoning laws in order to build new housing developments or new businesses. Developers came to be seen in many of the growing communities in the same way as employers were seen in the declining ones – as the villains and as the source of personal and community problems. In places across the Sunbelt, countless new neighborhood organizations arose among local residents to protest what seemed to be the relentless assault of the developers on old neighborhoods (Orum 2002). For many such organizations, the call to arms lay in the very notion of "growth" itself, and a variety of slow-growth, no-growth, and even "smart-growth" movements arose, all designed to limit the seemingly endless and inexorable expansion of the newer cities.

In brief, then, the broad changes in the form of industrialization and then deindustrialization greatly affected the fortunes of families as well as local institutions. People who lost jobs in Detroit found it more difficult to make home payments, while those people who lived in the neighborhoods of Austin, where developers came in and wished to create new housing developments, helped to create local neighborhood organizations to protect themselves. In other words, place as well as space continued to remain central to the lives of people, and in these perilous decades residents organized themselves politically and worked hard to protect the places where they lived and the neighborhoods to which they had become attached.

The emerging global economy
A brief overview

Just as the shifting population in the United States had signaled a profound movement in the energy and economy of that country, when the industries in US and European cities began to leave, seeking their fortunes in countries outside the West, it signaled a shift in the broader global economy. The countries of the West had for centuries been the dominant economic and political powers in the world. It was in England, France, and Holland, for example, that great wealth and enterprise began to emerge in the sixteenth century, and it was here too that major metropolitan areas such as London and Paris first developed. The whole sense of a modern metropolis emerged in this part of the world. And its emergence helped to give birth to the great social theories of the day, particularly the writings of Karl Marx and Friedrich Engels, who used these materials to fashion their view of the development of capitalism and the nature of economic and social inequality that accompanied its development.

For a variety of reasons, the world began to change after World War II. New markets began to open up outside the West, markets for the sale of commodities, of course, but primarily for the manufacture of goods (see Sklair 2002). At root, as Marx had predicted and followers such as V. I. Lenin had shown, the economic system of modern capitalism began to spread its tentacles across the world. The war in Vietnam, from one angle, was about the effort of the West to prevent the spread of Communism – to stop the so-called domino effect of one country after another falling under the dominion of the Communist ideology. But from another angle it was about the effort by Western business, aided by the authority of the state, to expand its reach across the globe and to create new markets where few had previously existed – at least not for the sale and purchase of commodities.

By the late 1960s and early 1970s, the pace of these developments had quickened. In the 1960s Japan was the first to rise as a major competitor to the United States, followed by the so-called "four little tigers" (Hong Kong, Singapore, South Korea, and Taiwan) as sources of manufactured products to be shipped to the United States (Vogel 1991). New firms were able to be opened in Taiwan and Hong Kong. The latter, a British protectorate until 1997, became a center of financial and banking capital, providing funds for new enterprises. New factories and firms began to arise in Asia as, compared to the United States and Western Europe, its countries offered labor at far lower wages. Profits under capitalism, of course, increase when either the cost of goods increases or the price of labor goes down; by the 1970s, there were sufficient numbers of new companies and an availability of labor that made it far cheaper and more profitable for US and other Western firms to produce goods in Asia than in the United States, for example. Leather goods that previously could be produced fairly cheaply in Milwaukee were now manufactured in firms and factories in Taiwan, where the cost of labor was far lower.

At the center of the early resurgence of Asia was the development of the Japanese economy in the post-World War II period. Japan provided a new model for the development of competitive capitalism. It was based on a close alliance of the government with the operation of new industries, something that enabled Japanese firms to recover and develop quickly after the war (Johnson 1982). As a result, the manufacture of high-quality goods in Japan took off in the 1970s, and such goods became highly competitive with the goods produced in the United States. The singular illustration of the rise of the Japanese economy came in the form of the manufacture of automobiles, a market once virtually dominated in the United States by Chrysler, Ford, and General Motors, all corporations in the United States. Mitsubishi, Nissan, and Toyota, leading automobile firms in Japan, soon became prime competitors of the US firms in the production of automobiles. And, by the end of the twentieth century, it would be these firms that gradually led to the decline and virtual collapse of the American automobile firms. But there were other firms as well, including Sony, which developed in the 1980s and eventually created a range of new technological products – the Walkman, among others – that opened up entirely new markets in the West (see Figure 7.4).

By the late 1970s, and after the death of Mao Tse-tung, yet another major nation, the People's Republic of China, joined the turn to capitalism. Deng Xiaoping, the successor to Mao, initiated a number of important reforms in China (Guthrie 2006). He and his allies insisted that the future lay in the development of China's economic power, a power that under Mao had been restrained by various ideological programs as well as obvious missteps by the Communist Party. Deng was a far more practical and pragmatic thinker who hoped to encourage the development of China's own economic resources and unleash the potential of its vast population of people. By the early 1980s, these reforms began to pay dividends. China embarked on a number of joint economic ventures with both Western and Asian countries. Western companies were encouraged to move their production facilities into China, where the cost of labor was considerably cheaper than in the West.

Figure 7.4 Industrial growth in Japan, particularly the manufacture of automobiles and consumer electronics, transformed its cities in the 1970s and 1980s. Here televisions are being made at Hitachi's Yokohama manufacturing facility in 1971. *Source: Photo © Associated Press/ PA Photos.*

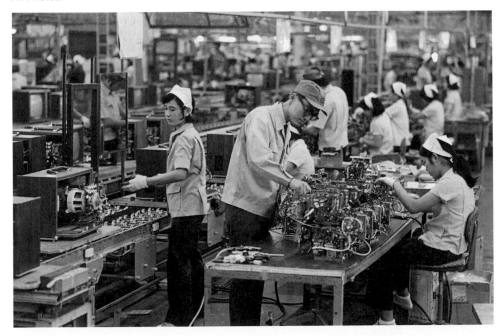

Soon the Chinese landscape was dotted with countless numbers of new production facilities, and tens of thousands of former Chinese peasants left their homes in the rural areas to take up residence in such newly booming metropolitan regions as Shenzhen and such older ones as Guangzhou (Canton). Furniture companies in small Indiana and Wisconsin cities could have their products made in Shenzhen and ship them all the way back to the US market and still save money. In effect, as the cities in the West, such as Milwaukee or Pittsburgh, began to decline, losing young people to cities such as Seattle or San Diego, the cities in China began to emerge and develop. Between 1979 and 2009, for example, the city of Shenzhen, on the southeastern coast of China, grew from 30 000 to over 10 million people (see Figure 7.5). Shenzhen's annual average growth rate of 30 percent over this period of time was unequaled anywhere in the world. It had a gross domestic product (GDP) of almost $100 billion in 2007, ranking fourth among all Chinese cities but without parallel elsewhere in the world. It was the first Chinese city in which GDP per capita surpassed $10 000. Its projected GDP per capita is expected to reach $20 000 in 2020, another first for China.[4]

The growth and development of new markets and industries that took place in Asia would happen in other parts of the world as well. In Latin America, both Argentina and Brazil became sites where new industries and markets took root, leading to the explosive growth of metropolitan areas such as São Paulo, Brazil. While national governments and political figures helped to promote and facilitate such growth, the emergence of powerful multinational corporations played a central part as well. By the early 1970s, it was evident that mobile and flexible corporations, such as General Electric, were now able to move their production facilities to one or two countries where labor was cheap and yet maintain their headquarters in the United States. There were a number of such firms that began to populate the world, and they seemed to many observers to represent a new and energetic form of modern capitalism, one in which the power and resources of the firm itself moved beyond the reach of any single nation and thus posed a potential challenge to the reigning order of nations in the world. General Electric is but one example of the range of such firms that emerged, especially in the 1980s, including Coca-Cola and Motorola. The power of such new multinational corporations was illustrated in the 1970s when it became known that

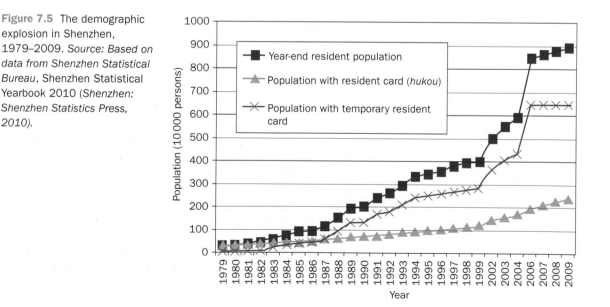

Figure 7.5 The demographic explosion in Shenzhen, 1979–2009. *Source: Based on data from Shenzhen Statistical Bureau,* Shenzhen Statistical Yearbook 2010 (*Shenzhen: Shenzhen Statistics Press, 2010).*

International Telephone and Telegraph, operating with the permission and consent of the United States government, had furnished some of the funds necessary to overthrow the Socialist regime of Salvador Allende in Chile.[5]

As this new and vibrant global economy emerged and expanded, certain sectors came to play an ever more important role. Whereas manufacturing capital lay behind the work of multinational corporations and the rise of new plants in Asia, far from their headquarters in the West, capital in the form of finance and banking eventually assumed a more prominent role. Capital itself, because it could easily be spread around the world, could be transferred from one country to another, taken out as a corporate investment, and then used to construct new plants and offices in one of the developing regions of the world in Asia or Latin America. Investment bankers became central agents and operatives in this process, and their banks became the organizations to which companies could turn to protect their profits as well as source financial backing for new industries. Moreover, once the technological revolution of the 1990s had occurred, in which the internet shrunk time and space, in David Harvey's apt metaphor, bankers in one part of the world could easily transfer funds to another part of the world (Harvey 1991). Business transactions that had once taken days, even months, to complete could now be done overnight, thereby making the marketplace truly global. Here the role of the new technology was truly revolutionary, speeding up processes and creating new kinds of connections and networks among businesses and people across the world.

The growing connections among people, firms, and cities across the globe created a new set of forces and factors that eventually would be felt in the workings of social institutions. Manuel Castells, who, along with Harvey, helped to usher in new theories about urban areas and the metropolis in the 1970s, argues, in fact, that the social world no longer should be

STUDYING THE CITY   7.1

Border metropolitan complexes

A border metropolitan complex, sometimes referred to as a **borderplex**, is a metropolitan area that spreads over a border between two countries. These borderplexes introduce a new, complex set of problems. Many urban issues, such as transportation, environmental protection, health, and public safety are concerns that are regional in nature and require the cooperation of municipal governments from both sides of the border.

borderplex A metropolitan area that crosses national boundaries.

For instance, on the United States–Mexico border, the cities of El Paso, Texas and Ciudad Juárez, Mexico come together to essentially form one metropolitan entity, a borderplex (see Figure 7.6). Many people daily cross over the border between the two cities to visit family or go to work, the economies of the cities are interdependent, and if one city has a problem the other city has a problem. Today, some of the major problems afflicting the El Paso–Ciudad Juárez metropolitan area include rapid unplanned growth as people have migrated to the border cities looking for work and seeking commercial opportunities as a result of the implementation of the North American Free Trade Agreement (NAFTA). This has caused heavy congestion in all traffic links between the two cities. This in turn results in serious air pollution plaguing the region.

Political scientists John Tuman and Grant Neely (2003) have examined the challenges associated with solving cross-border metropolitan issues. They found that many municipal leaders will attempt to

Figure 7.6 The Santa Fe Bridge border crossing between Ciudad Juarez and El Paso. These and other cities along the United States–Mexican border have experienced dramatic growth due to the development of *maquiladoras* on the Mexico side. *Source: Photo Jim Lyle/Texas Transportation Institute.*

cooperate across national borders to deal with problems regionally. The El Paso–Ciudad Juárez metropolitan region is no exception in this regard, as the cities have formed many agreements pertaining to issues such as environmental protection, tracking down criminals, and improving public health through the distribution of vaccines.

However, cooperation between municipal leaders is not always easy. In many cases, the countries that a borderplex stretches into will have different legal and political structures, cultural or language barriers, and sometimes even tense or hostile international relations (Alvarez 1995). Cooperating under these conditions can be difficult for city leaders, who may serve under different term limits, wield varying levels of political power, speak different languages, or have negative perceptions of one another. Beyond the challenges associated with political offices and office holders lie differences in what level of government takes charge of problems manifested in metropolitan areas. For instance, countries may approach problems such as transportation planning and environmental protection either at the national or local level, depending on how centralized their government is.

Despite the challenges, urban scholars have found that treating a borderplex like a single metropolitan entity through cooperation between the multiple cities involved makes solving regional problems much easier. But there are many more questions surrounding borderplexes, concerning topics of economics, public administration, social networks, and urban development, and it's up to new urban thinkers to come up with answers.

conceived in terms of institutions such as the state and corporation but rather in terms of the connections that both people and organizations have with one another. These connections, or networks, allow people to communicate easily across the globe, not only sharing information but also transferring funds easily from one site to another. Castells (1989, 2000) argues that such networks are the operating tools of society today and that they are so powerful that they actually challenge the integrity of nations as well as of corporations themselves. Whether this is entirely true or not, it is clear that one of the central tendencies of the period after World War II was to break down old state boundaries and create new alliances, ones that would help not only to integrate institutions and people in the global economy but also to transform the world in unexpected and potent new ways. Such was the case, for example, in the collapse of the old Soviet Union. There were various forces that came to disrupt the Soviet Union, but surely one of the most important was simply the televised information that penetrated the Iron Curtain, allowing people living in Moscow and St. Petersburg to become aware of the economic advances and luxury goods of people living in London or Paris or New York. Here was a case in which the new technology, and the information it furnished, helped to fuel the resistance that would eventually undermine a political regime that seemed as though it never could be toppled.

History and economic events, we believe, shape what happens within cities and what we, as individuals and in groups, can do as local residents. The developments in the postwar period have very much shaped the opportunities and the directions that our actions as urban residents can take. Just as the decline of local resources began to limit what local government officials could do, so the emergence of new resources and competition from firms abroad began to shape the actions that could be taken by firms and industries within the metropolitan region. Most of all, these broad changes in the economy and in politics began to reshape the urban landscape. Geographic scale, as geographer Neil Brenner argues, would become a very important factor in the analysis of the growing metropolitan areas. Analysts could no longer think merely about the qualities of interdependence or the hinterlands within a metropolitan region; they were compelled to think about the role of the federal or national government, even the powerful and wide-ranging multinational corporations, in altering the landscapes of cities and hence their residents – you and us.

People, place, and space in a global world

In the chapters that follow, we shall fill in many more details about how the changes since the 1960s have reshaped the nature of cities and of the people who live within them. One thing is certain: people spread across the globe are increasingly living in or around cities. In a world in which cities and people are now so closely connected across the globe, in which time and space seem, as David Harvey has suggested, to have become compressed, how have the lives of people been influenced and how have the places and spaces within which they make their lives been shaped? How are your lives different today, living within a metropolitan region, than were those of metropolitan residents, say, 50 years ago?

The one most obvious fact is that the forces and structures that influence our lives in cities no longer reside simply within the conventional boundaries of cities themselves. In the 1930s, in a city such as Muncie (recall the Lynds' study from Chapter 4), the one factory in the town, which produced glass jars and employed most of the working men and women, intimately affected the lives of everyone. If business was good, so were the wages of the local workers and residents, but if it was bad people would be thrown out of work. And, of course, terminated employees and their families could directly connect their changing circumstances to the declining fortunes of the glass jar company. The same was true in Pittsburgh, Pennsylvania, where many men were employed in the steel industry. Their entire lives were caught up in the fortunes of the local steel mills, and as those fortunes changed so, too, did the lives of the local residents and their families. Likewise, the same portrait could be painted in Detroit, where automobiles were the dominant industry and where the lives of most local residents revolved around the success, or failure, of companies such as Ford and General Motors. If these companies did well – as they managed to do for many years – it was not only the owners of the plants that did well but also the men and women who worked for those firms. Life in the metropolis, in other words, was relatively transparent and simple, and people could count on remaining in those places – those neighborhoods – from one generation to the next.

But, as the world has become more complicated and yet more tightly integrated, as people and metropolitan areas have come to be connected more closely to one another in the postwar period, the structures and events that lie outside the immediate metropolitan area have taken on an ever greater importance. New competition in the manufacture of steel or leather goods or electronic apparatus, whether in China or Korea or Japan, mean that the fortunes of local industries are no longer simply determined by economic circumstances in Detroit or Middletown or Pittsburgh but rather by the operations of businesses and economies that lie thousands of miles away. Thus, while Henry Ford might have been able to deal with the circumstances of an economic downturn in Detroit and Walter Reuther (the head of the American Federation of Labor and Congress of Industrial Organizations (AFL-CIO) during the 1940s and 1950s) might have been able to address the concerns of American auto workers, those who now run Ford or head the AFL-CIO have seen their authority diminish and, with it, their ability to influence circumstances so as to improve the lives of people living in these metropolitan areas.

The worldwide recession of 2007–2010 was a perfect example of how the scale of events in the metropolis has changed. Back in the 1930s, John Doe and his family could take out a mortgage at the local bank on Main Street. If John had a problem making payments, he could take a five-minute walk, meet with his local banker, Mr. Jones, and make some kind of arrangement to perhaps modify the loan or even delay payments for a short while. But that is no longer the case. The complexity and range of economic conditions today mean that the company that holds a home mortgage is not down the street but is in all likelihood in Brussels or London or Paris. Thus, if John Doe could not make his home payment today, he would be compelled to talk to someone over the phone located in a different city, if not a different country. Take, for example, the experience of Susan Hall, related in the *New York Times* in February 2012:

> Susan Hall, a homeowner in Cotati, Calif., who has been trying to modify the terms of her mortgage since October 2009, thought she was in luck last October when she got a letter informing her that a single person had been assigned to her case by her servicer, Bank of America. Within weeks, she got three more letters, all with different names as her ostensible point of contact. None of them proved able to help.
>
> "I just keep getting passed from one person to another," she said. To make matters worse, her house is now valued at less than her mortgage, putting her among the 10.7 million American mortgage holders who are so-called underwater borrowers. "Nobody is willing to talk to me." (Schwartz 2012)

Banks themselves have become larger and more global by way of their acquisitions and growth before the recession. Moreover, while in the United States this economic crisis may have originated on Wall Street, it has had a distant effect on the interior of the United States – in the older, manufacturing regions whose heydays are long past as well as in the newer, shallow-rooted Sunbelt economies whose recent economic booms have been fueled in part by real estate speculation, overdevelopment, and fictitious housing wealth (Florida

2009). We will address how some of these processes have played out in and around Chinese megacities such as Shanghai in Chapter 11.

It is often said by people who are deeply interested in helping residents with their homes, mortgages, or other problems in their local neighborhoods that we should all "think globally and act locally." What that means is that we must be aware of the degree to which our local circumstances, as neighbors, workers, and friends, living in the places to which we are attached, are caught in a web of circumstances that weave together the threads of our metropolitan region with those of our country, indeed our world. This thought might at first terrify you, but it is a reminder, as C. Wright Mills (2000 [1959]) said so many years ago, that our personal – that is to say, our *local everyday* – concerns have a greater import because they reflect causes and issues made outside our own local worlds. One might even conclude that in such a complicated world, where the actions of corporations or nations in one part can have an impact on the lives of families far away, we should simply throw up our hands and declare ourselves helpless victims. But that would be the wrong conclusion. Inasmuch as we all continue to live in specific places where we make our lives and find our security, it is all the more imperative that we actively remain connected to our friends and neighbors, and together with them work hard to improve life in the places where we live. Visit the book's companion website at www.wiley.com/go/cities for examples, case studies, and discussion questions, plus a list of useful films and other media, on how the metropolis changed during this era.

Critical thinking questions

1 Events after World War II, such as the loss of industries from major manufacturing cities and regions in the West, greatly reshaped the landscapes of many cities across the world. How, in particular, did those changes affect life in the city that you are from?

2 The economic recession of 2007–2010 has shown how closely interconnected are the fortunes of metropolitan areas in different part of the world. Do you think that these connections between different sites in the world will grow stronger or weaker in the coming years? And how might these connections reshape the ways in which nations work and people live?

3 Can you think of other metropolitan areas that resemble Los Angeles today in terms of the diversity of their residents as well as the multiple and different localities contained within their regions?

4 How are the global processes that have emerged in the wake of World War II, such as the movement of capital and the migration of people from one metropolitan area to another, likely to challenge national governments, such as that of the United States, as well as influence the attitudes of citizens?

Suggested reading

Robert Fogelson, *The Fragmented Metropolis: Los Angeles, 1850–1930* (Berkeley: University of California Press, 1993). This engaging history of Los Angeles shows how and why the city developed with its many fragments and areas rather than in the form of older industrial cities such as New York City and Chicago.

Anthony Orum, *City-Building in America* (Boulder, CO: Westview Press, 1995). A systematic comparison of the history and growth of four cities (Milwaukee, Minneapolis-St. Paul, Cleveland, and Austin), the book shows how history and agency matter to the growth as well as decline of particular cities.

Saskia Sassen, *The Global City: New York, London, Tokyo*, 2nd edition (Princeton, NJ: Princeton University Press, 2001).The second edition of Sassen's imaginative theory about the global city furnishes more facts about how the global city emerged and operates in the world today.

Leslie Sklair, *Globalization: Capitalism and Its Alternatives*, 3rd edition (Oxford: Oxford University Press, 2002). An excellent introduction to and analysis of the nature of globalization, and the world economy, today.

Edward Soja, *Postmetropolis: Critical Studies of Cities and Regions* (Oxford: Blackwell, 2000). A brilliant analysis of postmodern thought and the metropolis. Soja explores six different ways, or discourses, for thinking about the city.

Notes

1. See any of the following excellent works: Bluestone and Harrison (1984, 1990) and Teaford (1994).
2. For a superb book on Los Angeles and different ways of treating it, see Soja (2000).
3. For two excellent books on Los Angeles, see Fogelson (1993) and Fulton (2001).
4. These calculations exclude the six million temporary migrants who helped to build Shenzhen's industrial machine. See Chen and de' Medici (2010).
5. The seminal writing here is Barnet and Muller (1974).

PART III
THE METROPOLIS AND SOCIAL INEQUALITIES

CHAPTER 8

The early metropolis as a place of inequality

KEY TOPICS

→ Why racial/ethnic and class differences are fundamental to urban life.

→ Ways in which colonial powers used urban design and segregation as a means of exercising their authority.

→ The experiences of urban immigrants, and those immigrants' impact on neighborhoods and cities as places.

→ How racial segregation between blacks and whites was accomplished in US cities, and its impact on individuals' lives.

→ Early responses to urban inequality and deprivation, and how these relate to contemporary social welfare initiatives.

Contents

Introduction to Cities: How Place and Space Shape Human Experience,
First Edition. Xiangming Chen, Anthony M. Orum, and Krista E. Paulsen.
© 2013 Xiangming Chen, Anthony M. Orum, and Krista E. Paulsen.
Published 2013 by Blackwell Publishing Ltd.

Figure 8.1, which shows two distinct experiences of one London street, captures an important truth about cities: they are markedly different places for different people. On the left, a wealthy man gazes across the street, perhaps engaging in conversation with the man who stands beside him. At his feet, another man kneels on the sidewalk, intent on the work of shining shoes. Though these men shared the same *space* in the instant captured by the photographer, we can safely assume that they dwelt in two very different *places*, two Londons – from the landmarks they used to find their ways to the sites that held the most meaning to the kinds of opportunities that living in this great city afforded them. And their disparity was by no means unique: cities have, for centuries, been spaces where those of varying means and backgrounds have often lived vastly different lives.

Though urban density brings together disparate populations, their experiences of the city – even of the very same sidewalk – can be worlds apart. The same city can be clean or dirty, chaotic or orderly, bountiful or desolate – all depending on the neighborhoods one frequents, the resources one has, and the opportunities that one finds available to people like oneself. This chapter takes up just how larger structural inequalities of race/ethnicity, gender, and social class become embedded in cities, with an emphasis on the kinds of spaces that those inequalities produce in the urban environment and the ways in which inequalities affect the meanings and experiences of urban places.

Diversity has long been hailed as one of the distinctive qualities of urban settings. In his influential work "Urbanism as a Way of Life" (1938), the Chicago School's Louis Wirth specified large populations, density, and diversity (or heterogeneity) as the qualities responsible for making urban living unique. Jane Jacobs, too, has championed diversity as one of the keys to cities' vitality and economic success. But, while diversity can lead to innovation and economic expansion as new ideas are matched with the talent needed to

Figure 8.1 As this 1935 photograph of a London street shows, the experiences of the same place are very different for different individuals – in this case, the man who has his shoes shined and the man who shines shoes. *Source: Photo: General Photographic Agency/Getty Images.*

develop them and with markets that will appreciate them, this benefit of a diverse environment is often overlooked. Instead, diversity can be seen as a threat to important cultural norms and thus greeted with hostility. Similarly, the great disparities between the urban rich and poor have often been viewed as the result of individual or group shortcomings. The poor – particularly if they look, speak, or act differently from others – are often seen as creating their own troubles. That their poverty might be a byproduct of the same processes that create great wealth in cities is often overlooked. Because urban spaces bring diverse populations together – rich and poor, immigrant and native, dominant racial/ethnic groups and minorities – cultural differences between them are not only noticeable but also create tension. This is particularly true in urban neighborhoods, where the details of daily living are on full display.

As you will recall from Chapter 6, on suburbs, and as we detail further in this chapter, urban spaces and places take the forms that they do in part because of efforts to manage social differences. Wealthy and powerful individuals have often sought to insulate themselves from those of other social classes or racial/ethnic groups. They restricted where immigrants or minorities could buy or rent property and secluded themselves in neighborhoods and dwellings made inaccessible by physical or economic barriers. The urban poor were compelled to survive in substandard dwellings in crowded neighborhoods (recall Friedrich Engels' description of Manchester in Chapter 2), conditions that affected the everyday routines of their lives and even their life expectancies. Since economic inequality is often bound up with racial/ethnic differences, many poorer neighborhoods

immigrant enclaves
Neighborhoods where immigrants settle and are involved in local social institutions.

ghetto neighborhood
An area where a racial or ethnic minority group is forced to live by poverty or discrimination.

were also highly segregated, resulting in uniquely urban forms such as the **immigrant enclave** and the **ghetto neighborhood**. But, as we will show, these neighborhoods to which poor, minority, and immigrant populations were relegated became a new kind of resource for their residents, as well as for their cities.

We focus in this chapter on urban diversity and inequality before World War II. Examining this early period, we can see the ways in which differences among city residents began to be mapped onto urban space, resulting in patterns of racial/ethnic segregation and pronounced inequality that persist in cities today. We will take up more recent manifestations of urban diversity and inequality in Chapter 9, but here we feel it is important to set the stage by examining just how those patterns came to be. In doing so, we present not only the historic roots of current urban problems but also early efforts to make cities more humane places. We begin with a short discussion of difference and inequality in colonial cities, where racial/ ethnic differences could determine access to power and opportunity. The bulk of the chapter is then devoted to industrial cities of North America and Europe, where unprecedented numbers of very diverse migrants came seeking opportunity. While many found this, they also found a stratified landscape in which they would try to make their own place.

Colonial cities as unequal places

In colonial cities, the urban centers from which predominantly European colonialists oversaw their empires, large numbers of the ruling state's citizens lived near even larger indigenous populations. For the most part, they were "cities laid out by the rulers, not the ruled" (King 1976: p. xii). These populations typically differed not only by the amount of power they wielded but also by class and race (though not always in straightforward or predictable ways). Colonial cities therefore offer a distinct view of how race, class, and power have been mapped onto urban places because populations were segregated from one another and lived in distinctly different kinds of urban environments. This typically included a small but well-appointed district where colonial elites made their homes and conducted business and administrative tasks, a military outpost or **cantonment** with colonial and/or indigenous soldiers, and a larger indigenous city located in an old, precolonial area or in informal or self-built districts at the city's edge.

> **cantonment**
> A temporary or military encampment, particularly associated with colonial rule.

Sociologist Anthony King has explored the ways in which colonial power and privilege shaped Delhi as a distinct place. Like many Indian cities, Delhi (the area known as Old Delhi) predated Britain's colonial rule. A small walled city dating from the seventeenth century (other cities called Delhi had occupied the same location for hundreds of years prior), it was known for its jewelry, silverware, and other artistic goods. The British captured the city in 1803, marking the beginning of nearly 150 years of British rule. The military cantonment moved several times during this era, from outside the city to inside and back outside. As it did, the military confiscated and cleared properties in order to provide for its own needs. Among these needs were large, open parcels that would ensure adequate views and firing distance for defensive purposes, as well as serving as parade grounds and camps for visiting troops. Not only did the military spaces serve as symbols of colonial power but the associated open spaces also kept Delhi's different social groups separated. British governmental elites also segregated themselves during this era, building large bungalows on the outskirts of the walled city. The grand scale of their homes and lots contrasted sharply with the crowded walled city, and trees planted for cooling gave the colonial district a distinctly suburban feel (King 1976). Architectural differences between colonial and indigenous urban settlements were not unique to India. Half a world away in Quito, white-mestizo elites distinguished their urban space from rural, indigenous townships through the use of modern sanitation technologies and architectural adornments (Capello 2008).

The patterns of separation and segregation seen in nineteenth-century Delhi were in many ways typical of colonial cities. But it was in 1911, when Delhi was made the capital of the British Indian Empire, that patterns of segregation would be most formally and precisely inscribed. Construction of the capital required the development of areas lying further outside the old city. Nearly every dimension of the new city's construction, from the plotting and naming of streets to the size and location of individual estates and homes, reflected the social and political hierarchy of the city. For instance, the streets nearest the Government House were named for the king and his immediate family; those further away were named for figures central to establishing British colonial power; the next set were named for historic Indian rulers; and so on. Members of government were assigned estates whose location and sizes matched their rank and, again, proximity to the Government House was key. This system ensured that the residential areas of New Delhi were segregated with great precision: not only were British and Indian households, and working classes and elites, separated but also on a given block one would only find officers or officials of a specific rank. This practice took to extremes the tendency to associate neighborhoods or districts with differing social classes or racial groups – a key way in which the meanings associated with places confer status upon residents.

While the regimented segregation of Delhi might have been extreme, it showcased the rational, ordered approach to planning typical of many colonial cities. British and European colonial powers not only imposed systems of social and racial hierarchies but also brought with them plans for urban development that replaced indigenous forms of development. The Spanish were perhaps the most coherent in these efforts, employing the Laws of the Indies, a 1573 code that specified the use of a gridded street design and the creation of a central plaza surrounded by institutions of colonial power including government buildings and the city's main church (see Figure 8.2). Cities throughout Latin America conformed to this code, which inscribed into social space the power differences between the colonizer and the colonized (for the sociological theory that conceptualized social space and power see our discussion of the Chicago School in Chapter 2) (Rybczynski 1996).

It is important to keep in mind that cities such as Delhi, Mexico City, or Quito were not merely sites of colonial power but also hubs of industry and trade. In calling attention to some distinct patterns of racial/ethnic and class inequality we do not intend to paint a one-dimensional picture of life in these places or to suggest that the existence of a colonial power structure determined every aspect of urban life. Indeed, many cities in former Asian and Latin American colonies shared many qualities with the industrial cities of Europe. For instance, in a study of Ahmedabad in western India, Siddhartha Raychaudhuri describes the pronounced class inequality that followed expansion of the local textile mill industry, as well as other familiar urban problems such as congestion and environmental degradation (Raychaudhuri 2001). We turn now to the patterns of inequality found in cities marked by rapid urban and industrial expansion.

Early urban diversity

Industrialization and urbanization worked hand in hand. As factories grew, so did opportunities for industrial labor and the need for an ever-growing labor force of people. In Europe and Great Britain, this labor force typically included peasants who had long toiled in subsistence agriculture or who had been forced from agricultural pursuits due to the spread of enclosure laws that privatized common pasturelands. In the United States and Canada, they were immigrants, largely of similar rural backgrounds. Some made stops in British or European cities before migrating to North America, while others came more directly from small villages and rural areas in their home countries. Hundreds of thousands of Irish, pushed from their home country by the famine of the 1840s, made their homes in English and Scottish cities, often in the most run-down ghetto neighborhoods. In 1851, around 20 percent of the populations of Dundee, Glasgow, and Liverpool were Irish-born

Figure 8.2 Mexico City's Zócalo, or Plaza de la Constitución, bordered by the Metropolitan Cathedral and National Palace, illustrates the type of central plaza dictated by Spain's Laws of the Indies. Here, as in other colonial cities, the forms that spaces took symbolized just what groups and institutions held power. *Source: Photo © Kari/Alamy.*

(Tuataigh 1985). The opportunities they found were mixed: work was often abundant but required long hours and paid wages that again provided only for the most meager forms of subsistence.

The employers, on the other hand – industrialists whose fortunes grew with their cities – lived very different lives. Before the nineteenth-century expansion of suburbanization, wealthy merchants and industrialists lived in central cities. Like everyone else, they depended on muscle power to get to work – walking or travel by horse and carriage – which gave central locations a distinct advantage. But, if geographically close to their workforces, the homes of the great industrialists were otherwise far from the hovels in which their workers lived. Their large townhouses were designed to insulate the family from the challenges of urban life through design features such as private courtyards. A sizable staff, from chauffeurs to maids to governesses to footmen, and quarters for the staff were common as well. Homes also became a means of displaying wealth and accomplishment. As earnings came to replace inherited position as the marker of social status, the home took on an important role in affirming and announcing that status to colleagues and callers. A large home with many features and opulent décor suggested that the owner had truly arrived.

Urban affluence also gave rise to the kinds of cultural institutions that make cities interesting and vital places. Urban historian Lewis Mumford called attention to the ways in which the amenities of urban life, whether theaters, gardens, or hotels, provided spaces mimicking royal palaces and courts. Here the wealthy had opportunities to meet one another and display their affluence, often in areas segregated from the poor or working class. Museums, too, whether the British Museum in London or Paris' Louvre, not only reflected palaces in their architecture but also drew upon the power of the aristocracy to secure vast collections through military might or outright purchase. In turn, these institutions and their descendents in cities around the world have become important anchors of urban elites' social lives and networks (Mumford 1961).

But gardens, parks, dance halls, and other public or semi-public spaces often became sites of conflict as city dwellers of different racial/ethnic and national backgrounds brought with them different languages and dialects as well as distinct cultural norms. Gardens or dance halls might be used for the same general purposes by different groups – for instance, as a place for young, single people to see and meet one another – but in culturally distinct ways. Norms of acceptable courtship behaviors varied by social class and ethnic group, and what was acceptable to one might have been considered indecent by another. Other leisure activities also differed, making parks into spaces where struggles over the "proper" uses of space were routinely fought. Tompkins Square Park, on New York City's Lower East Side, was first developed in 1834 as a way to encourage middle-class settlement in the area. Instead, a national depression combined with increasing immigration led to unprecedented density in the neighborhood, and working-class residents used the park for both recreation and protests. The city aimed to discourage such practices by using the park as a military parade ground, but residents demanded that the park remain "open to the public for free assembly" (Abu-Lughod 1994). In other parts of New York City, such as Gramercy Park, green spaces were privately owned, requiring a key for access. This prevented conflicts over proper use of space, as only those who could afford to live in the area would be eligible to enter the park. To this day, only the owners and tenants of buildings on Gramercy Park have the privilege of using this rare patch of green.

The anonymity and diversity of cities changed their moral quality relative to that of small towns or villages. The presence of many different religious traditions created competing views of right and wrong. Weaker forms of informal social control meant that failure to comply with norms carried lighter penalties, if any. In addition, the large populations living in cities permitted those who were outcasts in their homes to find kindred spirits. Subcultures of many stripes, including sexual minorities, thus took root in cities. In addition, the large numbers of single men immigrating to cities created markets for female companionship and impersonal sex. Businesses developed to meet these needs, whether brothels or the "taxi dance halls" studied by the Chicago School's Paul Cressey (1932), often clustering in districts that fed a number of vices. For some, these districts were places of relief and liberation; for others, they were signs of moral decline and of the city's inherently wicked nature.

For those who could afford it, the solution to conflicts over the proper use of space was a retreat to the suburbs. As we discussed in Chapter 6, early suburbanization, particularly by the wealthiest city dwellers, was due in large part to families' desires to retreat from urban vices and from social difference. The larger homes and lots of the suburbs allowed families to buffer themselves from one another, and the homogeneous character of suburbs helped to ensure that neighbors were of similar status. The retreat of these households – which began with the wealthy in the nineteenth century and extended to the middle class in the twentieth – changed the character of cities as places. More and more, the central areas of cities became a mix of commercial and industrial spaces and residences for those with the fewest alternatives. Immigrants and the working class continued to make their homes there, transforming their neighborhoods as they did so.

Cities of immigrants

The diversity found in cities is paramount among the qualities that attracted the attention of early social theorists (see Chapter 2, especially the writings of the Chicago School social theorists). Unlike most small towns, cities are home to populations drawn from across their nations or around the globe. During the Industrial Revolution, peasants flocked to cities from rural areas in search of economic opportunities. As immigrants left their home countries, pushed out by famine, poverty, or persecution, cities were the first places in which they landed, and often where they stayed. This process transformed cities not only by dramatically increasing their size but also by imbuing neighborhoods with the traits of the varied immigrant groups who made their lives there. Immigrant neighborhoods became culturally rich and distinct places, and these hyper-local cultures have endured in many neighborhoods even after the immigrants who created them have moved on or assimilated.

Waves of immigrant settlements left a second, less positive, imprint on cities. As groups followed one another, patterns of social stratification favored those who arrived earlier and penalized those who arrived later. Those who were the newest residents of the city and country often worked in the least desirable jobs at the lowest wages (Lieberson 1981). As a result, they lived in the poorest housing, typically overcrowded and lacking in proper sanitation. Perhaps even worse, native-born citizens and earlier immigrants associated newcomers' poverty with personal failings or poor character, often extending these judgments to entire ethnic groups. In this way, social class became tightly bound up with race and ethnicity, which in turn either facilitated or hampered future opportunities for **social mobility**.

social mobility The capacity of a group or individual to move from one social class to another.

To illustrate these processes and provide a glimpse into the everyday lives of urban immigrants, we focus here on one neighborhood in particular: New York City's Five Points area. We might have chosen others – Chicago, as you know by now, is filled with neighborhoods in which new immigrants to the United States made their homes; Canadian cities such as Toronto and Montreal also gained substantial populations through immigration, particularly from Britain and Ireland but also significant numbers from other European countries. We offer Five Points as an *archetypical case* that illustrated important patterns in urban inequality in part because they were particularly pronounced here (see our discussion of archetypes in Chapter 4).

Immigrant lives: New York's Five Points

When you picture the lives of immigrants in the urban United States during the nineteenth or early twentieth century, particularly those of poor immigrants, it is likely that the picture in your head was taken by Jacob Riis. A Danish immigrant who alternated odd jobs and abject poverty before finding work as a journalist, Riis became one of the foremost chroniclers of the worst conditions in which the United States' immigrants lived. Much of his work centered on Mulberry Bend (see Figure 8.3), part of New York's notorious Five Points neighborhood (now Chinatown; we will explain this transition below). Riis first came to Five Points as an immigrant himself, seeking some sort of job that might ensure his success in America or fund his passage home. Later, having secured work as the *New York Tribune*'s police reporter, Riis found himself in the neighborhood as he covered various crimes and routinely walked its streets after work to see "the slum when off its guard"

Figure 8.3 Mulberry Bend, as photographed by Jacob Riis circa 1888. Initially an Irish neighborhood, Mulberry Street later became the heart of New York's Italian immigrant community. Italian-owned groceries and banks lined the street, and new immigrants knew to find their way here to look for work. *Source: Photo by Jacob A. Riis/Getty Images*.

(Anbinder 2001: p. 426). He soon came to see the problems that marked this area as the shortcomings not of inferior individuals or "races" but of the social and physical conditions in which those individuals and groups were forced to make their homes. In 1890, Riis shared this message in *How the Other Half Lives* (1914), a chronicle of urban poverty that pioneered the use of documentary photography and galvanized reform movements.

Riis' photography reveals two sides of immigrant life in American cities: the vitality and strength of communities and the deplorable conditions in which immigrants lived. While Five Points is in some ways an exceptional neighborhood – since the 1830s it had been known throughout New York City as a center of vice and crime – its notoriety generated the wealth of attention and documentation that allows us a glimpse into its past. In other ways it is typical of immigrant neighborhoods in the industrial cities of the United States. It has seen a succession of immigrant populations, beginning with the Irish in the 1820s and then later Italians and Poles and eventually Chinese. A glimpse into this neighborhood also provides some insight into immigrants' everyday lives and the efforts of reformers who sought to improve them.

Five Points, named for the intersection of Baxter, Park, and Worth Streets at its center, was once a bucolic spot on the northern outskirts of New York City. In the mid-eighteenth century, picnickers could perch on Bunker Hill and watch wildlife drink at the Collect Pond. But, as was a common occurrence on the outskirts of cities of that era, the area became home to slaughterhouses, tanneries, and other industries that city dwellers deemed noxious neighbors. By 1802 the Collect Pond had been filled, the tanneries had moved even further out, and breweries, pottery works, and artisan shops had moved in. The workshops then closed as industrialization displaced artisans and landlords subdivided these buildings to make apartments for a growing urban population. By 1825, "tenant houses" – what would come to be called "**tenements**" – provided shelter to a population with twice the proportion of immigrants and blacks as the rest of New York and constituting the poorest ward in the city. The per capita income at the time was about 40 percent lower than that of the average New York resident (Anbinder 2001: pp. 14–16). The neighborhood's notoriety, in part the result of being the capital of New York's sex industry, attracted notable visitors, including Charles Dickens, who remarked on the "lanes and alleys, paved with mud knee deep; underground chambers, where they dance and game … hideous tenements which take their name from robbery and murder" (from *American Notes*, as cited in Anbinder 2001: p. 33). Certainly some reports of neighborhood life contain sensational flourishes and exaggeration; they also reflect the biases and prejudices of the observers at the time.

tenement A term used for buildings containing multiple small, low-cost housing units.

Though the area was poorer than other neighborhoods, life here was much like that in other immigrant enclaves throughout the nineteenth century. Residents made their homes in crowded tenements constructed for maximum profitability. Most tenements constructed for housing (as opposed to those in buildings converted from other uses) were three to five stories tall, with four apartments on each floor. Miniscule by contemporary US standards, these dwellings included a 12 by 12 foot main room for cooking, dining, and sitting plus a windowless "sleeping closet" (about 8 by 10 feet). The typical occupancy of these 225 square foot (21 square meter) units was five persons, though almost half housed more than that. Water had to be carried up several flights of dark and rickety stairs from wells or hydrants on the street level, making cooking, cleaning, and laundry additionally difficult and dangerous. Toilet facilities, such as they were, were also located outside (often not too distant from the fresh water supply, leading to cholera and other diseases). For the privilege of these accommodations a family might pay four to five dollars a month – lower than rents elsewhere in the city but still steep for a seamstress who might make only a dollar a week

(Anbinder 2001: Chapter 3). To make ends meet, many families took in boarders, often young, single men or those who had immigrated without their families. While this practice may have helped both the boarders and their landlords, it offended middle-class American notions of privacy and morality and would later provide one of many motivations for the tenement reform movement.

Five Points residents worked in many of the lowest-paying occupations available. Women primarily worked in the needle trades, sewing shirts, pillowcases, and other products inside their apartments. About a quarter of the women worked as household servants, far less than the proportion of working women elsewhere in New York. (Most domestics lived with their employers during this time, therefore making their homes in more affluent parts of the city.) The men of the area were overwhelmingly employed as skilled and unskilled laborers, including tailors, shoemakers, watchmen, dock workers, and carters. These employment patterns, recorded in 1855, reveal not only the roots of the area's relative poverty but also an ethnic segregation of New York's labor force. For instance, over half of the neighborhood's unskilled workers were Irish immigrants while only 1 in 25 Germans worked in these jobs; and, even in diverse Five Points, all of the butchers (a higher-paying trade) were native-born Americans (Anbinder 2001: pp. 112–113). As Italians came to replace the Irish in the area (see Figure 8.4), some took up the same kinds of unskilled positions the Irish had held; the majority of non-laborers were peddlers or otherwise self-employed (see Figure 8.5). A common trajectory for Italian immigrants was to begin selling fruit on the street from a pushcart and then save enough to open a storefront. Indeed, Italian-owned produce markets became so common throughout New York that they were credited with changing the local diet (Anbinder 2001: Chapter 12).

But, beyond the squalor that made Five Points infamous, we can see the qualities that give immigrant neighborhoods their strength. Immigrant enclaves provide those new to a country with the social connections necessary to find housing and work. Many immigrants chose their destinations based on existing social connections – for instance, family members or neighbors in the home country might follow one another to a city, a neighborhood, or even the same building in the destination country – but others struck

Figure 8.4 Birthplaces of Five Points adults, 1855 and 1880. *Source: From the 1880 US manuscript census, National Archives.*

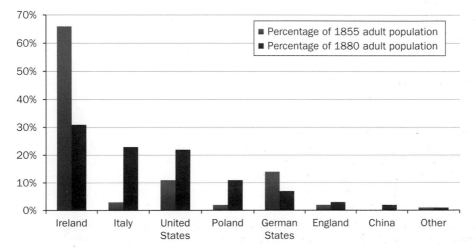

out on their own. Without knowledge of the language or economic system, they depended on fellow immigrants to ease their transition into a new society. For many Italian immigrants to New York, particularly those who came alone, Mulberry Street in Five Points was *the* place to go to find a job. Here, in exchange for a fee extracted from the immigrant's future wages, employment brokers called *padroni* placed men on jobs ranging from local public works crews to distant coalmines and railroads. A few blocks away on Mott Street, Chinese making their way from California found the support they needed to establish themselves in a new city. Chinese-owned groceries provided not only familiar foodstuffs but also a fixed address to receive mail and the opportunity to socialize over a game of dominoes. Like the Italians, many Chinese sought to start their own businesses, including laundries and restaurants, and often depended on funds raised within the community to do so. Small groups of immigrants established rotating lending pools, or *wheys*, that could quickly raise the funds needed to strike out on one's own. These were a variant on a common institution within early immigrant communities, **mutual aid societies**, that also became common among Korean immigrants. Through these associations immigrants could support one another's entrepreneurial aspirations as well as provide financial resources in times of need.

mutual aid societies
Organizations developed to provide insurance and other services to members of immigrant and minority communities.

Figure 8.5 Jacob Riis, "Italian Mother and Baby, Ragpicker, New York," circa 1889–1890. In one of his most famous images, Riis simultaneously reveals the struggle and humanity of his subjects. This woman worked as a ragpicker, sorting through trash for usable bits of cloth, paper, bone, or other materials. Tenement apartments routinely provided storage for the gleanings before they were sold. *Source: Photo by Jacob Riis.*

The changing population of Five Points illustrates the dynamism that characterizes many immigrant neighborhoods. The composition of immigrant populations, as we discuss below, changes in response to a number of forces, particularly the political and economic conditions in the home and destination countries and policies dictating who can enter the destination country. Economic success and cultural assimilation may then shift immigrants from their original landing places to other kinds of neighborhoods. Irish immigrants fleeing poverty and privation began arriving in the 1820s; within a generation or two, they were on their way to more desirable neighborhoods. Italians followed a similar path, with most arriving from southern Italy. Again, many moved to other parts of the city, and to the suburbs, as opportunities presented themselves. The Chinese story was a bit different. While a desire for economic success drew them to the United States, most came first to California, where they worked in mining and railroad construction. Anti-Chinese sentiment – much of it driven by Irish immigrants seeking to ensure their own status – along with the completion of major railroad projects then propelled Chinese immigrants east to New York, and a small number of them to the American South. In another twist, Chinese residents did not dominate the local population in the way that other immigrant groups had. Chinese immigrants operated laundries and other businesses throughout the city, though they used immigrant enclaves such as Five Points as a type of cultural base. The neighborhood became a center of Chinese social and entrepreneurial activity, and Chinese-owned groceries, restaurants, and nightclubs continue to dominate New York's Chinatown – the area formerly known as Five Points – while, a few blocks north, Little Italy provides a cultural touchstone to the area's other immigrant past.

STUDYING THE CITY   8.1

Canada's Chinatowns

As in the United States, Chinese immigrants to Canada were sought after as laborers in gold fields and railways but often treated with open hostility by white workers, employers, and property owners. As a result, they tended to cluster in segregated districts – what would become known as Chinatowns – on the outskirts of established urban areas. These enclaves allowed Chinese immigrants to avoid whites' periodic violence and racial slurs and to enjoy the benefits of strong social networks and of a familiar language and culture.

Examining Chinatowns from British Columbia to the Canadian prairies to Ontario and Quebec, geographer David Chuenyan Lai (1988) recognizes four distinct phases in their trajectories: budding, blooming, withering, and reviving. These roughly correspond to periods when Chinese migration was open (budding and blooming), then restricted through the use of head taxes and outright exclusion (withering), and finally renewed (reviving) following immigration reforms and the transfer of Hong Kong back to China (see Chapter 9).

Victoria's Chinatown illustrates this process. The community began as a small cluster of buildings owned by Chinese merchants working in import and export trades. Throughout the late nineteenth century, Chinese land holdings expanded through several blocks of central Victoria, and included a school and hospital among other institutions. By the early 1900s, the city's Chinese population numbered around 3000 and was becoming increasingly gender-balanced as men earned enough to bring their wives and families over from China. But, despite these successes, Chinese still faced discrimination in terms of civil rights (they were denied provincial voting rights through 1947) and in employment (many unions denied membership to Chinese). Poverty and discrimination led to pronounced overcrowding in Victoria's Chinatown, which was alleviated only when exclusion laws ended Chinese immigration in 1923 and the remaining Chinese died or dispersed. Revival began in the 1970s, as attitudes toward the district shifted from fear to fascination and community leaders worked together to identify the area's needs and strengths. These included construction of a ceremonial gate (see Figure 8.6) and signage to mark Victoria's Chinatown as a distinct place, and the development of cultural organizations such as folk dance groups. Today the area is a tourist and shopping destination as well as a residential neighborhood. This revitalization reflects a greater acceptance of the distinct cultures that immigrant groups bring to their new countries, and a shift from compulsory assimilation to multiculturalism.

Figure 8.6 The Gate of Harmonious Interest marks one boundary of Victoria's Chinatown. Like many Chinese enclaves in North America, Victoria's Chinatown was once viewed by outsiders as a dangerous and unsanitary place, but has since become a symbol of vital and desirable urban diversity. *Source: © Paul Thompson Images/Alamy.*

The Five Points case in context

While the story of Five Points is certainly iconic, and the accounts and photographs by Riis and others are compelling, how typical was this neighborhood of immigrant life in the United States and elsewhere? What general patterns of immigration, ethnicity, and inequality are illustrated by this case, and which require further exploration?

Figure 8.7 presents patterns of immigration to the United States from 1850 to 1930, with birth countries grouped by region. As you can see, many of the regions from which most contemporary immigrants come to the United States are not even represented here: immigrants from Africa numbered under 10 000 per decade until 1920, and even though Asian immigrants are part of the picture during this era the countries of origin were different from those we see today (for instance, fewer than 25 000 immigrated from India during the period covered by this graph). Latin American immigration was modest relative to contemporary levels, though we should keep in mind that some Latinos "entered" the

United States when it annexed what were Mexican territories in 1848. You will also notice that, while immigrants from the British Isles (England, Northern Ireland, Scotland, and Wales in this tally) and Western Europe (Austria, Belgium, France, Germany, Luxembourg, The Netherlands, and Switzerland) constituted a significant proportion throughout this timeframe, a shift among the other dominant groups occurred around 1900. At this time, Irish immigration declined, replaced by a steep increase in immigration from Southern and Eastern Europe – primarily from Italy, Poland, and Russia (later the Soviet Union).

While many of these migrants made their ways to farms and rural areas, our concern lies with those who lived in, and transformed, cities. As Table 8.1 reveals, the US immigrant population was unevenly distributed across American cities. Some cities – New York, most famously – served as major ports of entry for immigrants during the height of US immigration in the late nineteenth and early twentieth century. Many immigrants remained there, while others made their way to the expanding industrial cities of the upper Midwest, particularly Chicago but also cities such as Cleveland, Milwaukee, and Minneapolis. Cities that have since come to have thriving immigrant communities – particularly in the US South and southwest – saw relatively little influx of immigrants during this era.

Figure 8.7 Immigrants to the United States by birth country region, 1850–1930. *Source: based on data from the US Census.*

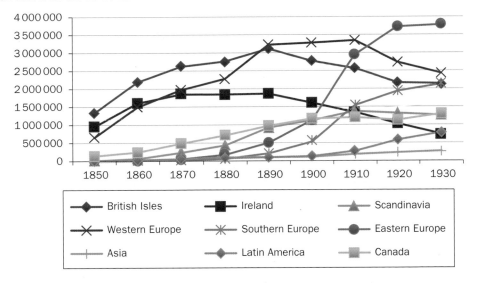

Table 8.1 Percentage of residents born outside the US, 1870–1930. *The New York City data for prior to 1898, when the city of Brooklyn and the outer boroughs of New York City were annexed, include only Manhattan.

	1870	1880	1890	1900	1910	1920	1930
New York City*	44.5	39.7	42.2	37.0	40.8	36.1	34.0
Chicago	48.4	40.7	41.0	34.6	35.9	29.9	25.5
Atlanta	5.0	3.8	2.9	2.8	2.9	2.4	1.8
Los Angeles	35.0	28.7	25.3	19.5	20.7	21.2	20.0

Canadian cities such as Montreal, Toronto, and Vancouver, now known for their multicultural character and vibrant immigrant enclaves, have long depended on immigrants for growth. However, the vast diversity of these immigrant populations is relatively new. Up to World War II, many of these immigrants came from the United Kingdom and Ireland (around 40 percent from the 1890s through the 1920s, then around 30 percent through the 1950s). Those from other nations, including the Chinese discussed in Studying the city 8.1, were routinely referred to as "foreigners" and not wholly welcomed into Canadian cities. National immigration policies contributed to this pattern by encouraging non-Anglo Saxon immigrants to work in railroad construction, mining, and other occupations located outside urban centers. Some immigrants did make their way to cities, working in occupations familiar to immigrants everywhere – construction, textile mills, domestic service, and the like (Troper 2003). Among these urban immigrants were significant numbers of Canada's Jewish population. An area known simply as the Ward was Toronto's first Jewish enclave, providing not only the goods and services that residents needed but also a strong sense of ethnic identity. Social organizations including mutual aid societies and trade unions provided support to residents, as did numerous synagogues and schools. Nevertheless, the Ward was viewed by outsiders as a slum (Siemiatycki et al. 2003).

From the mid-nineteenth century through World War I, immigration to the United States and Canada absorbed populations that might have otherwise moved within or among British or European countries. In Chapter 9, as you will discover, many European countries saw large waves of international immigration occur only after World War II. There were some exceptions, of course. As noted above, many Irish settled in English and Scottish cities in the nineteenth century, finding conditions and reactions similar to those of new immigrants to the United States They lived close to their work, which meant in central cities or near docks (typical occupations included construction, textile work, and stevedoring). Housing conditions were typical of nineteenth-century urban slums, with poor construction and sanitation, compounded by overcrowding. As reformers of the time noted, these conditions fostered a number of social ills: child neglect, vagrancy, alcoholism, and epidemics of disease among them. But, as is the case with many immigrant communities, not all members of the majority group took a structural perspective, and the sufferings of Irish immigrants were often blamed on poor character or lack of intelligence. Particularly after Ireland's famine sent increased numbers to British cities, cartoons caricaturing Irish features and occupations advanced negative stereotypes and hindered opportunities for assimilation and social mobility. By some accounts, these negative characterizations may have strengthened immigrants' resolve to retain their distinct cultures, as evidenced in the durability of Irish neighborhoods within British cities and cultural displays such as Saint Patrick's Day parades (Tuataigh 1985).

The pattern we saw in Five Points, in which one immigrant group yields to another, newer, group, is a common across cities. As groups become more financially secure and culturally assimilated, they move into neighborhoods that correspond to their new means. In some instances, these new neighborhoods may retain a distinct ethnic character as the descendents of one immigrant group continue to cluster together. Thus, we may see suburban neighborhoods in which second-, third-, or fourth-generation descendents of Irish, Italian, or Polish immigrants predominate. Despite this migration, the "old neighborhood" may remain a cultural touchstone. As the descendents of immigrants seek to reconnect with their heritage they may a visit a restaurant or shop in a city's "Little Italy," "Chinatown," or "Ukrainian Village." Transformed immigrant neighborhoods thus continue to play an important role in fostering identity, even for those who do not live there.

Early reform and intervention efforts

The living and working conditions in Five Points also reveal important, if exaggerated, dimensions of urban inequality. Housing conditions were deplorable, as they were in many of the neighborhoods where new immigrants made their homes. These conditions not only motivated the movement of more established immigrant families away from these areas but also inspired those with means to improve living conditions in poor areas. Their motives were, in part, self-serving. The piecework conducted in tenement apartments essentially brought middle-class consumers into contact with these places, even though they may never have set foot there. Consumers who bought the shirts or handkerchiefs sewn by an immigrant in her home worried that diseases might be transmitted on items of clothing. Although concerns about disease often reflected misperceptions of just how poor living conditions led to epidemics (see Making the city better 12.1), the quality of tenement housing certainly did little to advance public health. In addition, the crowding common in tenement dwellings (recall that entire families typically slept in one room, multiple families might share a bathroom, and single male roomers might share a dwelling already inhabited by a large family) constituted an affront to middle-class norms of privacy and morality.

The **Tenement Reform Movement** sought to address all these ills by providing decent, purpose-built housing stock to accommodate poor city residents and educating residents of existing structures about "proper" housekeeping and hygiene. Some of the advances were admirable, such as the development of tenement plans that allowed more natural light and air and provided water and sanitary facilities to all units. But the movement included explicit efforts at cultural assimilation as well: the décor of tenement units, which often included wallpaper and carpets as well as mementos from the home country, was viewed as unhygienic compared to the hard surfaces preferred in middle-class homes (see also Making the city better 8.1 on Chicago's settlement houses). New housing developments were often constructed in ways that discouraged street or sidewalk play, and without potentially "contaminating" neighborhood amenities such as pubs and saloons. We can see the shadow of the tenement reform movement in the ways in which public and council housing are provided even today. While these housing units are designed to provide minimum standards of safe and decent shelter, they often come with strings attached. Residents are subjected to rules and restrictions that residents of market-rate housing do not necessarily need to abide by, and that often reflect a desire to impose middle-class standards of behavior.

> **Tenement Reform Movement** A social movement in New York City and elsewhere designed to improve the safety and conditions of tenements.

Making the American ghetto

Integrated beginnings

It is difficult to look at the racial arrangements in US cities today and imagine them another way. One might easily conclude that cities have always been highly segregated and that black residents have always lived in central (and degraded) urban areas and whites in affluent suburbs. Given the history of race relations in the United States, we might also assume that cities in the South reflect the legacy of slavery and **Jim Crow**, manifested in pronounced levels of residential segregation. Alternatively, we might imagine a history of racial progress,

> **Jim Crow** A set of laws and customs in the United States that enforced segregation and compromised civil rights.

MAKING THE CITY BETTER   8.1

Jane Addams and Chicago's settlement houses

While Park, Burgess, Wirth, and others pursued theories of urban life based on their studies of Chicago, Jane Addams was engaged in what we might now call an applied scholarly enterprise: founding the settlement house movement. Settlement houses were often established in neighborhoods with large populations of immigrants in order to provide services and to help bridge the gap between rich and poor.

Jane Addams founded Hull House in 1889, in a once-grand home that found its Chicago neighborhood transformed from affluence to a largely immigrant population. Hull House aimed to be a center for all types of learning. There, neighborhood residents could take classes in art and literature as well as basic domestic and career skills. Childcare and kindergarten classes were offered, which allowed the children's mothers to work.

According to scholars such as Dolores Hayden (1982) and Kathryn Sklar (1985), Hull House was the major feminist reform institution of the Progressive Era due to its emphasis on the power of women to affect social change in the inner cities. Many young women were attracted to the idea of helping the urban poor and hindering social disorganization to beget improved human development among immigrant communities. Hull House instructors, called residents, included ambitious young women from a range of backgrounds with interests in social reform; many, like Addams, jointly worked for the University of Chicago as researchers and educators.

Some more recent scholars have critiqued the intentions and effects of the settlement house movement. Rivka Shpak Lissak (1989) argues that Addams did not value pluralism or the preservation of immigrant cultures, further arguing that the programs and services offered at Hull House were indicative of the organization's commitment toward the complete assimilation of immigrant cultures into the dominant Anglo-American culture.

However, an Eastern European immigrant living near Hull House, Hilda Satt Polacheck, seemed to appreciate the services provided. In her autobiography (which ended upon Jane Addams' death instead of Polacheck's own, 32 years later), Polacheck described Hull House as an avenue of upward mobility that allowed her to escape the limitations of her old culture and eventually become a writer and activist (Polacheck 1989).

While the settlement houses approached inner-city poverty among immigrant communities in an ethnocentric way, attempting to erase the rich backgrounds of immigrant cultures in favor of a more homogenous city, many immigrants (especially second-generation immigrants) were able to take advantage of the services provided in order to advance economically and politically in an ethnocentric American society.

---

de jure segregation
Racial/ethnic segregation achieved through laws governing who can live where.

de facto segregation
Racial/ethnic segregation achieved through informal means, such as preferences to live with one's own kind.

continually moving from more to less segregated cities as racist stereotypes diminished and civil rights expanded. The history of blacks and whites in American cities reveals a much more complex story, however. Urban race relations have been shaped by political and economic forces, and have played out differently in the different parts of American cities.

The segregation of blacks and whites in American cities, whether *de jure* **segregation** (through law) or *de facto* **segregation** (through custom), is largely a twentieth-century problem. Before then, small numbers of black residents in northern cities limited the development of what we would recognize as pronounced ghetto neighborhoods. Blacks tended to be overrepresented among the urban poor, but did not live in neighborhoods or conditions distinct from poor whites. Southern cities, with larger black populations, practiced a distinct form of spatial integration. In the South, many urban blacks worked in domestic service occupations, a fact that required their proximity to the households they served. This resulted in what is called a street-alley pattern, wherein wealthy white families lived in large houses facing well-traveled streets and their black employees lived in smaller dwellings facing rear alleys. While these arrangements were certainly far from equal, they provided an important type of geographic integration (Massy and Denton 1993). These rear dwellings, once used by chauffeurs, maids, nannies, and cooks, still form a distinctive architectural feature of historically affluent neighborhoods in the American South (though now they are largely used as guest houses, studios, or rentals).

New neighbors, new tensions

This era of relatively integrated neighborhoods and peaceful race relations began to unravel as more African Americans made their way north during the Great Migration. Starting during World War I and continuing through the 1940s, southern blacks sought freedom from the laws and customs that enforced their second-class status. Such customs ranged from enforced segregation on busses and in restaurants to prohibitions on voting; the name Jim Crow is often given to both the practices and the era in which they were common. At the same time, agricultural mechanization and crop failures were limiting economic opportunities for southern blacks. In northern US states, however, particularly in the northeast and upper Midwest, World War 1 increased demand for factory labor as it simultaneously squelched the steady stream of European immigrants who might provide it. A combination of factors thus pushed African Americans out of the South and pulled them toward a region that had been overwhelmingly white. Figure 8.8 reveals the volume of this truly epic migration. While the black population of the United States increased by about 7 to 15 percent every 10 years and the southern black population was relatively *stagnant* at some points during this era, the Midwest and northeastern populations increased by about 40 percent between 1920 and 1930 – or by nearly one million people. The black population of the American West (not shown here) was quite small at this time, so although the growth rate was steep this represents only tens of thousands of people. In some cities, the growth was far more pronounced: Detroit's black population, for instance, grew by some 600 percent between 1910 and 1920.

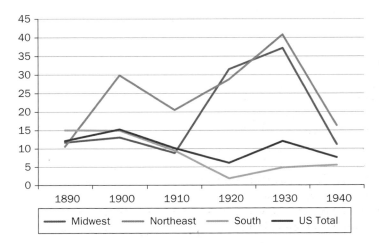

Figure 8.8 Percentage change in black population over the preceding 10 years, by US Census region, 1890–1940.
Source: Campbell Gibson and Kay Jung, "Historical Census Statistics on Population Totals by Race, 1790 to 1990, and by Hispanic Origin, 1970 to 1990, for the United States, Regions, Divisions, and States" (US Census Working Paper Number 56).

sundown towns
Small towns and
suburbs that prohibited
African Americans from
residing within the
municipal limits.

It is important to keep in mind that this was an overwhelmingly urban migration. African Americans who had lived in small towns and rural areas made their ways to the industrial cities of the North. The allure of manufacturing jobs provided one incentive, but equally important were the efforts of rural and small-town whites to preserve the racial homogeneity of their places. Historian James Loewen has documented the proliferation of **sundown towns**, small towns that prohibited African Americans from residing within their municipal boundaries. The name refers to laws and customs that permitted blacks to work in town but required that they be gone by sundown. Some towns purportedly used sirens or whistles to signal that it was time for black workers to leave; others posted signs at the city limit or relied upon law enforcement and citizen groups to warn people of color that they were not welcome. In some cases, a smaller black municipality might develop adjacent to a sundown town, similar to the townships of South Africa during Apartheid. Loewen argues that these rules kept blacks from settling in rural areas, particularly in the Midwest and West, and also that as sundown practices increasingly spread during the early twentieth century they encouraged blacks who had initially settled in rural areas to make their way to cities (Loewen 2006).

Although cities are typically more diverse than small towns, northern US cities were not always more welcoming to black migrants. Cultural differences were one part of the reason. Poor and often uneducated, rural black migrants brought with them cultural norms different from those of northern whites (and many northern blacks, for that matter). Another factor was that black migrants were also used as strike breakers during a time when the American labor movement was otherwise making strong strides. African Americans were excluded from many labor unions, and so often had no choice but to work as non-union replacements. Even when blacks and whites worked for the same firms, they often worked different, unequal, jobs. In the automotive industry, for instance, black workers took on especially hazardous jobs such as spray painting and foundry work (Boyle 2004).

White residents' animosity toward blacks manifested itself in restrictions on where blacks could live. Blacks had lived in northern cities throughout their history, but low numbers had resulted in sorting primarily by class. Affluent black families had lived in areas populated by their economic peers. With the Great Migration and the backlash against black migrants, *all* blacks – new migrants and longtime residents; rich and poor – found themselves confined to relatively small areas of the city. The resulting ghettos came to occupy otherwise undesirable areas that were near industry, prone to flooding, or had some other objectionable feature. The behavior of ghetto landlords made the neighborhoods even less desirable. Recognizing that blacks had little choice but to live in ghetto areas, landlords could charge high prices while investing little in improvements or upkeep. Buildings were subdivided into ever-smaller units, leading to overcrowding. As a result, black ghettos took on an unkempt appearance that, while no fault of the occupants, was nevertheless associated with their character. This provided a third source of tension between urban blacks and whites. In the view of whites, families that lived in such squalor must have been somehow inferior.

The perpetuation and implications of black ghettos

The development of black ghettos in cities of the northern United States ushered in an era of increased segregation throughout the country. Southern cities, in which segregation levels had been moderate throughout the early twentieth century, became more highly segregated. In 1940, Baltimore and Jacksonville, once well-integrated, ranked among the most highly segregated cities in America, with other southern cities close behind them. In the Midwest, Chicago, Cleveland, and St. Louis were just as terrible. More and more, blacks and whites

STUDYING THE CITY   8.2

W. E. B. Du Bois' *The Philadelphia Negro*

W. E. B. Du Bois, one of the most distinguished sociologists of the early twentieth century, laid out a broad and ambitious goal for his study titled *The Philadelphia Negro* (2007 [1899]). His goal was to find out more about urban life for African Americans living in Philadelphia: where in the city they lived, what their homes were like, where they worked, what types of organizations they were involved with, and other key bits of information necessary to inform efforts to better the living conditions of African Americans in the city (see Figure 8.9).

Some of Du Bois' most important findings had to do with the early identification of structural causes of crime, the roots of prejudice and racism against African Americans in American cities, and African American social life. He pointed out after 15 months of living with African American families in Philadelphia that there were clear links between a person being poor and out of work and turning to a life of crime. By pointing out that structural factors caused black Americans, who were not on an equal economic level with whites, to be more engaged in criminal activity, Du Bois essentially developed the sociological concept of stratification.

He also examined African American social structure extensively during his study, and found that many African Americans within Philadelphia used local churches as their primary social meeting spaces. While spirituality was obviously important, Du Bois argued that the ability to form social bonds took precedence, and that the lack of these bonds could also lead to increased criminality.

Du Bois also criticized the welfare system for benefiting the wrong types of African American families, leaving many deserving families without any assistance and promoting inaccurate and negative stereotypes about African Americans among the white population. He stated that the city's institutions and charities only reached out to "the criminal, the lazy and the shiftless," and that these types of people came to inaccurately represent the entirety of the African American people to white Philadelphians.

Du Bois' study was one of the earliest attempts at understanding the urban life of African Americans, and Du Bois himself was one of the earliest African American scholars to be accepted by the white American academic community. He was the first African American to graduate with a PhD from Harvard and the first African American to speak in front of the American Historical Association, and he taught at several universities and wrote many books. Du Bois took great strides in advancing his cause and improving the quality of life for African Americans through urban scholarship.

Figure 8.9 What were then called the "negro quarters" of Philadelphia (probably the Seventh Ward), around 1900. This area was at the heart of Du Bois' study.

social isolation The lack of regular interaction between groups, particularly between a minority group and the majority population.

culture of poverty Oscar Lewis' term for the cultural traits of impoverished people living together in dense settlements.

were living separate lives in the city, leading to what sociologists call **social isolation**. Social isolation refers to a lack of regular interaction between groups, particularly between a minority group and the majority population. As a result, the isolated group develops its own distinct cultural patterns, whether dialects of speech, norms of behavior, or traditions and celebrations. As in the case of the immigrant neighborhoods discussed above, these distinct patterns can lend places a unique character and serve as a basis for group solidarity. However, particularly in the postwar period discussed in Chapter 9, the social isolation of America's black ghettos led to cultural patterns associated with the perpetuation of inequality (see Exploring further 9.1 on the **culture of poverty**).

Maintaining these separate neighborhoods was not merely a matter of preference – at least not the preference of African Americans. Varied forms of interpersonal and institutional discrimination limited blacks' housing choices.

Violence was routinely used to keep black residents confined to ghetto areas. Buying a home in a white area posed a substantial risk of violence and intimidation, but even walking through the "wrong" neighborhood could lead to physical assault as whites attempted to curtail the movements of blacks. Other, less brutal, means of enforcing segregation were also employed. As we discussed in Chapter 6, African Americans' movement to the suburbs was largely prohibited through the use of deed clauses restricting the sale of properties to racial/ethnic and religious minorities. They remained legal through 1948. Lending guidelines for the inexpensive home loans that fueled the expansion of the suburbs also privileged white homebuyers, providing another challenge for blacks who sought new homes. Banks considered mortgages in uniformly white areas to be less risky, and so routinely refused loan applications for homes in mixed or minority areas. As a result, the rates of homeownership for African Americans are far lower than for whites, a gap that continues to contribute to unequal wealth accumulation for the two groups.

The experience of Detroit resident Ossian Sweet illustrates how all these forces worked together not only to enforce segregation but also to create substantial burdens for black homebuyers. Sweet, a physician, and his wife Gladys sought to buy a home in Detroit that would reflect their middle-class status. Such homes tended to be in newer developments at the city's edge, but a number of the Sweets' enquiries into properties were rebuffed by realtors unwilling to sell homes in white areas to black families, or by formal deed restrictions that accomplished the same task. In the spring of 1925, they finally located a suitable house (albeit in a working-class neighborhood) and – more importantly – an owner who was willing to sell to a black family. Indeed, the owner understood the Sweets' predicament and priced the home at a premium: about 50 percent above market value. When word of the Sweets' purchase of the property became known, white neighbors organized a homeowner's association that sought to protect property values by restricting the deeds of their properties. That fall, just days after the Sweets moved in, a mob surrounded the home, lobbing stones and insults. Sweet, who had seen other black professionals face the same treatment after buying homes in white neighborhoods, had assembled a group of friends armed to resist. They fired on the mob, injuring one man and killing another. Ossian and Gladys Sweet faced murder charges but were eventually acquitted. Shortly thereafter, Gladys died of tuberculosis, which she had contracted in jail (Boyle 2004).

The Sweets' story is tragic and well-documented, but by no means isolated. These kinds of tactics continued throughout the twentieth century, and milder forms of discrimination can still be seen today. For instance, renters who speak with a recognizably African American dialect are less likely to have their calls returned, and realtors routinely direct black buyers to dwellings in or near established black neighborhoods. These kinds of obstacles add significant costs to the search for a residence – thousands of dollars by some estimates (Yinger 1997; Massey and Lundy 2001). They also ensure that black ghettos remain entrenched elements of US cities.

EXPLORING FURTHER 8.1

Defining and measuring segregation

What is segregation? **Segregation** and **integration** describe the degree to which the diversity of a given population is mirrored in smaller social units – particularly schools, workplaces, and neighborhoods. Segregation exists when the smaller units do not reflect the lager population, and integration exists when they do. The types of segregation of greatest concern to sociologists tend to be those that mirror and reinforce social inequality. Thus, they are particularly concerned with the segregation of majority and minority groups within neighborhoods and schools, and gender segregation in workplaces and occupations, because these constrain opportunities. For instance, regarding neighborhoods, we see that majority and minority groups – typically whites and non-whites – live in different areas with different access to services and opportunities and different exposure to hazards.

segregation In cities, the degree to which different racial/ethnic groups or social classes live in different areas.

integration In cities, the degree to which different racial/ethnic groups or social classes live in the same areas.

Sociologists use a number of different measures to take stock of the degree of segregation. Regardless of the measure used, the analysis must always specify the boundaries that constrain the unit it seeks to understand and the larger population to which that unit will be compared. Thus, to understand racial segregation in a given city, we need to first know the racial composition of the city. In a city that is 30 percent black and 70 percent white, full integration would mean that each neighborhood is also 30 percent black and 70 percent white (we would see other groups represented in the real world, but for the sake of explanation we'll keep things simple). The degree to which neighborhoods deviate from that internally derived standard – the amount of segregation present – is typically measured using the **index of dissimilarity**. This statistical device measures the percentage of either racial group that would have to move to achieve integration. Table 8.2 shows levels of black–white segregation in selected US cities from 1980 to 2000. Values over 60 are considered high, as these indicate that 60 percent of a given group would need to change neighborhoods (operationalized here as census tracts) in order to achieve integration; values between 30 and 60 are considered moderate, and those under 30 low (though some of you are probably struck – and rightly so – by the implications of relocating even 30 percent of a population). As you can see here, many cities continue to have very high levels of segregation, and the trend is not always positive.

index of dissimilarity Reveals the percentage of a racial group that would have to move to achieve integration.

Index of exposure Indicates the degree to which people live near members of a different racial/ethnic group.

Index of isolation Indicates the degree to which people live near others of the same race/ethnicity.

Important as the index of dissimilarity is for revealing levels of segregation, it provides a relatively limited view. For instance, we may know that a city is segregated overall, but we know little about the degree to which this prevents interracial contact in day-to-day life. To better understand the latter, sociologists employ a number of other statistical devices, alone and in combination. **Indices of exposure** and **isolation**, for instance, can help us to see the degree to which residents of a given area are surrounded by people who are of their own racial group or another. Table 8.3 shows these indices for the year 2000 for the same cities listed in Table 8.2 (again, restricted to black and white populations). To make sense of these data, you can use the following sentence, inserting the racial categories in the column headings and the figure from the relevant column: "The average _____ person lives in a census tract that is __ percent _____." Thus, for Atlanta, Georgia, we can say that the average white person lives in a census tract that is 76.5 percent white – and also 20 percent black. The average black resident of Atlanta lives in a census tract that is 88.9 percent black and only 9.6 percent white.

Using the indices of isolation, exposure, and dissimilarity, we begin to obtain a clearer understanding of just how segregated a city is. To round out the picture, we might also ask how neighborhoods are arranged geographically within a city. Are predominantly minority areas concentrated together or interspersed with white areas? Are they clustered at the urban core or found on the periphery? Are they small and dense or large and sprawling? The answers to these questions allow us to understand whether a city is what sociologists Douglas Massey and Nancy Denton (1993) refer to as **hypersegregated**, meaning that minority areas have high dissimilarity and isolation indices and are also clustered together, spatially concentrated, and centralized. This type of segregation is the most damaging as it tends to concentrate the poverty and social problems that can beset minority areas.

hypersegregated
Massey and Denton's term for central-city ghetto neighborhoods that are highly segregated, isolated, and concentrated.

To investigate segregation further, you can access these indices yourself – at least for cities and metropolitan areas in the United States. See the American Communities Project website at http://www.s4.brown.edu/cen2000.

Table 8.2 Indices of dissimilarity for black and white populations, select US cities, 1980–2000. *Source: Based on data from the American Communities Project, Brown University.*

	1980	1990	2000
Atlanta	79.6	81.3	81.6
Chicago	90.6	87.4	85.5
Los Angeles	88.0	78.4	71.5
New York City	82.8	83.5	83.2
Washington, DC	76.8	78.2	79.9

Table 8.3 Indices of exposure and isolation, black and white populations, select US cities, 2000. *Source: Based on data from the American Communities Project, Brown University.*

	White with White	White with Black	Black with Black	Black with White
Atlanta	76.5	20.0	88.9	9.6
Chicago	77.8	5.3	89.9	5.8
Los Angeles	72.4	3.9	66.6	11.1
New York City	78.2	6.1	66.4	13.3
Washington, DC	68.3	23.8	88.2	8.8

The significance of urban diversity and inequality

We opened this chapter with the long-held assertion that diversity is a necessary element of urban life. In closing, we return to that claim, examining just how it is that this diversity and the associated inequality have made cities into the kinds of places that they are.

At the level of the city or metropolitan area, it is the diversity of cities that sets these places apart from smaller towns and rural areas. Individuals from across the globe congregate here, bringing new ideas and recombining them in creative ways. Distinct skills and specializations contribute to cities' robust economies, and the vast array of languages, traditions, and cuisines make for a vital urban culture. But difference can present challenges, particularly as residents try to negotiate their day-to-day lives and secure their futures. City dwellers may become frustrated by neighbors who speak different languages or dialects, or whose cultural norms differ in seemingly important ways. This tension is often most pronounced when difference and inequality intertwine. If residents understand their fates as tenuous – their ability to get and keep a job, for instance, or to secure high-quality education for their children – they may perceive that threats to these basic goals stem from unfamiliar others. Stereotypes and prejudices advance these types of divisions and create obstacles to social mobility.

Neighborhoods in which one racial/ethnic or immigrant group dominates historically have provided spaces in which to avoid these tensions. The *padroni* in New York City's Five Points, for instance, provided paths to employment for new immigrants who would otherwise have had few resources in seeking employment. Black neighborhoods in American cities provided their residents with security and freedom from the harassment of whites, particularly in times of heightened racial tensions. But, beyond providing residents with such basic needs, these neighborhoods also provided a physical manifestation of social solidarity. They were not merely neighborhoods but places that furnished their residents with identity, security, and community. Whether they retained these functions as immigrant populations dispersed has varied. Some, like the Chinatowns in Victoria and elsewhere, have undergone revitalization, and new generations have recognized and redefined the significance of those places. Other areas have not been so fortunate. Often labeled as "slums," areas that were onetime immigrant enclaves or black ghettos have often been targeted for the types of urban renewal schemes described in Chapter 5. Boston's West End, the Italian-American neighborhood discussed in Studying the city 3.1, was characterized as blighted and razed to the ground in the 1950s. The Chinese government pushed the same fate onto the migrant worker villages in major cities such as Beijing in the 1990s. The demolition of poor neighborhoods, repeated time and time again, suggests the ongoing struggle to recognize enclaves and ghettos as places where poor people have established important social resources, and as important sites of local history. This challenge is compounded as the residents who remain in these areas lack the power to speak up on their own behalf and the residents who have left now see their fortunes tied to other places. All of these processes play a part in the continual remaking of urban places.

In suggesting that poor and minority neighborhoods were important sites of *identity*, *community*, and *security*, we do not wish to romanticize the quality of life that they provided. Housing was substandard and unsanitary and, as reformers pointed out, standards of decency demanded that residents should have had something better. Levels of public services were often lower as well. For instance, because communities of color often doubled as vice districts, law enforcement tended to be lax or corrupt. The status of these areas relative to other neighborhoods created additional disadvantages. For instance, African Americans who bought homes in predominantly black areas saw their homes appreciate far less than those in comparable white areas, largely because the market for homes in black neighborhoods was (and typically is) more limited. As a result, homeownership is not the secure path to wealth accumulation that it has been for many white homeowners. Thus, when considering how urban places have shaped the fates of those who live there, it is important to recognize the ways in which places have both helped and hindered the progress of individuals and groups, often in ways that are not immediately visible.

Finally, we should keep in mind that much of what we know of our contemporary social welfare apparatus has its roots in the assessment and treatment of social ills brought about by urban inequality. Progressive reformers recognized the kinds of problems suffered by the "other half" – whether crime, disease, poor housing, or low levels of education – not merely as creating suffering for the urban poor but also as marring the image of entire societies. These individuals, often women of means and education, began to articulate for the rights of all city dwellers, and put their visions into action through government reforms and private agencies. It is possible to look back on their efforts as motivated in part by ethnocentrism, but they nevertheless improved the lives of many and continue to do so today. Chicago's Hull House, for instance, continues to offer job training and literacy classes among other services.

Our discussion of urban inequality does not end here. You can visit the book's companion website at www.wiley.com/go/cities for examples, case studies, and discussion questions, plus a list of useful films and other media, that are relevant to this chapter. Chapter 9 turns to issues of diversity and inequality in light of the dramatic transformation of cities following World War II – social and economic upheavals that different types of neighborhoods were more or less prepared to weather.

Critical thinking questions

1 Why would colonial powers seek to remake cities in the places that they ruled? What does this suggest about the importance of space and place?

2 How were the opportunities of racial minorities such as the Chinese or African Americans different from those of European immigrants? What does this suggest about the role of race as a barrier to assimilation or social mobility?

3 How were the tenement districts of nineteenth-century cities similar to or different from the kinds of places where immigrants now settle?

4 Why might early social reformers have sought to change the cultural norms of new immigrants? What does this suggest about how they understood social mobility?

5 In what ways have laws regulating immigration changed cities and urban neighborhoods?

Suggested reading

W. E. B. DuBois, *The Philadelphia Negro* (New York: Cosimo Classics, 2007 [1899]). One of the first thorough accounts of life in a US ghetto neighborhood, conducted by a founder of US sociology (see also Studying the city 8.2).

John Higham, *Strangers in the Land: Patterns of American Nativism, 1860–1925* (New Brunswick, NJ: Rutgers University Press, 2002). Higham examines responses to the great period of US immigration, particularly the backlash against immigrants and attempts to define who was an American.

Anthony D. King, *Colonial Urban Development: Culture, Social Power and Environment* (London: Routledge & Kegan Paul, 1976). Through a thorough examination of Dehli, King points to ways in which colonial rulers maintained and displayed power through the management of space.

Douglas Massey and Nancy Denton, *American Apartheid* (Cambridge, MA: Harvard University Press, 1993). Considered the definitive account of the history of black ghettos in US cities, the measurement of segregation, and the implications of segregation for racial inequality.

Gwendolyn Wright, *Building the Dream: A Social History of Housing in America* (Cambridge, MA: MIT Press, 1983). Wright provides an exhaustive but highly readable social history of US housing, including single-family homes, apartments, and public housing.

CHAPTER 9

Inequality and diversity in the post-World War II metropolis

KEY TOPICS

→ The two major themes that characterized the metropolis after World War II: growing inequality between residents and a growth in social diversity.

→ How and why urban problems such as poverty and homelessness increased during this era.

→ The ways in which gentrification began to remake the metropolis.

→ The rapid expansion of migration across the globe, which in turn led to the reconstitution and reshaping of many metropolitan areas.

Contents

Introduction to Cities: How Place and Space Shape Human Experience,
First Edition. Xiangming Chen, Anthony M. Orum, and Krista E. Paulsen.
© 2013 Xiangming Chen, Anthony M. Orum, and Krista E. Paulsen.
Published 2013 by Blackwell Publishing Ltd.

The emerging global economy and the vast network of social connections among people across the world that began in the 1970s had a profound impact on the metropolis. They not only reshaped broad contours of the metropolis in the West, leaving many cities in the United States and Western Europe with diminished resources, but also reshaped the metropolis in other parts of the world – in Africa, Asia, and Latin America. In Chapter 10 and Chapter 11 we shall examine some of these patterns in the non-Western world, particularly in Asia. In this chapter we want to explore more thoroughly the changes that occurred within the metropolis in Western nations.

There was, to begin with, a growing concentration of poverty in metropolitan areas, and with it conditions such as homelessness. Simultaneously, affluent parts of the metropolis grew, as was evident both in the emergence of upper-middle-class areas in the central cities and in the explosive growth of new suburban places (see Chapter 6). In the midst of all of this was a rapid and broad expansion and change in the movement of people from one country to another – immigration. This in itself transformed the character of the *places* and *spaces* of the metropolis, and of people's connections to them, in important ways. A shorthand way of capturing these various changes is to speak of them in terms of two broader transformations of the metropolis: a *growing inequality*, evident in the sharpening differences of wealth in different sites, and a *growth in the social diversity* of the residents, in terms of racial and ethnic diversity but also in terms of sexual diversity as well as in the tendency for new gay and lesbian communities to become place-based.

In this chapter we will provide you with an overview of the emerging inequalities within the city on the one hand and the growing social diversity on the other. These inequalities and the new diversity were not merely a matter of changing the character of the people who lived in the metropolis; they significantly altered the very character of the places and the spaces where people lived. Place and space themselves – the buildings, the streets, the sidewalks, the manner of transportation – would become reconfigured as new groups of people took up residence in the city. Yet in other respects they would remain invulnerable to change – as is evident especially in the continuing and flourishing pockets of social segregation in the metropolis, not only in America but also in European cities such as Amsterdam, Berlin, London, and Paris.

Inequality and the metropolis

Poverty and race

As the fortunes of the metropolis declined, with more and more industries departing for other sites, people living in metropolitan areas suffered. And some suffered far more profoundly than others. Among those who were hurt the most by the changing economic circumstances were African Americans. African Americans had moved by the tens of thousands into US cities in the early part of the twentieth century. By the middle of the twentieth century they had come to constitute substantial proportions of people living in the central cities of the American metropolis. In places such as Chicago they had fashioned communities for themselves across the city, in notable areas such as Hyde Park and Kenwood as well as on the near West Side. Many of these communities were home to prosperous groups of African Americans and to the formation of a distinctive and vital African American culture. In New York City, Harlem developed during the 1920s and 1930s and became a prominent center of African American culture in the United States. Similar communities of African Americans had taken root in other cities across the United States such as the Near East Side of Detroit.

Beginning in the 1950s and 1960s, however, these areas would become profoundly transformed and enter a period of steep economic and social decline. As the sociologist William Julius Wilson would argue in his famous series of works on African Americans in the city, the changes in the global economy and particularly the loss of jobs affected the black population more than many other segments of American society. As industries began to move to other parts of the United States or even abroad, the industrial jobs that many people had taken in the plants of automobile factories, such as those in Detroit, began to disappear. As they left, in their wake they left tens of thousands of people who could no longer make a decent living for themselves and their families. In some places, such as Milwaukee, the loss of jobs was especially tragic: here, just as the population of African Americans began to grow during the course of the 1960s, industries decided to depart for other places. This made the situation all the worse for the new residents of the city.

The effect of the loss of jobs crossed racial and ethnic lines, of course. But it proved especially painful for African Americans. They were not simply the victims of a declining economy but also continued to be the victims of an entrenched system of racial segregation. As we discussed in Chapter 8, racial segregation and the resulting inequalities it entailed were brutally evident across America. Blacks and whites lived in separate neighborhoods, with more and more whites moving to suburbs while blacks were denied this opportunity through the widespread use of restrictive covenants. These areas were not "separate but equal" – black neighborhoods had more than their share of substandard housing and were deprived of the public services common in white neighborhoods. Black neighborhoods as well as immigrant neighborhoods were also the targets of urban renewal schemes of the 1950s and 1960s that displaced residents and disrupted social networks. By the mid-1960s, the tensions between blacks and whites became overheated. When the Reverend Martin Luther King, Jr. came to Chicago in 1966 in an effort to draw attention to the racism that existed in the city, he was pummeled by rocks by local white residents (see Figure 9.1).

Urban ghetto neighborhoods declined even further in the 1970s and 1980s. The passage of the Fair Housing Act in 1968 eliminated the legal forms of housing discrimination responsible for a great deal of segregation. Before this legislation took effect, black residents of varying economic statuses lived together in racially segregated areas. The historian Alan

Figure 9.1 Martin Luther King Jr. after being hit by a stone at an event in Chicago, 1966. Although the US South was the site of pronounced civil rights struggles at this time, tensions were at least as high in the segregated communities of the northeast and Midwest. *Source: Photo © Bettmann/ CORBIS.*

Spear (1967) refers to these areas as **institutional ghettos**, where patterns of social organization closely resembled those of the larger society. In the years after the Fair Housing Act removed barriers to blacks' mobility, many affluent blacks left inner-city ghettos and moved to more suburban areas, just as whites had decades before. The neighborhoods they left behind might have remained vital communities were it not for the simultaneous decline in the industrial jobs available in US cities. The process of deindustrialization that we examined in Chapter 7 had devastating effects in these neighborhoods, as many residents had relatively little formal education and thus few opportunities once factory jobs moved overseas or to suburban areas. As cities hemorrhaged industrial jobs, ghetto neighborhoods became increasingly poorer and more residents began to depend on various forms of public assistance or the **informal economy** in order to get by. By the early 1990s, the institutional ghettos of the past had been replaced by what sociologist William Julius Wilson (1997) calls **jobless ghettos**: places where, on an average day, fewer than half of the working-age adults are actually working.

Industries in decline, growing unemployment, and the intractable character of racial segregation in the United States combined to produce sites in the metropolis that were, in the words of some observers, *dangerous places*. Poverty – indeed, persistent poverty that lasted across several generations of families – came to characterize these sites and to influence the daily life of people living within them. Crime rates were much higher in these spaces than in other sites of the city. The mortality rates, especially of young people between the ages of 18 and 30, were also noticeably higher. In many places murders happened on a routine and daily basis. Whereas for most people the places of the metropolis provided a sense of security and community, in these danger zones the very opposite was true. People could not feel safe living in them, and young people were more likely to die there than in other areas of the city. By the late 1990s and first decade of the twenty-first century, it had become almost routine for residents to gather and march the streets of these danger zones, calling upon other local residents, the police, and especially the gangs to bring a halt to the violence – and to make the streets and the neighborhoods safe places in which people could live.

institutional ghettos
Highly segregated neighborhoods where the social organization closely corresponds to that of the larger society.

informal economy
Economic activity that is not officially recorded, regulated, or taxed.

jobless ghettos
William Julius Wilson's term for the high-poverty minority neighborhoods where fewer than half of the working-age adults work.

EXPLORING FURTHER   9.1

The "culture of poverty" debate

The concept of the culture of poverty was first introduced by Oscar Lewis in his 1959 book entitled *Five Families: Mexican Case Studies in the Culture of Poverty*. Lewis suggested that impoverished people from all across the globe were taking on similar negative characteristics as a result of their misfortune, and essentially forming their own culture – the culture of poverty. As he explained,

Poverty becomes a dynamic factor which affects participation in the larger national culture and creates a subculture of its own. One can speak of the culture of the poor, for it has its own modalities and distinctive social and psychological consequences for its members. It seems to me that the culture of poverty cuts across regional, rural–urban, and even national boundaries. For example, I am impressed by the remarkable similarities in family structure, the nature of kinship ties, the quality of husband–wife and parent–child relations, time orientation, spending patterns, value systems, and the sense of community found in lower-class settlements in London, in Puerto Rico, in Mexico City slums and Mexican villages, and among lower class Negroes in the United States. (Lewis 1959: p. 2)

According to Lewis, cultural characteristics such as feelings of hopelessness and marginality, or fragile family structures, are taken on by poor individuals as poverty is inflicted upon them by larger structures of socioeconomic systems. Therefore, this culture of poverty that paralyzes poor individuals economically could be discontinued and obliterated through the proper structuring of public policy.

This theory greatly influenced public policy makers, especially in the United States. President Johnson's "War on Poverty" and much of the policy created during this era were crafted in such a way as to address the culture of poverty. One important example of this is the Moynihan Report, which was released by the US Department of Labor in 1965. The actual title of this report, "The Negro Family: The Case for National Action," makes it perfectly clear that the government believed that there was a major problem with African American family structure that required governmental intervention. As the report stated,

The evidence – not final, but powerfully persuasive – is that the Negro family in the urban ghettos is crumbling. A middle class group has managed to save itself, but for vast numbers of the unskilled, poorly educated city working class the fabric of conventional social relationships has all but disintegrated … So long as this situation persists, the cycle of poverty and disadvantage will continue to repeat itself. (United States Department of Labor 1965: p. 1)

Although the Moynihan report drew attention to structural factors that created widespread poverty, many policy makers seized upon cultural explanations for these families' plight. If cultural patterns were to blame for poverty and related social problems, then the families themselves could alleviate their poverty by adopting different norms and values – or so the argument went. Scholars with more structural approaches saw this line of thinking as "blaming the victim," and largely abandoned cultural explanations in favor of explanations that focused on the broad economic restructuring (such as the work of Wilson (1997), discussed above) and segregation (the focus of Massey and Denton, among others). Only relatively recently have cultural examinations of inner-city poverty received sustained attention. The work of Elijah Anderson (1999), who aims to explain violence in poor minority communities, and of Edin and Kafelas (2005), who study poor, unmarried mothers, are excellent examples of this line of inquiry.

In one of his most recent works, *More than Just Race* (2009), Wilson attempts to reconcile cultural and structural theories. He reveals the ways in which structural forces lead to certain kinds of cultural adaptations – a finding suggested by both Lewis and Moynihan but neglected in most debates on the culture of poverty. He also calls attention to the way in which cultural patterns among dominant groups produce the structural forces that perpetuate poverty (e.g., the racist stereotypes held by many white employers that contribute to black–white disparities in unemployment rates). By looking at culture in relation to structure, Wilson points to a means of giving culture its due without blaming the poor for their own misfortune.

Poverty and homelessness

One of the major consequences of the new poverty that overtook many metropolitan areas in the latter part of the twentieth century was the growth in the homeless population. Across many cities in Canada, the United States, and Western Europe, the streets became populated by countless numbers of people who no longer had permanent residences. Many set up new shelters for themselves in the back alleys and under the expressways of cities. A new generation of the homeless emerged, living in shelters or make-shift structures such as that seen in Figure 9.2. The homeless had few possessions, perhaps a plastic bag of clothing, a shopping cart they had found at a nearby grocery store, or a small piece of luggage they could use to transport their belongings from one place to another.

What made the situation particularly grim was that this new condition of homelessness emerged at a time when the fortunes of many other people were growing and flourishing. As the social critic and advocate for the poor Michael Harrington (1997 [1964]) once put it, the new homeless population represented "the other America." At a time when many Americans were enjoying prosperity, others lacked even the most basic of needs. Without shelter or a permanent address, they endured extraordinarily severe risks to their physical and mental health as well as facing distinct challenges in improving their situation. Lacking a fixed address, these individuals often could not successfully apply for work or for social services. The stigma associated with homelessness compounds these challenges: people who are homeless are scorned and avoided, and often become the targets of hate crimes.

Various theories were offered to account for the dramatic rise in homelessness in the 1980s. Some observers argued that the condition happened because, in the United States, many state governments changed the way in which they cared for the

Figure 9.2 A woman in a make-do shelter beneath the Manhattan Bridge in New York City. While homelessness is often regarded as a timeless and pervasive problem, the rate of homelessness increased dramatically in the 1980s. *Source: Photo: Mario Tama/Getty Images.*

deinstitutionalization
A shift from large, formal, state-run mental health facilities to smaller, less-formal, community-based facilities.

mentally ill. Rather than placing mentally ill persons in large, state-run facilities far from families, governments aimed to treat this population in smaller-scale and potentially more humane community-based facilities. This well-intentioned process – called **deinstitutionalization** – was unsuccessful because the community-based facilities were not funded adequately to meet the needs of the population. While some believe that the homeless are primarily the deinstitutionalized mentally ill, others see drugs and alcohol playing a major role in making – or keeping – people homeless. Both stances are somewhat correct. Just as many homeless people do face mental health issues (about one third), many also struggle with drugs and alcohol. These populations overlap, as, lacking adequate health services, some individuals try to treat mental illness by using drugs or alcohol. In his work *Sidewalk*, sociologist Mitchell Duneier describes the ways in which drug and alcohol use – and particularly crack cocaine use – led some of his subjects to take up residence on the streets. Addiction often led to unemployment, then to depression and withdrawal from friends and family, and eventually to a profound retreatism. Unable to see how their lives might return to a more manageable state, some of the people he studied gave up their homes and belongings and began a new kind of life on the streets and sidewalks. Although these men often said that they "chose" to be homeless, Duneier sees this statement as an attempt by the men to preserve their dignity and sense of self-determination, not as evidence that homelessness is a freely made "choice" (Duneier et al. 2000).

Although they are important factors to examine, mental health issues and drug and alcohol abuse cannot fully explain the contemporary homelessness problem. Another important cause is the loss of housing units that might have been used by the poor. In the 1970s and 1980s, urban renewal programs in the United States demolished around one million low-income apartment units, and, while many of these plans promised to replace "slum" housing with higher-quality dwellings, far fewer units were built than were torn down. A similar fate befell another low-cost housing option: single room occupancy hotels (or SROs), which provided shelter to those without the savings, credit, or employment history necessary to secure a long-term rental. About one million of these rooms were also lost in the 1970s and 1980s. Other types of housing remained standing but became financially out of reach as rents increased, salaries stagnated, and social welfare payments decreased. To make matters worse, the number of public housing units being constructed dramatically decreased in the 1980s (Gans 1994).

To complicate things further – *and this is a very complicated story* – we should also consider the role of social vulnerability in making individuals homeless. In studying homeless people in Austin, Texas, sociologists David Snow and Leon Anderson (1993) found that many people using the Salvation Army shelter there had moved to Austin looking for work. When they arrived, however, work was nowhere to be found, and without social networks they had nowhere else to turn. Some of Snow and Anderson's subjects blamed "bad luck" for their state. For instance, one might have suffered an injury or had a car stolen, and this event precipitated their turn to the streets. An important thing to keep in mind, however, is that people have different capacities to weather bad luck. While a stolen car might be an inconvenience for a middle-class person with insurance, it is disastrous to someone with no job, no savings, and no support network. Families, the primary support networks for most of us, are a final place we might look for the roots of homelessness. Many homeless men, and especially women and teenagers, found themselves on the streets after fleeing abusive homes. Others have been turned out of their homes as a result of drug, alcohol, or other behavioral problems. These patterns of abuse in turn contribute to mental health problems, where we began this complex account.

The economic recession that began in 2008 increased the numbers of homeless people in the United States and Western Europe even more. As businesses declined in the West, incomes dropped, and home loans were foreclosed, the number of people who were left homeless and living on the streets grew as well. Stories of middle-class men and women, and even families, who had lost their savings and their homes appeared in the news almost daily. The number of people who were compelled to turn to various social service agencies and shelters for food and housing also increased. More people were compelled to live out of their cars, putting all of their worldly possessions in the back seats. Since homes are so much a part of our lives as human beings – *a central part of our identity, as*

MAKING THE CITY BETTER   9.1

Organizations that aid the homeless

While homelessness has been a problem in cities since the Industrial Revolution, it was not until the problem increased in the 1980s that homelessness received any significant level of attention from academics and the popular press. Since then, scholarly assessments of homelessness have continued, but media attention has waned. Still, many organizations make it their business to aid the homeless every day.

A closer look at what types of organizations are aiding the homeless reveals that, in the United States, secular non-profits provide roughly 51 percent of homeless assistance programs, religious non-profits offer about 34 percent, government agencies account for another 14 percent, and for-profit organizations provide the remaining 1 percent. Of housing-related programs specifically, such as shelters and transitional housing programs, 60 percent are offered by secular non-profits. It is not uncommon to see that religiously affiliated non-profits will mandate attendance at religious services in order to receive food and shelter from the organization. Conversely, secular service providers will oftentimes require that homeless individuals attend job-training programs or substance-abuse rehabilitation classes in order to receive benefits. Secular organizations receive the majority of federal grants, with only about 13 percent of federal grant money being channeled through religious organizations (Aron and Sharkey 2002).

Organizations of each of these different classifications are working day to day to aid the homeless and to end this major urban problem in a variety of ways. Many provide meals and shelter, including transitional housing, while others may offer job-placement programs or mental and physical health treatment (homeless individuals face unique health challenges related to exposure as well as intermittent healthcare) (Leticq et al. 1998; Burt et al. 1999). These services significantly improve the day-to-day experiences of homeless people but do little to address structural barriers to housing access such as low wages and high rents. Some programs, such as those that provide job training, may provide clients with a means to gain permanent housing, but broader-scale changes to housing markets and attention to the factors leading to homelessness are necessary in order to truly eradicate this problem (McChesney 1990; Seltser and Miller 1993).

we have earlier argued – the loss proved devastating to the self-esteem of many people across Western cities.

The number of the homeless at this time tells the story. In the United States, on any given day, about 650 000 people were homeless in 2009. This represented an increase of 3 percent over the number who were homeless in 2008. Between 2008 and 2009, the number of homes in foreclosure went up by 21 percent. In 2009, moreover, about 40 percent of the people who were homeless lived on the street, in a car, or in some other place not meant for human habitation. In the state of Wisconsin, for example, there were twice as many homeless people living without a shelter in 2008 than in 2009. In England, a country with roughly one-sixth of the population of the United States, it was estimated that about 800 000 people were homeless on any given day in 2009, many concentrated in London but others to be found spread across the country (Crisis 2008; National Alliance to End Homelessness 2011).

Yet homelessness at this time was not a condition simply of people who had lost their fortunes and residences in the West. It also was a circumstance and condition that prevailed in many of the metropolitan areas of developing countries. Many of the people who were homeless were newly arrived to the metropolis, immigrants pushed to the metropolis because of tribal warfare or simply lured by the possibility of making a living. The homeless in the developing countries, in and around cities such as Johannesburg, Mumbai, Rio de Janeiro, and Shanghai built large squatter settlements in these areas – villages of poor people like themselves. And these areas, as we show in detail in Chapter 10 and Chapter 11, became in effect "shadow cities," places where poor people could at least find a shelter and rely on others to help them survive from day to day.

Gentrification and the remaking of the metropolis

Poverty, segregation, and homelessness were one side of the emerging and growing economic inequalities that helped to reshape metropolitan spaces and places after World War II. The other side was something that became known as gentrification. At the same time that industries were being lost and wealth was declining among many people living in the heart of the metropolis, new development began to take place. Warehouses that formerly were home to industries producing clothing or garments or other goods became vacated and, in their place, new enterprises arose. Sociologist Sharon Zukin (1982) has traced the transformation of an area in New York City known as SoHo. In the early decades of the twentieth century, the warehouses in SoHo were home to factories that produced clothing and created a great deal of wealth in the city. With the decline of industry and loss of jobs, however, many of the warehouses and factories came to stand empty (see also our discussion of Zukin and gentrification in Chapter 3).

Owing to the interest of local government as well as advantages provided to real estate developers, some of the vacant warehouses were transformed into new upscale residential developments. The first residential occupants in SoHo were young artists, many among them painters. They refashioned the area of SoHo into a new artist colony, right in the heart of Manhattan, giving a new vitality to the area and compensating in some ways for the loss of the older industries. The boom in new residences, upscale apartments, and handsome lofts took off. The prices of housing in the area skyrocketed, and new, immensely wealthy residents moved in. Paradoxically, Zukin notes, the very boom that the artists helped to unleash led to their own displacement.

This process whereby wealthy people moved into an area previously inhabited by factories or even many working-class residents was called "gentrification." The name was meant to recall the old-fashioned gentry, or middle-class residents, who had once lived in cities and who pursued an urban lifestyle singularly identifiable by their handsome homes. It was first used by Ruth Glass in London in the early 1960s. She observed that older residences in working-class areas were undergoing massive renovation and change, and that wealthier residents were moving into older working-class areas. She wrote:

> One by one, many of the working-class quarters of London have been invaded by the middle classes – upper and lower. Shabby, modest mews and cottages – two rooms up and two down – have been taken over, when their leases have expired, and have become elegant, expensive residences. Larger Victorian houses, downgraded in an earlier or recent period – which were used as lodging houses or were otherwise in multiple occupation – have been upgraded once again … Once this process of "gentrification" starts in a district, it goes on rapidly until all or most of the original working-class occupiers are displaced, and the whole social character of the district is changed. There is very little left of the poorer enclaves of Hampstead and Chelsea: in those boroughs, the upper-middle class take-over was consolidated some time ago. (Glass 2010: pp. 22–23)

In fact, this whole process of remaking the older industrial city eventually became part and parcel of the reconstruction of the central areas of cities both in Europe and in the United States after the end of World War II.

The process itself followed a fairly typical scenario. An older area would undergo decline in terms of the quality of its housing or other buildings. Then, depending on availability, new residents or real estate developers would step in and begin to renovate the housing. Local governments frequently helped to initiate these changes, largely because they stood to gain in taxes and spending from the new residents who came to occupy the housing. It was especially helpful, from the point of view of the local governments, to find some use for the old vacant buildings, as otherwise they simply would have to be demolished and it was often unclear whether anything else would be built on the land. Detroit became a prime illustration of how a city once home to many hundreds of thousands of people and a number of factories could turn almost overnight into an urban desert – empty lots and chain-link fences put up to protect the empty properties (see our extended discussion of Detroit in Chapter 13). It is this fate that urban governments seek to avoid by backing the gentrification efforts of private developers.

But, while this process seemed clear enough, it was also evident that the interests and wishes of wealthier residents won out over those of the poor. Local governments wanted the taxes provided by the new residents or new businesses, and sometimes would provide special tax incentives in order to lure developers and businesses back into the city (see Exploring further 9.2). At the same time, just as the artists had been displaced from SoHo because of their very success in revitalizing the area, so, too, the working class suffered from the wealth and power of the rich to transform their neighborhoods.

EXPLORING FURTHER   9.2

Tax increment financing

Many funding sources from the US state and federal government that cities once used for redevelopment projects have disappeared, and cities now have to seek out new ways to finance the restoration of economically distressed areas. One funding option for local governments who wish to attract businesses for redevelopment purposes is to set up tax increment financing (TIF) districts.

The basic way in which TIF districts work is to allow municipalities to stimulate private investment in blighted areas without raising taxes. Once a city has designated an area as a TIF district, the property tax rates and contributions to the city's general fund are designated and frozen for 15 to 50 or so years. As TIF district property is improved, the area's increased property tax revenues would normally go into the city's general fund. But in TIF districts those "tax increments" over and above the old tax revenues are instead funneled directly back into district-level redevelopment projects. These may include infrastructure projects, purchases of land, or other investments made through municipal bonds that the city will repay using the "tax increments" (Cullingworth and Caves 2009). In other words, increased tax revenues are used to subsidize mainly private development in TIF districts.

Like any other municipal funding mechanism, the power to designate TIF districts is given to cities by their corresponding state governments. The Council of Development Finance Agencies (2008) has compiled the enabling legislation for the 49 states, and the District of Columbia, that permit their municipalities to utilize TIF (Arizona repealed its enabling legislation in 1999). Within these pieces of enabling legislation, states lay out the regulations and guidelines cities have to abide by while funding redevelopment through the use of TIF districts.

The states regulate many aspects of the TIF funding process, including what types of areas can be designated as TIF districts, how long TIF districts can last, what types of projects can be funded, what specific uses the revenues can be used to fund, what must be included in the redevelopment plan put forward by the city, whether public hearings are required for the creation of TIF districts or for development deals, and what types of financing options are available to municipal governments. All of these regulations vary widely from state to state, though there is some common ground throughout the legislation.

Many states require cities to conduct a feasibility study or a "but for" analysis on an area before designating it as a TIF district. These types of studies try to determine whether the investments (bonds, loans, etc.) will pay for themselves in time and whether private investment would not occur in the area "but for" the creation of a TIF district. Cities may look at factors such as how long the area has been "blighted" (definitions vary from state to state) or has experienced significant vacancies, the success rate of previous redevelopment attempts and the types of projects attempted, or whether a prospective developer has the funds necessary to complete the project in its entirety. One last common trend worth mentioning is that most states require public hearings when a municipality creates a TIF district, but many do *not* require public hearings regarding deals for individual redevelopment projects within the districts. This shows that, while in many states the public may agree that some sort of redevelopment is desired within TIF districts, cities are permitted to decide behind closed doors just what types of redevelopment will occur, thus enabling them to avoid lengthy and therefore costly negotiations with the public (Weber and Goddeeris 2007).

While TIF districts have been around since the 1950s, they have become more popular in recent years as other funding sources for urban redevelopment have disappeared. According to Weber and Goddeeris (2007), "TIF revenue accounted for 38% of Minneapolis' revenues for economic development between 1991 and 2001." As an example of how widespread TIF districts are, Weber and Goddeeris also report that 78 percent of all local governments in the State of California had a community redevelopment agency (what TIF districts are called in California) in 2003 – a total of 386 active TIF districts. TIF districts are perhaps the most widespread in Illinois, which hosted 550 TIF districts, with 130 of them in Chicago alone (City of Chicago 2011).

Chicago uses the revenue generated from TIF districts to improve its neighborhoods in a variety of ways. To give a better idea of the types of projects funded through TIF district revenues in Chicago, following are some figures regarding publicly funded TIF investments taken directly from the city's website (2011):

- $762 million over several years to rehabilitate and construct new public schools as part of the Modern Schools Across Chicago plan;
- $560 million for improvements for streets, alleys, and other neighborhood infrastructure since 1997;
- $278 million to support nearly 11 000 affordable housing units;
- $198 million for capital improvements in 2008 alone (including Chicago Transport Authority improvements);
- $13 million in grants to help more than 400 businesses in more than 40 TIF districts through the Small Business Improvement Fund (SBIF); and
- $11.5 million through 181 grants to train 10 417 workers and hire 840 new employees.

Chicago is just one of many cities that are beginning to fund necessary urban redevelopment projects through the use of TIF districts. As the use of this funding mechanism spreads to more urban areas, researchers should continue to analyze its effectiveness as an investment tool to promote economic redevelopment.

Middle- and upper-class professional residents simply could exercise much more clout than poor residents.[1]

Gentrification has come to be a process that today happens across the globe. It occurs not only in London and in New York City but also in cities as different as Pittsburgh and Adelaide; indeed, according to some accounts, it occurs almost everywhere. Older areas in cities are ripe for change and redevelopment, and there are countless developers willing to come in, rehabilitate older residential structures or warehouses, and then make a great profit by their sale. A number of scholars, drawing on the writings of Karl Marx for their inspiration, highlight these changes because they view them as a new way in which capitalism can exercise its power over the transformation and development of the evolving metropolis. Geographer Neil Smith (1979) speaks of the gap in rent values that occurred in some of the areas left to decline, and how such areas inevitably became the sites where developers stood to gain great profits. Indeed, there is a good deal of evidence to suggest that both local governments and developers have often conspired to ramp up the value of such properties, thereby benefiting both the local developers and the local governments.

Over time, the process of gentrification radically reshaped certain areas of the postwar metropolis. Some places became like SoHo in New York City: they were fashionable and upscale; they hosted numerous high-end retail outlets where the wealthy could shop; they possessed fabulous restaurants; and they displayed the standard array of businesses in such areas – a local Starbucks, a Gap clothing store, even Dolce & Gabbana or Chanel boutiques. All of this did in fact transform the metropolis. But the question often raised by the critics was: *at what cost to the other residents of the city?*

This kind of transformation eventually had wholesale consequences for the landscape and the people of the city. A little-noted one is that of the process of displacement itself. Geographer Mark Davidson, attentive to the importance of place to people, observed that the fundamental issue involved in gentrification is not so much that capitalism reinvents itself but that some people become displaced as a result of these changes, and that place itself is deeply meaningful to them. Unlike the Marxist critics, who condemn the fact that the rich, because of their wealth, are able to force the poor residents out of an area, Davidson (2009) argues that it is the very fact that families are forced to leave their homes and neighborhoods that is in itself deeply disruptive of their daily lives.

Many people did not take their displacement lightly, simply standing by as their homes and neighborhoods were taken over. Across many cities, local residents mobilized in order to counter gentrification. For example, in Austin, Texas neighborhood associations across the city became regular and vocal critics at meetings of the local city council, resisting efforts to build new commercial or residential housing in their neighborhoods. In New York City, local residents engaged in rent strikes in the late 1970s in order to counter the owners of real estate who wished to raise the cost of local housing. In some New York City neighborhoods, such as the Lower East Side, gentrification efforts had to adapt to the resistance posed by residents, and developers packaged this as a dimension of the area's edgy, "bohemian" character (Mele 2000).

STUDYING THE CITY   9.1

Mary Pattillo's *Black on the Block*

Most of the studies done on gentrification have shown how when white middle-class residents move into a redeveloped area it often leads to the displacement of the working-class and/or minority residents. These studies reveal how the process of gentrification tends to advance the interests of the middle classes over those of the working classes. But a few studies have looked at the gentrification that has taken place in primarily African American neighborhoods in the United States. More and more middle-class African Americans seem to be moving back into the city and helping to restore the older, declining areas that many of them, and their parents, left.

Correcting this oversight is sociologist Mary Pattillo, who in *Black on the Block* (2007) examined the changes that took place over a period of several decades in the North Kenwood–Oakland neighborhood of Chicago. At one time, this area had been the pride of the African American community. Nightclubs and various kinds of cultural activities dotted the landscape; the population expanded and young people were motivated to remain in the area; and the neighborhood became home to the wealthiest and most successful black residents in Chicago. But, beginning in the 1960s, decline set in rapidly. Wealthier residents moved out, leaving behind lower-income families. The area became a hot spot for drug traffickers, gangs took over, and the neighborhood became one of those *dangerous places* in Chicago.

By the 1980s, the North Kenwood–Oakland area was a place that people wanted to avoid rather than to embrace. Eventually efforts were made by the federal government and local authorities to improve the area. This meant an effort to provide housing for middle-class residents, both white and black, as well to enhance the quality of the local schools. Among progressive social scientists, this was seen as an experiment both in gentrification and in bringing together people of different classes to see whether they could live in harmony with one another.

Pattillo's book considers the gentrification and redevelopment period in detail as she seeks to answer whether this new model of neighborhood growth can work. In some ways it does. The older, poorer black residents begin to enjoy the better stores and public services. Yet at the same time difficult issues arise. While one would expect that African Americans might unite on the issues of common racial concern, the class issues often prove divisive. The middle-class black residents often will express prejudice toward their poorer black counterparts. Moreover, the effort to improve public education in the area tends to benefit the middle classes, both white and black, far more than the poorer black households.

Pattillo's work represents an incredibly important and rich narrative of how gentrification occurs: how the best of intentions are put forth but how social conflict and struggle nevertheless ensue. It is one of the best recent ethnographies of race and place by any social scientist.

Social diversity and the transformed metropolis

The new immigration and the transformation of the metropolis

As we noted earlier, in the post-World War II period the composition of many cities began to change in significant ways. The beginnings of an integrated global economy began to emerge in the 1960s and had reached full-scale intensity by the 1980s. Nations began to open their doors to more and more trade. And, along with the movement of goods there also began a major movement of people from one nation to another. The effect was to create a brand new mix of people in many major metropolitan areas. In the first part of this section we discuss some of the important historical background to these changes. We begin with European nations and then move on to the United States and Canada. Then, having laid out in the broadest strokes the nature of these changes, we turn to a depiction of the effects they had on the demographic composition of the metropolis and the ways in which the postwar metropolis has been remade by peoples from around the world.

Europe

The world changed dramatically in the period after World War II, especially in the 1970s and the 1980s. One of the most significant changes was the increase in the movement of immigrants across national borders. There were various reasons for these changes. For one thing, old struggles between different nations began to diminish. The end of the war in Europe brought about economic and political efforts to mediate the old conflicts that had been its source. In the early 1960s, diplomatic efforts were made to create a new European Union, one that would consist of many of the nations that had been members of the allied forces during World War II. They included Belgium, France, and Norway, among others. Though there was considerable resistance to these efforts, the years of intense negotiations and deliberations paid off. A new European Union was established in 1993 with its governing body in Brussels. New rules and regulations were created that tied each country to the others. Border regulations were loosened for individuals wishing to cross from one country to another. Eventually a new currency, the euro, was created in 1995, recognizing the economic interdependence of the several nations and replacing the old individual currencies of each nation; it is now in use by 17 of the 27 EU countries. The United Kingdom is the only major European country that has refused to adopt the new currency.

A major impetus to the union was the effort to consolidate the economic forces of the various European countries of the West. After the war, more trade developed among the various countries, thereby overcoming the old political battles between nations such as France and Germany. In addition, it became easier for individuals to cross the national boundaries – this was greatly facilitated by the signing of the Schengen Agreement in 1985, which would eventually encompass 25 EU countries. Thus, for example, in the early part of the twenty-first century, when job opportunities were more plentiful in Germany than in England, many workers would travel from England to obtain jobs there.

Germany became the leading economic power and engine for the growth of the new European Union. Like other European nations, its population had begun to age. As a result, in order to keep its factories going and to maintain its high rate of productivity, Germany turned to other nations to find younger and cheaper labor. One key target was Turkey. Beginning in the late 1950s, Germany embarked on an effort to import labor from Turkey, where the economy was not nearly so robust. By the end of the 1990s, there were approximately two million Turks living in Germany, concentrated mainly, though not exclusively, in industrial regions and especially in Berlin, where the Kreuzberg area is known as Little Istanbul. They furnished a good deal of the labor necessary to keep some of the leading German industries booming.

Germany was only one example of the growth of the new transnational labor force that crossed national boundaries with far greater frequency and far more easily than in the past, when such boundaries were essentially impenetrable. France, too, began to encourage far more immigrants to settle within its borders. By the early 1960s, Algerians had in large numbers begun to migrate to France. There, many young students could attend some of the most famous and important universities in the world. Again, by the 1990s there were thousands of immigrants who had settled in France, gaining access to education and employment but at the same time posing major challenges for the French state. Many immigrants came from entirely different cultures. A great many were Muslims, and represented a religious tradition entirely new to and different from the Catholicism of France.

Similar changes in patterns of migration happened elsewhere in Europe as well. More and more immigrants came to the Netherlands, looking for jobs and offering younger and cheaper labor than the Dutch themselves. As in France and Germany, many of the new immigrants were Muslims and they settled in some of the larger urban settlements such as Amsterdam. In the United Kingdom, too, the same thing happened: in the 1960s, its restrictions of entry were eased. Many new immigrants took up residence there – in particular, large numbers of Afro-Caribbeans who exercised their rights as citizens in the British colonies. In the early 1960s, the proportion of the British population that was foreign-born was relatively small, but by the first decade of the twenty-first century that proportion had grown considerably larger. Between 1991 and 2008, the percentage of the British population that was foreign-born doubled, reaching 11 percent in 2008 (Whitehead 2009). Many immigrants settled into the heart of England, into sections of London but also into older working-class cities such as Manchester. The new immigrants began to dramatically refashion the face of London and England. As early as 1994, Bernie Grant, the Labor Member of Parliament who represented the district of Tottenham in London, would observe that his district had become completely multi-racial and multi-ethnic. It consisted of migrants from across the world: Africans, Bangladeshis, Cypriots, Hassidic Jews, Irish,

Kurdistan immigrants, and many others. Grant estimated that in the early 1990s at least 97 languages were being spoken among the residents and in the schools of Tottenham.[2]

The United States and Canada

The changing patterns of migration and the trend toward increasingly large numbers of foreign-born residents that were seen in Europe became evident in the United States as well. In 1965, the Hart-Celler Act was passed to reform immigration policy in the United States; this went into effect in 1968. After immigration laws became more restrictive in the late 1920s, only a relatively small number of foreign-born residents moved into the United States. And, because of biases in the laws at that time, the new Americans were very much like the old Americans: they came from Western Europe and often were English or Scottish or German. Their only contribution to the mix of nationalities in the United States was to increase the numbers of those peoples already there. But the 1965 law, in its effort to be progressive and to embrace more and different people from abroad, altered the criteria used to permit migrants to enter the United States and then to become citizens. Residents of Asian and African nations, who formerly had been severely limited in number, now were granted easier entry into the United States – as were their families, who often were permitted to join husbands, brothers, or sons who were the first to come to America. The same thing happened too for residents from many Latin American countries. As in Europe, the borders opened, and more and increasingly diverse people, intent on joining family and/or getting jobs, entered the United States.

The composition of the population in the United States eventually began to change as well. In 1970, for example, 4.7 percent of the US population was foreign-born; by 2009, this had increased to fully 12.5 percent. The largest percentage of immigrants came from Mexico. In 2009, about three of every ten foreign-born immigrants living in the United States were from Mexico (Batalova and Terrazas 2010).

Many of the immigrants to the United States settled, as they had in Europe, in major metropolitan areas. These places had the most employment opportunities, plus they were the sites of already well-established communities of fellow nationals. Historically, this had been the pattern of immigrant settlement in the United States. At the end of the nineteenth century and beginning of the twentieth, when many European immigrants came to America they settled in the central portions of major metropolitan areas because these were the sites of factories. Yet there were also new wrinkles and patterns to immigrant settlement in the period after the 1960s. Many of the new enclaves grew up at the periphery of the major metropolitan areas. They took root in smaller cities or even suburban areas of the metropolis, places that previously had been occupied by long-time native residents (see Table 9.1).

Canada also became home to more and more immigrants in the post-World War II period. By 2001, about 18 percent of the Canadian population represented foreign-born immigrants. Many of them came from places such as India, Hong Kong, and the Philippines, and elsewhere in Southeast Asia, and most live in three Canadian cities – Montreal, Toronto, and Vancouver (see Table 9.2). In 1997, when Hong Kong shifted from British authority to that of the People's Republic of China, a number of Hong Kong residents moved themselves, their families, and their assets to Canada (Ray 2005).

Canada possesses a much more careful and precise set of regulations and laws governing immigration than the United States. It created a system that sought to permit the entry of people into the country based, in large part, upon the labor needs of the nation as well as the specific skills and talents of those who wished to migrate to Canada. In 2004, for example, almost six of every ten admissions to Canada were based on the skills and abilities

Table 9.1 Immigrant (foreign-born) populations of select US metropolitan areas by city and suburbs, 1980 and 2005. *Source: Audrey Singer.* "Twenty-First Century Gateways: An Introduction." In Audrey Singer, Susan W. Hardwick, and Caroline B. Brettell, eds. Twenty-First-Century Gateways: Immigrant Incorporation in Suburban America (Washington, DC: Brookings Institution, 2008, pp. 1–28).

Metropolitan Statistical Area	City Population, Foreign-Born				Suburban Population, Foreign Born			
	1980		2005		1980		2005	
Atlanta–Sandy Springs–Marietta	9 777	2.3%	26 413	6.7%	38 038	2.0%	586 346	13.2%
Washington–Arlington–Alexandria	73 764	8.2%	149 955	17.8%	181 675	11.6%	867 477	20.3%
Chicago–Naperville–Joliet	442 199	16.3%	633 167	21.3%	344 484	7.0%	992 482	15.8%
New York–Northern New Jersey–Long Island	1 717 938	28.1%	2 991 395	36.4%	1 011 278	13.9%	2 125 895	21.0%
Los Angeles–Long Beach–Santa Ana	918 388	37.8%	1 801 618	40.1%	1 003 599	26.6%	2 605 735	31.8%

Table 9.2 Percentage distribution of total immigrants to Canada living in key cities and provinces, 1981 and 2000. *Source: Statistics Canada: Feng Hou,* Summary Of: The Initial Destinations and Redistribution of Canada's Major Immigrant Groups: Changes over the Past Two Decades *(Analytical Studies Branch Research Paper Series; PDF version; catalogue number 11F0019MIE-No. 255; 2005).*

City or Province	1981	2000
Vancouver	10.0	13.5
Remainder of British Columbia	6.4	5.1
Totonto	29.7	37.3
Remainder of Ontario	23.3	18.7
Montreal	11.9	11.4
Remainder of Quebec and Atlantic Provinces	3.6	2.6
Other Provinces	15.2	11.4

of the applicant rather than on any specific racial or ethnic criteria. In general, Canada is regarded as offering a more tolerant and inclusive climate for foreign-born residents than the United States, particularly in its major cities of Montreal, Toronto, and Vancouver.

Reconstructing the contemporary metropolis
New ethnic enclaves

When immigrants first entered major cities in Europe and the United States during the last great wave of migration (late nineteenth and early twentieth centuries), they settled in the central areas. Over time and as their numbers grew they created new **ethnic enclaves**, small communities where they lived and where many of them worked. And there were a variety of such enclaves – places such as German Town, Little Italy, and Chinatown – where immigrants and their friends and families could settle. They found support from one another. They established new churches, typically at the center of the immigrant enclave. They felt comfortable because they could speak the language of their home, and did not have to speak English, a language difficult for many immigrants to learn.

ethnic enclaves
Areas of cities where immigrants of the same ethnic background congregate to create social and economic opportunities for themselves.

When more restrictive immigration laws came into effect in early decades of the twentieth century, shutting the doors on immigration to countries such as the United States and Canada, many of these enclaves disappeared. They remained in name only for the most part as their residents died off, and the second and third generations moved to the outer portions of the city (see Studying the city 8.1). As we have noted in earlier chapters, this movement became part of the assimilation and integration of immigrants into the national fabric of their new countries. The later generations could speak English, and therefore they could blend into the older, native parts of the new country. Typically they also were better educated than their parents and grandparents, and, as a result, they had better jobs and higher incomes. In effect, they became Americans in America, Canadians in Canada, and British in Great Britain: all traces of their native homelands – or at least many of the material traces of them, such as the urban villages they had created – tended to be erased.

But when the doors reopened to new immigrants, in New York City, in Toronto, and in London, among other sites, the immigrants as a class once again began to create small enclaves. As various pieces of research show (e.g., Massey 1985), immigrants tend to follow a pattern of social networks: people from one village in Mexico, for example, move to those sites where their fellow villagers have settled, and eventually create dense new settlements of people who share a common homeland and ethnicity. Through this process, whether in Germany or the United States or elsewhere, the metropolitan landscape became dotted with a variety of new places, of new villages, of people who knew one another and, as in the case of their predecessors, could rely on one another for social support. This same process unfolded in Miami, with the creation of a new Cuban enclave, Little Havana, and in London, with the creation of new and lively enclaves that consisted of immigrants from the Caribbean islands.

But there were some very important differences, differences that left a decided impact on the landscape of the larger metropolis. For one thing, as we have already noted, many of the new enclaves did not arise in the central areas of the city, where earlier generations of immigrants had settled because they could live closer to factories, but rather in the outskirts of the metropolis. Now, as the means of transportation changed – as people began to arrive in the city by car, for example – new settlements could be established outside the central city. Eventually a host of immigrant enclaves arose in the outskirts of many urban areas. Such enclaves grew up across the Los Angeles metropolitan region. They also arose in the larger New York City metropolitan region as well as in small towns and older cities in the greater Chicago metropolitan region. Their effect was to change the apparent dynamics of the spatial and social trajectory of assimilation in countries such as the United States. Whereas prior groups of immigrants moved over time to outer portions of the metropolis, becoming in Douglas Massey's words "spatially assimilated," many recent immigrants have immediately settled in the outermost portions of the city.

So, it would seem that large groups of immigrants in the United States – for example, Mexicans and Russians – have taken a major step toward becoming integrated into the American mainstream. But have they actually? This is one of the major questions that students of immigration are now studying. There is some evidence that suggests that some of the new immigrant enclaves are in fact small communities of fellow immigrants who, even though they possess high levels of education and considerable wealth, have chosen to remain living with their fellow co-ethnics. A major examination of the Chinese immigrants in the greater New York City metropolitan region by Min Zhou, for instance, reveals that there are sites in Flushing, outside Manhattan in the borough of Queens, with relatively dense congregations of Chinese immigrants and their children. While by all measures these groups have achieved the education and income consistent with the American Dream, they also appear to continue to draw on the social support and community they find among their fellow co-ethnics from China. In other words, they recreate key features of their homelands as a way of blending into the American landscape – and they apparently do not simply blend into the places and spaces occupied by white Americans. They assimilate in terms of their economic and social achievements, but they retain a strong attachment to their homelands in terms of their spatial location (Zhou 2009).

Wherever one looks, similar patterns of creating new ethnic enclaves and special ethnic places are currently occurring in the United States and other countries. In a recent work, sociologist Jan Lin investigates the "making of ethnic places" in several cities in America. In Miami, for example, he finds a booming and expansive Cuban community, inhabited by several generations of Cubans who trace their original settlement to their forced exile to Miami. Cubans have established their own specific economic and cultural places in the city. They are also active in local politics. And they have made considerable economic gains since they came to America in the late 1950s and early 1960s. Both in New York City and Los Angeles, Lin has uncovered vibrant and significant congregations of Chinese immigrants along with their children. In each city, there is a Chinatown with its various small businesses. These communities replicate the earlier dense settlements of immigrants from China, but with important distinctions. Now they may consist of people who arrive not only from mainland China but also from Taiwan and Hong Kong. More than that, the people in these new Chinatowns are not inclined simply to abandon them in order to assimilate into American society. Instead, they work actively to sustain and invigorate these "ethnic places," in part to retain connections to their national heritages but also to furnish ways to profit from the cultural artifacts they can sell to an endless stream of tourists. The effect is to create a new ethnic place for recent immigrants as well as their children – a place that, like all places, furnishes its residents with a sense of community and security (Lin 2011).

Similar new ethnic places have been created in Boston and Orange County by the refugees who arrived from Vietnam in 1975 and beyond, and their children. As Karin Aguilar-San Juan shows in her compelling study of these two communities, the immigrants have carved out special places for themselves in these two major American regions, though they are places that differ from one another. In Boston, the immigrants have created a smaller community and have done so in a city whose cultural traditions can be traced to the American Revolution. The kind of place they have established reflects in part the nature of the broader metropolis: the ethnic community occupies a smaller space and it also sits among a larger group of native residents who have very different memories and conceptions of the Vietnam War and the Vietnamese people. Yet the Vietnamese here have carved out a strong and viable place just for themselves. Little Saigon in Orange County is a much larger settlement of people, consisting of about a quarter of a million residents. It houses a number of different restaurants and shops, and, like other ethnic places across the United States, it has also become a site that tourists like to visit. Moreover, it lies in an area that consists not merely of one set of immigrants but of immigrants of different national backgrounds. Indeed, Little Saigon possesses a large and thriving Chinese immigrant community, one that provides it with a strong and viable ethnic economy. Thus, it has become something like a community of different nations, where people of different nationalities live in proximity to one another (Aguilar-San Juan 2009).

A similar social space of diverse immigrants can be found on the Near North Side of Chicago along Devon Avenue. This has become well-known in Chicago as the space of recent immigrants and ethnic diversity, as well as entrepreneurial activity. Indeed, there are several streets in the area named after particular national heroes or heroines of dominant immigrant populations. There are Orthodox Jews and their children who left Russia in the 1980s and 1990s and settled here. They can be seen walking the streets daily, and they have their own local stores, including delicatessens, in the area. In addition, there are recent Indian immigrants from the subcontinent of Asia who have clothing stores here as well as restaurants that cater to their co-ethnics, but also many tourists. And, in a pattern that is not entirely unusual, while many Indians have their business establishments here, many of them actually reside in the western suburbs and make a regular commute to Devon Avenue to work. Besides the Russian Jews and the Indians, there are various other groups that either live or work in the area. In effect, just as in Orange County, a variety of groups have remade this social space of Chicago into an *ethnic space*, one where they obviously feel comfortable but that has also become known as a site where tourists interested in ethnic food and/or clothing may come and shop.

This social reconstruction of the metropolitan landscape is not only a US phenomenon; it has happened in European cities as well. In London, for example, there are areas such as Brixton and the East End where thousands of recent immigrants and their children live. One of the more notable features of Brixton is the open market, where people can come and shop. Such markets not only represent an important ethnic place but also furnish a public space where people can see one another regularly. Thus, they help to establish a community of fellow immigrants, people who have experienced similar instances of displacement.

In Germany, too, similar kinds of ethnic enclaves have arisen that have helped to reshape the nature of the metropolitan space, creating important new and significant places for their residents. Berlin, as we noted earlier, has been the recipient of thousands of Muslim migrants from Turkey. Many began to arrive in the 1960s as part of the German effort to attract labor. As in other countries and cities, they have established their own settlements and enclaves.

Across the world, then, among different groups of immigrants and in various cities and countries, the new flows of immigrants to the city are remaking the social landscape of the city itself. New ethnic enclaves arise almost overnight, furnishing their residents with an important sense of security and community that helps to shelter them against a larger society that often targets them for hostility and discrimination. Will today's new residents eventually become integrated into the larger social fabric, respectively becoming Americans, British, or Germans? Or will they remain marginal, on the fringes both of the national order and the metropolis?

STUDYING THE CITY   9.2

Annika Hinze on Turkish Muslims and their neighborhoods in Berlin

Since the second half of the twentieth century, the metropolis has increasingly become a home for immigrant populations (Judd and Swanstrom 2011). In Western countries, they came as political refugees, immigrants from former colonies, or as "guest workers," temporary migrants in search of higher incomes and better lives (Marcuse and van Kempen 2000). In Western Europe, many of these "guest worker" immigrants ended up staying for good. However, their permanent incorporation into the societies of Western Europe has proven difficult. In the case of Germany, for instance, guest worker immigrants, who were predominantly from rural areas in Eastern Turkey, could not naturalize as German citizens.

By the time Germany's citizenship law was finally revised in the year 2000 to include, under certain conditions, immigrants of non-German descent, the former Turkish guest workers had children and grandchildren who had been born in Germany and had never lived in Turkey. Yet these children and grandchildren had never been made to feel as though they were Germans, for two main reasons. One was Germany's exclusionary descent-based citizenship law, and the other was the fact that they felt stigmatized as "the other" in Germany based on their different cultural and religious customs and the different language many of them spoke in their homes, whether they were citizens or not. However, while they had never really felt like Germans, they had never really felt like Turks either. Most of them only knew Turkey from their families' summer vacations, and from their parents' and grandparents' stories. In personal interviews and conversations, many German Turks reported that they were approached by young people in Turkey who asked them whether they were Germans or *almancı*, even though their Turkish was flawless. *Almancı* is a somewhat derogatory term used in Turkey referring to former Turkish guest worker immigrants and their descendants in Germany. It literally means "those whose business is in Germany," which has slightly opportunist undertones in the sense that the "German Turks" have turned their backs on Turkey for better socioeconomic opportunities in Germany.

In interviews conducted in Berlin in 2008 and 2009, many second-generation German Turks reported that they had a "neither-here-nor-there" identity and that they felt they did not fit into either German or Turkish societies. For example, when asked about her identity, one woman of Turkish descent who was born in Germany explained:

> My mother says you are at home where you eat. I think that is true. Because otherwise we would not really be at home anywhere. Neither here in Germany, nor at home in Turkey, where we are being looked at in this way "Look at those Germans."

Another noted:

> To be honest, I feel in the middle. Why? Let me tell you: For example, when we are in Turkey they [the Turks in Turkey] often say, "yeah, those are Germans, well, German-Turks who live in Germany" – well, like tourists, so to say. When we come here [to Germany], we are foreigners. [...] So, where are we supposed to live, this is our state – for example, I am a German citizen. But still I am a foreigner because my name is different and my family, and Islam [my religion], everything. [...] When I travel to Turkey and say I am Turkish, that's not true either – I was born in Berlin. And went to school here. And I can speak German [...]. So because of all this I have no idea where we [German Turks] belong.

This "neither-here-nor-there" notion is a common way in which sociologists have described the second generation of immigrants, who belong in both the country of origin and the country of immigration while at the same time being permanently unable to reach a sense of complete belonging and acceptance anywhere.

This quality is apparent in the ways in which scholars have described immigrant enclaves as intrinsically "hybrid" – Edward Soja's (1999) term – or "creolized" – from Betigül Argun (2003). This means that immigrant minorities do not necessarily seek to recreate a piece of their home country in the ethnic enclave. Rather, their own identity is quite often so hybrid within itself – or, as we have seen, "neither here nor there" – that it is precisely this hybridity that is reflected in the culture and life of the enclave. This, again, became quite clear in the interviews with second-generation Turkish immigrants in Berlin. In reference to reconciling identity and place, for example, one woman said:

> Those children [our children] will not leave [Germany] because they did not come from Turkey, so they're not going to Turkey; they may not see Germany as their home but they relate to the [specific] place – for example, I can tell you about the children [of Turkish immigrants] in Berlin, who say "we are Berliners, not Germans, Berliners!" That is their identity, it's place-related, not nation-related.

Another interviewee related specifically to the neighborhood, noting that the hybridity of the neighborhood remedied her position as an outsider in Germany. In the enclave itself, she is not different but just another human being:

When you know everything, when you get along with the people [in the neighborhood] … when I go outside here, I do not feel like I am in Germany [...]. I can go shopping here and I have no problems, nothing. I don't feel like a Turk, *I just feel like a human being*.

The strong local identity becomes a substitute for the lack of national belonging. Specific places and neighborhoods in the city acquire an almost mythical status, as life stories and memories are tied to them. The immigrant neighborhood represents a safe haven in which immigrants acquire the status of belonging and acceptance they fail to find in either German or Turkish society. Despite the fact that every immigrant may interpret the personal meaning of the neighborhood differently, it appears that the traditional neighborhood itself provides a place of hybrid belonging that neither German nor Turkish identity can provide. The immigrant neighborhood becomes a spatialized representation of the different ways in which Turkish immigrants integrate themselves into the city, reconciling the seemingly irreconcilable differences between German and Turkish identities (see Figure 9.3).

Figure 9.3 Shops in Berlin-Kreuzberg, an immigrant neighborhood, cater to the area's Turkish population. *Source: Photo: Sean Gallup/Getty Images.*

Other dimensions of urban diversity

The new urban immigration was certainly not the only force leading to greater diversity within cities. As observed by early theorists such as Simmel and Tönnies as well as contemporary scholars such as Richard Florida and Sharon Zukin, cities are home to a great deal of cultural and subcultural diversity. This includes art, music, and other cultural expressions – including relatively esoteric or avant-garde art movements, concentrations of students and other young people who push cultural boundaries (recall our discussion of the social upheavals of the 1960s, many of which began in cities such as Paris), political outsiders, and sexual minorities.

In cities, ideas from across space and time converge, leading to tremendous creativity. When this combines with the large populations found in cities, great cultural innovations can occur that in turn attract their own followings. Consider music scenes. Typically the products of young musicians and their fans, these subcultures not only form in cities but also take their names from the cities in which they originate, and in turn transform the meanings associated with those places. Think of Detroit in the 1960s ("Motown"), Manchester and Seattle in the 1980s and 1990s, or Brooklyn and Montreal today. Richard Florida also credits these music scenes with enhancing cities' appeal to the creative class, as they not only provide a source of entertainment but also contribute to a spirit of creativity and innovation (Florida 2002). Music scenes, and other art scenes as well (literature, theater, visual art, and so on), also attract individuals whose interests and tastes are not satisfied in small towns and rural areas, further contributing to cities' rich diversity.

Another facet of urban diversity is lesbian, gay, bisexual, and transgender (LGBT) populations. As part of a relatively small and often marginalized facet of the population, LGBT individuals have often found small towns and rural areas difficult places to live. Not only do these places often tend toward more socially conservative values but they also have small populations, and even smaller LGBT populations. Finding community, companionship, and romance is a challenge for LGBT residents. In cities, however, LGBT populations are able to be more open about their identities and reach significant numbers. This has changed the lives of LGBT residents as well as the places where they live (see Making the city better 9.2). Many cities have well-known gay or lesbian neighborhoods, which include bookstores, cinemas, coffee houses, and nightclubs catering to distinct populations. Many of these are found in urban core areas, including gentrifying districts. In some of these places, lesbian and especially gay male populations are among the early gentrifying groups, although many are sensitive to potential negative impacts of gentrification and do what they can to mitigate these (Brown-Saracino 2009). The vitality that characterizes many lesbian and gay areas has significantly transformed cities, and many of these places are now considered among cities' most interesting and desirable neighborhoods.

MAKING THE CITY BETTER   9.2

Spaces and places of the LGBT community

Though lesbian, gay, bisexual, and transgender (LGBT) people were not able to openly stake a claim to communities within their cities around the world until after World War II, the roots of many postwar social movements go significantly further back in history.

In many countries, laws curtailing sexual practices were derived from religious contexts and used to oppress gay and lesbian individuals. However, in 1791, France became the first country to repeal these laws, shortly after the beginning of the French Revolution. Other major cultural and political breakthroughs gave the LGBT community more equitable and open access to metropolitan areas in Germany, Poland, and Russia before World War II, only for this to be halted and reversed by the rise of Nazism and Stalinism (Plant 1988).

After World War II, however, the gay rights movement exploded onto the political and cultural scene of many Western countries. The movements started out based around assimilation, and adapted to more radical stances during the late 1960s to the 1980s. One major turning point in the gay rights movement happened during the very early morning of June 28, 1969 at the Stonewall Inn of New York City's Greenwich Village neighborhood. Police raided this gay bar in the early morning hours, as they routinely did at similar establishments. As the New York Public Morals Squad attempted to arrest and transport the bar patrons, a large crowd formed and began shouting them down. Hundreds of protestors confronted police on that night and subsequent evenings, catalyzing the gay and lesbian movement. Many pride parades (see Figure 9.4) take place in June to commemorate the anniversary of the Stonewall Rebellion (Duberman et al. 1989; Blasius and Phelan 1997).

Movements such as these resulted in a number of places in cities across the world becoming representations of marginalized identities and also becoming safe places for the LGBT community to make full and open use of the city they live in. One example of this sort of neighborhood is The Castro in San Francisco. The neighborhood includes several landmarks, including one of the first gay bars, the camera shop and political headquarters of pioneering gay activist Harvey Milk, and a LGBT Historical Society exhibit. A rainbow flag flies proudly in the middle of a major intersection for all to see.

Across the world, there are many other examples of spaces and places being heavily influenced by marginalized identities, making the city safe for groups who have had a very limited right to the city in the not-so-distant past. Neighborhoods such as Barrio Norte in Buenos Aires, Clifton in Cape Town, Le Marais in Paris, and Darlinghurst in Sydney are all places where members of the LGBT community have been able to leave a cultural mark on the city.

Figure 9.4 Toronto's 2008 Gay Pride Parade. Gay and lesbian populations are creating neighborhood enclaves and recognition through formal celebrations in more and more cities. *Source: http://commons. wikimedia.org/wiki/File:Toronto_ Gay_Pride_2008.jpg, photo by Neal Jennings. Licensed under the Creative Commons Attribution-Share Alike 2.0 Generic license.*

The Western metropolis in flux

Since the end of World War II, metropolitan areas across the world have undergone major transformations. Two concepts that are useful for thinking about these changes are those of social inequality and social diversity. Owing to the broad structural changes that occurred during this period, tens of thousands of urban residents have become impoverished. Certain groups, such as African Americans, have suffered more from poverty. As William Julius Wilson and his students have shown, the loss of jobs in the urban cores of many US cities was felt particularly harshly by black Americans. At the same time, the character of the city, and its residents, was changing. In an effort to promote the central city as a place for new residents as well as tourists, many cities turned to a variety of ways to lure the rich and wealthy back into the cities. This whole process became known as the process of gentrification. There have been winners and losers in this transformation as well. The city, at least for a time, managed to secure more tax revenues as new, wealthier residents moved into older areas left by the manufacturing firms as they moved from Western cities to those in Asia and other parts of the world. The wealthier residents gained as well. Parts of the central city in sites such as London, New York City, Chicago, and many other similar metropolitan areas have been refashioned into upscale places, each with its own Starbucks, an array of boutiques, and the other cultural paraphernalia of the postmodern city. The losers, however, have been the poor and the working classes. Wherever gentrification has occurred, it has left in its wake countless people who have been displaced – who have lost their homes to wealthier residents, and who have thus been forced to abandon the neighborhoods they have known so well. These struggles have been well-documented, and they have taken place across the globe.

But the story of the postwar Western metropolis does not end there. Indeed, just as black Americans were beginning to become impoverished in growing numbers, and as the new gentry were moving back into the central cities, yet another set of events unfolded that began to change the very character of many Western metropolises. This was the process of immigration, a broad and expansive wave of migration that brought into many European and North American cities a whole host of new migrants. They came for the jobs but they also came for the opportunities for children and young people. They arrived in Berlin, Chicago, Paris, Toronto, and elsewhere: they spread across the globe, looking for new opportunities and ways to support their families. The result of this new, postwar migration has been to change the ethnic character of the Western metropolis and to set the demographic stage for a new phase of urban politics in the city. Latinos now dominate among the urban migrants in the United States, and they have begun to shift the potential balance of power among the various racial and ethnic minorities. In Berlin, Turkish immigrants have posed challenges to the meaning of citizenship and national identity, resulting in important policy changes but also producing a continuing source of tension between the native Germans and their Turkish counterparts. In Amsterdam, large groups of Muslims have entered, bringing with them of course a new source of labor for an aging workforce but also new questions about identity and about how to weave together religions with very different images of the past as well as the future.

The postwar Western metropolis, in other words, has become a place of continuing forms of inequality but also of competing sources of identity and national aspirations. European cities, in particular, face challenges that North American ones have faced for centuries: how to integrate disparate peoples from all parts of the world and maintain a kind of national integrity. It is a challenge that will continue to confront the nations and the new immigrants, but particularly the civil and political life of the Western metropolis.

In the following two chapters, we turn the page and consider the story of the postwar period in developing nations and the emerging metropolitan behemoths that now rival those of the West. Visit the book's companion website at www.wiley.com/go/cities for examples, case studies, and discussion questions, plus a list of useful films and other media, that are relevant to this chapter.

Critical thinking questions

1 Since the late 1980s the social and economic inequalities within metropolitan areas seem to have increased and show no sign of declining any time in the near future. What problems does this pose for the future of cities and for the governance of them, in particular?

2 Are the issues of inequality that face the cities in the older industrial world different from those that face cities and their residents in the developing world? How are they different?

3 Are there any things that local governments might do to help lower- and working-class residents as they face more challenging economic circumstances in the near future?

4 How might the growing ethnic and racial diversity of cities reshape the lives of residents in the future?

5 Looking around where you live, what signs are there of recent gentrification? And what are the ways, if any, that residents are attempting to counter the efforts of developers and local governments to gentrify older areas?

6 What does the presence of ethnic enclaves suggest regarding "melting pot" theories of immigrant assimilation? Are these ethnic places a positive or negative development for cities and societies?

Suggested reading

Karin Aguilar-San Juan, *Little Saigons: Staying Vietnamese in America* (Minneapolis: University of Minnesota Press, 2009). Aguilar-San Juan contrasts the place-making efforts of Vietnamese communities in Boston and Orange County, providing insights into how ethnic enclaves form and function in a multicultural era.

Japonica Brown-Saracino, ed., *The Gentrification Debates* (New York: Routledge, 2010). This exhaustive collection includes the works of some of the most important scholars, examining gentrification and studying accounts from a variety of types of gentrifying places.

Jan Lin, *The Power of Urban Ethnic Places: Cultural Heritage and Community Life* (New York and London: Routledge, 2011). Using a variety of case studies, Lin examines the changing status of urban enclaves in a global era, emphasizing positive impacts on cities and urban life.

William Julius Wilson, *More than Just Race: Being Black and Poor in the Inner City* (New York: W. W. Norton & Company, 2009). In this succinct volume, Wilson weaves structural and cultural explanations of inner-city poverty with an emphasis on African Americans.

Min Zhou, *Contemporary Chinese America: Immigration, Ethnicity and Community Transformation* (Philadelphia, PA: Temple University Press, 2009). A comprehensive examination of Chinese immigrants to the United States and their offspring that calls into question past assumptions about assimilation.

Notes

1. Not everyone agrees that gentrification will always lead to the displacement of poor and lower-income households. Recent research by the sociologist Lance Freeman suggests that lower-income households may be less, rather than more, likely to move from gentrifying neighborhoods. He also argues that disadvantaged residents may remain in the gentrifying neighborhoods precisely because they have more to gain from the better retail stores and public services that arise. See Freeman and Braconi (2004).

2. Anthony Orum, coauthor of this text, visited London regularly in the mid-1990s as the director of a study-abroad program at his university. He had the opportunity to observe many of these changes first-hand in London as well as to hear and visit with Members of Parliament such as Bernie Grant and Diane Abbott, among the first people of color to be elected as MPs. The observations here are based upon lectures he attended at the Institute of European Studies in central London.

PART IV
THE METROPOLIS IN THE DEVELOPING WORLD

CHAPTER 10

Urbanization and urban places in developing-country cities

KEY POINTS

→ The meaning of place and space in the context of urbanization.

→ The urban pyramid as a way of understanding the city system found in developing countries.

→ The concept of urban primacy and its influence on a country's urban system and urban places.

→ The difference between over-urbanization and under-urbanization and the implications of both urban places, particularly in developing countries.

→ The concept of the megacity and its strategic importance for places and spaces.

→ The rise of slums and the opportunities and challenges they pose for restructuring urban places.

Introduction to Cities: How Place and Space Shape Human Experience,
First Edition. Xiangming Chen, Anthony M. Orum, and Krista E. Paulsen.
© 2013 Xiangming Chen, Anthony M. Orum, and Krista E. Paulsen.
Published 2013 by Blackwell Publishing Ltd.

Contents

If the main storyline of the Western metropolis during the postwar period centers around inequality and diversity, it has some parallels in the cities of many developing countries in Asia, Africa, and Latin America. The developing-country cities are, however, quite distinctive in how they have been altered as urban places in the striking context of accelerated urbanization and the emergence of cities much larger than those in the West. In this chapter we present the various distinctive facets of urbanization in developing countries and demonstrate how they affect cities, especially megacities as urban places.

According to the World Bank (2009: p. 12), between 1985 and 2005 the urban population in developing countries grew by more than 8.3 million annually, almost three times the annual increase of today's high-income countries between 1880 and 1900. Another big difference is that the world's largest developing cities today have much larger populations. London had fewer than seven million people in 1900, while the largest city among low-income countries today (Mumbai) is three times that size, and Mexico City is about the same. The world's largest 100 cities are now almost 10 times the size of the largest 100 cities in 1900, and almost two-thirds of these cities are in developing countries, as are 15 of the world's 20 largest city-regions (Burdett 2008).

These numbers reveal a momentous shift of the world's urban population from the Western industrialized countries to the less developed countries. One simple way to describe this shift is to view cities in the industrialized economies, especially those of the United States and Europe, as "shrinking" and those in most developing countries as "expanding." Yet even this characterization misses a lot of the complexity of the rapidly urbanizing parts of the world, where the larger but poorer cities now challenge how social scientists think about place and space. This population shift is a defining story of the late twentieth and early twenty-first centuries that will unfold with significant implications far into the remainder of this century.

Before addressing the details concerning cities in developing countries, we must emphasize that these cities no longer belong to the old, more or less homogeneous, category of "Third World countries." A fair number of cities – some large, others not so large – in developing countries have experienced continuous economic booms such that they now approach the status of major cosmopolitan cities in developed countries, with a handful of them, such as Shanghai, being recognized as global cities. We begin with a general discussion of urbanization in developing countries and then examine a small number of individual cities that stand out as interesting case studies of place and space.

Urbanization
The basic path and its impact on place

Cities and places are the essential product of **urbanization**, the process by which a country becomes urbanized. Measured simply as the percentage of a country's total population that lives urban areas (however officially defined), urbanization unfolds in the same basic manner in all countries: populations move from rural starting points to increasingly urban destinations. Along the way, an urbanizing country builds more cities, particularly larger cities that house a growing proportion of the population. There is also a temporal dimension to urbanization; that is, all countries tend to become more urbanized over time. Moreover, although all countries will urbanize sooner or later, they do so and have done so differently. Consequently, this variation produces highly diverse cities and places in developing countries.

urbanization The process by which a country becomes urbanized from its rural origins.

level of urbanization A numerical measure of urbanization of a country that ranges from zero to 100 percent along a continuum.

We explore urban places in developing cities in greater detail later in this chapter and Chapter 11, but for now we ask you to imagine urbanization as a macro process of and context for urban growth. Ranging from zero percent at one (the left) end to 100 percent at the other (the right), the path of the **level of urbanization** is marked with many points or stations between the two extremes, with each of the points representing a certain level of urbanization of a given country at any given stage of its development (see Figure 10.1). Counties move along a continuum between the theoretical possibilities of zero and 100 percent (or complete) urbanization and eventually reach a terminal station of stabilized urbanization. While the United States and Western European countries have obtained an almost permanent level of urbanization of around 80 percent, China has just reached the middle point of 50 percent urbanization, with the developing countries in Africa being the least urbanized. The city-states of Singapore (Figure 10.2) and Hong Kong (the latter before its return to China in 1997) are exceptional cases of complete urbanization. In comparison, developing countries in Asia and Africa, especially China and India, have been rapidly urbanizing, making their large cities major sites for our study of urban places.

The developing countries are rapidly catching up with the highly urbanized Western countries, but they have used different strategies in navigating the process. Some countries such as China drive urbanization with strong government directives and incentives, whereas other countries are less interventionist, allowing urbanization and city growth to proceed more "naturally" through demographic and market mechanisms. As a result, the urbanizing

Figure 10.1 Level of urbanization. *Source: Based on an original diagram drawn by Curtis Stone and data compiled by the author.*

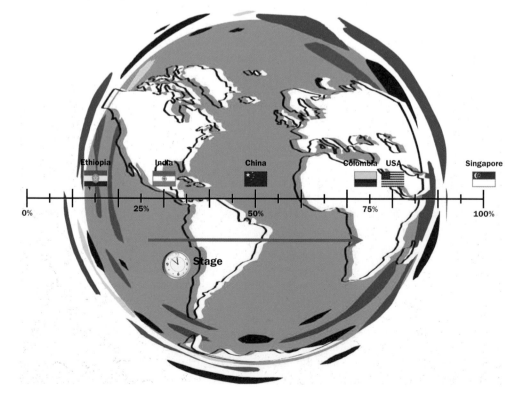

trajectories of developing countries vary greatly, further differentiating their cities. More importantly, urbanization in the developing world has many intersected macro–micro influences on place and space through reordering the economic structure, the built environment, and the cultural fabric of cities.

Developing-country cities in historical perspective

The accelerated urbanization seen today in developing countries is by no means a recent phenomenon. The irony, in fact, is that urbanization began centuries ago in today's developing regions. If we go back many years, we can identify the earliest form of urban life as beginning in the Middle and Near East – in and around present-day southern Iraq – around 3500 BCE. In other words, the oldest urban communities or ancient cities known in history began approximately 6000 years ago and later emerged with the Maya culture in Mexico and in the river basins of China and India (see Studying the city 10.1). In fact, as early as the thirteenth century, the largest cities in the world were the Chinese cities of Chang'an (Xi'an today) and Hangzhou, as well as perhaps the ancient kingdom located at Angkor Wat in present-day Cambodia, which held about one million people. In the Western world, the city of London did not reach one million people until around 1800 (Clark 2003).

Figure 10.2 Singapore's financial district. A city-state, Singapore is arguably the only fully urbanized country. *Source: http://commons.wikimedia.org/wiki/File:Singaporedt.jpg.*

STUDYING THE CITY   10.1

Ancient cities

Since urbanization refers to the process by which rural areas become urban, we must take you all the way back to the beginning of the process by looking at ancient cities, including some of the earliest cities in the world. It is generally acknowledged that the world's first cities emerged in Mesopotamia during the fourth millennium BCE. The actual location of the very first city was in what is South Iraq today, at the site of Uruk (Warka). Most of the Mesopotamian cities had histories of emergence stretching back even further: most began as undifferentiated villages in the Neolithic or Chalcolithic period of the sixth millennium BCE or earlier. Like all cities up to the present day, the Mesopotamian cities grew as a combined result of natural internal population increase and immigration. While most of them reached a plateau of 100–150 hectares (250–370 acres), later imperial cities expanded to as large as 300 to 700 hectares (740 to 1730 acres). Some of these larger ancient cities – for example, Neo-Babylonian Babylon – might have incorporated gardens and little-used spaces (McMahon forthcoming 2013).

Other ancient cities, in China and elsewhere, developed later. The very first Chinese city was a walled settlement that was founded around the time of the sixth millennium BCE. However, these early Chinese walled cities did not become larger and more complex until the second millennium BCE and Emperor Qin Shi Huangdi's unification in 221 BCE. The two great capitals of Han China (206 BCE–220 CE) – located in Chang'an (present-day Xi'an) and Luoyang (in Henan Province, central China today) – had walls surrounding them of 25 kilometers (15 miles) in diameter and multiple palaces that were as large, covering six square kilometers (2.3 square miles). Chang'an's and Luoyang's populations reached roughly 250000 and 500000 respectively during that time. In fact, Chang'an grew to become the world's first city, containing one million people around the thirteenth century. Besides their large scale for the times, these Chinese cities had become vibrant places for daily residential life and commercial activities (see Steinhardt forthcoming 2013).

Of the ancient cities in the Mediterranean, the ancient Greek city-states or *polis* (meaning "city" in Greek) flourished and persisted from the Archaic period through the Hellenistic and Roman periods (from 800 BCE to about 500 CE). Although not typical of the city-states, Athens was quite large in both population and territory and known for its early adoption of democratic politics and governance that were based on the diversity of experience of those who served in the political process.

To summarize the profile of ancient cities, they developed as cultural crossroads, economic hubs, political and religious centers, and transport nodes and links. Urban space was sometimes clearly differentiated from, yet dependent on, an agricultural hinterland. In these cases, cities were maintained by systems of rule that extracted wealth from that hinterland and exploited its labor. In other cases, cities and their surrounding regions were more closely integrated economically and culturally. Within many empires and states, the city was a religious center or pilgrimage site that provided a metaphysical identity and the cement for the meaning that bonded subjects to the urban center. Surviving texts and artifacts have identified ancient cities as places with layered meanings, power, and connections. More importantly, from the orientation of this book, ancient cities developed into rich and lively places of everyday life that became increasingly varied and complex, regardless of how their external functions and connectivities changed.

Sparse and sometimes ambiguous archeological and historical records (Grauman 1976) indicate that the world's urban population fluctuated between 4 and 7 percent from the beginning of the Christian era until to about 1850, when the urban population consisted of people dispersed over hundreds of urban places worldwide. In 1850, only three cities – Beijing, London, and Paris – had more than a million inhabitants while another 110 held more than 100 000 inhabitants. Of the 25 largest cities at the time, 11 were in Europe, eight were in East Asia, four were in South Asia, and only two were in North America (Golden 1981).

After reaching about 10 percent of the world's population in 1900, urbanization in the first half of the twentieth century occurred most rapidly in Europe, the Americas, and Australia. The number of large cities – defined as places holding more than 100 000 inhabitants – in the world increased to 946, and the largest city (New York) had a population of 2.3 million in 1950 (Davis 1965). In the rest of the world, however, urbanization proceeded very slowly. Although only a quarter of the world's total population lived in urban places in 1950, urbanization in the developed countries began to approach its peak three decades later, around 1980, when Tokyo became the first metropolitan region of 20 million people.

The urbanization of the developing world began to pick up in the late twentieth century. According to the United Nations, the levels of urbanization in 1995 were high (around 70 percent) across the Americas, parts of Europe, western Asia, and Australia. South America was the most urban continent with the population in all but one of its countries – Guyana – being more urban than rural. Levels of urban development were low throughout most of Africa, South Asia, and East Asia. Less than one person in three in sub-Saharan Africa was an urban dweller (Peng et al. 2010). The transition from the twentieth to the twenty-first century marked a new and more striking era of urbanization. In 2008 the world crossed a long-awaited demographic watershed: half of the earth's population now lived in urban areas. A further acceleration of urbanization in the near future is apt to raise the world's urban population to around 70 percent by 2050. Moving along a steeper upward trajectory, China is on course to urbanize from less than 20 percent in 1980 to over 60 percent by 2030, as predicted by the United Nations (Soja and Kanai 2007), whereas China itself has the more ambitious plan of reaching 67 percent by 2030 by shifting another 280 million people to cities in less than two decades (Kwan 2010).

It is evident from this broad historical picture of urbanization that the current developing countries and regions were the first to become urbanized but were surpassed by the early industrializing countries in the West. Only now are they once again taking over the urbanization engine. Can we say that urban history is coming full circle? The evidence not only confirms that we can but also compels us to ask the next big question: how do we fully understand the new and serious consequences of the ongoing wave of urbanization in the developing world?

The basic dimensions of urbanization

Urbanization is a "master" process of sweeping social and spatial changes, but it by no means has been or will ever be a monolithic process. On the contrary, urbanization, as it proceeds further and deeper into developing countries, brings about challenging consequences that shape everyday places and everyday life, especially those of the urban poor. These consequences are shaped by a few basic dimensions of urbanization that we introduce here.

Urban hierarchy

Because national definitions of urban areas vary greatly, for many countries, especially developing countries with an unreliable base of data, we will use an early United Nations definition of urban localities (population greater than 20 000) and cities (population greater than 100 000) (United Nations Commission for Africa 1980) to create standard comparisons of urban development across nations and over time. The cities of all countries are arranged into a hierarchy of horizontal segments on an **urban pyramid** (see Figure 10.3). At the higher levels of the hierarchy are larger cities and the size of the urban places decreases toward the bottom of the pyramid. The shape of a national urban hierarchy (pyramid) at any given time reflects the progress of urbanization up to that point in time by showing the respective numbers of cities of varying sizes at each level of the hierarchy. The shape of a country's urban pyramid changes as its urban population grows more and moves in and out of different-sized cities, or up or down the pyramid.

What, then, drives this dimension of urbanization? Generally speaking, a higher level of economic development – measured by greater **gross national product (GDP)** per capita – leads to a higher level of urbanization (see Preston 1979; London 1986; Bairoch 1988). Wage differences between manufacturing and agriculture also affect

urban pyramid A hierarchical structure with the smaller number of larger cities at the top and the larger number of smaller cities at the bottom.

gross domestic product (GDP) The basic and standard measure of a country's or a city's total economic output and performance.

Figure 10.3 The urban pyramid. *Source: Diagram drawn by Curtis Stone.*

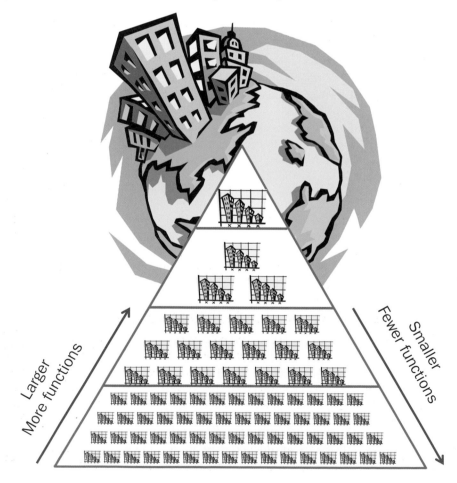

urbanization, as do government employment, informal economy employment (more on this later), education, and migration (see Connell et al. 1976; Kelly and Williamson 1984; Henderson 1986). As these factors draw more people into cities, especially large cities, small cities may begin to be outnumbered by the large ones. Thus, the urban hierarchy may widen from the middle sections to the top faster than at the lower levels. Nevertheless, a hierarchy or system of urban places remains a salient dimension of urbanization in any country over time.

That the process of urbanization in a country changes the hierarchy of its cities is a familiar phenomenon. Yet this relationship is increasingly affected by global forces, which leads to more economic and socio-spatial disparities among the cities and towns that comprise a national or regional hierarchy of urban places.

Urban primacy

Strongly related to the hierarchical aspect of urbanization is urban primacy, which is assumed to have undesirable effects on national development. Since the **primate city** absorbs a disproportionately large share of resources, causing uneven growth and wealth distribution, Hauser labeled it "parasitic" rather than "generative" (see Hauser 1957). Since its early formulation, the concept of urban primacy has been modified to include the notions and measures of two-city primacy, regional multiple-city primacy, and multi-centric urban systems (Kasarda and Crenshaw 1991). Transportation, the location of cities, government services, and the characteristics of rural hinterlands influence the growth of the largest city relative to that of other cities, which may lead to urban primacy. Urban primacy also tends to emerge in developing countries that have administrative centralization and a concentration of government social services and expenditures (see Mutlu 1989; Petrakos and Brada 1989).

Are there forces that mitigate or pre-empt urban primacy? Urban primacy is not usually present in more developed countries, and there are also developing countries where urban primacy is absent. In China, urban primacy at the national level has not developed because of the entrenched positions of major cities across an expansive landmass. While colonial rule contributed to urban primacy in Latin America and Africa, it did not do so in India. Some urban policies such as promoting small towns and secondary cities have helped to moderate urban primary. Conversely, though, partial strategies such as relocating the national capital, creating alternative growth centers, and encouraging border-focused regional development have had limited success in reducing urban primacy because they have high initial costs, slow investment returns, and minimal long-term impact (Richardson 1987).

> **primate city** A city that is both the largest in a country and disproportionately larger than the second and lower-ranked cities.

Over-urbanization versus under-urbanization

We will now introduce the two polar opposites of urbanization in developing countries: "over-urbanization" (too much) and "under-urbanization" (not enough). **Over-urbanization** refers to the excessive growth of the urban population relative to the amount of industrial employment available to accommodate it. The idea dates back to Hoselitz (1954), who advanced the thesis that urbanization in developing nations might become too strong as a result of the industrial mix of their economies. The symptoms of over-urbanization include substandard living conditions for urban residents (including **slums**), the failure of municipal governments to provide the infrastructure and services that make urban life more efficient

> **over-urbanization** The process whereby urban population growth outpaces that of urban jobs.

> **slum** A run-down city area characterized by substandard, makeshift housing, lack of tenure security, and the presence of poverty.

under-urbanization The process whereby urban population growth lags behind the growth of urban jobs.

and comfortable, urban unemployment and low wages, and the need to import food from abroad in order to sustain the urban population (Lowry 1990). While over-urbanization occurs in many developing countries, where urban population growth tends to outpace industrial jobs, the term can be misleading if applied to postindustrial societies such as the United States, where urban populations outnumber manufacturing jobs because of deindustrialization and the rapid growth of service industries.

The flip side of over-urbanization – **under-urbanization** – features a much faster expansion of industrial employment than the growth of the urban population. This situation characterized the Stalinist period in the former Soviet Union and the policy of balanced urban–rural development in China in the 1960s and 1970s (Chen and Parish 1996). Under-urbanization, according to Murray and Szelényi (1984), is typical of formerly socialist countries, with their tendency to prioritize industrial production in cities over those cities' residents' demands for commercial and social services. Taken to its extreme, under-urbanization turns into deurbanization or zero urban growth, which became the official policy of Cambodia in the wake of its socialist revolution in the early 1970s, when the Khmer Rouge government killed or expelled about two million residents from the capital city of Phnom Penn (Figure 10.4). Ironically, China may be experiencing a new form and stage of under-urbanization today, as it has an official level of urbanization (about 50 percent) that is lower than the proportion of the labor force that is non-agricultural (about 65 percent) due to the legacy of urban population and migration controls through **household registration** (also see Chapter 11). This form of under-urbanization amounts to "shallow" or "lagging" urbanization, in which rural migrant workers (including those permanently living

household registration A system created by China in 1958 to register city residents, entitling them to housing, education, healthcare, and food.

Figure 10.4 Phnom Penh, Cambodia's capital, was forcibly emptied by the Khmer Rouge in an attempt to recreate an agrarian state. *Source: Photo: Marcus Thompson/Oxfam.*

in cities) are not "urbanized" as full-fledged city residents. To overcome this under-urbanization or to achieve catch-up urbanization, the Chinese central government has, in an unprecedented experiment, designated Chongqing in southwestern China as the location for the urbanization of approximately 10 million rural residents in a matter of one decade (see Studying the city 10.2). Together, over-urbanization and under-urbanization, as well as their permutations, offer more nuanced accounts for the speed and form of urbanization in developing countries.

STUDYING THE CITY   10.2

An unprecedented experiment with urbanization and megacity building in Chongqing, China

The city of Chongqing in southwestern China, which has approximately 32 million people living within its municipal boundaries of about 82 000 square kilometers (31 660 square miles), may be the largest city in the world that few people know. An inland port city located some 2250 kilometers (1400 miles) up the Yangtze River from the sea, Chongqing lacks the access to the most lucrative markets and trading routes that accelerated Shanghai's evolution as a major city from the mid-1800s onward. Chongqing was not cosmopolitan until the outbreak of the war against the Japanese in 1937 and the transfer of the Nationalist capital from Nanjing (to which it subsequently returned in 1946). China's government faced daunting challenges on many fronts when it assumed control of Chongqing after Liberation in November of 1949, lacking as it did both the expertise and the resources to rapidly restore Chongqing to health. And, while energetic efforts were made to relieve the major social ills that were an outgrowth of decades of war, chaotic population transfer, and neglect, Chongqing languished for a period of time before the task of reinvigorating the city began later (though when it did it was for political and military reasons).

From 1964 to the late 1970s, concerned about the possibility of attacks by the United States and subsequently the Soviet Union, China set out to create a secure "Third Front" (literally the "great third line") to shield strategic industries by moving factories from the "First Front" along the coast to the deep interior. The irony, in retrospect, was the attribution to Chongqing of the role of leading the nation in developing defense-related machinery and ship-building industries. Of the 212 new projects in defense-related industries that arose during the "Third Front" period, Chongqing received 122, and all of them were relocated from Shanghai, which had a large pool of human talent in engineers and technical professionals. The central government also invested around 4.2 billion Chinese yuan (US$646 million), a huge sum at that time, to upgrade Chongqing's transport infrastructure, including rebuilding the major railway from Hubei Province. By the end of the 1970s, the massive influx of capital and human resources had turned Chongqing into a considerably upgraded major industrial center with strong capacities in defense, chemicals, natural gas, machinery, and shipbuilding. In 1974, heavy industries accounted for 90 percent of Chongqing's total fixed assets and 48.5 percent of its total GDP

It is in the post-reform era beginning in the early 1980s, however, that Chongqing has come closest to characterizing a model of state-driven urbanization and megacity building of unprecedented scale. Following the construction of the Three Gorges Dam nearby (from 1994 to 2006), during which time it had had to relocate the large number of displaced rural residents, Chongqing was tasked by the central government with undertaking an unprecedented experiment: using a proportionally smaller urban core to attract and absorb a vast rural hinterland and population into an integrated metropolis. The early evidence of this orchestrated experimental urbanization is reflected in the fast rise of Chongqing's non-agricultural population, which remained below the national average until about 1997, when Chongqing was designated as a central government municipality (like Shanghai). The planned conversion of about 10 million rural residents of Chongqing into urban dwellers in 20 years (by around 2020) is the first of its kind in the country and of symbolic importance for China's overall urbanization through the reform of the household registration system, or *hukou*. However, Chongqing faces a real challenge in making the large rural population into urban residents in the real sense of providing them with the welfare benefits such as healthcare insurance, education, and pensions accorded to urban people. As the first phase of this ambitious plan, the municipal government planned to make 3.8 million first- and second-generation migrant workers residents of the urban districts they work in by 2012. This group, which would receive the full *hukou* status, also includes demobilized servicemen and college graduates who were originally from rural areas. While the nearly four million new urban residents have been working in Chongqing's urban areas for years, creating enough jobs for seven million more villagers by 2020 will be a daunting challenge. By presenting the mechanism and outcomes of this unprecedented experiment with urbanization and urban–rural integration, we offer Chongqing as a test case that illuminates the consequences of state-orchestrated urbanization and massive city building for large Chinese and other cities.

Natural increase and in-migration

We cannot understand urbanization and cities in developing countries without identifying the demographic sources of urban growth: natural increase and **in-migration** (also see our discussion of these issues in Chapter 5). In general, natural increase is positively related to urban population growth. Conversely, high levels of urbanization may lead to a somewhat lower rate of growth in urbanization as urban growth slows down when urban proportions increase and rural populations first stabilize and then decline (Rogers and Williamson 1982). Constraints on land ownership and rural overpopulation tend to push surplus populations toward cities, and rural underdevelopment is an additional impetus to rural-to-urban migration (Firebaugh 1979, 1984).

in-migration Population gain in a city from more people moving in than moving out.

It is usually difficult to fully separate out the effects of natural increase and in-migration on urbanization – this has been the case in some developing and urbanizing countries. However, there have been recent cases in which natural increase and in-migration have gone separate ways due to special policy and economic circumstances. Take China as an example. Migration to cities has surged at the same time as fertility in cities has dropped to a very low level, largely as a result of the one-child family policy, introduced in 1979. In addition, rural migrants in Chinese cities, most of whom are relatively young and of child-producing ages, have not had measurably more children (than local urban residents) due to the one-child family policy as well as their limited income, marginal living conditions, and lack of access to childcare, education, and healthcare, all of which were created by restrictive government policies.

If some kind of under-urbanization kept the share of China's urban population under 20 percent from roughly 1960 to 1980, much faster urbanization through large-scale rural-to-urban migration has raised that (official) percentage to about 50 today. In fact, if the huge numbers of temporary or floating rural migrants in Chinese cities and towns are counted, China may have already crossed the demographic milestone of half urbanization, bringing it in line with the figure for the world as a whole. Looking forward, of the estimated 350 million people that China will add to its urban population by 2025, more than 240 million will be migrants (McKinsey Global Institute 2009).

From process and system to place

By now you should have a basic grasp of the multiple dimensions of urbanization as a dynamic process in developing countries. Yet you should not lose sight of individual developing-country cities as they are molded by the urbanization process. In this section we will guide you from a broader and deeper understanding of urbanization in the developing world to a fuller appreciation of real urban places as the structure and content of community and everyday life. As we make this transition, we remind you to keep in mind the basic concepts of place and space introduced in Chapter 1.

A basic profile with multiple wrinkles

What is the city of the developing world like? Do you know you are in a developing-country city when you visit Shanghai these days? Since you don't see visible poverty in Shanghai, you may wonder whether it is a developing-country city, even though it is part of China, which is still considered a developing country. Conversely, the South Side of Chicago has for some time seemed to match the profile of a developing-country city, as has much of Detroit since the 2008 global economic crisis. Shanghai has been booming while Detroit has been "bleeding," and this fact presents us with a sharp contrast of striking irony. If Shanghai represents the "expanding city" of the developing world then Detroit typifies the "shrinking city" of the developed world as profiled by *TIME* magazine in October 2009 (see "Notown" 2009). This reversal of fortune makes it difficult to characterize the developing-country city and its places.

Since the early 1980s, if not before, the scholarship on the developing-country city has portrayed it as belonging to a general category of cities that differ considerably from those in developed countries. Developing-country cities have been growing much faster, reaching much larger sizes, becoming increasingly unequal at the social-economic level, and becoming more and more integrated into the global economy. But they have been moving with these trends in very different ways and at highly uneven speeds. As a result, categorical labels such as "Third World" appear to have faded whereas other terms have come to be used more frequently. These terms include "megacities," focusing on size, and "cities of the Global South," with its explicit reference to the global dimension of developing-country cities (see Chapter 11).

A basic element of the general profile of the developing-country city is size and its continued enlargement. While many developing-country cities are and will remain relatively small, the explosion of a large number of these cities, some from very small bases, has become a defining feature of what they are and why they are called megacities. For example, South Asia will host five of the world's ten biggest cities in about ten years – namely, Delhi, Dhaka, Karachi, Kolkata, and Mumbai (see Figure 10.5).

What is the first image that we tend to associate with the huge and continuously expanding developing-country city? Poverty and the resultant lack of basic amenities come to mind. In the Pakistani city of Lahore, an open drain is reported to be causing health problems for nearby residents. Originally planned to channel storm water, this drain is now, like the 16-odd other open drains in the city, a floating cesspool of raw and untreated sewage (Alam 2008). The coupling of mega size and much poverty appears to be a dominant feature of the landscape of the developing-country city.

Not all developing-country cities are very large and very poor. Shanghai and a number of other coastal Chinese cities are huge and yet seem to be without the obvious poverty that characterizes many South Asian and African cities. But, if you look more closely at many local places and communities in Shanghai, you will notice not only physical and social signs of poverty but also clear evidence of tremendous wealth, as well as the large disparity between them. This reflects the continued influx of migrants, which in turn helps to sustain the basic source of fast growth and persistent poverty in cities such as Shanghai. In a sense, the more these cities change, the more they stay the same at some fundamental level.

Another major ingredient in constructing a complex profile of the developing-country city is how its connection to the global economy has evolved. The era during which most

Figure 10.5 The 10 largest cities by 2020. *Source: Plotted and drawn by Curtis Stone using United Nations data.*

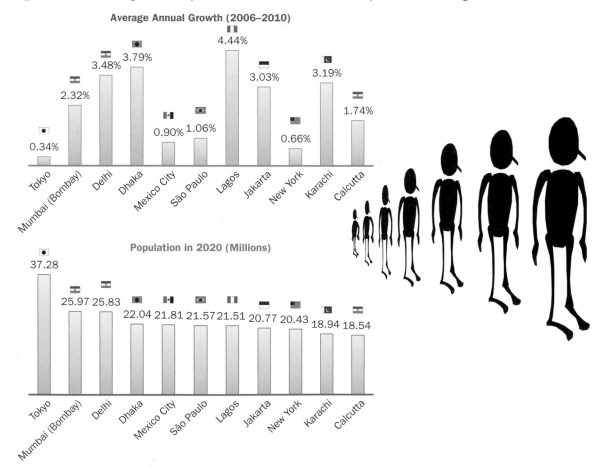

developing countries served primarily as exporters of raw commodities to Western industrial economies may be passing. As more and more developing countries experience more rapid economic growth, the cities within them have become the specific nodes and places of manufacturing activities and processes on a global scale. The growing concentration of factories and the massive number of low-paid workers, including many rural migrants who live marginalized lives, have characterized the demographic, economic, and socio-spatial aspects of developing-country cities for a long time. This depiction aside, many developing-country cities, especially those in Latin America, have long had a flourishing informal economic sector that encompasses myriad small-scale service jobs and activities as an indispensable part of the urban landscape (see Portes et al. 1989). More recently, some of these manufacturing-based developing-country cities, most notably those that are the most dominant economic centers of their respective countries, have taken on a new economic dimension by developing global financial service functions. Buenos Aires, Mumbai, and Shanghai are positioning themselves to do so and making uneven progress toward this goal (see Sassen 2006, 2009). This development adds an extra layer of complexity to the profile of the developing-country cities.

To complicate this picture further, more developing-country cities have grown beyond or deviated from their national norms to a like and stand as new places that have taken on more mixed but globally oriented forms, functions, and identities. This is not a totally new phenomenon in the history of cities. The early Renaissance cities such as Bruges and Antwerp created the legal framework for the first transnational stock exchanges, independent and way ahead of the modern nation-state government. As a contemporary parallel, since the early 1990s, many Chinese cities have tried to bypass Beijing to engage in economic diplomacy by sending large numbers of officials and businessmen to international conferences and fairs (Khanna 2010). In the remainder of this chapter, we turn to a more detailed discussion of the characteristics of developing-country cities with reference to a number of specific cases.

Megacities as places
Opportunities and challenges

Size and density

We take up the subject of size/scale again to highlight how some developing-country cities have become very large strikingly quickly. Looking back through a comparative lens, we saw that it took New York City (the world's largest metropolis in 1950) nearly a century and a half to expand by eight million residents. Mexico City and São Paulo would match this growth in less than 15 years (Kasarda and Parnell 1993). In another example, the Chinese city of Shenzhen grew even more dramatically, from a village of 30 000 to a city of approximately 10 million people in less than 20 years (see Figure 7.5 and more on Shenzhen in Chapter 11). All three of these cities and many more in the developing world have passed the threshold of a **megacity**, with 10 million or more people; a few are already approximately double that size. Not coincidentally, a number of today's developing megacities have histories as the primate cities of their respective countries (e.g., Mexico City) and are much larger than the other cities in their respective countries.

> **megacity** A city containing 10 million or more people.

City size by itself does not mean very much. It matters a great deal more in the context of urban places and urban life through interaction with other economic, geographic, and social factors. At a smaller scale, geography and other conditions pose different challenges than at a larger scale. Although rural villages and small towns generally lag behind large cities in terms of economic development and available amenities, very large developing cities may have more drawbacks, such as congestion and poverty, relative to the great efficiency of cities of the same size in developed countries. Millions of rural migrants have moved into large cities and ended up living in very poor urban slums, and more will continue to do so to escape wretched poverty. According to the World Bank, a child born in a village outside Zambia's capital, Lusaka, will live only half as long as a child born in New York City and, during that short life span, will earn just one cent for every two dollars the New Yorker earns (World Bank 2009). Besides other difficult conditions such as the lack of education, the desire to escape extreme poverty for perhaps slightly better economic opportunities drives millions of villagers to cities such as Lagos and Mumbai.

While millions of poor migrants may get a small portion of the economic pie produced in developing megacities and their surrounding regions, these city-regions generate a disproportionately large share of the national wealth. In Brazil, the south-central states of Minas Gerais, Rio de Janeiro, and São Paulo (which are anchored to the megacities of the latter two names) occupy less than 15 percent of the national land area but account for more than 52 percent of the country's GDP. In the Arab Republic of Egypt, Greater Cairo generates 50 percent of the country's GDP using just 0.5 percent of its land area (World Bank 2009: p. 5).

These cases are clear reminders of urban primacy, discussed above.

agglomeration The economic benefits that accrue from industries and firms that are located near one another or tightly clustered

What makes these megacities so productive? Besides the traditional explanation of economic efficiency through **agglomeration**, these cities host heavy concentrations of particular industries that employ the very productive workforce of less- or least-developed countries. For example, the nine million people who live in Kano in Northern Nigeria provide the skilled labor and infrastructure for the concentration of tanneries in and around the city that make the area's economic density (GDP per square kilometer) 35 times the national average of Nigeria (World Bank 2009: p. 6). While density can help to raise the spatial productivity of megacities, it also tends to generate some social costs that can translate into persistent poverty.

Creating wealth and sustaining poverty

Megacities are the richest cities in developing countries, which are generally poor as a whole. A long-standing explanation for this concentration of wealth goes back to the urban primacy of some megacities. It is the very size of megacities, some argue, that accounts for the fact that they draw a disproportionately large share of national economic resources through government-prioritized investment and infrastructure (Hoselitz 1954). Today's rapidly urbanizing developing countries are experiencing the fastest-growing concentration of people and economic activity at the local scale as opposed to the national scale. Like the earlier trajectory of today's developed countries, growth came to some cities in developing countries before and faster than others and led the wealth to concentrate in certain places first, in some cases spreading to other places later (World Bank 2009: p. 8). But the megacities of the developing countries in the late twentieth and early twenty-first centuries, as earlier and faster growing urban centers, are tending to accumulate wealth exponentially. This phenomenon challenges the "the world is flat" thesis of Thomas Friedman (2005), who contends that computers and information technology give countries and companies a sort of equal playing field on which to compete globally.[1] More so than the large cities of developed countries, developing-country megacities represent "peaks" of wealth on a highly differentiated economic landscape where poor cities and regions lag behind as "valleys."

How do we reconcile the two contrasting images of poor developing countries and their wealthy megacities? We can do this by looking at a few striking examples of the megacities' shares in their national economic pies. Though its share dropped from that of its peak years (1960 to 1980), from the 1990s to the early 2010s Mexico City accounted for about one-third of Mexico's GDP. In another example, though not a megacity in population, Johannesburg accounted for 16.4 percent of South Africa's GDP in 2002.[2] From a longer historical perspective, a few developing-country megacities today have lost a lot of their relative shares of national GDP as other cities and regions have caught up. In the 1930s, Shanghai accounted for more than half of China's industrial output, but in 2003 this figure was only 5.4 percent (see Chen and Orum 2009). This relative shift of megacities' positions does not, however, alter their top standing in the national hierarchy of wealth. With GDP per capita at or over US$10 000, both São Paulo and Shanghai triple Brazil's and China's GDP per capita, respectively. This level of wealth concentration in a few top cities, according to the World Bank, is expected to happen at a per capita national income of US$3500, which marks a threshold for becoming upper-middle countries (World Bank 2009: p. 8). Although Brazil and China, as a whole, are not close to the upper-income ranks, their megacities have already become quite wealthy places and significant producers or generators of national economic growth.

If we return momentarily to the systemic view presented earlier of cities arranged in a pyramid, it is easy to see that the megacities, with their tremendous scale, functions, and wealth, occupy the top rung of the urban pyramid. If we examine these megacities as local places, they have the visible symbols and appearances of prosperity and even glamour – for example, iconic skyscrapers and gated communities. In both São Paulo and Shanghai, there are hundreds of millionaires who live in mansions and can afford to drive Ferraris (see Figure 10.6). In addition to their super-rich residents, these cities have a larger and continuously growing number of well-educated professionals with an upper-middle income. In China, these talents

Figure 10.6 A Ferrari showroom in downtown Shanghai. *Source: Photo © Robert Wallis/Corbis.*

and spending power are concentrated in a few centers such as Shanghai and Shenzhen, which rise above not only vast, impoverished rural areas but also many smaller cities. These glitzy places lead the way in terms of wealth creation, knowledge innovation, and modern lifestyle (see Florida 2008). Without them, it would be easy to imagine a lower level of urbanization in today's developing countries.

With the bright side of the megacities thus presented, you can easily anticipate the exposure of their "dark underbelly" – the massive concentrations of poverty in the wealthiest cities of the rapidly urbanizing developing countries. This juxtaposition of wealth and poverty in cities is nothing new: the working class who created wealth in eighteenth-century British industrial cities such as Manchester lived an existence of misery. Fast forward in time and we find that the boom of Chicago's Loop district in the 1990s occurred only a few miles from the entrenched poverty of the city's South Side. What is different about poverty in today's developing megacities is its novel scale and the way in which it has grown in step with the rapid creation of wealth in these very same cities. This has resulted in a wider and deeper gap between the rich and poor in the megacities of the developing world and in similar cities in the developed world.

Gini index A measure of income inequality. A measurement closer to 1.00 means a larger gap between poor and rich.

Economists have a measure called the **Gini index**. Basically, it provides a statistical measure ranging from zero to one of the degree of income inequality in a country, or the gap between the incomes of the very poor and those of the very rich. If we use this index to compare inequality in various megacities, Buenos Aires, Mexico City, Rio de Janeiro, and São Paulo all rank higher than London and New York (see Figure 10.7). Despite its egalitarian roots in socialist China, Shanghai's Gini index rose from 0.37 in 1994 to 0.45 in

Figure 10.7 The Gini index for 12 world cities and national averages. *Source: "South American Cities" (Urban Age South America conference newspaper, December 2008, p. 20); LSE Cities, London School of Economics, http://www2.lse.ac.uk/LSECities. Reprinted with permission.*

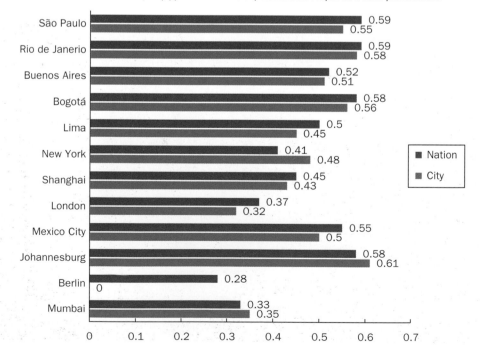

2001 (reported in *The Pudong Social Development Report* 2002). Standing behind this simple statistical index is the more graphic reality of the residential juxtaposition of the rich and poor in these megacities. The image of luxury homes right next to slums (see Figure 10.8) epitomizes the residential landscape of São Paulo, where over 10 percent of its population live in *favelas* such as Paraisopolis, which is the largest *favela* (at 60 000 residents) and is located in and surrounded by the very wealthy Morumbi.[3] In Mumbai, about one million poor people live in Dharavi (Asia's largest slum), which is nested in the central city. With a bird's-eye view of Dharavi, Mukesh Ambani, an Indian billionaire and the world's fourth-richest person, is reportedly spending close to US$2 billion to build his 27-story home, equipped with hanging gardens, a health center, and helicopter pads.

> *favela* A Brazilian Portuguese word that generally refers to a slum or shanty town in Brazil.

The ironic situation of the wealthy living immediately alongside the poor can be found in megacities across the developing world. This reality suggests that the recent economic growth is itself so pervasive and significant a phenomenon that it overrides any possible and important differences based upon culture or nationhood. The developing megacities are teeming with millions of urban poor working in the so-called informal economy. In Mexico City, for instance, 60 percent of all home construction takes place in the informal economy, over 60 percent of the jobs are informal, 25 percent of the 100 000 taxis are unofficial, and 65 percent of the music sold is pirated (Castillo Olea 2006). In Jakarta, nearly 70 percent of the jobs are located in the informal sector. In Mumbai, the overwhelming majority of the Dharavi residents labor away in small, family-owned workshops or through street vending. Even in the once state-dominated Shanghai economy, informal employment has risen to over half a million (see Exploring further 10.1 on the informal economy in African cities and elsewhere).

Figure 10.8 A striking contrast between São Paulo's Paraisopolis *favela* and a gated condominium in Morumbi. *Source: Photo © Tuca Vieira.*

EXPLORING FURTHER   10.1

The informal economy in African cities and beyond

The informal economy of major cities is often ignored in macro-scale economic figures and public policy discussions on poverty or unemployment, but the informal economy can often serve as a valuable avenue of economic development. While a small segment of the informal economy includes illegal goods and services, the vast majority of economic activity involves legal entrepreneurial ventures that take place on a very small scale – under the radar of the government and not included in gross national product (GNP) or producer price index (PPI) figures. The size of the informal economy can range from an estimated quarter of the GNP or higher in countries such as Canada, Germany, and the United States up to over a massive 95 percent of economic activity in developing countries when the agricultural sector is included. The urban informal sector is elusive and problematic to define given the wide range of economic activities that run the whole gamut of elementary production, simple distribution, basic services, and daily consumption.

The informal economy is most prevalent in African countries, which are the least urbanized globally, but it also varies greatly among African cities. In Johannesburg, arguably Africa's most advanced city or "most global city," the informal sector accounts for about one-sixth of all jobs. Regarding male employment, which is more informal than females' employment, this share appears to vary from an extremely high 93.2 percent in Douala, the largest city in Cameroon, to a medium of 54.7 percent in Niamey, the capital and largest city of Niger, to a very low 2.8 percent in Nairobi, the capital and largest city of Kenya.[4]

While the informal economy in African cities is generally unregistered, unregulated, small-scale, and often illegal, it is frequently connected to the formal economy in varied ways. As in other developing-country cities, the informal and formal economies can be mutually interdependent through subcontracting and other transactions. In Chinese cities, the informal or "private" economy, which was eliminated under the socialist planned economy before 1980, has since grown rapidly. It has absorbed surplus employment and taken over more service functions from the declining state (formal) sector. This is most visible in the retailing sector, where small street vendors have filled the spaces vacated by inefficient state-owned stores.

Moving beyond the simplistic dichotomy between the informal and formal economy, Garth Myers, in his recent book *African Cities*, takes a broader and more nuanced view of the informal sector in African cities. He takes into account the long history of informal settlements in urban Africa and the rising importance of social networks in the built environment, livelihood strategies, social reproduction, cultural organization, and political mobilization. He has shown that the activities of the informal economy in African cities are heavily mediated by social networks and that the locations of informal work and settlement in the urban core and the peri-urban or semi-rural areas are sometimes not aligned as expected (Myers 2011).

Research by Myers and others has revealed a much more complex and differentiated picture of the informal economic sector in African cities, and in developing-country cities more generally. This research leads us to question the established assumption of many governments and planners that the informal sector, often tied to informal or slum settlements, should be reduced or "formalized" through planning and redevelopment schemes. On the contrary, many people in developing-country cities fully rely on the informal economy to make a living. It can also be said that the informal economy is simply a way of life in many developing-country cities. Even in developed societies, informal economic activities through social networks allow friends, colleagues, and neighbors to rely on one another for goods and services without having to participate in the formal economy. While they probably won't be able to pay their doctor with chickens, many do pay a friend to watch their children or take in unreported income from neighbors at yard sales, along with numerous other informal economic activities (Leonard 1998).

Toiling in low-paying and unstable informal-sector jobs, millions of the urban poor, whether born and raised locally or immigrants from villages, play a critical role in building the wealth of developing-country megacities. Relative to their large numbers and indispensable positions, the poor city-builders benefit little from the wealth they create. Those who have done well in the informal economy continue to face tremendous constraints on financing their own business ventures. This makes microlending, which is limited but effective, more desirable and even necessary as a cheap source of financing for entrepreneurial activities in large urban economies (see Making the city better 10.1). Microfinancing provides a practical means for many urban poor to earn a basic living and thus become part these cities, living in them more or less permanently and raising the next generation in them. While some will gradually move up the social ladder to obtain a larger share of the economic pie, many more, including the never-ending inflow of rural migrants, will continue to replenish the pool of cheap labor in the informal sector, add to the aggregate wealth of these megacities, and sustain the megacities' global competitiveness, but they will struggle to avoid being trapped in permanent poverty.

MAKING THE CITY BETTER   10.1

Microlending and urban economies

In places where the informal economy makes up the majority of economic activity, "microlending" (also called microfinance) has proven to be an exceptionally effective method of economic development. Microlending was pioneered by Muhammad Yunus when he founded Grameen Bank in his native Bangladesh in 1976; he won the Noble Peace Prize for this accomplishment in 2006 (Grameen Bank 2011).

Microlending involves giving extremely small loans to people who would normally have no access to credit of any kind. For people in poverty living outside the boundaries of the formal economy, microlending offers a chance to act upon entrepreneurial ideas that would not have been possible using conventional avenues of credit (Yunus and Jolis 1999). Often, microloans lead to successful small-business ventures, and recipients are often able to receive larger loans to improve and expand their businesses after paying off their microloan in full. Kiva is one of the most successful and widely known organizations to extend microloans to impoverished people today, and its work has empowered countless entrepreneurs through the use of recycled donations (Kiva n.d.).

Women's empowerment is a core focus of many microlending organizations: 97 percent (over 100 million) of Grameen Bank's clients are women (Grameen Bank 2011). Women entrepreneurs are often shut out of more formal means of securing credit, but with microloans they have developed enterprises including weaving and sewing shops, produce sales, food preparation, and retailing. Single mother Patricia Palle is one success story. With an initial loan of US$200 from microlender BancoSol (part of the Accion lending network), she was able to purchase yarn and supplies to begin a small knitting business in La Paz, Bolivia. She then continued to expand her business with loans for equipment and capital improvements, paying off each loan as her business grew. She now employs and trains other women in La Paz, increasing their human capital. Not only have poor women shown strong returns in the success of their businesses but they have also consistently demonstrated high loan-repayment rates and reinvest in their families and their communities.

As microlending has become more successful in bringing much-needed income into developing-world cities, increasing the financial security of entrepreneurs as well as their communities, it has also been extended into rural communities. In China, a French microfinance organization has been providing small loans of about US$500 to each peasant household in some of the poorest and most barren villages in northwestern China, helping them to start a small business or set up an energy-efficient gas tank for cooking and heating.

While microfinance has a successful track record in alleviating poverty and aiding development, it has recently faced some difficult challenges. Muhammad Yunus is fighting in court the Bangladeshi government's attempts to remove him from Grameen Bank, which he founded over three decades ago. Greed is also infiltrating microfinance as some people try to make money out of it through commercial investors. A report released by the Microcredit Summit Campaign in early 2011 called for appropriate laws to be adopted to enable microfinance institutions to attract and accept local deposits and lend out those deposits rather than seeking loan funds from commercial investors. The report also stressed that the microfinance sector needs to address the issue of over-indebtedness that may be affecting some segments of borrowers, and not lose sight of its development focus.

The developing megacity as a lived place

Megacities in the developing world, we have argued, are sites where great wealth and great poverty exist side by side. They are also, in the words of Saskia Sassen, "strategic places for a range of new political, economic, and cultural operations and … a prominent nexus where the transformation of old practices and formation of new claims, involving both the powerful and the disadvantaged, unfold and take hold" (see back cover of Chen 2009c). As places, of course, they also exhibit the fundamental qualities of all places – sites where communities are established among and between people and where people's identities become rooted. Moreover, they are also places of great social diversity, just as are the cities of the developed countries covered earlier in this book.

If you think back to our argument about the linked logic of size/scale and density as keys to understanding the developing megacity, you will expect to find considerable diversity in the megacity. When cities reach upwards of 10 million people, the image they project is one of a sea of humanity. In addition, megacities that pack as many as 100 000 people into a square kilometer, as in central Mumbai, challenge us to imagine the kinds and depth of individual, group, and communal interactions across varied local places and spaces. The closeness and density of human encounters can make these interactions appear chaotic and even confrontational. And, when modernist urban design and architecture – for example, high-rise blocks – also hamper these interactions, as suggested by Richard Sennett, the city is made brittle and social divisions are reinforced instead of bridged (Sennett 2005).

In China, the government has focused on reducing central city density through spatial relocation and expansion in megacities such as Beijing, Chongqing, and Shanghai, where the population count has surpassed 60 000 per square kilometer (155 400 per square mile), in contrast to the world's average of just 10 000 people per square kilometer (25 900 per square mile). Despite the already generous provision for 120 square meters (1296 square feet) of living space per person (which includes housing, parks, roads, schools, and other public utilities), the Chinese government advocates doubling the per capita living and public space standard on the grounds that urban residents should not live a crowded life represented by high-rise apartment buildings. This will mean expanding the land coverage of China's cities from 80 000 square kilometers (31 200 square miles) to 160 000 square kilometers (62 400 square miles), which contradicts a simultaneous policy to protect the rapidly shrinking arable land and declining food supply of the huge and expanding urban population (Fu 2009).

Policy intervention in the rapid and complex process of building up and then restructuring megacities is bound to produce new policy opportunities and dilemmas. On one hand, the local government, as in Shanghai, has produced a huge number of green and public spaces over the past decade or so. On the other, the same Shanghai government has constructed many highways, elevated overpasses, and massive bridges (across the Huangpu River) that have led to the displacement of hundreds of thousands of city residents who would otherwise have been able to enjoy the green and public spaces.

While government intervention in some developing megacities such as those in China remains strong, the privatization of urban space has gained more speed and scope, fueled by state-initiated market reforms and the influx of global capital. In Shanghai, this process involves rapid large-scale urban redevelopment, some of which ends up as gated communities and massive residential towers with larger living space and better indoor amenities. With wealth and poverty rubbing shoulders, the rich people's perception, if not the reality, of any crime against them leads to their withdrawal or retreat into fortressed residential spaces. These redevelopments erode the meanings and functions of places as sites of community and security based on collective identities and mutual trust that existed in traditional *linong* houses. In Jakarta, the newly completed mega-blocks of luxury residential towers have severed the communal path and access of nearby poor residents. In Johannesburg, São Paulo, and even in relatively safe Shanghai, fenced compounds with private security guards and cameras dot the cityscapes. Shanghai's residents yearn for public space and make full and routinized use of public parks, some socializing as individuals, others performing collectively, and still others talking politics in groups (Orum et al. 2009). Some Shanghainese residents, however, frown upon migrants in park and street spaces as if they, as outsiders, are less deserving of using them. Private vendors from outside of Shanghai move around sidewalks to dodge sporadic police intervention. In Mumbai, removing unruly private vending is linked to an official vision and policy aiming at building a world-class city (see Chen 2009b).

> **linong (Chinese)**
> Traditional courtyard houses in Shanghai that extend in rows through lanes and alleys.

An even more contested arena of the developing megacity as a lived place is the slums, where millions of the poor are confined. Growing in tandem with the accumulated wealth in the recent past and near future, the slums of developing cities, especially the megacities, will be hosting the majority of the world's projected urban population over the next two or three decades. One billion people are living in slums today, and this figure will rise by 25 million per year until 2030, when every third urban resident on the planet will be a slum dweller. While this is a depressing prospect, the picture today is already alarming. About 80 percent of Nigeria's urban population, according to Mike Davis, lives in slums, as does over half of India's urban population, ranging from 41 percent in Ahmedabad to 56 percent in Mumbai (see Davis 2006). Even at the low end, more than 10 percent of São Paulo's population lives in *favelas*. Slum dwellers don't have a secure lease or title. They are missing durable walls, adequate living space, access to electricity, safe drinking water, and toilets, which together add up to a horrible picture of grinding poverty and squalid living (see Figure 10.9). But, to their dwellers, these slums function as daily living and working places. As one community activist in a slum of Caracas, Columbia once said, "while it may be a slum to you [the outsider], it is home for us" (Brillembourg et al. 2005). Moreover, thriving economies actually exist in a few of the most crowded and notorious slums. With one million people packed into its 172 hectares (430 acres) of land, Dharavi in Mumbai makes and sends textile products such as cloth and T-shirts to the United States (Huggler 2006).

Figure 10.9 Water is delivered by truck in Lomo de Corvina slum in Lima. In many poor urban areas in the developing world, public services such as water, power, sewage, and trash removal are limited or nonexistent. *Source: Photo © Martin Mejia / AP / PA Photos.*

Although slums like Dharavi possess some degree of collective vitality and communal existence in squalid conditions, their prime locations, often in the central parts of megacities, frequently make them vulnerable targets for urban redevelopment that is driven by either government or market or both. Though they are quite different from the slums in Mumbai, many of the old and substandard houses in Shanghai have been torn down as part of government-orchestrated urban renewal facilitated by powerful development companies. As a result, over one million residents in central Shanghai have relocated to its expanding suburbs, although some of them have done so reluctantly after weighing up their gains (government compensation and more spacious new housing) and losses (lost social networks and a longer commute). It is Dhavari that exemplifies the conflict between slum dwellers defending their place and the private–public interest in redeveloping the slum. With a severe shortage of land and rents reaching New York and London levels in central Mumbai, in 2004 the government announced a plan to regenerate Dharavi from a slum into a modern city quarter (see Making the city better 10.2). But the local residents are not happy about the government's intention of selling three quarters of the land to developers and leaving just one quarter for new but smaller apartments to rehouse many large families on the same sites. Their organized resistance has stalled the Dharavi redevelopment project. Regardless of the different redevelopment mechanisms and outcomes in Shanghai versus Mumbai, the urban poor in both megacities have experienced a loss of and a threat to their housing rights as a result of urban renewal, actual or planned. While the lost housing right is permanent for many residents, more so in Shanghai than in Mumbai, the residents' use of different resistance tactics allows them to make a strong claim to the cities as urban citizens (see Weinstein and Ren 2009).

MAKING THE CITY BETTER 10.2

The Dharavi redevelopment project

Dharavi is currently home to roughly one million of Mumbai's poorest residents, but a major redevelopment project orchestrated by Mumbai's state government of Maharashtra may displace many of these residents. The land in Dharavi has become very valuable with increased competition for land in central Mumbai. As a response to this increase in land values, the Maharashtra state government implemented a redevelopment project through which the land would be sold by the government to developers, leaving current residents without a place to stay.

The process to redevelop Dharavi began in 2004 when the state government first planned the project. Since then, the state government's housing agency, the Maharashtra Housing and Area Development Authority (Mhada), has run into various problems implementing the project caused by a combination of the global economic crisis, which limited the amount of foreign investment money coming in, and local resistance to the redevelopment project (Kamath 2011).

Mhada has tried to overcome this local resistance by giving some current residents a place to stay free of charge after their old home is bulldozed. The government's Slum Rehabilitation Authority (SRA) website states that residents of old households in the slum will be given carpeted units that are 225 square feet in size either within or near Dharavi for free ("Dhavari Redevelopment Project" n.d.). However, the SRA website also says that the only residents eligible for new housing to compensate for their loss are "the slum dweller whose name appears in the voters list as on 01.01.1995 & who is actual occupant of the hut." It is safe to assume that relying on old voter records from 1995 to determine who is compensated for bulldozed housing is going to leave a lot of people on the streets. In fact, a survey in 2009 found that 63 percent of Dharavi residents would not be eligible for new homes. In response, Mhada released their own survey that sampled a different sector of Dharavi in 2010 that found that only 31 percent of Dharavi residents would not be eligible for new homes (Kamath 2011).

Because of this apparent effort to force out slum residents in the pursuit of profit, the state has faced a lot of criticism. Akbar Patel, who runs a local residents' group, argues that 225 square feet is not enough space to accommodate the large families who currently live in Dharavi, even if they are eligible for new housing (Huggler 2006). Combined with the fact that only 25 percent of the original land is set aside to house current residents while the rest is sold to developers, this leaves very little housing for poor families in Dharavi.

And, aside from the extremely small size of the units, architect P. K. Das criticizes SRA building regulations, claiming that "the present SRA model, with its permanent structures which cannot be redone for years, is only slumming the city further." Architects and other experts in the field worry that the redeveloped Dharavi, for those slum residents who were not left homeless, will simply consist of a series of "vertical slums" and "depressing concrete monoliths" (Thirani 2010).

Governing the megacities

Developing megacities present mega-challenges, which seem to render these cities almost ungovernable and unsustainable. The speed of growth and the scale of in-migration are stretching and straining the capacity of governments to respond to the myriad needs, especially the most glaring and urgent. For example, only 1 percent of housing and urban aid in developing world cities goes to urban slums. Of this limited aid, little priority is given to chronic water and sanitation shortages in slums, which exacerbates health, educational, and economic or labor force problems. The non-governmental organization Wateraid has called for city authorities and national governments to make water and sanitation a priority in urban reform plans, with an explicit focus on the growing urban slums ("World's Slums Need Water Infrastructure," 2008). This is easier said than done. Due to the lack of reliable water supply infrastructure, as much as 70 percent of the water pumped into cities is lost before it can reach consumers, leaking out of faulty water mains, pipes, and faucets ("Towards Sustainable Cities," 2008). In Ho Chi Minh City, the number of public toilets falls far short of serving its eight million people. Although the city's Department of Natural Resources and Environment planned to build 40 more public restrooms in 2008, it had to reduce the number to 16 due the complicated procedures for surveying the locations and getting approvals at the district and household levels ("Toilet Trouble" 2008). The inability of municipal governments to provide basic water and sanitation facilities is one of the major constraints facing developing megacities.

It is tempting to view the megacities as being too big to govern, but the argument is more complex. One of the key reasons that the governance of megacities is hampered, as Gerald Frug sees it, is the fragmentation of the metropolitan regions in which the cities are located (see Frug 2006). No matter how large these cities are, they are not large enough to encompass the ever-expanding regions around them that tend to misalign political governance and the shifting boundaries demarcating that power. In Mexico City, governance is compromised by 79 executive bodies in three areas of government legislating for 63 legislative zones and at least 80 territorial plans and programs. In India, urban planning and administrative functions not only are vested in different departments but also reside in different tiers of government. Take transportation, for example: rail services are managed nationally, road building is controlled at the state level, and bus services, street lighting, and repair are municipal responsibilities (Rode et al. 2008). This splintered administrative system, which is often found in democratic countries, unintentionally hampers integrated transport planning in Mumbai in the State of Maharashtra. In contrast, the more consistent and top-down administration of China made it easier to implement an ambitious program in Liaoning Province in which more than one million low-income citizens in the shanty houses in two large coal-mining cities were moved en masse into brand new and much better residential communities; the plan was accomplished over two years and was completed by 2007. As another example, while some low-income tenants in Johannesburg have benefited from the social housing created by the Johannesburg Housing Company (JHC) under the post-Apartheid government, the stronger real estate market forces have created more socio-spatial stratification that favors the rich at the expense of the poor and has made Johannesburg more difficult to govern (see Studying the city 10.3).

STUDYING THE CITY   10.3

Martin Murray on Johannesburg

One example of an urban area that changed dramatically within a short time frame is Johannesburg after the fall of Apartheid. Martin Murray writes about many of the changes that took place in the city in his book *Taming the Disorderly City: The Spatial Landscape of Johannesburg After Apartheid* (2008).

Murray argues throughout much of his book that Johannesburg is an excellent counter-example to the sustainable city. Instead of planning for the efficient use of the city center, the complex system of freeways around the downtown urban core has diverted businesses and wealthy residents to several exclusive suburbs north of the city. Murray presents several reasons why Johannesburg is lacking in terms of both the sustainable use of resources and social sustainability. One is that capitalism manifested through the real estate market causes land in different areas to undergo very different rates of economic development and change. This huge spatial variation in the rates of economic development produces areas that are growing at a ruthlessly effective pace in one section of the city while other sections of the city suffer from limited mobility and underdeveloped and neglected space, with little capital for development. Murray rejects the notion that these negative characteristics plaguing poor areas of many cities are in any way unanticipated or temporary in nature, and instead argues that this underutilization of urban land is a direct consequence of real estate capitalism.

While the system of Apartheid may be over in South Africa, Murray finds many ways in which social stratification is still enforced in Johannesburg through the influence that real estate capitalism has on land use and planning principles to create spatial inequity throughout the city. He links the redevelopment and economic progress of wealthy, primarily white areas of the city to the economic degradation of poor areas on the urban fringe and run-down areas of the inner city.

Murray includes the example of the Johannesburg Housing Company (JHC), which became a victim of its own success. While the JHC was initially very successful in creating social housing options for low-income tenants by finding out where tenants wanted to live and connecting them to necessary amenities, the presence of this sort of housing and the prospect of constructing similar housing in the area caused property values to steadily increase in the inner-city areas until the JHC was not able to afford to house only poor residents. Gentrification effects such as these on top of the already extensive wealth gap between white and black residents in post-Apartheid Johannesburg led to increased economic prosperity for wealthy white residents while poor black residents were pushed to shanty towns on the outskirts of town – even though the original beneficiaries were supposed to be low-income black tenants.

Throughout his book, Murray uses Johannesburg as an excellent illustration of just how severely market forces that create spatial economic disparity can threaten the sustainability of a city and limit the social and economic rights of the most vulnerable populations in an urban area.

The governance challenge facing the developing megacity sheds light on the megacity's complexity beyond the simple duality of wealth and poverty. A recent survey of 25 megacities ("Megacity Isn't Necessarily a 'Good' Word Survey" 2007) in both developed and developing countries indicates that, while the sheer size of the megacity makes it a powerful economic engine connecting the flow of goods, people, and culture, the fragmented systems of metropolitan governance have yet to catch up with diverse challenges such as large slums, woefully lacking services, and environmental sustainability. As the survey also shows, the so-called development stakeholders (business executives, government officials) in these megacities are concerned with striking a balance between the three cornerstones of governance: competitiveness, quality of life, and the environment. To be more specific, being competitive can demand lowering high unemployment, improving quality of life calls for dealing with poor housing and the lack of water and sanitation, and air pollution needs to be reduced to make the environment cleaner. These tend to be competing goals, but they should not be: their successful implementation requires a lot political will and an effective governance structure in order to allocate limited resources more efficiently. While resources are generally more limited for developing countries, they are more concentrated in their relatively wealthier megacities. It is these megacities that are really testing the national and local governments of developing countries on whether and how those governments will be up to the governance challenges.

We have been focusing on the developing-country megacity, but it is important to note that not all developing-country cities are megacities, and in fact most of them are not. While we are alarmed by the prospect of developing-country megacities becoming even larger in the coming decades, we also need to take into account that even greater urban growth is likely to take place in developing-country cities of 500 000 people or less. In India, where the megacities of Bangalore, Kolkata, and Mumbai dominate the news reports and research agenda on urban issues, about half of the population lives in over 2000 small and medium towns, some of which are still villages on their way to becoming urbanized. Half of the 285 million urban Indians in 2001 lived in cities with populations ranging from 100 000 to megacities of over 10 million. About a quarter of India's population in the small and medium towns, which lack jobs and urban planning, live in slums (Sharma 2009). In China, many of the small and medium cities, especially those in the interior, lag far behind the big booming coastal cities in economic development, infrastructure, and standard of living. Ironically, the fact is that many of the small and medium cities and towns in developing countries, often located near the megacities, are no less important in terms of their connections to the global economy. We will bring these cities back into focus as part of a more extensive look at cities in the global economy in Chapter 11.

Reassessing the developing city

As we bring this chapter to a close, you may be feeling somewhat pessimistic about the current state of developing-country cities, in light of the whole host of current problems and challenges that will only become more daunting for the governments involved. But there is also an underlying sense of optimism for these cities if we look at the fundamental conditions for their continued growth and vitality. Cities concentrate poverty, and developing-country cities amass more poverty, as illustrated by the slums we portrayed earlier. But, at the same time, these cities also represent the best hope of escaping poverty. Dismal as the slums may be, they continue to attract millions of the rural poor. As noted by a study on migration and poverty in Asia by the International Organization of Migration in 2005, the gains to be made in the risky informal sector can be several times higher than wages in rain-fed agriculture ("Towards Sustainable Cities" 2008). In Mumbai, the small factories lodged in the squalor of Dharavi export leather belts directly to Wal-Mart, while one Johannesburg slum hosts 335 000 small business, one in seven home-based, that include everything from hairdressers and bars to welders and furniture makers (see Husock 2009). This reaffirms our point that the developing megacity is truly a lived place in a broad sense in that it is also a working place for economic survival.

When we consider the intersection between living and working of the urban poor, we also need to be aware of their broader and more diverse communities to understand the developing megacity. Home ownership is a critical factor in the collective identity and viability of these communities. To debunk the conventional perception and wisdom that *favelas* are where the poor in São Paulo live illegally, Brazilian-born urban scholar Teresa Caldeira pointed to the fact that, in 2000, the majority (69 percent) of the city's poor owned their homes (up considerably from 19 percent in 1920) on the cheap lands without infrastructure that they had previously bought in the peripheral areas (Caldeira 2008). This high rate of home ownership creates and sustains a strong sense of collective interest and stake in these communities. More importantly, it provides a clear perspective on the local resilience and dynamism of these cities from the ground up. It is not surprising that even those residents of Dharavi who don't have a legal right to their shanty residences (the majority) generally resist the government's redevelopment efforts for fear that they will lose out financially while the politicians and developers will profit handsomely.

Gross-roots resistance to redevelopment in Mumbai reveals the global aspirations and dimensions of the developing megacities that we will explore in depth in Chapter 11. Mumbai has unveiled the ambitious goal of becoming "a city of the millennium" and achieving annual GDP growth of 8 to 10 percent while reducing slums from 50–60 percent of housing to 10–20 percent (Mathur 2009). Is the latter objective a necessary condition for realizing the former? The answer appears to be "no" because many of the poor residents, especially those slum dwellers, are not connected to or willing to support the official decision to build a global city at their expense. As an alternative, local urban spaces can be used to reduce poverty and promote sustainability if public–private partnerships work for the benefit of all residents in developing-country cities. This again calls for political will as well as managerial and technical competencies in protecting poor people from the abusive practices of developers and in investing available resources into more equitable and sustainable urban development. However, any effective approaches to improving the current conditions of developing cities are constrained by the global economy, which impinges on the wellbeing of all cities. We turn to this broad topic in the following chapter. Visit the book's companion website at www.wiley.com/go/cities for examples, case studies, and discussion questions, plus a list of useful films and other media, that are relevant to this chapter.

Critical thinking questions

1 What are the salient characteristics of urbanization that are both common and distinctive across countries, particularly developing countries at lower and more varied levels of urbanization?

2 What are the main factors that can push or induce developing countries to either follow along or diverge from the path of urbanization traveled by industrialized countries?

3 How can one critically assess the full range of consequences of urbanization, focusing on its presumed benefits versus costs?

4 How can one fully examine and understand the dominant influence of megacities in developing countries today in comparison to that of the colonial primate cities of the past?

5 What are the most important lessons that developing megacities can teach us about the past and present of urban development?

Suggested reading

David W. Drakakis-Smith, *Third World Cities* (London: Routledge, 2000). Using case studies of cities drawn from around the world, this book addresses three main questions: is there still a Third World city, does it have a common urban form, and what is the relationship between urbanization and sustainability?

Josef Gugler, ed., *The Urban Transformation of the Developing World* (Oxford: Oxford University Press, 1996). This edited book provides careful investigations and comparisons of the major regions now experiencing rapid urbanization, focusing on global transition and its social, political, and economic consequences for these regions.

Joel Kotkin, *The City: A Global History* (London: Weidenfeld and Nicolson, 2005). Kotkin offers his readers a history of the city from the first urban centers of the "Fertile Crescent" in 5000 BC to post-9/11 New York City, arguing that three key factors distinguish successful cities: commerce, security, and power.

David A. Smith, *Third World Cities in Global Perspective: The Political Economy of Uneven Urbanization* (Boulder, CO: Westview Press, 1996). The book links what happens in the neighborhoods where people live to the larger political and economic forces at work, putting these connections in a historical framework with a focus on global inequality and dependency.

Notes

1. For a strong counter-argument, see Florida (2005b).
2. See the various conference research reports on Shanghai, Mexico City, Johannesburg, São Paulo, and Mumbai of the Urban Age Project, London School of Economics and Alfred Herrhausen Society, 2005–2009.
3. See note 2.
4. UN-Habitat data cited in Myers (2011: Table 3.1).

CHAPTER 11

Cities in the global economy

KEY TOPICS

→ The city as a node in a global grid.

→ The importance of place in the emergence and survival of cities.

→ Ways in which cities integrate themselves into the global economy.

→ The rise and fall of several European, Asian, and Middle Eastern cities.

→ How the 2008 financial crisis has affected certain key cities.

→ The role regions play in mediating how cities and the global economy are related.

→ The role of cities in balancing global, regional, and national urban systems.

→ Understanding cities as the link between the global and the local.

→ The emergence of a transnational corporate elite and their influence on the architecture of globalizing cities.

Introduction to Cities: How Place and Space Shape Human Experience,
First Edition. Xiangming Chen, Anthony M. Orum, and Krista E. Paulsen.
© 2013 Xiangming Chen, Anthony M. Orum, and Krista E. Paulsen.
Published 2013 by Blackwell Publishing Ltd.

Contents

How can we approach something as seemingly complex and complicated as cities in the global economy today? In previous chapters of this book we have devoted our attention to cities as places as well as spaces, and talked about these issues with a sense of the urban residents in mind. We have addressed the particulars of cities, in terms of who lives there and the neighborhoods and settlements that people create. This image, of the city from the bottom up, is crucial, we believe, to understanding the social features of cities – of who moves into the cities, how people develop their attachments to cities, and how people contest their rights to particular sites in cities. But now we move on from this very concrete and human image of the city to talk about cities in a somewhat more abstract way. We shift our focus from the ways in which we as human beings connect to cities as places to the ways in which cities operate today in a more complex – indeed, global – world. This shift calls for the use of a somewhat different lens for understanding the city: we must shift from seeing the city in terms of its internal and social dynamics to seeing it in terms of the way it works in a large and expanding global economy. Finally, we will bring you back to seeing the essential flexibilities and constraints facing cities in the globalized urban world.

In this chapter, then, we will introduce some additional ideas that are required to understand how cities work within the larger global system. We will continue to talk about cities, but we also will talk about regions and countries. We will explain how the elements of cities work in a large global economy, and how some cities have become more significant in this economy than others. We also will talk more about some key features of our world – of how matters such as economic inequality have grown even worse as the global economy has emerged. More than this, we will also move our focus from many of the metropolitan areas in the West to bring in other metropolitan areas across the world – in places such as China and India. In addition, we will examine life in smaller, out-of-the-way cities, cities that scholars overlook when they talk about urban expansion and growth in the global economy today.

Yet, while we shift our focus a bit, our intent is to broaden your perspective as a reader and student of cities. We must continue to think about the importance of cities as places, but also about how the workings of those places are today affected by powerful forces that lie outside them: economic decisions made in countries and by people who do not themselves reside in those cities. Most of you who read this book will reside in or near a city today, while others may live in a suburb far away from a city. You get up; you go to school or work; you come home; you wave to your neighbors next door. You do things that all urban dwellers do, but your actions today are also influenced by the workings of the economy of the metropolis in which you reside, and beyond that by the significance of that metropolis, and its key economic and political players, in the broader global arena. It is these interconnections – between you, the places where you live and work, and the broader structures in which you live – that we hope to illuminate and explain in this chapter. This is a chapter about cities in the global economy, but at the same time it is also a chapter about your life and your connections to the major urban places in the world, and how the fortunes of those places are changing as the economy of the world itself becomes transformed.

Cities in a globalizing world
Theoretical background

The person who laid the groundwork for global perspectives on cities was the eminent British geographer Peter Hall (1984). He focused on eight of what he termed "world cities." They were Hong Kong, London, Mexico City, Moscow, New York City, Paris, Randstad Holland (the sprawling urban complex that includes Amsterdam, Rotterdam, and The Hague), and Tokyo. He portrayed these cities as national centers of government, trade, and professional talents of all kinds. Hall's ideas had caught on more by the early 1980s, when the geographer John Friedmann proposed a more refined and productive research agenda for understanding world cities. Friedmann (Friedmann and Wolff 1982; Friedmann 1986) argued that world cities represent a small number of urban regions, and that they lie at the top of an urban hierarchy, or hierarchy of places, that exercises worldwide power over production and the expansion of markets. With their control over production and employment, world cities also become the major sites for the concentration and accumulation of international finance. Friedmann identified several world cities, including Hong Kong, London, Mexico City, New York, Paris, Randstad Holland, and Tokyo – all originally identified by Peter Hall – but also a number of major international cities (Friedmann and Wolff 1982; Friedmann 1986).

A few years later, the sociologist Saskia Sassen, with the publication of *The Global City: New York, London, Tokyo* in 1991, brought a definitive touch to the study of the global city. According to Sassen, global cities function as: (1) highly concentrated command points in the organization of the global economy; (2) key locations for finance and specialized services, which have replaced manufacturing as the leading industries; (3) innovative sites of production in these leading industries; and (4) markets for the products and innovations of these industries (Sassen 1991: pp. 3 4). From her perspective, the hallmark of a global city is the growth and extent of its producer services, which include accounting, banking, financial services, legal services, insurance, real estate, and computer and information processing. Producer services, she argues, are highly concentrated in the central locations in cities of considerable size because they require diversified resources, the centralization of information, and easy access to the concentration of the headquarters of large manufacturing firms (Sassen 1991: Chapters 5–6). Having identified these clear criteria and characteristics of the global city, Sassen also went on to examine such major international cities as Miami, Sydney, and Toronto, which, she claims, exercise global-city functions but are not full-fledged global cities (Sassen 2006). Of a number of insights and contributions from Sassen's work one central proposition stands out: the dominant influence of global cities coexists with undesirable local consequences such as the growing income inequality between white-collar professionals in high-paying producer services jobs and minority workers in low-end commercial services and the striking spatial disparity between the downtown booming through renewal and the physical decay of peripheral areas (illustrative examples will follow below) (Sassen 1991: Chapters 8–9, 2006: Chapters 3 and 6).

By taking a global perspective on the city, Sassen as well as other scholars questioned the tacit assumption that a city represents a bounded territory of the sovereign state. Sassen has thus pointed to the need to reimagine the relationship between local places and space in a globalizing world.[1] While they acknowledge the powerful impact of globalization, some geographers and sociologists insist on the persistence of local diversity and identities. The British geographers Ash Amin and Nigel Thrift, for example, suggest that global dynamics, such as the flow of capital, or money, across borders, inevitably encounter places that are themselves distinctive, with unique histories and complex patterns of economic institutions and cultural traditions. Thus, according to some alternative views to Sassen's, the process of globalization does not imply homogeneity among places but instead a continuation of the significance of territorial diversity and difference. Sociologist McMichael labels this local diversity in the global order "local cosmopolitanism" (see Amin and Thrift 1994; McMichael 1996).

This emphasis on the local/cosmopolitan angle is fully consistent with our understanding and approach to the nature of *places* in this book. Places are indeed unique and special, having their own traditions and histories. But more than that, as we have argued, it is because of the way in which people establish their own *identities* and find *communities* in places that the local/cosmopolitan emphasis is important to us as a means of understanding how cities work in a globalizing world. We turn now then to consider how very different kinds of cities have emerged and become connected to the workings of the global economy today.

Emerging cities in the global economy

Yiwu, China

To consider how cities become a part of the larger global economy, we begin with a short journey through the Chinese city of Yiwu, located in coastal Zhejiang province. Few people outside China have heard about Yiwu and how it has become one of the most globalized cities in China today. Yet Yiwu possesses a variety of global connections, many of which spring from the connections that people in Yiwu have to the global economy. Take the case of Mr. Azimi, a young man from Afghanistan. He attended a university in Beijing and, after graduating, came to Yiwu to begin his own business. Like some other foreign businesspeople in the city, he now owns a trading company here and speaks fluent Mandarin. Reflecting on his quick business success, Azimi remarked, "When my cousin told me there was a city in China called Yiwu, which sounds like YOU, I had no idea where it was." During his first visit to Yiwu in 2001, Azimi saw the early phase of the small commodity market and this impressed him a lot. After finishing his studies, he decided to start his business career in Yiwu. The rapid development of the city has brought him big profits. At first, Azimi planned to stay in Yiwu for a year to earn some extra money before continuing his studies, but later he decided to continue to stay in Yiwu because his business was going well. Azimi's company sells various products for daily use to people in many countries, including the United States. Like many other foreign businesspeople in the city, Azimi has come to see Yiwu as the place where he will stay and pursue his business career (CRIENGLISH.com 2007).

Yiwu furnishes an early example of how decentralization and a more autonomous local government in post-reform China jump-started rapid economic development, urban growth, and global economic integration through careful planning and flexible policies from the early 1980s. Yiwu has sustained its top ranking among all the city-based merchandise markets in China up to today. In addition, Yiwu illustrates how local as well as personal global connections have played a key role in turning a small city from an unknown local place into an integral part of today's global economy (see Figure 11.1). As the city plays out its role in forming and sustaining its global–local production and trade networks, foreigners like Azimi have come to embrace the city as a place to live and work, while native Chinese entrepreneurs have also become an integral part of the global economy. Indeed, the story of Azimi vividly illustrates how the connection between people and places develop: he chose to live in the city in order

Figure 11.1 Egyptian traders outside a Palestinian-run restaurant in Yiwu. Although Yiwu is not well-known outside international trade and manufacturing businesses, it is one of the most globalized cities in China. *Source: Photo: Mark Ralston/AFP/Getty Images.*

to pursue his business, but now he also sees the city as a place crucial to his own pursuits and personal identity.

Rajarhat, India

From Yiwu in southeastern China we now take you to the outskirts of Kolkata, India where a new suburban town called Rajarhat has emerged as a different kind of local place that possesses global connections. Planners have designed Rajarhat New Town (see Figure 11.2 and Figure 11.3) to be an integrated township with an expected population of one million people. It lies just to the northeast of the existing city of Kolkata. In the early 1990s urban planners conceived Rajarhat New Town as a self-contained growth center that would help to diminish the population density of the core city of Kolkata. Spread across 3075 hectares (7598 acres) of land, the new city will serve as a major hub for information technology, educational institutions, and cultural centers, all of which are to be located within its central business district.

Real estate ventures and the information technology industry dominate the design, layout, and planning of all the township projects in Kolkata. In Rajarhat, in particular, the Housing and Infrastructure Development Corporation has taken the lead in planning and developing this township, and it has given considerable attention to the growing and specialized needs of the information technology sector. Located adjacent to the Nabadiganta Industrial Township – also known as Salt Lake Electronic City – where the bulk of the information technology industry is found, Rajarhat will provide the much-needed residences as well as retail enterprises for people who work in this growing sector. In addition, planners intend it to serve as a center for the new regional-level community

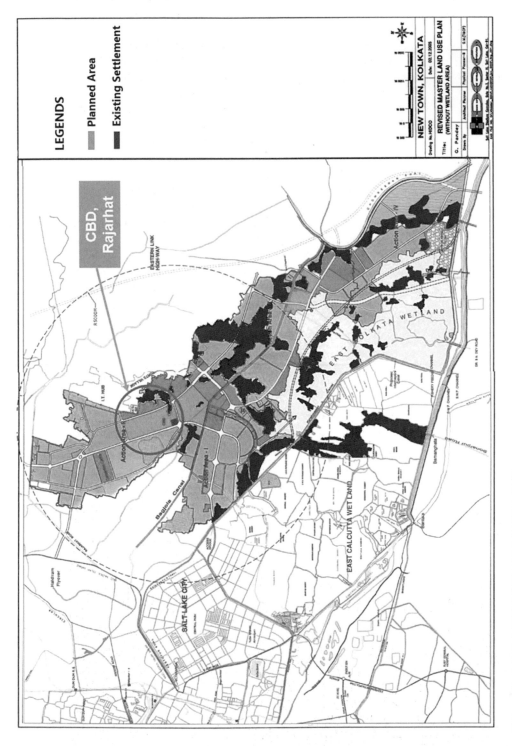

Figure 11.2 Rajarhat New Town, near Kolkata, India.

facilities, to furnish land for environmentally safe industries, and to become an environmentally friendly and attractive settlement that is fully integrated into the future metropolis of Kolkata.

Rajarhat has thus been conceived to be a self-sufficient urban center but one that also pays heed to people's need for a desirable place in which they can live and work. This is reflected in the overall master plan and the land use pattern for the township. Open spaces have been given top priority by local officials. In addition, because of the rapidly expanding growth of the local information technology industry, the plans for Rajarhat are constantly being updated. In the original land use plan that was created in May 1999, the residential space accounted for 51 percent, industrial land for 6 percent, commercial land for 5 percent, and open spaces for 28 percent. In the recently revised land use plan adopted in 2006, residential space now occupies only 38 percent of the land while open spaces account for 24 percent. The space for industrial land remains the same, and commercial space has grown to 10 percent. It is indicative of the importance of information technology that in the latest official plan 4 percent of the land has been set aside for information technology sector users. With major international real estate companies such as Jones Lang La Salle and C. B. Richard Ellis operating actively in the local real estate market, Rajarhat today has been touted as an attractive residential location for high-income professionals who work in the information technology sector. At the same time, however, many of the local residents are becoming priced out of the real estate market – part and

Figure 11.3 Construction in Rajarhat New Town, near Kolkata, India. Here development is oriented toward the needs of a rapidly growing information technology sector. *Source: Photo by Ratoola Kundu, April 9, 2009.*

parcel of the process of gentrification evident across the world (see our discussion of gentrification in Chapter 9) (Chen et al. 2009).

Further reflections on Yiwu

In helping you to understand how cities have grown to become an integral part of the global economy, we have used two places – Yiwu, China and Rajarhat, India – to show the spatial width and depth of global–local economic and social connections. We now want to dwell a bit longer on cities like Yiwu to probe more deeply into the processes and mechanisms by which small and previously shielded urban places have today become what we can call world cities.

The conventional view about cities in the global economy insists that cities, as local places, are shaped and constrained by the operations of the global economy. This perspective emphasizes the power of international forces such as foreign investment in bringing about local change. It pays very little attention to the internal sources, such as individuals as well as local officials, that prompt cities to change in the first place. Following the logic of the standard view, one would expect to find strong local evidence of a global economic imprint that may take the form of such elements as export-producing factories. A striking example of just such a scenario is the city of Dongguan in southern China (see the section on Dongguan below). Here there are massive numbers of young women who labor away in major export industries for long hours but who also strive to advance themselves by taking a computer or English class (Chang 2008). In this manner, Dongguan not only serves as a globally oriented local production platform but also furnishes a crucial link between the global market and the life chances of rural migrants who see the "factory-city" as a place where they may trade their rural poverty for a more prosperous urban life. This trade-off, however, is not easy to secure for most rural migrant workers because of the entrenched barrier of the household registration system (*hukou*) in China (see its definition in Chapter 10 and the Glossary). This system, put into place by the Communist government in the 1950s, compels people to have their residence fixed and registered in the places where they live. It prevents them from moving to another site. Even today, when the force of the household registration system has begun to erode, it continues to keep most rural migrant workers from becoming permanent residents in cities.

The city of Yiwu has become connected to the global economy in a different way from Dongguan. Instead of building rows of factories in spatially distinctive industrial districts as a response to the influx of foreign investment, Yiwu has chosen a commercial route and thus charted a new path to globalize its own local economy. The local government, from the very outset in the 1980s, focused on promoting spatially centralized and specialized markets and vending stalls for small merchandise such as handicraft items and hand tools. By furnishing the necessary economic infrastructure as well as financial incentives, the local government officials built Yiwu as China's hub of small merchandise markets. As these markets grew in number and density, they attracted thousands and thousands more merchants from near and far, both from within China and from abroad. People like Azimi, a native of Afghanistan, have come and settled in large numbers in Yiwu because it is the place where they can buy and sell the widest range of small merchandise. A vast and interconnected array of such local enterprises has gradually emerged in Yiwu. Economists refer to such growth and development as "agglomeration" (see the definition in Chapter 10 and the Glossary). The increase in commercial transactions led to the emergence and expansion of small factories within and beyond the city. These factories process and assemble more small-merchant products to be sold at and exported from the central markets. The entire process, which was created and shaped by local officials, fueled the economic and demographic boom of Yiwu. Today, its population numbers almost one million people, including over 10 000 long-term foreign residents like Azimi. This represents a tenfold increase since 1990. There are few, if any, cities in the Western world that have grown as rapidly or as much as Yiwu. It has become the world's leading center for small merchandise with a market index that is widely regarded as a barometer of prices and performance.

Yiwu represents a sort of "commerce-factory-city" in the global economy that has grown naturally from the combination of local-government incentives and the workings of markets. Although unlikely to become a global city in the sense employed by Saskia Sassen, Yiwu's central position in the global network of small merchandise makes it a vitally important world city today. Its critical significance in the emerging global economy is evident in the thousands of overseas merchants and buyers who annually attend the trade fairs in the city – and of course in the individual stories of people like Azimi who have come to embrace the people and commerce of the city, and who make it their home.

Re-emerging cities in the global economy

If Yiwu shows that small cities can rise from unlikely backgrounds to become important centers of the global economy, we would expect that cities that became part of the world economy in an earlier time would be even more intensively connected to the global economy today. There is no shortage of such cities. Generally, they are the larger and more established metropolises, but they can vary considerably in their relative standings in and connections to the global economy. While some are once-great world cities that have since lost their former luster and influence, many others have undergone a renaissance. We do not intend to resurrect the familiar argument about the rise and fall of major cities of the distant past – for example, Rome – that once ruled the world. Instead we offer you a more nuanced and historically concrete view of how major and significant metropolitan centers have become transformed and how their connections to the global economy have changed in the process. We will now turn to the stories of a few of these major cities.

Berlin, Germany: A once-prosperous, then challenged, and now re-emerging local culture

The metropolis of Berlin offers a striking example of a dominant world city of the past that fell to a low point but in recent times has been undergoing a revival in a new regional and global environment. At the height of the German Weimar Republic in the 1920s, Berlin was the world's third-largest city, ranking only behind London and New York. Its demographic and territorial growth had stemmed from the unification of dozens of suburban cities, villages, and estates around Berlin into a vastly expanded city of four million people. Though not as glamorous as London or Paris, Berlin was a major center of cultural cosmopolitanism where the arts, architecture, film, literature, and music flourished. The city epitomized Germany's significant presence in and contribution to the so-called "Golden Twenties" in Europe, which were characterized by political stability, economic prosperity, and cultural diversity. However, the good times for Berlin came to an end with the Wall Street crash in 1929 and Adolf Hitler's rise to power in 1933. The Nazi government suppressed what it saw as Berlin's cultural decadence and destroyed the large and culturally vibrant Jewish community. Ruined by bombings during World War II and the subsequent split into East versus West Berlin in 1945, the once-prosperous and dynamic Berlin fell into a long period of decline and marginality until the fall of the Berlin Wall in 1989.

Shortly thereafter, Berlin became the new capital of a reunified Germany. The event brought about high hopes and expectations for Berlin to rise again and to serve as a linchpin that would knit together the former East Germany with its counterpart in the West. This ambition became manifest as Berlin turned itself into a large construction site in the early 1990s, seeking a balance between the preservation of its historical neighborhoods and the construction of modern buildings for the future. The redeveloped Potsdamer Platz represented an innovative architectural attempt at bridging the tension between these two aims. However, an economic collapse in the early 1990s brought the revival to a sudden halt. Today it numbers about 3.4 million people, while roughly 100 000 apartments in the city stand empty (Bisky 2006). This tortured past, coupled with a spatial fragmentation into occupation zones after World War II and then the division into Eastern and Western sectors, helps to explain why Germany, unlike England and France, never developed an enduring metropolis like London or Paris (Läpple 2006).

Nonetheless, Berlin is a lively and thriving metropolis today, as is evident in its creative and alternative local culture and the forms of its art. Different forms of music and art with an anti-authoritarian – sometimes even an anarchist – bent exist and survive in marginal and somewhat unregulated, albeit often lively, public spaces across the city. In Berlin, the local alternative cultural scene, with its mixture of punk and New Wave musicians, community and gay activists, and rebellious students, has thrived in the abandoned industrial sites and empty residential buildings in the former West Berlin district adjacent to the old Berlin Wall. One of the abandoned buildings in the Tacheles neighborhood became a central gathering space for the local alternative culture: it was occupied by East and West German neo-punks, artists, and activists. After Germany and Berlin were reunified in 1989, Tacheles became a more visible and dominant center for the alternative culture as it attracted growing numbers of artists (see Figure 11.4).

Seizing on the opportunity presented to redevelop this area, the Berlin municipal government tried to evict some occupants from the buildings, but it failed and the ensuing confrontation between the government and the artists, and their allies, made headline news in Germany. In the end, municipal authorities permitted Tacheles to engage in a combination of heritage and planning protection, coupled with private commercial establishments that helped to support the alternative artists. While local officials made this decision in order to be viewed as supporting inclusion and cultural diversity, it has also enabled Berlin to attract tourists and to convince middle-class residents to stay. It has helped, in other words, to allow Berlin to remain as a competitive world city.[2] It is the small local spaces of alternative culture and artists, through somewhat successful urban regeneration, that have helped to enhance the growth of the city and to wire Berlin back into the world cultural circuits.

Figure 11.4 The Art House Tacheles (Kunsthaus Tacheles) in Berlin. Built at the turn of the twentieth century and occupied by diverse tenants throughout its history, Tacheles has become a central point in Berlin's art and cultural scene. *Source: Photo © John MacDougall/AFP/Getty Images.*

Shanghai, China: Local change in a rising renaissance city

Though it has some uncanny historical similarities to Berlin as a world city in the 1920s and thereafter, the metropolis of Shanghai has fared very differently since the early 1990s. In the 1920s, Shanghai achieved the status of a top-tier world city. It became known across the world as "the Paris of the Orient." At the time, Shanghai ranked as the world's sixth-largest city, after London, New York, Berlin, Tokyo, and Chicago (in that order). In addition, it had become by far the most dominant financial, industrial, and cosmopolitan center in China. By 1936, Shanghai held half of all the banks, money stores, and trust companies – both foreign and domestically owned – in China. It also accounted for more than half of China's total industrial output. From 1886 to around 1930, Shanghai consistently handled about half of China's foreign trade. During that period, Shanghai's publishing houses accounted for 69 percent of the Western books translated into Chinese in China (Chen and Orum 2009). Behind these statistical indicators lurked the harsh reality that Shanghai was subject at the same time to Western colonial domination through the local foreign representatives who occupied the British, American, and French **concessions**. Shanghai thus projected an external image of economic prosperity and cosmopolitan glamour but was effectively ruled by foreign powers. All of this almost made it seem as if Shanghai was a distant Asian extension of the "Roaring Twenties" that engulfed the major US and European cities, including Berlin.

Like Berlin, too, Shanghai underwent a period of political and social misfortune spanning the late 1930s to the late 1980s. The city and its residents were consumed by the turmoil of Japanese occupation in the 1930s and later by

> **concession** An area within a weaker country conceded to a stronger one, such as the French Concession in post-1842 Shanghai.

**Nationalists
(*Kuomintang* or KMT in
Chinese)** The Chinese
Nationalist Party,
founded in 1911 by Sun
Yat-sen shortly after the
Xinhai Revolution.

the Civil War that raged between the Communists and Nationalists in the 1940s. From 1949 to 1980, the city was remade into an overwhelmingly industrial center by the rigid socialist central planning practiced by the Chinese Communist Party. The Party emphasized production rather than consumption, while in the world outside China more countries had begun to emphasize the development of a consumption economy. This reshaping of Shanghai in the period after the ascendance of the Communist Party to power in 1949 was partly motivated by the Communist perception of the city's cultural decadence in the 1920s – incidentally, the very same reason that the Nazis had singled out Berlin and its residents for some of the purges that took place under Hitler.

In Shanghai, economic growth became stagnant until the late 1970s due to the central government's policy of redistributing its economic and technical surplus to help finance the development of poor interior cities. Shanghai turned over 350 billion yuan, or the equivalent of US$40 billion, in revenue to the central government during the period 1949 to 1985, but in return it received only 3.5 billion yuan, or about US$44 million, to help build its own municipal facilities, such as roads. Shanghai decidedly languished behind the booming coastal cities of Shenzhen and Guangzhou in South China, cities that were favored by the central government's open-door policy during the 1980s (Chen 2009a).

Unlike Berlin, whose ambition to regain its past glory after 1989 has largely gone unfulfilled, Shanghai has followed a historically unprecedented path and risen again almost a century after its most glorious and cosmopolitan era. This rise is, in a sense, also a renaissance. A few statistics suffice to tell the story of its return. Shanghai experienced the fastest economic growth of any megacity from the early 1990s, averaging 12 percent annually. It attracted over US$120 billion in total foreign direct investment after 1992, including US$14.6 billion in 2006, or 23 percent of China's total foreign direct investment (Chen 2009a). In the 1980s, the row of European-style buildings along the Bund by the Huangpu River – the most visible architectural legacy of past Western influence (see Figure 11.5a) – looked distinctively tall against the sea of traditional houses nested along and into narrow alleys. Today they are far overshadowed by more than 4000 modern high-rises that have sprung up since the early 1990s. Rumor had it that in the mid-1990s half of the world's cranes were working in the Pudong New Area (east of the Huangpu River) of Shanghai, turning it into the "world's largest construction project," one that dwarfed the postreunification build-up in Berlin and the much more grandiose construction in Dubai. Figure 11.5a shows Pudong with its agricultural land, scattered state-owned factories, and low-rise buildings around 1980; today, in contrast, Pudong's skyline sparkles with high-rise towers and includes the world's tallest hotel: the new World Financial Center tower (the tallest building in the top-right quarter of Figure 11.5b). Thus, despite their similar size and international standing in the 1920s, as well as their common economic stagnation through to the 1980s, Berlin and Shanghai have diverged sharply in terms of pace, scale, and process of change and transformation since the early 1990s.

But in some respects Shanghai, especially its new and flourishing cultural scene, bears important parallels to the growth today in Berlin. The counterparts to Berlin's Tacheles' vibrant and alternative cultural spaces are spaces in Shanghai such as 50 Moganshan Road, where many artists have set up their galleries in recent years. Here some Western-oriented and avant-garde as well as traditional Chinese artists have congregated to form an important hub for their creative work. Attracted by the cheap rent and location in an old factory complex in the center of a rapidly growing, cosmopolitan city, artists have opened galleries of contemporary Chinese art. They are now able to display work that until recently had not only been discouraged but even banned by the government and Party leaders.

50 Moganshan Road
A 1930s-era factory
complex near the
Suzhou Creek
converted into an art
district.

Figure 11.5 Pudong (east of the Huangpu River), Shanghai around 1980 (a) and 2010 (b). *Source: Photos: The skyline of Pudong, Shanghai in 1990 [sic]; http://www.bricoleurbanism.org/ wp-content/uploads/2011/01/Pudong-Bund_Shanghai-1990vs2010.jpg. Contemporary view of the skyline of Pudong, Shanghai; photo: Staffan Holgersson/flickr/Getty Images.*

(a)

(b)

The government had even banned the work of foreign artists who have studios and galleries in similar surroundings in SoHo or the East End in New York City (Zukin 2012). Today the creative output of the Chinese artists who inhabit 50 Moganshan Road is powerfully distinctive. More than that, however, it connects the local practices of Shanghai artists to the broader artistic and cultural voices beyond Shanghai.

As an Asian metropolis, Shanghai is ironically more interconnected with the global economy than cities such as Berlin, located in the heart of Western Europe. Much of the community-oriented participation in Shanghai is organized by the local Communist government. It employs top-down procedures to recruit local volunteers, thus blurring the usual distinction – in Western countries – between volunteer activity and government organization. Despite the government's strong hand in pushing community volunteer activities, however, there is empirical evidence that community participation may increase as local Shanghai residents become even more concerned with major domestic and global events (see Figure 11.6). This trend points to the interest of local residents in linking their community concerns to national and global dynamics and attempting to address them in a global–local context.

Using direct measures of personal global connections – including working in foreign companies, having traveled abroad, having overseas relatives, and surfing foreign websites – Jiaming Sun and Xiangming Chen have shown that, for Shanghai's residents, having global links is associated with having had fast foods and having bought foreign brand-name clothes in Shanghai itself. Higher percentages of those people with personal global connections have bought food at McDonald's or Kentucky Fried Chicken (KFC) and purchased foreign brand-name clothes (see Figure 11.7). Personal global connections also make people more likely to buy foreign brand-name clothes than eating American fast foods, taking educational and income differences into account.[3] The lesson from this recent study is clear and emphatic: local community participation and consumer behavior by Shanghai residents are associated with being tied to the world outside China. Here, in other words, we have evidence of the powerful ways in which global changes have promoted local decisions by the residents of a rising global city.

Figure 11.6 Community participation and concerns for domestic and global events, Pudong, Shanghai, 2001. *Source: Figure 9.4 from Hanlong Lu, Yuan Ren, and Xiangming Chen, "Downward Pressure and Upward Bubbling: Global Influence and Community (Re)Building in Shanghai." In Xiangming Chen, ed.* Shanghai Rising: State Power and Local Transformations in a Global Megacity *(Minneapolis: University of Minnesota Press, 2009, pp. 191–213). Reprinted with permission of University of Minnesota Press.*

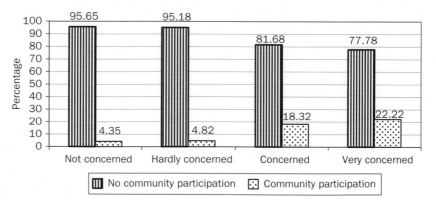

Figure 11.7 Personal global connections and eating McDonald's or KFC and buying foreign brand-name clothes, Shanghai, 2001. *Source: Figure 10.6 from Jiaming Sun and Xiangming Chen, "Fast Foods and Brand Clothes in Shanghai: How and Why Do Locals Consume Globally?" In Xiangming Chen, ed.* Shanghai Rising: State Power and Local Transformations in a Global Megacity *(Minneapolis: University of Minnesota Press, 2009, pp. 215–235). Reprinted with permission of University of Minnesota Press.*

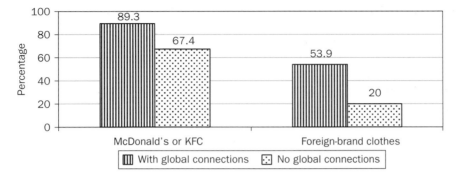

Moving more deeply into the global economy

The preceding sections of this chapter have shown you how different cities, large and small, past and present, have become inserted into the global economy today. The ways in which the cities become part of and have an impact on this global economy vary. It may be through trade ties or chains of economic production. Or it may be through the flow of culture – for example, the practices of artists – or even through personal links, such as the travel of individuals from one country to another. Given that these ways of linking local to global practices are varied, and that their strengths often vary, there are many ways in which local changes may happen in cities today. Moreover, they cover a wide and seemingly expanding range of circumstances: economic transformations, rebuilding the landscapes of cities, and even everyday changes in the consumer habits of local residents, as in Shanghai. As more cities become connected to as well as interconnected through the world economy, the connections become mediated by a variety of local as well as non-local conditions. We now want to share with you some of this greater complexity. We hope it will furnish you with an even deeper understanding of how cities, and their residents, are involved in the global economy today.

Dongguan, China: A place transformed from a rural township into a global factory-city

We begin our discussion by returning to the Chinese city of Dongguan, mentioned earlier in this chapter. Besides improving the life chances of poor rural migrant workers as a "factory-city," Dongguan has become deeply embedded in the world economy. It has emerged as one of the world's major hubs for a few specialized products in the computer and electronics industries. In 2002, the workers in Dongguan made 40 percent of the world's magnetic heads and computer cases, 30 percent of the world's copper-clad boards and disk drives, 25 percent of the world's AC capacitors and fly-back transformers, and 20 percent of the world's scanners and mini-motors (World Bank 2009: p. 127). With 16 percent of the world market share in keyboards and 15 percent of the same in motherboards, Dongguan has become the world's largest supplier of computer peripherals and components. Among those in the information technology industry it is known as the "global capital of personal computers." Not surprisingly, the export of personal computer-related products accounts for over 40 percent of Dongguan's total exports. Dongguan now ranks third in exports among Chinese cities, just behind Shanghai and Shenzhen. How can this be possible for a place that in the 1980s was a quiet rural township surrounded by a collection of villages and rice fields and known primarily for growing lychees (a tropical fruit)?

One way to explain the sudden rise to prominence of Dongguan is in location and economic terms. In this regard, the primary factor in accounting for Dongguan's economic "miracle" seems also to be the most obvious. The city is located midway between the Hong Kong–Shenzhen border and Guangzhou, the provincial capital of Guangdong province. Dongguan is thus in an ideal location to attract investment from both Hong Kong and Taiwanese manufacturing firms, which began to build factories en masse in the Pearl River Delta region (see Figure 11.8), where Dongguan lies, in the early 1980s. Earlier in China's recent economic expansion, investors either concentrated their capital in the border city of Shenzhen, known for its more convenient location and **Special Economic Zone** status, or in Guangzhou, which had a larger population, a more established economic base, and other local amenities.

Then, in the 1990s, Dongguan became a magnet for labor-intensive manufacturing investment. Why? Mainly because it offered less expensive and

Special Economic Zone (or SEZ) An area designated under market-oriented regulations that offers special economic incentives unavailable elsewhere in a country.

Figure 11.8 The Pearl River Delta region, Guangdong Province, China. *Source: Figure 2 in Xiangming Chen, "A Tale of Two Regions in China: Rapid Economic Development and Slow Industrial Upgrading in the Pearl River and the Yangtze River Deltas"* (International Journal of Comparative Sociology 48(2–3): 174; 2007). *Based on data from* The Guangdong Statistical Yearbook *2001.*

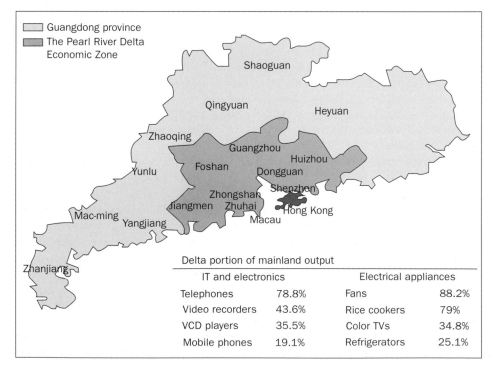

Delta portion of mainland output			
IT and electronics		Electrical appliances	
Telephones	78.8%	Fans	88.2%
Video recorders	43.6%	Rice cookers	79%
VCD players	35.5%	Color TVs	34.8%
Mobile phones	19.1%	Refrigerators	25.1%

more plentiful land and labor than either Shenzhen or Guangzhou. In this respect, the rise of Dongguan typifies the story of how cities in China came to compete successfully for the attention of the industries of the West: manufacturing firms were drawn to locate their plants there because of the great availability of land on which to build and the abundance of cheap labor. The millions of people who made up the region's cheap labor, primarily female workers from interior China, have been portrayed in lively human dimensions by Leslie Chang in *Factory Girls* (see Studying the city 11.1). This massive influx of migrant labor fueled Dongguan's population explosion and wealth expansion. Its annual growth rate averaged over 20 percent from 1980 through the 1990s. In 2004 the GDP, or the total value of the goods produced in Dongguan, reached US$14 billion – this was larger than the gross domestic product of the entire country of Ireland!

Yet there is much more to the story of how Dongguan became such a powerful center for the production of technological goods in China. And here the story takes us into the important social and political factors involved in its rise. Over the course of economic reform in China, which began in about 1979, the Chinese central government has permitted some local municipal governments to embark on their own administrative and fiscal decision-making. Unlike federalist systems such as the United States, where the constitution permits both state and local governments to exercise an important degree of autonomy over such matters as taxes and law enforcement, in Communist China the central government historically has been the key source of authority and the institutional source of power throughout the country. This changed around the early 1980s. As part of the effort to promote economic growth, the central government began to permit some local municipalities, such as Shanghai, to make decisions about local matters, such as transportation and the construction – as well as destruction – of local housing.

Officials in the city of Dongguan at both the municipal and the township levels of government were and continue to be eager to offer manufacturing enterprises lucrative financial incentives. (Similar incentives were offered years ago to lure businesses from the North to the South in the United States, and some states such as Texas still offer incentives in the form of lower local taxes.) In Dongguan, the local officials, eager to recruit business enterprises from Taiwan, offer such incentives as reduced taxes, lower land prices, long-term factory leases, and lower utility charges. Today there even is an agency called the Taiwan Affairs Office located in Dongguan. It expedites such services as entry and exit visas for investors from Taiwan. It also helps to settle economic disputes that sometimes arise between the Taiwan industrialists working in Dongguan and the Chinese authorities, and arranges for the education of the children of the Taiwanese families that have chosen to settle in Dongguan.

However, the recent history of Dongguan reveals problems as well. As in other places in the world today, the residents of Dongguan have suffered during the current economic crisis. While many people have seen their fortunes prosper, millions of others, especially migrant workers, have not. The growing economic inequality among residents was magnified. The crisis forced 856 factories in Dongguan to shut down in 2008, according to an official government report. Among these closures, there were 673 instances in which the owners had fled the city, some to overseas, in order to avoid paying money they owed to their workers and to their own supply firms. The Hong Kong-based owner of a toymaker that sold its products to Walt Disney and Mattel closed down two sprawling factories in Dongguan. It ended up owing US$29 million to about 800 suppliers and US$3.5 million to several thousand workers. In response, the local government actually paid the wages for the laid-off employees after many of them held a political protest at the town hall (Roberts 2009). The several million migrant workers, in particular, in Dongguan have proven very

STUDYING THE CITY   11.1

Leslie Chang's *Factory Girls*

In a China that is rapidly urbanizing and expanding economically to meet the needs of a global economy, journalist Leslie Chang was able to chronicle the lives of young Chinese women seeking the personal economic opportunities that come with urbanization, migration, and export-oriented production in China's coastal cities. Many Chinese residents have moved and continue to move from rural areas into cities in order to increase their quality of life and to seek new opportunities in an expanding and globally connected economy. In the early 1990s, Dongguan in Guangdong province was a rural county of less than 100 000 people, but it has today become a booming factory city of approximately eight million people (also see the discussion of Shenzhen in this chapter). A considerable proportion of this rapidly expanded and largely temporary population is made up of young women who are in transition from a slow-paced rural life to the grueling conditions of the factories.

One of the themes that Chang touches on continuously is that many of the women working in the factories of Dongguan seem to have adopted a position of rugged individualism. In contrast to both the traditional philosophies of ancient China and the principles of collective wellbeing touted by Communist China, they adopt a more Western outlook on capitalism and individual gain. Many of the women working in the factories of Dongguan frequently change jobs as new openings become available, and a sizable portion of the workers try to teach themselves new skills (computer usage or English) in their downtime to improve their chances of being hired for better-paying positions.

Unfortunately, many of the women who Chang talked to over the course of her study did not enjoy a high quality of life as a result of their forward-thinking ambitions. Working conditions in many of the factories were substandard, and the large number of migrants constantly arriving from rural areas made it difficult for the factory girls to set themselves apart and improve their economic standing. In addition, many of the women working in Dongguan suffered from a severe lack of social connections. High turnover rates in the factories made it difficult to sustain workplace friendships, and the distance between themselves and any family members they left behind in rural China strained those relationships. This lonely lifestyle for workers in Dongguan could also explain why Chang was able to find employees willing to divulge so much personal information to her.

After the publication of *Factory Girls* in 2008, the global financial crisis took a heavy toll on factory cities like Dongguan, putting millions of young female (and male) migrant workers out of work and sending many of them back to the villages in the interior, albeit only temporarily. China's quick economic rebound in 2009 recreated the millions of lost manufacturing jobs in the coastal cities, although more and more jobs have begun to migrate to second-tier cities in the interior. Despite this huge swing in China's globalized manufacturing economy and labor market, the millions of young women workers portrayed by Leslie Chang continue trying to find a more steady presence and settled life in urban centers such as Dongguan. The strong appeal of the prosperous cities makes the rural villages that the young women have left increasingly unfamiliar and unattractive places to return to and resume living.

vulnerable to the global economic downturn. Most of those who were laid off during the initial crisis in 2008 were forced to return to their rural hometowns. The misfortune for migrant workers became highlighted on the eve of the 2009 Chinese New Year holiday, when the Dongguan government decided to offer 230 million Chinese yuan, or about $34 million, through the symbolic **red envelope** (*hongbao*) to local residents – primarily those living in the local towns and villages. This symbolized a rich local government using a traditional practice of sharing wealth to pacify and stabilize a potentially restless local population. However, unfortunately only those with official household registration were eligible to receive the subsidies, which varied based on per capita income and economic losses during the crisis (*New Beijing Daily* 2009).

> **red envelope**
> (*hongbao* **in Chinese**)
> A small amount of cash given as a gift on special celebratory occasions.

In brief, the story of Dongguan, China, adds greater depth to our understanding of cities, and their residents, in the global economy today. Dongguan burst on to the global scene in a short space of time. It has become a major center for the production of computer products. It has generated huge revenues that the central Chinese government permits the local authorities to use for funding the education of its children as well as furnishing health insurance for its local citizens. At the same time, however, its inhabitants have suffered during the recent economic recession. The most harmed have been the millions of migrant workers who, left unemployed by the closure of factories, have been forced to return to their homes in the rural areas. The workers have not always been compliant; at times they have engaged in political protests against the local authorities. In China this, in itself, is unusual.

China as a country and Dongguan as a booming metropolis have been relatively prosperous in the current global economy. But, as we have seen, they and their residents have not been entirely sheltered from the world's major economic downturns. This is a case where the increasing connections between a city and the global economy have, in fact, had bittersweet consequences: in good times, prosperity for some and substantial government revenues, but, in tough times, a loss of jobs and a return to the countryside for the migrant workers. We turn now to another illustration and another place that has become connected to the global economy.

Dubai, United Arab Emirates: From desert to urban miracle to mirage

Now let us consider a very different city: Dubai, which lies in the United Arab Emirates. Dubai, like Singapore, is a city-state: it is an urban concentration of people that also has the territorial powers of a nation-state. In some ways its recent history parallels that of Dongguan, though its local features and cultural traditions are very different. Long a backwater in the desert and in the nineteenth century trapped in the British colonial orbit, Dubai was known as a port city for piracy and smuggling in the Indian Ocean maritime trade. Despite the Gulf oil booms between the 1930s and the 1970s, Dubai remained relatively underdeveloped. Its political independence from the British, achieved in 1971, ironically did not eliminate the dynastic and autocratic rule to which it had historically been subject – instead, different autocrats assumed control of its fortunes.

During the 1990s, Dubai really took off as a booming metropolis. It did so by building itself out and up, both literally and figuratively, as a global city. It featured billion-dollar projects such as Palm Jumeirah (see Figure 11.9) and the Burj Dubai, as of 2012 the world's tallest building. The boom in construction and the economic vitality it generated eventually attracted many Western expatriates, Russian traders, and tourists, as well as Iranian merchants. Some came as temporary visitors, others as permanent residents. In 2004 and 2005, half of its re-exports (goods imported and then exported out again) as an **entrepôt** went to Iran.[4] But what really made Dubai into an international presence in the global economy were the hundreds of thousands of poor migrant laborers who came from South Asia

> **entrepôt** A trading post, usually a seaport, for transferring goods at a profit between other ports.

to seek their fortunes in the city. They worked on Dubai's construction sites and helped to build it up into a major global economic hub and tourist destination. Today, these workers account for the bulk of the foreign or expatriate residents in Dubai – and the foreigners represent fully 90 percent of Dubai's population – but they do not enjoy the same rights and protection as their more wealthy counterparts. The treatment of Dongguan's rural migrant population, in other words, is repeated in a slightly different form in Dubai.

What is most distinctive about Dubai is how its open character, coupled with a bold program for fueling its market and linking the market to the global economy, has become interwoven with traditional Arab values and practices. This unique mix of history, culture, and economics has helped to produce its own special form of local social change and personal consequences. Dubai's ruler and his Executive Council view the city as a corporation; the ruler refers to himself the "CEO of Dubai, Inc." This amounts to the branding of Dubai as a "city-corporation" with the obvious intent to compete with other countries and cities for the dollars of tourists and the funds of investors. When a city-state is run as a corporation, it becomes subject to a political strategy that is global in its ambitions and local in its market-based policy and practices. While Dubai's rulers have always had global interests, its **neoliberal ideology** has trickled down to the local young professionals who work for Dubai's companies. Instead of thinking and acting exclusively as globally oriented economic citizens, young Dubai residents take a more pragmatic and flexible approach: they define the sense they have of themselves by balancing a global identity with a strong attachment to their traditional social values of ethics and gender (Kanna 2010).

neoliberal ideology
Making the free market work successfully by letting it naturally balance itself via the pressures of market demands.

Dubai World An investment company that manages and supervises a portfolio of businesses and projects for the Dubai government.

With their mixed identities, the young local citizens enjoyed a good time in booming Dubai well through the 1990s and into the early part of the twenty-first century. This all abruptly ended in 2008, when the global financial crisis shook up Dubai's urban miracle. The local shock came to a head in November 2009, when the state-controlled investment firm **Dubai World** sought to reschedule its payments on about US$26 billion of debt it owed to other countries (Reed 2009). The news sent a shockwave around the world, causing stock

Figure 11.9 Dubai Palm Jumeirah and adjacent development, as seen from a satellite. *Source: NASA, http://commons.wikimedia. org/wiki/File:Dubai_from_NASA_ ASTER_2010-02-08.jpg.*

markets to dive and the business media to panic. Underlying the broader global concern were the amount of real estate speculation and Dubai's excessive construction projects. The widely acclaimed Palm Jumeirah project – the iconic palm island real estate development off the coast (Figure 11.9), built by the property arm of Dubai World – itself soon stood deeply in debt to its investors as well as to its suppliers. Dubai World had also bought a 50 percent stake in CityCenter, the multi-billion-dollar resort and casino development in Las Vegas and the single largest and most expensive such project in the world. Today, Dubai World is overextended and saturated with debt. Dubai's ruler, the Sheikh Mohammed bin Rashid Al Maktoum (or Sheikh Mo), had come to rely heavily on this dominant and diversified state-owned company to help realize his goal of building Dubai into the next London or Hong Kong, a global hub for finance and tourism in the Middle East. The interconnectedness of the Dubai state, its ruling elite, and Dubai World has made it difficult to solve the financial mess and the debt crisis surrounding Dubai today (Keehner and Saitto 2009).

As the leadership of the United Arab of Emirates begins to ponder whether or not to bail out Dubai World and how to tighten the leash on Dubai, the city-state of Dubai is confronting the critical question of whether the path it chose for prosperity can be sustained in the future. The international business media continue to tout Dubai's strengths in favor of it bouncing back. They note the millions of young and underemployed laborers in the Gulf Region who are willing to work – not even accounting for the millions of migrants from South Asia and beyond – plus the millions more eager young consumers and the billions of dollars that continue to flow into Dubai from oil sales. Truly these are advantages that could help Dubai to recover once the current economic crisis ends (Reed 2009: p. 37). However, Dubai's autocracy appears either incapable of or unwilling to rein in the powerful global economic forces. The same fate has befallen Dongguan, which, as we learned above, took a similarly big hit from the global economic crisis. In yet another unexpected parallel, both Dongguan and Dubai are boomtowns that have been built by the labor and on the shoulders of a disproportionately large number of poor migrants. In the end, both cities offer compelling illustrations of how, once fashioned, the local–global connection can bring not only prosperity but also sudden decline and economic hardship.

Cities in a fully networked global economy

As we have taken you around and through several Asian, European, and Middle Eastern cities, we have also moved between the different levels of cities and countries as well as between cities and the people who live there. But this does not complete our inquiry into the extensive and complex connections between cities and the layered environments of which they are a part. We now will take you up yet two more analytical ladders – or scales, if you wish – so that you can gain an even broader view of the systems within which cities, and people, are embedded. We do so (to repeat a point we made earlier in this chapter) to allow you to form a full and complete picture of how your life today, as an urban resident, is shaped not just by your neighborhood or your city but also by even larger and broader territorial units, such as regions.

The regional dimension and mediation of cities

Besides the features of globalization already examined here, cities also are becoming part and parcel of other territories. Urban scholars have identified some of these new territories as regions – as larger places such as the Midwest in the United States and the Pearl Delta

Region of China. These regions play a significant role in how globalization is playing out across the world and how it is affecting the lives of people. Regionalization of cities can vary a great deal. It varies in terms of the scale or size of regions; the types and kinds of interactions between cities and their regions; the types or degree of networks that develop among the cities within a region; and, finally, the reach of city-regional systems.

Let us consider one prominent example closely. This is the case of Berlin. One can think of Berlin as a city, with its own special history and current dynamics. But one can also think of Berlin in terms of its larger territorial region and the other cities to which it is connected. There are four major metropolitan regions within Germany: Berlin, Hamburg, Cologne, and Munich. Across these four regions the growth of people and industry has varied greatly since the reunification of Germany in 1989. Despite strong connections between the regions, each is more autonomous and less hierarchical in a systemic sense than you would expect from a highly industrialized and connected economy. The older, heavy-industrial city-region around Leipzig–Halle–Bitterfeld in the former East Germany experienced a population decline of 8 percent from 1995 to 2004. This loss was principally caused by the closure of businesses as well as broader regional suburbanization and its associated loss of population. By comparison, the major metropolitan centers within and along the corridor stretching from Stuttgart to the Ruhr Basin in the south and southwest, including Munich, managed to keep a more or less stable population during the same time period (Urban Age Project 2006).

The Stuttgart–Ruhr Basin region highlights yet another way in which the global economy operates today: it can cross the boundaries that separate one nation from another. This particular region of Germany has become a part of the massive and cross-border European territory that begins in London in southeastern England, runs through northern France, the Benelux countries, and the Rhine Valley in Switzerland, and terminates in Milan in northern Italy. This broad region has become known as the "Blue Banana" (see Figure 11.10). It is the site of important historical, commercial, and cultural ties that have grown up between neighboring countries. These ties were promoted and encouraged with the development of the European Union (EU), which made the borders of Europe much more open and connected (Newhouse 1997). It can be said that one largely domestic city-region has evolved into a more expansive cross-national region as Europe has become more united territorially, economically, and politically through the EU. On the margin of Europe, in spite of not being in the region's core, Istanbul has become the city with the highest population (15 million) of the 78 metropolitan cities of Western Europe. Despite occupying the strategic intersection between Europe and Asia, Istanbul and Turkey have had limited trade relations with their immediate neighbors and have traded more with further-away countries such as China, Germany, and Russia.

European Union (EU)
An economic and political union of 27 member states located in Europe.

Let us consider another example of an emerging territorial region in the global economy. In doing so we will return to the case of the factory-city of Dongguan, in China. While it trails behind the thriving city of Shenzhen in terms of its investments from Hong Kong businesses, Dongguan has benefited from its later historical rise to urban and economic prominence. It lies very close to Shenzhen and thus is able to attract some of the surplus investment funds that left Shenzhen because of the rising costs of labor there. The repositioning of investment dollars has even accelerated since the global economic crisis began in 2008. Despite the major economic incentives the officials of Shenzhen continue to offer to businesses, investors still prefer to open their plants and factories in nearby Dongguan.

For instance, in 2009, the Taiwanese-owned Guangdong Nai Li Shoes in Shenzhen moved its factory to nearby Dongguan because of the availability of cheaper land and lower labor costs. "We had tax privileges for five years," said

Figure 11.10 Europe's "Blue Banana" economic region. *Source: Wikimedia Commons, http:// commons.wikimedia.org/wiki/File:Blue_Banana.png.*

owner Mr. Li. "Then we realized that Shenzhen was getting very expensive, so we moved our factory of 30 000 square meters [98 400 square feet] and 4000 workers to Dongguan." Even Shenzhen's home-grown powerhouse, Huawei – China's largest telecommunications company – decided to build its new production facility at a park established especially for new technology centers in Dongguan. Huawei, which employs 22 000 people worldwide (including around 1000 in Bangalore, India) and which still maintains about 4000 workers in Shenzhen, invested almost half a billion US dollars in the Dongguan project (Chen and de' Medici 2010). Given the density of export manufacturing in the Pearl River Delta region in which it is located, the city of Dongguan seems to be well-positioned to maintain its growth and expansion in coming years, perhaps even at a faster pace than that of the nearby city of Shenzhen, which is one of the urban economic miracle cities of China. All of this has happened because of the significance of regional growth and urban connections (and competition), which continues to emerge as an important pattern of the new global economy today.

This kind of economic synergy that links and enhances the development of cities that lie in the same geographic regions – and even across borders, as we showed above in the case of Europe – appears to be largely absent in Africa. The flow of trade between cities and between neighboring countries is severely restricted by different kinds of barriers. In the West African region of Burkina Faso, Ghana, Mali, and Togo, trucks carrying exports and originating from Mali's capital city of Bamako have to face countless obstacles. These include many checkpoints at the borders of countries as well as additional costs required by particular governments. All of this makes the transportation of goods and the flow of economic trade and traffic highly inefficient. Observers estimate that more than half an hour is wasted for every 62 miles traveled as goods make their to Ghana's port city of Tema on the Gulf of Guinea in the Atlantic Ocean. Besides costs such as the inefficiency of Africa's major ports, there are others including the money that must be paid to various police officials as well as large costs charged by transport services along the trade corridor between Bamako and Tema (World Bank 2009: p. 187). Disadvantaged by weak manufacturing capacities, the cities in West Africa are further hampered by the absence of connections among their various transportation and economic firms, links that in other areas would promote development simply because of the significant effects of geographic proximity.

While there is mixed evidence on how distance makes regional connections and integration easier and more important in the global economy today, we can gain even greater insight into these issues by examining the importance of the regional networking that goes on among business and firms in different countries. Let's consider one significant case, that of the networks that developed among the international financial centers of London and Frankfurt, Germany. For a long time, it was assumed that London and New York were the premier financial centers in the world and that every other urban center of finance would have to fight hard for third place. By the late 1990s, however, the European Monetary Union had been established. It created the euro as a common currency that would help to unite various European nations in an economic partnership. In addition, the European Central Bank became relocated in Frankfurt. The United Kingdom, however, chose to remain outside the Union and not to employ the euro as its currency.

European Monetary Union (EMU) The policies for moving the economies of members of the European Union (EU) to a single currency, the euro.

A concern arose that London might lose its prominence as a center of international finance relative to Frankfurt. But this did not happen. Instead, London solidified its dominance as the top international finance center even though Frankfurt did become more prominent. Two conditions accounted for this, each of which further illustrates the regional roles that cities have come to play in the global economy. One simply is the size of London's financial markets and the concentration of its financial firms, both of which bring about efficiency through **economy of scale**. The second is London's great attraction for skilled financial workers. Workers in the financial services congregate in London in order to take advantage of the density of jobs available in the global financial industries. Both factors combine to give London a distinct relational advantage as the central node for the European as well as global financial network. Frankfurt, by comparison, has gained some strength because of the higher number of financial transactions that occur there as the result of the relocation of the European Central Bank. The gain in relative importance as a result of the more unified European monetary system was enough to propel Frankfurt to become a true global financial center.[5]

economy of scale The efficiency gains and cost reductions that a firm obtains due to expansion in scale.

To summarize the regional effect on London versus Frankfurt as cities in a system, the more established and networked regional financial ties have strengthened London's continued dominance, while the enhanced European regional role for Frankfurt has elevated its position and influence relative to London's. In a way, the two financial centers have become more complementary to rather than competitive with each other because of different old and new ties between them and other cities in the European regional financial network.

Becoming globally networked

A regional view of cities in the global economy takes you closer but not all the way to a truly global understanding of cities. To get you all the way there, we must step back briefly to remind you of the pyramid-shaped urban hierarchy introduced in Chapter 10. This system has implicit national boundaries, but now we want to move outside these boundaries and to shift our attention to a broader perspective on the notion of an urban hierarchy. By doing so we hope you will come to understand not only the broader hierarchy, or ordering, of metropolitan areas across the world today but also the roles that industries, individual firms, and people play within this new global order.

Building on John Friedmann's and Saskia Sassen's seminal work on global cities, David Smith and Michael Timberlake have proposed that there exists today a single world city system. Some world cities, they argue, have risen above and beyond the national political and economic spaces wherein they lie (see Exploring further 11.1). As in any system, there are three key elements: (1) the number and scale of the parts in the system; (2) the connections as well as the integration among the parts; and (3) the functional differences as well as the hierarchy among the different parts of the system. The combination of these three dimensions affects both the individual parts of the system and the system as a whole. Since, as Smith and Timberlake argue, the world system of cities is a spatial result of global capitalist development, some cities are more important than others because they represent the principal locations of concentrated and centralized economic power. The major implication of this notion of a world city system is that cities, themselves, become more important actors relative to countries. Moreover, the networks among cities have become more crucial to understanding cities in the global system today (Orum and Chen 2003: Chapter 2). To simplify why this is so, consider that cities depend more heavily now than in the past on their trade and travel links with other cities around the world, rather than their own internal economic activities, for growth and performance as well as competition with other cities.

Imagining and conceptualizing the structure of the world city system is one thing, but visualizing and converting it into measurement and analysis is quite another. This challenge, however, has not prevented a small number of urban scholars from attempting to conduct rigorous analyses of different dimensions of the world city system. Here we want to share some of this new and highly important work with you. Smith and Timberlake chose to use air passenger flows as a measure of the connection among and the centrality of about 100 world cities at six time points – 1977, 1980, 1985, 1991, 1994, and 1997. They assumed that

EXPLORING FURTHER   11.1

World cities versus global cities

You have by now heard about both world cities and global cities and may wonder what the differences between them are. Is New York both a world and a global city? What about Shanghai, which we have discussed on a number of occasions thus far? More interestingly, is the smaller city of Yiwu in China, which we will examine again below, a world city or a potential global city? Scholars often use the terms "world city" and "global city" interchangeably. The two concepts also suggest the same or a similar kind of city, and this can be confusing to students. However, there are several important distinctions that can be made. These distinctions stem from the different scholarly origins of the two concepts and have evolved from how other scholars have applied them. To outline these distinctions clearly, we draw from one of the most prominent urban scholars, Saskia Sassen, who not only invented the term "global city" but also set it apart from "world city."[6]

Sassen first chose to use "global city" in 1984, with the deliberate purpose of naming a crucial difference from "world city." She argued that "world city" refers to a type of city that we have seen over the centuries, and most probably also in much earlier periods in Asia and in European colonial centers than in the West. In a way, we can say that the cities mentioned in Studying the city 10.1 – the Mesopotamian cities, Xi'an and Beijing in China, and the Greek city-states – were the early world cities because they were the first hubs and crossroads of civilizational development, primitive politics, and long-distance trade. European port cities such as Genoa and Antwerp during the Renaissance era would qualify as later world cities as they facilitated intra-regional trade and overseas colonial expansion. Other world cities, such as Istanbul, developed from their origins as political capitals of either empires or states.

In contrast to world cities in those times and terms, Sassen originally defined global cities as those that have been key organizing nodes of the global economy for at least three decades; she names only three such cities – London, New York City, and Tokyo – in her book *The Global City*, published in 1991. She defined global cities as: (1) highly concentrated command points in the organization of the global economy; (2) key locations for financial and specialized service firms, which have replaced manufacturing as the leading economic sectors; (3) innovative sites of production in the advanced service industries of banking, accounting, and law; and (4) markets for the products and innovations of these service industries. Given this definition, which focuses on concentrated and advanced economic service functions, it is easy to see why London, New York, and Tokyo were the only cities to qualify as "global cities." In fact, New York and London together still account for 40 percent of global market capitalization. Sassen later expanded the list of global cities to about 40, reflecting a broader conception of what is a global city.

In light of the above, we can characterize one important difference between world cities and global cities in terms of timing; that is, world cities have been around for a long time while global cities are of more recent provenance, developing in tandem with an increasingly global economy. Regarding a related difference, we can say that world cities have existed in both developed and developing countries, perhaps more in the latter, while global cities are generally found in developed countries today.

Sassen also suggested that most of today's major global cities have been world cities at one time or another. This is certainly true of London and Tokyo, which were once world economic, political, and cultural centers. But some global cities today, such as New York, are not world cities in a broad sense because their natures and functions were narrower, partly for not being national capitals. London and Tokyo are exceptions in this regard. Sassen also suggested that, while Miami has since the late 1980s developed global-city functions as a result of becoming the site of the Latin American headquarters for many US multinational corporations, it is not a full-fledged global city in the sense of London or New York. She also indicated that the absence (at least until very recently) of global-city functions in Kolkata (Calcutta) acts to diminish its status as a historically and culturally rich world city during the period of its development as the cultural capital of India during the British colonial rule.

Although it is useful to present the distinctions between world and global cities based on Sassen's definition, we see some blurring between them and it can be challenging to differentiate them empirically. As the global economy expands further, more and more world cities in developing countries today such as Mexico City and Kolkata will become potential or future global cities. We can characterize these as "globalizing" cities, of which Shanghai is an example. As more cities become more global or develop global functions, we will need to establish more varied and flexible criteria and indicators to confirm their true status.

air passenger flows and the role of airports would furnish important indicators of how people move between origin and destination cities – and, further, that the combination of both measures constitutes a crucial aspect of a linked world city system and the power and influence of cities in that system. Smith and Timberlake found that a few cities showed up as being the most central within the pattern of flights between cities, and they concluded that these represented the most powerful cities in the world city system. They were, as one might say, the usual suspects: London, Frankfurt, Paris, and New York (in that order).

Given that it had the largest number of passenger arrivals and departures as well as the widest air links to other world cities, London, Smith and Timberlake claimed, sat at the top of the world city hierarchy. In addition to being a major hub for long-distance connecting flights via Europe, Frankfurt also dominated the world travel network as the business and financial center of Germany – notably, Germany was Europe's most powerful economy and the world's largest exporter until 2010. This finding also confirms Frankfurt's standing in the European financial network we mentioned above. In the years between 1977 and 1997, several East Asian cities, including Beijing, Hong Kong, Seoul, and Singapore, rose in the rankings to the top tier of the world city hierarchy, based upon air passenger flows.[7] In addition, this study found evidence of continuity and stability regarding dominant European centers such as London and Frankfurt but also important change and movement in the cases of the rising Asian cities such as Seoul and Beijing.

While air passenger flows are an obvious relational feature of the world city system, Arthur Alderson and Jason Beckfield chose to examine the relations between multinational corporations and their subsidiaries in different cities as another way to understand the networks among world cities. They built upon Stephen Hymer's earlier argument. Hymer claimed that the increasing globalization of corporate activities and production across localities would lead to a more hierarchical, diffused, and specialized organization of cities with high-level corporate decision-making concentrated in a few dominant cities such as London, New York, and Tokyo. Using data on the headquarters and subsidiaries of 2000 Fortune 500 companies, Alderson and Beckfield performed a network analysis of the power and prestige of the 3692 cities where the corporations were located. They discovered that (1) a small number of cities monopolized the power of the strongly hierarchical world city system and (2) the positions of cities such as London, New York, and Tokyo at the apex of the world system in their analysis confirmed earlier claims about the importance of these cities. In a subsequent and improved study that incorporated data for 1981, Alderson and Beckfield uncovered not only instability in terms of the rise and fall of specific cities in the world system but also increased inequality in the power of cities between 1981 and 2000.[8] For a further discussion of cities in global networks, see Studying the city 11.2.

Interdependence between cities and the global economy

Having looked at different kinds of cities in different parts of the global economy, we conclude this chapter by re-emphasizing the strong similarities between these places in terms of their tight connections to and integration with the global economy. We view the current relationship between cities and the global economy as interdependent and mutually reinforcing: cities help to shape the emerging global economy but they are also shaped by it. What we want to make most clear to you is that cities are no longer local places in the ways they once were. If the cities that were unlikely to be global have already become part

STUDYING THE CITY   11.2

Cities in global networks

The study of world and/or global cities (see Exploring further 11.1) has in recent years moved from an individual case-oriented or comparative approach examining the cities' attributes and functions in the global system to an increasingly networked perspective and methodology. This shift reflects important theoretical and analytical advances in the study of cities. Throughout this book, we have dealt with the city as a collection of concrete places and spaces at the local and national scale, but have included numerous examples from a variety of countries with global references. Building on the systemic treatment of cities in Chapter 10, we present here a succinct view on understanding cities as more stretched and connected places in global networks.

Spurred on by the ideas of John Friedmann about a hierarchical world city system and Saskia Sassen about the few global cities anchoring the global economy (see Chapter 3), the study of cities in global networks took off in the 1990s. Reflecting this approach and using data on passenger flows between Asian cities, David Smith and Michael Timberlake (1993) found that the growing role of major Chinese cities such as Beijing and Shanghai was as key nodes in an imbalanced network of intercity air links. This approach became more systematic, comprehensive, and rigorous through the birth and maturity of the Globalization and World Cities (GaWC) research network. This is a non-institutionalized, collaborative venture between researchers in different parts of the world. One analytical approach to GaWC's study of world city networks (WCNs) is the "interlocking network model," which looks at WCNs through the analysis of interorganizational ties, especially those between advanced service firms such as financial institutions and their subsidiaries in those important cities that form global networks. For instance, Ronald Sean Wall and G. A. van der Knapp (2011) recently found that 84 percent of the network connections among multinational corporations occur between cities and not within them, and that approximately 70 percent of European and North American ties extend beyond their respective regions. This finding supports the claim that cities have become dissociated from their local geographies as their positions in worldwide networks have grown. The main gateway of GaWC is its website (http://www.lboro.ac.uk/gawc), where everyone is welcome to share ideas, publications, and data on WCNs without favoring particular theoretical readings, geographical foci, or conceptual and empirical approaches (Taylor 2004). (The article by Wall and Knaap was first published as Bulletin 295 on the GaWC website.)

Heavily shaped by GaWC, research on WCNs has become empirically very informative and sophisticated, and also includes more and more cities, particularly those in developing countries. In response, Sassen (2010) has recently broadened the discussion that pertains to WCNs. She suggested that using the city as a broader context can allow the inclusion of all conditions and actors that interfere with the WCN as a somewhat narrow phenomenon. More importantly, Sassen argued that world city and global city analyses are not urban theories per se but explain a new phase of global capitalism that features some key cities, such as London and New York, as strategic spaces and others, such as some small cities and towns in the less developed world, as excluded places.

In summary, while presenting cities in global networks helps you to see the complex connections between many cities on a global scale, it should not blind you from viewing the cities as places and spaces that are becoming more and more linked by and through various global forces and flows such as trade and immigration.

of the global economy, the cities expected to be an inherent part of the global economy have become even more globalized than they were, with more interconnections and even greater wealth and prominence. The growing hierarchical and networked nature of the world city system has only reinforced the interdependence and inequality among the units or members that make up different layers of that system.

Systematic constraint and individual flexibility

If there is one key thread that can help to bring together what we have covered in this chapter, it is the balance and tension between the constraints of the global, regional, and national urban systems and the flexibility or autonomy of individual cities to grow or stagnate in response to these constraints. This tension can lead some cities to do better than others by overcoming these constraints or turning them into opportunities. It may even allow a few cities, especially those from more marginal starting points, to move up in the system.

The Chinese city of Yiwu, introduced at the beginning of this chapter, is an important example. By aggressively developing a heavy concentration of small merchandise vendors and distributors, a prominent international trade fair, and then factories and suppliers in geographic proximity, Yiwu has climbed from almost nowhere to become a central hub for the global distribution and purchase of small-merchandise products in China. Without this global economic reach, Yiwu would have grown and urbanized far more slowly. Likewise, despite its different economic base and industrial focus, the southern Chinese city of Dongguan has similarly ascended to a far higher spot in the global system of export-intensive manufacturing than one would have anticipated based upon its rural past and late start in the processes of industrialization and urbanization.

While the upward mobility of cities such as Yiwu and Dongguan is evidence of the flexibility in the world city system, the continuing prominence of global financial centers such as London and New York reflects a different kind of city-specific flexibility. According to the **Global Financial Centres Index (GFCI)**, London and New York have consistently ranked as the top two global financial centers in recent years. In their head-to-head competition, London moved further ahead of New York between 2005 and 2007 in such areas as its business environment, market access, and infrastructure. In September 2009, London maintained a small lead over New York. Even in the face of a deep global financial crisis, London and New York remain numbers one and two in terms of the GFCI. Moreover, the strong links between their economies and corporations seem to have helped to strengthen their cooperation with one another.

Global Financial Centres Index (GFCI) A ranking of global financial centers based on such factors as professional workforce, business climate, market access, and basic infrastructure.

The crisis that rocked the system of global financial centers in 2008 provided an opening for the less-affected and faster-recovering Asian centers to become more prominent in the global economy – and they did. By 2009, Hong Kong and Singapore had respectively attained third and fourth places in the GFCI rankings, and Shanghai had entered the top 10. Beijing, which had been in 36th place in 2007, jumped to 22nd place, while Seoul moved up to 35th from 43rd place. One of the great surprises was that the dominant manufacturing center of Shenzhen in China shot up to fifth place, coming out of nowhere. Shenzhen and Shanghai were rated as being likely to become even more significant as financial centers in the next few years.[9] The rise of these several Asian financial centers provides further evidence of the opportunity and flexibility of the global economy to accommodate the changing prospects of individual cities even in the face of a major financial crisis.

The global restructuring of cities

As we draw this chapter's global tour through cities and their systems to a close, we return to the early segment of the journey by taking a final look at the local urban spaces and the occupants of cities that have become globalized. We want to drive home the point that, regardless of the powerful, transforming forces of globalization that can restructure cities, the real changes in local socio-spatial places reflect complex factors deeply embedded in national and local contexts. Globalization takes hold in cities, but cities are made up of multiple layers of local places that either persist or change in response to external and internalized global influences. Cities are the sites where global forces ultimately meet local circumstances.

The globalization of cities, if you will, happens not just through the long production and supply chains or heavy flows of financial capital but through human movement and clustering, which make the chains and flows actually connect cities as concrete places. London has held its top ranking in global finance because of its combined advantages of liberal immigration controls, a favorable but sound regulatory system, and its similarity to New York. Of this mix, the key factor probably is the influx and concentration of skilled financial professionals into the City of London. Here this class of workers can benefit from face-to-face interactions with one another. This phenomenon has led some scholars to talk about the emergence of a transnational corporate elite as the critical ingredient of an emerging transnational capitalist class. Leslie Sklair defined this class in terms of four segments: corporate elites, state officials, skilled professionals, and merchants (consumers) and media (Sklair 2005). One clear example is the competition among celebrity architects Rem Koolhaas and Jean Nouvel, who belong to the third segment in Sklair's typology. Architects such as these have worked on renewal projects such as Les Halles (see Figure 11.11), a declined, water-sodden, and garbage-filled central area in Paris that is rich in history, exhibits urban centrality and commercial culture, and represents the authentic Parisian and French identity (Wakeman 2007). The revival of Les Halles, ironically, parallels the recent build-up of La Défense – a new inner-ring clustered development of commercial and residential projects outside Paris. These renewal and new projects, including Canary Wharf in London, both confirm and deviate from the pattern of the traditional European city, with its compact, dense, and diverse center and rich mixture of people and activities. Beyond Europe, in developing-country cities large and small, urban renewal, global capital, and rural in-migration have had a displacement effect on local places on one hand and have unleashed strong bottom-up responses from grassroots non-governmental organizations on the other (see Making the city better 11.1).

Figure 11.11 Les Halles, long the site of markets in Paris, continues to provide shopping space but in a completely redeveloped place. *Source: Photo: Altrendo Panoramic/Getty Images.*

MAKING THE CITY BETTER   11.1

Global urban growth, displacement, and the role of non-governmental organizations

As global economic and political forces touch down locally, cities grow more quickly and sometimes in unpredictable ways. As you have seen in this chapter, expanding economic opportunities draw rural migrants to cities like Dongguan and Yiwu, resulting in rapid population growth and development. But growth can happen in less predictable ways: during times of war, genocide, or other forms of oppression, many cities will see sudden influxes of racial, ethnic, or religious groups as a result of refugees fleeing areas in turmoil.

One example of this can be found in McLeod Ganj, India, where many refugees from Chinese-occupied Tibet, including the fourteenth Dalai Lama, have taken up residence since the failed 1959 Tibetan uprising that followed China's invasion in 1951. Interviews with several monks and nomads who fled Tibet to live in McLeod Ganj have revealed that Tibetans were not free to practice their religion or express their culture in their own homeland any longer, and many people risked their lives crossing the mountains and avoiding Chinese soldiers to seek religious freedom in India. While not all of the refugees made it to India, those who did were greeted by non-governmental organizations (NGOs) such as the Lha Charitable Trust that seek to meet the needs of incoming refugees by offering language classes, skill-building workshops, and medical services.

The Indian government accepted the Tibetan refugees with open arms. And, because of the Dalai Lama's presence and the strength of the Tibetan culture that subsequently took root, the tiny mountain city of McLeod Ganj and greater Dharamsala benefit from a small but steady tourist industry. However, many urban areas have been changed by global forces across the world, and McLeod Ganj may be a special case in terms of its smooth transition. Other groups forced from their homes who have settled in nearby urban areas include refugees from regions of Afghanistan, Iraq, Myanmar (Burma), Palestine, and Sudan, among others.

In the megacity of Chongqing in southwestern China, which has 32 million people bounded by its expansive rural hinterland and increasing global economic connections, the Chongqing Green Volunteering Alliance has been operating as one of the first environmental-protection NGOs in China. It is officially sanctioned by the municipal government, and has been pressing the government to create and enforce more stringent environmental regulations for foreign and domestic industrial enterprises. It has managed to get one formerly polluting factory to relocate to the outskirts of Chongqing and upgrade its waste treatment system. Whether in a small city such as McLeod Ganj or a megacity such as Chongqing, NGOs, small and underfunded as they are, play a growing role in mediating the impact of global forces on local urban life.[10]

Any concept of a normative or typical city of national origin is less valid today than it once was. Johannesburg has taken on Los Angeles-like attributes, with its new and upscale business center, Sandton City, which overshadows the hollowed-out city core from a distance, and its spatial spread of malls and gated communities that resemble Southern California (see Studying the city 10.3) (Sudjic 2006). The redeveloped glamour zone in central Shanghai, coupled with its overdeveloped and underoccupied suburban new towns, presents similarities to and differences from European and US cities and defies any effort to characterize Shanghai as a typical Chinese city. This blurring of city types based on national traditions and systematic constraints enriches the evidence that cities are intensively globalized and reinventing what it means to be local. While the process of globalization is a force for city change through local penetration, the world city system imposes constraints on the changes that can make cities ascend or descend in the system. However, there is opportunity and flexibility for individual cities to take advantage of, and it ultimately takes human agency, local or trans-local, to make or break a city and change its various places. One can easily picture this happening through the thousands and thousands of vendors and traders, both local and global, who run or visit the seemingly endless rows of merchandise stalls in the center of Yiwu in China, a local place that is now intimately linked to the core of the global economy. Visit the book's companion website at www.wiley.com/go/cities for examples, case studies, and discussion questions, plus a list of useful films and other media, that are relevant to this chapter.

Critical thinking questions

1 What are the varied ways by which cities are linked and integrated into the world economy?

2 How can one make a meaningful comparison of the conditions and consequences of cities' places and functions in the world economy?

3 What lessons can be learned from the impact of globalization on cities as local places through the 2008 financial crisis?

4 How can one differentiate between and assess the growing influence of regional integration on cities versus the continued local impact of globalization?

5 How does the notion of place help you to understand the essence of the city as the global–local nexus?

Suggested reading

Josef Gugler, ed., *World Cities Beyond the West: Globalization, Development and Inequality* (New York: Cambridge University Press, 2004). The book provides an original perspective on world cities and the impact of globalization upon them through case studies of major cities in countries outside the industrialized West: Bangkok, Cairo, Mumbai, Jakarta, Johannesburg, Mexico City, São Paulo, Seoul, Shanghai, and Singapore.

Peter Hall, *The World Cities,* 3rd edition (London: Weidenfeld and Nicolson, 1984). Originally published in 1966, the book was probably the first authoritative and yet readable account of several world cities (e.g., London, Mexico City, New York, Paris, Tokyo, and the Randstad-Holland). The book helped to put the term "world city" on the map.

Saskia Sassen, *The Global City: New York, London, Tokyo*, 2nd edition (Princeton, NJ: Princeton University Press, 2001). Originally published in 1991, this seminal book chronicles how London, New York, and Tokyo became command centers for the global economy and underwent massive and parallel changes such as growing spatial inequality and new forms of local politics. The book launched the term "global city."

Allen J. Scott, *Regions and the World Economy: The Coming Shape of Global Production, Competition, and Political Order* (Oxford: Oxford University Press, 1998). A wide-ranging exploration of the economic logic and political meaning of the renewed importance of regions in national development and global economic integration and competitiveness. It helped to set a new research agenda on city-regions as an emerging mosaic of global systems of production and exchange.

Notes

1. For another illustrative example of this global perspective, see Rosenau (1997).
2. Our reference to Sassen here is based primarily on.
3. This paragraph draws heavily from Shaw (2005).
4. The data and analysis in this paragraph are taken from Lu et al. (2009) and Sun and Chen (2009).
5. This and the following paragraph draw heavily from Kanna (2012).
6. This paragraph draws heavily from Faulconbridge (2004).
7. This paragraph is largely based on Smith and Timberlake (2001).
8. This empirical discussion in this paragraph draws from Alderson and Beckfield (2004, 2007).
9. The information on these financial centers is derived from Zyen (2007, 2009).
10. The information in this box is derived from interviews held by David Boston while volunteering at Lha Charitable Trust in McLeod Ganj, India, March 2010. See http://www.forcedmigration.org/browse/regional and http://www.lhasocialwork.org.

PART V
CHALLENGES OF TODAY AND THE METROPOLIS OF THE FUTURE

CHAPTER 12

Urban environments and sustainability

KEY TOPICS

→ The ways in which cities depend on features of the natural environment, and the ways in which the natural environment's shortcomings are reinterpreted or manipulated.

→ The reasons that cities are prone to so-called natural disasters, and why the economic and human tolls of these disasters are increasing.

→ Reasons for rebuilding in the same place following a natural disaster.

→ The types of environmental concerns common within cities and urban areas.

→ Patterns of environmental risk distribution in cities and neighborhoods.

→ How social movements are working to improve urban environmental problems and ensure the equitable distribution of risks.

→ Impacts of increasing urbanization on global environmental issues, including climate change.

→ Some strategies for diminishing the environmental impacts of urbanization and making cities more sustainable.

Introduction to Cities: How Place and Space Shape Human Experience,
First Edition. Xiangming Chen, Anthony M. Orum, and Krista E. Paulsen.
© 2013 Xiangming Chen, Anthony M. Orum, and Krista E. Paulsen.
Published 2013 by Blackwell Publishing Ltd.

Imagine yourself walking through a city. Your feet most likely travel along a concrete sidewalk, perhaps dodging a piece of litter or discarded gum. If you are in the urban core, much of your walk may be in the shadows if tall buildings block the sun; wind may buffet you in the canyons created by block after block of skyscrapers. The air itself may be clean or foul, depending on how briskly, and from what direction, the wind is blowing. The water features of this landscape may include rivers or waterfronts (likely kept in place by seawalls or concrete channels), fountains adorning squares and corporate plazas, or dirty rivulets making their ways through the gutter to storm drains. The creatures you meet on this urban safari are most likely other humans, with a few other scorned species – the pigeon, rat, or cockroach – thrown in for good measure. The city, you may conclude, is a decidedly unnatural place.

Seeking a refuge from the "concrete jungle," you may amble toward a public park. Here trees, lawns, and ponds offer a glimpse of the natural world designed to soothe the city dweller's soul. But this is not truly nature, either, one might argue. The landscapes you will find are carefully designed to communicate a cultural *ideal* of nature: the mowed, monoculture lawns, for instance, are a far cry from woodland meadows. Moreover, the species of animals in urban parks, whether swans in Boston Common or pelicans in London's St. James's Park, do not represent indigenous fauna. Throw in infrastructure such as band shells, restrooms, and concession stands and you begin to see how removed from nature we are.

Or are we? Philosophers have long considered the question of whether humans are *a part of* nature or *apart from* nature. Do humans rely on nature in the way that other animals do, or do our intellects and technologies successfully distance us from the natural world? Once we have the answer to this question, we might ask whether the works of humankind are an extension of natural processes or somehow contrary to them. These are heady questions, and we will leave the philosophical implications for you to ponder. This chapter will, however, take up the question of *just how cities relate to the natural world*. Given the content of our idealized urban tour above, we might assume that they relate very little. But, as we will argue here, cities have an *interdependent relationship* with the natural world, the stakes of which are becoming more apparent and pressing each day. Cities depend upon natural resources and processes, and the natural world is constantly – and increasingly – affected by what happens in cities. We will begin by examining the ways in which cities depend on nature: the resources nature provides such as water, and the ability of nature to foster intensive human development through stable climates and topographies. We will then turn to the impacts of urban development at the local, regional, and global levels. In doing so we will see the ways in which race and class shape urban dwellers' experiences of the environment, particularly environmental hazards. Finally, we will examine ways to ease the burdens placed on natural systems by ever-increasing urbanization.

Making use of nature

Natural attributes and urban development

Conventional thinking suggests that cities develop in places that are, based on natural attributes, well-suited for human habitation. This was indeed the case for many premodern cities, where hilltop locations provided means of defense, or bays and rivers facilitated trade (think of London, poised on the Thames, or Manhattan, located at the confluence of the

East and Hudson Rivers). In cases where nature did not provide, human ingenuity and effort might compensate. Walls, for instance, aided in cities' defense, and aqueducts brought fresh water (see Figure 12.1).

But in the case of premodern cities we must keep in mind issues of scale: most early cities were typically limited to a few thousand inhabitants, what we might consider a small town by today's standards, and the technologies available to manipulate nature were relatively limited. In the modern era, humans' capacity to manipulate their environment has increased dramatically: steam-powered dredges allow for the expansion or creation of harbors, railroads shift trade routes to new corridors, and even the course of rivers can be altered (or reversed) to suit human needs. Just as importantly, the kinds of players involved in urban development have changed, as have the stakes of city building. Logan and Molotch's theory of the city as a growth machine (see Chapter 3) emphasizes that real estate development and speculation, as well as the increasing mobility of capital, have encouraged place entrepreneurs to lure investment and growth to their locales. Their desire to generate profits can prove more powerful than forces of nature. When nature has neglected to provide something an urban population might need, the environment itself can be manipulated. And, when a place's natural endowments seem unappealing, they can be reinterpreted.

Interpreting and manipulating nature

The development of a number of cities illustrates these processes. Take Los Angeles, for example. The Los Angeles metropolitan area is now home to some 16 million people, but

Figure 12.1 Aqueducts, like these built by the Romans in Segovia, provided an early means of harnessing natural resources to serve urban populations. *Source: http://upload.wikimedia.org/ wikipedia/commons/6/63/AcueductoSegovia04.jpg.*

at the time of its initial settlement the place that would become the city of Los Angeles lacked almost all the qualities that would *naturally* predispose a location to urban development. It had no port, no timber, and no mineral deposits that were recognized at the time (though oil production would flourish in the 1920s). Most importantly, it lacked water. Although the existence of the Los Angeles River had initially attracted Spanish settlers to the area, its flow fluctuated with the seasons, and was substantially diminished by pumping. Conservation measures helped to stretch the supply a bit, but to grow beyond its 100 000 or so population at the turn of the twentieth century Los Angeles would require a more reliable, and ample, supply. Los Angeles **boosters** – those who promote a city's advantages to attract growth – faced other challenges as well. In enticing migrants to Southern California, they could not assume that the area's warm, dry climate would be attractive: a century ago, heat was often associated with malaria, and arid lands were considered unproductive. In a clever move, boosters characterized the climate as "Mediterranean," allowing them to associate otherwise negative qualities with romantic images of Italy or Spain (Davis 1998). Of course, their efforts met with great success, and now Southern California's climate is popularly regarded as among the world's most desirable. This irony calls attention to another important consideration regarding places' so-called natural advantages: a disadvantage in one time and place may be an advantage in another, and vice versa.

> **boosters** Those that encourage development in a particular city or place, often because they will profit from intensified development.

Unlike the climate, Los Angeles' lack of water posed a problem that could not be solved through rhetoric alone. Boosters' dreams of a great city were constrained by the river's ability to provide adequate water for drinking and bathing, let alone industry and landscaping. But, rather than shift their efforts to some other locale endowed with adequate water, a coalition of men whose fortunes were tied in various ways to the city's growth sought to endow Los Angeles with a more abundant water supply. Harrison Gray Otis, publisher of the *Los Angeles Times*, was perhaps the most active advocate, relying on his newspaper to promote the cause while he and others busied themselves purchasing land that would dramatically increase in value if a water supply was secured. Given the arid quality of the immediate region, city water superintendent William Mulholland looked east to the snows of the Sierra Nevada range for a source. The Owens Valley, some 200 miles to the northeast, provided ample water that might flow toward the city using the power of gravity. Mulholland would lead construction of the 231 mile (372 kilometer) Los Angeles Aqueduct, which brought Owens River water to the San Fernando Valley, just outside the city. As the aqueduct initially supplied more water than city residents needed, the abundant supply was used to irrigate land surrounding Los Angeles, providing for the citrus orchards that became iconic of the region. Soon tract homes would grow where the citrus groves had been, replacing one icon of Southern California landscape with another. Indeed, one of Otis' allies in bringing Owens Valley water to Los Angeles was Henry Huntington, operator of the Pacific Electric Railway and developer of suburban communities along its routes (see Chapter 6). They, and other members of the city's growth coalition, profited handsomely as the main obstacle to Los Angeles' growth was successfully surmounted (see Figure 12.2).

As water from the Owens River made its way to Los Angeles, the farms and orchards of the Owens Valley slowly turned to dust. In essence, moving the river had eliminated one desert as it created another. Owens Valley farmers resisted, going so far as to dynamite the aqueduct and occupy its floodgates. In turn, Los Angeles officials found that the most effective way to quell the violence was to buy out the farmers. By the mid-1920s, the city controlled 90 percent of the Owens Valley's land and water (Walton 1992: p. 189). The story of Los Angeles' water wars is not only the stuff of Hollywood films (*Chinatown*, starring Jack Nicholson and Faye Dunaway lent a *film noir* interpretation) and much local folklore but is also illustrative of the conflicts that arise when cities and rural areas eye the same resources.

Los Angeles' quest for water reveals an important pattern in understanding natural resource use among cities. Until very recently, urban development has been predicated upon the acquisition of substantial natural resources. Boosters and developers gave relatively little regard to the long-term or global availability of those resources, or to the best ways to steward and preserve them. In Los Angeles, the arrival of Owens River water made possible entirely new landscaping practices, such as the planting of orange groves, palm trees, and other tropical flora never before seen there. The "California Dream" – one punctuated by orange blossoms and green lawns – attracted new migrants with additional water needs (including more lawns and so on), thus escalating the rate at which Los Angeles exhausted its new water supply. The availability of the resource effectively created new demands that

Figure 12.2 Headline from the *Los Angeles Times*, July 29, 1905. The article continues, "The cable that has held the San Fernando Valley vassal for 10 centuries to the arid demon is about to be severed by the magic scimitar of engineering skill. Back to the headwaters of the Los Angeles River will be turned the flow of a thousand mountain streams that ages ago were tributaries of the current that swept past the site of the ancient pueblo of Los Angeles to the ocean. The desert has yielded up its wealth. The problem of Los Angeles' water supply has been solved for the next hundred years." While it is difficult to imagine such an unabashedly positive account of such an event in today's news media, the tone here provides insight into the strong desire of Los Angeles' boosters to obtain water.

would only be fulfilled by locating new supplies (in this case, water collected by damming the Colorado River). The lessons here extend even further than Los Angeles' thirst: first, increasing supplies of resources often increases demand for them, creating the need to again locate new supplies, and second, meeting needs instead of questioning them rewards robust appetites. As we will see in the concluding section of this chapter and Studying the city 12.1, behavioral "fixes" can provide more long-term solutions.

STUDYING THE CITY   12.1

Man-made disasters

On February 26, 1972, a West Virginia dam holding back some 130 million gallons of wastewater and coal slurry collapsed, flooding the Buffalo Creek valley. A wall of black water rushed down the valley picking up vehicles, buildings, and people as it went. Within hours, 125 people had been killed, 1000 injured, and some 4000 left homeless. While the dam collapse was precipitated by four days of rain, the US Department of the Interior had long recognized the dam (and others) as unstable, and the mine operator – Pittston Coal – had been cited for its failure to maintain its slurry dams as well as for other safety violations. The Buffalo Creek Flood, as it is known, was thus not a natural disaster in the typical sense but instead reflected the capacity of industry and government to create situations that endanger, harm, and even kill citizens. Sociologist Kai Erikson (1995) called this type of man-made disaster "a new species of trouble." Erikson argues that, whereas natural disasters can actually bring communities together as they rebuild, man-made disasters undermine community solidarity. Oftentimes it is the very institutions that citizens had relied upon for their livelihood, comfort, or safety that cause these man-made disasters. Man-made disasters thus leave in their wake a sense of betrayal as well as a fear of what the future might bring.

Following Hurricane Katrina, Kai Erikson worked with fellow environmental sociologists William Freudenburg, Robert Gramling, and Shirley Laska (Freudenburg et al. 2008) to ogate just how human actions contributed to the devastation in New Orleans and elsewhere. Disasters such as this, they conclude, can be understood as the outcome of engineering and development projects that generate wealth for a relative few while subjecting large numbers of individuals to grave risk. Not only do disasters disproportionately impact individuals with a lower socioeconomic status but the systems that create these disasters also have disproportionate benefits and risks. In the case of Hurricane Katrina, the authors point to the 75 mile Mississippi River Gulf Outlet (MRGO, or "Mr. Go," as it is called) channel that parallels the Mississippi, creating a shortcut from New Orleans to the Gulf of Mexico. They argue that the channel actually acted as an inlet for salt water, killing plants and cypress trees in the wetlands that had long buffered the city from hurricanes. Without the vegetation, surrounding wetlands slumped into the channel, leading to more dredging and continuing the vicious cycle of wetland decay. As a result, up to 100 of the 500 square miles of wetlands southeast of New Orleans had been destroyed before Katrina approached the city from this direction. Had the MRGO channel facilitated increased ship traffic, an economic argument could be made for this added risk, but the channel carried less than half of one percent of southern Louisiana's ship cargo in the year before the hurricane. The millions of dollars spent dredging and maintaining the now-defunct channel (MRGO was closed to ships in April 2009) can be seen as funding little *but* disaster.

Inviting "disaster"

While water may appear to be the most basic of resources, we can trace cities' dependence upon nature back to an even more fundamental set of needs. When humans intensively develop land by constructing buildings – particularly large, tall, or expensive buildings, plus the accompanying infrastructures that provide for transportation, distribution of water, energy, and information – they do so with the assumption that the land upon which they build today will still be there tomorrow. While such an assumption may appear a relatively safe bet, events such as earthquakes, storms, floods, fires, and even droughts reveal the inherent dynamism of natural systems. While these events are often called **natural disasters**, they are more accurately understood as instances in which humans' plans and projects get in the way of natural processes that have occurred for millennia. The human lifespan is simply too short, or the stakes of building in a chosen location are too high, for humans to take into account the potential dangers posed by tectonic movement, shifting river courses, and similar events that endanger urban infrastructures. Moreover, as development expands and intensifies, so-called natural disasters become more common, more costly, and more deadly.

natural disasters
Natural events that cause significant damage to human structures and/or loss of life.

Earthquakes provide a useful example here. As urban development intensifies, the human and economic toll of earthquakes increases dramatically. This trend is compounded as we see more urban development in cities where buildings are not constructed to withstand the stresses of earthquakes (or hurricanes, typhoons, and other challenges that nature sends their way). In many societies, building codes attempt to anticipate the stresses associated with these potential disasters and harden against them; in other places, particularly in the developing world, building codes are insufficient or poorly enforced. In the 2010 earthquake in Haiti, for example, many concrete structures that appeared to be strong turned to dust during the temblor, crushing those inside. Some 230 000 lost their lives in the Haiti quake, and a similar number of fatalities was associated with the earthquake that brought down most of the shoddy buildings and houses in the city of Tangshan in northern China in 1976.

While the strongest earthquakes on record include some of the deadliest (and also, due to their remote locations, some of the *least* deadly), as Table 12.1 below reveals, the strength of an earthquake does not neatly predict its economic or human toll. Instead, these reflect an untidy function of the intensity and cost of structures, the density of the population, and the capability of structures to withstand damage. Note that Table 12.1 ranks quakes in terms of their economic costs, so the exceptionally deadly 2010 Haiti quake is not listed there (damage estimates range from $US 8.1 to 13.8 billion) (Associated Press 2010). Early damage estimates for the 2011 Tōhoku earthquake and tsunami – over US$200 billion – easily top those listed in Table 12.1, even though this figure does not take into account the unprecedented secondary disaster at the Fukushima nuclear power plant (Reuters 2011).

Though the earliest boosters of cities such as San Francisco or Seattle might reasonably be excused for failing to recognize the seismic risks that those locations pose, in many locales the very features that attracted development also brought with them serious hazards. Take rivers, for example. As we have noted in several places throughout this book, rivers provided essential transportation routes in the era before rail. As such, many of the oldest cities are located on riverbanks, locations both strategic and precarious. A typical example is the city of Winnipeg in central Canada, which lies at the junction of the Assiniboine and Red Rivers (in the United States, the latter is called the Red River of the North to distinguish it from the river of the same name that forms the border between Texas and Oklahoma). This location appealed to the trappers and traders who first established outposts there, and secured the place's role as a trade hub when agriculture spread through western Canada. Though rail and

Table 12.1 The ten costliest earthquakes, 1980–2010. *Source: Adapted from NatCatSERVICE, Münchener Rückversicherungs-Gesellschaft, GeoRisks Research. Reprinted with permission.*

Location	Year	Strength	Economic Losses (Billions of US Dollars)	Fatalities
Kobe, Japan	1995	6.8	100.0	6430
Wenchuan, Sichuan Province, China	2008	7.9	85.0	70 000
Los Angeles, California, United States (Northridge)	1994	6.8	44.0	61
Bió Bió, Chile	2010	8.8	30.0	520
Niigata, Japan	2004	6.9	28.0	46
Nantou, Taiwan	1999	7.6	14.0	2368
Spitak, Armenia	1988	6.9	14.0	25 000
Niigata, Japan (Chuetsu-Oki)	2007	6.8	12.5	11
Izmit, Turkey	1999	7.6	12.0	17 118
Iprinia, Italy	1980	6.9	11.8	2914

highways came to replace the rivers for the bulk of transportation, the rivers remained. Each year, as winter snows melt, the rivers swell, and, when conditions are right – when snows are heavy, the thaw is quick, and so on – they flood. In 1950, 100 000 people (about one third of Winnipeg's residents) fled floodwaters, and 10 000 homes flooded (see Figure 12.3). The waters rose again in 1966 and 1979, but during the so-called "flood of the century" in 1997 the Red River would crest at record heights in Fargo and Grand Forks, North Dakota as it made its way to Winnipeg – at that point protected by a major flood diversion system. This, and some 8.1 million sandbags, spared the city the extensive damage suffered in 1950 (Canadian Broadcasting Corporation 1950; United States Geological Survey 1952, 2005; City of Winnipeg 2008). When viewed through a longer lens, catastrophic floods like this can be seen as common, even routine. But imagine the settler or developer who arrives during the drier years: to his or her eyes, perhaps glossed over by visions of the metropolis that might someday lie upon these banks, the river presents only an advantage.

Why rebuild?

Hardening cities against disasters – whether through temporary means such as sandbags or more permanent structures such as levees, dikes, and spillways – is an expensive proposition. Add to this the cost of caring for displaced populations and rebuilding when defensive measures fail and one can reasonably wonder why we continue to rebuild in what seem to be very precarious places. The answers to such a question might vary depending on just what we are rebuilding. A useful analogy is the case of a family that rebuilds a beach house destroyed by hurricane winds. They might be seeking to recover the memories and sentiments associated with holidays at the shore. Or perhaps they have doubts about rebuilding but find themselves tied to this particular seaside parcel through the legal bonds of ownership and, lacking a willing buyer, have little choice but to again cast their lot in the same place. Alternatively, an insurance settlement may have provided them with the financial means to rebuild with relatively little in the way of out-of-pocket costs. Finally, their house may be

Figure 12.3 The Kingston Crescent area of Winnipeg during the 1950 Red River Flood. The river crested at its highest level in some 90 years, breaking levees, destroying bridges, and submerging 600 square miles of urban and rural land. Over 100 000 people were evacuated. *Source: Photo: Courtesy of manitobaphotos.com.*

among few destroyed, while other elements of this seaside community – shops and restaurants, friends' homes (and the friends who dwell in them), and recreational attractions – are still intact. In short, everything that had made their beach house enjoyable *is still there*.

The beach house analogy is simple but useful, calling attention to a number of the factors that compel rebuilding in the face of disaster. First, sentiments and memories cannot be underestimated in their power to connect people to places, even when those places have been radically altered by flood, fire, or other catastrophes. Recall our discussion of Walter Firey's work in Chapter 2 (see Studying the city 2.2). He found that sentiment and symbolism – the meanings associated with places – were just as important to understanding the "ecological" patterns of the city as economic concerns (Firey 1947). Second, legal structures bind us to places. Through the apparatuses associated with private property, humans dissect, label, and price pieces of land and then attach them to individuals, corporations, and organizations that have vested interests in preserving the value and utility of those parcels. Insurance policies are one important means of preserving value. While policyholders pay premiums based upon the risks associated with their insured properties – higher in risky areas, lower in safer areas – they pay far less in premiums than the actual cost of rebuilding. Often it is policyholders in low-risk areas who subsidize reconstruction of riskier dwellings, whether beach houses on Atlantic barrier islands or mansions in the canyons of Orange County.

While any of these rationales would provide a compelling incentive to rebuild, perhaps the last in our beach house analogy, the continued existence of the physical and social infrastructures that interact with the disaster site, is most interesting. In his examination of Chicago's growth, historian William Cronon illustrates this point particularly well. By the time of the Great Fire in 1871, Chicago was well-established as a trade center for lumber, wheat, and meat. Rail lines spread from this place like tentacles into the hinterland, bringing agricultural goods into the city and shipping manufactured goods out to the prairies. Chicago's port on Lake Michigan provided a central node in a water–rail system: once offloaded from their rail cars, goods could be shipped along the Great Lakes and Erie Canal to profitable eastern markets and, again, manufactured goods would take their place on the return trip (see Figure 4.6). When the Great Fire destroyed the city in 1871, the rail–water system *remained intact*, linking the prairie to the east coast via Chicago. Buildings or no buildings, Chicago remained the most profitable trade hub for the increasing production of the American West. Rebuilding in place made good economic sense (Cronon 1991).

But a fire, you may counter, is the kind of disaster that could happen anywhere. Chicago had no special predisposition to fire, and indeed fires of this scale were common when cities were built primarily of wood (Seattle burned in 1889; Jacksonville, Florida in 1901; Baltimore in 1904; and so on). Why rebuild cities in locations that seem poised for destruction, such as San Francisco, teetering on the San Andreas Fault, or New Orleans, lying below sea level and routinely in the path of hurricanes?

Let's consider New Orleans in greater depth. New Orleans sits at the juncture of the Mississippi River and the Gulf of Mexico. For its part, the Mississippi drains the center of the United States, winding its way from Minnesota to the Gulf, collecting on its way the waters of the Missouri, Ohio, and Arkansas Rivers, among others. In doing so it has provided an inexpensive transit route for the goods produced in much of the country's most productive farmland and coalfields, as well as for the region's industrial production. The Mississippi carries a lot of goods – half a billion tons of cargo a year, according to the Port of New Orleans (n.d.) – and *a lot* of water – 520 cubic kilometers a year, or about 18.4 trillion cubic feet (Meade 1995). The terrain through which the river follows is largely flat, and when it was left to its own devices the river meandered here and there, its banks shifting as climate and topography subtly changed through the millennia. As it did so, deposits of silt created the fertile soil that would bring the farms that in turn relied upon the river for access to markets. But trouble arose as towns and cities began to pepper the banks of the river. A meandering behemoth like the Mississippi poses a risk to urban infrastructure, threatening grain elevators and wharves, warehouses and shops, and the homes and families of their workers. The solution, in the case of the Mississippi, was to make the river's course more predictable by building high levees along its current banks. These levees offer some protection to the urban infrastructure, although they create hazards as well. In constraining the river upstream, water that might have otherwise spilled into nearby terrain is instead sent downstream in a giant chute: preventing floods in one place causes floods in another (this pattern is actually called the "levee effect") (McPhee 1989; Freudenburg et al. 2008).

The Mississippi remains unwieldy as it continues toward New Orleans. In central Louisiana, the Mississippi occupies one of many channels that fan across a broad delta. Though a dominant channel persists, every few hundred years it builds up enough silt and sediment to effectively obstruct itself; a smaller but now less obstructed channel becomes the swiftest route to the Gulf, captures the Mississippi's massive flow, and becomes the new dominant channel. In an undeveloped landscape such changes might matter little. But, when a major port and an industrial infrastructure rely upon a particular dominant channel, that channel cannot be allowed to move. Such is the case with the Mississippi near New Orleans. A series of dams and locks preserve the channel as it was in 1950, forestalling its shift to a new channel at the Atchafalaya. Delivering the Mississippi to New Orleans thus requires continual human intervention, with positive and negative impacts. The economy of a city is preserved at the same time that the distribution of silt across the Mississippi Delta – the geologic process that lifted southern Louisiana out of the Gulf – is forestalled (McPhee 1989). In simplest terms, preserving New Orleans' economy undermines its topography. As this case illustrates, we not only find ourselves compelled to rebuild cities in place but we are also compelled to preserve the land, water, and other natural features as they were when cities – and their dependent systems throughout the hinterlands – developed. The costs are high, economically and environmentally – US$12.9 billion in flood control planning, construction, and operations since 1928 for the Mississippi and its tributaries (United States Army Corps of Engineers 2009); see also Studying the city 12.1 – but entire regional infrastructures depend upon cities remaining in place.

For the same reasons that the Mississippi "must" continue to flow through New Orleans, New Orleans "must" be rebuilt after – and defended against – hurricanes. But the New Orleans case raises important questions regarding just what it means to rebuild. In the aftermath of Hurricane Katrina, the 2005 storm that unleashed what is arguably the greatest urban disaster in US history (see Table 12.2), government officials, planners, and academics struggled over what it would mean to rebuild New Orleans. Should the city be rebuilt at all? If so, should it take the same form or should some particularly vulnerable areas be off-limits to development? How large would the city be? What would its population look like? How would the city's rich culture change as a result? Issues of race and class were central in this debate, as communities with much of the worst damage, and the fewest resources for rebuilding, tended to be poor, minority communities.

Hurricane Katrina revealed not only that disasters disproportionately affect poor and minority communities but also that the rebuilding that follows disasters can perpetuate or exacerbate these inequalities. Some of these disparities are fairly obvious: households with insurance, and with the knowledge and social skills needed to ensure that their insurance pays in the wake of a disaster, fare better than those that lack one or both of these. Similarly, individuals working to remove or repair structures after the storms had different levels of access to protective equipment such as respirators. This was particularly important in New Orleans, where floodwaters spread toxic sludge across much of the city and facilitated the growth of hazardous mold in inundated structures. Still other problems reveal how disaster recovery compounds longstanding environmental inequalities. To facilitate the removal of storm debris from the city of New Orleans, formerly closed landfills in surrounding rural areas were reopened and soon began emitting noxious odors and "black ooze." This replicates a pattern that occurred in the 1960s following another hurricane (Betsy). At that time, storm debris was burned at the Agriculture Street Landfill, formerly closed due to citizen complaints.

Table 12.2 Damage and displacement from Hurricane Katrina (August 29, 2005). *Source: Based on data from Richard D. Knabb, Jamie R. Rhome, and Daniel P. Brown, "Tropical Cyclone Report Hurricane Katrina 23–30 August 2005" (NOAA National Hurricane Center, 2006).*

Storm Strength	Category 5 maximum (at Sea); category 3 at landfall in Florida and Louisiana
Fatalities	1833 (1577 in Louisiana)
Persons Ordered to Evacuate	1.2 million
Damage Estimate	US$81 billion
Insured Losses	US$40.6 billion (63 percent in Louisiana)

As a result, soil in the area contains elevated amounts of lead, arsenic, and carcinogens. Nevertheless, the same site would later be developed as affordable housing sold primarily to families, and would include an elementary school. After sustained pressure from resident groups, the US Environmental Protection Agency remediated the area by removing and replacing two feet of contaminated soil (Allen 2007; Environmental Protection Agency n.d.). The viability of this solution has come into question following the latest storm, however, as Katrina's floodwaters may have again exposed the toxic remains of Hurricane Betsy.

So, how might we sum up the ways in which cities rely upon nature? First, cities are often built in places that offer **natural advantages**, but those advantages are in turn enhanced by human hands. It is also important to keep in mind that all places have their share of **natural disadvantages**, which can be reinterpreted through boosters' narratives or overcome through engineering projects. Second, intensive and permanent development requires stable environments, which nature does not typically provide. Although climates may appear constant and the ground solid enough, infrequent but dramatic events remind us of Earth's dynamism. Third, for the most part, the disasters that occur when dynamic nature meets static urban development do not destroy the geographic, economic, and social systems of which cities are a part. Although rebuilding may seem foolish on the one hand, on the other we can see the logic and necessity of picking up the pieces. Finally, the inequalities present before disasters tend to be amplified during and after these events, lending an important social dimension to these purportedly "natural" catastrophes.

> **natural advantages**
> Qualities of a place's geography and/or climate that appear to predispose it to intensive human habitation.
>
> **natural disadvantages**
> Qualities of a place's geography and/or climate that threaten intensive human habitation.

Urban environments

Let's return to the walk through the city we imagined at the beginning of this chapter. Depending on how far we walk, we may wander through a number of very different physical environments. We may begin in the urban core, where commercial development is dense, traffic is thick, and greenery sparse. Moving through an industrial area, we confront a different environment. While traffic is still heavy, private cars, busses, and taxis may be replaced by trucks of all sizes, with their associated noise and dust, or by rail spurs and train cars. Factories may discharge air pollution containing visible particulates and noxious odors, or water pollution that leaves the health of nearby rivers and creeks in question. The residential neighborhoods through which we pass may also vary a great deal – from dense apartment districts with the occasional pocket park to leafy suburbs with vast lawns and a fair share of wildlife. If we pay close attention, we may notice that the quality of these neighborhoods' environments in terms of noise, dust, traffic, litter, and pollution varies depending on who lives there. Affluent and white neighborhoods may be cleaner and quieter, while poor neighborhoods and communities of color are saddled with more environmental hazards. Finally, if we walk at night, we may notice another form of pollution throughout the city and suburbs – light emitted by streetlamps, vehicles, and buildings obscures the night sky. In many cities one can never see the stars.

Such a walk would prime us to examine many of the most pressing issues regarding urban environments. Are urban environments healthful for their residents? And are all residents exposed to the same levels of environmental risk? Looking at your own city as one of many, you may wonder what happens when you multiply its environmental impacts several-thousand-fold. What burdens do cities and increased urbanization place on the *global* environment? As cities become home to more and more of the Earth's population, this question becomes all the more pressing and should lead us to ask how those burdens can be minimized. Let's take up these issues in turn.

Local environmental concerns

As we saw in Chapter 6, part of the impetus for suburban expansion lay in the desire to provide a healthy environment for children and families. Cities, it was feared, were hotbeds of disease due to stale air, foul water, and exposure to multitudes of people. Some of these fears were baseless: for instance, many diseases associated with "bad air," such as cholera, are not transmitted through the air at all (cholera is caused by water-borne bacteria; see Making the city better 12.1). Other fears were the by-product of racism and xenophobia, as the immigrant populations found in cities were often blamed for epidemics. For instance, in San Francisco, an outbreak of bubonic plague in 1900 led to the temporary quarantine of the city's Chinatown. But fleas carried by rats – not humans of any particular racial-ethnic group – are responsible for the spread of this disease (Chase 2004). Though sometimes misplaced, concerns for the health of urban residents led to a number of important reforms. New York's Tenement Law of 1901, for example, addressed very real hazards associated with urban living including fire danger and insufficient sanitation (Wright 1983).

Cutting through the misplaced fears and exaggerations, we can see cities as places with distinct advantages and disadvantages vis-à-vis health. "Bad air" certainly does not cause

MAKING THE CITY BETTER   12.1

London's cholera epidemic and the beginning of epidemiology

During the mid-nineteenth century, two major cholera outbreaks in the city of London ended up changing the face of urban public health for ever. John Snow, a medical doctor and researcher, studied the cholera epidemic of 1854 in an attempt to figure out why more people from certain areas of the city were dying of cholera than others (over 600 died in the 1854 outbreak) and linked the source of the increased deaths to the water supply ("John Snow: Anaesthetist and Epidemiologist" 1946; Snow 1857).

By ascertaining where each area of the city was getting its water, through his own inquiries and by working with a registrar of Southwark to double-check data, Snow was able to identify a clear difference between areas serviced by two different water companies. After discovering that "impure water" was being supplied by the Southwark and Vauxhall Waterworks Company, especially through one particular well on Broad Street, he located the well, dismantled the pump, and attempted to purify the water – leading to the end of the epidemic.

Snow's actions and research effectively founded the science of epidemiology, and other medical researchers began to take up the task of locating and ending deadly epidemics at their roots. And, in the process of ending epidemics, many researchers began to find that poor public health conditions in dense industrial urban areas were at the root of many deadly diseases. Aside from the development of artificial vaccines, epidemiology also provoked interest in public health in order to prevent outbreaks of infectious diseases before they began.

Efforts to make cities more healthy and clean involved the development of public sewer systems, emphasizing cleaner water supplies, improvement of public trash disposal, and higher standards of health in housing construction and maintenance. Many areas of major industrial cities were intensely polluted by factories and mills, densely populated in poor housing stock, and completely void of sewage or trash disposal services. While many major cities have drastically improved their public health conditions, many others in developing and recently industrialized countries around the world are facing public health crises similar to, or worse than, what John Snow observed in London in 1854.

cholera, but urban air pollution is responsible for increases in asthma, lung cancer, and other respiratory ailments. Transportation contributes its fair share of pollution, as does industrial production. The latter may call to mind images of tall stacks belching black smoke over the landscape, but poor urban air quality often results from an accumulation of less substantial polluters such as small plating, manufacturing, and printing plants. Risks of cancer and other diseases can thus be understood as a by-product of urban density and industrial land uses (which often exist alongside housing, retail, and schools). In some places, such as the south Los Angeles neighborhoods studied by Raul Lejano and C. Scott Smith, concentrations of small polluters can elevate cancer risks to four times those found in the city as a whole (see Figure 12.4) (Lejano and Smith 2006). We must also account for less obvious forms of pollution. For instance, noise pollution can lead to hearing damage as well as high blood pressure, heart disease, and mental illnesses including depression and anxiety. Urban environments, particularly those with railroads, freeways, airports, and manufacturing plants are especially loud (Fitzpatrick and LaGory 2000). Violence, too, can

Figure 12.4 When many small polluters are found in the same neighborhood, the cumulative risks to residents' health can become quite high. Here Lejano and Smith have plotted the cancer risks for a small Los Angeles neighborhood (Huntington Park). The vertical axis indicates lifetime risk (e.g., 400 in one million). *Source*: Raul P. Lejano and C. Scott Smith, "Incompatible Land Uses and the Topology of Cumulative Risk." (*Environmental Management* 37(2): 230–246 at p. 239; 2006). Published by Springer Science & Business Media. Reprinted with permission.

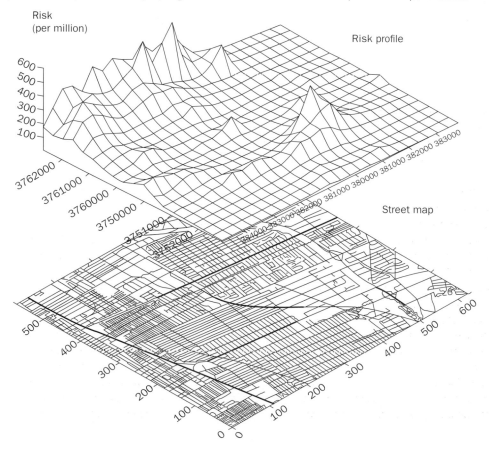

be considered an urban health hazard, although cities by no means have a monopoly here. On the positive side, cities typically have greater resources than rural areas in terms of their ability to treat disease and other health problems. Small towns and rural areas lack the healthcare specialists and technologies found in cities and suburbs. For some rural residents, treating a serious health concern such as cancer or AIDS may mean relocating to an urban area, at least temporarily.

Environment and inequality

While most city dwellers experience some environmental risks, social scientists have documented that these risks are not evenly distributed geographically or socially. It likely comes as no surprise to you to learn that poor and minority communities experience greater exposure to environmental hazards than do wealthier and white communities. For instance, in Los Angeles, Latinos and African Americans are two to three times more likely than whites to live near a hazardous waste facility and nearly twice as likely to live near reported releases of cancer-causing chemicals (Pastor et al. 2001). In the impoverished slums of Asian, African, and South American cities, homes are rarely served by municipal sewer lines or regular trash collection, so the wastes produced through routines of everyday life create environmental hazards. Interior spaces present their own hazards, such as asbestos, a fire-retarding material that can cause serious respiratory ailments, and lead paint, a leading cause of lead poisoning in children. Poor neighborhoods with older and neglected housing stock have higher concentrations of lead paint and present higher risks for the potentially devastating effects of lead toxicity on young populations (Fitzpatrick and LaGory 2000: p. 55). Trends such as these reveal that cities' most vulnerable residents, who are often those with the fewest resources available to treat the health effects of environmental pollutants, face an overabundance of environmental hazards.

Part of this disproportionate risk is the result of discrimination in the siting of industrial or waste facilities in poor communities and communities of color. One might reasonably ask whether these facilities – often referred to as **LULUs**, or locally unwanted land uses – are deliberately placed where the poor and minorities live or whether these groups move near LULUs because surrounding property values have declined and have thus made housing more affordable. Although some of each likely occurs, a number of scholars have documented that the owners of these facilities as well as the government officials who oversee their placement have routinely targeted poor communities and communities of color. For instance, in Los Angeles, sociologist Manuel Pastor and his colleagues (2001) found that disproportionate numbers of Latinos and African Americans lived in neighborhoods near toxic storage and disposal facilities *before* those facilities arrived. Another sociologist, Mary Pardo, documented how consultants suggested that Los Angeles County should locate a new prison in predominantly Latino East Los Angeles because the community was, in their perception, too disorganized to offer effective resistance (Pardo 1990).

We can see this process at the regional and global levels as well. Robert Bullard is perhaps the best-known scholar of what is called **environmental racism** – the enactment of policies and practices that create greater environmental burdens for poor and minority communities, whether intentionally or unintentionally. Bullard chronicles the disproportionate share of chemical manufacturing and toxic storage that is conducted in the southern United States, often in predominantly African American towns. This region, as well as the cities and towns therein, invited these

LULU Locally unwanted (or undesirable) land use. Industrial and infrastructure projects considered detrimental to their neighborhoods, despite their necessity.

environmental racism "Any policy, practice or directive that differentially affects or disadvantages ... individuals, groups or communities based on race or color" (Bullard 2000).

businesses in the interest of economic development. In doing so, they followed a common practice of creating a "friendly business climate," with low levels of environmental and labor regulations and low tax rates (Bullard 2000). Although long considered a reasonable strategy for attracting investment, scholars are now pointing to the capacity of ever more lax regulatory regimes to foster a **race to the bottom**. This means that cities, regions, and even countries out-do one another in providing the fewest hindrances to business. They may succeed in attracting investment, but the social and environmental costs are high as workers have long hours, low pay, and few rights; wastes may be discharged with little concern for their effects on the environment; and governments receive little in the way of taxes with which they might address these problems. This phenomenon has become quite prevalent among many cities in China, especially those smaller inland cities that, in competing for economic growth and foreign investment, have attracted heavily polluting factories and paid the considerable price of severe local environmental degradation. As we will see below and in Chapter 13, many governments, whether at the city or national level, are turning away from these practices and toward those that will instead attract investment through enhanced environments.

> **race to the bottom**
> A pattern in which places vie to attract investment by providing the most permissible regulatory environment.

MAKING THE CITY BETTER   12.2

The environmental justice movement

For many years, the environmental movement was understood as primarily a middle-class, white movement. Its early focus on the preservation of wild places and endangered plant and animal species seemed largely irrelevant to individuals who wanted for basic necessities or who were excluded from democratic and economic opportunities. This changed in the 1980s and 1990s, as activists began to formally recognize patterns that had existed for centuries: poor and minority communities shouldered a disproportionate burden in terms of exposure to toxic materials and undesirable land uses. In the United States, framing environmental issues as civil rights issues was key: if all citizens were granted equal protection under the law, why were they all not equally protected from environmental hazards? Armed with this new perspective, activists have successfully protested new hazards such as proposed landfills, garbage incinerators, toxic storage facilities, prisons, and even the use of diesel busses for public and school transportation. They have also demanded the cleanup of existing hazards such as the contaminated soil from New Orleans' Agriculture Street Landfill, discussed in this chapter. Success has extended beyond the streets, too: in 1994 President Bill Clinton signed Executive Order 12898, requiring federal agencies to consider any disproportionate and adverse impacts their projects might have on minority and low-income populations.

Successful **environmental justice** struggles rely on the efforts of many individuals new to political activism. Take the case of the prison siting conflict in East Los Angeles discussed in this chapter. For years both the state of California and the city of Los Angeles operated on the assumption that affluent and well-educated residents would successfully oppose LULUs while older persons and the less educated would not do so. But, when a 1700-bed prison was slated for the Boyle Heights neighborhood of East Los Angeles, within two miles of 34 schools, the very types of people presumed to be most passive became active and organized protestors. Out of the prison protests grew Mothers of East Los Angeles, a group of primarily Mexican American women aged 40 to 60 with at most high-school

> **environmental justice** A social movement seeking equity in terms of the environmental risks and benefits experienced by different groups

educations. They understood their activism as an extension of their roles as mothers and grandmothers: to protect their children, they felt compelled to also protect their communities from harm (Pardo 1990).

Environmental racism and the responses of the environmental justice movement are not only US phenomena. Across the globe we find instances of disproportionate exposure to hazards based on race and class. Many of these are not explicitly urban struggles: conflicts between indigenous and rural peoples and those seeking to extract natural resources are also typical. For example, the Ogoni people of Nigeria have long struggled against oil producers whose wells and pipelines pollute their farms and fishing grounds. The oil, and profits, flow to developed countries, while the wastes remain in the Niger Delta. Urban movements have also addressed the impacts of industrial accidents and routine pollution. Prominent examples include the efforts to secure medical care and cleanup in the aftermath of the 1984 gas release at Union Carbide's plant in Bhopal, India (see Figure 12.5) (International Campaign for Justice in Bhopal n.d.) and the coalitions working to halt inequitable pollution from petroleum refineries in Durban, South Africa.

Figure 12.5 Protestors mark the 25th anniversary of the gas leak in Bhopal that killed some 8000 and injured 150 000 others. Not only do toxic industries disproportionately locate in poor and minority areas but these communities also have a difficult time gaining redress for illnesses and injuries suffered as a result of exposure. Victims of the Bhopal accident and their families are still seeking what they feel is adequate compensation. *Source: Photo: AP Photo/Altaf Qadri/PA Photos.*

Global environmental concerns

Cities concentrate not only the positive and productive elements of human society but also the raw materials needed to sustain human life and the byproducts of everyday activities and economic production. As the case of Los Angeles related at the beginning of this chapter reveals, the amount of resources – such as water, but also food, raw materials, manufactured goods, and energy – needed to support dense human settlements creates an **ecological footprint** far larger than the city limits. The same is true of the emission of waste, whether air pollution created by vehicles, factories, and power plants or the water pollution created by domestic uses, street

ecological footprint
The environmental impact of a city's resource needs and waste production.

runoff, and industry. Our increasingly global economy has the potential to stretch a city's footprint around the world, as does the global nature of pollution problems such as climate change and ozone depletion (Bugliarello 2006). Here we present two particularly pressing global concerns: the environmental effects of urbanization itself and the complex role of cities in global climate change.

Urbanization's environmental impacts

The continuing growth and urbanization of the world's population poses distinct challenges to both local and global environments. Over the past 50 or so years we have seen rapid urbanization in regions of the world that were once primarily rural – Africa, Asia, and Latin America – and population experts project that this trend will continue apace for the foreseeable future. Indeed, the United Nations projects that by 2050 some 60 percent of Africans and Asians will live in urban areas, along with nearly 90 percent of those in the Americas (United Nations 2007). To provide housing and economic opportunities for these new residents, cities must expand far beyond their former boundaries, a pattern already seen in the megacities of Tokyo and Mumbai, urban agglomerations that may include some 36 and 26 million residents, respectively, by 2025 (see Chapter 7 and Chapter 10 for more details on urbanization in developing countries) (United Nations 2007).

To assess the extent to which the environmental impacts of this growth are felt locally or globally, we must first understand the character of daily life in these cities. In technologically advanced cities with strong economies, consumption of resources such as water and energy may increase, thus increasing the city's ecological footprint (see Kahn 2006). The city's infrastructure may determine just how far these impacts spread; for instance, a city with efficient public transportation can curb demands on petroleum and the generation of greenhouse gasses, thus minimizing its global impact. The density of development is relevant here as well, as sprawling cities take the place of agricultural land and wildlife habitat while dense development can preserve those same resources. Cities in which populations are underserved by municipal infrastructure – such as those where large numbers live in slums – pose a separate set of challenges. Underserved by sewers and trash collection, slums generate untreated wastes that contaminate local waterways and soils. These same wastes pose hazards for slum dwellers who lack regular access to clean water for drinking, cooking, and hygiene. Tokyo and Mumbai, mentioned above, provide an illustration of this contrast. While Tokyo is known worldwide for its dense residential development and public transportation, about half of Mumbai's residents live in slums and only 44 percent have access to latrines (Desai 2009). The proliferation of slums poses immediate hazards to residents and cumulative hazards at the regional level. When governments fail to ensure that infrastructure keeps up with growth, they imperil not only their citizens but entire natural and social systems. Untreated sewage and storm water from urban areas flow into nearby rivers, fouling natural habitats as well as increasingly scarce sources of fresh water, and the extreme lack of access to toilets in the massive slums of Indian megacities such as Mumbai contributes to poor health, especially among women and children (see Figure 12.6; Chapter 11).

Cities and climate change

Climate change poses dual threats to cities. First, as average temperatures rise, the threats posed by seasonal heat waves increase. While they lack the drama of disasters such as earthquakes, floods, and tornadoes, in the United States heat waves kill more citizens each year, on average, than these other disasters, and they are particularly deadly in urban environments (Klinenberg 2003: p. 17). Chicago faced a particularly deadly heat disaster in July 1995 when an estimated 700 people lost their lives (exact figures are difficult to come by, as the means for measuring heat-related deaths – and deaths from other disasters – are open to some interpretation). Sociologist Eric Klinenberg found that many of these deaths occurred in the city's most vulnerable neighborhoods, where residents lacked air conditioning and lived in relative social isolation due to their neighborhoods' high crime rates and diminished infrastructure (Klinenberg 2003). Horrifying as Chicago's heat disaster may have been, it was dwarfed by a much longer and more severe heat wave affecting most of Europe in the summer of 2003. Record highs were recorded in the United Kingdom (38.1 °C/100.5 °F), France (40 °C/104 °F), and Switzerland (41.5 °C/106.7 °F), where June was the hottest month in over 250 years of meteorological record keeping. This heat disaster claimed some 30 000 lives and, as in Chicago, most of the victims were elderly. The European heat wave posed a challenge to energy infrastructure as well: water levels in the rivers that France's nuclear reactors rely upon for cooling dropped so low that plants had to shut down or reduce their capacity. This occurred at the same time that demand for electricity increased due to air conditioning and refrigeration needs (United Nations Environmental Programme/GRID Europe 2004).

Other climate-related threats are generated by rising sea levels and increasingly severe storms. Much of the world's urban development is found in coastal areas, and coastal cities tend to be fast-growing cities. The appeal is both economic and cultural, as global trade makes shipping and port activity ever more important to urban economies, and coastal living takes on a cachet that is, in historic terms, relatively new (believe it or

Figure 12.6 In slum areas where access to water is limited, residents often have little choice but to use rivers to meet basic sanitation needs. Bathing and washing in urban rivers are common in developing-world cities; pictured here is the Buriganga River in Dhaka, which is polluted by industrial as well as human wastes. *Source: Photo © Rafiqur Rahman/Reuters/ Corbis.*

not, living at the beach – particularly year-round – was not always seen as appealing). Climate change puts all of this in peril by increasing sea levels as ice sheets melt and creating conditions in which hurricanes, cyclones, and related storm surges thrive. The inundation of cities by seawater may come as a relatively slow creep, as in the case of Venice, Italy, where tidal flooding submerges the old city for some 50 days a year (a condition locals refer to as *acqua alta*), or with brutal force, as when 2007's Cyclone Sidr destroyed some 1.5 million homes in Bangladesh (Chafe 2007; Dasgupta et al. 2009). Indeed, Bangladesh is one of the countries most threatened by rising sea levels, as a one-meter rise could inundate 14.5 percent of the nation's land (Chafe 2007). In poor flood-prone cities such as Ho Chi Minh City, Kolkata, Dhaka, and Manila, the rise in sea level and the increased frequency and intensity of extreme weather events pose enormous adaptation challenges. Projecting current population trends into the future, economists predict that only a handful of coastal cities will be particularly vulnerable to the combined threats of sea level rise and storm surge but that this represents increased risk for millions of inhabitants. For example, in the year 2100 the number of Manila residents in storm surge zones will have increased by some 3.4 million (Dasgupta et al. 2009). If the historic patterns continue, many of these residents will be those with the fewest resources to withstand such a disaster or rebuild in its wake.

For cities in an ever-warmer world, a key question is just how to address their increasing vulnerability. One alternative is to treat the specific threats posed by heat emergencies, storms, and sea-level rise through new infrastructure and revamped social institutions. Floodgates, such as the MOSE (Modulo Sperimentale Elettromeccanico) project in Venice, may keep rising tides at bay and social services may be able to reach out to elderly and vulnerable populations during heat emergencies. The price, however, is high: Venice's MOSE project is projected to cost some €4.2 billion (Chafe 2007), and, while social services are often less expensive, they are also often vulnerable to municipal budget cuts. The second alternative is to address the *causes* of climate change. Cities are major producers of carbon emissions, whether from transportation, industry, or power generation. By changing how these processes occur, cities might diminish their contribution to global greenhouse gases and thus reduce the hazards of climate change. While doing so involves costs, it also promises efficiencies and long-term savings that infrastructure projects cannot necessarily deliver. Developing-country cities face a bigger dilemma. While contributing an increasing amount of global greenhouse gases through a growing number of factories and cars, they have made little attempt to address climate change systematically as part of their decision-making processes. Facing major climate risks but serving as drivers of regional economic growth, large coastal cities of Asian developing countries must make adaptation a core element of long-term urban planning (World Bank 2010).

Addressing environmental issues
Toward sustainability

All of this can paint a gloomy picture. Are we moving toward a hot, wet planet where city dwellers must fight to keep their heads above water? Toward what urban critic Mike Davis has called a "planet of slums," where trash piles ever higher while infrastructure fails to keep up with the generation of waste? Toward a world of environmental haves and have-nots, stratified by race, class, and region? If so, what happens to our sense of places as sites of safety and security? What happens to our connections to others within cities as places? It is important to keep in mind that, as insurmountable as these problems may seem, they are the product of human actions and, thus, potentially also capable of being unmade by human actions.

With the environmental movement, which gained widespread support in the 1970s, urban residents and planners began shifting their views about the relationship between cities and nature. Rather than continually seeking and securing new natural resources, they increased attention to the conservation of existing resource supplies. While this shift occurred in part as a result of diminishing supplies (for instance, in the arid western United States there were simply no more rivers to dam), it also reflected a shifting environmental ethos. As a result, contemporary urban planning and management increasingly attends to

sustainable development
Development that meets current needs without compromising the needs of future generations.

sustainable development. In general terms, "sustainability" refers to the ability of systems to endure, and sustainable development seeks to meet current needs without compromising the needs of future generations (Brundtland et al. 1987). At the level of cities and metropolitan areas, this means not only ensuring the long-term viability of the city itself but also minimizing the degree to which the city threatens the larger systems upon which it depends. As Exploring further 12.1 reveals, sustainable urban transportation requires ensuring cities' economic vitality, preserving their local environmental quality, and minimizing their impact upon the global environment.

Cities are places where decisions are made every day about how to accommodate growth, how to support the economy, and how to provide vital services to residents. The key to sustainable development is accomplishing all of these things in ways that maximize benefits and minimize impacts, and doing so requires that we have a thorough understanding of just what those impacts are. Sustainable development advocates ask that we expand our assessment of technological, natural, and social systems in both time and space so that we recognize all of a development proposal's impacts. These impacts may be conceptualized in terms of costs, although some impacts are easier to price than others (for instance, the price of building a new road is relatively easy to calculate, while the habitat lost or harmed by the new road has a less readily calculable value). As we stretch our notion of impacts, and costs, we may find that seemingly simple and inexpensive proposals are actually complex and costly.

Take for instance the development patterns associated with suburban sprawl. Rural land is typically available in large parcels owned by a single party; these parcels can be quickly and easily bought and cleared; and the buildings associated with sprawl such as chain stores and subdivisions are mass-produced with minimal customization. All of this makes for low expense on the part of the developer. But, if we consider perspectives other than those of the developer, this type of project has significant impacts as well as costs. Farmland and wildlife habitat are lost, resources are used and wasted in the construction process, roads and sewers must be built to serve the new development, automobile and fuel use will increase as customers and residents drive to the development, and so on. At the same time, on the other side of town, a neighborhood may be declining if this development does not serve excess demand for housing or retail but instead shifts fixed demand to a new area. Finally, if these buildings are not made to last – to withstand the forces of fickle nature or culture – they may become abandoned, blighted, and eventually fodder for a landfill. Taking this longer, broader view, our cheap and easy development seems to be neither (see also Exploring further 12.1). Elements of sustainable urban development, on the other hand, can seem expensive and complicated. Renewable energy technologies have high up-front costs, as do public transit systems,

EXPLORING FURTHER   12.1

Transportation and sustainability

The increasing use of, and the growing number of alternatives to, private automobiles provide a useful illustration of the local and global impacts of urban routines. The beginning of the twenty-first century has been marked by dramatic increases in automobile use worldwide. In the United States, this reflects longstanding patterns of sprawling, low-density development as well as policies that keep the price of gasoline low, a long history of automobile manufacturing, and a cultural love affair with the car. These factors, and others, are leading to increased private automobile use worldwide. In the 1970s, Asian automakers began their eclipse of the United States, and automobile manufacturing has since spread from Japan and Korea to India and China, where companies such as Tata and Mahindra (in India) and Chery and Geely (in China) are selling more and more vehicles in their home markets. As a result, the once bicycle-clogged streets of cities such as Shanghai are instead increasingly choked with automobiles, with a resulting decline in air quality. While automobiles are certainly not the only source of emissions that lead to higher ground ozone levels (the pollution that causes visibly dirty air, eye irritation, and respiratory distress) and global climate change, they are certainly among the leading causes. In the United States, 33 percent of greenhouse gas emissions from fossil fuels result from transportation, and 60 percent of that is from private automobiles (United States Environmental Protection Agency 2009). Increased automobile use also extends the resource footprint of cities into petroleum-producing regions around the world, resulting in potential environmental hazards in those locales as well (see Making the city better 12.2).

Attempts to address the environmental impacts of automobile use have led to a number of innovative technologies and policies. Many of these seek to improve the automobile itself, particularly in the areas of fuel efficiency and emissions. Hybrid and electric cars represent important moves in this direction. But a number of other environmental and public health concerns remain. Switching to a different *type* of vehicle does little to curb injuries and fatalities from accidents or diminished health as a result of less walking and cycling. Moreover, as automobiles proliferate, so do the types of infrastructure they require, such as roads, highways, and parking lots, all of which contribute to urban sprawl.

How, then, can we truly minimize the negative effects of automobile use while still efficiently moving people and goods from one place to another? For many years, urban planners and boosters looked to expensive infrastructure projects for solutions. In the United States, freeways were seen as a means of reducing traffic created as increasing numbers of automobiles swamped streets built for entirely different vehicles. The shortsightedness of this approach seems obvious now: creating faster roads encouraged more people to drive, and new freeways met or exceeded their capacities long before projections predicted they would. Another common infrastructure-based solution is the construction of subway and light rail systems. While these can succeed in taking vehicles off the road and motivating more efficient transit-centered development designs, construction is typically expensive and disruptive (see Making the city better 3.1).

When rapid transit services use existing infrastructure, the expenses and disruptions associated with construction are minimized. Bus rapid transit (BRT) systems aim to move travelers throughout metropolitan areas as quickly and efficiently as possible by using dedicated travel lanes and special traffic signals to give priority to busses, and by increasing rider-friendliness through integrated transfer points, coordinated fare systems, and more accessible rider information. Curitiba, Brazil, is considered among the pioneers of successful BRT planning and implementation (see Figure 12.7).

The system is highly efficient: by paying fares at a station rather than on the bus itself, typical stops are reduced to under 20 seconds; riders on some heavily used routes can expect a bus to arrive every 90 seconds. Curitiba's BRT is credited with saving 27 million auto trips per year and lowering per capita fuel consumption by 30 percent relative to eight comparable Brazilian cities (United States Department of Transportation n.d.). Curitiba's model is being implemented in a number of other cities, including Beijing, Bogotá, Jakarta, and Quito. Although the degree of success has varied as elements of the system are adapted and perfected in these locations, the potential to move riders quickly and at low costs shows great promise (Hook 2007).

Another set of potential solutions relies on policy changes to reduce traffic at minimal costs. One reason we have witnessed such an explosion of automobile use is the low cost to the user. Consider all the costs associated with automobile use that the driver *does not* pay. What about the costs of increased pollution? When pollution leads to respiratory disease, the costs are borne by the ill, by members of health insurance pools, or by taxpayers, and the dirt associated with vehicle emissions

external(ized) costs
Costs associated with the production of a good or service that are not borne by the producers.

creates expenses for property owners. And what about the economic costs of time lost to traffic congestion? Or the costs of building and maintaining parking lots? Increasingly, transportation policy is seeking to charge drivers for what have been, up to now, **external(ized) costs** – costs not borne by the users of automobiles. The implementation of congestion pricing is probably the best-known example. Drivers must pay a daily fee of £8 in central London; cameras enforce compliance, and the proceeds are used to enhance public transit. To date the scheme has been almost too successful – drivers have avoided the fee, and the area, resulting in less-than-expected benefits to the transit fund (Goldman and Gorham 2006).

Policy efforts to reduce the detrimental effects of city traffic extend beyond the internalization of automobile expenses. A number of Scandanavian cities prohibit older and less efficient trucks from using downtown loading zones, and construction projects such as Potsdamer Platz in Berlin require the production of many materials on-site to minimize truck traffic (a move that helped the project to be completed six months ahead of schedule) (Wheeler 2007). No single policy or technology will solve this problem, but innovative initiatives on multiple fronts are showing some promise.

Figure 12.7 Bus rapid transit (or BRT) in Curitiba, Brazil, which is often looked to as a model of public transit efficiency. Dedicated bus lanes, "tube" stations where riders pay before boarding the bus, and a mix of local and regional routes contribute to the system's success. *Source: © Marcelo Rudini/Alamy.*

dense, in-town developments, reclaimed water irrigation systems, and on and on. But each of these – and others like them – promises lower costs over the long run or in some other part of a larger system.

Cities (and metropolitan areas, as we learned in Chapter 7) will face great challenges in the years to come. They will face immediate environmental hazards – whether toxic landfills from the last century or rising temperatures of a new climate epoch – and many of these will require significant financial and social resources. Cities will also face challenges to the normal order of things: taken-for-granted practices will become untenable as resources decline and populations increase. But cities – and their citizens – also face a wealth of opportunities as places are remade under these changing conditions. Chapter 13, on the future of cities, begins to paint a picture of just how we might make the most of this moment. Visit the book's companion website at www.wiley.com/go/cities for examples, case studies, and discussion questions, plus a list of useful films and other media, that are relevant to this chapter.

Critical thinking questions

1   Consider the way in which the importation of Owens River water to Los Angeles was heralded in the early twentieth century. How might such a project be greeted today? Under what circumstances might a city now be allowed to so exploit the resources of its hinterland?

2   Reflecting on recent disasters in the news, to what extent were these natural or man-made? Were the disasters characterized in this way in the media?

3   Consider the ecological footprint of your household, neighborhood, or city. How does this connect your life to places around the world?

What kinds of local environments are found in those places?

4   What constitute the LULUs (locally unwanted land uses) in your town or city? What kinds of people live closest to these?

5   Consider the types of environmental problems faced in slum areas. How are these different from the kinds of conditions Engels documented in nineteenth-century Manchester? Do you see the same trajectory for change in these areas?

6   How do concerns about the local and global environment complicate places' ability to provide for the security of their residents?

Suggested reading

Mike Davis, *Ecology of Fear: Los Angeles and the Imagination of Disaster* (New York: Vintage, 1998). In this engaging volume, Davis examines the myriad ways in which nature threatens Los Angeles and its residents (earthquakes, fires, floods, predatory animals, and even tornadoes) as well as the presentation of disaster in Hollywood films.

Kevin Fitzpatrick and Mark LaGory, *Unhealthy Places: The Ecology of Risk in the Urban Landscape* (New York: Routledge, 2000). A thorough account of the kind of health risks found in urban places, and their distribution.

Chester Hartman and Gregory D. Squires, eds., *There is No Such Thing as a Natural Disaster: Race, Class and Hurricane Katrina* (New York: Routledge, 2006). This edited volume provides a number of views of Hurricane Katrina and its aftermath, giving special attention to the ways in which race and class shaped outcomes for New Orleans residents.

Matthew E. Kahn, *Green Cities: Urban Growth and the Environment* (Washington, DC: Brookings Institution Press, 2006). A global look at the environmental impact of cities, drawing extensively on literature in economics.

John McPhee, *The Control of Nature* (New York: Farrar, Straus and Giroux, 1989). McPhee provides accounts of three largely futile attempts to bend nature to human (and urban) needs, including efforts to keep the Mississippi in its historic channel.

CHAPTER 13

The remaking and future of cities

KEY POINTS

→ The reasons and rationales for thinking about remaking cities into better places for the future.

→ How to be really clear about why and how place and space are related yet distinct.

→ How cities can be remade by macro-level forces and at critical moments.

→ How and why the remaking of cities from the bottom up occurs all the time.

→ The daunting scale of the future megacities in China and India.

→ Inclusivity, sustainability, and creativity as keys to better future cities.

Introduction to Cities: How Place and Space Shape Human Experience,
First Edition. Xiangming Chen, Anthony M. Orum, and Krista E. Paulsen.
© 2013 Xiangming Chen, Anthony M. Orum, and Krista E. Paulsen.
Published 2013 by Blackwell Publishing Ltd.

Contents

As we approach the end of the book, it is time to pose the most fundamental question regarding the city, a question that is central to the human experience now and into the future: can cities be remade in any way to make them more inhabitable and enjoyable for future city dwellers? This is both a theoretical and a practical question. Having moved from concept and theory (especially in Chapter 1, Chapter 2, and Chapter 3) through the bulk of empirical discussion to this conclusion, we now lean more heavily toward the practical side of the city, or the real process of making and remaking cities. The choice of this way of concluding this book stems from our joint conviction that the city is fundamentally a lived place for its ordinary residents. If this lived place is not good or good enough for most of its inhabitants, it should and can be remade for the better. This statement immediately triggers a consideration of concepts of "good cities," "ideal cities," and "caring cities," and the question of how to build one such city, let alone many of them. Since it is rarely possible to make a brand new cities, as happened in Shenzhen in China, mentioned earlier in the book, it is more realistic to talk about how to make existing cities better. Since any existing cities, especially those of a large scale, are entrenched and complex places, remaking them to achieve measurable improvements in either quality of life or the built environment can be a very long and challenging process.

How long is meaningfully long enough for us to expect to see much better cities in the future? Who will remake cities into better places in the future, and how? While people and policy are the obvious drivers of remaking cities, other existing and emerging conditions, such as growth momentum and new technology, will impinge heavily and yet unpredictably on the process. For instance, the explosive growth of megacities in China and India since the early 1990s is already creating supercities of 20 million or more people that will challenge any effort to provide better municipal infrastructure, and massive city-regions of as many as 50 million people are likely to emerge in the near future. Reciprocally, more energy-efficient and green-building technology will help make these gigantic cities more environmentally and socioeconomically sustainable. But the fragile ecological environment and expanding role of material technology will be up against variously strong or weak governments and entrenched urban culture in determining the future of the metropolis.

Unlike in China, the US federal, state, and local governments have a limited mandate and coffer for dealing with the remaking of weak cities that have been damaged by natural or man-made disasters (e.g., post-Hurricane New Orleans, or Detroit after the recent global economic crisis). The generally vibrant New York City confronts the tension between the accumulation of real estate wealth via continued renewal and gentrification versus displacement, inequality, and the loss of authenticity at the neighborhood level. Both sides of this process have been remaking New York from below with macro-structural forces. Before assessing how the balance between them will play out and reshape cities over a longer time horizon, it is necessary to reiterate our theoretical perspective in light of the recent spatial thinking as an anchor for discussing the opportunities for and constraints on remaking cities.

Between place and space
Reinforcing a theoretical vision

In Chapter 1, we introduced *place* and *space* as a pair of foundational concepts for studying cities. We discussed identity, community, and security as three salient attributes of place that define specific cities and specific sites in cities as material and emotional anchors to the lived human experience. We saw private and public as the two halves of space that are functionally distinctive but interdependent for urban life. Because of its more concrete and existential qualities, place is preferable and takes a conceptual and analytical priority over space in our treatment of cities. Since place is more concrete than space, it is easy to see places in the more abstract urban space, and identity sometimes overlaps between their conceptual boundaries. In this sense, we are not necessarily privileging place over space. More importantly, we have tried to use the conceptual power of place and space to examine cities throughout the book.

In working with and between both place and space, we also attempt to connect with Ed Soja's recent call for "putting space first" – that is, giving more attention to space than to time in studying urban change. Challenging the view that all spaces are socially constructed, Soja (2010) emphasizes that spatial processes also shape social relations and experiences. While we have looked into the social construction of physical space through a variety of empirical examples, we have largely sided with Soja's position by stressing the social characteristics and dimensions of both place and space. In doing so, we have gone beyond just saying that place and space are important to social life, making the two concepts the twin pillars of the city and its full dimensions.

We heed Ed Soja's plea for the clarification of the influence of spatial processes on social outcomes by stressing how place affects human experience in cities. Place is by no means a pre-existing cause for social life and human experience. Place instead is a collection of many sites lodged in and extending out from larger urban spaces. When we talked about China's booming manufacturing centers or factory-cities, such as Shenzhen and Dongguan (see Chapter 11), we were really conveying the reality of an intensive and expansive industrial space that dominates these dynamic centers. This industrial space contains specific places such as the humming factory floors and crammed dormitories where young migrant women maintain their meager daily existence, as portrayed in Leslie Chang's book *Factory Girls* (2008) (see Studying the city 11.1 and Figure 13.1). Furthermore, these places provide both an escape from the daily grind in the countryside and a barrier to more

Figure 13.1 Chinese workers sew T-shirts at the Bo Tak garment factory in Dongguan city in Guangdong province, southern China, May 27, 2005. *Source: © KIN CHEUNG/Reuters/Corbis.*

upward mobility for these young women, who have yet to be accepted as the cities' permanent residents. In this sense, these places exert a mixed effect on the identities and life chances of migrant workers. Created by larger economic forces such as foreign investment triggered by earlier government policies, these places function both as spatial and social opportunities and as constraints on the newly arrived migrant workers who have left rural life behind, often for good.

More than space, place distinguishes our orientation and approach to the understanding of the city. As previous chapters have indicated, the city has so many facets that no single textbook of any length can cover them all. But, when presented as comprising variegated places, the city's complexity is distilled into its simpler components, which can be made and remade. This means that when we study cities we really study places. More important to our place-centric treatment of cities is that places are not passive geographic locales or sites where urban life is lived. Instead, they contain and constitute the most engrained attributes of urban experience, such as identity and community. Since places are constantly reshaped by urban conditions that are both internal and external to the city, they are capable of sustaining a strong influence on how our identity and sense of community with the city change over time.

Remaking cities from above and at critical moments

In reinforcing our conceptual emphasis on place, and space to a lesser extent, we stress the dynamic nature of place and its pliability and resilience as both the object to be shaped and the source of influence. Places change or persist in response to how the larger and encompassing spaces around them are reorganized by local and extra-local forces. This turns places and spaces into a process of place-making that involves multiple actors, as well as events and shocks that are difficult to predict and almost impossible to control. In other words, the short- and long-term social impact of existing and evolving places is often contingent on how they are made in the first place and remade subsequently. Regardless of how vibrant some cities or places may be in their early formation, they can become very different places, either revitalized or eroded, depending on the severity of broader economic conditions and the effectiveness of government policy responses. This place-remaking comes into sharp relief at some critical moments in history, when forces of change that are invisible and gradual over long periods of time are unleashed and then restructure certain places permanently. When this happens, it presses us to dig deeper for more generalizable lessons about how cities can be remade, with profound social consequences. Again, a few examples illustrate what we mean.

The crisis of Detroit

We could easily have used Detroit throughout the book to make a number of important points, but we have saved it for the end to illustrate our central argument about remaking cities as places. Detroit after the 2008 global economic crisis tells a compelling story of how a once-powerful city has fallen and lost many of the important elements of "placeness." As a city known from the 1940s as the "Arsenal of Democracy" and the "car capital of the world," Detroit remained the fourth- or fifth-largest US city up to the 1970s and the top-ranked US city in total export value as recently as the early 1990s due to its massive amounts of automobile manufacturing. But, by 2006, at the peak of the booming stock and real estate markets, Detroit had lost more than half of its population (which peaked at almost two million around 1960) and had dropped out of the top 10 largest US cities. By the time the crisis hit in 2008 and worsened in 2009, Detroit had fallen US$300 million short of the funds needed to provide basic municipal services and had an unemployment rate of 28.9 percent, the highest of any major US city. Beyond these strikingly depressing figures was the even more tragic physical cityscape. A *TIME* magazine reporter who grew up in Detroit described his old neighborhood, his familiar place, in these haunting words:

> The neighborhood where I lived as a child, where for decades orderly rows of sturdy brick homes lined each block, is now the urban equivalent of a boxer's mouth, more gaps than teeth. Some of the surviving houses look as if the wrecker's ball is the only thing that could relieve their pain. On the adjacent business streets, commercial activity is so palpably absent you'd think a neutron bomb had been detonated. (Okrent 2009)

As more and more of Detroit's neighborhoods have deteriorated in this way, they have added up to a city-wide amalgamation of hollowed spaces that make Detroit's 357 square kilometers (138 square miles) "a post-apocalyptic nightmare," as lamented by the *TIME* reporter above (see Figure 13.2). Today, Detroit is the poorest major city in America, with a poverty rate of 34 percent, nearly triple the national average (Gray 2010).

For Detroit and other cities already on a downward spiral, the economic toll of the 2008 crisis was magnified. By the end of 2008, the average home price in Detroit stood at a very low US$18 513, and some 45 000 properties were in some form of foreclosure. A listing of tax foreclosures in Wayne County, which encompasses Detroit, ran to 137 pages in the *Detroit Free Press*. The city's public school system, facing a budget deficit of US$408 million, was taken over by the state. The crime rate, high for quite some time, rose further. For the residents of Detroit, place-based identity, community, and security were eroded at their roots, while a new dilemma was now staring them in the face: choosing between staying put in an unsellable property and walking away because their property value had fallen so low (see Florida 2009). Either option, if it is an option at all, hurts a great deal and further weakens or completely severs a Detroit resident's ties to his or her neighborhood as a place.

Figure 13.2 Vacant lots outnumber homes in some Detroit neighborhoods. Residents, planners, and government officials are now trying to reimagine and remake a city with only a fraction of its former population. *Source: © Zach Fein.*

This clear "lose-lose" situation for the people involved stands in contrast to the positive/ negative side of place attachment (see Exploring further 1.1). As Detroit illustrates, while the negative impact of the crisis on an already suffering city originated from a macroeconomic source afar – the subprime mortgages manipulated by Wall Street in Manhattan – it was felt at the very local place level by individual residents. This place-remaking by the crisis is particularly intense and consequential.

The remaking of Detroit

Post-crisis Detroit is the most extreme example, or an archetypical case (see Table 4.1), of the fallen deindustrialized US city. If it has clarified the local place-remaking effect of a global crisis, it also raises the critical question of how the worst-affected cities and places can be remade once again through effective policy responses or other means. A good answer, or even a partial one at that, can reinforce our claim about the central importance of place and how it can be remade with a more positive human experience. In declaring that the crisis will "reset" the geography of the United States' economic landscape, Richard Florida recently predicted that Detroit's population will shrink faster in the next few years than it has in the past few, and, as its population density dips further, the city's struggle to provide services and prevent blight across an ever-emptier landscape will intensify. He contends further that we cannot stop the decline of some places, and that we would be foolish to try (see Florida 2009).

The Mayor of Detroit has tried to save the city by turning to the federal government for support and was quoted as saying at the White House that "it's going to be very difficult for us to come back without some massive federal support." Yet this plea was met by a very reluctant response by Congressman Pete Hoekstra, a Republican representing western Michigan, who cautioned that "federal money shouldn't be used to prop up a broken Detroit, and should be used for a new Detroit" (Gray 2010). It is ironic that the old Detroit, wedded almost exclusively to automobile manufacturing, was propped up by persistent federal support through the championship and lobbying of John Dingell (the longest-serving Congressman) for his home district of southeastern Michigan. By resisting tougher safety regulations, more stringent mileage standards, and freer trade, Dingell believed that he served whole-heartedly the interests of his main constituencies (the three big auto-makers and their unionized workers and families), not realizing that his political and legislative efforts ended up weakening the competitiveness of the US automobile industry and thus contributing to the long decline of Detroit (Okrent 2009).

If the federal government's role is suspect at a time when it is most needed, who and what else can help Detroit now? First of all, should Detroit reduce its footprint since its municipal services can't be delivered effectively to the large uninhabited areas (nearly one-third of the land is empty and some 80 000 homes are vacant)? With plentiful available land, much of it brownfields, and depressed wages, Detroit is a prime candidate for new federal money to stimulate its revival. With US$2 billion in grants from the Obama Administration, Mayor David Bing tried to bring in battery makers to build plants on a large tract of abandoned land. Furthermore, the federal government did in fact spend US$18.4 billion on Detroit and the surrounding county in 2008, but this huge outlay lacked a broader purpose. Bruce Katz, director of Brookings Institution's Metropolitan Policy Program, argues that obtaining a much better return on the federal money would require Detroit to place its most dysfunctional agencies in receivership and to cooperate with its neighboring suburban municipalities on issues that cross political boundaries. Katz envisioned the federal government supporting the physical regeneration of Detroit through a new city plan for retrofitting economic and social activities to a much smaller demographic base: a city of more dense neighborhoods, large and small urban gardens, arts facilities, and entertainment parks built on old factory sites (Katz and Bradley 2009).

Following the spirit if not the detail of this proposal, Mayor Bing has implemented the so-called Detroit Works, which aims to relocate residents from supposedly vacant neighborhoods to "seven or nine urban villages" through incentives – for example, continued city services such as fire engines, water, and electricity. The hollowed-out areas are then set aside for "future development." This clean or blank slate approach may amount to a large-scale remaking of a major American city, and, more importantly, of the many smaller living places in the city. Some businesspeople have proposed an alternative and perhaps controversial way to reuse and remake empty urban spaces (see Making the city better 13.1 for details).

While reducing Detroit's footprint through a sort of strategic contraction seems to make some sense based on economics, it smacks of the old urban-renewal practice of ghetto

MAKING THE CITY BETTER   13.1

Urban agriculture in Detroit and beyond

In Detroit and other cities, the purpose of urban farms has as much to do with recreation and education as it has to do with the actual production of food. Small urban farms are encouraged in poor areas of cities to give young residents something productive to devote time toward, to educate residents on the importance of healthy eating, and to provide some healthy food options in areas of the city that are typically lacking a wide variety of healthy groceries for residents to choose from (Urban Farming 2011).

However, in Detroit, where the city's population is rapidly shrinking and vacancy is becoming a major problem, people are beginning to turn toward urban agriculture as a solution to another host of economic problems. John Hantz, a wealthy Detroit resident, proposed urban agriculture as a possible way to solve the city's problem of being too big for its current population. The hope is that turning much of the vacant city land into urban farms will artificially create scarcity and raise property values in the city so that the real estate market can begin to operate under normal circumstances again. While the idea faced a decent amount of criticism from Detroit residents and community activists arguing that the idea was a land grab scheme, other organizations, such as the American Institute of Architects, came forward to support the idea by affirming that "Detroit is particularly well suited to become a pioneer in urban agriculture at a commercial scale" (Whitford 2009). Hantz Farms propose to provide hundreds of green jobs; a supply of fresh, healthy foods for many residents living under "food desert" conditions in the city; better environmental quality in the city; tourists from outside the city who will patronize other local businesses; and the consolidation of city resources now that emergency services and utilities no longer have to be stretched so thinly across sparsely populated neighborhoods (Hantz Farms Detroit 2011).

Hantz Farms is not the only urban agriculture project in Detroit, and there are many smaller, community-based efforts with similar goals in mind. For example, a community group called Distributed Power is also maintaining urban farms on vacant land in the city in order to both put the empty land to good use and provide affordable and healthy food to local residents who otherwise might not have access to them (Connolly 2011). Another example can be found in Baltimore, where city schoolchildren, city agencies, and small non-profits are working together to create sustainable urban agriculture in order to improve health and employment levels in their city (Shenot 2010).

removal that goes back to the 1960s. It has re-emerged conveniently in post-crisis Detroit with an intended goal or unintended consequence of deconcentrating poverty. This policy has also been attempted in Detroit for the purpose of removing concentrated poverty through the dispersal or emptying of poor, flooded neighborhoods, yet it has been met with uneven resistance by activists and residents.

Beyond the limited attempts of the government, people, primarily young people, have begun to remake Detroit by seeking new opportunities in the city. As *The New York Times* reported in July 2011 (Conlin 2011), set against the general decline of the city's population over the past decade, downtown Detroit had experienced a 59 percent increase in the number of college-educated residents under the age of 35 – nearly 30 percent more than two-thirds of the US's 51 largest cities. This influx of socially aware hipsters and artists roams the streets of Detroit. As in Berlin, which was revitalized in the 1990s by young artists migrating there for the cheap studio space (as discussed in Chapter 11), Detroit's city leaders may have this new generation of "creatives" to thank if they can help to revive the city core, which is already regaining trappings of a thriving youth culture: trendy bars and restaurants that have brought pedestrians back to once-empty streets. A group of real estate brokers have begun to pitch the units in a 1920s office tower called the Broderick, which may be turned into a 127-unit apartment building with a restaurant, lounge, and retail stores. Detroit became attractive again due to simple economics. Real estate is cheap by urban standards, and the city is so eager to attract educated young residents that it offers strong subsidies to new arrivals. In April 2011, *Blueprint America*, a National Public Radio program, profiled an effort called "Live Midtown," an incentive program created to lure some of the 30 000 employees of the midtown's major anchor institutions (Wayne State University, Detroit Medical Center, and Henry Ford Health System) to move from the suburbs back into the city. By the end of June, 178 people were reported to have taken advantage of deep discounts on rent (US$2500 in the first year and $1000 in the second) or purchases (US$20 000 toward the purchase of their primary residence). This upbeat news triggered the media to make an unfair comparison to gentrified Brooklyn in New York City (Hughes 2011; see below).

Place-remaking on a larger scale

The lesson learned from Detroit – that its areal size is too big for its shrunk population, especially when its main economic engine is dead – sheds light on the contrasting territorial and demographic expansion of already very large cities and city-regions in developing countries (see Chapter 11). This opposite trend to Detroit, ironically, exerts a similar place-remaking pressure on the smaller spatial components within and around developing megacities. Megacities, those with 10 million or more people, can cloud our view of the micro-level pressure of scale and density on the meaning of place. With 20 million or more people, "**metacities**" (or supercities) may obscure the deeper reality of place even more. These cities force us to search harder for how place is made, used, and remade by peeling away layers of intersected economic, political, and social spaces. Looking through the bi-focal lens of industrialized or postindustrial versus developing, Rem Koolhaas, the renowned Dutch architect, sees the megacities of tomorrow as more Lagos-like and less Tokyo-like (see Figure 13.3) (Heathcote 2010). This view seems logical in light of the faster and more expansive growth of megacities like Lagos and the severe contraction of cities like Detroit. A broader and more nuanced look across the world, however, yields a more complex crossover picture of the shifting

metacities A new term used to describe cities that have 20 million or more people.

mega-scaled urban forms that both continues and deviates from earlier patterns. As the urban cores of mature industrialized cities have declined or hollowed out, their outlying areas – more distant suburbs – have stretched the metropolitan boundaries and stitched them together. This massive metropolitan spread was envisioned by Jean Gottmann in the classic book *Megalopolis* as early as 1961 for the northeastern United States, an area also known as **BosWash** (see Exploring further 7.1).

On the other side of the Atlantic around the same time, Israeli/French architect and planner Yona Friedman predicted a European transnational version of the BosWash corridor of contiguous urbanization that would extend from Oxford through London, northern France, and the Benelux countries to the Ruhr valley in Germany (see Figure 11.10) (Heathcote 2010). Again ironically, while the central cores of all developing megacities such as Shanghai and Mumbai have been the heart of the urban explosion, these cities have grown out, albeit unevenly, toward and beyond their rural hinterlands, reinforcing an earlier form of extended metropolitan region of mixed urban–rural landscapes that emerged in Southeast Asia in the 1960s. But it is the much larger scale of the megacity regions in rapidly urbanizing China that deserves the final scrutiny regarding place-remaking and its consequences.

Moving from Detroit to China's large cities to see the remaking of place is like traveling from one end of the urban spectrum to the other. This shift reveals every facet of the contrast between shrinking and expanding cities, but the fundamental difference is the abundant and powerful urban investment that accounted for over half of China's overall GDP growth from the early 1990s onward. This massive investment drove China's cities to expand at a rapid pace: the incorporation of neighboring land and its resident

> **BosWash** The expansive region stretching 500 miles from Boston to Washington, DC. The focus of Jean Gottmann's book *Megalopolis*.

Figure 13.3 Crowded and chaotic Lagos provides one model of what the future might look like for the majority of city dwellers. *Source: Photo: Pius Utomi Ekpei/AFP/Getty Images.*

population accounted for 130 million people, while rural-to-urban migration was responsible for about 113 million (Devan et al. 2008). The process allowed local governments to build up much infrastructure and services for the newly incorporated land and population. If the shrinking and economically depressed physical landscape of Detroit reminds us of a so-called Third World city, with its poor slums, the large Chinese city today is remarkably free of these conditions. But, in terms of place-remaking, the exploding cities of China, especially the megacities, have undergone a greater transformation of their central cores and outlying areas, which in turn has remade many specific places of everyday life.

We return briefly to Shanghai to summarize the drastic, planned remaking of both central-city and peripheral areas. As a result of Shanghai having the most densely populated central city area and the highest housing prices of China's cities, its municipal government drew up a massive plan to build "one new city and nine new towns" with a combined population of 5.4 million, plus 60 new small towns with populations of around 50 000 each. Millions of Shanghainese may soon have to choose, if they haven't already, between moving out to the new and more spacious suburban housing or staying put in the old and crowded central-city dwellings. Those who have moved enjoy the lower mortgage payments, larger living spaces, better air quality, green parks, modern facilities, and reduced noise in the suburban towns of Pudong, but they miss their familiar social networks and the more convenient shopping and transportation. Despite the fairly generous compensation offered by the government and/or property developers for vacating housing units slated for demolition, some residents refuse to move because they do not like the idea of the inconvenience of a long commute to and from downtown Shanghai. Others are put off by the lack of commercial facilities and social services. However, as more amenities such as shopping centers, schools, and hospitals become available in the suburbs, more families are likely to relocate there. While this will reduce the high density in the city center, it may trigger the US-style suburban sprawl that has contributed to the decline of cities such as Detroit. The growing population pressure calls for 200 000 new housing units per year to be added in Shanghai for the next 10 years, and so the city is looking to spread and stretch out further sooner rather than later (Chen 2007; Chen et al. 2009). The displaced residents in central Shanghai make it easy to trace how places can be remade, especially during periods of disrupting urban redevelopment.

Daily place-remaking from below

Most places in mature developed-country cities do not change very often or very drastically unless they are altered by powerful external shocks such as the global financial crisis, as in the case of Detroit. In comparison, developing-country cities such as those in China experience rapid change unleashed by powerful government policies. There are, however, places in both developed and developing cities that are stable and resilient in the face of shocking events and disruptive policies. The existence of these places suggests that the remaking of place does not occur only as a result of macro or top-down influences emanating from external sources, far or near. Indeed, there are bottom-up ways of changing places that involve a variety of local actors at the community and neighborhood levels, although these actors do not always act independently and with full autonomy. A brief look at how places can be made from below offers a complementary and more nuanced perspective on the key attributes of place (identity, community, and security) and, more importantly, on their profound meanings and symbiotic relationships with human experience.

Remaking neighborhoods and communities

Cities as places are fundamentally socio-spatial collections of living and lived neighborhoods and communities where the most emotional (deep) and practical (surface) human experiences are rooted and extended out into the larger world. In a truly local sense, many of these places have in the past been shielded from the full force of external influence and thus have been able to sustain their more or less self-contained existence. But this is no longer possible in our current age, in which cities and communities simply do not exist and function as independent and self-referential local places. They instead have become part of larger and more globally and regionally linked economic and social spaces, and therefore are more vulnerable to being remade from above. However, we recognize the strong relative capacity of local places – stemming from joint individual, organizational, and communal sources and resources – to remake themselves. We will turn briefly to New York City for some grounded insights into the remaking of neighborhoods as microspaces.

The remaking of Brooklyn, New York

While the gentrification of Brooklyn has been a familiar story since the mid-twentieth century, it has taken on a new twist in recent years with the creation of names for amalgamated neighborhoods; for example, "ProCro" (for Prospect and Crown Heights) and "BoCoCa" (for Brooklyn Heights, Cobble Hill, and Carroll Gardens). *The New York Times*, on April 3, 2011, reported on this phenomenon with a feature on "twenty under-the-radar microneighborhoods." One of them, the Gowanus area, or what *The New York Times* named "Superfund South," has been undergoing a renaissance from an old center of industrial and shipping activity since the 1860s and problems associated with industrial zoning and sewage overflow through a toxic canal. As a result of renters seeking more space for less rent and shopkeepers needing bigger footprints, Gowanus has turned into a bustling nightlife district. Not long ago, neighborhoods such as Gowanus, or Superfund South, were part of the larger and less differentiated South Brooklyn (Osman 2011). In various ways – through an overhaul of cultural space or the opening of a fancy building or a restaurant – these neighborhoods have become more lively, upscale, and even glamorous microspaces (Robledo 2011).

But not all is good and simple about this micro-scale remaking of these old Brooklyn neighborhoods. The early gentrifiers from the 1960s onward were, paradoxically, tied to modernity by education and occupation but looking for premodern authenticity in their private lives. Middle-class, white gentrifiers – in an interesting dimension to their politics – supported the nascent Reform Democrat movement in New York City in the 1960s and 1970s. These "white ethnic" residents were also conservative in trying to preserve the low-scale, emerging middle-class character of these neighborhoods. Sharon Zukin – a leading urban sociologist and keen observer of New York's cityscape – has followed this phenomenon for decades and has recently brought her earlier work on the subject up to date in her book, *Naked City*. Zukin (2010) has observed the loss of the small scale and local identity of these microplaces as increasing numbers of wealthy gentrifiers, cocktail bars, Starbucks, and chain merchandisers have moved in and replaced tenement dwellers, "mom and pop" store owners, and groups of artists. Her analysis is that this phenomenon boils down to a loss of "authentic" New York, or of the city's soul.[1]

From Detroit and New York to China and Shanghai – again

We have learned something about the remaking of cites and places by looking at Detroit in the context of the external shock of a severe economic crisis and at New York from the ground up in terms of small-scale and cumulative gentrification and renewal. China and Shanghai, again, will teach us about a very different kind of remaking of communities.

Between the Chinese city of the first 30 years after the founding of the People's Republic in 1949 and the Chinese city of the three decades following the 1979 reform, there was an initially gradual and subsequently accelerated breakdown of the structure and meaning of community. In the pre-reform Chinese city, community, if there was one, existed as self-contained organizational and geographic places around the socialist work unit (**danwei**), which provided living quarters, educational and healthcare facilities, and all social services to its mostly lifelong employees and their families (see Figure 13.4). Although this communal arrangement fostered – or, more accurately, forced – a sense of politicized identity and even loyalty, it served as a governance mechanism that ensured grassroots social control and political stability. Despite the lack of individual freedom and mobility, the arrangement created and sustained interpersonal familiarity and a sense of communal existence and life.

danwei **(Chinese)**
Generally translated as *work unit*; any state-owned enterprise or agency acting as both employer and self-contained community in pre-reform China.

Figure 13.4 The entrance to a work unit (*danwei*) named North China Optico-Electric Co. The *danwei* provided workers with housing and needed services, and a compulsory type of community. New urban forms have eroded that old model of community, without yet replacing it with a new one. *Source: Photo © Jeanne Boden (www.chinaconduct.com).*

All this began to shift with the reform and restructuring of state-owned enterprises in the 1980s, which first loosened and later dropped the lifetime employment system as the anchor for the *danwei*-based community. The introduction of contractual employment facilitated individual mobility within and between cities. More importantly, the accelerated privatization of state and public housing pulled the carpet from under the residential structure of the old community. The end of the welfare housing system, coupled with increasing job mobility, moved most city dwellers onto the track of buying market housing in the high-rise apartment blocks dotting the urban landscape. In addition, the growing number of migrants from small cities and rural areas, either in white- or blue-collar jobs, have become new city residents, joining the majority of homeowners and apartment renters. The emergence and expansion of gated low-rise residential communities or villas, some built to luxury standards and with Western names, has further diversified and fragmented living choices. The combination of all these conditions has culminated in the end of the *danwei* community as both a residential unit and a governance mechanism (Bray 2006).

What could possibly replace the old *danwei* community in the exploding cities in China? The answer is very little, in terms of creating a new kind of community to which people could attach their identity. In fact, as a result of the faster pace of life and the fact that residents now live alongside people with different employers and from diverse backgrounds, they do not know their neighbors well and have little interaction with them. Although the politicized community of the pre-reform era did not allow full and trusting relations, neighbors bonded on the basis of their equal socioeconomic status and extended families maintained strong connections, especially in the *linong* houses (see Chapter 11). In comparison, the alienated strangers in the new dense residential spaces create new barriers to communication with one another, which is reminiscent of the paradox of crowding and isolation in the tradition of Louis Wirth (see Figure 2.6). During Xiangming Chen's fieldwork in Shanghai, he heard about a tragedy in which a death in a high-rise residential building was not discovered by neighbors until odors from the decomposing body began to spread down the hallway. He also met Chinese planners and architects who have lamented the loss of community and struggled to fill that void. Using survey data in 2001, Chen and his Shanghai-based collaborators found that local residents with the most personal global connections (having been overseas, having worked for foreign companies locally, and so on; see Chapter 11) were less satisfied with community safety, air quality, and the environment than those with fewer or no global connections. With regard to community-based cultural, organizing, and participatory activities, the level of satisfaction for the people with the most global connections was lower than that for those without these connections. This suggests that global connections and their implied frame of reference might stimulate a higher level of local community participation (Lu et al. 2009). At two levels, this research shows that the lost community in rapidly urbanizing China can be regained as meaningful places even and especially when their residents bring a global reference to bear on their perception of and potential participation in the local community.

The entry of the global into Shanghai's local context is not surprising, given the retreat of the state in shaping community spaces. However, the state remains very relevant and present in other national and local settings where places are made and remade by individual residents in seemingly non-state ways. The Brazilian *favela* community provides an example of this that helps us to understand how the state penetrates poor and informal living spaces that lack much material evidence of formal state institutions and practices. This differs considerably from the Chinese state-driven model of city and community rebuilding, which has prevented slum communities of the *favela* kind from emerging. Through detailed ethnographic research on the *favela* community of Pirambu in the northeastern Brazilian *favelados* Dwellers in a *favela*, a Portuguese term for slums in Brazilian cities.

city of Fortaleza, geographer Jeff Garmany produced varied evidence on the long-standing practices of residents and community-based organizations that carry out the state's functions. By mobilizing local non-governmental organizations or churches, both the residents and community organizations address health, legal, political, infrastructure, zoning, and environmental issues (Garmany 2009). While we recognize this grounded insight, we also see it as reflecting the limits of the state in terms of making and remaking the reality of the *favela* as a lived community. In practical terms, it is the *favelados* (*favela* dwellers) who make the real difference to how the identity, community, and security associated with their places are socially constructed and experientially felt. The very fact that the state is indirectly involved in shaping local places reinforces our point here that places can be remade from below at any and all times.

Remaking cities for the future

We have tried to demonstrate that cities can be and have been remade by both powerful macro-forces from above and outside and grounded individual and community efforts from below and within. Now we turn to a discussion of why and how to remake cities into better places for the future. The rationale starts with a full recognition that cities of the past and present, especially developing megacities, have engendered a host of problems and challenges such as poverty, inequality, housing shortages, traffic congestion, and environmental degradation, to name a few. While these may be seen in narrowly problematic terms and may be labeled as "urban pathologies or ills" (Dogan and Kasarda 1988), we prefer to see them as being accompanied by or associated with the adaptive capacity and spirit of cities during the course of their development. This process itself is inherently one of remaking places either by more "natural" evolution and growth or drastic intervention and redesign. If the wretched living conditions of the British working class in eighteenth-century Manchester could be and indeed were improved (see Studying the city 2.1) through growth, wealth accumulation, and institutional responses, it should give us hope for addressing the daunting problems confronting twenty-first-century Detroit and Lagos.

As some may be disillusioned about the living conditions of slums in many developing megacities as a result of their portrayal by Mike Davis (2006), we have presented evidence on the vibrant activities of slum dwellers in Mumbai (see Chapter 11) and the relatively orderly existence in the Brazilian *favela* (earlier in this chapter). It is not simply that we are more optimistic about the future of cities than others. Rather, we view cities as places overlaid with the deepest human attachment to identity, community, and security, which should stimulate desires and actions of all kinds to make or remake cities into better places. To probe deeper into how to remake future cities better for the human experience, we revisit the projected scenarios of the urban future featuring large developing cities using China and India as two illustrative cases.

Scaling up and looking forward

To clearly see how cities today can become better cities in the future, we must place the efforts and policies for achieving this goal in the context of the global urban future. As we pointed out in Chapter 10, the hallmark of global urban growth for the next two or three decades will be accelerated urbanization in developing countries marked by the continued enlargement of already very large cities. New York, London, and Tokyo, generally regarded as the top global cities in terms of economic dominance and influence (see Chapter 3), were among the world's largest cities from 1950 to 2010. In 2020, while Tokyo (plus its extended metropolitan region) will hold its top ranking, the top 10 megacities will also include (in descending order of size) Mumbai, Karachi, Dhaka, Shanghai, Mexico City, São Paulo, and Lagos (see Figure 10.3). Lesser-known cities in the urban developing world, such as Tianjin in China, will also move up the size hierarchy to catch up with New York and London. While there will be few cities or metropolitan regions of 10 million or more people in the industrialized world, the developing countries will supply and sustain the lion's share of the world's most populous cities in the future. As a caveat to this scenario, a large group of developing-country cities that will enter the world's top 600 cities (which will generate 60 percent of global GDP growth from 2010 to 2025) will have populations of between 150 000 and 10 million (McKinsey Global Institute 2011). To anticipate the full scale of future urban growth, it is important to understand how to project this growth (see Studying the city 13.1).

STUDYING THE CITY   13.1

Projecting urban growth

In order for planners and scholars to understand what their community is going to need in the future, it is critical for them to be able to accurately predict how fast their population is growing. With this information, planners are more effectively able to project and plan for urban growth, so that the city is able to accommodate new residents with the proper amount and effective placement of infrastructure and other amenities.

For starters, the most basic way to project urban growth is to calculate the absolute and percentage change of population in an area. To do this, one simply finds the difference between populations in two given years. This can be done over 5, 10, 20, or even 50 years, depending on the scope of the project. The difference is the absolute change in population. Alternatively, one can look at the percentage change in population, which is calculated by dividing the absolute change in population by the population in the beginning year. For instance, if the population in Frederick County, Maryland in 2000 was 195 277 and it grew to 233 385 by 2010, the absolute change in population between 2000 and 2010 was

$$233\,385 - 195\,277 = 38\,108$$

And the percentage change in population between 2000 and 2010 was

$$38\,108 \div 195\,277 = 0.1951 \approx 19.5\,\text{percent}$$

Now, the simplest population projection derives from the researcher assuming that the population will continue to grow linearly. More complicated projections can be done with more complex formulas, such as a logistic growth formula, if the researcher has reason to believe that the population may be just beginning to rise exponentially or will eventually plateau. However, for the simplest of linear projections, a researcher can simply multiply the percentage change by the most recent population and add that number to the most recent population. For example, if the population in Frederick County, Maryland was 233 385 in 2010 and the percentage change between 2000 and 2010 was 19.5 percent, then the population in 2020 (10 years later, because the percentage change being used in this particular case is for a period of 10 years) could be projected to be

$$233\,385 + (233\,385 \times 0.195) = 278\,895$$

The researcher could then find the population for 2030 by simply going a step further:

$$278\,895 + (278\,895 \times 0.195) = 333\,280$$

It behooves many urban researchers to use software such as SPSS or even Excel to calculate these projections with improved efficiency when handling a large number of population estimates, or when using more complex formulas. In most cases, however, urban growth projections need to be taken to a higher level of analysis in order to be useful. To do this, many scholars and planners incorporate spatial and explanatory elements into their urban growth projections. By explaining where and why the population in a community is changing, it becomes easier to understand what areas of the city are going to experience more growth in the future.

Much of the information pertinent to this kind of analysis can be presented through the use of maps and GIS (geographic information systems) software. By looking at changes in population, property values, local employment opportunities, nearby amenities, population density, vacancy rates, and other indicators of urban growth spatially through the use of maps and other visual tools, it becomes easier to draw conclusions about why certain areas may be growing faster than others and therefore easier to predict how much longer the current growth rate can be expected to last. It is also helpful to look at the community's zoning map to find what the current density limitations are in any particular area, and to track potential changes in the zoning code or map to know when and where that density cap, and therefore population cap, could be changed (Wang and Hofe 2007).

The China and India scenarios and their wider implications

Given the population sizes of China and India and their rapid urban and economic growth, the two countries will obviously be integral to charting the global urban future. As China and India urbanize, a large chunk of the world will urbanize with it. But there are wrinkles in this easily identifiable and seemingly linear trend that will reveal the most striking challenges facing cities everywhere, especially large developing-country cities. Let's start with China, which may more than India furnish the most instructive lessons about both the short and long term, and the direct and indirect influences of huge urban scale on cities as places.

While we may be struck by how fast China has urbanized, from less than 20 percent urbanization around 1980 to about 50 percent officially in 2012 (see Figure 10.1), this process has only served to position China well to sustain additional widespread growth in its large cities and megacities, which is being driven much more by migration than by natural increase. Take Shanghai as a somewhat extreme example: in-migration accounted for the entirety of demographic growth from 1995 to 2006, while natural increase remained negative due to the city's extremely low fertility rate of about 0.08 – well below replacement level (see Figure 13.5 and the definition of natural increase in Chapter 5). The McKinsey Global Institute (2009) has projected that China will gain 221 cities of over one million people by 2025 – a huge gain when it is considered that today Europe has only 35 such cities and the United States only nine. Twenty-three of the new million-plus cities will have five million or more people. By 2015, the million-plus cities will account for approximately

70 percent of China's total urban population, which will rise to 926 million from less than 572 million in 2005. Of the 350 million new urbanites (more than the entire US population today), 240 million (about 70 percent) will be rural migrants. This momentum will push China's urban population to past the billion mark around 2030. China's massive urban transformation since 1979, which is historically unprecedented in its combined scale and speed, puts a host of challenges to place and human experience in the spotlight. At this point of the book, we look to the future to capture some glimpses of the projected impact of such a massive agglomeration of people and activities on specific places and individual experience. This goal will partly be accomplished via identifying the key pressure points that cities will have to deal with in terms of the supply of resources that are important for people and places.

The McKinsey report mentioned above has projected a set of stunning demands for residential development, transport infrastructure, and consumer goods from the urban forecast. China will need to build 40 billion square meters (431 billion square feet) of floor space over the next two decades, which will translate into the construction of 20 000–50 000 new skyscrapers of more than 30 floors each, equal to 10 New York Cities. China also will need to build five billion square meters (54 billion square feet) of road and up to 28 000 kilometers (17 398 miles) of commuter rail. With 170 Chinese cities that will need mass-transit systems by 2025, this may lead to the largest boom in mass-transit construction in history. On the energy front, the projected urban growth will call for the construction of scores of new coal-fired power plants before 2025. The urban trends will also lead to a five-fold increase in water consumption that could worsen the existing water shortage created by ongoing heavy agricultural usage on the one hand and water pollution on the other (60 percent of China's river water is already below international potable standards). These demands will require a huge pool of investment capital, but China's projected growth and GDP over the next two decades – the latter of which may well surpass that of the United States by 2020 and account for one-fifth of the world's total – will be capable of furnishing what is required. Regarding the likely distribution of this huge amount of created wealth, the estimate of the McKinsey Global Institute (2009) is that 40 percent of China's higher-income class will be concentrated in the eight megacities of 10 million-plus people by 2025. This projected demographic, infrastructure, and economic growth appears to put China at the

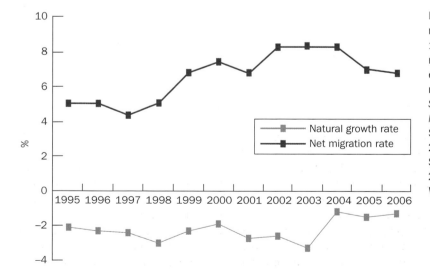

Figure 13.5 Net migration and natural growth rate in Shanghai, 1995–2006. Net migration rate = in-migration rate minus out-migration rate. Natural growth rate = birth rate minus death rate. *Source: Data from Shanghai Municipal Statistics Bureau,* Shanghai Statistical Yearbook 2007. *Adapted from UN-HABITAT,* State of the World's Cities 2008/2009 (London and Sterling, VA: Earthscan).

forefront of the unsettling urban future, but some similarly staggering projections for India suggest that China's prominence will not be unrivaled.

According to projections in another, comparable study by the McKinsey Global Institute (2010), by 2030 India will have 68 cities of over a million people (up from 42 today) and will reach a total urban population of 590 million by 2030. While these figures seem to pale in comparison with the projected numbers for China, they herald an urban future that will require a massive outlay of US$1.2 trillion for 700–900 million square meters (7.5–9.7 billion square feet) of commercial and residential space (or a new Chicago every year); 2.5 billion square meters (27 billion square feet) of roads; and 7400 kilometers (4600 miles) of metros and subways – these figures represent 20 times the capacity in each category added in the first decade of the twenty-first century. India will find these targets more difficult to meet than China, as it has been lagging behind China severely in terms of building up infrastructure. However, in the McKinsey Global Institute's somewhat optimistic economic and human resource projections, India's GDP will multiply by five times, fueled by the net increase of approximately 270 million in the working-age population, and 70 percent of new jobs will be concentrated in cities. This scale of economic growth will produce 91 million urban middle-class households, up from 22 million around 2010 (McKinsey Global Institute 2010). These scenarios will keep India right on the heels of China throughout the next phase of their urban expansion, which will continue to dwarf that of the rest of the developing world.

Before assessing what this China- and India-dominated future urban world may mean for the making and remaking of their cities and those of other countries, let us touch on the huge demand for steel, cement, and other building materials that construction on this scale entails. As a result of two decades of building cities, factories, and factory-cities on a massive scale, China now consumes about 40 percent of the world's total output of steel, cement, and copper annually. The projected scaling up of city construction in China will impose great upward pressure on the prices of these materials. It will also strain the sources of energy needed to run the sprawling factories and to heat and cool the huge office and residential towers, considering that buildings in cities account for 40 to 50 percent of the world's total energy use. Given the limited availability of these resources within China, it is easy to envision China further stepping up the effort to purchase energy and materials from other countries. While this is not a main focus of this book, you should not lose sight of the strong impact of rapid urbanization and city-building in China on the price and availability of energy and commodities on a global scale.

While these overall projections point to a greater presence and dominance of Chinese and Indian cities on the world stage, varied scenarios regarding the uneven growth of Chinese cities are more useful for understanding the differential economic and social consequences of China's national and local development. The McKinsey Global Institute has offered four scenarios: (1) supercities (a few very large cities); (2) hub and spoke (clusters of small and mid-sized cities around large cities); (3) distributed growth (a large number of mid-sized cities); and (4) proliferation of towns (a large number of small cities). Based on data analysis, the McKinsey Global Institute favors a more concentrated model based on either of the first two scenarios for China's future urban growth. The reasons for this advocacy include: China's ability to exploit efficiencies of scale, its more developed infrastructure, some China-specific advantages relating to more seasoned administrators, the concentration of multinationals in China, and its much-developed higher-educational institutions in large cities. The concentrated approach would lead to advantages of 20 percent higher GDP per capita and 18 percent higher energy efficiency by 2025. However, more concentrated urban growth could also lead to mixed environmental consequences including saving more farmland and mitigating water pollution on the one hand and increasing water usage, traffic congestion, and transport emission problems on the other (Hantz Farms Detroit 2011). Regardless of how the growth trends thus far may induce one scenario over another, the powerful central and local levels of Chinese government are capable of intervening in future growth in ways that could change its course.

Interventions suggested by the McKinsey Global Institute include more transparent and consistent enforcement of control over already tightened land use, more infrastructure investment in supercities and hub–spoke clusters, and more incentives and disincentives that will force local officials to balance their performance in economic growth with that in regional cooperation, energy efficiency, and environmental protection (Hantz Farms Detroit 2011). Once local officials see their political careers as tied to advocating and promoting more balanced and sustainable cities, they will be more likely to deliver a higher quality of life to the residents of their cities. The **supercity** and the hub–spoke scenarios would place the strongest political pressure on these future municipal leaders to be more strategic and balanced in approaching the planning and governance of these massive connected urban places. The decentralization and localization of political power may offset the deficiency of state-driven urban growth by redirecting some attention to everyday life. In the light of this kind of politics of place-making, the Chinese context and its urban future become less exceptional and more relevant to understanding the relationship between urban scale, political power, and quality of place. With a future urban scale that is almost as massive as China's, India reinforces the same lesson – that denser development in the growing megacities can improve the quality of the lived environment by increasing the energy efficiency of buildings and appliances, industry, power distribution, agriculture, and transportation (Osman 2011). The Chinese and Indian urban scenarios point to another source of place-remaking beyond the power of the state and the pressure of scale, respectively.

> **supercity** A term used by McKinsey Global Institute to refer to cities with a population of 20 million or more

How will the hundreds of millions of current and future Chinese and Indian rural migrants live their lives in these megacities? In the Chinese context, they have lived and will continue to live in substandard and marginal residential spaces due to the residual constraint of the household registration system (*hukou*; see Chapter 10 and Chapter 11) and the lack of affordable housing. Yet they will not be crammed into large slums in the same way as will the majority of Indian migrants and migrants to Latin American and African large cities and megacities. Regardless of the role of the state, other non-state actors and actions will affect whether rural migrants will be living a fully or partially inclusive life in cities, or experiencing exclusion. These include professional planners/architects, private developers, community organizations, local residents, and early and already settled migrants. While their relative roles vary considerably across national and local contexts, each of them exerts a distinctive influence on the inclusiveness of cities and thus their quality of life and social meaning as lived places. Despite their main function of countering the state, they sometimes play a complementary role, as illustrated by the following Indian example.

We return here briefly to the Dharavi slum in Mumbai mentioned in Chapter 11. This is a complex and potentially lucrative place (given its central location) being remade jointly by the State (of Maharashtra) government and private developers to turn it into a desirable neighborhood that will offer market-rate residential real estate and provide improved housing and services to its longtime residents. The goal of balancing government planning and private development may be achieved through this private–public partnership formed in Dharavi. Private developers have struggled to manage the costs of capital and construction in trying to meet minimum government bids and deciding who will receive the 28 square meters (300 square feet) of free housing that is only available for families who took up residence before January 2000. Given the dilemma involved in weighing profitable development against unpopular evictions and shutting down thriving but unregistered businesses, which could trigger large-scale resistance, the Dharavi slum project has recently made its way into a rare case at the Harvard Business School (Hanna 2010). Setting aside the foray of private–public partnerships into slum redevelopment, it should be remembered that the residents of these places have built massive-scale informal housing and economic activities from within, and by doing so have built up a large swath of cities such as Mumbai and Kolkata. As the slum dwellers are the largest and habitual builders of their communities, they are the most important makers and stakeholders of the places they call and experience as home. Although their city- and community-building is often overshadowed by the construction of large office towers in Mumbai (see Figure 13.6), it represents a true bottom-up practice that may change how outsiders perceive urban slums (see Making the city better 13.2). This is ultimately a process that should be left to and driven by the cooperative effort of their residents and other parties such as the government.

Cities of the future and the future of cities

Inclusive cities are better cities. At the Future of Cities Pavilion at the 2010 Shanghai World Expo, the motto of which was "Better City, Better Life," a striking sign read "Imaging the Cities of the Future is Imaging the Future of Our Cities." At the Expo's

Figure 13.6 Construction on the Imperial Towers in Mumbai. In the coming years, the volume of new construction in Indian and Chinese cities will dwarf all cities in the West. However, large Chinese cities like Shanghai are much taller and more vertical than their Indian counterparts, such as Mumbai. *Source: Photo © Frédéric Soltan/ Corbis.*

MAKING THE CITY BETTER 13.2

Remaking slum housing

Many instances in which a city government slates slum housing reflect a focus on the improvement of places over lives, resulting in an overall decrease in the amount of affordable housing available in the city and the displacement of countless poor residents. Sociologist Sudhir Venkatesh wrote about such a pattern when the Robert Taylor Homes project was built in the place of former slum housing in Chicago. When it was built in the 1960s, the housing project upended social ties and relationships that had thrived on the streets of the slums; new ties that developed in the projects were later shattered when the Robert Taylor Homes were demolished in the 2000s (Venkatesh 2000). The same thing happened when Boston's West End slums were demolished in the early 1960s (see Studying the city 3.1). Slum housing is routinely demolished to prepare for mega-events such as the Olympics or the World Cup in order for cities to save face by hiding their problems from the international community. While some new units are built, these do not approach the number of units lost. There have been many other instances of the sort of disregard for the wellbeing of poorer residents that occurs when slums are remade or redeveloped. Influential activists and scholars such as Jane Jacobs and Mike Davis have written about how urban renewal movements throughout the world have actually done more harm than good to poor urban residents.

However, there are ways in which slum housing can be remade responsibly in order to best serve the needs of residents. One organization that has devoted a significant amount of research toward finding ways to effectively improve slum housing is the Development Innovations Group. By looking at slum transformation in São Paulo as an example of best practices, Development Innovations Group researcher David Smith has found conditions that must be met in order to successfully remake slum housing. São Paulo's program wasn't perfect, but Smith has analyzed the pros and cons of the city's approaches in the neighborhoods of Cingapura and Guarapiranga to pick apart what works and what doesn't (Smith 2008).

Smith argues that successful programs must strive to do the following: benefit entire slum areas as opposed to selected beneficiaries; create dense and pedestrian-friendly streets; never relocate the community for an extended construction period; more effectively induce investment in slum housing through incentives such as housing formalization or infrastructure improvements as opposed to imposing formal building standards on pre-existing homes; and, perhaps most importantly, bring in genuine community participation (Smith 2008). By taking steps away from the days of urban renewal and rampant demolition, instead moving toward methods of slum improvement, city governments can begin to utilize many of these suggestions and strategies to improve the lives of poor families while at the same time saving money previously wasted on urban renewal projects.

Theme Pavilion, a huge banner displayed "People Are the City." Together, these two signs point to a nice way of bringing this concluding chapter, and the central idea of the book as a whole, to a fitting end. In introducing you to cities and guiding you through how to understand them, we have put the human experiential aspects of place and space at the front and center of the book. Without humans as their inhabitants, cities are empty physical spaces. Human experience is the essence of cities everywhere. Improving cities is making the human experience better, and future cities should be better and more livable places for the human experience.

To imagine how future cities could improve the human experience, we have tried to clarify the forces and conditions that shape the spatial and social processes and outcomes that leave varied imprints on city dwellers. Much of the urban influence on the human experience has been favorable – for example, the beneficial effects of construction and transportation technologies on residence and mobility in modern cities. As a result of massive investment in new residential housing with amenities, the average Shanghai resident now has over 20 square meters (215 square feet) of living space – a five-fold increase from the four square meters (43 square feet) he or she had around 1980 and a significant improvement from the dilapidated housing without indoor toilets long occupied by millions. Unfortunately, though, not all urban growth has had a positive effect on all facets of the human experience. Sprawl in the United States, for example, has brought about a number of undesirable social and ecological consequences for suburban residents such as long and costly commutes, residential isolation, erosion of community, and high energy consumption (see Chapter 8 and Chapter 12). By describing the scope and locating the sources of these negative social and spatial effects on the human experience in this book, we intend to identify the critical domains where the remaking of our existing cities into better future places should take place.

As we see it, future cities should and must be better in terms of inclusivity, sustainability, and creativity. The current barriers against cities' increased inclusivity have been built up and entrenched into class and racial divisions, spatial inequalities of all kinds, and the unbalanced power of governance and planning discussed throughout the book. These barriers have kept most of the past and present cities deeply divided into stratified places and spaces of wealth versus poverty and of power versus powerlessness (see Chapter 6 and Chapter 7). They range, widely and ironically, from the permanent underclass in the South Side of Chicago and many parts of post-crisis Detroit to luxury gated compounds next to marginalized migrant settlements outside Shanghai to the sheer poverty in the slums of Mumbai and Lagos and finally to the segregated immigrant communities in suburban Paris. These differentiated places include their more privileged occupants in the realms of the good urban life but exclude other groups of city dwellers from accessing it. Cities that are more exclusive tend to be more contested and less stable places with eroded identity, community, and safety, while more inclusive cities possess and preserve these three valuable attributes of place much better. In this sense, the inclusivity of cities has a fundamental influence on whether their residents feel a sense of community and safety where they live. Inclusivity is therefore the first key to improving the cities of today, creating the better cities of tomorrow.

How do we make future cities more inclusive? Who and what mechanisms will be the most effective for this remaking of cities? Some may view the task itself as impossible, given the deep-seated causes of spatial inequality and exclusion. We, however, are more optimistic about the prospect of more inclusive cities, which we argue may originate from two sources, one somewhat unexpected (architects and planners) and the other more familiar (the state). The former possibility concerns the more active role of architects, designers, and planners in reshaping cities into more inclusive living places. By planning and designing the residential environment to accommodate people of more diverse backgrounds and conditions, and to improve their access to nearby public spaces, service facilities, and entertainment outlets, professional planners and architects can help to strengthen wide-ranging social interactions that can translate into collective trust, communal sentiment, and place identity. While some may view architects as merely technical actors in the building of cities, they make a critical difference to the most practical and microscopic details of residents' lived environments. Architects and urban designers, according to Richard Sennett

(2005), can do a lot to make cities less brittle and more inclusive. If we were to evaluate the inclusiveness of cities based only on the presence or absence of slums, we would give high marks to the megacities of China – especially Shanghai – that have been discussed extensively in this book. But there is more to the issue than meets the eye. Millions of migrant workers and their children in booming cities such as Shenzhen are excluded from full and equal access to housing, healthcare, and education in spite of the fact that they have already become de facto residents and contributors. This is an example of where and when the Chinese state, which led and drove this kind of city-building, could step up with more targeted and accommodating policies and resources for incorporating the large number of migrants into these cities as local residents. Bold state policy is capable of making the future Chinese city more inclusive from above, just as the living places in other cities can be remade by socially conscious architects and planners from below.

Inclusive cities also are more sustainable cities, but making future cities more sustainable goes beyond that. It primarily involves fully learning the lessons about the main sources of unsustainable urban growth in both (de)industrialized and rapidly industrializing countries. One such lesson concerns the increasingly unsustainable characteristics of the sprawling, car-driven, and energy-inefficient US cities, which in these aspects differ considerably from many European cities (see Figure 13.7 and Making the city better 13.3). Post-crisis Detroit is also not sustainable in terms of economic stagnation, severe deterioration in social service delivery, and permanently depressed housing stock. The 2008 crisis also exposed and amplified the economic malaise, namely large budgetary shortfalls, resulting from the simultaneously overstretched metropolitan region and its internal political fragmentation into small and autonomous municipalities that compete more fiercely for ever-dwindling resources. On the more encouraging side, the crisis appears to be revitalizing the long-

Figure 13.7 A woman and child bicycle through Vauban, a German suburb designed to be largely car-free. Homes are also constructed for maximum energy efficiency to enhance sustainability on multiple fronts. *Source: Photo © Martin Specht.*

MAKING THE CITY BETTER   13.3

Vauban, an auto-free suburb

Urban planners and local elected officials have often tried to limit the amount of automobile use in newly planned or redeveloped areas of the city by implementing traffic calming measures, designing higher-density and mixed-use neighborhoods, lowering the availability of free parking, and other strategies that coincide with the principles of smart growth. Suburbs are rarely considered to be part of the smart growth equation, except in the context of limiting their existence.

However, the German suburb of Vauban has changed this perception for the better. Leading by example, Vauban was constructed in 2006 to show the world that suburbs can exist without having to rely on private automobiles for transportation. By using a tram that runs down a main street through the center of town and connects to downtown Freiburg, as well as parking garages on the outskirts of town, Vauban is able to keep the rest of its narrow roads pedestrian-friendly and free of cars. Since the neighborhood is long and narrow, all residents are able to stay within a short walk from the main street (which supports a variety of businesses) and the tram, in order to access all of the amenities the nearby city has to offer.

Residents living in Vauban praise the design of the suburb and claim that being without a car has improved their quality of life by keeping stress levels down. Other residents enjoy the fact that they can let their children play in the streets without having to worry about their safety. In fact, the suburb seems to be doing so well that it has attracted the attention of planners and developers in other countries. In the United States, the Hayward Area Planning Association has made plans for a suburb called Quarry Village outside Oakland, which is intended to be relatively car-free, following the example set by Vauban.

Though both Vauban and the planned suburb of Quarry Village are excellent examples of environmental responsibility due to the way in which their designs encourage less driving, both suburbs are also very financially exclusive. If these communities prove to be successful and sustainable, the next step that planners and policy makers should take is to make these communities affordable (Rosenthal 2009).

standing, albeit limited, efforts to create more regionalist policies and programs for delivering services more efficiently and sustainably. The slow recovery as well as the more uneven performance of cities and regions in the wake of the recent crisis are likely to reinforce the growing momentum and tendencies toward sustainable urban development.

Regardless of the global financial crisis of 2008, sustainable urban development has gained new urgency and saliency from the demographic realities that are dawning on the world. With over 60 percent of its population projected to be living in cities by as early as 2020, China again is leading in the uphill battle against the limits of supportive resources such as energy and water. Besides trying to reduce energy intensity per unit of its economic output, China will need to use recycled water effectively for purposes other than drinking in order to ward off the water scarcity that already affects 90 percent of its cities, mostly those in the arid north. These efforts, however, will not be very effective in the light of China's contradictory practice of building large brand-new cities that stand as ghost towns, such as those on the Mongolian steppes. Other rapidly urbanizing countries face the same unsustainable urban future. Ho Chi Minh City – the capital city of Vietnam – has an infrastructure designed for only three million people and yet has eight million residents today and will grow to 20 million by 2020, thus becoming a supercity. There are simply not enough roads to accommodate the surging number of cars in the city, which holds 30 percent of the total number of cars in Vietnam but only 8 percent of the total national road surface. With about nine million people already, Jakarta, Indonesia's Capital, swells to almost 12 million from Mondays to Fridays due to the large influx of mostly poor commuters. This has prompted the municipal government to encourage these commuters to register as residents so that they can receive more public services such as small loans. In 1964, Singapore, recognizing that the lack of adequate and affordable housing is a major barrier to making large cities sustainable, had the foresight to construct public housing and make it available to its citizens through very low interest mortgages, with grants to those earning low wages. It is currently upgrading the old public housing to avoid its degeneration. As building sustainable cities has become more urgent and imperative, the pressure on governments and other players to act, both immediately and strategically, has been mounting – and will continue to grow. This urgency casts a worrying light on the projected and probably unsustainable scenario of urban growth and construction of China and India mentioned earlier.

What complicates the collective effort to remake cities into more sustainable places is the more complex, intertwined, and continuously evolving meaning and practice of urban sustainability. While it used to and still largely refers to ensuring enough material resources for the cities of today and the future, there are more distinctive economic, social, and cultural dimensions, both internal and external, to sustainable cities. Having attracted millions of rural migrants, the rapidly growing export-oriented factory-cities on China's booming coast, such as Shenzhen, must now confront the challenge of planning and delivering more badly needed services to sustain themselves. Ironically, while they need to provide considerably lower levels of service to a shrinking population, severely depressed postindustrial cities such as Detroit still face problems in terms of sustaining themselves due to the further loss of revenue from depopulation and poor residents becoming stuck in properties they can't sell. This also raises the question of whether to help poor people or poor places, which Edward Glaeser answered in his 2010 book *The Triumph of the City*, favoring the former. Economically deprived cities that are socially divided and exclusive are even more difficult to sustain. Even if gated communities and shanty towns have managed to exist side by side in and around some large Latin American cities, the ongoing friction and inevitable conflict between them will eventually spill over their narrow spatial divides. If cities lose their cultural traditions and fabric through rampant redevelopment without proper preservation, as has already happened in some cities in China, they will be without a sustainable foundation on which to build new and better urban environments.

Finally, we come to the crucial connection between sustainability and creativity as a key to remaking cities into better future places for the human experience. More sustainable cities need to be much more creative, but the question is what makes cities more creative in a lasting fashion. Looking back, it is easy to admire the creative role of new building and transport technologies, such as elevators and cars, in unleashing the rapid vertical and horizontal expansions of cities in the late nineteenth and early twentieth centuries. The same creative spirit and energy lasted through to the early twenty-first century, when energy-efficient buildings and electric cars helped to provide more sustainable and healthier environments in cities. In the cultural realm, creativity has enriched and enlivened the quality of life for city residents in successive generations. While these kinds of creativity are often associated with the educated (such as engineers or artists, or what Richard Florida has termed "the creative class"), much creative city living has originated from ordinary people, often in poor communities. For example, a community organization in a poor neighborhood on the outskirts of Mexico City has transformed a former waste dump into a well-used public space for renewed social interaction. This project reflects the deep belief of the community residents in their right to live an inclusive, sustainable, and healthy life (see Exploring further 13.1). For this and other achievements in cultural, health, environmental, educational, and employment programs, this Mexico City community organization received the fourth Deutsche Bank Urban Age Award in July 2010. It is these kinds of grassroots creative practices concerning the right to the city that contribute the most to the remaking of cities and communities into better and more humane places for the future.

EXPLORING FURTHER   13.1

The right to the city

A major breakthrough in the way in which scholars thought about the quality of urban life was the concept that residents living in an urban area had a *right* to the city. This idea was first developed in 1968 by Henri Lefebvre, a French sociologist who frequently wrote from the philosophical and sociological perspective of neo-Marxism.

Lefebvre emphasized the importance of urban social movements in bringing about individual rights to the city for vulnerable populations, and sought to provide a framework for those social movements in his book, *Le droit à la ville* (*The Right to the City*). The book was highly influential within social movements across the world, and especially in Latin America, where the right to the city was touted as a political slogan for debates and social movements promoting rights for the disenfranchised in urban areas (Reclaiming Spaces 2009).

However, even while the concept of poor and vulnerable populations having a right to access the resources and services that cities have to offer became increasingly popular, it was still not clear in many academic circles precisely what it meant for urban residents to have a "right to the city." In order to clarify the concept and to shed light on how this right could be exercised by urban dwellers to improve their quality of life, Mark Purcell (2002) closely examined and analyzed "the intellectual roots of the idea" in the writings of Henri Lefebvre.

Many of the problems that Lefebvre was trying to address through his book were linked to the growing disenfranchisement of poor laborers as the economy became increasingly globalized. As the globalization of markets expanded, so did the presence and influence of major international corporations such as the World Bank, the International Monetary Fund (IMF), and the World Trade Organization (WTO). As these organizations became increasingly influential in the global economy, national governments began to cede power both to these international corporations through financial agreements and other processes and to local governments via the devolution of power concerning economic affairs. And, as international corporations began to have more say over the economic decisions of countries and local governments began to focus more on exports than on ensuring a high quality of life and access to resources for their residents, citizens in some places across the world began to worry that democracy had fallen to the might of capitalism (Purcell 2002).

For Lefebvre, a solution lay in giving urban inhabitants a right to the city. By this, Lefebvre meant not only a right to access urban resources but also a right to full democratic control over decisions that would alter residents' urban space. Purcell describes Lefebvre's breakdown of urban space in the following three categories:

1. Perceived space: the relatively objective, concrete space people encounter in their daily environment.
2. Conceived space: mental constructions of space, and creative ideas about and representations of space.
3. Lived space: the complex combination of perceived and conceived space. It represents a person's actual experience of space in everyday life.

By showing just how expansive Lefebvre's definition of urban space is, we can begin to understand how radically different society would be if this version of the "right to the city" was embraced. Lefebvre stressed the importance of use value over exchange value, and argued that citizens have a right to full and complete usage of urban space, therefore eliminating the commoditization of space completely and giving inhabitants complete control over any decisions that would alter their urban space (Purcell 2002).

While many of the ideas that Lefebvre advocated when he introduced the concept of the right to the city are rather radical in nature, other writers and advocates have since altered the idea of urban inhabitants' right to the city to fit current political contexts. One of the most influential scholars to adopt and popularize the "right to the city" concept is David Harvey. Instead of a radically different anti-capitalist society in which urban inhabitants exercise complete control over every change to their urban space, Harvey focuses on giving urban inhabitants control over financial surplus. He recognizes the city as an agglomeration of trade that must bring in a fiscal surplus to exist. And, instead of wealthy individuals and organizations having complete control over the changes that occur in the urban area, this version of the "right to the city" would give urban inhabitants complete democratic control over how those surpluses are used to transform their urban space (Harvey 2008).

But the right to the city is not only a concept being debated by urban scholars. Many cities have now elevated the right to the city to the status of law. For example, the European Charter for the Safeguarding of Human Rights in the City (ECSHRC) had been ratified by 350 cities in 21 countries as of 2006. Since the ECSHRC is now law in many cities, it provides a more concrete framework for the right to the city than the idea's conceptual origins, and even cites urban residents' right to the city as one of its primary overarching principles (Brown and Kristiansen 2009).

Another major example of how the "right to the city" concept has taken root in reality is through the City Statute in Brazil. This statute took several decades of political movements to create, and some cities even crafted their own policies ahead of time. For example, the city of Porto Alegre experimented with participatory budgeting before the City Statute was passed. Now passed, the statute adds a social dimension to the right to urban property and promotes democratic participation in urban management. One of the ways in which the government enforces this statute is by taking vacant or underused lands from absent property owners and subdividing those parcels for alternative uses (Brown and Kristiansen 2009).

A final look at the twenty-first-century city

It is not yet possible to determine whether the twenty-first-century city will become the more inclusive, sustainable, and creative place of our vision. One obvious reason for this is that the twenty-first century is still young and thus the long view on something as complex as the city is undoubtedly cloudy. A more synthetic reason is that our forward view is complicated by the myriad challenges collectively and individually facing all three ideal features of the future city. The city has been and will continue to be full of divides and disparities – manifested in gated communities, open slums, and general socio-spatial inequality – that test our will and efforts to make it fully inclusive. While it is naïve to hope for the end of entrenched urban inequalities, the inherently creative and innovative capacities of cities, which stem from human density and proximity, reinforce our optimism that we will develop more effective solutions to ameliorate, if not eradicate, some exclusionary features of the future city. To the extent that the forces conducive to inclusivity and creativity can converge, they will help to counter a set of more pressing challenges that make sustainable urban development the most difficult and worthy long-term goal to achieve.

To place you in the best position to think about the future city, we will end by highlighting and reiterating a few of the most daunting challenges to urban sustainability identified by the United Nations. Demographically speaking, almost all of the urban growth through 2050 will occur in developing countries, and the bulk of this growth will take place in smaller and often institutionally weak settlements of 100 000–250 000 people, while the megacities of 10 million or more people will continue to multiply in number, spatial scope, and functional influence. A major environmental challenge will come from climate change and cities' excessive dependence on cars powered by fossil fuels. For example, higher temperatures may cause sea level to rise, making large coastal cities more vulnerable to natural hazards such as flooding, which disproportionally hurt the poor living in slums. Economic challenges will continue to arise from uncertain future growth, widespread doubt about market-led approaches (reinforced by the 2008 global financial crisis), and increasingly informal economic activity and semi- or quasi-urban settlement, primarily in and around large developing-country cities. In institutional terms, the challenge will continue to revolve around the shift from government to governance along a pair of coupled dimensions. On one hand, the rescaling of urban decision-making from the geographically bounded unit of the city to the multi-level context of the globalizing city-region has been accelerating in both developed and developing countries. But, on the other hand, urban decision-making has become and will continue to be more decentralized and democratic and attuned to the rights of the ordinary city resident (UN-Habitat 2009). Daunting as they are and insurmountable as they seem to be, these challenges could also be new opportunities for building the future city. The opportunities, according to the same United Nations report, converge on the central positive role of improved urban planning, which will involve recognizing the existence of informal economic activity and urban settlement, linking spatial and land use plans to infrastructure and transport planning to facilitate more compact development, setting up better monitoring and evaluation of the planning process and its outcomes, and updating and improving the planning curriculum in developing countries.

While we recognize the powerful interventionist role of planning in shaping the future city, we instead have taken a sociological approach, bringing out the essential qualities of cities as malleable and remakeable places that are deeply lodged in our collective senses of community, identity, and security. These are enduring attributes of our places of work, life, and play that make up the city of today and tomorrow. They motivate us to be involved in participatory or bottom-up planning, which can work well with governmental and professional approaches to planning. Most importantly, when we sense the threat of exclusive and unsustainable cities to the fundamental values we attach to place, we are more likely to be motivated to remake these cities so that we can enjoy better places in the future. We hope that we have made this critical connection clear to you through this book. Visit the book's companion website at www.wiley.com/go/cities for examples, case studies, and discussion questions, plus a list of useful films and other media, that are relevant to this and all the other chapters.

Critical thinking questions

1 How do you respond to our conceptualization of place versus space?

2 What is your assessment of the possible scenarios for future cities?

3 In light of our discussion of how cities have been remade and will be remade as places, can you

suggest other ways in which this has happened and could happen?

4 In addition to our emphases on inclusivity, sustainability, and creativity as critical to the future wellbeing of cities, what else will be as significant in your judgment?

Suggested reading

Jeb Brugmann, *Welcome to the Urban Revolution: How Cities Are Changing the World* (New York: Bloomsbury Press, 2010). Through detailed case studies of Bangalore, Dharavi in Mumbai, Detroit, and Chicago, Brugmann shows that urban advantages such as density, scale, and association can be harnessed to achieve sustainable development on a global scale.

Ricky Burdett and Deyan Sudjic, eds., *The Endless City* (London: Phaidon, 2007). This book details an authoritative survey of cities now and the prospects for our urban future. Over 30 contributors from Africa, China, Europe, South America, and the United States set the agenda for the city, detailing its successes as well as its failures.

Edward Glaeser, *The Triumph of the City* (New York: Penguin, 2011). This book provides a comprehensive survey of how cities around the world thrive and falter. It makes a convincing case for why the once-successful Industrial Age model may not work in the service-age economy and why and how denser

cities are greener and can militate against global warming.

Jean Gottmann, *Megalopolis: The Urbanized Northeastern Seaboard of the United States* (Cambridge: MIT Press, 1961). Now a classic, the book was a pioneering study of urban sprawl along the Boston–Washington corridor, which stretches about 500 miles as a connected political, economic, and social entity. The author gained wide acclaim for his insights into the emergence of large-scale metropolitan urbanism.

Witold Rybczynski, *Makeshift Metropolis: Ideas About Cities* (New York: Scribner, 2010). This book integrates history and prediction in its survey of the development of the US city from the early twentieth century. Rybczynski examines the trend toward arcades, malls, and big-box retail stores and critiques mixed-use development projects in a variety of US cities in order to find the right mix of aesthetics and practical, user-friendly spaces in an era of scarce resources and daunting environmental challenges.

Note

1. Additional points in this paragraph were provided by Sharon Zukin during personal communication.

Glossary

50 Moganshan road A 1930s-era factory complex near the Suzhou Creek, owned by Shangtex, a large textile and apparel holding company that had moved to a new development zone in Pudong, east of the Huangpu River. Artists in Shanghai, attracted by the cheap rents and location in the center of a rapidly growing, cosmopolitan city, rapidly moved into the Shangtex site. Shangtex became an eager patron and landlord of new artists, and the art district also enjoys the support of local party and government officials.

Agglomeration The economic benefits that accrue from industries and firms that are clustered together or near each other over an extended metropolitan area that encompasses the built-up area of a central city plus some surrounding regions.

Barrio (Spanish) A term used to describe a poor urban settlement, or slum area. See also *Favela*.

Boosters Individuals and organizations that encourage development in a particular city or place, often because they will profit from intensified development.

Borderplex A metropolitan area that crosses national boundaries.

BosWash The expansive region stretching 500 miles from Boston in the north to Washington, DC, in the south. It was the focus of Jean Gottmann's book, *Megalopolis*, published in 1961. See also *Megalopolis*.

Cantonment A temporary or military encampment, particularly associated with colonial rule.

Case study A clear and well-defined example that furnishes evidence of the particular phenomenon that a researcher is studying.

City as a growth machine The concept developed by Harvey Molotch, and later enlarged and enriched in work with John Logan. It refers to the idea that cities are primarily concerned with growth and development, something that leads to a bifurcation of the city into an alliance of key leaders and officials, on the one side, and residents and neighborhood groups, on the other.

Common-interest development (CID) A residential community that uses fees levied on homeowners to fund privately held infrastructure and amenities.

Concentric zones theory The theory developed by Ernest Burgess and Robert Park that claimed that all metropolitan areas develop in terms of a set of circular areas radiating out from the center of the city. Inhabitants of each zone tend to be similar and different from those inhabitants in other spatially distinctive parts or rings of the city. Two such zones are those of the warehouse district and the zone of commuters.

Concession An area within a weaker country conceded to and administered by a stronger one. As a result of the defeat of China by the Western powers during the Opium Wars and the unequal Treaty of Nanking in 1842, Shanghai was one of the five treaty ports forced to open to Western trade and political domination through the Shanghai International Settlements of the various European countries. The French separated its own Concession in 1862, after which the British and Americans united to become the Shanghai International Settlement.

Culture of poverty A term invented by the anthropologist Oscar Lewis to describe the cultural traits of people who are impoverished and live together in dense settlements. Lewis later

Introduction to Cities: How Place and Space Shape Human Experience, First Edition. Xiangming Chen, Anthony M. Orum, and Krista E. Paulsen.
© 2013 Xiangming Chen, Anthony M. Orum, and Krista E. Paulsen.
Published 2013 by Blackwell Publishing Ltd.

came under attack from sociologists such as William Julius Wilson, who believed that it was the economy – and, in particular, the absence of regular and stable employment – that led to the lifestyles as well as problems characterizing poor communities, especially those of African Americans. The debate, about whether it is the absence of structural opportunities or the presence of a set of particular cultural traits that is responsible, continues to animate the analysis and discussion of many scholars of poverty today.

Danwei (Chinese) Generally translated as *work unit*. Refers to any state-owned enterprise or agency that existed and functioned pre-reform (before 1980) as both an employer and self-contained community that offered comprehensive welfare benefits and social services.

De jure segregation Racial/ethnic segregation achieved through laws governing who can live where.

De facto segregation Racial/ethnic segregation achieved through informal means, such as preferences to live with one's own kind, economic barriers experienced by minority groups, or hostility, resistance, and illegal discrimination on the part of majority-group residents.

Deindustrialization The movement of industrial enterprises out of older metropolitan areas during the period after World War II.

Deinstitutionalization A shift from large, state-run mental health facilities to smaller community-based facilities, accompanied by an increase in the number of mentally ill people who do not receive formal treatment.

Dubai World An investment company that manages and supervises a portfolio of businesses and projects for the Dubai government across a wide range of industry segments and projects that promote Dubai as a hub for commerce and trading. It is the Dubai government's flag bearer in global investments and has a central role in the direction of Dubai's economy.

Ecological footprint The environmental impact of a city's resource needs and waste production in terms of a standard measurement of a unit's influence on its habitat.

Economy of scale The efficiency gains and cost reductions that a firm obtains due to expansion. A producer's average cost per unit falls as the scale of output is increased. At the micro level, economy of scale can be obtained by a single firm's expansion, while there can be economy of scale efficiency gains as a result of the collective and mutually reinforcing or synergistic growth of a group or cluster of firms.

Edge city Journalist Joel Garreau's term for clusters of development at the urban periphery that include substantial commercial as well as residential land uses. Edge cities are typically located along major transportation routes, especially Interstate highways.

Entrepôt A trading post, usually a seaport, for transferring goods at a profit between other ports. The term dates back to the Middle Ages and the early modern period, when long-distance shipping between the European colonial empires and colonies would be trans-shipped via different entrepôts.

Environmental justice A social movement seeking equity in terms of the environmental risks and benefits experienced by different groups.

Environmental racism "Any policy, practice or directive that differentially affects or disadvantages (whether intended or unintended) individuals, groups or communities based on race or color" (Bullard 2000).

Ethnic enclaves Areas of cities where recent immigrants of the same ethnic background tend to settle and create various social and economic opportunities for themselves (e.g., Little Havana in Miami). While such enclaves frequently consist only of immigrants of similar national origins, in some places – as in Little Saigon in Orange County, California – the enclave can consist of large numbers of people from different national backgrounds.

Ethnographic case study A case study using field research methods of a particular social phenomenon evident in the more or less contemporary circumstances of a group.

European Monetary Union (EMU) The policies for moving the economies of members of the European Union (EU) through three stages so as to allow them to adopt a single currency, the euro. As such, it is largely synonymous with the Eurozone. All member states, except Denmark, Sweden, and the United Kingdom, have committed themselves by treaty to join the EMU. Seventeen member states of the European Union have entered the third stage and have adopted the euro as their currency. The five remaining (post-2004) states have yet to achieve sufficient convergence to participate. Altogether, 10 of the 27 EU members currently still use their own currencies.

European Union (EU) An economic and political union of 27 member states located in Europe. The EU traces its origins from the European Coal and Steel Community (ECSC) and the European Economic Community (EEC), formed by six countries (Belgium, France, Italy, Luxembourg, the Netherlands, and West Germany) in 1958. In the intervening years, the European Union has grown in size by the accession of new member states that in recent years have come primarily from the former Soviet bloc. The newest members, Romania and Bulgaria, joined the European Union on January 1, 2007. The Maastricht Treaty established the European Union under its current name in 1993. The last amendment to the constitutional basis of the EU, the Treaty of Lisbon, came into force in 2009 and created a permanent President of the European Council.

Exchange value A concept defined by Karl Marx as the market value of commodities, the products produced under capitalism. Used by John Logan and Harvey Molotch to identify the interest of real estate developers in the lands and neighborhoods of city residents, and used to contrast with use values.

External(ized) costs Costs associated with the production or consumption of a good or service that are not borne by the individual or group engaged in that production or consumption but that instead typically are borne by the larger group or society (called "social costs"). For example, the manufacturers of products that will eventually require landfill space do not pay for creating that landfill space.

Favela A Brazilian Portuguese word that generally refers to a slum or shanty town in Brazil. The Spanish term *barrio* is used to refer to the same poor urban settlement in other Latin American countries, such as Colombia.

Favelados Dwellers in a *favela*.

First-ring suburbs The older suburbs of metropolitan areas. Such suburbs in recent years have shown some evidence of decline in population and housing stock – the same kind of decline that has taken place in the central areas of the metropolis.

Gated community A residential community surrounded by walls, fences, gates, water, and/or natural barriers to restrict entry and access. These are typically (though not exclusively) affluent communities, and represent a key way whereby groups of people can seclude themselves from others in the metropolis.

Gemeinschaft **(German)** The term used by Ferdinand Tönnies to refer to community. It depicts the close and intimate relationships between people as compared to those relationships that are fleeting and impersonal.

Gentrification Redevelopment of older residential and/or industrial districts of the metropolis with the intention of bringing more wealth into an urban area. Many older industrial cities have resorted to gentrification in recent years as a way of enhancing themselves and adding more revenue to their tax base. In many instances, it appears that gentrification leads to the displacement of older and poorer residents, but newer research suggests that this might not always be true.

Gesellschaft **(German)** The term used by Ferdinand Tönnies to refer to society. It depicts the partial and impersonal relationships between people as compared to those relationships that are close and intimate.

Ghetto neighborhood An area where members of a racial or ethnic minority group are forced to live because of an absence of other viable options. Such neighborhoods arise primarily due to the poverty of residents and/or outright hostility and discrimination by the dominant group.

Gini index A basic statistical measure of the degree of income inequality in a country, or the gap between the incomes of the very poor and those of the very rich. The closer the index is to 1.00, the more unequal is the gap between them.

Global city A term invented by Saskia Sassen to refer to those major cities in the world in which the most powerful and influential institutions are located – such as investment banks, insurance companies, and real estate development firms – making these cities the controlling nodes of the global economy. The term refers specifically to London, New York, and Tokyo, with a more recent and wider reference to such cities as Mexico City, Mumbai, São Paulo, Shanghai, and a few others.

Global Financial Centres Index (GFCI) An index that ranks global financial centers based on several instrumental factors, including availability of a professional workforce, business climate, market access, basic infrastructure, general competitiveness, availability of capital, and digitization. The index has been compiled and published twice a year by the City of London in the United Kingdom since March 2007.

Globalization The growing integration of countries, firms, and individuals across the world, coupled with the compression of space and time such that information about events in one part of the world can rapidly be transmitted to and have consequences in other parts. It is especially evident today in financial markets, manufacturing, and human migration.

Great Migration The movement of large numbers of African Americans from the southern United States to the north and Midwest, especially during the 1920s and 1930s.

Gross domestic product (GDP) The basic and standard measure of a country's or city's total economic output and performance – that is, the value of all goods and services produced by that country or city.

Growth coalition A group of individuals and organizations who come together in support of urban growth. It may include real estate agents and developers, local government, business owners, utility companies, and even sports franchises and universities.

Hinterland The area outside the central and most dense zones of population in the metropolis. Typically the hinterlands consist of farmlands and forests, and are far more sparsely populated than the central parts of the metropolis. The central city and the hinterlands are clusters that depend on one another for the flow and exchange of commodities as well as information.

Historical case study A study of a particular area or city that focuses on how historical circumstances or temporal processes have shaped life in that setting.

Household registration (*hukou* in Chinese) A system created by the Chinese government in 1958 to officially register every city resident with an identification number that entitled him or her to housing, education, healthcare, and food. The system prevented rural residents from entering cities and thus created a dual, or bifurcated, society. Although it was modified somewhat after China's reform in 1980, the household registration system continues to exist today and to restrict the full integration of migrant workers into cities.

Human ecology The view, originally developed by Robert Park and his colleagues, that change in cities can be construed in terms of the rivalries among different population groups. It drew on ideas from ecology and used the imagery of Charles Darwin to characterize the ongoing struggle for dominance of groups in cities.

Hypersegregated Douglas Massey and Nancy Denton's term for ghetto neighborhoods that are highly segregated and isolated (see the specific measures in Studying the city 8.2), clustered close together, spatially concentrated, and located in the center of the city. These areas provide residents with the least amount of exposure to affluent or majority-group individuals and places.

Immigrant enclaves Neighborhoods where immigrants of similar backgrounds settle, typically on their initial arrival in a new country. These places provide social and economic opportunities. See also *Ethnic enclaves*.

Index of dissimilarity A statistical device that measures segregation by calculating the percentage of one of two racial groups that would have to move in order to achieve integration between the two.

Index of exposure A statistical measure indicating the degree to which the average person of a given race/ethnicity lives near people of a different racial/ethnic group. A higher number indicates more exposure to members of the different group.

Index of isolation A statistical measure indicating the degree to which the average person of a given race/ethnicity lives near people of his or her own racial/ethnic group. A higher number indicates that this statistically average person lives near more people of the same race/ethnicity.

Industrial suburbs Developments on the metropolitan periphery that are anchored by manufacturing or other industrial facilities, typically including worker housing as well.

Informal economy Economic activities that (1) fall outside regulations concerning registration, tax payments, conditions of employment, and operating licenses, (2) involve self-employment not recognized and protected by legal or regulatory frameworks and (3) are performed at home, on the street, in season or in between. This three-pronged definition is based on a report prepared by the Swedish International Development Cooperation Agency (Sida) in 2004.

In-migration Population gain in a city from more people moving in than moving out, or a higher rate of in-migration than of out-migration.

Institutional ghettos Highly segregated neighborhoods where the social organization closely corresponds to that of the larger society.

Integration Exists when groups with different social statuses live or work together. In the context of cities, this refers to the degree to which different racial/ethnic groups or social classes live in the same areas.

Jim Crow A set of laws and customs in the United States that enforced segregation in public and private spaces and services (separate dining areas and so on) and compromised voting and other civil rights.

Jobless ghettos William Julius Wilson's term for the high-poverty minority neighborhoods where, on an average day, fewer than half of the working-age adults are actually working. The joblessness in these areas has resulted primarily from urban deindustrialization.

Level of urbanization A numerical measure of urbanization of a country that ranges from zero to 100 percent along a continuum.

Linong **(Chinese)** Traditional courtyard houses in Shanghai that extend one after the other in rows crammed through lanes and alleys like Western duplexes or condos. Many of the *linong* houses have been torn down today as a result of the rapid leveling and redevelopment in Chinese cities.

LULU Locally unwanted (or undesirable) land use. Industrial and infrastructure projects that, despite their necessity, are considered detrimental to the neighborhoods where they are located. Examples include jails and prisons, manufacturing plants, rail yards, and the like.

Megacity A city containing 10 million or more people.

Megalopolis A highly dense population site, stretching across thousands of acres of land and connecting people and enterprises in different cities and towns. The term originally was invented by Jean Gottmann to describe the area in the United States that ran from Boston to Washington, DC.

Metacity A new term used to describe cities that have 20 million or more people. An equivalent term, proposed by the McKinsey Global Institute, is "supercity."

Metropolis A vast settlement of people and various organizations that can range over many square miles and can consist of countless cities and towns, as the examples of Los Angeles and New York City illustrate.

Metropolitan expansion (or contraction) The growth (or decline) of a city-region. It depends both on the net natural increase (births versus deaths) and the overall addition (or subtraction) of migrants (immigrants versus emigrants).

Multiple nuclei The claim that metropolitan areas consist of different centers rather than a single center, and that such centers, like a shopping district, may themselves attract and sustain new residential developments. It represents an alternative view of the metropolis, often associated with Los Angeles, to that of the concentric zone theory, which was developed and based upon the city of Chicago.

Mutual aid societies Organizations developed to provide insurance and other services to members of immigrant and minority communities. They range from relatively informal to ones that are formally and bureaucratically organized.

Nationalists (*Kuomintang* **or KMT in Chinese)** The Chinese Nationalist Party, founded by Sun Yat-sen shortly after the Xinhai Revolution, which overthrew the last Emperor of China in 1911. Later led by Chiang Kai-shek, the Nationalists ruled much of China from 1928 until their retreat to Taiwan in 1949 after being defeated by the Communist Party of China (CPC) during the Chinese Civil War.

Natural advantages Qualities of a place's geography and/or climate that appear to predispose it to intensive human habitation. They may include access to a natural harbor, ample freshwater, or a defensible position. The specific qualities that are considered advantageous will vary as human needs and preferences change.

Natural areas of the metropolis Those specific spaces in the metropolis where distinctive groups of people and/or organizations congregate – for example, the central city or specific ethnic neighborhoods.

Natural disadvantages Qualities of a place's geography and/or climate that threaten intensive human habitation or cast it in a negative light. Examples include tectonic instability or susceptibility to flooding. Such qualities are not always apparent at the time a particular place is developed.

Natural disasters Natural events that cause significant damage to human structures and/or loss of life. They are best understood as the result of interactions between human structures and dynamic natural processes.

Natural increase The crude birth rate minus the death rate of a population. It can be either positive or negative, though generally it is positive. As a rule, a country or city needs a fertility rate of 2.1, or slightly more than two children per couple, relative to its death rate to replace its population naturally.

Neoliberal ideology Essentially about making the free market work successfully by letting it naturally balance itself via the pressures of market demands. It includes making trade between nations easier through the freer movement of goods, resources, and enterprises to maximize profits and efficiency. This entails the removal of various controls deemed as barriers to free trade, such as regulations and tariffs.

Over-urbanization The process whereby urban population growth outpaces that of urban jobs.

Owner-built suburb Areas outside cities where property owners have constructed their own dwellings.

Place attachment The emotional connections that people feel toward specific places such as buildings, neighborhoods, or cities.

Places Specific sites in cities, and sometimes the whole ensemble of cities, that are shaped by human beings and shape the lives of human beings. They are the sites of human identity, security, and community.

Postmodern metropolis A postindustrial city characterized by social fragmentation.

Postmodernism The movement in contemporary scholarship that emphasizes fragmentation and de-centering both in intellectual thought and material projects. It is evident in, among other things, many of the recent architectural additions to cities.

Primate city A city that is both the largest in a country and disproportionately larger than the second and lower-ranked cities.

Private spaces Spaces to which access is restricted by those who own the property.

Privatization (of space) The shift in ownership of spaces from public to private, whether corporations, management companies, or homeowners' associations, typically in efforts to reduce access to places.

Prototypical case A case that serves to define the special and unique elements of a city, community, or area on the grounds that this particular setting furnishes insight into how other places will, or can, eventually develop the same features.

Public spaces Spaces that are open and accessible to every person in a society, in particular its citizens.

Race to the bottom A pattern in which places vie to attract investment by providing the most permissible regulatory environment in terms of labor, environment, and taxes. As a result, places succeed in attracting businesses that exploit workers, foul the environment, and contribute little to the tax base of a city.

Red envelope (*hongbao* **in Chinese**) A small amount of cash given as a gift on special celebratory occasions, especially during the Chinese Lunar New Year or Spring Festival.

Redlining The systematic denial of mortgages and other forms of lending in minority communities.

Reliability Measures of, or information about, a particular phenomenon that can be replicated by observers.

Restrictive covenants Agreements prohibiting the sale of property to members of racial, ethnic, or religious minorities.

Segregation Exists when groups with different social statuses live or work separately. In the context of cities, this refers to the degree to which different racial/ethnic groups or social classes live in different areas.

Sentiment Walter Firey's term for a set of attachments people have to places, whether aesthetic, historical, or familial.

Slum A run-down area of a city characterized by substandard, makeshift housing, lack of tenure security, and the presence of poverty. See also *Ghetto*.

Social isolation The lack of regular interaction between groups, particularly between a minority group and the majority population. Residents of ghetto neighborhoods, particularly *hypersegregated* areas, are often socially isolated.

Social mobility The capacity of a group or individual to move from one social class to another – for instance, moving up from the working class to the middle class. Upward mobility is common and desirable, but downward mobility also occurs.

Social space The ways in which the spatial patterns and areas of cities are shaped, and influenced, by their residents.

Spaces Geographic entities with distinct shapes, scales, and other properties that set the stage for certain kinds of human activities.

Special Economic Zone (or SEZ) An area designated under market-oriented regulations that offers special economic incentives such as lower taxes that are not available elsewhere in a country. Also includes other types of zones such as export-processing zones (EPZs) and free trade zones (FTZs). In China, the SEZs, of which Shenzhen was the first (created in 1980), marked spatially and institutionally shielded areas or enclaves for experimenting with bold market reforms and attracting the first wave of foreign investment, especially from Hong Kong.

Sprawl The extensive growth and spread of people and institutions across metropolitan areas. Particularly evident in the period after World War II as more and more people moved out of central cities and into the suburban and fringe areas of the metropolis.

Streetcar suburbs A concept invented by Samuel Bass Warner, Jr. to describe communities that are developed as a result of streetcar, tram, or light rail lines.

Suburbs Areas on the periphery of cities containing primarily low-density residential development. This definition is continually challenged, however, as suburbs come to have more commercial development, and autonomy from adjacent urban areas.

Sunbelt The southern and western portions of the United States where many people and firms relocated after World War II.

Sundown towns Small towns and suburbs that prohibited African Americans from residing within the municipal limits. Blacks could work in these places but needed to leave before nightfall, hence the name.

Supercity A term used by McKinsey Global Institute to refer to cities with a population of 20 million or more.

Sustainable development The United Nations' 1987 Bruntland Commission defines this as the ability of systems to endure or to meet current needs without compromising the needs of future generations. Subsequent scholars have critiqued that definition as anthropocentric and overly dependent on the subjective concept of "needs." An alternative definition offered by Wheeler defines "sustainable" as "development that improves the long-term health of human and ecological systems" (Wheeler 2007 [1998]: pp. 438–439).

Symbolism In Walter Firey's conception, what a place represents as compared to other places.

Technoburb Robert Fishman's term for areas on the urban periphery that have developed their own socioeconomic viability. Just like *edge cities*, technoburbs combine residential, commercial, and institutional land uses.

Tenement A term used for buildings containing multiple small, low-cost housing units. Purpose-built or converted from other uses such as factories, they were poorly constructed, with few safety features or sanitary facilities. The three- to six-story brick apartment buildings in cities in the Eastern United States, such as those that still stand in New York City's Lower East Side, are typical.

Tenement Reform Movement A social movement in New York City and elsewhere designed to increase the safety of tenements and improve the living conditions of their residents.

Tourist spaces Highly controlled areas that cater specifically to the experiential, consumption, service, and aesthetic demands of tourists.

Typical case A case that represents the typical, or common, features of all cities, or communities, at that time and/or in that country.

Under-urbanization The process whereby urban population growth lags behind the growth of urban jobs.

Uneven growth of the city The unequal spatial development of cities, with older portions often sitting idle and left to decline while newer growth occurs in the outer rings of the city. An extension of Karl Marx's ideas by David Harvey that is intended to show how urban growth inevitably produces inequalities and injustice.

Urban enclaves Settlements and communities created by new immigrants to a country.

Urban fragmentation The proliferation of municipalities and other governmental units within a metropolitan area. It often complicates political efforts to furnish services at a regional or metropolitan level of government.

Urban limit line A planning device that aims to curtail sprawl by designating boundaries between developed and undeveloped, or rural, areas.

Urban pyramid A hierarchical structure and shape of a country's layered city system in which the smaller number of larger cities is arrayed toward the top while the larger number of smaller cities is positioned toward the bottom.

Urban renewal Large-scale, government-funded efforts to remake older areas of cities. The structures that are removed usually include slum housing, thus effectively displacing poor residents of color, while new structures include highways, sports stadiums, convention centers, office buildings, and a small amount of low-income housing.

Urbanism as a way of life Louis Wirth's view of life in the city as impersonal and anonymous. Wirth drew on some of the ideas of Georg Simmel.

Urbanization The process by which a country becomes urbanized. Usually represented by the growing proportion of the total population living in urban areas (cities and towns), however such settlements are defined in a particular country. Measured by the share of a country's population in urban areas, which has a theoretical range from zero to 100 percent but typically falls in between these extremes.

Use value A concept defined by Karl Marx as the use or utility of a thing, and employed by John Logan and Harvey Molotch to depict the uses that residents make of their neighborhoods. The concept is the opposite of the exchange value (or the market value) of commodities or places.

Validity The verifiable assumption that the measures of, or information about, a particular phenomenon actually represent that phenomenon.

Walking city The dense, compact forms that cities took before the wide adoption of powered transportation technologies.

References

Abu-Lughod, Janet. 1994. *From Urban Village to East Village: The Battle for New York's Lower East Side* (Cambridge, MA: Blackwell).

Aguilar-San Juan, Karin. 2009. *Little Saigons: Staying Vietnamese in America* (Minneapolis: University of Minnesota Press).

Alam, Ahmad Rafay. 2008, April 8. "Facing the Urban Challenges Ahead." http://lahorenama.wordpress.com/tag/lda.

Alderson, Arthur and Jason Beckfield. 2004. "Power and Position in the World City System." *American Journal of Sociology* 109: 811–851.

Alderson, Arthur and Jason Beckfield. 2007. "Power and Position in the World City System: 1981–2000." In Peter Taylor, Ben Derudder, Pieter Saey, and Frank Witlox, eds. *Cities in Globalization: Practices, Policies and Theories* (London: Routledge, pp. 21–37).

Allen, Barbara L. 2007. "Environmental Justice, Local Knowledge and After-Disaster Planning in New Orleans." *Technology in Society* 29: 153–159.

Alvarez, Robert R. Jr. 1995. "The Mexican–US Border: The Making of an Anthropology of Borderlands." *Annual Review of Anthropology* 24(1): 447–470.

Amin, Ash and Nigel Thrift. 1994. "Living in the Global." In Ash Amin and Nigel Thrift, eds. *Globalization, Institutions and Regional Development in Europe* (Oxford: Oxford University Press, pp. 1–22).

Anbinder, Tyler. 2001. *Five Points: The Neighborhood that Invented Tap Dance, Stole Elections, and Became the World's Most Notorious Slum* (New York: The Free Press).

Anderson, Elijah. 1990. *Streetwise: Race, Class and Change in an Urban Community* (Chicago, IL: University of Chicago Press).

Anderson, Elijah. 1999. *Code of the Street* (New York: W.W. Norton & Company).

Anderson, Nels. 1923. *The Hobo: The Sociology of the Homeless Man* (Chicago, IL: University of Chicago Press).

Argun, Betigül Ercan. 2003. *Turkey in Germany: The Transnational Sphere of Deutschkei* (New York and London: Routledge).

Aron, Laudan Y. and Patrick T. Sharkey. 2002. "The 1996 National Survey of Homeless Assistance Providers and Clients: A Comparison of Faith-Based and Secular Non-Profit Programs." *The Urban Institute*. http://aspe.hhs.gov/hsp/homelessness/NSHAPC02.

Associated Press. 2010, February 16. "Haiti Quake Damage Could Cost $14B US." *CBC News Online*. http://www.cbc.ca/news/world/story/2010/02/16/haiti-quake-damage016.html.

Avila, Eric. 2004. *Popular Culture in the Age of White Flight: Fear and Fantasy in Suburban Los Angeles* (Berkeley: University of California Press).

Bairoch, Paul. 1988. *Cities and Economic Development from the Dawn of History to the Present* (Chicago, IL: University Chicago Press).

Barnet, Richard J. and Ronald E. Muller. 1974. *Global Reach: The Power of Multinational Corporations* (New York: Touchstone).

Batalova, Jeanne and Aaron Terrazas. 2010, December 9. "Frequently Requested Statistics on Immigrants and Immigration in the United States." *Migration Policy Institute*. http://www.migrationinformation.org/USfocus.

Baumgartner, M. P. 1988. *The Moral Order of a Suburb* (New York: Oxford University Press).

Baxandall, Rosalyn Fraad and Elizabeth Ewen. 2001. *Picture Windows: How the Suburbs Happened* (New York: Basic Books).

BBC News. 2005, November 17. "French Violence 'Back to Normal.'" *BBC News*. http://news.bbc.co.uk/2/hi/europe/4445428.stm.

Introduction to Cities: How Place and Space Shape Human Experience, First Edition. Xiangming Chen, Anthony M. Orum, and Krista E. Paulsen.
© 2013 Xiangming Chen, Anthony M. Orum, and Krista E. Paulsen.
Published 2013 by Blackwell Publishing Ltd.

Beauregard, Robert S. 2003 "City of Superlatives." *City & Community* 2(3): 183–199.

Bernard, Richard A. and Bradly R. Rice, eds. 1984. *Sunbelt Cities: Politics and Growth Since World War II* (Austin: University of Texas Press).

Binford, Henry C. 1985. *The First Suburbs: Residential Communities on the Boston Periphery, 1815 1860.* (Chicago, IL: University of Chicago Press).

Bisky, Jens. 2006, November. "Berlin: A Profile." In *Berlin An Urban Experiment* (Urban Age Project, London School of Economics and Alfred Herrhausen Society of Deutsche Bank).

Blakely, Edward J. and Mary Gail Snyder. 1997. *Fortress America: Gated Communities in the United States* (Washington, DC: Brookings Institution Press).

Blakely, Edward J. and Mary Gail Snyder. 1998. "Forting Up: Gated Communities in the United States." *Journal of Architectural and Planning Research* 15(1): 61–72.

Blasius, Mark and Shane Phelan, eds. 1997. *We Are Everywhere: A Historical Sourcebook of Gay and Lesbian Politics* (New York: Routledge).

Bluestone, Barry and Bennett Harrison. 1984. *The Deindustrialization of America: Plant Closings, Community Attachment and the Dismantling of Basic Industry* (New York: Basic Books).

Bluestone, Barry and Bennett Harrison. 1990. *The Great U-Turn: Corporate Restructuring and the Polarizing of America* (New York: Basic Books).

Boyle, Kevin. 2004. *Arc of Justice: A Saga of Race, Civil Rights, and Murder in the Jazz Age* (New York: Henry Holt and Company).

Bray, David. 2006. "Building 'Community': New Strategies of Governance in Urban China." *Economy and Society* 35(4): 530–549.

Brechin, Gray. 2006. *Imperial San Francisco* (Berkeley: University of California Press).

Brenner, Neil. 2003. "Stereotypes, Archetypes and Prototypes: Three Uses of Superlatives in Contemporary Urban Studies." *City & Community* 2(3): 205–216.

Brillembourg, Alfred, Kristin Feireiss, and Hubert Klumpner, eds. 2005. *The Informal City: Caracas Case* (New York: Prestel Publishing).

Brown, Alison and Annali Kristiansen. 2009. "Urban Policies and the Right to the City: Rights, Responsibilities and Citizenship." *UNESCO.* http://unesdoc.unesco.org/images/0017/001780/178090e.pdf.

Brown-Saracino, Japonica. 2009. *A Neighborhood That Never Changes: Gentrification, Social Preservation, and the Search for Authenticity* (Chicago, IL: University of Chicago Press).

Brown-Saracino, Japonica, ed. 2010. *The Gentrification Debates* (New York: Routledge).

Bruegmann, Robert. 2005. *Sprawl: A Compact History* (Chicago, IL: University of Chicago Press).

Brundtland, Gro Harlem et al. 1987. "Report of the World Commission on Environment and Development: Our Common Future." *United Nations.* http://www.un-documents.net/wced-ocf.htm.

Bugliarello, George. 2006. "Urban Sustainability: Dilemmas, Challenges and Paradigms." *Technology in Society* 28: 19–26.

Bullard, Robert D. 2000. *Dumping in Dixie: Race, Class and Environmental Quality* (Boulder, CO: Westview Press).

Bulmer, Martin. 1986. *The Chicago School of Sociology* (Chicago, IL: University of Chicago Press).

Burdett, Ricky, ed. 2008. *South American Cities: Securing an Urban Future* (Urban Age Project, London School of Economics and Alfred Herrhausen Society of Deutsche Bank).

Burgess, Ernest W. 1961 [1925]. "The Growth of the City: An Introduction to a Research Project." In Robert E. Park, Ernest W. Burgess, and Roderick D. McKenzie, eds.; with a bibliography by Louis Wirth. *The City* (Chicago, IL: University of Chicago Press, pp. 47–62).

Burt, Martha R., Laudan Y. Aron, Toby Douglas, Jesse Valente, Edgar Lee, and Britta Iwen. 1999. "Homelessness: Programs and the People they Serve – Findings from the National Survey of Homeless Assistance Providers and Clients." *The Urban Institute.* http://www.urban.org/url.cfm?ID=310291.

Caldeira, Teresa. 2001. *City of Walls: Crime, Segregation, and Citizenship in São Paulo* (Berkeley: University of California Press).

Calderia, Teresa. 2008, December. "Worlds Set Apart." *South American Cities: Securing an Urban Future* (Urban Age Project, London School of Economics and Alfred Herrhausen Society of Deutsche Bank).

Canadian Broadcasting Corporation. 1950, 10 May. "Red River Rising: Manitoba Floods." http://archives.cbc.ca/environment/extreme_weather/topics/670.

Capello, Ernesto. 2008. "Public Spheres, Crónicas and Heterogeneous Landscapes: New Works in Latin American History." *Latin American Research Review* 43(2): 251–259.

Caplow, Theodore, Bruce A. Chadwick, Howard M. Bahr, and Reuben Hill. 1982. *Middletown Families: Fifty Years of Change and Continuity* (Minneapolis: University of Minnesota Press).

Caro, Robert. 1975. *Power Broker: Robert Moses and the Fall of New York* (New York: Vintage).

Castells, Manuel. 1977. *The Urban Question: A Marxist Approach* (Cambridge, MA: The MIT Press).

Castells, Manuel. 1989. *The Informational City: Information Technology, Economic Restructuring, and the Urban–Regional Process* (Cambridge, MA: Basil Blackwell).

Castells, Manuel. 2000. *The Rise of the Network Society*, 2nd edition (New York: Blackwell).

Castillo Olea, Jose Manuel. 2006. "The Informal Economy as a Way of Life." In *Mexico City: Growth at the Limit?* (Urban Age Project, London School of Economics and Alfred Herrhausen Society of Deutsche Bank).

Centre on Housing Rights and Evictions. 2007. "Fair Play for Housing Rights: Mega-Events, Olympic Games and Housing Rights." http://www.cohre.org/news/documents/fair-play-for-housing-rights.

Chafe, Zoë. 2007. "Reducing Natural Disaster Risk in Cities." In Linda Starke, ed. *State of the World 2007: Our Urban Future* (New York: W. W. Norton & Company, pp. 112–129).

Chang, Leslie T. 2008. *Factory Girls: From Village to City in a Changing China* (New York: Spiegel & Grau).

Charles, Camille Zubrinsky. 2003. "The Dynamics of Racial Residential Segregation." *Annual Review of Sociology* 29: 167–207.

Chase, Marilyn. 2004. *The Barbary Plague: The Black Death in Victorian San Francisco* (New York: Random House).

Chen, Xiangming. 2007. "*The Urban Laboratory.*" In Ricky Burdett and Deyan Sudjic, eds. *The Endless City* (London: Phaidon, pp. 118–125).

Chen, Xiangming. 2009a. "A Globalizing City on the Rise: Shanghai's Transformation in Comparative Perspective." In Xiangming Chen, ed. *Shanghai Rising: State Power and Local Transformations in a Global Megacity* (Minneapolis: University of Minnesota Press, pp. xv–xxxv).

Chen, Xiangming. 2009b. "Introduction: Why Chinese and Indian Megacities?" *City & Community* 8(4): 363–368.

Chen, Xiangming, ed. 2009c. *Shanghai Rising: State Power and Local Transformations in a Global Megacity* (Minneapolis: University of Minnesota Press).

Chen, Xiangming and Tomas de' Medici. 2010. "The 'Instant City' Coming of Age: Production of Spaces in China's Shenzhen Special Economic Zone in Thirty Years." *Urban Geography* 31(4): 1141–1147.

Chen, Xiangming and Anthony A. Orum. 2009. "Shanghai as a New Global(izing) City: Lessons for and from Shanghai." In Xiangming Chen, ed. *Shanghai Rising: State Power and Local Transformations in a Global Megacity* (Minneapolis: University of Minnesota Press, pp. 237–249).

Chen, Xiangming and William Parish. 1996. "Urbanization in China: Reassessing an Evolving Model." In Josef Gugler, ed. *The Urban Transformation of the Developing World* (Oxford: Oxford University Press, pp. 61–90).

Chen, Xiangming, Lan Wang, and Ratoola Kundu. 2009. "Localizing the Production of Global Cities: A Comparative Analysis of New Town Developments around Shanghai and Kolkata." *City & Community* 8(4): 433–465.

Church, Andrew. 1988. "Urban Regeneration in London Docklands: A Five-Year Policy Review." *Environment and Planning C: Government and Policy* 6(2): 187–208.

City of Chicago. 2011. *TIF Projection Reports*. http://www.cityofchicago.org/city/en/depts/dcd/supp_info/tif_projection_reports.html.

City of Winnipeg. 2008. "Flood of the Century." http://www.winnipeg.ca/services/CityLife/HistoryOfWinnipeg/TOC/floodofcentury.stm.

Clark, David. 2003. *Urban World/Global City*, 2nd edition (London: Routledge).

Conlin, Jennifer. 2011, July 3. "Detroit Pushes Back with Young Muscles." *The New York Times*, p. ST6.

Connell, J., B. Dasgupta, R. Laishley, and M. Lipton. 1976. *Migration from Rural Areas: The Evidence from Village Studies* (Delhi: Oxford University Press).

Connolly, Cory. 2011. "Community-Based Urban Agriculture in Detroit – Candler Farms – Highland Park Movement Center." *DoSomething.org*. http://www.dosomething.org/project/community-based-urban-agriculture-detroit-candler-farms-highland-park-movement-center.

Council of Development Finance Agencies. 2008. *Original Research: 2008 TIF State-by-State Report*. http://www.cdfa.net/cdfa/cdfaweb.nsf/pages/tifstatestatutes.html.

Cressey, Paul G. 1932. *The Taxi Dance Hall: A Sociological Study in Commercialized Recreation and City Life* (Chicago, IL: University of Chicago Press).

CRIENGLISH.com. 2007, December 28. "Yiwu: A Flourishing City." *CRIENGLISH.com*. http://english.cri.cn/4026/2007/12/28/1481@308852.htm.

Crisis: The National Charity for Single Homeless People. 2008. "Official Homelessness Statistics." *Crisis*. http://www.crisis.org.uk/policywatch/pages/homelessness_statistics.html.

Cronon, William. 1991. *Nature's Metropolis: Chicago and the Great West* (New York: W. W. Norton & Company).

Cullingworth, Barry and Roger W. Caves. 2009. *Planning in the USA: Policies, Issues, and Processes*, 3rd edition (London and New York: Routledge).

Dasgupta, Susmita, Benoit Laplante, Siobhan Murray, and David Wheeler. 2009. "*Climate Change and the Future Impacts of Storm-Surge Disasters in Developing Countries.*" Washington, DC: Center for Global Development (Working Paper 182).

Davidson, Mark. 2009. "Displacement, Space and Dwelling: Placing Gentrification Debate." *Ethics, Place and Environment* 12(2): 219–234.

Davis, Kinsley. 1965. "The Urbanization of the Human Population." *Scientific American* 213: 40–53.

Davis, Mike. 1990. *City of Quartz: Excavating the Future in Los Angeles* (New York: Vintage).

Davis, Mike. 1998. *Ecology of Fear: Los Angeles and the Imagination of Disaster* (New York: Vintage).

Davis, Mike. 2006. *Planet of Slums* (London and New York: Verso).

Dear, Michael. 2002. *From Chicago to LA: Making Sense of Urban Theory* (Thousand Oaks, CA: Sage Publishers).

Demsteader, Christine. 2007, February 9. "Concrete Jungle: Sweden's Suburbs Become Cool." *The Local: Sweden's News in English.* http://www.thelocal.se/6356/20070209.

Desai, Shweta. 2009, September 1. "Half of City Lives in Slums, Without Clean Water, Sanitation or Security." *IndianExpress.com.* http://www.indianexpress.com/news/half-of-city-lives-in-slums-without-clean-w/509741.

de Tocqueville, Alexis. 1945. *Democracy in America, the Henry Reeve Text as Revised by Francis Bowen, with Notes and an Interpretive Essay by Phillips Bradley,* vols. 1 and 2 (New York: Vintage Books).

Devan, Janamitra, Stefano Negri, and Jonathan R. Woetzel. 2008. "Meeting the Challenges of China's Growing Cities." *The McKinsey Quarterly* 3: 107–116.

DeWilt, David. 2006. "Suburbia." In Peter Rollins, ed. *The Columbia Companion to American History on Film: How the Movies Have Portrayed the American Past* (New York: Columbia University Press, pp. 480–486).

Dogan, Mattei and John D. Kasarda, eds. 1988. *The Metropolis Era: A World of Giant Cities* (Newbury Park, CA: Sage Publications).

Drake, St. Clair and Horace R. Cayton. 1945. *Black Metropolis: A Study of Negro Life in a Northern City,* vols. 1 and 2 (New York: Harcourt, Brace & Company).

Duberman, Martin B., Martha Vicinus, and George Chauncey Jr., eds. 1989. *Hidden From History: Reclaiming the Gay and Lesbian Past* (New York: Penguin Books).

DuBois, W. E. B. 2007 [1899]. *The Philadelphia Negro* (New York: Cosimo Classics).

Duneier, Mitchell, Hakin Hassan, and Ovie Carter. 2000. *Sidewalk* (New York: Farrar, Straus and Giroux).

Edin, Katherine and Maria Kafelas. 2005. *Promises I Can Keep: Why Poor Women Put Motherhood Before Marriage* (Berkeley: University of California Press).

E Magazine. 2001, April 30. "Whose Grass is Greenest? Building a Pretty Lawn Without Toxic Chemicals." *E: The Environmental Magazine.*

Engels, Friedrich. 2010 [1845]. "The Great Towns." *The Condition of the Working Class in England in 1844* (Cambridge: Cambridge University Press, pp. 23–74).

Environmental Protection Agency, n.d. "About Superfund" [Region 6 Superfund Program]. http://www.epa.gov/region6/6sf/6sf.htm.

Erikson, Kai T. 1995. *A New Species of Trouble: The Human Experience of Modern Disasters* (New York: W. W. Norton & Company).

Faulconbridge, James R. 2004. "London and Frankfurt in Europe's Evolving Financial Centre Network." *Area* 36: 235–244.

Feagin, Joe R., Anthony M. Orum, and Gideon Sjoberg, eds. 1991. *A Case for the Case Study* (Chapel Hill: University of North Carolina Press).

Firebaugh, Glenn. 1979. "Structural Determinants of Urbanization in Asia and Latin America, 1950–1970." *Annual Reviews of Sociology* 44(2): 199–215.

Firebaugh, Glenn. 1984. "Urbanization of the Non-Farm Population: A Research Note on the Convergence of Rich and Poor Nations." *Social Forces* 62(3): 775–783.

Firey, Walter. 1947. "Sentiment and Symbolism as Ecological Variables." *American Sociological Review* 10(2): 140–148.

Fishman, Robert. 1987a. "American Suburbs/English Suburbs: A Transatlantic Comparison." *Journal of Urban History* 13(3): 237–251.

Fishman, Robert. 1987b. *Bourgeois Utopias: The Rise and Fall of Suburbia* (New York: Basic Books).

Fitzpatrick, Kevin and Mark LaGory. 2000. *Unhealthy Places: The Ecology of Risk in the Urban Landscape* (New York: Routledge).

Florida, Richard. 2002. *The Rise of the Creative Class: And How It's Transforming Work, Leisure, Community and Everyday Life* (New York: Basic Books).

Florida, Richard. 2005a. *Cities and the Creative Class* (New York: Routledge).

Florida, Richard. 2005b. "The World Is Spiky." *The Atlantic Monthly* (October).

Florida, Richard. 2008. *Who's Your City? How the Creative Economy is Making Where You Live the Most Important Decision of Your Life* (New York: Basic Books).

Florida, Richard. 2009. "How the Crash Will Reshape America." *The Atlantic Monthly* (March). http://www.theatlantic.com/magazine/archive/2009/03/how-the-crash-will-reshape-america/7293.

Fogelson, Robert R. 1993. *The Fragmented Metropolis: Los Angeles, 1850–1930* (Berkeley: University of California Press).

Fong, Eric and Rima Wilkes. 1999. "The Spatial Assimilation Model Reexamined: An Assessment by Canadian Data." *International Migration Review* 33(3): 594–620.

Freeman, Lance and Frank Braconi. 2004. "Gentrification and Displacement: New York City in the 1990s." *Journal of the American Planning Association* 70(1): 39–52.

Freudenburg, William, Robert Gramling, Shirley Laska, and Kai T. Erikson. 2008. "Organizing Hazards, Engineering Disasters? Improving Recognition of Political-Economic Factors in the Creation of Disasters." *Social Forces* 87(2): 1015–1038.

Frey, William. 2002. "Escaping the City – and the Suburbs." *American Demographics* 24(6): 20–24.

Fried, Marc. 2000. "Continuities and Discontinuities of Place." *Journal of Environmental Psychology* 20: 193–205.

Friedan, Betty. 2001 [1963]. *The Feminine Mystique* (New York: W. W. Norton & Company).

Friedman, Thomas L. 2005. *The World Is Flat: A Brief History of the Twenty-First Century* (New York: Farrar, Straus and Giroux).

Friedmann, John. 1986. "The World City Hypothesis." *Development and Change* 17(1): 69–83.

Friedmann, John and Goetz Wolff. 1982. "World City Formation: An Agenda for Research." *International Journal of Urban and Regional Research* 6: 304–344.

Frisbie, W. Parker and John D. Kasarda. 1988. "Spatial Processes." In Neil J. Smelser, ed. *The Handbook of Sociology* (Newbury Park, CA: Sage Publications, pp. 629–666).

Frug, Gerald. 2006. "Governance and Legal Structures." *Towards an Urban Age* (Urban Age Project, London School of Economics and Alfred Herrhausen Society of Deutsche Bank).

Fu, Jing. 2009, August 27. "China's Cities to Receive Massive Influx." *China Daily*. http://www.chinadaily.com.cn/china/2009-08/27/content_8621552.htm.

Fulton, William. 2001. *The Reluctant Metropolis: The Politics of Urban Growth in Los Angeles* (Baltimore, MD: The Johns Hopkins University Press).

Gans, Herbert J. 1967. *The Levittowners: Ways of Life and Politics in a New Suburban Community*. (New York: Vintage).

Gans, Herbert. 1982 [1962]. *The Urban Villagers: Group and Class in the Life of Italian Americans* (New York: The Free Press).

Gans, Herbert. 1994. *People, Plans, and Policies: Essays on Poverty, Racism, and Other National Urban Problems* (New York: Columbia University Press).

Garmany, Jeff. 2009. "The Embodied State: Governmentality in a Brazilian Favela." *Social & Cultural Geography* 10(7): 721–739.

Garreau, Joel. 1992. *Edge City: Life on the New Frontier* (New York: Anchor Books).

Glaser, Mark A., Lee E. Parker, and Hong Li. 2003. "Community of Choice or Ghetto of Last Resort: Community Development and the Viability of an African American Community." *Review of Policy Research* 20(3): 525–548.

Glass, Ruth. 2010. "Aspects of Change." In Japonica Brown-Saracino, ed. *The Gentrification Debates* (Routledge: New York and London).

GlimmerGuy. 2010, 13 April. "Why Fritz Haeg Wants to Eat your Lawn." *GlimmerSite*. http://glimmersite.com/2010/04/13/why-fritz-haeg-wants-to-eat-your-lawn/ever-green.

Golden, H. H. 1981. *Urbanization and Cities: Historical and Comparative Perspectives on Our Urbanizing World* (Lexington, MA: D. C. Heath).

Goldman, Todd and Roger Gorham. 2006. "Sustainable Urban Transport: Four Innovative Directions." *Technology in Society* 28: 261–273.

Gordon, L. A. David. 1996. "Planning, Design and Managing Change in Urban Waterfront Redevelopment." *The Town Planning Review* 67(3): 261–290.

Gottdiener, Mark. 1994. *The Social Production of Urban Space*, 2nd edition (Austin: University of Texas Press).

Gottmann, Jean. 1957. "Megalopolis or the Urbanization of the Northeastern Seaboard." *Economic Geography* 33(3): 189–200.

Gottmann, Jean. 1961. *Megalopolis: The Urbanized Northeastern Seaboard of the United States* (Cambridge, MA: MIT Press).

Grameen Bank. 2011, October. "Grameen Bank at a Glance." *Grameen Bank*. http://www.grameen-info.org/index.php?option=com_content&task=view&id=26&Itemid=175.

Grant, Richard. 2005. "The Emergence of Gated Communities in a West African Context: Evidence from Greater Accra, Ghana." *Urban Geography* 26(8): 661–683.

Grauman, J. V. 1976. "Orders of Magnitude of the World's Urban Population in History." *Population Bulletin of the United Nations* 8: 16–33.

Gray, Steven. 2010, April 24. "Fixing Detroit: A Laboratory for Saving America's Cities." *TIME*. http://www.time.com/time/nation/article/0,8599,1983609,00.html.

Guthrie, Doug. 2006. *China and Globalization: The Social, Economic and Political Transformation of Chinese Society* (New York: Routledge).

Hall, Peter. 1984. *The World Cities*, 3rd edition (London: Weidenfeld and Nicolson).

Hall, Peter. 2002. *Cities of Tomorrow*, 3rd edition (Oxford and Malden, MA: Blackwell).

Hall, Thomas and Sonja Vidén. 2005. "The Million Homes Programme: A Review of the Great Swedish Planning Project." *Planning Perspectives* 20(July): 301–328.

Hanna, Julia. 2010, March 15. "HBS Cases: Developing Asia's Largest Slum." *HBS Working Knowledge*.

Hantz Farms Detroit. 2011. "Introducing Hantz Farms." *Hantz Farms Detroit*. http://www.hantzfarmsdetroit.com/introduction.html.

Harrington, Michael. 1997 [1964]. *The Other America: Poverty in the United States* (New York: Scribner).

Harris, Chauncy D. and Edward L. Ullman. 2005 [1945]. "The Nature of Cities." In Nicholas R. Fyfe and Judith T. Kenny, eds. *The Urban Geography Reader* (London and New York: Routledge, pp. 46–55).

Harris, Richard. 1996. *Unplanned Suburbs: Toronto's American Tragedy, 1900–1950* (Baltimore, MD: Johns Hopkins University Press).

Harvey, David. 1973. *Social Justice and the City* (Baltimore, MD: Johns Hopkins University Press).

Harvey, David. 1989. *The Urban Experience* (Baltimore, MD: Johns Hopkins University Press).

Harvey, David. 1991. *The Condition of Postmodernity: An Enquiry into the Origins of Cultural Change* (Cambridge, MA: Blackwell).

Harvey, David. 2008. "The Right to the City." *New Left Review* 53: 23–40.

Hauser, Philip M. 1957. "World and Asian Urbanization in Relation to Economic Development and Social Change." In Philip M. Hauser, ed. *Urbanization in Asia and the Far East* (Calcutta: UNESCO).

Hayden, Dolores. 1982. *The Grand Domestic Revolution: A History of Feminist Designs for American Homes, Neighborhoods, and Cities* (Cambridge: MIT Press).

Hayden, Dolores. 2003. *Building Suburbia: Green Fields and Urban Growth, 1820–2000* (New York: Vintage Books).

Hayden, Dolores. 2006. "Building the American Way: Public Subsidy, Private Space." In Becky M. Nicolaides and Andrew Wiese, eds. *The Suburb Reader* (New York: Routledge, pp. 273–280).

Heathcote, Edwin. 2010, April 7. "Mega to Meta." *Financial Times*, part 1, pp. 12–15.

Henderson, John V. 1986. "Efficiency of Resource Usage and City Size." *Journal of Urban Economics* 19: 47–70.

Hook, Walter. 2007. "Bus Rapid Transit: The Unfolding Story." In Linda Starke, ed. *State of the World 2007: Our Urban Future* (New York: W. W. Norton & Company, pp. 80–81).

Hoselitz, Bert. 1954. "Generative and Parasitic Cities." *Economic Development and Culture Change* 32: 277–302.

Hou, Feng. 2005. *Summary Of: The Initial Destinations and Redistribution of Canada's Major Immigrant Groups: Changes over the Past Two Decades* (Analytical Studies Branch Research Paper Series; PDF version; catalogue number 11F0019MIE-No. 255).

Howard, Ebenezer. 1902. *Garden Cities of To-Morrow* (London: Swan Sonnenschein & Co., Ltd.).

Hoyt, Homer. 1939. *The Structure and Growth of Residential Neighbourhoods in American Cities* (Washington, DC: Federal Housing Administration).

Huggler, Justin. 2006, July 25. "Alternative Tourist Trail: Slumming it in Mumbai." *Independent News and Media*. http://www.johnnydepp-zone.com/boards/viewtopic.php?f=40&t=28334.

Hughes, Kathy. 2011, July 7. "Is Detroit the New Brooklyn?" *National Public Radio*. http://www.pbs.org/wnet/nccd to-know/the-daily-need/is-detroit-the-new-brooklyn/10290.

Husock, Howard. 2009. "Slum of Hope," *City Journal* 19(1). http://www.city-journal.org/2009/19_1_slums.html.

International Campaign for Justice in Bhopal. n.d. http://bhopal.net.

Jackson, Kenneth T. 1985. *Crabgrass Frontier: The Suburbanization of the United States* (New York and Oxford: Oxford University Press).

Jacobs, Jane. 1961. *The Death and Life of Great American Cities* (New York: Random House).

Jazbinsek, Dietmar. 2003. "The Metropolis and the Mental Life of Georg Simmel: On the History of an Antipathy." *Journal of Urban History* 30(1): 102–125.

Jenkins, Virginia Scott. 1994. *The Lawn: A History of an American Obsession* (Washington, DC: Smithsonian Institution Press).

"John Snow: Anaesthetist and Epidemiologist." 1946. *British Medical Journal* 2(4475): 535.

Johnson, Chalmers. 1982. *MITI and the Japanese Miracle: The Growth of Industrial Policy, 1925–1975* (Stanford: Stanford University Press).

Judd, Dennis R. 1999. "Constructing the Tourist Bubble." In Dennis R. Judd and Susan S. Fainstein, eds. *The Tourist City* (New Haven, CT: Yale University Press, pp. 35–53).

Judd, Dennis and Todd Swanstrom. 2011. *City Politics: The Political Economy of Urban America* (New York: Pearson).

Kahn, Matthew H. 2006. *Green Cities: Urban Growth and the Environment* (Washington, DC: Brookings Institution Press).

Kamath, Naresh. 2011. "More Stumbling Blocks for Dharavi Revamp." *Hindustan Times*. http://epaper.hindustantimes.com/PUBLICATIONS/HT/HM/2011/01/22/ArticleHtmls/More-stumbling-blocks-for-Dharavi-revamp-22012011006015.shtml?Mode=image# and http://www.hindustantimes.com/More-stumbling-blocks-for-Dharavi-revamp/Article1-653247.aspx.

Kanna, Ahmed. 2010. "Flexible Citizenship in Dubai: Neoliberal Subjectivity in the Emerging 'City-Corporation.'" *Cultural Anthropology* 15(1):100–129.

Kanna, Ahmed. 2012. "The Trajectories of Two 'Asian Tigers': The Imperial Roots of Capitalism in Dubai and Singapore." In Xiangming Chen and Ahmed Kanna, eds. *Rethinking Global Urbanism: Comparative Insights from Secondary Cities* (New York: Routledge, pp. 35–52).

Kasarda, John D. and Edward M. Crenshaw. 1991. "Third World Urbanization: Dimensions, Theories, and Determinants." *Annual Reviews Sociology* 17: 467–501.

Kasarda, John D. and Allan M. Parnell. 1993. "Introduction: Third World Urban Development Issues." In John D. Kasarda and Allan M. Parnell, eds. *Third World Cities: Problems, Policies, and Prospects* (Newbury Park, CA: Sage Publications, pp. ix–xvii).

Katz, Bruce and Jennifer Bradley. 2009, December 9. "The Detroit Project: A Plan for Solving America's Greatest Urban Disaster." *The New Republic*. http://www.tnr.com/article/metro-policy/the-detroit-project.

Keehner, Jonathan and Serena Saitto. 2009, December 14. "Dubai's Crazy Quilt of Assets." *Business Week*, pp. 38–40.

Kelly, Allen C. and Jeffrey Williamson. 1984. *What Drives Third World City Growth: A Dynamic General Equilibrium Approach* (Princeton, NJ: Princeton University Press).

Khanna, Parag. 2010. "Beyond City Limits." *Foreign Policy* (September/October): 122–128.

King, Anthony D. 1976. *Colonial Urban Development: Culture, Social Power and Environment* (London: Routledge & Kegan Paul).

Kiva. n.d. "About Us." *Kiva*. http://www.kiva.org/about.

Klinenberg, Eric. 2003. *Heat Wave: A Social Autopsy of Disaster in Chicago* (Chicago, IL: University of Chicago Press).

Knox, Paul L. and Peter J. Taylor, eds. 1995. *World Cities in a World-System* (Cambridge: Cambridge University Press).

Kusenbach, Margarethe. 2003. "Street Phenomenology: The Go-Along as Ethnographic Research Tool." *Ethnography* 4(3): 455–485.

Kwan, Clarence. 2010. "Urbanization in China – Another 280 Million People by 2030." *Deloitte Chinese Service Group*. http://www.deloitte.com/assets/Dcom-UnitedStates/Local%20Assets/Documents/us_csg_UrbanizationInChina_060410.pdf.

Lai, David Chuenyan. 1988. *Chinatowns: Towns within Cities in Canada* (Vancouver: University of British Columbia Press).

Läpple, Dieter. 2006, November. "An Alternative to the Global City?" In *Berlin: An Urban Experiment* (Urban Age Project, London School of Economics and Alfred Herrhausen Society of Deutsche Bank).

Leinberger, Christopher B. 2008. "The Next Slum?" *Atlantic Monthly* (March). http://www.theatlantic.com/magazine/archive/2008/03/the-next-slum/6653.

Lejano, Raul P. and C. Scott Smith. 2006. "Incompatible Land Uses and the Topology of Cumulative Risk." *Environmental Management* 37(2): 230–246.

Lemann, Nicholas. 1992. *The Promised Land: The Great Black Migration and How it Changed America* (New York: Vantage Publishers).

Leonard, Madeline. 1998. *Invisible Work, Invisible Workers: The Informal Economy in Europe and the US* (New York: St. Martin's Press).

Letiecq, Bethany L., Elaine A. Anderson, and Sally A. Koblinsky. 1998. "Social Support of Homeless and Housed Mothers: A Comparison of Temporary and Permanent Housing Arrangements." *Family Relations* 47(4): 415–421.

Lewicka, Maria. 2005. "Ways to Make People Active: The Role of Place Attachment, Cultural Capital, and Neighborhood Ties." *Journal of Environmental Psychology* 25: 381–395.

Lewis, Oscar. 1959. *Five Families: Mexican Case Studies in the Culture of Poverty* (New York: Basic Books).

Lewis, Robert D. 2001. "A City Transformed: Manufacturing Districts and Suburban Growth in Montreal, 1850–1929." *Journal of Historical Geography* 27(1): 20–35.

Lieberson, Stanley. 1981. *A Piece of the Pie* (Berkeley: University of California Press).

Light, Ivan and Edna Bonacich. 1991. *Immigrant Entrepreneurs: Koreans in Los Angeles, 1905–1982* (Berkeley: University of California Press).

Lin, Jan. 2011. *The Power of Urban Ethnic Places: Cultural Heritage and Community Life* (New York and London: Routledge).

Lissak, Rivka Shpak. 1989. *Pluralism and Progressives: Hull House and the New Immigrants, 1890–1919* (Chicago, IL: University of Chicago Press).

Loewen, James. 2006. *Sundown Towns: A Hidden Dimension of American Racism* (New York: Simon and Schuster).

Logan, John R. and Harvey L. Molotch. 1987. *Urban Fortunes: The Political Economy of Place* (Berkeley: University of California Press).

London, Bruce. 1986. "Ecological and Political Economic Analyses of Migration to a Primate City: Bangkok, Thailand ca. 1970." *Urban Affairs Quarterly* 21: 501–526.

Low, Setha. 2003. *Behind the Gates: Life, Security and the Pursuit of Happiness in Fortress America* (New York: Routledge).

Low, Setha. 2005. "Towards a Theory of Urban Fragmentation: A Cross-Cultural Analysis of Fear, Privatization and the State." *CyberGeo: European Journal of Geography* (February 28–March 3). http://cybergeo.revues.org/3207.

Lowry, I. S. 1990. "World Urbanization in Perspective." *Population and Development Review* 16: 148–176.

Lu, Hanlong, Yuan Ren, and Xiangming Chen. 2009. "Downward Pressure and Upward Bubbling: Global Influence and Community (Re)Building in Shanghai." In Xiangming Chen, ed. *Shanghai Rising: State Power and Local Transformations in a Global Megacity* (Minneapolis: University of Minnesota Press, pp. 191–213).

Lynd, Robert S. and Helen Merrell Lynd. 1959. *Middletown: A Study in American Culture* (New York: Harcourt, Brace & Company).

Lynd, Robert S. and Helen Merrell Lynd. 1965. *Middletown in Transition: A Study in Cultural Conflicts* (New York: Harcourt, Brace Jovanovich).

MacDonald, Michael Patrick. 2000. *All Souls: A Family Story from Southie* (New York: Ballantine Books).

Mah, Alice. 2006. "Devastation but Also Home: Place Attachment in Areas of Industrial Decline." *Home Cultures* 6(3): 287–310.

Marcuse, Peter and Ronald van Kempen. 2000. "Introduction." In Peter Marcuse and Ronald van Kempen, eds. *Globalizing Cities: A New Spatial Order?* (Oxford and Malden, MA: Blackwell, pp. 1–21).

Markusen, Ann, Peter Hall, Scott Campbell, and Sabina Deitrick. 1991. *The Rise of the Gunbelt: The Military Remapping of Industrial America* (New York: Oxford University Press).

Marx, Karl and Friedrich Engels, with an introduction by Eric J. Hobsbawm. 1998 [1848]. *The Communist Manifesto: A Modern Edition* (New York: Verso).

Massey, Douglas S. 1985. "Ethnic Residential Segregation: A Theoretical and Empirical Synthesis." *Sociology and Social Research* 69(3): 315–350.

Massey, Douglas S. and Nancy A. Denton. 1985. "Spatial Assimilation as a Socioeconomic Outcome." *American Sociological Review* 50(1): 94–106.

Massey, Douglas S. and Nancy Denton. 1993. *American Apartheid* (Cambridge, MA: Harvard University Press).

Massey, Douglas S. and Garvey Lundy. 2001. "Use of Black English and Racial Discrimination in Urban Housing Markets: New Methods and Findings." *Urban Affairs Review* 36(4): 452–469.

Massey, Douglas S. and Brendan P. Mullan. 1984. "Processes of Hispanic and Black Spatial Assimilation." *American Journal of Sociology* 89(4): 836–873.

Mathur, Om Prakash. 2009. *Slum-Free Cities.* (New Delhi: National Institute of Public Finance and Policy).

McChesney, Kay Young. 1990. "Family Homelessness: A Systematic Problem." *Journal of Social Issues* 46(4): 191–205.

McKenzie, Roderick D. 1968. *On Human Ecology: Selected Writings* (Chicago, IL: University of Chicago Press).

McKinsey Global Institute. 2009. "Preparing for China's Urban Billion." *McKinsey Global Institute.* http://www. mckinsey.com/Insights/MGI/Research/Urbanization/Preparing_for_urban_billion_in_China.

McKinsey Global Institute. 2010. "India's Urban Awakening: Building Inclusive Cities, Sustaining Economic Growth." *McKinsey Global Institute.* http://www.mckinsey.com/Insights/MGI/Research/Urbanization/Urban_awakening_in_India.

McKinsey Global Institute. 2011. "Urban World: Mapping the Economic Power of Cities." *McKinsey Global Institute.* http://www.mckinsey.com/Insights/MGI/Research/Urbanization/Urban_world.

McMahon, Augusta. Forthcoming 2013. "Mesopotamian Cities." In Peter Clark, ed. *Handbook of Cities in World History* (Oxford: Oxford University Press).

McMichael, Philip. 1996. "Globalization: Myth and Realities." *Rural Sociology* 61: 25–55.

McPhee, John. 1989. *The Control of Nature* (New York: Farrar, Straus and Giroux).

Meade, Robert H., ed. 1995. "Contaminants in the Mississippi River, 1987–1992." US Geological Survey Circular 1133. US Department of the Interior. Denver, CO: United States Geological Survey.

"Megacity Isn't Necessarily a 'Good' Word Survey." 2007, May 26. *Daily Times* [Pakistan]. http://www.dailytimes.com.pk/default.asp?page=2007%5C05%5C26%5Cstory_26-5-2007_pg12_7.

Mele, Christopher. 2000. *Selling the Lower East Side: Culture, Real Estate, and Resistance in New York City* (Minneapolis: University of Minnesota Press).

Miller, David Y. 2002. *The Regional Governing of Metropolitan America* (Boulder, CO: Westview Press).

Mitchell, Don. 2003. *The Right to the City: Social Justice and the Fight for Public Space* (New York: Guilford Press).

Molotch, Harvey. 1976. "The City as a Growth Machine." *American Journal of Sociology* 82(2): 309–332.

Mumford, Lewis. 1961. *The City in History: Its Origins, Transformations, and Its Prospects* (San Diego, CA and New York: Harcourt Brace Jovanovich).

Murray, Martin J. 2008. *Taming the Disorderly City: The Spatial Landscape of Johannesburg After Apartheid* (Ithaca, NY and London: Cornell University Press).

Murray, P. and Ivan Szelényi. 1984. "The City in the Transition to Socialism." *International Journal of Urban and Regional Research* 8: 90–108.

Mutlu, S. 1989. "Urban Concentration and Primacy Revisited: An Analysis and Some Policy Conclusions." *Economic Development and Cultural Change* 37: 611–639.

Myers, Garth. 2011. *African Cities: Alternative Visions of Urban Theory and Practice* (London: Zed Books).

Nagle, Garrett. 1998. *Changing Settlements* (Cheltenham, UK: Nelson Thornes).

National Alliance to End Homelessness. 2011. "The State of Homelessness in America 2011." *Policy Watch 2009. National Alliance to End Homelessness.* http://www.endhomelessness.org/content/article/detail/3668.

New Beijing Daily. 2009, January 11. p. A10.

Newhouse, James. 1997. "Europe's Rising Regionalism." *Foreign Affairs* 76: 67–84.

Nicolaides, Becky M. and Andrew Wiese. 2006. *The Suburb Reader* (New York: Routledge).

"Notown." 2009, October 5. *Time*, pp. 26–34.

Okrent, Daniel. 2009, September 24. "Detroit: The Death – and Possible Life – of a Great City." *TIME*. http://www.time.com/time/magazine/article/0,9171,1926017,00.html.

Oldenburg, Ray. 1997. *The Great Good Place* (New York: Marlowe and Company).

Oliver, Melvin L and Thomas M. Shapiro. 1997. *Black Wealth, White Wealth: A New Perspective on Racial Inequality* (New York: Routledge).

Orum, Anthony M. 1995. *City-Building in America* (Boulder, CO: Westview Press).

Orum, Anthony M. 2002. *Power, Money & The People: The Making of Modern Austin* (Portland, OR: Resource Publications).

Orum, Anthony M., Sidney Bata, Shumei Li, Jiewei Tang, Yang Sang, and Nguyen Thanh Trung. 2009. "Public Man and Public Space in Shanghai." *City & Community* 8(4): 369–389.

Orum, Anthony and Xiangming Chen. 2003. *The World of Cities: Places in Comparative and Historical Perspective* (Oxford: Blackwell Publishers).

Orum, Anthony M. and John G. Dale. 2008. *Political Sociology: Power and Participation in the Modern World*, 5th edition (New York: Oxford University Press).

Osman, Suleiman. 2011. *The Invention of Brownstone Brooklyn: Gentrification and the Search for Authenticity in Postwar New York* (Oxford: Oxford University Press).

Pardo, Mary. 1990. "Mexican-American Women Grassroots Community Activists: 'Mothers of East Los Angeles.'" *Frontiers: A Journal of Women's Studies* 9(1): 1–7.

Park, Robert E. 1936. "Human Ecology." *American Journal of Sociology* 42(1): 1–15.

Park, Robert E. and Ernest W. Burgess. 1924. *Introduction to the Science of Sociology* (Chicago, IL: University of Chicago Press).

Park, Robert E., Ernest W. Burgess, and Roderick D. McKenzie; with an introduction by Morris Janowitz. 1967. *The City* (Chicago, IL: University of Chicago Press).

Pastor Jr., Manuel , Jim Sadd, and John R. Hipp. 2001. "Which Came First? Toxic Facilities, Minority Move-In, and Environmental Justice." *Journal of Urban Affairs* 23(1): 1–21.

Pattillo, Mary. 2007. *Black on the Block: The Politics of Race and Class in the City* (Chicago, IL: University of Chicago Press).

Paulsen, Krista E. 2008, April. "Making a Market Feel at Home: Assumptions and Implications of Model Home Merchandising." Presented at the conference *A Suburban World?* in Reston, VA.

Peng, Xizhe, Xiangming Chen, and Yuan Cheng. 2010. "Urbanization and Its Consequences." In UNESCO and the EOLSS Joint Committee, *The Encyclopedia of Life Support Systems* (EOLSS) (New York: United Nations).

Peterson, Paul. 1981. *City Limits* (Chicago, IL: University of Chicago Press).

Petrakos, G. and J. C. Brada. 1989. "Metropolitan Concentration in Developing Countries." *Kyklos* 42: 557–578.

Plant, Richard. 1988. *The Pink Triangle: The Nazi War against Homosexuals* (New York: Henry Holt and Company).

Polacheck, Hilda Satt. 1989. *I Came a Stranger: The Story of a Hull-House Girl* (Champaign: University of Illinois Press).

Port of New Orleans. n.d. "Port of New Orleans Overview." *Port of New Orleans.* http://www.portno.com/pno_pages/about_overview.htm.

Portes, Alejandro, Manuel Castells, and Lauren A. Benton, eds. 1989. *The Informal Economy: Studies in Advanced and Less Developed Countries* (Baltimore, MD: Johns Hopkins University Press).

Preston, Samuel. 1979. "Urban Growth in Developing Countries: A Demographic Reappraisal." *Population and Development Review* 11: 344–348.

The Pudong Social Development Report 2002. 2002. (Shanghai: People's Press of Shanghai).

Puentes, Robert and David Warren. 2006, February. *One-Fifth of America: A Comprehensive Guide to America's First Suburbs* (Washington, DC: Brookings Institution Survey Series).

Purcell, Mark. 2002. "Excavating Lefebvre: The Right to the City and its Urban Politics of the Inhabitant." *GeoJournal* 58(2–3): 99–108. http://faculty.washington.edu/mpurcell/geojournal.pdf.

Putnam, Robert D. 2000. *Bowling Alone: The Collapse and Revival of American Community* (New York: Simon & Schuster).

Race: The Power of An Illusion; Episode Three – The House We Live In. 2003. California Newsreel, in association with the Independent Television Service (ITVS). http://www.pbs.org/race/000_About/002_04-about-03.htm.

Rajaram, Shireen S. 2007. "An Action-Research Project: Community Lead Poisoning Prevention." *Teaching Sociology* 35(2): 138–150.

Ray, Brian. 2005. "Canada: Policy Changes and Integration Challenges in an Increasingly Diverse Society." *Migration Policy Institute.* http://www.migrationinformation.org/Profiles.

Raychaudhuri, Siddhartha. 2001. "Colonialism, Indigenous Elites and the Transformation of Cities in the Non-Western World: Ahmedabad (Western India), 1890–1947." *Modern Asian Studies* 35: 677–726.

Rebar. 2011. "About Park(ing) Day." http://parkingday.org/about-parking-day.

Reclaiming Spaces. 2009. "'Right to the City' as a Response to the Crisis: 'Convergence' or Divergence of Urban Social Movements?" http://www.reclaiming-spaces.org/crisis/archives/266.

Reed, Stanley. 2009, December 14. "Why Dubai Matters." *BusinessWeek*, pp. 25–38.

Reich, Robert B. 1991, January 20. "Secession of the Successful." *New York Times Magazine*. http://www.nytimes.com/1991/01/20/magazine/secession-of-the-successful.html?pagewanted=all&src=pm.

Reisner, Marc. 1986. *Cadillac Desert: The American West and its Disappearing Water* (New York: Viking).

Reuters. 2011, June 23. "Japan Estimates Quake Damage at 16.9 Trln Yen." *Reuters*. http://www.reuters.com/article/2011/06/24/japan-economy-estimate-idUSL3E7HN3CM20110624.

Richardson, Harry W. 1987. "Whither National Urban Policy in Developing Countries?" *Urban Studies* 23: 227–244.

Riis, Jacob. 1914. *How the Other Half Lives: Studies Among the Tenements of New York* (New York: Charles Scribner and Sons).

Roberts, Dexter. 2009, April 13. "As Factories Fail, So Does Business Law." *BusinessWeek*, pp. 46–48.

Robledo, S. Jhoanna. 2011, April 3. "Today's Gowanus Is Tomorrow's Tribeca." *New York Times*, Real Estate Section. http://nymag.com/realestate/features/microneighborhoods.

Rode, Phillip et al. 2008. *Integrated City Making: Governance, Planning and Transport* (Urban Age Project, London School of Economics and Alfred Herrhausen Society of Deutsche Bank).

Rogers, A. and John G. Williamson. 1982. "Migration, Urbanization, and Third World Development: An Overview." *Economic Development and Cultural Change* 30: 463–482.

Rosenau, James N. 1997. *Along the Domestic–Foreign Frontier: Exploring Governance in a Turbulent World* (New York: Cambridge University Press).

Rosenthal, Elisabeth. 2009, May 11. "In German Suburb, Life goes on Without Cars." *New York Times*. http://www.nytimes.com/2009/05/12/science/earth/12suburb.html?pagewanted=1.

Ross, Andrew. 2000. *The Celebration Chronicles: Life, Liberty, and the Pursuit of Property Value in Disney's New Town* (New York: Ballantine Books).

Rybczynski, Witold. 1996. *City Life* (New York: Simon and Schuster).

Sassen, Saskia. 1991. *The Global City: New York, London, Tokyo* (Princeton, NJ: Princeton University Press).

Sassen, Saskia. 2001. *The Global City: New York, London, Tokyo*, 2nd edition (Princeton, NJ: Princeton University Press).

Sassen, Saskia. 2006. *Cities in a World Economy*, 3rd edition (Thousand Oaks, CA: Pine Forge Press).

Sassen, Saskia. 2009. "The Global City Perspective: Theoretical Implications for Shanghai." In Xiangming Chen, ed. *Shanghai Rising: State Power and Local Transformations in a Global Megacity* (Minneapolis: University of Minnesota Press, pp. 3–29).

Sassen, Saskia. 2010. "Global Inter-City Networks and Commodity Chains: Any Intersections?" *Global Networks* 10(1): 150–163.

Saunders, Peter. 1981. *Social Theory and the Urban Question* (New York: Holmes & Meier Publishers).

Schwartz, Alex F. 2006. *Housing Policy in the United States: An Introduction* (New York: Routledge).

Schwartz, Nelson D. 2012, February 21. "Some Doubt a Settlement Will End Mortgage Ills." *New York Times*, Business Day, B1.

Seltser, Barry J. and Donald E. Miller. 1993. *Homeless Families: The Struggle for Dignity* (Chicago, IL: University of Illinois Press).

Sennett, Richard. 2005. "The Open City." *Towards an Urban Age* (Urban Age Project, London School of Economics and Alfred Herrhausen Society of Deutsche Bank).

Shapira, Philip. 1990. "Industrial Restructuring and Economic Development Strategies in a Japanese Steel Town: The Case of Kitakyushu." *Town Planning Review* 61(4): 389–411.

Sharma, Kalpana. 2009, April. "Slumdogs and Small Towns." *InfoChange News and Features*. http://infochangeindia.org/Urban-India/Cityscapes/Slumdogs-and-small-towns.html.

Shaw, Clifford. 1966. *The Jack Roller: A Delinquent Boy's Own Story* (Chicago, IL: University of Chicago Press).

Shaw, Kate. 2005. "The Place of Alternative Culture and the Politics of its Protection in Berlin, Amsterdam and Melbourne." *Planning Theory & Practice* 6: 149–169.

Shenot, Christine. 2010, August 10. "Baltimore seeds city farms as path to sustainability, jobs." *Grist*. http://www.grist.org/article/food-baltimore-seeds-city-farms-as-path-to-sustainability-jobs.

Short, John R. 1989. "Yuppies, Yuffies and the New Urban Order." *Transactions of the Institute of British Geographers* 14(2): 173–188.

Siemiatycki, Myer, Tim Rees, Ronanna Ng, and Kahn Rahi. 2003. "Integrating Community Diversity in

Toronto: On Whose Terms?" In Paul Anisef and C. Michael Lanphier, eds. *The World in a City* (Toronto: University of Toronto Press, pp. 373–456).

Simmel, Georg. 1964 [1903]. "The Metropolis and Mental Life," trans. H. H. Gerth and C. Wright Mills. In Kurt H. Wolff, ed. *The Sociology of Georg Simmel* (New York: Free Press of Glencoe, pp. 409–424).

Sklair, Leslie. 2002. *Globalization: Capitalism and Its Alternatives*, 3rd edition (Oxford: Oxford University Press).

Sklair, Leslie. 2005. "The Transitional Capitalist Class and Contemporary Architecture in Globalizing Cities." *International Journal of Urban and Regional Research* 29: 485–500.

Sklar, Kathryn Kish. 1985. "Hull House in the 1890s: A Community of Women Reformers." *Signs* 10(4): 658–677.

Slum Rehabilitation Agency. n.d. "Dharavi Redevelopment Project." *Slum Rehabilitation Agency*. http://www.sra.gov.in/htmlpages/Dharavi.htm.

Smith, David A. 2008. "Best Practices in Slum Improvement: The Case of São Paulo, Brazil." *Development Innovations Group*. http://www.affordablehousinginstitute.org/resources/library/DS_saopaulo_best_practices_2008.pdf.

Smith, David A. and Michael Timberlake. 1993. "World Cities: A Political Economy/Global Network Approach." In Ray Hutchinson, ed. *Research in Urban Sociology*, vol. 3: *Urban Sociology in Transition* (New Jersey: JAI Press, pp. 179–205).

Smith, David A. and Michael F. Timberlake. 2001. "World City Networks and Hierarchies, 1977–1997: An Empirical Analysis of Global Air Travel Links." *American Behavioral Scientist* 44: 1656–1678.

Smith, Neil. 1979. "Toward a Theory of Gentrification: A Back to the City Movement by Capital, Not People." *Journal of the American Planning Association* 45(4): 538–548.

Snow, David and Leon Anderson. 1993. *Down on Their Luck: A Study of Homeless Street People* (Berkeley: University of California Press).

Snow, John. 1857. "Cholera, and the Water Supply in the South Districts of London." *British Medical Journal* 2(42): 864–865.

Soja, Edward W. 1999. "Thirdspace: Expanding the Scope of the Geographical Imagination." In Doreen Massey, John Allen, and Phillip Sarre, eds. *Human Geography Today* (Cambridge: Polity Press, pp. 260–278).

Soja, Edward W. 2000. *Postmetropolis: Critical Studies of Cities and Regions* (Oxford: Blackwell).

Soja, Edward W. 2010. *Seeking Spatial Justice* (Minneapolis: University of Minnesota Press).

Soja, Edward W. and Miguel Kanai. 2007. "The Urbanization of the World." In Ricky Burdett and Deyan Sudjic, eds. *The Endless City* (London: Phaidon, pp. 54–69).

Spain, Daphne. 1992. *Gendered Spaces* (Chapel Hill: University of North Carolina Press).

Spear, Alan. 1967. *Black Chicago: The Making of a Negro Ghetto* (Chicago, IL: University of Chicago Press).

Steinhardt, Nancy. Forthcoming 2013. "China." In Peter Clark , ed. *The Oxford Handbook of Cities in World History* (Oxford: Oxford University Press).

Sudjic, Deyan. 2006, July "The View from Outside." In *Johannesburg: Challenges of Inclusion*? (Urban Age Project, London School of Economics and Alfred Herrhausen Society of Deutsche Bank).

Sugrue, Thomas. 2005. *The Origins of the Urban Crisis: Race and Inequality in Postwar Detroit* (Princeton, NJ: Princeton University Press).

Sun, Jiaming and Xiangming Chen. 2009. "Fast Foods and Brand Clothes in Shanghai: How and Why Do Locals Consume Globally?" In Xiangming Chen, ed. *Shanghai Rising: State Power and Local Transformations in a Global Megacity* (Minneapolis: University of Minnesota Press, pp. 215–235).

Swanstrom, Todd. 1985. *The Crisis of Growth Politics: Cleveland, Kucinich, and the Challenge of Urban Populism* (Philadelphia, PA: Temple University Press).

Tan, Minghong, Xiubin Li, Hui Xie, and Changhe Lu. 2005. "Urban Land Expansion and Arable Land Loss in China – A Case Study of Beijing–Tianjin–Hebei Region." *Land Use Policy* 22(3): 187–196.

Taylor, Peter J. 2004. *World City Network: A Global Urban Analysis* (London: Routledge).

Teaford, Jon C. 1994. *Cities of the Heartland* (Bloomington, IN: Indiana University Press).

Teyssot, Georges, ed. 1991. *The American Lawn* (Princeton, NJ: Princeton Architectural Press).

Thirani, Neha. 2010, December 12. "The SRA is Further Slumming the City." *Times of India*. http://dharavi.org/F._Press/2010/12.12.2010_The_SRA_is_further_sluming_the_city.

Tilly, Charles. 1990. *Coercion, Capital and European States, AD 990–1990* (Cambridge, MA: Blackwell).

"Toilet Trouble." 2011, July 8. *Thanh Nien Daily*. http://www.thanhniennews.com/2010/pages/20110710161239.aspx.

"Towards Sustainable Cities." 2008, January 26. *People and the Planet*. http://www.peopleandplanet.net/?lid=27116&topic=26&section=40.

Troper, Harold. 2003. "Becoming an Immigrant City: A History of Immigration into Toronto Since the Second World War." In Paul Anisef and C. Michael Lanphier, eds. *The World in a City* (Toronto: University of Toronto Press, pp. 19–62).

Tuataigh, M. A. G. Ó. 1985. "The Irish in Nineteenth Century Britain: Problems of Integration." In Roger Swift and Gilley Sheridan, eds. *The Irish in the Victorian City* (London: Croom Helm, pp. 13–36).

Tuman, John P. and Grant W. Neeley. 2003. "Public Management in the United States–Mexico Border Region: Toward Increased Cooperation between Texas and Mexican Officials?" *State & Local Government Review* 35(1): 38–47.

UN-Habitat. 2009. "Planning Sustainable Cities: Global Report on Human Settlements 2009." United Nations Human Settlements Programme (Sterling, VA: Earthscan).

United Nations. 2007. "World Urbanization Prospects: The 2007 Revision Population Database." http://esa.un.org/unup.

United Nations Commission for Africa. 1980. *Demographic Handbook for Africa* (Addis Ababa: United Nations).

United Nations Environmental Programme/GRID Europe. 2004. "Environmental Alert Bulletin: Impacts of Summer 2003 Heat Wave in Europe." Nairobi, Kenya: UNEP.

United States Army Corps of Engineers, Mississippi Valley Division. 2009. "Mississippi River & Tributaries Project." http://www.mvd.usace.army.mil/mrc/mrt/index.php.

United States Department of Labor. 1965. "The Negro Family: The Case for National Action" [also known as "The Moynihan Report"] (Washington: Office of Policy Planning and Research).

United States Department of Transportation. n.d. *Issues in Bus Rapid Transit*, Chapter 3: "Curitiba Experience." http://www.fta.dot.gov/4391.html.

United States Environmental Protection Agency. 2009. "2008 Inventory of US Greenhouse Gas Emissions and Sinks, Executive Summary." *United States Environmental Protection Agency*. http://www.epa.gov/climatechange/emissions/usgginv_archive.html.

United States Geological Survey. 1952. "US Geological Survey Flood Photos: Red River of the North Flooding 1950." *United States Geological Survey*. http://nd.water.usgs.gov/photos/1950RedFlood/index.html.

United States Geological Survey. 2005. "US Geological Survey Flood Photos: Red River of the North Flooding 1997." *United States Geological Survey*. http://nd.water.usgs.gov/photos/1997RedFlood.

Urban Age Project. 2006, May 9–10. "German Cities: Success Beyond Growth?" Paper for the Berlin conference, organized by Urban Age at London School of Economics and supported by Alfred Heehausen Society in partnership with the City of Halle on the Saale, the Bauhaus Dessau Foundation, HafenCity University Hamburg and the German Association of Cities.

Urban Farming. 2011. "Urban Farming Mission Statement." *Urban Farming*. http://www.urbanfarming.org/about.html.

Venkatesh, Sudhir. 2000. *American Project: The Rise and Fall of a Modern Ghetto* (Cambridge, MA: Harvard University Press).

Vogel, Ezra F. 1991. *The Four Little Dragons: The Spread of Industrialization in East Asia* (Cambridge, MA: Harvard University Press).

Wakeman, Rosemary. 2007. "Fascinating Les Halles." *French Politics, Culture & Society* 25: 46–72.

Waldie, D. J. 1996. *Holy Land: A Suburban Memoir* (New York: W. W. Norton & Company).

Waldinger, Roger and Mehdi Bozorgmehr, eds. 1996. *Ethnic Los Angeles* (New York: Russell Sage).

Wall, Ronald Sean and G. A. van der Knaap. 2011. "Sectoral Differentiation and Network Structure Within Contemporary Worldwide Corporate Networks." *Economic Geography* 87(3): 267–308.

Walton, John. 1992. *Western Times and Water Wars: State, Culture and Rebellion in California* (Berkeley: University of California Press).

Wang, Xinhao and Rainer Hofe. 2007. *Research Methods in Urban and Regional Planning* (New York: Springer).

Weber, Max. 2011. *The Methodology of the Social Sciences*, trans. and ed. Edward A. Shils and Henry A. Finch (Piscataway, NJ: Transaction Publishers Reprint).

Weber, R. and L. Goddeeris. 2007. "Tax Increment Financing: Process and Planning Issues." *Lincoln Institute of Land Policy* (working paper). http://www.lincolninst.edu/subcenters/teaching-fiscal-dimensions-of-planning/materials/goddeeris-weber-financing.pdf.

Webster, Chris. 2001. "Gated Cities of Tomorrow." *Town Planning Review* 72(2): 149–170.

Weinstein, Liza and Xuefei Ren. 2009. "The Changing Right to the City: Urban Renewal and Housing Rights in Globalizing Shanghai and Mumbai." *City & Community* 8(4): 407–432.

Wheeler, Stephen. 2007. "Planning Sustainable and Livable Cities." In Richard T. Legates and Frederic Stout, eds. *The City Reader*, 4th edition (New York: Routledge, pp. 500–509).

Whitehead, Tom. 2009, December 8. "Record Level of British Population is Foreign-Born." *The Telegraph*. http://www.telegraph.co.uk/news/uknews/immigration/6762299/Record-level-of-British-population-is-foreign-born.html.

Whitford, David. 2009. "Can Farming Save Detroit?" *Fortune Magazine*. http://money.cnn.com/2009/12/29/news/economy/farming_detroit.fortune.

Whyte, William H. 1956. *The Organization Man* (New York: Simon and Schuster).

Whyte, William H. 2000. "Selection from 'The Social Life of Small Urban Spaces.'" In Albert LaFarge, ed. *The Essential William H. Whyte* (New York: Fordham University Press).

Wiese, Andrew. 2004. *Places of Their Own: African American Suburbanization in the Twentieth Century* (Chicago, IL: University of Chicago Press).

Wilson, William Julius. 1997. *When Work Disappears* (New York: Vintage Books).

Wilson, William Julius. 2009. *More than Just Race: Being Black and Poor in the Inner City* (New York: W. W. Norton & Company).

Wirth, Louis. 1928. *The Ghetto* (Chicago, IL: University of Chicago Press).

Wirth, Louis. 1938. "Urbanism as a Way of Life." *American Journal of Sociology* 44(1): 1–24.

World Bank. 2009. *World Development Report 2009: Reshaping Economic Geography* (Washington, DC: World Bank).

World Bank. 2010. *Climate Risks and Adaptation in Asian Coastal Megacities: A Synthesizing Report* (Washington, DC: World Bank).

"World's Slums Need Water Infrastructure." 2008, November 11. *edieWater*. http://www.edie.net/news/news_story.asp?id=15590.

Wright, Gwendolyn. 1983. *Building the Dream: A Social History of Housing in America* (Cambridge, MA: MIT Press).

Wright Mills, C. 2000 [1959]. *The Sociological Imagination*, 40th anniversary edition (New York: Oxford University Press).

Yin, Robert K. 2008. *Case Study Research: Design and Methods*, 4th edition (Thousand Oaks, CA: Sage Publishers).

Yinger, John. 1997. *Closed Doors, Opportunities Lost: The Continuing Costs of Housing Discrimination* (New York: Russell Sage Foundation).

Yunus, Muhammad and Alan Jolis. 1999. *Banker to the Poor: Micro-Lending and the Battle Against World Poverty* (New York: Public Affairs).

Zhou, Min. 2009. *Contemporary Chinese America: Immigration, Ethnicity and Community Transformation* (Philadelphia, PA: Temple University Press).

Zorbaugh, Harvey. 2005 [1926]. "The Natural Areas of the City." In Jan Lin and Christopher Mele, eds. *The Urban Sociology Reader* (New York: Routledge, pp. 82–88).

Zorbaugh, Harvey. 1983 [1929]. *The Gold Coast and the Slum: A Sociological Study of Chicago's Near North Side* (Chicago, IL: University of Chicago Press).

Zukin, Sharon. 1982. *Loft Living: Culture and Capital in Urban Change* (Baltimore, MD: Johns Hopkins University Press).

Zukin, Sharon. 1991. *Landscapes of Power: From Detroit to Disney World* (Berkeley: University of California Press).

Zukin, Sharon. 1995. *The Cultures of Cities* (Oxford: Blackwell).

Zukin, Sharon. 2010. *Naked City: The Death and Life of Authentic Urban Places* (Oxford: Oxford University Press).

Zukin, Sharon. 2012. "Competitive Globalization and Urban Change: The Allure of Cultural Strategies." In Xiangming Chen and Ahmed Kanna, eds. *Rethinking Global Urbanism: Comparative Insights from Secondary Cities* (New York: Routledge, pp. 17–34).

Zyen. 2007, March. Global Financial Centres Index 1. City of London. http://www.zyen.com/PDF/GFCI.pdf.

Zyen. 2009, September. Global Financial Centres Index 6. City of London. http://www.mfc-moscow.com/assets/files/analytics/GFCI6.pdf.

Index

Introduction to Cities: How Place and Space Shape Human Experience,
First Edition. Xiangming Chen, Anthony M. Orum, and Krista E. Paulsen.
© 2013 Xiangming Chen, Anthony M. Orum, and Krista E. Paulsen.
Published 2013 by Blackwell Publishing Ltd.